34th
Annual Meeting
of the
Association for
Computational Linguistics

Proceedings of the Conference

24-27 June 1996
University of California, Santa Cruz
Santa Cruz, California, USA

Published by the Association for Computational Linguistics

Order copies of this and other ACL proceedings from:

Morgan Kaufmann Publishers
340 Pine Street, 6th Floor
San Francisco, CA 94104
1-800-745-7323

PREFACE

On behalf of the Program Committee for ACL96 we are pleased to present you with this volume containing the papers accepted for presentation at the 34th Meeting of the Association for Computational Linguistics, June 23-28, 1996, at UCSC, Santa Cruz, California. This volume also contains the papers that were selected by the student program committee for presentation at the student poster session.

We received a gratifyingly large number of papers (many of them electronically without having to resort to subsequent hard-copy backups), and of unusually high quality. This, of course, made the program committee's job that much more difficult because of the number of papers needing to be read (25 - 30 each), but also because of the onerous task of having to choose between many equally interesting and convincing papers. The encouraging response we had to our request in the call for a wider range of papers also resulted in greater demands on the reviewing process, requiring an unusually wide range of expertise. The hard work of the authors and the committee have produced the stimulating document before you, a broad selection of much of the best work in the field.

Special praise goes to our outstanding invited speakers, Mike Tanenhaus and Hiyan Alshawi, who have begun a new precedent by including written versions of their talks in the proceedings. We thank Johanna Moore, the tutorial chair, who put together an excellent slate of tutorial instructors: Alison Cawsey, Larry Fagan, Bonnie Webber, Ido Dagan, Eduard H. Hovy, Kevin Knight, Alex Lascarides, and Ann Copestake, whom we also thank for preparing their alluring and informative tutorials. We are very grateful to Mettina Veenstra and Christy Doran, the student session co-chairs, who ably organized the student poster session. In addition, we are most appreciative of the exemplary job performed by Doug Appelt and Geoffrey Pullum, the local arrangements co-chairs, who have provided us with our delightful "California" experience.

Our hard working program committee and the additional external reviewers cannot be thanked too much for the conscientious and painstaking job they performed in reviewing a prodigious number of papers which covered a wide spectrum of topics. They are also to be commended for the professional judgment that they brought to the program committee meeting in Philadelphia which made it such a pleasant experience. Their names, and the names of the student session reviewers, are listed on the following page. In the interests of including a somewhat larger number of clearly acceptable papers, the committee decided to experiment with a new organization format, namely parallel sessions. The ACL executive committee and the next program chair will be very interested in your feedback on these sessions and their organization as well as on the poster sessions organized by the students.

We are extremely grateful to Trisha Yannuzzi, who is the one person most responsible for handling the myriad tasks associated with the proceedings preparation, including our successful attempt at automating most of the electronic submissions process, the program committee meeting at the University of Pennsylvania, communications with authors and reviewers, and finally the submission of the proceedings itself to the publisher. She has been very ably assisted by Susan Deysher and by Mark-Jason Dominus, the implementer of our automated submission handler, to whom we also owe a debt of gratitude. In addition we thank the Institute for Research in Cognitive Science and the Department of of Computer and Information Science at the University of Pennsylvania for providing internal financial support for both administrative and technical tasks related to this conference.

Finally, we would like to express our gratitude to Kathy McKeown and Priscilla Rasmussen, who as usual provided the consistent and efficient support and guidance that we have all come to rely on, and to the ACL Executive Committee.

Welcome to ACL96 at Santa Cruz!

Aravind Joshi and Martha Palmer,
Program Co-Chairs
May, 1996
University of Pennsylvania, Philadelphia, PA

ACL96 Program Committee members

Anne Abeillé (Université Paris 7)
Steve Abney (University of Tübingen)
Susan Armstrong (ISSCO, University of Geneva)
Madeleine Bates (BBN Systems & Technologies)
Sandra Carberry (University of Delaware)
Claire Cardie (Cornell University)
David Carter (SRI International)
Kenneth W. Church (AT&T Research)
Ann Copestake (CSLI, Stanford)
Pierre Isabelle (CITI, Montreal)
Kevin Knight (USC/Information Sciences Institute)
Sadao Kurohashi (Kyoto University)
John Lafferty (Carnegie Mellon University)
Klaus Netter (DFKI, Saarbrücken)
Cécile Paris (University of Brighton)
Fernando Pereira (AT&T Research)
Emmanuel Roche (Mitsubishi Electric Research Laboratories)
Candy Sidner (Lotus Development Corporation)

Additional Reviewers

Afzal Ballim (Swiss Federal Institute of Technology at Lausanne)
Tilmann Becker (DFKI, Saarbrücken)
Pierrette Bouillon (ISSCO, University of Geneva)
Richard Crouch (Defence Research Agency, Malvern, UK)
Louis des Tombe (University of Utrecht)
Greger Erbach (DFKI, Saarbrücken)
Julia Hirschberg (AT&T Research)
Stephen Isard (University of Edinburgh)
Walter Kasper (DFKI, Saarbrücken)
Bernd Kiefer (DFKI, Saarbrücken)
Steven Krauwer (University of Utrecht)
Hans-Ulrich Krieger (DFKI, Saarbrücken)
Ian Lewin (SRI International, Cambridge)
Mitch Marcus (University of Pennsylvania)
Paola Merlo (University of Geneva)
Mehryar Mohri (AT&T Research)
Günter Neumann (DFKI, Saarbrücken)
Richard Oerhle (University of Arizona)
Dominique Petitpierre (ISSCO, University of Geneva)
Stephen Pulman (SRI International, Cambridge)
Graham Russell (ISSCO, University of Geneva)
Mark Steedman (University of Pennsylvania)

CONFERENCE PROGRAM

SUNDAY EVENING, 23 JUNE

7:00– 9:00 REGISTRATION

7:00– 9:00 RECEPTION

MONDAY, 24 JUNE

8:30–12:00 Tutorial registration

9:00–12:30 TUTORIAL SESSIONS
NLP for Health Care Applications
Alison Cawsey, Lawrence Fagan, and Bonnie Webber

Bilingual Word Alignment and Lexicon Construction
Ido Dagan

2:00– 5:30 TUTORIAL SESSIONS
Machine Translation
Eduard H. Hovy and Kevin Knight

Lexical Semantics: Where Linguistics Meets the Real World
Alex Lascarides and Ann Copestake

2:00– 6:00 Conference Registration

7:00–10:00 RECEPTION

TUESDAY, 25 JUNE

8:30– 5:00 Conference Registration

8:45– 9:05 OPENING REMARKS AND ANNOUNCEMENTS

9:05– 9:30 *Higher-Order Coloured Unification and Natural Language Semantics*
Claire Gardent and Michael Kohlhase

9:30– 9:55 *A Model-Theoretic Framework for Theories of Syntax*
James Rogers

9:55–10:20 *Noun Phrase Analysis in Large Unrestricted Text for Information Retrieval*
David A. Evans and Chengxiang Zhai

10:20–11:00 BREAK

11:00–11:25 *Morphological Cues for Lexical Semantics*
Marc Light

11:25–11:50 *From Submit to Submitted via Submission: On Lexical Rules in Large-Scale Lexicon Acquisition*
Evelyne Viegas, Boyan Onyshkevych, Victor Raskin and Sergei Nirenburg

11:50–12:15 *Integrating Multiple Knowledge Sources to Disambiguate Word Sense: An Exemplar-Based Approach*
Hwee Tou Ng and Hian Beng Lee

12:15– 1:45 LUNCH (Student Poster Sessions)

1:45– 2:50 **INVITED TALK**
Using Eye Movements to Study Spoken Language Comprehension: Evidence for Incremental Interpretation
Michael K. Tanenhaus

2:50– 3:30 *A Fully Statistical Approach to Natural Language Interfaces*
Scott Miller, David Stallard, Robert Bobrow and Richard Schwartz

3:15– 3:40 *A Robust System for Natural Spoken Dialogue*
James F. Allen, Bradford W. Miller, Eric K. Ringger and Teresa Sikorski

3:40– 4:20 BREAK

4:20– 4:45 *Combining Trigram-Based and Feature-Based Methods for Context-Sensitive Spelling Correction*
Andrew R. Golding and Yves Schabes

4:45– 6:30 STUDENT POSTER SESSION AND RECEPTION
See separate student session program.

WEDNESDAY, 26 JUNE

Parallel Session Ia

9:05– 9:30 *Efficient Normal-Form Parsing for Combinatory Categorial Grammar*
Jason Eisner

9:30– 9:55 *Another Facet of LIG Parsing*
Pierre Boullier

9:55–10:20 *Parsing with Semidirectional Lambek Grammar is NP-Complete*
Jochen Dörre

10:20–11:00 BREAK

11:00–11:25 *Computing Optimal Descriptions for Optimality Theory Grammars with Context-Free Position Structures*
Bruce Tesar

11:25–11:50 *Directed Replacement*
Lauri Karttunen

11:50–12:15 *Synchronous Models of Language*
Owen Rambow and Giorgio Satta

Parallel Session Ib

9:05– 9:30 *Coordination as a Direct Process*
Augusta Mela and Christophe Fouqueré

9:30– 9:55 *High-Performance Bilingual Text Alignment Using Statistical and Dictionary Information*
Masahiko Haruno and Takefumi Yamazaki

9:55–10:20 *An Iterative Algorithm to Build Chinese Language Models*
Xiaoqiang Luo and Salim Roukos

10:20–11:00 BREAK

11:00–11:25 *Pattern-Based Context-Free Grammars for Machine Translation*
Koichi Takeda

11:25–11:50 *A Polynomial-Time Algorithm for Statistical Machine Translation*
Dekai Wu

11:50–12:15 *SẸMHẸ: A Generalised Two-level System*
George Anton Kiraz

12:15– 1:45 LUNCH

1:45– 2:50 **INVITED TALK**
Head Automata and Bilingual Tiling: Translation with Minimal Representation
Hiyan Alshawi

2:50– 3:30 *Parsing Algorithms and Metrics*
Joshua Goodman

3:15– 3:40 *A New Statistical Parser Based on Bigram Lexical Dependencies*
Michael John Collins

3:40– 4:20 BREAK

4:20– 4:45 *Two Sources of Control Over the Generation of Software Instructions*
Anthony Hartley and Cécile Paris

4:45– 5:10 *Chart Generation*
Martin Kay

5:10– 5:35 *Evaluating the Portability of Revision Rules for Incremental Summary Generation*
Jacques Robin

5:35– 6:30 FREE TIME

7:00–10:00 RECEPTION AND BANQUET

Presidential Address: Oliviero Stock

THURSDAY, 27 JUNE

Parallel Session IIa

9:05– 9:30 *Compilation of Weighted Finite-State Transducers from Decision Trees*
Richard Sproat and Michael Riley

9:30– 9:55 *Fast Parsing Using Pruning and Grammar Specialization*
Manny Rayner and David Carter

9:55–10:20 *An Efficient Compiler for Weighted Rewrite Rules*
Mehryar Mohri and Richard Sproat

10:20–11:00 BREAK

11:00–11:25 *Efficient Tabular LR Parsing*
Mark-Jan Nederhof and Giorgio Satta

11:25–11:50 *Magic for Filter Optimization in Dynamic Bottom-Up Processing*
Guido Minnen

11:50–12:15 *Efficient Transformation-Based Parsing*
Giorgio Satta and Eric Brill

Parallel Session IIb

9:05– 9:30 *Resolving Anaphors in Embedded Sentences*
Saliha Azzam

9:30– 9:55 *Functional Centering*
Michael Strube and Udo Hahn

9:55–10:20 *Mechanisms for Mixed-Initiative Human-Computer Collaborative Discourse*
Curry I. Guinn

10:20–11:00 BREAK

11:00–11:25 *A Prosodic Analysis of Discourse Segments in Direction-Giving Monologues*
Julia Hirschberg and Christine H. Nakatani

11:25–11:50 *An Information Structural Approach To Spoken Language Generation*
Scott Prevost

11:50–12:15 *The Rhythm of Lexical Stress in Prose*
Doug Beeferman

12:15–1:45 LUNCH and STUDENT MEMBER LUNCH
See separate notice on student member lunch

1:45–2:50 ACL ANNUAL BUSINESS MEETING

2:50–3:30 *An Empirical Study of Smoothing Techniques for Language Modeling*
Stanley F. Chen and Joshua Goodman

3:15–3:40 *Minimizing Manual Annotation Cost in Supervised Training from Corpora*
Sean P. Engelson and Ido Dagan

3:40–4:20 BREAK

4:20–4:45 *Unsupervised Learning of Word-Category Guessing Rules*
Andrei Mikheev

4:45–5:10 *Linguistic Structure as Composition and Perturbation*
Carl de Marcken

5:10–6:30 FREE TIME

TUTORIALS

NLP for Health Care Applications

Alison Cawsey, Herriot Watt University; Larry Fagan, Stanford University; and Bonnie Webber, University of Pennsylvania

Health care practitioners and their patients rely on Natural Language. But for health care payers, health care providers' insistence on using Natural Language seems to be a luxury, compared with their using fixed terminologies and non-NL formats. Given the parallel thrusts in health care towards outcomes-based practice and cost reductions, Natural Language may be a luxury that health care payers will reject unless the cost of its use can be reduced.

Efforts to develop and apply NLP techniques to health care delivery have been going on for the past 25 years, many of these efforts initiated and carried out by the health care providers themselves. Over this period, there have been many developments in both computational techniques and NLP research that are applicable to solving the Natural Language needs of health care. This tutorial will provide a review of issues and techniques, including: efforts to codify and link terminologies used in health care; how Natural Language information ("free text") becomes part of a patient's record, and input technology that can support it; symbolic and statistical techniques for extracting information from free text; and efforts to customize health care information to the specific needs of individual patients.

Bilingual Word Alignment and Lexicon Construction

Ido Dagan, Bar Ilan University

Bilingual alignment is the task of identifying corresponding segments in a bilingual pair of parallel texts, where one is the translation of the other. This tutorial will focus on alignment methods that identify correspondences at the word level. The output produced by these methods can be used for searching translation archives and for constructing domain-specific bilingual lexicons of the type needed for human and machine translation and for multilingual information retrieval.

The tutorial will include a short review of alignment methods and a detailed description of two practical word-level algorithms: (1) The word align algorithm by Dagan, Church and Gale, which consists of two components. The first learns a probabilistic bilingual lexicon, based on the IBM statistical translation models 1&2. The second finds an optimal alignment using a dynamic programming technique. (2) A version of the pattern-matching DK-Vec algorithm by Fung, which was developed for aligning languages with different alphabets, but is useful for any language pair. The algorithm handles incompatibilities between the two texts, such as skipping sections that appear in one of the texts and are missing in the other.

I will describe simple implementations of both algorithms in AWK, and demonstrate them on a pair of documents taken from the ACL European Corpus Initiative CD-ROM.

Lexical Semantics: Where Linguistics Meets the Real World

Alex Lascarides, University of Edinburgh; Ann Copestake, Stanford University

This tutorial focuses on the representation of lexical semantic information, and the links between this and other knowledge resources that are used during text processing. Our ultimate aim is to examine how words can be interpreted effectively in a discourse context. In particular, we consider how lexical processing should integrate and communicate with more open-ended pragmatic reasoning.

The tutorial will include an overview of several approaches to lexical semantics, including work by Fillmore, Nunberg, Clark, Levin, Pustejovsky, Schütze, Hobbs, and researchers involved in the ACQUILEX project. We concentrate on linguistic phenomena involving polysemy in various guises, since this is central to both theoretical work and also to the problem of building wide-coverage lexicons for practical work in NLP. We will illustrate the need to represent partial regularities in the lexicon, and discuss some approaches to formalizing defaults which allow for exceptions to lexical generalizations. This discussion will be grounded using examples of representations expressed in the LKB typed default feature structure language. We will examine the interrelationship between syntax and lexical semantics within lexicalist linguistic theories and illustrate some ways in which statistical and symbolic approaches can be effectively integrated. Finally, we will critically assess existing proposals for integrating lexical and pragmatic information.

Machine Translation

Eduard H. Hovy and Kevin Knight, USC/Information Sciences Institute

Machine Translation (MT) is one of the oldest large-scale applications of computer science. The need for MT continues to increase: in today's networked world, the need for systems to help humans read documents written in a variety of languages is constantly growing. But despite optimistic predictions in the 60's, and despite the fact that worldwide, over 50 companies perform or sell MT, MT technology is not yet capable of fully automated, high-quality, wide-domain performance. Moreover, evaluating systems and measuring the quality of MT remain problematic issues. Still, MT research continues to push the boundaries of the automation-quality-scope continuum. New techniques, such as statistics- and example-based methods, add new capabilities and possibilities to the older linguistics-based methods and theories. This tutorial covers the issues of MT, taking various perspectives and including both the older and the latest theories, techniques, and technology. Course topics include: the history and development of MT, the theoretical foundations of MT, traditional and modern MT techniques, newest MT research, the thorny questions of evaluating MT systems, current MT systems and technology on the market. The lecturers are actively involved in the construction of MT systems and the ongoing activities of the MT world at large.

TABLE OF CONTENTS

PREFACE TO THE STUDENT SESSION PAPERS

These proceedings include the extended abstracts for the poster presentations at the Student Session of the *34th Annual Meeting of the Association for Computational Linguistics.* The goal of the Student Session is to provide a forum for student members to present work in progress, rather than completed work, and to receive feedback from other members of the computational linguistics community, particularly senior researchers. The response to the ACL Student Sessions held during the previous years was very positive. The student authors consistently report that they find the Student Sessions valuable, and answers to questionnaires filled out by ACL members (most recently in 1995) indicate that the audiences find the sessions interesting and of high quality.

Last year, a new format was adopted on a trial basis. Instead of brief ten-minute presentations in parallel sessions, student authors had the opportunity to present their work in a special poster session. Answers to questionnaires indicate that this approach is appreciated by a majority of the respondents, although most of the student respondents showed a preference for talks or a combination of posters and talks over posters alone. This year, the poster format will be tried again and then re-evaluated. Thirty-two papers were submitted to the ACL Student Session in 1996 (as compared with forty-eight submissions last year), and we accepted fourteen of these. We thank all the authors for their submissions, and hope that the reviews provide constructive criticism and encourage them in their research.

We thank all of the reviewers for their detailed and often stimulating reviews of the submissions.

Student members of the ACL 1996 Student Session Program Committee: Johan Bos, *University of the Saarland*; Lidia Fraczak, *Université Paris-Sud*; Pamela Jordan, *University of Pittsburgh*; V. Kṛpāsundar, *SUNY at Buffalo*; Deryle Lonsdale, *Carnegie Mellon University*; Dragomir R. Radev, *Columbia University*; Stefan Riezler, *University of Tübingen*; Eric Ringger, *University of Rochester*; Frank Schilder, *University of Edinburgh*; Matthew Stone, *University of Pennsylvania*; Cynthia A. Thompson, *University of Texas at Austin*; Marc Verhagen, *Brandeis University*; Karen Ward, *Oregon Graduate Institute*; Cheng-Xiang Zhai, *Carnegie Mellon University*.

Non-student members of the Student Session Program Committee: Pierrette Bouillon, *ISSCO/University of Geneva*; Miriam Butt, *University of Stuttgart*; John Carroll, *University of Sussex*; Crit Cremers, *University of Leiden*; Bruce Croft, *University of Massachusetts*; Walter Daelemans, *University of Tilburg*; Douglas Jones, *University of Maryland*; Ellen Riloff, *University of Utah*; Giorgio Satta, *University of Padua*; Ed Stabler, *UCLA*; Leo Wanner, *University of Waterloo*.

Last year's Student Session chairs, Vasileios Hatzivassiloglou and Peter Heeman, were extremely generous with their advice. Finally, we thank Geoffrey Pullum for his help in finding an appropriate space for the poster session.

Mettina Veenstra, *University of Groningen*
Student Session Chair

Christine Doran, *University of Pennsylvania*
Student Session Vice-Chair

STUDENT SESSION TABLE OF CONTENTS

AUTHOR INDEX

STUDENT AUTHOR INDEX

Higher–Order Coloured Unification and Natural Language Semantics

Claire Gardent
Computational Linguistics
Universität des Saarlandes
D–Saarbrücken
claire@coli.uni-sb.de

Michael Kohlhase
Computer Science
Universität des Saarlandes
D–Saarbrücken
kohlhase@cs.uni-sb.de

Abstract

In this paper, we show that Higher–Order Coloured Unification – a form of unification developed for automated theorem proving – provides a general theory for modeling the interface between the interpretation process and other sources of linguistic, non semantic information. In particular, it provides the general theory for the Primary Occurrence Restriction which (Dalrymple et al., 1991)'s analysis called for.

1 Introduction

It is well known that Higher–Order Unification (HOU) can be used to construct the semantics of Natural Language: (Dalrymple et al., 1991) – henceforth, DSP – show that it allows a treatment of VP–Ellipsis which successfully captures the interaction of VPE with quantification and nominal anaphora; (Pulman, 1995; Gardent and Kohlhase, 1996) use HOU to model the interpretation of focus and its interaction with focus sensitive operators, adverbial quantifiers and second occurrence expressions; (Gardent et al., 1996) shows that HOU yields a simple but precise treatment of corrections; Finally, (Pinkal, 1995) uses linear HOU to reconstruct underspecified semantic representations.

However, it is also well known that the HOU approach to NL semantics systematically over–generates and that some general theory of the interface between the interpretation process and other sources of linguistic information is needed in order to avoid this.

In their treatment of VP–ellipsis, DSP introduce an informal restriction to avoid over–generation: the *Primary Occurrence Restriction* (POR). Although this restriction is intuitive and linguistically well–motivated, it does not provide a general theoretical framework for extra–semantic constraints.

In this paper, we argue that *Higher–Order Coloured Unification* (HOCU, (cf. sections 3,6), a restricted form of HOU developed independently for theorem proving, provides the needed general framework. We start out by showing that the HOCU approach allows for a precise and intuitive modeling of DSP's Primary Occurrence Restriction (cf. section 3.1). We then show that the POR can be extended to capture linguistic restrictions on other phenomena (focus, second occurrence expressions and adverbial quantification) provided that the notion of *primary occurrence* is suitably adjusted (cf. section 4). Obviously a treatment of the interplay of these phenomena and their related notion of primary occurrence is only feasible given a precise and well–understood theoretical framework. We illustrate this by an example in section 4.4. Finally, we illustrate the generality of the HOCU framework by using it to encode a completely different constraint, namely Kratzer's binding principle (cf. section 5).

2 Higher–Order Unification and NL semantics

The basic idea underlying the use of HOU for NL semantics is very simple: the typed λ–calculus is used as a semantic representation language while semantically under–specified elements (e.g. anaphors and ellipses) are represented by free variables whose value is determined by solving higher–order equations. For instance, the discourse (1a) has (1b) as a semantic representation where the value of R is given by equation (1c) with solutions (1d) and (1e).

(1) a. *Dan likes golf. Peter does too.*
b. $like(dan,golf) \wedge R(peter)$
c. $like(dan,golf) = R(dan)$
d. $R = \lambda x.\ like(x,golf)$
e. $R = \lambda x.\ like(dan,golf)$

The process of solving such equations is traditionally called unification and can be stated as follows:

given two terms M and N, find a substitution of terms for free variables that will make M and N equal. For first order logic, this problem is decidable and the set of solutions can be represented by a single most general unifier. For the typed λ–calculus, the problem is undecidable, but there is an algorithm which – given a solvable equation – will enumerate a complete set of solutions for this equation (Huet, 1975).

Note that in (1), unification yields a linguistically valid solution (1d) but also an invalid one: (1e). To remedy this shortcoming, DSP propose an informal restriction, the **Primary Occurrence Restriction**:

> Given a labeling of occurrences as either primary or secondary, the POR excludes of the set of linguistically valid solutions, any solution which contains a primary occurrence.

Here, a **primary occurrence** is an occurrence that is *directly associated* with a *source parallel element.* Neither the notion of direct association, nor that of parallelism is given a formal definition; but given an intuitive understanding of these notions, a **source parallel element** is an element of the source (i.e. antecedent) clause which has a parallel counterpart in the target (i.e. elliptic or anaphoric) clause.

To see how this works, consider example (1) again. In this case, *dan* is taken to be a primary occurrence because it represents a source parallel element which is neither anaphoric nor controlled i.e. it is directly associated with a source parallel element. Given this, equation (1c) becomes (2a) with solutions (2b) and (2c) (primary occurrences are underlined). Since (2c) contains a primary occurrence, it is ruled out by the POR and is thus excluded from the set of linguistically valid solutions.

(2) a. $like(\underline{dan}, golf) = R(dan)$
b. $R = \lambda x.like(x, golf)$
c. $R = \lambda x.like(\underline{dan}, golf)$

Although the intuitions underlying the POR are clear, two main objections can be raised. First, the restriction is informal and as such provides no good basis for a mathematical and computational evaluation. As DSP themselves note, a general theory for the POR is called for. Second, their method is a generate–and–test method: all logically valid solutions are generated before those solutions that violate the POR and are linguistically invalid are eliminated. While this is sufficient for a theoretical analysis, for actual computation it would be preferable never to produce these solutions in the first place. In what follows, we present a unification framework which solves both of these problems.

3 Higher–Order Coloured Unification (HOCU)

There is a restricted form of HOU which allows for a natural modeling of DSP's Primary Occurrence Restriction: Higher–Order Coloured Unification developed independently for theorem proving (Hutter and Kohlhase, 1995). This framework uses a variant of the simply typed λ-calculus where symbol occurrences can be annotated with so-called *colours* and substitutions must obey the following constraint:

> For any colour constant c and any c–coloured variable V_{c}, a well-formed coloured substitution must assign to V_{c} a c–monochrome term i.e., a term whose symbols are c–coloured.

3.1 Modeling the Primary Occurrence Restriction

Given this coloured framework, the POR is directly modelled as follows: Primary occurrences are pe-coloured whilst free variables are $\neg\mathsf{pe}$-coloured. For the moment we will just consider the colours pe (primary for ellipsis) and $\neg\mathsf{pe}$ (secondary for ellipsis) as distinct basic colours to keep the presentation simple. Only for the analysis of the interaction of e.g. ellipsis with focus phenomena (cf. section 4.4) do we need a more elaborate formalization, which we will discuss there.

Given the above restriction for well–formed coloured substitutions, such a colouring ensures that any solution containing a primary occurrence is ruled out: free variables are $\neg\mathsf{pe}$-coloured and must be assigned a $\neg\mathsf{pe}$-monochrome term. Hence no substitution will ever contain a primary occurrence (i.e. a pe-coloured symbol). For instance, discourse (1a) above is assigned the semantic representation (3a) and the equation (3b) with unique solution (3c). In contrast, (3d) is not a possible solution since it assigns to an $\neg\mathsf{pe}$-coloured variable, a term containing a pe-coloured symbol i.e. a term that is not $\neg\mathsf{pe}$-monochrome.

(3) a. $like(dan_{\mathsf{pe}}, golf) \wedge R_{\neg\mathsf{pe}}(peter)$
b. $like(dan_{\mathsf{pe}}, golf) = R_{\neg\mathsf{pe}}(dan_{\mathsf{pe}})$
c. $R_{\neg\mathsf{pe}} = \lambda x.like(x, golf)$
d. $R_{\neg\mathsf{pe}} = \lambda x.like(dan_{\mathsf{pe}}, golf)$

3.2 HOCU theory

To be more formal, we presuppose a finite set $\mathcal{C} = \{\mathsf{a}, \mathsf{b}, \mathsf{c}, \mathsf{pe}, \neg\mathsf{pe}, \ldots\}$ of **colour constants** and a countably infinite supply $\mathcal{CV} = \{\mathsf{A}, \mathsf{B}, \ldots\}$ of **colour variables**.

As usual in λ-calculus, the set *wff* of **well-formed formulae** consists of (coloured[1]) constants $c_{\mathsf{a}}, runs_{\mathsf{b}}, runs_{\mathsf{A}}, \ldots$, (possibly uncoloured) variables $x, x_{\mathsf{a}}, y_{\mathsf{b}}, \ldots$ (function) **applications** of the form MN and λ-abstractions of the form $\lambda x.M$. Note that only variables without colours can be abstracted over. We call a formula M c-**monochrome**, if all symbols in M are bound or tagged with c.

We will need the so-called **colour erasure** $|M|$ of M, i.e. the formula obtained from M by erasing all colour annotations in M. We will also use various elementary concepts of the λ-calculus, such as **free** and **bound** occurrences of variables or substitutions without defining them explicitly here. In particular we assume that free variables are coloured in all formulae occuring. We will denote the substitution of a term N for all free occurrences of x in M with $[N/x]M$.

It is crucial for our system that colours annotate symbol occurrences (i.e. colours are not sorts!), in particular, it is intended that different occurrences of symbols carry different colours (e.g. $f(x_{\mathsf{b}}, x_{\mathsf{a}})$) and that symbols that carry different colours are treated differently. This observation leads to the notion of coloured substitutions, that takes the colour information of formulae into account. In contrast to traditional (uncoloured) substitutions, a coloured substitution σ is a pair $\langle \sigma^t, \sigma^c \rangle$, where the **term substitution** σ^t maps coloured variables (i.e. the pair x_{c} of a variable x and the colour c) to formulae of the appropriate type and the **colour substitution** σ^c maps colour variables to colours. In order to be legal (a **$\mathcal{C}$-substitution**) such a mapping σ must obey the following constraints:

- If a and b are different colours, then $|\sigma(x_{\mathsf{a}})| = |\sigma(x_{\mathsf{b}})|$, i.e. the colour erasures have to be equal.
- If $\mathsf{c} \in \mathcal{C}$ is a colour constant, then $\sigma(x_{\mathsf{c}})$ is c-monochrome.

The first condition ensures that the colour erasure of a $\mathcal{C}$-substitution is a well-defined classical substitution of the simply typed λ-calculus. The second condition formalizes the fact that free variables with constant colours stand for monochrome subformulae, whereas colour variables do not constrain the substitutions. This is exactly the trait, that we will exploit in our analysis.

[1]Colours are indicated by subscripts labeling term occurrences; whenever colours are irrelevant, we simply omit them.

Note that $\beta\eta$-reduction in the coloured λ-calculus is just the classical notion, since the bound variables do not carry colour information. Thus we have all the known theoretical results, such as the fact that $\beta\eta$-reduction always terminates producing unique normal forms and that $\beta\eta$-equality can be tested by reducing to normal form and comparing for syntactic equality. This gives us a decidable test for *validity* of an equation.

In contrast to this, higher-order unification tests for *satisfiability* by finding a substitution σ that makes a given equation $M = N$ valid ($\sigma(M) =_{\beta\eta} \sigma(N)$), even if the original equation is not ($M \neq_{\beta\eta} N$). In the coloured λ-calculus the space of (semantic) solutions is further constrained by requiring the solutions to be $\mathcal{C}$-substitutions. Such a substitution is called a **$\mathcal{C}$-unifier** of M and N. In particular, $\mathcal{C}$-unification will only succeed if comparable formulae have unifiable colours. For instance, $intro_{\mathsf{a}}(p_{\mathsf{a}}, j_{\mathsf{b}}, x_{\mathsf{a}})$ unifies with $intro_{\mathsf{a}}(y_{\mathsf{a}}, j_{\mathsf{A}}, s_{\mathsf{a}})$ but not with $intro_{\mathsf{a}}(p_{\mathsf{a}}, j_{\mathsf{a}}, s_{\mathsf{a}})$ because of the colour clash on j.

It is well-known, that in first-order logic (and in certain related forms of feature structures) there is always a most general unifier for any equation that is solvable at all. This is not the case for higher-order (coloured) unification, where variables can range over functions, instead of only individuals. Fortunately, in our case we are not interested in general unification, but we can use the fact that our formulae belong to very restricted syntactic subclasses, for which much better results are known. In particular, the fact that free variables only occur on the left hand side of our equations reduces the problem of finding solutions to higher-order matching, of which decidability has been proven for the subclass of third-order formulae (Dowek, 1992) and is conjectured for the general case. This class, (intuitively allowing only nesting functions as arguments up to depth two) covers all of our examples in this paper. For a discussion of other subclasses of formulae, where higher-order unification is computationally feasible see (Prehofer, 1994).

Some of the equations in the examples have multiple most general solutions, and indeed this multiplicity corresponds to the possibility of multiple different interpretations of the focus constructions. The role of colours in this is to restrict the logically possible solutions to those that are linguistically sound.

4 Linguistic Applications of the POR

In section 3.1, we have seen that HOCU allowed for a simple theoretical rendering of DSP's Primary Occurrence Restriction. But isn't this restriction fairly idiosyncratic? In this section, we show that the restriction which was originally proposed by DSP to model VP–ellipsis, is in fact a very general constraint which far from being idiosyncratic, applies to many different phenomena. In particular, we show that it is necessary for an adequate analysis of focus, second occurrence expressions and adverbial quantification.

Furthermore, we will see that what counts as a primary occurrence differs from one phenomenon to the other (for instance, an occurrence directly associated with focus counts as primary w.r.t focus semantics but not w.r.t to VP–ellipsis interpretation). To account for these differences, some machinery is needed which turns DSP's intuitive idea into a fully–blown theory. Fortunately, the HOCU framework is just this: different colours can be used for different types of primary occurrences and likewise for different types of free variables. In what follows, we show how each phenomenon is dealt with. We then illustrate by an example how their interaction can be accounted for.

4.1 Focus

Since (Jackendoff, 1972), it is commonly agreed that focus affects the semantics and pragmatics of utterances. Under this perspective, **focus** is taken to be the semantic value of a prosodically prominent element. Furthermore, focus is assumed to trigger the formation of an additional semantic value (henceforth, the **Focus Semantic Value** or FSV) which is in essence the set of propositions obtained by making a substitution in the focus position (cf. e.g. (Kratzer, 1991)). For instance, the FSV of (4a)[2] is (4b), the set of formulae of the form *l(j,x)* where x is of type e, and the pragmatic effect of focus is to presuppose that the denotation of this set is under consideration.

(4) a. *Jon likes SARAH*
    b. $\{l(j,x) \mid x \in wff_e\}$

In (Gardent and Kohlhase, 1996), we show that HOU can successfully be used to compute the FSV of an utterance. More specifically, given (part of) an utterance U with semantic representation Sem and foci $F^1 \dots F^n$, we require that the following equation, the **FSV equation**, be solved:

$Sem = Gd(F^1)\dots(F^n)$

On the basis of the Gd value, we then define the FSV, written $\overline{Gd}$, as follows:

Definition 4.1 *(Focus Semantic Value)*
Let Gd be of type $\alpha = \vec{\beta_k} \rightarrow t$ and n be the number of foci ($n \leq k$), then the Focus Semantic Value derivable from Gd, written $\overline{Gd}$, is $\{Gd(t^1 \dots t^n) \mid t^i \in wff_{\beta_i}\}$.

This yields a focus semantic value which is in essence Kratzer's presupposition skeleton. For instance, given (4a) above, the required equation will be $l(j,s) = Gd(s)$ with two possible values for Gd: $\lambda x.l(j,x)$ and $\lambda x.l(j,s)$. Given definition (4.1), (4a) is then assigned two FSVs namely

(5) a. $\overline{Gd} = \{l(j,x) \mid x \in wff_e\}$
    b. $\overline{Gd} = \{l(j,s) \mid x \in wff_e\}$

That is, the HOU treatment of focus over–generates: (5a) is an appropriate FSV, but not (5b). Clearly though, the POR can be used to rule out (5b) if we assume that occurrences that are directly associated with a focus are primary occurrences. To capture the fact that those primary occurrences are different from DSP's primary occurrences when dealing with ellipsis, we colour occurrences that are directly associated with focus (rather than a source parallel element in the case of ellipsis) pf. Consequently, we require that the variable representing the FSV be ¬pf coloured, that is, its value may not contain any pf term. Under these assumptions, the equation for (4a) will be (6a) which has for unique solution (6b).

(6) a. $l(j,s_{\mathsf{pf}}) = FSV_{\neg\mathsf{pf}}(s_{\mathsf{pf}})$
    b. $FSV_{\neg\mathsf{pf}} = \lambda x.l(j,x)$

4.2 Second Occurrence Expressions

A second occurrence expression (SOE) is a partial or complete repetition of the preceding utterance and is characterised by a de-accenting of the repeating part (Bartels, 1995). For instance, (7b) is an SOE whose repeating part *only likes Mary* is deaccented.

(7) a. *Jon only likes MARY.*
    b. *No, PETER only likes Mary.*

In (Gardent, 1996; Gardent et al., 1996) we show that SOEs are advantageously viewed as involving a deaccented anaphor whose semantic representation must unify with that of its antecedent. Formally, this is captured as follows. Let $SSem$ and $TSem$ be the semantic representation of the source and target clause respectively, and $TP^1 \dots TP^n, SP^1 \dots SP^n$

[2]Focus is indicated using upper–case.

be the target and source parallel elements[3], then the interpretation of an SOE must respect the following equations:

$An(SP^1, \ldots, SP^n) = SSem$
$An(TP^1, \ldots, TP^n) = TSem$

Given this proposal and some further assumptions about the semantics of *only*, the analysis of (7b) involves the following equations:

(8) $An(j) = \forall P[P \in \{\lambda x.like(x,y) \mid y \in wff_e\} \wedge P(j) \rightarrow P = \lambda x.like(x,m)]$
$An(p) = \forall P[P \in FSV \wedge P(p) \rightarrow P = \lambda x.like(x,m)]$

Resolution of the first equation then yields two solutions:

$An = \lambda z \forall P[P \in \{\lambda x.like(x,y) \mid y \in wff_e\} \wedge P(z) \rightarrow P = \lambda x.like(x,m)]$
$An = \lambda z \forall P[P \in \{\lambda x.like(x,y) \mid y \in wff_e\} \wedge P(j) \rightarrow P = \lambda x.like(x,m)]$

Since An represents the semantic information shared by target and source clause, the second solution is clearly incorrect given that it contains information (j) that is specific to the source clause. Again, the POR will rule out the incorrect solutions, whereby contrary to the VP–ellipsis case, all occurrences that are directly associated with parallel elements (i.e. not just source parallel elements) are taken to be primary occurrences. The distinction is implemented by colouring all occurrences that are directly associated with parallel element ps, whereas the corresponding free variable (An) is coloured as ¬ps. Given these constraints, the first equation in (8) is reformulated as:

$An_{\neg ps}(j_{ps}) = \forall P[P \in \{\lambda x.like(x,y) \mid y \in wff_e\} \wedge P(j_{ps}) \rightarrow P = \lambda x.like(x,m)]$

with the unique well–coloured solution

$An_{\neg ps} = \lambda z.\forall P[P \in \{\lambda x.like(x,y) \mid y \in wff_e\} \wedge P(z) \rightarrow P = \lambda x.like(x,m)]$

4.3 Adverbial quantification

Finally, let us briefly examine some cases of adverbial quantification. Consider the following example from (von Fintel, 1995):

Tom always takes SUE to Al's mother.
Yes, and he always takes Sue to JO's mother.

In (Gardent and Kohlhase, 1996), we suggest that such cases are SOEs, and thus can be treated as involving a deaccented anaphor (in this case, the anaphor *he always takes Sue to _'s mother*). Given some standard assumptions about the semantics of *always*, the equations constraining the interpretation An of this anaphor are:

$An(al) = always$ *(Tom take x to al's mother) (Tom take Sue to al's mother)*
$An(jo) = always$ FSV *(Tom take Sue to Jo's mother)*

Consider the first equation. If An is the semantics shared by target and source clause, then the only possible value for An is

$\lambda z.always$ *(Tom take x to z's mother) (Tom take Sue to z's mother)*

where both occurrences of the parallel element m have been abstracted over. In contrast, the following solutions for An are incorrect.

$\lambda z.always$ *(Tom take x to al's mother) (Tom take Sue to z's mother)*
$\lambda z.always$ *(Tom take x to al's mother) (Tom take Sue to al's mother)*
$\lambda z.always$ *(Tom take x to z's mother) (Tom take Sue to al's mother)*

Once again, we see that the POR is a necessary restriction: by labeling as primary, all occurrences representing a parallel element, it can be ensured that only the first solution is generated.

4.4 Interaction of constraints

Perhaps the most convincing way of showing the need for a theory of colours (rather than just an informal constraint) is by looking at the interaction of constraints between various phenomena. Consider the following discourse

(9) a. *Jon likes SARAH*
b. *Peter does too*

Such a discourse presents us with a case of interaction between ellipsis and focus thereby raising the question of how DSP' POR for ellipsis should interact with our POR for focus.

As remarked in section 3.1, we have to interpret the colour ¬pe as the concept of being not primary for ellipsis, which includes pf (primary for focus). In order to make this approach work formally, we have to extend the supply of colours by allowing boolean combinations of colour constants. The semantics of these ground colour formula is that of propositional logic, where ¬d is taken to be equivalent to the disjunction of all other colour constants.

Consequently we have to generalize the second condition on $\mathcal{C}$-substitutions

- For all colour annotations d of symbols in $\sigma(x_c)$ $d \models c$ in propositional logic.

Thus $X_{\neg d}$ can be instantiated with any coloured formula that does not contain the colour d. The

[3] As in DSP, the identification of parallel elements is taken as given.

HOCU algorithm is augmented with suitable rules for boolean constraint satisfaction for colour equations.

The equations resulting from the interpretation of (9b) are:

$l(j_{\mathsf{pe}}, s_{\mathsf{pf}}) = R_{\neg\mathsf{pe}}(j_{\mathsf{pe}})$
$R_{\neg\mathsf{pe}}(p) = FSV_{\neg\mathsf{pf}}(F)$

where the first equation determines the interpretation of the ellipsis whereas the second fixes the value of the FSV. Resolution of the first equation yields the value $\lambda x.l(x, s_{\mathsf{pf}})$ for $R_{\neg\mathsf{pe}}$. As required, no other solution is possible given the colour constraints; in particular $\lambda x.l(j_{\mathsf{pe}}, s_{\mathsf{pf}})$ is not a valid solution. The value of $R_{\neg\mathsf{pe}}(j_{\mathsf{pe}})$ is now $l(p_{\mathsf{pe}}, s_{\mathsf{pf}})$ so that the second equation is[4]:

$l(p, s_{\mathsf{pf}}) = FSV_{\neg\mathsf{pf}}(F)$

Under the indicated colour constraints, three solutions are possible:

$FSV_{\neg\mathsf{pf}} = \lambda x.l(p, x), F = s_{\mathsf{pf}}$
$FSV_{\neg\mathsf{pf}} = \lambda O.O(p), F = \lambda x.l(x, s_{\mathsf{pf}})$
$FSV_{\neg\mathsf{pf}} = \lambda X.X, F = l(p, s_{\mathsf{pf}})$

The first solution yields a *narrow focus* reading (only *SARAH* is in focus) whereas the second and the third yield *wide focus* interpretations corresponding to a VP and an S focus respectively. That is, not only do colours allow us to correctly capture the interaction of the two PORs restricting the interpretation of ellipsis of focus, they also permit a natural modeling of focus projection (cf. (Jackendoff, 1972)).

5 Another constraint

An additional argument in favour of a general theory of colours lies in the fact that constraints that are distinct from the POR need to be encoded to prevent HOU analyses from over-generating. In this section, we present one such constraint (the so-called *weak-crossover constraint*) and show how it can be implemented within the HOCU framework.

In essence, the main function of the POR is to ensure that some occurrence occuring in an equation appears as a bound variable in the term assigned by substitution to the free variable occurring in this equation. However, there are cases where the *dual* constraint must be enforced: a term occurrence appearing in an equation must appear unchanged in the term assigned by substitution to the free variable occurring in this equation. The following example illustrates this.

(Chomsky, 1976) observes that focused NPs pattern with quantified and wh–NPs with respect to pronominal anaphora: when the quantified/wh/focused NP precedes and c–commands the pronoun, this pronoun yields an ambiguity between a co-referential and a bound–variable reading. This is illustrated in example

(10) *We only expected HIM$_i$ to claim that he$_i$ was brilliant*

where the presence of the pronoun he_i gives rise to two possible FSVs[5]

$FSV = \{\lambda x.ex(x, y, i) \mid y \in \mathit{wff}_e\}$
$FSV = \{\lambda x.ex(x, y, y) \mid y \in \mathit{wff}_e\}$

thus allowing two different readings: the **corefential** or **strict** reading

$\forall P[P \in \{\lambda x.ex(x, y, i) \mid y \in \mathit{wff}_e\}$
$\quad \wedge P(we) \rightarrow P = \lambda x.ex(x, i, i)]$

and the **bound-variable** or **sloppy** reading.

$\forall P[P \in \{\lambda x.ex(x, y, y)) \mid y \in \mathit{wff}_e\}$
$\quad \wedge P(we) \rightarrow P = \lambda x.ex(x, i, i))]$

In contrast, if the quantified/wh/focused NP does not precede and c–command the pronoun, as in

(11) *We only expected him$_i$ to claim that HE$_i$ was brilliant*

there is no ambiguity and the pronoun can only give rise to a co-referential interpretation. For instance, given (11) only one reading arises

$\forall P[P \in \{\lambda x.ex(x, i, y) \mid y \in \mathit{wff}_e\}$
$\quad \wedge P(we) \rightarrow P = \lambda x.ex(x, i, i)]$

where the FSV is $\{\lambda x.ex(x, i, y) \mid y \in \mathit{wff}_e\}$.

To capture this data, Government and Binding analyses postulate first, that the antecedent is raised by quantifier raising and second, that pronouns that are c–commanded and preceded by their antecedent are represented either as a λ–bound variable or as a constant whereas other pronouns can only be represented by a constant (cf. e.g. (Kratzer, 1991)'s *binding principle*). Using HOCU, we can model this restriction directly. As before, the focus term is pf- and the *FSV* variable ¬pf-coloured. Furthermore, we assume that pronouns that are preceded and c–commanded by a quantified/wh/focused antecedent are variable coloured whereas other pronouns are ¬pf-coloured. Finally, all other terms are taken to

[4]Note that this equation falls out of our formal system in that it is untyped and thus cannot be solved by the algorithm described in section 6 (as the solutions will show, we have to allow for *FSV* and *F* to have different types). However, it seems to be a routine exercise to augment HOU algorithms that can cope with type variables like (Hustadt, 1991; Dougherty, 1993) with the colour methods from (Hutter and Kohlhase, 1995).

[5]We abbreviate $exp(x, cl(y, blt(i)))$ to $ex(x, y, i)$ to increase legibility.

be ¬pf-coloured. Given these assumptions, the representation for (10) is $ex_{\neg pf}(we_{\neg pf}, i_{pf}, i_{A})$ and the corresponding FSV equation

$$R_{\neg pf}(i_{pf}) = \lambda x.ex_{\neg pf}(x, i_{pf}, i_{A})$$

has two possible solutions

$$R_{\neg pf} = \lambda y.\lambda x.ex_{\neg pf}(x, y, i_{\neg pf})$$
$$R_{\neg pf} = \lambda y.\lambda x.ex_{\neg pf}(x, y, x)$$

In contrast, the representation for (11) is $ex_{\neg pf}(we_{\neg pf}, i_{\neg pf}, i_{pf})$ and the equation is

$$R_{\neg pf}(i_{pf}) = \lambda x.ex_{\neg pf}(x, i_{\neg pf}, i_{pf})$$

with only one well–coloured solution

$$R_{\neg pf} = \lambda y.\lambda x.ex_{\neg pf}(x, i_{\neg pf}, y)$$

Importantly, given the indicated colour constraints, no other solutions are admissible. Intuitively, there are two reasons for this. First, the definition of coloured substitutions ensures that the term assigned to $R_{\neg pf}$ is ¬pf-monochrome. In particular, this forces any occurrences of i_{pf} to appear as a bound variable in the value assigned to $R_{\neg pf}$ whereas i_{A} can appear either as $i_{\neg pf}$ (a colour variable unifies with any colour constant) or as a bound variable – this in effect models the sloppy/strict ambiguity. Second, a colour constant only unifies with itself. This in effect rules out the bound variable reading in (11): if the $i_{\neg pf}$ occurrence were to become a bound variable, the value of $R_{\neg pf}$ would then $\lambda y.\lambda x.ex_{\neg pf}(x, y, y)$. But then by β–reduction, $R_{\neg pf}(i_{pf})$ would be $\lambda x.ex_{\neg pf}(x, i_{pf}, i_{pf})$ which does not unify with the right hand side of the original equation i.e $\lambda x.ex_{\neg pf}(x, i_{\neg pf}, i_{pf})$.

For a more formal account of how the unifiers are calculated see section 6.1.

6 Calculating Coloured Unifiers

Since the HOCU is the principal computational device of the analysis in this paper, we will now try to give an intuition for the functioning of the algorithm. For a formal account including all details and proofs see (Hutter and Kohlhase, 1995).

Just as in the case of unification for first-order terms, the algorithm is a process of recursive decomposition and variable elimination that transform sets of equations into solved forms. Since $\mathcal{C}$-substitutions have two parts, a term– and a colour part, we need two kinds ($M =^t N$ for term equations and $c =^c d$ for colour equations). Sets $\mathcal{E}$ of equations in solved form (i.e. where all equations are of the form $x = M$ such that the variable x does not occur anywhere else in M or $\mathcal{E}$) have a unique most general $\mathcal{C}$-unifier $\sigma_{\mathcal{E}}$ that also $\mathcal{C}$-unifies the initial equation.

There are several rules that decompose the syntactic structure of formulae, we will only present two of them. The rule for abstractions transforms equations of the form $\lambda x.A =^t \lambda y.B$ to $[c/x]A =^t [c/y]B$, and $\lambda x.A =^t B$ to $[c/x]A =^t Bc$ where c is a new constant, which may not appear in any solution. The rule for applications decomposes $h_{a}(s^1, \ldots, s^n) =^t h_{b}(t^1, \ldots, t^n)$ to the set $\{a =^c b, s^1 =^t t^1, \ldots, s^n =^t t^n\}$, provided that h is a constant. Furthermore equations are kept in $\beta\eta$-normal form.

The variable elimination process for colour variables is very simple, it allows to transform a set $\mathcal{E} \cup \{\mathsf{A} =^c \mathsf{d}\}$ of equations to $[\mathsf{d}/\mathsf{A}]\mathcal{E} \cup \{\mathsf{A} =^c \mathsf{d}\}$, making the equation $\{\mathsf{A} =^c \mathsf{d}\}$ solved in the result. For the formula case, elimination is not that simple, since we have to ensure that $|\sigma(x_{A})| = |\sigma(x_{B})|$ to obtain a $\mathcal{C}$-substitution σ. Thus we cannot simply transform a set $\mathcal{E} \cup \{x_{d} =^t M\}$ into $[M/x_{d}]\mathcal{E} \cup \{x_{d} =^t M\}$, since this would (incorrectly) solve the equations $\{x_{c} = f_{c}, x_{d} = g_{d}\}$. The correct variable elimination rule transforms $\mathcal{E} \cup \{x_{d} =^t M\}$ into $\sigma(\mathcal{E}) \cup \{x_{d} =^t M, x_{c_1} = M^1, \ldots, x_{c_n} =^t M^n\}$, where c_i are all colours of the variable x occurring in M and $\mathcal{E}$, the M^i are appropriately coloured variants (same colour erasure) of M, and σ is the $\mathcal{C}$-substitution that eliminates all occurrences of x from $\mathcal{E}$.

Due to the presence of function variables, systematic application of these rules can terminate with equations of the form $x_{c}(s^1, \ldots, s^n) =^t h_{d}(t^1, \ldots, t^m)$. Such equations can neither be further decomposed, since this would loose unifiers (if G and F are variables, then $Ga = Fb$ as a solution $\lambda x.c$ for F and G, but $\{F = G, a = b\}$ is unsolvable), nor can the right hand side be substituted for x as in a variable elimination rule, since the types would clash. Let us consider the uncoloured equation $x(a) =^t a$ which has the solutions $(\lambda z.a)$ and $(\lambda z.z)$ for x.

The standard solution for finding a complete set of solutions in this so-called **flex/rigid** situation is to substitute a term for x that will enable decomposition to be applicable afterwards. It turns out that for finding all $\mathcal{C}$-unifiers it is sufficient to bind x to terms of the same type as x (otherwise the unifier would be ill-typed) and compatible colour (otherwise the unifier would not be a $\mathcal{C}$-substitution) that either

- have the same head as the right hand side; the so-called **imitation** solution ($\lambda z.a$ in our example) or
- where the head is a bound variable that enables the head of one of the arguments of x to become head; the so-called **projection** binding ($\lambda z.z$).

In order to get a better understanding of the situation let us reconsider our example using colours.

$x(a_c) = a_d$. For the imitation solution $(\lambda z.a_d)$ we "imitate" the right hand side, so the colour on a must be d. For the projection solution we instantiate $(\lambda z.z)$ for x and obtain $(\lambda z.z)a_c$, which β-reduces to a_c. We see that this "lifts" the constant a_c from the argument position to the top. Incidentally, the projection is only a $\mathcal{C}$-unifier of our coloured example, if c and d are identical.

Fortunately, the choice of instantiations can be further restricted to the most general terms in the categories above. If x_c has type $\overline{\beta_n} \rightarrow \alpha$ and h_d has type $\overline{\gamma_m} \rightarrow \alpha$, then these so-called **general bindings** have the following form:

$$\mathcal{G}_d^h = \lambda z^{\alpha_1} \ldots z^{\alpha_n}.h_d(H_{e_1}^1(\overline{z}), \ldots, H_{e_m}^m(\overline{z}))$$

where the H^i are new variables of type $\overline{\beta_n} \rightarrow \gamma_i$ and the e_i are either distinct colour variables (if $c \in \mathcal{CV}$) or $e_i = d = c$ (if $c \in \mathcal{C}$). If h is one of the bound variables z^{α_i}, then $\mathcal{G}_d^h$ is called an **imitation binding**, and else, (h is a constant or a free variable), a **projection binding**.

The general rule for flex/rigid equations transforms $\{x_c(s^1, \ldots, s^n) =^t h_d(t^1, \ldots, t^m)\}$ into $\{x_c(s^1, \ldots, s^n) =^t h_d(t^1, \ldots, t^m), x_c =^t \mathcal{G}_c^h\}$, which in essence only fixes a particular binding for the head variable x_c. It turns out (for details and proofs see (Hutter and Kohlhase, 1995)) that these general bindings suffice to solve all flex/rigid situations, possibly at the cost of creating new flex/rigid situations after elimination of the variable x_c and decomposition of the changed equations (the elimination of x changes $x_c(s^1, \ldots, s^n)$ to $\mathcal{G}_c^h(s^1, \ldots, s^n)$ which has head h).

6.1 Example

To fortify our intuition on calculating higher-order coloured unifiers let us reconsider examples (10) and (11) with the equations

$R_{\neg pf}(i_{pf}) =^t \lambda x.ex_{\neg pf}(x, i_{pf}, i_A)$
$R_{\neg pf}(i_{pf}) =^t \lambda x.ex_{\neg pf}(x, i_{\neg pf}, i_{pf})$

We will develop the derivation of the solutions for the first equations (10) and point out the differences for the second (11). As a first step, the first equation is decomposed to

$R_{\neg pf}(i_{pf}, c) =^t ex_{\neg pf}(c, i_{pf}, i_A)$

where c is a new constant. Since $R_{\neg pf}$ is a variable, we are in a flex/rigid situation and have the possibilities of projection and imitation. The projection bindings $\lambda xy.x$ and $\lambda xy.y$ for $R_{\neg pf}$ would lead us to the equations $i_{pf} =^t ex_{\neg pf}(c, i_{pf}, i_A)$ and $c =^t ex_{\neg pf}(c, i_{pf}, i_A)$, which are obviously unsolvable, since the head constants i_{pf} (and c resp.) and $ex_{\neg pf}$ clash[6]. So we can only bind $R_{\neg pf}$ to the imitation binding $\lambda yx.ex_{\neg pf}(H_{\neg pf}^1(y,x), H_{\neg pf}^2(y,x), H^3(y,x))$. Now, we can directly eliminate the variable $R_{\neg pf}$, since there are no other variants. The resulting equation

$$\begin{aligned} & ex_{\neg pf}(H_{\neg pf}^1(i_{pf}, c), H_{\neg pf}^2(i_{pf}, c), H^3(i_{pf}, c)) \\ =^t\ & ex_{\neg pf}(c, i_{pf}, i_A) \end{aligned}$$

can be decomposed to the equations

$$(17)\quad \begin{aligned} H_{\neg pf}^1(i_{pf}, c) &=^t c \\ H_{\neg pf}^2(i_{pf}, c) &=^t i_{pf} \\ H_{\neg pf}^3(i_{pf}, c) &=^t i_A \end{aligned}$$

Let us first look at the first equation; in this flex/rigid situation, only the projection binding $\lambda zw.w$ can be applied, since the imitation binding $\lambda zw.c$ contains the forbidden constant c and the other projection leads to a clash. This solves the equation, since $(\lambda zw.w)(i_{pf}, c)$ β-reduces to c, giving the trivial equation $c =^t c$ which can be deleted by the decomposition rules.

Similarly, in the second equation, the projection binding $\lambda zw.z$ for H^2 solves the equation, while the second projection clashes and the imitation binding $\lambda zw.i_{pf}$ is not $\neg$pf-monochrome. Thus we are left with the third equation, where both imitation and projection bindings yield legal solutions:

- The imitation binding for $H_{\neg pf}^3$ is $\lambda zw.i_{\neg pf}$, and not $\lambda zw.i_A$, as one is tempted to believe, since it has to be $\neg$pf-monochrome. Thus we are left with $i_{\neg pf} =^t i_A$, which can (uniquely) be solved by the colour substitution [$\neg$pf/A].
- If we bind $H_{\neg pf}^3$ to $\lambda zw.z$, then we are left with $i_{pf} =^t i_A$, which can (uniquely) be solved by the colour substitution [pf/A].

If we collect all instantiations, we arrive at exactly the two possible solutions for $R_{\neg pf}$ in the original equations, which we had claimed in section 5:

$R_{\neg pf} = \lambda yx.ex_{\neg pf}(x, y, i_{\neg pf})$
$R_{\neg pf} = \lambda yx.ex_{\neg pf}(x, y, x)$

Obviously both of them solve the equation and furthermore, none is more general than the other, since $i_{\neg pf}$ cannot be inserted for the variable x in the second unifier (which would make it more general than the first), since x is bound.

In the case of (11) the equations corresponding to (17) are $H_{\neg pf}^1(c, i_{pf}) =^t c$, $H_{\neg pf}^2(c, i_{pf}) =^t i_{\neg pf}$ and $H_{\neg pf}^3(i_{pf}) =^t i_{pf}$. Given the discussion above, it is immediate to see that $H_{\neg pf}^1$ has to be instantiated with the projection binding $\lambda zw.w$, H^2 with the imitation

[6]For (11) we have the same situation. Here the corresponding equation is $i_{pf} =^t ex_{\neg pf}(c, i_{\neg pf}, i_{pf})$.

binding $\lambda zw.i_{\neg\mathsf{pf}}$, since the projection binding leads to a colour clash ($i_{\neg\mathsf{pf}} =^t i_{\mathsf{pf}}$) and finally $H^3_{\neg\mathsf{pf}}$ has to be bound to the projection binding $\lambda zw.z$, since the imitation binding $\lambda zw.i_{\mathsf{pf}}$ is not ¬pf-monochrome. Collecting the bindings, we arrive at the unique solution $R_{\neg\mathsf{pf}} = \lambda yx.ex_{\neg\mathsf{pf}}(x, i_{\neg\mathsf{pf}}, x)$.

7 Conclusion

Higher–Order Unification has been shown to be a powerful tool for constructing the interpretation of NL. In this paper, we have argued that Higher–Order Coloured Unification allows a precise specification of the interface between semantic interpretation and other sources of linguistic information, thus preventing over–generation. We have substantiated this claim by specifying the linguistic, extra–semantic constraints regulating the interpretation of VP–ellipsis, focus, SOEs, adverbial quantification and pronouns whose antecedent is a focused NP.

Other phenomena for which the HOCU approach seems particularly promising are phenomena in which the semantic interpretation process is obviously constrained by the other sources of linguistic information. In particular, it would be interesting to see whether coloured unification can appropriately model the complex interaction of constraints governing the interpretation and acceptability of gapping on the one hand, and sloppy/strict ambiguity on the other.

Another interesting research direction would be the development and implementation of a monostratal grammar for anaphors whose interpretation are determined by coloured unification. Colours are tags which decorate a semantic representation thereby constraining the unification process; on the other hand, there are also the reflex of linguistic, non-semantic (e.g. syntactic or prosodic) information. A full grammar implementation would make this connection more precise.

8 Acknowledgements

The work reported in this paper was funded by the Deutsche Forschungsgemeinschaft (DFG) in Sonderforschungsbereich SFB–378, Project C2 (LISA).

References

Christine Bartels. 1995. Second occurrence test. Ms.

Noam Chomsky. 1976. Conditions on rules in grammar. *Linguistic Analysis*, 2(4):303–351.

Mary Dalrymple, Stuart Shieber, and Fernando Pereira. 1991. Ellipsis and higher-order-unification. *Linguistics and Philosophy*, 14:399–452.

Daniel Dougherty. 1993. Higher-order unification using combinators. *Theoretical Computer Science B*, 114(2):273–298.

Gilles Dowek. 1992. Third order matching is decidable. In *Proc. LICS92*, pages 2–10. IEEE Computer Society Press.

Claire Gardent and Michael Kohlhase. 1996. Focus and higher–order unification. In *Proc. COLING96* forthcoming.

Claire Gardent, Michael Kohlhase, and Noor van Leusen. 1996. Corrections and higher–order unification. CLAUS report 77, University of Saarland.

Claire Gardent. 1996. Anaphores parallèles et techniques de résolution. *Langages.*

Gérard Huet. 1975. A unification algorithm for typed λ–calculus. *Theoretical Computer Science 1*, pages 27–57.

Ulrich Hustadt. 1991. A complete transformation system for polymorphic higher-order unification. Technical Report MPI-I-91-228, MPI Informatik, Saarbrücken, Germany.

Dieter Hutter and Michael Kohlhase. 1995. A coloured version of the λ-calculus. SEKI-Report SR-95-05, Universität des Saarlandes.

Ray S. Jackendoff. 1972. *Semantic Interpretation in Generative Grammar.* The MIT Press.

Angelika Kratzer. 1991. The representation of focus. In Arnim van Stechow and Dieter Wunderlich, editors, *Semantik: Ein internationales Handbuch der zeitgenoessischen Forschung.* Berlin: Walter de Gruyter.

Manfred Pinkal. 1995. Radical underspecification. In *The 10th Amsterdam Colloquium.*

Christian Prehofer. 1994. Decidable higher-order unification problems. In Alan Bundy, editor, *Proc. CADE94*, LNAI, pages 635–649, Nancy, France.

Steve G. Pulman. 1995. Higher-order unification and the interpretation of focus. Paper submitted for publication.

Kai von Fintel. 1995. A minimal theory of adverbial quantification. Unpublished draft Ms. MIT, Cambridge, March.

A Model-Theoretic Framework for Theories of Syntax

James Rogers
Institute for Research in Cognitive Science
University of Pennsylvania
Suite 400C, 3401 Walnut Street
Philadelphia, PA 19104
jrogers@linc.cis.upenn.edu

Abstract

A natural next step in the evolution of constraint-based grammar formalisms from rewriting formalisms is to abstract fully away from the details of the grammar mechanism—to express syntactic theories purely in terms of the properties of the class of structures they license. By focusing on the structural properties of languages rather than on mechanisms for generating or checking structures that exhibit those properties, this model-theoretic approach can offer simpler and significantly clearer expression of theories and can potentially provide a uniform formalization, allowing disparate theories to be compared on the basis of those properties. We discuss $L^2_{K,P}$, a monadic second-order logical framework for such an approach to syntax that has the distinctive virtue of being superficially expressive—supporting direct statement of most linguistically significant syntactic properties—but having well-defined strong generative capacity—languages are definable in $L^2_{K,P}$ iff they are strongly context-free. We draw examples from the realms of GPSG and GB.

1 Introduction

Generative grammar and formal language theory share a common origin in a procedural notion of grammars: the grammar formalism provides a general mechanism for recognizing or generating languages while the grammar itself specializes that mechanism for a specific language. At least initially there was hope that this relationship would be informative for linguistics, that by characterizing the natural languages in terms of language-theoretic complexity one would gain insight into the structural regularities of those languages. Moreover, the fact that language-theoretic complexity classes have dual automata-theoretic characterizations offered the prospect that such results might provide abstract models of the human language faculty, thereby not just identifying these regularities, but actually accounting for them.

Over time, the two disciplines have gradually become estranged, principally due to a realization that the structural properties of languages that characterize natural languages may well not be those that can be distinguished by existing language-theoretic complexity classes. Thus the insights offered by formal language theory might actually be misleading in guiding theories of syntax. As a result, the emphasis in generative grammar has turned from formalisms with restricted generative capacity to those that support more natural expression of the observed regularities of languages. While a variety of distinct approaches have developed, most of them can be characterized as *constraint based*—the formalism (or formal framework) provides a class of structures and a means of precisely stating constraints on their form, the linguistic theory is then expressed as a system of constraints (or principles) that characterize the class of well-formed analyses of the strings in the language.[1]

As the study of the formal properties of classes of structures defined in such a way falls within domain of Model Theory, it's not surprising that treatments of the meaning of these systems of constraints are typically couched in terms of formal logic (Kasper and Rounds, 1986; Moshier and Rounds, 1987; Kasper and Rounds, 1990; Gazdar et al., 1988; Johnson, 1988; Smolka, 1989; Dawar and Vijay-Shanker, 1990; Carpenter, 1992; Keller, 1993; Rogers and Vijay-Shanker, 1994).

While this provides a model-theoretic interpretation of the systems of constraints produced by these formalisms, those systems are typically built by derivational processes that employ extra-logical mechanisms to combine constraints. More recently, it has become clear that in many cases these mechanisms can be replaced with ordinary logical operations. (See, for instance:

[1]This notion of *constraint-based* includes not only the obvious formalisms, but the formal framework of GB as well.

Johnson (1989), Stabler, Jr. (1992), Cornell (1992), Blackburn, Gardent, and Meyer-Viol (1993), Blackburn and Meyer-Viol (1994), Keller (1993), Rogers (1994), Kracht (1995), and, anticipating all of these, Johnson and Postal (1980).) This approach abandons the notions of grammar mechanism and derivation in favor of defining languages as classes of more or less ordinary mathematical structures axiomatized by sets of more or less ordinary logical formulae. A grammatical theory expressed within such a framework is just the set of logical consequences of those axioms. This step completes the detachment of generative grammar from its procedural roots. Grammars, in this approach, are purely declarative definitions of a class of structures, completely independent of mechanisms to generate or check them. While it is unlikely that every theory of syntax with an explicit derivational component can be captured in this way,[2] for those that can the logical re-interpretation frequently offers a simplified statement of the theory and clarifies its consequences.

But the accompanying loss of language-theoretic complexity results is unfortunate. While such results may not be useful in guiding syntactic theory, they are not irrelevant. The nature of language-theoretic complexity hierarchies is to classify languages on the basis of their structural properties. The languages in a class, for instance, will typically exhibit certain closure properties (e.g., pumping lemmas) and the classes themselves admit normal forms (e.g., representation theorems). While the linguistic significance of individual results of this sort is open to debate, they at least loosely parallel typical linguistic concerns: closure properties state regularities that are exhibited by the languages in a class, normal forms express generalizations about their structure. So while these may not be the right results, they are not entirely the wrong *kind* of results. Moreover, since these classifications are based on structural properties and the structural properties of natural language can be studied more or less directly, there is a reasonable expectation of finding empirical evidence falsifying a hypothesis about language-theoretic complexity of natural languages if such evidence exists.

Finally, the fact that these complexity classes have automata-theoretic characterizations means that results concerning the complexity of natural languages will have implications for the nature of the human language faculty. These automata-theoretic characterizations determine, along one axis, the types of resources required to generate or recognize the languages in a class. The regular languages, for instance, can be characterized by finite-state (string) automata—these languages can be processed using a fixed amount of memory. The context-sensitive languages, on the other had, can be characterized by linear-bounded automata—they can be processed using an amount of memory proportional to the length of the input. The context-free languages are probably best characterized by finite-state tree automata—these correspond to recognition by a collection of processes, each with a fixed amount of memory, where the number of processes is linear in the length of the input and all communication between processes is completed at the time they are spawned. As a result, while these results do not necessarily offer abstract models of the human language faculty (since the complexity results do not claim to characterize the human languages, just to classify them), they do offer lower bounds on certain abstract properties of that faculty. In this way, generative grammar in concert with formal language theory offers insight into a deep aspect of human cognition—syntactic processing—on the basis of observable behavior—the structural properties of human languages.

In this paper we discuss an approach to defining theories of syntax based on $L^2_{K,P}$ (Rogers, 1994), a monadic second-order language that has well-defined generative capacity: sets of finite trees are definable within $L^2_{K,P}$ iff they are strongly context-free in a particular sense. While originally introduced as a means of establishing language-theoretic complexity results for constraint-based theories, this language has much to recommend it as a general framework for theories of syntax in its own right. Being a monadic second-order language it can capture the (pure) modal languages of much of the existing model-theoretic syntax literature directly; having a signature based on the traditional linguistic relations of domination, immediate domination, linear precedence, etc. it can express most linguistic principles transparently; and having a clear characterization in terms of generative capacity, it serves to re-establish the close connection between generative grammar and formal language theory that was lost in the move away from phrase-structure grammars. Thus, with this framework we get both the advantages of the model-theoretic approach with respect to naturalness and clarity in expressing linguistic principles and the advantages of the grammar-based approach with respect to language-theoretic complexity results.

We look, in particular, at the definitions of a single aspect of each of GPSG and GB. The first of these, Feature Specification Defaults in GPSG, are widely assumed to have an inherently dynamic character. In addition to being purely declarative, our reformalization is considerably simplified wrt the definition

[2]Whether there are theories that cannot be captured, at least without explicitly encoding the derivations, is an open question of considerable theoretical interest, as is the question of what empirical consequences such an essential dynamic character might have.

in Gazdar et al. (1985),[3] and does not share its misleading dynamic flavor.[4] We offer this as an example of how re-interpretations of this sort can inform the original theory. In the second example we sketch a definition of chains in GB. This, again, captures a presumably dynamic aspect of the original theory in a static way. Here, though, the main significance of the definition is that it forms a component of a full-scale treatment of a GB theory of English S- and D-Structure within $L^2_{K,P}$. This full definition establishes that the theory we capture licenses a strongly context-free language. More importantly, by examining the limitations of this definition of chains, and in particular the way it fails for examples of non-context-free constructions, we develop a characterization of the context-free languages that is quite natural in the realm of GB. This suggests that the apparent mismatch between formal language theory and natural languages may well have more to do with the unnaturalness of the traditional diagnostics than a lack of relevance of the underlying structural properties.

Finally, while GB and GPSG are fundamentally distinct, even antagonistic, approaches to syntax, their translation into the model-theoretic terms of $L^2_{K,P}$ allows us to explore the similarities between the theories they express as well as to delineate actual distinctions between them. We look briefly at two of these issues.

Together these examples are chosen to illustrate the main strengths of the model-theoretic approach, at least as embodied in $L^2_{K,P}$, as a framework for studying theories of syntax: a focus on structural properties themselves, rather than on mechanisms for specifying them or for generating or checking structures that exhibit them, and a language that is expressive enough to state most linguistically significant properties in a natural way, but which is restricted enough to have well-defined strong generative capacity.

2 $L^2_{K,P}$—The Monadic Second-Order Language of Trees

$L^2_{K,P}$ is the monadic second-order language over the signature including a set of individual constants (K), a set of monadic predicates (P), and binary predicates for immediate domination ($\triangleleft$), domination ($\triangleleft^*$), linear precedence ($\prec$) and equality ($\approx$). The predicates in P can be understood both as picking out particular subsets of the tree and as (non-exclusive) labels or features decorating the tree. Models for the language are labeled *tree domains* (Gorn, 1967) with the natural interpretation of the binary predicates. In Rogers (1994) we have shown that this language is equivalent in descriptive power to SωS—the monadic second-order theory of the complete infinitely branching tree—in the sense that sets of trees are definable in SωS iff they are definable in $L^2_{K,P}$. This places it within a hierarchy of results relating language-theoretic complexity classes to the descriptive complexity of their models: the sets of strings definable in S1S are exactly the regular sets (Büchi, 1960), the sets of finite trees definable in SnS, for finite n, are the recognizable sets (roughly the sets of derivation trees of CFGs) (Doner, 1970), and, it can be shown, the sets of finite trees definable in SωS are those generated by generalized CFGs in which regular expressions may occur on the rhs of rewrite rules (Rogers, 1996b).[5] Consequently, languages are definable in $L^2_{K,P}$ iff they are strongly context-free in the mildly generalized sense of GPSG grammars.

In restricting ourselves to the language of $L^2_{K,P}$ we are restricting ourselves to reasoning in terms of just the predicates of its signature. We can expand this by defining new predicates, even higher-order predicates that express, for instance, properties of or relations between sets, and in doing so we can use monadic predicates and individual constants freely since we can interpret these as existentially bound variables. But the fundamental restriction of $L^2_{K,P}$ is that all predicates other than monadic first-order predicates must be explicitly defined, that is, their definitions must resolve, via syntactic substitution, into formulae involving only the signature of $L^2_{K,P}$.

3 Feature Specification Defaults in GPSG

We now turn to our first application—the definition of Feature Specification Defaults (FSDs) in GPSG.[6] Since GPSG is presumed to license (roughly) context-free languages, we are not concerned here with establishing language-theoretic complexity but rather with clarifying the linguistic theory expressed by GPSG. FSDs specify conditions on feature values that must hold at a node in a licensed tree unless they are overridden by some other component of the grammar; in particular, unless they are incompatible with either a feature specified by the ID rule licensing the node (*inherited* features) or a feature required by one of the agreement principles—the Foot Feature Principle (FFP), Head Feature Convention (HFC), or Control Agreement Principle (CAP). It is the fact that the default holds

[3]We will refer to Gazdar et al. (1985) as GKP&S

[4]We should note that the definition of FSDs in GKP&S is, in fact, declarative although this is obscured by the fact that it is couched in terms of an algorithm for checking models.

[5]There is reason to believe that this hierarchy can be extended to encompass, at least, a variety of mildly context-sensitive languages as well.

[6]A more complete treatment of GPSG in $L^2_{K,P}$ can be found in Rogers (1996c).

just in case it is incompatible with these other components that gives FSDs their dynamic flavor. Note, though, in contrast to typical applications of default logics, a GPSG grammar is not an evolving theory. The exceptions to the defaults are fully determined when the grammar is written. If we ignore for the moment the effect of the agreement principles, the defaults are roughly the converse of the ID rules: a non-default feature occurs iff it is licensed by an ID rule.

It is easy to capture ID rules in $L^2_{K,P}$. For instance the rule:

$$\mathrm{VP} \longrightarrow \mathrm{H}[5],\ \mathrm{NP},\ \mathrm{NP}$$

can be expressed:

$$\begin{aligned}&\mathrm{ID}_5(x, y_1, y_2, y_3) \equiv\\ &\quad \mathrm{Children}(x, y_1, y_2, y_3) \wedge \mathrm{VP}(x) \wedge\\ &\quad \mathrm{H}(y_1) \wedge \langle \mathrm{SUBCAT}, 5\rangle (y_1) \wedge \mathrm{NP}(y_2) \wedge \mathrm{NP}(y_3),\end{aligned}$$

where $\mathrm{Children}(x, y_1, y_2, y_3)$ holds iff the set of nodes that are children of x are just the y_i and VP, $\langle\mathrm{SUBCAT}, 5\rangle$, etc. are all members of P.[7] A sequence of nodes will satisfy ID_5 iff they form a local tree that, in the terminology of GKP&S, is *induced* by the corresponding ID rule. Using such encodings we can define a predicate $\mathrm{Free}_f(x)$ which is true at a node x iff the feature f is compatible with the inherited features of x.

The agreement principles require pairs of nodes occurring in certain configurations in local trees to agree on certain classes of features. Thus these principles do not introduce features into the trees, but rather propagate features from one node to another, possibly in many steps. Consequently, these principles cannot override FSDs by themselves; rather every violation of a default must be licensed by an inherited feature somewhere in the tree. In order to account for this propagation of features, the definition of FSDs in GKP&S is based on identifying pairs of nodes that co-vary wrt the relevant features in all possible extensions of the given tree. As a result, although the treatment in GKP&S is actually declarative, this fact is far from obvious.

Again, it is not difficult to define the configurations of local trees in which nodes are required to agree by FFP, CAP, or HFC in $L^2_{K,P}$. Let the predicate $\mathrm{Propagate}_f(x, y)$ hold for a pair of nodes x and y iff they are required to agree on f by one of these principles (and are, thus, in the same local tree). Note that Propagate is symmetric. Following the terminology of GKP&S, we can identify the set of nodes that are prohibited from taking feature f by the combination of the ID rules, FFP, CAP, and HFC as the set of nodes that are *privileged* wrt f. This includes all nodes that are not Free for f as well as any node connected to such a node by a sequence of $\mathrm{Propagate}_f$ links. We, in essence, define this inductively. $\mathrm{P}'_f(X)$ is true of a set iff it includes all nodes not Free for f and is closed wrt $\mathrm{Propagate}_f$. $\mathrm{PrivSet}_f(X)$ is true of the smallest such set.

$$\begin{aligned}&\mathrm{P}'_f(X) \equiv\\ &\quad (\forall x)[\neg \mathrm{Free}_f(x) \rightarrow X(x)] \wedge\\ &\quad (\forall x)[(\exists y)[X(y) \wedge \mathrm{Propagate}_f(x, y)] \rightarrow X(x)]\end{aligned}$$

$$\begin{aligned}\mathrm{PrivSet}_f(X) \ \equiv\ & \mathrm{P}'_f(X) \wedge\\ & (\forall Y)[\mathrm{P}'_f(Y) \rightarrow \mathrm{Subset}(X, Y)].\end{aligned}$$

There are two things to note about this definition. First, in any tree there is a unique set satisfying $\mathrm{PrivSet}_f(X)$ and this contains exactly those nodes not Free for f or connected to such a node by $\mathrm{Propagate}_f$. Second, while this is a first-order inductive property, the definition is a second-order explicit definition. In fact, the second-order quantification of $L^2_{K,P}$ allows us to capture any monadic first-order inductively or implicitly definable property explicitly.

Armed with this definition, we can identify individuals that are privileged wrt f simply as the members of $\mathrm{PrivSet}_f$.[8]

$$\mathrm{Privileged}_f(x) \equiv (\exists X)[\mathrm{PrivSet}_f(X) \wedge X(x)].$$

One can define $\mathrm{Privileged}_{\neg f}(x)$ which holds whenever x is required to take the feature f along similar lines.

These, then, let us capture FSDs. For the default [−INV], for instance, we get:

$$(\forall x)[\neg \mathrm{Privileged}_{[-\,\mathrm{INV}]}(x) \rightarrow [-\,\mathrm{INV}](x)].$$

For [BAR 0] ⊃∼ [PAS] (which says that [Bar 0] nodes are, by default, not marked passive), we get:

$$\begin{aligned}(\forall x)[\ &([\mathrm{BAR}\,0](x) \wedge \neg \mathrm{Privileged}_{\neg[\mathrm{PAS}]}(x)) \rightarrow\\ &\neg[\mathrm{PAS}](x)].\end{aligned}$$

The key thing to note about this treatment of FSDs is its simplicity relative to the treatment of GKP&S. The second-order quantification allows us to reason directly in terms of the sequence of nodes extending from the privileged node to the local tree that actually licenses the privilege. The immediate benefit is the fact that it is clear that the property of satisfying a set of FSDs is a static property of labeled trees and does not depend on the particular strategy employed in checking the tree for compliance.

---

[7] We will not elaborate here on the encoding of categories in $L^2_{K,P}$, nor on non-finite ID schema like the iterating co-ordination schema. These present no significant problems.

[8] We could, of course, skip the definition of $\mathrm{PrivSet}_f$ and define $\mathrm{Privileged}_f(x)$ as $(\forall X)[\mathrm{P}'(X) \rightarrow X(x)]$, but we prefer to emphasize the inductive nature of the definition.

4 Chains in GB

The key issue in capturing GB theories within $L^2_{K,P}$ is the fact that the mechanism of free-indexation is provably non-definable. Thus definitions of principles that necessarily employ free-indexation have no direct interpretation in $L^2_{K,P}$ (hardly surprising, as we expect GB to be capable of expressing non-context-free languages). In many cases, though, references to indices can be eliminated in favor of the underlying structural relationships they express.[9] The most prominent example is the definition of the *chains* formed by move-α. The fundamental problem here is identifying each trace with its antecedent without referencing their index. Accounts of the licensing of traces that, in many cases of movement, replace co-indexation with government relations have been offered by both Rizzi (1990) and Manzini (1992). The key element of these accounts, from our point of view, is that the antecedent of a trace must be the closest antecedent-governor of the appropriate type. These relationships are easy to capture in $L^2_{K,P}$. For $\overline{\text{A}}$-movement, for instance, we have:

$\overline{\text{A}}$-Antecedent-Governs$(x, y) \equiv$

$\neg$A-pos$(x) \wedge$ C-Commands$(x, y) \wedge$ F.Eq$(x, y) \wedge$

—x is a potential antecedent in an $\overline{\text{A}}$-position

$\neg(\exists z)[\text{Intervening-Barrier}(z, x, y)] \wedge$

—no barrier intervenes

$\neg(\exists z)[\text{Spec}(z) \wedge \neg\text{A-pos}(z) \wedge$ C-Commands$(z, x) \wedge \text{Intervenes}(z, x, y)]$

—minimality is respected

where F.Eq(x, y) is a conjunction of biconditionals that assures that x and y agree on the appropriate features and the other predicates are are standard GB notions that are definable in $L^2_{K,P}$.

Antecedent-government, in Rizzi's and Manzini's accounts, is the key relationship between adjacent members of chains which are identified by non-referential indices, but plays no role in the definition of chains which are assigned a referential index.[10] Manzini argues, however, that referential chains cannot overlap, and thus we will never need to distinguish multiple referential chains in any single context. Since we can interpret any bounded number of indices simply as distinct labels, there is no difficulty in identifying the members of referential chains in $L^2_{K,P}$. On these and similar grounds we can extend these accounts to identify adjacent members of referential chains, and, at least in the case of English, of chains of head movement and of rightward movement. This gives us five mutually exclusive relations which we can combine into a single *link* relation that must hold between every trace and its antecedent:

$$\begin{aligned}\text{Link}(x, y) \quad \equiv \quad & \text{A-Link}(x, y) \vee \overline{\text{A}}\text{-}\overline{\text{Ref}}\text{-Link}(x, y) \vee \\ & \overline{\text{A}}\text{-Ref-Link}(x, y) \vee \text{X}^0\text{-Link}(x, y) \vee \\ & \text{Right-Link}(x, y).\end{aligned}$$

The idea now is to define chains as sequences of nodes that are linearly ordered by Link, but before we can do this there is still one issue to resolve. While minimality ensures that every trace must have a unique antecedent, we may yet admit a single antecedent that licenses multiple traces. To rule out this possibility, we require chains to be *closed* wrt the link relation, i.e., every chain must include every node that is related by Link to any node already in the chain. Our definition, then, is in essence the definition, in GB terms, of a discrete linear order with endpoints, augmented with this closure property.

Chain$(X) \equiv$

$(\exists! x)[X(x) \wedge \text{Target}(x)] \wedge$

—X contains exactly one Target

$(\exists! x)[X(x) \wedge \text{Base}(x)] \wedge$

—and one Base

$(\forall x)[X(x) \wedge \neg\text{Target}(x) \rightarrow (\exists! y)[X(y) \wedge \text{Link}(y, x)]] \quad \wedge$

—All non-Target have a unique antecedent in X

$(\forall x)[X(x) \wedge \neg\text{Base}(x) \rightarrow (\exists! y)[X(y) \wedge \text{Link}(x, y)]] \quad \wedge$

—All non-Base have a unique successor in X

$(\forall x, y)[X(x) \wedge (\text{Link}(x, y) \vee \text{Link}(y, x)) \rightarrow X(y)]$

—X is closed wrt the Link relation

Note that every node will be a member of exactly one (possibly trivial) chain.

The requirement that chains be closed wrt Link means that chains cannot overlap unless they are of distinct types. This definition works for English because it is possible, in English, to resolve chains into boundedly many types in such a way that no two chains of the same type ever overlap. In fact, it fails only in cases, like head-raising in Dutch, where there are potentially unboundedly many chains that may overlap a single point in the tree. Thus, this gives us a property separating GB theories of movement that license strongly context-free languages from those that potentially don't—if we can establish a fixed bound on the number of chains that can overlap, then the definition we sketch here will suffice to capture the theory in $L^2_{K,P}$ and, consequently, the theory licenses only strongly context-free languages.

[9] More detailed expositions of the interpretation of GB in $L^2_{K,P}$ can be found in Rogers (1996a), Rogers (1995), and Rogers (1994).

[10] This accounts for subject/object asymmetries.

This is a reasonably natural diagnostic for context-freeness in GB and is close to common intuitions of what is difficult about head-raising constructions; it gives those intuitions theoretical substance and provides a reasonably clear strategy for establishing context-freeness.

5 A Comparison and a Contrast

Having interpretations both of GPSG and of a GB account of English in $L^2_{K,P}$ provides a certain amount of insight into the distinctions between these approaches. For example, while the explanations of filler-gap relationships in GB and GPSG are quite dramatically dissimilar, when one focuses on the structures these accounts license one finds some surprising parallels. In the light of our interpretation of antecedent-government, one can understand the role of minimality in Rizzi's and Manzini's accounts as eliminating ambiguity from the sequence of relations connecting the gap with its filler. In GPSG this connection is made by the sequence of agreement relationships dictated by the Foot Feature Principle. So while both theories accomplish agreement between filler and gap through marking a sequence of elements falling between them, the GB account marks as few as possible while the GPSG account marks every node of the spine of the tree spanning them. In both cases, the complexity of the set of licensed structures can be limited to be strongly context-free iff the number of relationships that must be distinguished in a given context can be bounded.

One finds a strong contrast, on the other hand, in the way in which GB and GPSG encode language universals. In GB it is presumed that all principles are universal with the theory being specialized to specific languages by a small set of finitely varying parameters. These principles are simply properties of trees. In terms of models, one can understand GB to define a universal language—the set of all analyses that can occur in human languages. The principles then distinguish particular sub-languages—the head-final or the *pro*-drop languages, for instance. Each realized human language is just the intersection of the languages selected by the settings of its parameters. In GPSG, in contrast, many universals are, in essence, closure properties that must be exhibited by human languages—if the language includes trees in which a particular configuration occurs then it includes variants of those trees in which certain related configurations occur. Both the ECPO principle and the metarules can be understood in this way. Thus while universals in GB are properties of trees, in GPSG they tend to be properties of *sets* of trees. This makes a significant difference in capturing these theories model-theoretically; in the GB case one is defining sets of models, in the GPSG case one is defining sets of sets of models. It is not at all clear what the linguistic significance of this distinction is; one particularly interesting question is whether it has empirical consequences. It is only from the model-theoretic perspective that the question even arises.

6 Conclusion

We have illustrated a general formal framework for expressing theories of syntax based on axiomatizing classes of models in $L^2_{K,P}$. This approach has a number of strengths. First, as should be clear from our brief explorations of aspects of GPSG and GB, re-formalizations of existing theories within $L^2_{K,P}$ can offer a clarifying perspective on those theories, and, in particular, on the consequences of individual components of those theories. Secondly, the framework is purely declarative and focuses on those aspects of language that are more or less directly observable—their structural properties. It allows us to reason about the consequences of a theory without hypothesizing a specific mechanism implementing it. The abstract properties of the mechanisms that might implement those theories, however, are not beyond our reach. The key virtue of descriptive complexity results like the characterizations of language-theoretic complexity classes discussed here and the more typical characterizations of computational complexity classes (Gurevich, 1988; Immerman, 1989) is that they allow us to determine the complexity of checking properties independently of how that checking is implemented. Thus we can use such descriptive complexity results to draw conclusions about those abstract properties of such mechanisms that are actually inferable from their observable behavior. Finally, by providing a uniform representation for a variety of linguistic theories, it offers a framework for comparing their consequences. Ultimately it has the potential to reduce distinctions between the mechanisms underlying those theories to distinctions between the properties of the sets of structures they license. In this way one might hope to illuminate the empirical consequences of these distinctions, should any, in fact, exist.

References

Blackburn, Patrick, Claire Gardent, and Wilfried Meyer-Viol. 1993. Talking about trees. In *EACL 93*, pages 21–29. European Association for Computational Linguistics.

Blackburn, Patrick and Wilfried Meyer-Viol. 1994. Linguistics, logic, and finite trees. *Bulletin of the IGPL*, 2(1):3–29, March.

Büchi, J. R. 1960. Weak second-order arithmetic and finite automata. *Zeitschrift für mathematische Logik und Grundlagen der Mathematik*, 6:66–92.

Carpenter, Bob. 1992. *The Logic of Typed Feature Structures; with Applications to Unification Grammars, Logic Programs and Constraint Resolution.* Number 32 in Cambridge Tracts in Theoretical Computer Science. Cambridge University Press.

Cornell, Thomas Longacre. 1992. *Description Theory, Licensing Theory, and Principle-Based Grammars and Parsers.* Ph.D. thesis, University of California Los Angeles.

Dawar, Anuj and K. Vijay-Shanker. 1990. An interpretation of negation in feature structure descriptions. *Computational Linguistics*, 16(1):11–21.

Doner, John. 1970. Tree acceptors and some of their applications. *Journal of Computer and System Sciences*, 4:406–451.

Gazdar, Gerald, Ewan Klein, Geoffrey Pullum, and Ivan Sag. 1985. *Generalized Phrase Structure Grammar.* Harvard University Press.

Gazdar, Gerald, Geoffrey Pullum, Robert Carpenter, Ewan Klein, T. E. Hukari, and R. D. Levine. 1988. Category structures. *Computational Linguistics*, 14:1–19.

Gorn, Saul. 1967. Explicit definitions and linguistic dominoes. In John F. Hart and Satoru Takasu, editors, *Systems and Computer Science, Proceedings of the Conference held at Univ. of Western Ontario, 1965.* Univ. of Toronto Press.

Gurevich, Yuri. 1988. Logic and the challenge of computer science. In E. Börger, editor, *Current Trends in Theoretical Computer Science.* Computer Science Press, chapter 1, pages 1–57.

Immerman, Neil. 1989. Descriptive and computational complexity. In *Proceedings of Symposia in Applied Mathematics*, pages 75–91. American Mathematical Society.

Johnson, David E. and Paul M. Postal. 1980. *Arc Pair Grammar.* Princeton University Press, Princeton, New Jersey.

Johnson, Mark. 1988. *Attribute-Value Logic and the Theory of Grammar.* Number 16 in CSLI Lecture Notes. Center for the Study of Language and Information, Stanford, CA.

Johnson, Mark. 1989. The use of knowledge of language. *Journal of Psycholinguistic Research*, 18(1):105–128.

Kasper, Robert T. and William C. Rounds. 1986. A logical semantics for feature structures. In *Proceedings of the 24th Annual Meeting of the Association for Computational Linguistics.*

Kasper, Robert T. and William C. Rounds. 1990. The logic of unification in grammar. *Linguistics and Philosophy*, 13:35–58.

Keller, Bill. 1993. *Feature Logics, Infinitary Descriptions and Grammar.* Number 44 in CSLI Lecture Notes. Center for the Study of Language and Information.

Kracht, Marcus. 1995. Syntactic codes and grammar refinement. *Journal of Logic, Language, and Information*, 4:41–60.

Manzini, Maria Rita. 1992. *Locality: A Theory and Some of Its Empirical Consequences.* MIT Press, Cambridge, Ma.

Moshier, M. Drew and William C. Rounds. 1987. A logic for partially specified data structures. In *ACM Symposium on the Principles of Programming Languages.*

Rizzi, Luigi. 1990. *Relativized Minimality.* MIT Press.

Rogers, James. 1994. *Studies in the Logic of Trees with Applications to Grammar Formalisms.* Ph.D. dissertation, Univ. of Delaware.

Rogers, James. 1995. On descriptive complexity, language complexity, and GB. In Patrick Blackburn and Maarten de Rijke, editors, *Specifying Syntactic Structures.* In Press. Also available as IRCS Technical Report 95-14. cmp-lg/9505041.

Rogers, James. 1996a. *A Descriptive Approach to Language-Theoretic Complexity.* Studies in Logic, Language, and Information. CSLI Publications. To appear.

Rogers, James. 1996b. The descriptive complexity of local, recognizable, and generalized recognizable sets. Technical report, IRCS, Univ. of Pennsylvania. In Preparation.

Rogers, James. 1996c. Grammarless phrase-structure grammar. Under Review.

Rogers, James and K. Vijay-Shanker. 1994. Obtaining trees from their descriptions: An application to tree-adjoining grammars. *Computational Intelligence*, 10:401–421.

Smolka, Gert. 1989. A feature logic with subsorts. LILOG Report 33, IBM Germany, Stuttgart.

Stabler, Jr., Edward P. 1992. *The Logical Approach to Syntax.* Bradford.

Noun-Phrase Analysis in Unrestricted Text for Information Retrieval

David A. Evans, Chengxiang Zhai
Laboratory for Computational Linguistics
Carnegie Mellon Univeristy
Pittsburgh, PA 15213
dae@cmu.edu, cz25@andrew.cmu.edu

Abstract

Information retrieval is an important application area of natural-language processing where one encounters the genuine challenge of processing large quantities of unrestricted natural-language text. This paper reports on the application of a few simple, yet robust and efficient noun-phrase analysis techniques to create better indexing phrases for information retrieval. In particular, we describe a hybrid approach to the extraction of meaningful (continuous or discontinuous) subcompounds from complex noun phrases using both corpus statistics and linguistic heuristics. Results of experiments show that indexing based on such extracted subcompounds improves both recall and precision in an information retrieval system. The noun-phrase analysis techniques are also potentially useful for book indexing and automatic thesaurus extraction.

1 Introduction

1.1 Information Retrieval

Information retrieval (IR) is an important application area of natural-language processing (NLP).[1] The IR (or perhaps more accurately "text retrieval") task may be characterized as the problem of selecting a subset of documents (from a document collection) whose content is relevant to the information need of a user as expressed by a query. The document collections involved in IR are often gigabytes of unrestricted natural-language text. A user's query may be expressed in a controlled language (e.g., a boolean expression of keywords) or, more desirably, a natural language, such as English.

A typical IR system works as follows. The documents to be retrieved are processed to extract *indexing terms* or *content carriers*, which are usually single words or (less typically) phrases. The indexing terms provide a description of the document's content. Weights are often assigned to terms to indicate how well they describe the document. A (natural-language) query is processed in a similar way to extract *query terms*. Query terms are then matched against the indexing terms of a document to determine the relevance of each document to the query.

The ultimate goal of an IR system is to increase both *precision*, the proportion of retrieved documents that are relevant, as well as *recall*, the proportion of relevant document that are retrieved. However, the real challenge is to understand and represent appropriately the content of a document and query, so that the relevance decision can be made efficiently, without degrading precision and recall. A typical solution to the problem of making relevance decisions efficient is to require exact matching of indexing terms and query terms, with an evaluation of the 'hits' based on a scoring metric. Thus, for instance, in vector-space models of relevance ranking, both the indexing terms of a document and the query terms are treated as vectors (with individual term weights) and the similarity between the two vectors is given by a cosine-distance measure, essentially the angle between any two vectors.[2]

1.2 Natural-Language Processing for IR

One can regard almost any IR system as performing an NLP task: text is 'parsed' for terms and terms are used to express 'meaning'—to capture document content. Clearly, most traditional IR systems do not attempt to find structure in the natural-language text in the 'parsing' process; they merely extract word-like strings to use in indexing. Ideally, however, extracted structure would directly reflect the encoded linguistic relations among terms—capturing the conceptual content of the text better than simple word-strings.

There are several prerequisites for effective NLP in an IR application, including the following.

[1](Evans, 1990; Evans et al., 1993; Smeaton, 1992; Lewis & Sparck Jones, 1996)

[2](Salton & McGill, 1983)

1. Ability to process large amounts of text

   The amount of text in the databases accessed by modern IR systems is typically measured in gigabytes. This requires that the NLP used must be extraordinarily efficient in both its time and space requirements. It would be impractical to use a parser with the speed of one or two sentences per second.

2. Ability to process unrestricted text

   The text database for an IR task is generally unrestricted natural-language text possibly encompassing many different domains and topics. A parser must be able to manage the many kinds of problems one sees in natural-language corpora, including the processing of unknown words, proper names, and unrecognized structures. Often more is required, as when spelling, transcription, or OCR errors occur. Thus, the NLP used must be especially robust.

3. Need for shallow understanding

   While the large amount of unrestricted text makes NLP more difficult for IR, the fact that a deep and complete understanding of the text may not be necessary for IR makes NLP for IR relatively easier than other NLP tasks such as machine translation. The goal of an IR system is essentially to classify documents (as relevant or irrelevant) vis-a-vis a query. Thus, it may suffice to have a shallow and partial representation of the content of documents.

Information retrieval thus poses the genuine challenge of processing large volumes of unrestricted natural-language text but not necessarily at a deep level.

1.3 Our Work

This paper reports on our evaluation of the use of simple, yet robust and efficient noun-phrase analysis techniques to enhance phrase-based IR. In particular, we explored an extension of the phrase-based indexing in the CLARIT™ system[3] using a hybrid approach to the extraction of meaningful (continuous or discontinuous) subcompounds from complex noun phrases exploiting both corpus-statistics and linguistic heuristics. Using such subcompounds rather than whole noun phrases as indexing terms helps a phrase-based IR system solve the phrase normalization problem, that is, the problem of matching syntactically different, but semantically similar phrases. The results of our experiments show that both recall and precision are improved by using extracted subcompounds for indexing.

[3](Evans et al., 1991; Evans et al., 1993; Evans et al., 1995; Evans et al., 1996)

2 Phrase-Based Indexing

The selection of appropriate indexing terms is critical to the improvement of both precision and recall in an IR task. The ideal indexing terms would directly represent the concepts in a document. Since 'concepts' are difficult to represent and extract (as well as to define), concept-based indexing is an elusive goal. Virtually all commercial IR systems (with the exception of the CLARIT system) index only on 'words', since the identification of words in texts is typically easier and more efficient than the identification of more complex structures. However, single words are rarely specific enough to support accurate discrimination and their groupings are often accidental. An often cited example is the contrast between "junior college" and "college junior". Word-based indexing cannot distinguish the phrases, though their meanings are quite different. Phrase-based indexing, on the other hand, as a step toward the ideal of concept-based indexing, can address such a case directly.

Indeed, it is interesting to note that the use of phrases as index terms has increased dramatically among the systems that participate in the TREC evaluations.[4] Even relatively traditional word-based systems are exploring the use of multiword terms by supplementing words with statistical phrases—selected high frequency adjacent word pairs (bigrams). And a few systems, such as CLARIT—which uses simplex noun phrases, attested subphrases, and contained words as index terms—and New York University's TREC system[5]—which uses "head–modifier pairs" derived from identified noun phrases—have demonstrated the practicality and effectiveness of thorough NLP in IR tasks.

The experiences of the CLARIT system are instructive. By using selective NLP to identify simplex NPs, CLARIT generates phrases, subphrases, and individual words to use in indexing documents and queries. Such a first-order analysis of the linguistic structures in texts approximates concepts and affords us alternative methods for calculating the fit between documents and queries. In particular, we can choose to treat some phrasal structures as atomic units and others as additional information about (or representations of) content. There are immediate effects in improving precision:

1. Phrases can replace individual indexing words. For example, if both "dog" and "hot" are used for indexing, they will match any query in which both words occur. But if only the phrase "hot dog" is used as an index term, then it will only match the same phrase, not any of the individual words.

[4](Harman, 1995; Harman, 1996)

[5](Strzalkowski, 1994)

2. Phrases can supplement word-level matches. For example, if only the individual words "junior" and "college" are used for indexing, both "junior college" and "college junior" will match a query with the phrase "junior college" equally well. But if we also use the phrase "junior college" for indexing, then "junior college" will match better than "college junior", even though the latter also will receive some credit as a match at the word level.

We can see, then, that it is desirable to distinquish—and, if possible, extract—two kinds of phrases: those that behave as *lexical atoms* and those that reflect more general linguistic relations.

Lexical atoms help us by obviating the possibility of extraneous word matches that have nothing to do with true relevance. We do not want "hot" or "dog" to match on "hot dog". In essence, we want to eliminate the effect of the independence assumption at the word level by creating new words—the lexical atoms—in which the individual word dependencies are explicit (structural).

More general phrases help us by adding detail. Indeed, all possible phrases (or paraphrases) of actual content in a document are potentially valuable in indexing. In practice, of course, the indexing term space has to be limited, so it is necessary to select a subset of phrases for indexing. Short phrases (often nominal compounds) are preferred over long complex phrases, because short phrases have better chances for matching short phrases in queries and will still match longer phrases owing to the short phrases they have in common. Using only short phrases also helps solve the phrase normalization problem of matching syntactically different long phrases (when they share similar meaning).[6]

Thus, lexical atoms and small nominal compounds should make good indexing phrases.

While the CLARIT system does index at the level of phrases and subphrases, it does not currently index on lexical atoms or on the small compounds that can be derived from complex NPs, in particular, reflecting cross-simplex NP dependency relations. Thus, for example, under normal CLARIT processing the phrase "the quality of surface of treated stainless steel strip"[7] would yield index terms such as "treated stainless steel strip", "treated stainless steel", "stainless steel strip", and "stainless steel" (as a phrase, not lexical atom), along with all the relevant single-word terms in the phrase. But the process would not identify "stainless steel" as a potential lexical atom or find terms such as "surface quality", "strip surface", and "treated strip".

To achieve more complete (and accurate) phrase-based indexing, we propose to use the following four kinds of phrases as indexing terms:

1. Lexical atoms (e.g., "hot dog" or perhaps "stainless steel" in the example above)
2. Head modifier pairs (e.g., "treated strip" and "steel strip" in the example above)
3. Subcompounds (e.g., "stainless steel strip" in the example above)
4. Cross-preposition modification pairs (e.g., "surface quality" in the example above)

In effect, we aim to augment CLARIT indexing with lexical atoms and phrases capturing additional (discontinuous) modification relations than those that can be found within simplex NPs.

It is clear that a certain level of robust and efficient noun-phrase analysis is needed to extract the above four kinds of small compounds from a large unrestricted corpus. In fact, the set of small compounds extracted from a noun phrase can be regarded as a weak representation of the meaning of the noun phrase, since each meaningful small compound captures a part of the meaning of the noun phrase. In this sense, extraction of such small compounds is a step toward a shallow interpretation of noun phrases. Such weak interpretation is useful for tasks like information retrieval, document classification, and thesaurus extraction, and indeed forms the basis in the CLARIT system for automated thesaurus discovery.

3 Methodology

Our task is to parse text into NPs, analyze the noun phrases, and extract the four kinds of small compounds given above. Our emphasis is on robust and efficient NLP techniques to support large-scale applications.

For our purposes, we need to be able to identify all simplex and complex NPs in a text. Complex NPs are defined as a sequence of simplex NPs that are associated with one another via prepositional phrases. We do not consider simplex NPs joined by relative clauses.

Our approach to NLP involves a hybrid use of corpus statistics supplemented by linguistic heuristics. We assume that there is no training data (making the approach more practically useful) and, thus, rely only on statistical information in the document database itself. This is different from many current statistical NLP techniques that require a training corpus. The volume of data we see in IR tasks also makes it impractical to use sophisticated statistical computations.

The use of linguistic heuristics can assist statistical analysis in several ways. First, it can focus the use of statistics by helping to eliminate irrelevant structures from consideration. For example, syntactic category analysis can filter out impossible

[6] (Smeaton, 1992)

[7] This is an actual example from a U.S. patent document.

word modification pairs, such as [adjective, adjective] and [noun, adjective]. Second, it may improve the reliability of statistical decisions. For example, the counting of bigrams that occur only within noun phrases is more reliable for lexical atom discovery than the counting of all possible bigrams that occur in the corpus. In addition, syntactic category analysis is also helpful in adjusting cutoff parameters for statistics. For example, one useful heuristic is that we should use a higher threshold of reliability (evidence) for accepting the pair [adjective, noun] as a lexical atom than for the pair [noun, noun]: a noun–noun pair is much more likely to be a lexical atom than an adjective–noun one.

The general process of phrase generation is illustrated in Figure 1. We used the CLARIT NLP module as a preprocessor to produce NPs with syntactic categories attached to words. We did not attempt to utilize CLARIT complex-NP generation or subphrase analysis, since we wanted to focus on the specific techniques for subphrase discovery that we describe in this paper.

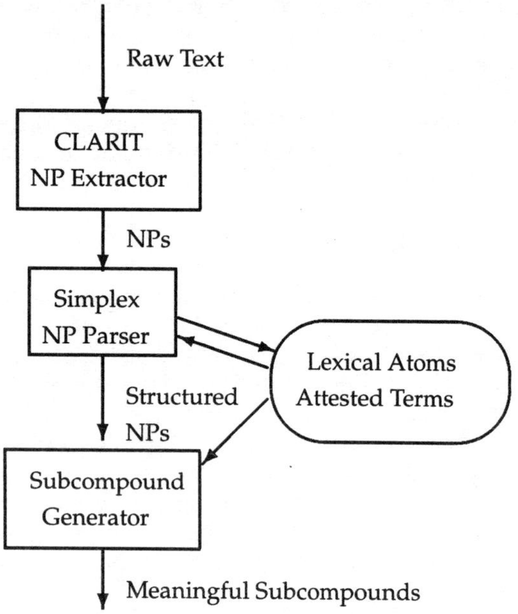

Figure 1: General Processing for Phrase Generation

After preprocessing, the system works in two stages—parsing and generation. In the parsing stage, each simplex noun phrase in the corpus is parsed. In the generation stage, the structured noun phrase is used to generate candidates for all four kinds of small compounds, which are further tested for occurrence (validity) in the corpus.

Parsing of simplex noun phrases is done in multiple phases. At each phase, noun phrases are partially parsed, then the partially parsed structures are used as input to start another phase of partial parsing. Each phase of partial parsing is completed by concatenating those most reliable modification pairs together to form a single unit. The reliability of a modification pair is determined by a score based on frequency statistics and category analysis and is further tested via local optimum phrase analysis (described below). Lexical atoms are discovered at the same time, during simplex noun phrase parsing.

Phrase generation is quite simple. Once the structure of a noun phrase (with marked lexical atoms) is known, the four kinds of small compounds can be easily produced. Lexical atoms are already available. Head–modifier pairs can be extracted based on the modification relations implied by the structure. Subcompounds are just the substructures of the NP. Cross-preposition pairs are generated by enumerating all possible pairs of the heads of each simplex NP within a complex NP in backward order.[8]

To validate discontinuous compounds such as non-sequential head–modifier pairs and cross-preposition pairs, we use a standard technique of CLARIT processing, viz., we test any nominated compounds against the corpus itself. If we find independently attested (whole) simplex NPs that match the candidate compounds, we accept the candidates as index terms. Thus for the NP "the quality of surface of treated stainless steel strip", the head–modifier pairs "treated strip", "stainless steel", "stainless strip", and "steel strip", and the cross-preposition pairs "strip surface", "surface quality", and "strip quality", would be generated as index terms only if we found independent evidence of such phrases in the corpus in the form of free-standing simplex NPs.

3.1 Lexical Atom Discovery

A lexical atom is a semantically coherent phrase unit. Lexical atoms may be found among proper names, idioms, and many noun–noun compounds. Usually they are two-word phrases, but sometimes they can consist of three or even more words, as in the case of proper names and technical terms. Examples of lexical atoms (in general English) are "hot dog", "tear gas", "part of speech", and "von Neumann".

However, recognition of lexical atoms in free text is difficult. In particular, the relevant lexical atoms for a corpus of text will reflect the various discourse domains encompassed by the text. In a collection of medical documents, for example, "Wilson's disease" (an actual rheumatological disorder) may be used as a lexical atom, whereas in a collection of general news stories, "Wilson's disease" (reference to the disease that Wilson has) may not be a lexical atom. Note that in the case of the medical usage, we would commonly find "Wilson's disease" as a bigram and we would not find, for example,

[8] (Schwarz, 1990) reports a similar strategy.

"Wilson's severe disease" as a phrase, though the latter might well occur in the general news corpus. This example serves to illustrate the essential observation that motivates our heuristics for identitying lexical atoms in a corpus: (1) words in lexical atoms have strong association, and thus tend to co-occur as a phrase and (2) when the words in a lexical atom co-occur in a noun phrase, they are never or rarely separated.

The detection of lexical atoms, like the parsing of simplex noun phrases, is also done in multiple phases. At each phase, only two adjacent units are considered. So, initially, only two-word lexical atoms can be detected. But, once a pair is determined to be a lexical atom, it will behave exactly like a single word in subsequent processing, so, in later phases, atoms with more than two words can be detected.

Suppose the pair to test is $[W_1, W_2]$. The first heuristic is implemented by requiring the frequency of the pair to be higher than the frequency of any other pair that is formed by either word with other words in common contexts (within a simplex noun phrase). The intuition behind the test is that (1) in general, the high frequency of a bigram in a simple noun phrase indicates strong association and (2) we want to avoid the case where $[W_1, W_2]$ has a high frequency, but $[W_1, W_2, W]$ (or $[W, W_1, W_2]$) has an even higher frequency, which implies that W_2 (or W_1) has a stronger association with W than with W_1 (or W_2, respectively). More precisely, we require the following:

$F(W_1, W_2) > MaxLDF(W_1, W_2)$

and

$F(W_1, W_2) > MaxRDF(W_1, W_2)$

Where,

$MaxLDF(W_1, W_2) =$

$Max_W(Min(F(W, W_1), DF(W, W_2)))$

and

$MaxRDF(W_1, W_2) =$

$Max_W(Min(DF(W_1, W), F(W_2, W)))$

W is any context word in a noun phrase and $F(X, Y)$ and $DF(X, Y)$ are the continuous and discontinuous frequencies of $[X, Y]$, respectively, within a simple noun phrase, i.e., the frequency of patterns $[...X, Y...]$ and patterns $[...X, ..., Y...]$, respectively.

The second heuristic requires that we record all cases where two words occur in simplex NPs and compare the number of times the words occur as a strictly adjacent pair with the number of times they are separated. The second heuristic is simply implemented by requiring that $F(W_1, W_2)$ be much higher than $DF(W_1, W_2)$ (where 'higher' is determined by some threshold).

Syntactic category analysis also helps filter out impossible lexical atoms and establish the threshold for passing the second test. Only the following category combinations are allowed for lexical atoms: [noun, noun], [noun, lexatom], [lexatom, noun], [adjective, noun], and [adjective, lexatom], where "lexatom" is the category for a detected lexical atom. For combinations other than [noun, noun], the threshold for passing the second test is high.

In practice, the process effectively nominates phrases that are true atomic concepts (in a particular domain of discourse) or are being used so consistently as unit concepts that they can be safely taken to be lexical atoms. For example, the lexical atoms extracted by this process from the CACM corpus (about 1 MB) include "operating system", "data structure", "decision table", "data base", "real time", "natural language", "on line", "least squares", "numerical integration", and "finite state automaton", among others.

3.2 Bottom-Up Association-Based Parsing

Extended simplex noun-phrase parsing as developed in the CLARIT system, which we exploit in our process, works in multiple phases. At each phase, the corpus is parsed using the most specific (i.e., recently created) lexicon of lexical atoms. New lexical atoms (results) are added to the lexicon and are reused as input to start another phase of parsing until a complete parse is obtained for all the noun phrases.

The idea of association-based parsing is that by grouping words together (based on association) many times, we will eventually discover the most restrictive (and informative) structure of a noun phrase. For example, if we have evidence from the corpus that "high performance" is a more reliable association and "general purpose" a less reliable one, then the noun phrase "general purpose high performance computer" (an actual example from the CACM corpus) would undergo the following grouping process:

general purpose high performance computer ⇒
general purpose [high=performance] computer ⇒
[general=purpose] [high=performance] computer ⇒
[general=purpose] [[high=performance]=computer] ⇒
[[general=purpose]=[[high=performance]=computer]]

Word pairs are given an association score (S) according to the following rules. Scores provide evidence for groupings in our parsing process. Note that a smaller score means a stronger association.

1. Lexical atoms are given score 0. This gives the highest priority to lexical atoms.
2. The combination of an adverb with an adjective, past participle, or progressive verb is given score 0.
3. Syntactically impossible pairs are given score 100. This assigns the lowest priority to those

pairs filtered out by syntactic category analysis. The 'impossible' combinations include pairs such as [noun, adjective], [noun, adverb], [adjective, adjective], [past-participle, adjective], [past-participle, adverb], and [past-participle, past-participle], among others.

4. Other pairs are scored according to the formulas given in Figure 2. Note the following effects of the formulas:
   When $F(W_1, W_2)$ increases, $S(W_1, W_2)$ decreases;
   When $DF(W_1, W_2)$ increases, $S(W_1, W_2)$ decreases;
   When $AvgLDF(W_1, W_2)$ or $AvgRDF(W_1, W_2)$ increases, $S(W_1, W_2)$ increases; and
   When $F(W_1) - F(W_1, W_2)$ or $F(W_2) - F(W_1, W_2)$ increases, $S(W_1, W_2)$ decreases.

$$S(W_1, W_2) = \frac{1 + LDF(W_1, W_2) + RDF(W_1, W_2)}{\lambda_1 \times F(W_1, W_2) + DF(W_1, W_2)} \times A(W_1, W_2)$$

$$AvgLDF(W_1, W_2) = \frac{\sum_{W \in LD} Min(F(W, W_1), DF(W, W_2))}{|LD|}$$

$$AvgRDF(W_1, W_2) = \frac{\sum_{W \in RD} Min(F(W_2, W), DF(W_1, W))}{|RD|}$$

$$A(W_1, W_2) = \frac{\lambda_2}{F(W_1) + F(W_2) - 2 \times F(W_1, W_2) + \lambda_2}$$

Where

- $F(W)$ is frequency of word W
- $F(W_1, W_2)$ is frequency of adjacent bigram $[W_1, W_2]$ (i.e., ...W_1 W_2 ...)
- $DF(W_1, W_2)$ is frequency of discontinuous bigram $[W_1, W_2]$ (i.e., ...W_1...W_2...)
- LD is all left dependents, i.e., $\{W | min(F(W, W_1), DF(W, W_2)) \neq 0\}$
- RD is all right dependents, i.e., $\{W | min(DF(W_1, W), F(W_2, W)) \neq 0\}$
- λ_1 is the parameter indicating the relative contribution of $F(W_1, W_2)$ to the score (e.g., 5 in the actual experiment)
- λ_2 is the parameter to control the contribution of word frequency (e.g., 1000 in the actual experiment)

Figure 2: Formulas for Scoring

The association score (based principally on frequency) can sometimes be unreliable. For example, if the phrase "computer aided design" occurs frequently in a corpus, "aided design" may be judged a good association pair, even though "computer aided" might be a better pair. A problem may arise when processing a phrase such as "program aided design": if "program aided" does not occur frequently in the corpus and we use frequency as the principal statistic, we may (incorrectly) be led to parse the phrase as "[program (aided design)]".

One solution to such a problem is to recompute the bigram occurrence statistics after making each round of preferred associations. Thus, using the example above, if we first make the association "computer aided" everywhere it occurs, many instances of "aided design" will be removed from the corpus. Upon recalculation of the (free) bigram statistics, "aided design" will be demoted in value and the false evidence for "aided design" as a preferred association in some contexts will be eliminated.

The actual implementation of such a scheme requires multiple passes over the corpus to generate phrases. The first phrases chosen must always be the most reliable. To aid us in making such decisions we have developed a metric for scoring preferred associations in their local NP contexts.

To establish a preference metric, we use two statistics: (1) the frequency of the pair in the corpus, $F(W_1, W_2)$, and (2) the number of the times that the pair is *locally dominant* in any NP in which the pair occurs. A pair is locally dominant in an NP iff it has a higher association score than either of the pairs that can be formed from contiguous other words in the NP. For example, in an NP with the sequence $[X, Y, Z]$, we compare $S(X, Y)$ with $S(Y, Z)$; whichever is higher is locally dominant. The preference score (PS) for a pair is determined by the ratio of its local dominance count (LDC)—the total number of cases in which the pair is locally dominant—to its frequency:

$$PS(W_1, W_2) = \frac{LDC(W_1, W_2)}{F(W_1, W_2)}$$

By definition all two-word NPs score their pairs as locally dominant.

In general, in each processing phase we make only those associations in the corpus where a pair's PS is above a specified threshold. If more than one association is possible (above theshold) in a particular NP, we make all possible associations, but in order of PS: the first grouping goes to the pair with highest PS, and so on. In practice, we have used 0.7 as the threshold for most processing phases.[9]

4 Experiment

We tested the phrase extraction system (PES) by using it to index documents in an actual retrieval task. In particular, we substituted the PES for the default NLP module in the CLARIT system and then indexed a large corpus using the terms nominated by the PES, essentially the extracted small compounds and single words (but not words within a lexical atom). All other normal CLARIT processing—weighting of terms, division of documents into subdocuments (passages), vector-space modeling, etc.—was used in its default mode. As a baseline

[9] When the phrase data becomes sparse, e.g., after six or seven iterations of processing, it is desirable to reduce the threshold.

for comparison, we used standard CLARIT processing of the same corpus, with the NLP module set to return full NPs and their contained words (and no further subphrase analysis).[10]

The corpus used is a 240-megabyte collection of Associated Press newswire stories from 1989 (AP89), taken from the set of TREC corpora. There are about 3-million simplex NPs in the corpus and about 1.5-million complex NPs. For evaluation, we used TREC queries 51–100,[11] each of which is a relatively long description of an information need. Queries were processed by the PES and normal CLARIT NLP modules, respectively, to generate query terms, which were then used for CLARIT retrieval.

To quantify the effects of PES processing, we used the standard IR evaluation measures of recall and precision. Recall measures how many of the relevant documents have been actually retrieved. Precision measures how many of the retrieved documents are indeed relevant. For example, if the total number of relevant documents is N and the system returns M documents of which K are relevant, then,

$Recall = \frac{K}{N}$

and

$Precision = \frac{K}{M}$.

We used the judged-relevant documents from the TREC evaluations as the gold standard in scoring the performance of the two processes.

5 Results

The results of the experiment are given in Tables 1, 2, and 3. In general, we see improvement in both recall and precision.

Recall improves slightly (about 1%), as shown in Table 1. While the actual improvement is not significant for the run of fifty queries, the increase in absolute numbers of relevant documents returned indicates that the small compounds supported better matches in some cases.

Interpolated precision improves significantly, as shown in Table 2. The general improvement in precision indicates that small compounds provide more accurate (and effective) indexing terms than full NPs.

Precision improves at various returned-document levels, as well, as shown in Table 3. Initial precision, in particular, improves significantly. This suggests that the PES could be used to support other IR enhancements, such as automatic feedback of the top-returned documents to expand the initial query for a second retrieval step.[12]

CLARIT	Retrieved-Rel	Total-Rel	Recall
Baseline	2,668	3,304	80.8%
PES	2,695	3,304	81.6%

Table 1: Recall Results

Recall	Baseline	PES	Rel.Improvement
0.00	0.6819	0.7099	4%
0.10	0.5535	0.5730	3.5%
0.20	0.4626	0.4927	6.5%
0.30	0.4098	0.4329	5.6%
0.40	0.3524	0.3782	7.0%
0.50	0.3289	0.3317	0.5%
0.60	0.2999	0.3026	0.9%
0.70	0.2481	0.2458	–0.9%
0.80	0.1860	0.1966	5.7%
0.90	0.1190	0.1448	21.7%
1.00	0.0688	0.0653	–5.0%

Table 2: Interpolated Precision Results

Doc-Level	Baseline	PES	Rel.Improvement
5 docs	0.4255	0.4809	13%
10 docs	0.4170	0.4426	6%
15 docs	0.3943	0.4227	7%
20 docs	0.3819	0.3957	4%
30 docs	0.3539	0.3603	2%
100 docs	0.2526	0.2553	1%
200 docs	0.1770	0.1844	4%
500 docs	0.0973	0.0994	2%
1000 docs	0.0568	0.0573	1%

Table 3: Precision at Various Document Levels

The PES, which was not optimized for processing, required approximately 3.5 hours per 20-megabyte subset of AP89 on a 133-MHz DEC alpha processor.[13] Most processing time (more than 2 of every 3.5 hours) was spent on simplex NP parsing. Such speed might be acceptable in some, smaller-scale IR applications, but it is considerably slower than the baseline speed of CLARIT noun-phrase identification (viz., 200 megabytes per hour on a 100-MIPS processor).

[10] Note that the CLARIT process used as a baseline does not reflect optimum CLARIT performance, e.g., as obtained in actual TREC evaluations, since we did not use a variety of standard CLARIT techniques that significantly improve performance, such as automatic query expansion, distractor space generation, subterm indexing, or differential query-term weighting. Cf. (Evans et al., 1996) for details.

[11] (Harman, 1993)

[12] (Evans et al., 1995; Evans et al., 1996)

[13] Note that the machine was not dedicated to the PES processing; other processes were running simultaneously.

6 Conclusions

The notion of association-based parsing dates at least from (Marcus, 1980) and has been explored again recently by a number of researchers.[14] The method we have developed differs from previous work in that it uses linguistic heuristics and locality scoring along with corpus statistics to generate phrase associations.

The experiment contrasting the PES with baseline processing in a commercial IR system demonstrates a direct, positive effect of the use of lexical atoms, subphrases, and other pharase associations across simplex NPs. We believe the use of NP-substructure analysis can lead to more effective information management, including more precise IR, text summarization, and concept clustering. Our future work will explore such applications of the techniques we have described in this paper.

7 Acknowledgements

We received helpful comments from Bob Carpenter, Christopher Manning, Xiang Tong, and Steve Handerson, who also provided us with a hash table manager that made the implementation easier. The evaluation of the experimental results would have been impossible without the help of Robert Lefferts and Nataša Milić-Frayling at CLARITECH Corporation. Finally, we thank the anonymous reviewers for their useful comments.

References

David A. Evans. 1990. Concept management in text via natural-language processing: The CLARIT approach. In: *Working Notes of the 1990 AAAI Symposium on "Text-Based Intelligent Systems"*, Stanford University, March, 27–29, 1990, 93–95.

David A. Evans, Kimberly Ginther-Webster, Mary Hart, Robert G. Lefferts, Ira A. Monarch. 1991. Automatic indexing using selective NLP and first-order thesauri. In: A. Lichnerowicz (ed.), *Intelligent Text and Image Handling. Proceedings of a Conference, RIAO '91*. Amsterdam, NL: Elsevier, pp. 624–644.

David A. Evans, Robert G. Lefferts, Gregory Grefenstette, Steven K. Handerson, William R. Hersh, and Armar A. Archbold. 1993. CLARIT TREC design, experiments, and results. In: Donna K. Harman (ed.), *The First Text REtrieval Conference (TREC-1)*. NIST Special Publication 500-207. Washington, DC: U.S. Government Printing Office, pp. 251–286; 494–501.

David A. Evans, and Robert G. Lefferts. 1995. CLARIT-TREC experiments *Information Processing and Management*, Vol. 31, No. 3, 385–395.

David A. Evans, Nataša Milić-Frayling, Robert G. Lefferts. 1996. CLARIT TREC-4 experiments. In: Donna K. Harman (ed.), *The Fourth Text REtrieval Conference (TREC-4)*. NIST Special Publication. Washington, DC: U.S. Government Printing Office.

Donna K. Harman, ed. 1993. *The First Text REtrieval Conference (TREC-1)* NIST Special Publication 500-207. Washington, DC: U.S. Government Printing Office.

Donna K. Harman, ed. 1995. *Overview of the Third Text REtrieval Conference (TREC-3)*, NIST Special Publication 500-225. Washington, DC: U.S. Government Printing Office.

Donna K. Harman, ed. 1996. *Overview of the Fourth Text REtrieval Conference (TREC-4)*, NIST Special Publication. Washington, DC: U.S. Government Printing Office.

Mark Lauer. 1995. Corpus statistics meet with the noun compound: Some empirical results. In: *Proceedings of the 33th Annual Meeting of the Association for Computational Linguistics*.

David Lewis and K. Sparck Jones. 1996. Natural language processing for information retrieval. *Communications of the ACM*, January, Vol. 39, No. 1, 92–101.

Mark Liberman and Richard Sproat. 1992. The stress and structure of modified noun phrases in English. In: I. Sag and A. Szabolcsi (eds.), *Lexical Matters*, CSLI Lecture Notes No. 24. Chicago, IL: University of Chicago Press, pp. 131–181.

Mitchell Maucus. 1980. *A Theory of Syntactic Recognition for Natural Language*. Cambridge, MA: MIT Press.

J. Pustejovsky, S. Bergler, and P. Anick. 1993. Lexical semantic techniques for corpus analysis. In: *Computational Linguistics*, Vol. 19(2), Special Issue on Using Large Corpora II, pp. 331–358.

P. Resnik, and M. Hearst. 1993. Structural Ambiguity and Conceptual Relations. In: *Proceedings of the Workshop on Very Large Corpora: Academic and Industrial Perspectives*, June 22, Ohio State University, pp. 58–64.

Gerard Salton and Michael McGill. 1983. *Introduction to Modern Information Retrieval*, New York, NY: McGraw-Hill.

Christoph Schwarz. 1990. Content based text handling. *Information Processing and Management*, Vol. 26(2), pp. 219–226.

Alan F. Smeaton. 1992. Progress in application of natural language processing to information retrieval. *The Computer Journal*, Vol. 35, No. 3, pp. 268–278.

T. Strzalkowski and J. Carballo. 1994. Recent developments in natural language text retrieval. In: Donna K. Harman (ed.), *The Second Text REtrieval Conference (TREC-2)*. NIST Special Publication 500-215. Washington, DC: U.S. Government Printing Office, pp. 123–136.

[14](Liberman et al., 1992; Pustejovsky et al., 1993; Resnik et al., 1993; Lauer, 1995)

Morphological Cues for Lexical Semantics

Marc Light
Seminar für Sprachwissenschaft
Universität Tübingen
Wilhelmstr. 113
D-72074 Tübingen
Germany
light@sfs.nphil.uni-tuebingen.de

Abstract

Most natural language processing tasks require lexical semantic information. Automated acquisition of this information would thus increase the robustness and portability of NLP systems. This paper describes an acquisition method which makes use of fixed correspondences between derivational affixes and lexical semantic information. One advantage of this method, and of other methods that rely only on surface characteristics of language, is that the necessary input is currently available.

1 Introduction

Some natural language processing (NLP) tasks can be performed with only coarse-grained semantic information about individual words. For example, a system could utilize word frequency and a word cooccurrence matrix in order to perform information retrieval. However, many NLP tasks require at least a partial understanding of every sentence or utterance in the input and thus have a much greater need for lexical semantics. Natural language generation, providing a natural language front end to a database, information extraction, machine translation, and task-oriented dialogue understanding all require lexical semantics. The lexical semantic information commonly utilized includes verbal argument structure and selectional restrictions, corresponding nominal semantic class, verbal aspectual class, synonym and antonym relationships between words, and various verbal semantic features such as causation and manner.

Machine readable dictionaries do not include much of this information and it is difficult and time consuming to encode it by hand. As a consequence, current NLP systems have only small lexicons and thus can only operate in restricted domains. Automated methods for acquiring lexical semantics could increase both the robustness and the portability of such systems. In addition, such methods might provide insight into human language acquisition.

After considering different possible approaches to acquiring lexical semantic information, this paper concludes that a "surface cueing" approach is currently the most promising. It then introduces morphological cueing, a type of surface cueing, and discusses an implementation. It concludes by evaluating morphological cues with respect to a list of desiderata for good surface cues.

2 Approaches to Acquiring Lexical Semantics

One intuitively appealing idea is that humans acquire the meanings of words by relating them to semantic representations resulting from perceptual or cognitive processing. For example, in a situation where the father says *Kim is throwing the ball* and points at Kim who is throwing the ball, a child might be able learn what *throw* and *ball* mean. In the human language acquisition literature, Grimshaw (1981) and Pinker (1989) advocate this approach; others have described partial computer implementations: Pustejovsky (1988) and Siskind (1990). However, this approach cannot yet provide for the automatic acquisition of lexical semantics for use in NLP systems, because the input required must be hand coded: no current artificial intelligence system has the perceptual and cognitive capabilities required to produce the needed semantic representations.

Another approach would be to use the semantics of surrounding words in an utterance to constrain the meaning of an unknown word. Borrowing an example from Pinker (1994), upon hearing *I glipped the paper to shreds*, one could guess that the meaning of *glib* has something to do with tearing. Similarly, one could guess that *filp* means something like *eat* upon hearing *I filped the delicious sandwich and now I'm full.* These guesses are cued by the meanings of *paper, shreds, sandwich, delicious, full,* and the partial syntactic analysis of the utterances that contain them. Granger (1977), Berwick (1983), and Hastings (1994) describe computational systems that implement this approach. However, this approach is hindered by the need for a large amount of initial lexical semantic information and the need for a robust natural language understanding system that produces semantic representations as output, since producing this output requires precisely the lexical semantic information the system is trying to acquire.

A third approach does not require any semantic information related to perceptual input or the input utterance. Instead it makes use of fixed correspondences between surface characteristics of language input and lexical semantic information: surface characteristics serve as cues for lexical semantics of the words. For example, if a verb is seen with a noun phrase subject and a sentential complement, it often has verbal semantics involving spatial perception and cognition, *e.g.*, *believe, think, worry,* and *see* (Fisher, Gleitman, and Gleitman, 1991; Gleitman, 1990). Similarly, the occurrence of a verb in the progressive tense can be used as a cue for the non-stativeness of the verb (Dorr and Lee, 1992); stative verbs cannot appear in the progress tense (*e.g.*,**Mary is loving her new shoes*). Another example is the use of patterns such as $NP, NP*$ *,and other*NP to find lexical semantic information such as hyponym (Hearst, 1992). *Temples, treasuries, and other important civic buildings* is an example of this pattern and from it the information that temples and treasuries are types of civic buildings would be cued. Finally, inducing lexical semantics from distributional data (*e.g.*, (Brown et al., 1992; Church et al., 1989)) is also a form of surface cueing. It should be noted that the set of fixed correspondences between surface characteristics and lexical semantic information, at this point, have to be acquired through the analysis of the researcher—the issue of how the fixed correspondences can be automatically acquired will not be addressed here.

The main advantage of the surface cueing approach is that the input required is currently available: there is an ever increasing supply of online text, which can be automatically part-of-speech tagged, assigned shallow syntactic structure by robust partial parsing systems, and morphologically analyzed, all without any prior lexical semantics.

A possible disadvantage of surface cueing is that surface cues for a particular piece of lexical semantics might be difficult to uncover or they might not exist at all. In addition, the cues might not be present for the words of interest. Thus, it is an empirical question whether easily identifiable abundant surface cues exist for the needed lexical semantic information. The next section explores the possibility of using derivational affixes as surface cues for lexical semantics.

3 Morphological Cues for Lexical Semantic Information

Many derivational affixes only apply to bases with certain semantic characteristics and only produce derived forms with certain semantic characteristics. For example, the verbal prefix *un-* applies to telic verbs and produces telic derived forms. Thus, it is possible to use *un-* as a cue for telicity. By searching a sufficiently large corpus we should be able to identify a number of telic verbs. Examples from the Brown corpus include *clasp, coil, fasten, lace,* and *screw.*

A more implementation-oriented description of the process is the following: (i) analyze affixes by hand to gain fixed correspondences between affix and lexical semantic information (ii) collect a large corpus of text, (iii) tag it with part-of-speech tags, (iv) morphologically analyze its words, (v) assign word senses to the base and the derived forms of these analyses, and (vi) use this morphological structure plus fixed correspondences to assign semantics to both the base senses and the derived form senses. Step (i) amounts to doing a semantic analysis of a number of affixes the goal of which is to find semantic generalizations for an affix that hold for a large percentage of its instances. Finding the right generalizations and stating them explicitly can be time consuming but is only performed once. Tagging the corpus is necessary to make word sense disambiguation and morphological analysis easier. Word sense disambiguation is necessary because one needs to know which sense of the base is involved in a particular derived form, more specifically, to which sense should one assign the feature cued by the affix. For example, *stress* can be either a noun *the stress on the third syllable* or a verb *the advisor stressed the importance of finishing quickly.* Since the suffix *-ful* applies to nominal bases, only a noun reading is possible as the stem of *stressful* and thus one would attach the lexical semantics cued by *-ful* to the noun sense. However, *stress* has multiple readings even as a noun: it also has the reading exemplified by *the new parent was under a lot of stress.* Only this reading is possible for *stressful.*

In order to produce the results presented in the next section, the above steps were performed as follows. A set of 18 affixes were analyzed by hand providing the fixed correspondences between cue and semantics. The cued lexical semantic information was axiomatized using Episodic Logic (Hwang and Schubert, 1993), a situation-based extension of standard first order logic. The Penn Treebank version of the Brown corpus (Marcus, Santorini, and Marcinkiewicz, 1993) served as the corpus. Only its words and part-of-speech tags were utilized. Although these tags were corrected by hand, part-of-speech tagging can be automatically performed with an error rate of 3 to 4 percent (Merialdo, 1994; Brill,

1994). The Alvey morphological analyzer (Ritchie et al., 1992) was used to assign morphological structure. It uses a lexicon with just over 62,000 entries. This lexicon was derived from a machine readable dictionary but contains no semantic information. Word sense disambiguation for the bases and derived forms that could not be resolved using part-of-speech tags was not performed. However, there exist systems for such word sense disambiguation which do not require explicit lexical semantic information (Yarowsky, 1993; Schütze, 1992).

Let us consider an example. One sense of the suffix *-ize* applies to adjectival bases (*e.g.*, *centralize*). This sense of the affix will be referred to as *-Aize*. (A related but different sense applies to nouns, *e.g.*, *glamorize*. The part-of-speech of the base is used to disambiguate these two senses of *-ize*.) First, the regular expressions "`.*IZ(E|ING|ES|ED)$`" and "`^V.*`" are used to collect tokens from the corpus that were likely to have been derived using *-ize*. The Alvey morphological analyzer is then applied to each type. It strips off *-Aize* from a word if it can find an entry with a reference form of the appropriate orthographic shape and has the features "uninflected," "latinate," and "adjective." It may also build an appropriate base using other affixes, *e.g.*,[[*tradition -al*] *-Aize*].[1] Finally, all derived forms are assigned the lexical semantic feature CHANGE-OF-STATE and all the bases are assigned the lexical semantic feature IZE-DEPENDENT. Only the CHANGE-OF-STATE feature will be discussed here. It is defined by the axiom below.

```
For all predicates P with features
CHANGE-OF-STATE and DYADIC:
∀x,y,e [P(x,y)**e ->
        [∃e1:[at-end-of(e1,e) ∧
              cause(e,e1)]
         [rstate(P)(y)**e1] ∧
         ∃e2:at-beginning-of(e2,e)
         [¬rstate(P)(y)**e2]]]
```

The operator ** is analogous to $\models$ in situation semantics; it indicates, among other things, that a formula describes an event. P is a place holder for the semantic predicate corresponding to the word sense which has the feature. It is assumed that each word sense corresponds to a single semantic predicate. The axiom states that if a CHANGE-OF-STATE predicate describes an event, then the result state of this predicate holds at the end of this event and that it did not hold at the beginning, *e.g.*, if one wants to formalize something it must be non-formal to begin with and will be formal after. The result state of an *-Aize* predicate is the predicate corresponding to its base; this is stated in another axiom.

Precision figures for the method were collected as follows. The method returns a set of normalized (*i.e.*, uninflected) word/feature pairs. A human then determines which pairs are "correct" where correct means that the axiom defining the feature holds for the instances (tokens) of the word (type). Because of the lack of word senses, the semantics assigned to a particular word is only considered correct, if it holds for all senses occurring in the relevant derived word tokens.[2] For example, the axiom above must hold for all senses of *centralize* occurring in the corpus in order for the *centralize*/CHANGE-OF-STATE pair to be correct. The axiom for IZE-DEPENDENT must hold only for those senses of *central* that occur in the tokens of *centralize* for the *central*/IZE-DEPENDENT pair to be correct. This definition of correct was constructed, in part, to make relatively quick human judgements possible. It should also be noted that the semantic judgements require that the semantics be expressed in a precise way. This discipline is enforced in part by requiring that the features be axiomatized in a denotational logic. Another argument for such an axiomatization is that many NLP systems utilize a denotational logic for representing semantic information and thus the axioms provide a straightforward interface to the lexicon.

To return to our example, as shown in Table 1, there were 63 *-Aize* derived words (types) of which 78 percent conform to the CHANGE-OF-STATE axiom. Of the bases, 80 percent conform to the IZE-DEPENDENT axiom which will be discussed in the next section. Among the conforming words were *equalize, stabilize,* and *federalize*. Two words that seem to be derived using the *-ize* suffix but do not conform to the CHANGE-OF-STATE axiom are *penalize* and *socialize (with the guests)*. A different sort of non-conformity is produced when the morphological analyzer finds a spurious parse. For example, it analyzed *subsidize* as *[sub- [side -ize]]* and thus produced the *sidize*/CHANGE-OF-STATE pair which for the relevant tokens was incorrect. In the first sort, the non-conformity arises because the cue does not always correspond to the relevant lexical semantic information. In the second sort, the non-conformity arises because a cue has been found where one does not exist. A system that utilizes a lexicon so constructed is interested primarily in the overall precision of the information contained within and thus the results presented in the next section conflate these two types of false positives.

[1] In an alternative version of the method, the morphological analyzer is also able to construct a base on its own when it is unable to find an appropriate base in its lexicon. However, these "new" bases seldom correspond to actual words and thus the results presented here were derived using a morphological analyzer configured to only use bases that are directly in its lexicon or can be constructed from words in its lexicon.

[2] Although this definition is required for many cases, in the vast majority of the cases, the derived form and its base have only one possible sense (*e.g.*, *stressful*).

4 Results

This section starts by discussing the semantics of 18 derivational affixes: *re-, un-, de-, -ize, -en, -ify, -le, -ate, -ee, -er, -ant, -age, -ment, mis-, -able, -ful, -less*, and *-ness*. Following this discussion, a table of precision statistics for the performance of these surface cues is presented. Due to space limitations, the lexical semantics cued by these affixes can only be loosely specified. However, they have been axiomatized in a fashion exemplified by the CHANGE-OF-STATE axiom above (see (Light, 1996; Light, 1992)).

The verbal prefixes *un-, de-*, and *re-* cue aspectual information for their base and derived forms. Some examples from the Brown corpus are *unfasten, unwind, decompose, defocus, reactivate*, and *readapt*. Above it was noted that *un-* is a cue for telicity. In fact, both *un-* and *de-* cue the CHANGE-OF-STATE feature for their base and derived forms—the CHANGE-OF-STATE feature entails the TELIC feature. In addition, for *un-* and *de-*, the result state of the derived form is the negation of the result state of the base (NEG-OF-BASE-IS-RSTATE), *e.g.*, the result of unfastening something is the opposite of the result of fastening it. As shown by examples like *reswim the last lap*, *re-* only cues the TELIC feature for its base and derived forms: the lap might have been swum previously and thus the negation of the result state does not have to have held previously (Dowty, 1979). For *re-*, the result state of the derived form is the same as that of the base (RSTATE-EQ-BASE-RSTATE), *e.g.*, the result of reactivating something is the same as activating it. In fact, if one reactivates something then it is also being activated: the derived form entails the base (ENTAILS-BASE). Finally, for *re-*, the derived form entails that its result state held previously, *e.g.*, if one recentralizes something then it must have been central at some point previous to the event of recentralization (PRESUPS-RSTATE).

The suffixes *-Aize, -Nize, -en, -Aify, -Nify* all cue the CHANGE-OF-STATE feature for their derived form as was discussed for *-Aize* above. Some exemplars are *centralize, formalize, categorize, colonize, brighten, stiffen, falsify, intensify, mummify*, and *glorify*. For *-Aize, -en* and *-Aify* a bit more can be said about the result state: it is the base predicate (RSTATE-EQ-BASE), *e.g.*, the result of formalizing something is that it is formal. Finally *-Aize, -en*, and *-Aify* cue the following feature for their bases: if a state holds of some individual then either an event described by the derived form predicate occurred previously or the predicate was always true of the individual (IZE-DEPENDENT), *e.g.*, if something is central then either it was centralized or it was always central.

The "suffixes" *-le* and *-ate* should really be called verbal endings since they are not suffixes in English, *i.e.*, if one strips them off one is seldom left with a word. (Consequently, only regular expressions were used to collect types; the morphological analyzer was not used.) Nonetheless, they cue lexical semantics and are easily identified. Some examples are *chuckle, dangle, alleviate*, and *assimilate*. The ending *-ate* cues a CHANGE-OF-STATE verb and *-le* an ACTIVITY verb.

The derived forms produced by *-ee, -er*, and *-ant* all refer to participants of an event described by their base (PART-IN-E). Some examples are *appointee, deportee, blower, campaigner, assailant*, and *claimant*. In addition, the derived form of *-ee* is also sentient of this event and non-volitional with respect to it (Barker, 1995).

The nominalizing suffixes *-age* and *-ment* both produce derived forms that refer to something resulting from an event of the verbal base predicate. Some examples are *blockage, seepage, marriage, payment, restatement, shipment*, and *treatment*. The derived forms of *-age* entail that an event occurred and refer to something resulting from it (EVENT-AND-RESULTANT)), *e.g.*, seepage entails that seeping took place and that the seepage resulted from this seeping. Similarly, the derived forms of *-ment* entail that an event took place and refer either to this event, the proposition that the event occurred, or something resulting from the event (REFERS-TO-E-OR-PROP-OR-RESULT), *e.g.*, a restatement entails that a restating occurred and refers either to this event, the proposition that the event occurred, or to the actual utterance or written document resulting from the restating event. (This analysis is based on (Zucchi, 1989).)

The verbal prefix *mis-*, *e.g.*, *miscalculate* and *misquote*, cues the feature that an action is performed in an incorrect manner (INCORRECT-MANNER). The suffix *-able* cues a feature that it is possible to perform some action (ABLE-TO-BE-PERFORMED), *e.g.*, something is enforceable if it is possible that something can enforce it (Dowty, 1979). The words derived using *-ness* refer to a state of something having the property of the base (STATE-OF-HAVING-PROP-OF-BASE), *e.g.*, in *Kim's fierceness at the meeting yesterday was unusual* the word *fierceness* refers to a state of Kim being fierce. The suffix *-ful* marks its base as abstract (ABSTRACT): *careful, peaceful, powerful*, etc. In addition, it marks its derived form as the antonym of a form derived by *-less* if it exists (LESS-ANTONYM). The suffix *-less* marks its derived forms with the analogous feature (FUL-ANTONYM). Some examples are *colorful/less, fearful/less, harmful/less*, and *tasteful/less*.

The precision statistics for the individual lexical semantic features discussed above are presented in Table 1 and Table 2. Lexical semantic information was collected for 2535 words (bases and derived forms). One way to summarize these tables is to calculate a single precision number for all the features in a table, *i.e.*, average the number of correct types for each affix, sum these averages, and then divide this sum by the total number of types. Using this statistic it can be said that if a random word is derived, its features have a 76 percent chance of being true and if it is a stem of a derived form, its features have a 82 percent chance of being true.

Computing recall requires finding all true tokens of a cue. This is a labor intensive task. It was performed for the verbal prefix *re-* and the recall was found to be 85 percent. The majority of the missed *re-* verbs were due to the fact that the system only looked at verbs starting with RE and not other parts-of-speech, *e.g.*, many nominalizations such as *reaccommodation* contain the *re-* morphological cue. However, increasing recall by looking at all open class categories would probably decrease precision. Another cause of reduced recall is that some stems were not in the Alvey lexicon or could not be properly extracted by the morphological analyzer. For example, *-Nize* could not be stripped from *hypothesize* because Alvey failed to reconstruct *hypothesis* from *hypothes*. However, for the affixes discussed here, 89 percent of the bases were present in the Alvey lexicon.

5 Evaluation

Good surface cues are easy to identify, abundant, and correspond to the needed lexical semantic information (Hearst (1992) identifies a similar set of desiderata). With respect to these desiderata, derivational morphology is both a good cue and a bad cue.

Let us start with why it is a bad cue: there may be no derivational cues for the lexical semantics of a particular word. This is not the case for other surface cues, *e.g.*, distributional cues exist for every word in a corpus. In addition, even if a derivational cue does exist, the reliability (on average approximately 76 percent) of the lexical semantic information is too low for many NLP tasks. This unreliability is due in part to the inherent exceptionality of lexical generalization and thus can be improved only partially.

However, derivational morphology is a good cue in the following ways. It provides exactly the type of lexical semantics needed for many NLP tasks: the affixes discussed in the previous section cued nominal semantic class, verbal aspectual class, antonym relationships between words, sentience, etc. In addition, working with the Brown corpus (1.1 million words) and 18 affixes provided such information for over 2500 words. Since corpora with over 40 million words are common and English has over 40 common derivational affixes, one would expect to be able to increase this number by an order of magnitude. In addition, most English words are either derived themselves or serve as bases of at least one derivational affix.[3] Finally, for some NLP tasks, 76 per-

[3]The following experiment supports this claim. Just

Feature	Affix	Types	Precision
TELIC	*re-*	164	91%
RSTATE-EQ-BASE-RSTATE	*re-*	164	65%
ENTAILS-BASE	*re-*	164	65%
PRESUPS-RSTATE	*re-*	164	65%
CHANGE-OF-STATE	*un-*	23	100%
NEG-OF-BASE-IS-RSTATE	*un-*	23	91%
CHANGE-OF-STATE	*de-*	35	34%
NEG-OF-BASE-IS-RSTATE	*de-*	35	20%
CHANGE-OF-STATE	*-Aize*	63	78%
RSTATE-EQ-BASE	*-Aize*	63	75%
CHANGE-OF-STATE	*-Nize*	86	56%
ACTIVITY	*-le*	71	55%
CHANGE-OF-STATE	*-en*	36	100%
RSTATE-EQ-BASE	*-en*	36	97%
CHANGE-OF-STATE	*-Aify*	17	94%
RSTATE-EQ-BASE	*-Aify*	17	58%
CHANGE-OF-STATE	*-Nify*	21	67%
CHANGE-OF-STATE	*-ate*	365	48%
PART-IN-E	*-ee*	22	91%
SENTIENT	*-ee*	22	82%
NON-VOLITIONAL	*-ee*	22	68%
PART-IN-E	*-er*	471	85%
PART-IN-E	*-ant*	21	81%
EVENT-AND-RESULTANT	*-age*	43	58%
REFERS-TO-E-OR-PROP-OR-RESULTANT	*-ment*	166	88%
INCORRECT-MANNER	*mis-*	21	86%
ABLE-TO-BE-PERFORMED	*-able*	148	84%
STATE-OF-HAVING-PROP-OF-BASE	*-ness*	307	97%
FUL-ANTONYM	*-less*	22	77%
LESS-ANTONYM	*-ful*	22	77%

Table 1: Derived words

Feature	Affix	Types	Precision
TELIC	*re-*	164	91%
CHANGE-OF-STATE	*Vun-*	23	91%
CHANGE-OF-STATE	*Vde-*	33	36%
IZE-DEPENDENT	*-Aize*	64	80%
IZE-DEPENDENT	*-en*	36	72%
IZE-DEPENDENT	*-Aify*	15	40%
ABSTRACT	*-ful*	76	93%

Table 2: Base words

cent reliability may be adequate. In addition, some affixes are much more reliable cues than others and thus if higher reliability is required then only the affixes with high precision might be used.

The above discussion makes it clear that morphological cueing provides only a partial solution to the problem of acquiring lexical semantic information. However, as mentioned in section 2 there are many types of surface cues which correspond to a variety of lexical semantic information. A combination of cues should produce better precision where the same information is indicated by multiple cues. For example, the morphological cue *re-* indicates telicity and as mentioned above, the syntactic cue the progressive tense indicates non-stativity (Dorr and Lee, 1992). Since telicity is a type of non-stativity, the information is mutually supportive. In addition, using many different types of cues should provide a greater variety of information in general. Thus morphological cueing is best seen as one type of surface cueing that can be used in combination with others to provide lexical semantic information.

6 Acknowledgements

A portion of this work was performed at the University of Rochester Computer Science Department and supported by ONR/ARPA research grant number N00014-92-J-1512.

References

Barker, Chris. 1995. The semantics of *-ee*. In *Proceedings of the SALT conference.*

Berwick, Robert. 1983. Learning word meanings from examples. In *Proceedings of the 8th International Joint Conference on Artificial Intelligence (IJCAI-83).*

Brill, Eric. 1994. Some advances in transformation-based part of speech tagging. In *Proceedings of the Twelfth National conference on Artificial Intelligence: American Association for Artificial Intelligence (AAAI).*

Brown, Peter F., Vincent J. Della Pietra, Peter V. deSouza, Jennifer C. Lai, and Robert L. Mercer. 1992. Class-based *n*-gram models of natural language. *Computational Linguistics*, 18(4).

Church, Kenneth, William Gale, Patrick Hanks, and Donald Hindle. 1989. Parsing, word associations and typical predicate-argument relations. In *International Workshop on Parsing Technologies*, pages 389–98.

over 400 open class words were picked randomly from the Brown corpus and the derived forms were marked by hand. Based on this data, a random open class word in the Brown corpus has a 17 percent chance of being derived, a 56 percent chance of being a stem of a derived form, and an 8 percent chance of being both.

Dorr, Bonnie J. and Ki Lee. 1992. Building a lexicon for machine translation: Use of corpora for aspectual classification of verbs. Technical Report CS-TR-2876, University of Maryland.

Dowty, David. 1979. *Word Meaning and Montague Grammar.* Reidel.

Fisher, Cynthia, Henry Gleitman, and Lila R. Gleitman. 1991. On the semantic content of subcategorization frames. *Cognitive Psychology*, 23(3):331–392.

Gleitman, Lila. 1990. The structural sources of verb meanings. *Language Acquisition*, 1:3–55.

Granger, R. 1977. Foulup: a program that figures out meanings of words from context. In *Proceedings of the 5th International Joint Conference on Artificial Intelligence.*

Grimshaw, Jane. 1981. Form, function, and the language acquisition device. In C. L. Baker and J. J. McCarthy, editors, *the logical problem of language acquisition.* MIT Press.

Hastings, Peter. 1994. *Automatic Acquistion of Word Meaning from Context.* Ph.D. thesis, University of Michigan.

Hearst, Marti. 1992. Automatic acquisition of hyponyms from large text corpora. In *Proceedings of the fifteenth International Conference on Computational Linguistics (COLING).*

Hwang, Chung Hee and Lenhart Schubert. 1993. Episodic logic: a comprehensive natural representation for language understanding. *Mind and Machine*, 3(4):381–419.

Light, Marc. 1992. Rehashing *Re-*. In *Proceedings of the Eastern States Conference on Linguistics.* Cornell University Linguistics Department Working Papers.

Light, Marc. 1996. *Morphological Cues for Lexical Semantics.* Ph.D. thesis, University of Rochester, Rochester, NY.

Marcus, Mitchell, Beatrice Santorini, and Mary Ann Marcinkiewicz. 1993. Building a large annotated corpus of English: The Penn Treebank. *Computational Linguistics*, 19(2):313–330.

Merialdo, Bernard. 1994. Tagging English text with a probabilistic model. *Computational Linguistics*, 20(2):155–172.

Pinker, Steven. 1989. *Learnability and Cognition: The Acquisition of Argument Structure.* MIT Press.

Pinker, Steven. 1994. How could a child use verb syntax to learn verb semantics? *Lingua*, 92:377–410.

Pustejovsky, James. 1988. Constraints on the acquisition of semantic knowledge. *International journal of intelligent systems*, 3:247–268.

Ritchie, Graeme D., Graham J. Russell, Alan W. Black, and Steve G. Pulman. 1992. *Computational Morphology: Practical Mechanisms for the English Lexicon.* MIT press.

Schütze, Hinrich. 1992. Word sense disambiguation with sublexical representations. In *Statistically-Based NLP Techniques (American Association for Artificial Intelligence Workshop, July 12-16, 1992, San Jose, CA.)*, pages 109–113.

Siskind, Jeffrey M. 1990. Acquiring core meanings of words, represented as Jackendoff-style conceptual structures, from correlated streams of linguistic and non-linguistic input. In *Proceedings of the 28th Meeting of the Association for Computational Linguistics.*

Yarowsky, David. 1993. One sense per collocation. In *Proceedings of the ARPA Workshop on Human Language Technology.* Morgan Kaufmann.

Zucchi, Alessandro. 1989. *The Language of Propositions and Events: Issues in the Syntax and the Semantics of Nominalization.* Ph.D. thesis, University of Massachusetts, Amherst, MA.

From *Submit* to *Submitted* via *Submission*: On Lexical Rules in Large-Scale Lexicon Acquisition.

Evelyne Viegas, Boyan Onyshkevych§, Victor Raskin§§, Sergei Nirenburg
Computing Research Laboratory,
New Mexico State University,
Las Cruces, NM 88003, USA
viegas,boyan,raskin,sergei@crl.nmsu.edu

Abstract

This paper deals with the discovery, representation, and use of lexical rules (LRs) during large-scale semi-automatic computational lexicon acquisition. The analysis is based on a set of LRs implemented and tested on the basis of Spanish and English business- and finance-related corpora. We show that, though the use of LRs is justified, they do not come cost-free. Semi-automatic output checking is required, even with blocking and preemtion procedures built in. Nevertheless, large-scope LRs are justified because they facilitate the unavoidable process of large-scale semi-automatic lexical acquisition. We also argue that the place of LRs in the computational process is a complex issue.

1 Introduction

This paper deals with the discovery, representation, and use of lexical rules (LRs) in the process of large-scale semi-automatic computational lexicon acquisition. LRs are viewed as a means to minimize the need for costly lexicographic heuristics, to reduce the number of lexicon entry types, and generally to make the acquisition process faster and cheaper. The findings reported here have been implemented and tested on the basis of Spanish and English business- and finance-related corpora.

The central idea of our approach – that there are systematic paradigmatic meaning relations between lexical items, such that, given an entry for one such item, other entries can be derived automatically – is certainly not novel. In modern times, it has been reintroduced into linguistic discourse by the Meaning-Text group in their work on lexical functions (see, for instance, (Mel'čuk, 1979). It has been lately incorporated into computational lexicography in (Atkins, 1991), (Ostler and Atkins, 1992), (Briscoe and Copestake, 1991), (Copestake and Briscoe, 1992), (Briscoe et al., 1993)).

Pustejovsky (Pustejovsky, 1991, 1995) has coined an attractive term to capture these phenomena: one of the declared objectives of his 'generative lexicon' is a departure from sense enumeration to sense derivation with the help of lexical rules. The generative lexicon provides a useful framework for potentially infinite sense modulation in specific contexts (cf. (Leech, 1981), (Cruse, 1986)), due to type coercion (e.g., (Pustejovsky, 1993)) and similar phenomena. Most LRs in the generative lexicon approach, however, have been proposed for small classes of words and explain such grammatical and semantic shifts as *+count* to *−count* or *−common* to *+common*.

While shifts and modulations are important, we find that the main significance of LRs is their promise to aid the task of *massive* lexical acquisition.

Section 2 below outlines the nature of LRs in our approach and their status in the computational process. Section 3 presents a fully implemented case study, the morpho-semantic LRs. Section 4 briefly reviews the cost factors associated with LRs; the argument in it is based on another case study, the adjective-related LRs, which is especialy instructive since it may mislead one into thinking that LRs are unconditionally beneficial.

2 Nature of Lexical Rules

2.1 Ontological-Semantic Background

Our approach to NLP can be characterized as ontology-driven semantics (see, e.g., (Nirenburg and Levin, 1992)). The lexicon for which our LRs are introduced is intended to support the computational specification and use of text meaning representations. The lexical entries are quite complex, as they must contain many different types of lexical knowledge that may be used by specialist processes for automatic text analysis or generation (see, e.g.,

§ also of US Department of Defense, Attn R525, Fort Meade, MD 20755, USA and Carnegie Mellon University, Pittsburgh, PA. USA. §§ also of Purdue University NLP Lab, W Lafayette, IN 47907, USA.

(Onyshkevych and Nirenburg, 1995), for a detailed description). The acquisition of such a lexicon, with or without the assistance of LRs, involves a substantial investment of time and resources. The meaning of a lexical entry is encoded in a (lexical) semantic representation language (see, e.g., (Nirenburg et al., 1992)) whose primitives are predominantly terms in an independently motivated world model, or ontology (see, e.g., (Carlson and Nirenburg, 1990) and (Mahesh and Nirenburg, 1995)).

The basic unit of the lexicon is a 'superentry,' one for each citation form holds, irrespective of its lexical class. Word senses are called 'entries.' The LR processor applies to all the word senses for a given superentry. For example, *pronunciar* has (at least) two entries (one could be translated as "articulate" and one as "declare"); the LR generator, when applied to the superentry, would produce (among others) two forms of *pronunciación*, derived from each of those two senses/entries.

The nature of the links in the lexicon to the ontology is critical to the entire issue of LRs. Representations of lexical meaning may be defined in terms of any number of ontological primitives, called *concepts*. Any of the concepts in the ontology may be used (singly or in combination) in a lexical meaning representation.

No necessary correlation is expected between syntactic category and properties and semantic or ontological classification and properties (and here we definitely part company with syntax-driven semantics–see, for example, (Levin, 1992), (Dorr, 1993) –pretty much along the lines established in (Nirenburg and Levin, 1992). For example, although meanings of many verbs are represented through reference to ontological EVENTs and a number of nouns are represented by concepts from the OBJECT sublattice, frequently nominal meanings refer to EVENTs and verbal meanings to OBJECTs. Many LRs produce entries in which the syntactic category of the input form is changed; however, in our model, the semantic category is preserved in many of these LRs. For example, the verb *destroy* may be represented by an EVENT, as will the noun *destruction* (naturally, with a different linking in the syntax-semantics interface). Similarly, *destroyer* (as a person) would be represented using the same event with the addition of a HUMAN as a filler of the agent case role. This built-in transcategoriality strongly facilitates applications such as interlingual MT, as it renders vacuous many problems connected with category mismatches (Kameyama et al., 1991) and misalignments or divergences (Dorr, 1995), (Heid, 1993) that plague those paradigms in MT which do not rely on extracting language-neutral text meaning representations. This transcategoriality is supported by LRs.

2.2 Approaches to LRs and Their Types

In reviewing the theoretical and computational linguistics literature on LRs, one notices a number of different delimitations of LRs from morphology, syntax, lexicon, and processing. Below we list three parameters which highlight the possible differences among approaches to LRs.

2.2.1 Scope of Phenomena

Depending on the paradigm or approach, there are phenomena which may be more–or less–appropriate for treatment by LRs than by syntactic transformations, lexical enumeration, or other mechanisms. LRs offer greater generality and productivity at the expense of overgeneration, i.e., suggesting inappropriate forms which need to be weeded out before actual inclusion in a lexicon. The following phenomena seem to be appropriate for treatment with LRs:

- Inflected Forms - Specifically, those inflectional phenomena which accompany changes in subcategorization frame (passivization, dative alternation, etc.).
- Word Formation - The production of derived forms by LR is illustrated in a case study below, and includes formation of deverbal nominals (*destruction*, *running*), agentive nouns (*catcher*). Typically involving a shift in syntactic category, these LRs are often less productive than inflection-oriented ones. Consequently, derivational LRs are even more prone to overgeneration than inflectional LRs.
- Regular Polysemy - This set of phenomena includes regular polysemies or regular non-metaphoric and non-metonymic alternations such as those described in (Apresjan, 1974), (Pustejovsky, 1991, 1995), (Ostler and Atkins, 1992) and others.

2.2.2 When Should LRs Be Applied?

Once LRs are defined in a computational scenario, a decision is required about the time of application of those rules. In a particular system, LRs can be applied at acquisition time, at lexicon load time and at run time.

- Acquisition Time - The major advantage of this strategy is that the results of any LR expansion can be checked by the lexicon acquirer, though at the cost of substantial additional time. Even with the best left-hand side (LHS) conditions (see below), the lexicon acquirer may be flooded by new lexical entries to validate. During the review process, the lexicographer can accept the generated form, reject it as inappropriate, or make minor modifications. If the LR is being used to build the lexicon up from scratch, then mechanisms used by Ostler and Atkins (Ostler and Atkins, 1992) or (Briscoe et al., 1995), such as blocking or preemption, are not available as automatic mechanisms for avoiding overgeneration.

- Lexicon Load Time - The LRs can be applied to the base lexicon at the time the lexicon is loaded into the computational system. As with run-time loading, the risk is that overgeneration will cause more degradation in accuracy than the missing (derived) forms if the LRs were not applied in the first place. If the LR inventory approach is used or if the LHS constraints are very good (see below), then the overgeneration penalty is minimized, and the advantage of a large run-time lexicon is combined with efficiency in look-up and disk savings.
- Run Time - Application of LRs at run time raises additional difficulties by not supporting an index of all the head forms to be used by the syntactic and semantic processes. For example, if there is an LR which produces ***abusive-adj2*** from ***abuse-v1***, the adjectival form will be unknown to the syntactic parser, and its production would only be triggered by failure recovery mechanisms — if direct lookup failed and the reverse morphological process identified ***abuse-v1*** as a potential source of the entry needed.

A hybrid scenario of LR use is also plausible, where, for example, LRs apply at acquisition time to produce new lexical entries, but may also be available at run time as an error recovery strategy to attempt generation of a form or word sense not already found in the lexicon.

2.2.3 LR Triggering Conditions

For any of the LR application opportunities itemized above, a methodology needs to be developed for the selection of the subset of LRs which are applicable to a given lexical entry (whether base or derived). Otherwise, the LRs will grossly overgenerate, resulting in inappropriate entries, computational inefficiency, and degradation of accuracy. Two approaches suggest themselves.

- LR Itemization - The simplest mechanism of rule triggering is to include in each lexicon entry an explicit list of applicable rules. LR application can be chained, so that the rule chains are expanded, either statically, in the specification, or dynamically, at application time. This approach avoids any inappropriate application of the rules (overgeneration), though at the expense of tedious work at lexicon acquisition time. One drawback of this strategy is that if a new LR is added, each lexical entry needs to be revisited and possibly updated.
- Rule LHS Constraints - The other approach is to maintain a bank of LRs, and rely on their LHSs to constrain the application of the rules to only the appropriate cases; in practice, however, it is difficult to set up the constraints in such a way as to avoid over- or undergeneration *a priori*. Additionally, this approach (at least, when applied after acquisition time) does not allow explicit ordering of word senses, a practice preferred by many lexicographers to indicate relative frequency or salience; this sort of information can be captured by other mechanisms (e.g., using frequency-of-occurrence statistics). This approach does, however, capture the paradigmatic generalization that is represented by the rule, and simplifies lexical acquisition.

3 Morpho-Semantics and Constructive Derivational Morphology: a Transcategorial Approach to Lexical Rules

In this section, we present a case study of LRs based on constructive derivational morphology. Such LRs automatically produce word forms which are polysemous, such as the Spanish *generador* 'generator,' either the artifact or someone who generates. The LRs have been tested in a real world application, involving the semi-automatic acquisition of a Spanish computational lexicon of about 35,000 word senses.

We accelerated the process of lexical acquisition[1] by developing morpho-semantic LRs which, when applied to a lexeme, produced an average of 25 new candidate entries. Figure 1 below illustrates the overall process of generating new entries from a citation form, by applying morpho-semantic LRs.

Generation of new entries usually starts with verbs. Each verb found in the corpora is submitted to the morpho-semantic generator which produces all its morphological derivations and, based on a detailed set of tested heuristics, attaches to each form an appropriate semantic LR label, for instance, the nominal form *comprador* will be among the ones generated from the verb *comprar* and the semantic LR "agent-of" is attached to it. The mechanism of rule application is illustrated below.

The form list generated by the morpho-semantic generator is checked against three MRDs (Collins Spanish-English, Simon and Schuster Spanish-English, and Larousse Spanish) and the forms found in them are submitted to the acquisition process. However, forms not found in the dictionaries are not discarded outright because the MRDs cannot be assumed to be complete and some of these "rejected" forms can, in fact, be found in corpora or in the input text of an application system. This mechanism works because we rely on linguistic clues and

[1] See (Viegas and Nirenburg, 1995) for the details on the acquisition process to build the core Spanish lexicon, and (Viegas and Beale, 1996) for the details on the conceptual and technological tools used to check the quality of the lexicon.

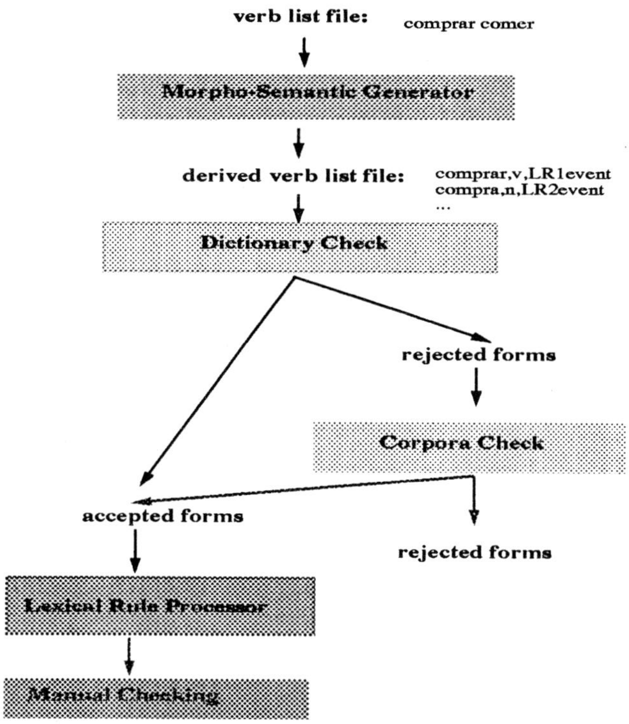

Figure 1: Automatic Generation of New Entries.

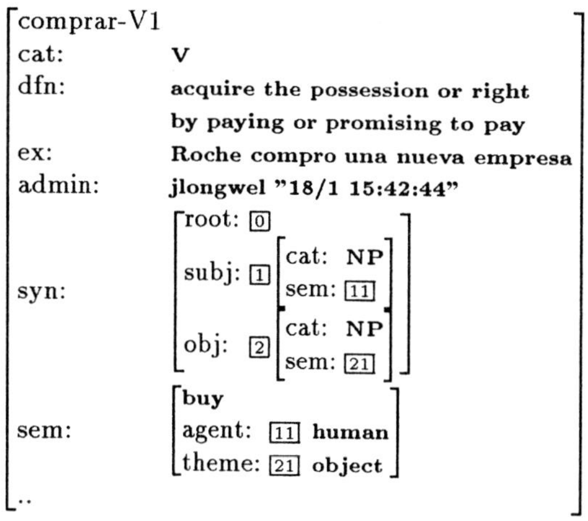

Figure 2: Partial Entry for the Spanish lexical item *comprar*.

therefore our system does not grossly overgenerate candidates.

The Lexical Rule Processor is an engine which produces a new entry from an existing one, such as the new entry *compra* (Figure 3) produced from the verb entry *comprar* (Figure 2) after applying the LR2event rule.[2]

The acquirer must check the definition and enter an example, but the rest of the information is simply retained. The LEXical-RULES zone specifies the morpho-semantic rule which was applied to produce this new entry and the verb it has been applied to.

The morpho-semantic generator produces all predictable morphonological derivations with their morpho-lexico-semantic associations, using three major sources of clues: 1) word-forms with their corresponding morpho-semantic classification; 2) stem alternations and 3) construction mechanisms. The patterns of attachement include unification, concatenation and output rules[3]. For instance *beber* can be derived into *beb[e]dero, bebe[e]dor, beb[i]do, beb[i]da, volver* into *vuelto*, and *communicar* into *telecommunicación*, etc... All affixes are assigned semantic features. For instance, the morpho-semantic rule *LRpolarity_negative* is at least attached to all verbs belonging to the -AR class of Spanish verbs, whose initial stem is of the form 'con', 'tra', or 'fir' with the corresponding allomorph *-in* attached to it (*incontrolable, intratable, ...*).

Figure 4 below, shows the derivational morphology output for *comprar*, with the associated lexical rules which are later used to actually generate the entries. Lexical rules[4] were applied to 1056 verb citation forms with 1263 senses among them. The rules helped acquire an average of 25 candidate new entries per verb sense, thus producing a total of 31,680 candidate entries.

From the 26 different citation forms shown in Figure 4, only 9 forms (see Figure 5), featuring 16 new entries, have been accepted after checking.[5]

For instance, *comprable, adj, LR3feasibility-attribute1*, is morphologically derived from *comprar*,

[2]We used the typed feature structures (tfs) as described in (Pollard and Sag, 1997). We do not illustrate inheritance of information across partial lexical entries.

[3]The derivation of stem alternations is beyond the scope of this paper, and is discussed in (Viegas et al., 1996).

[4]We developed about a hundred morpho-semantic rules, described in (Viegas et al., 1996).

[5]The results of the derivational morphology program output are checked against existing corpora and dictionaries, automatically.

compra-N1	
cat:	**V**
dfn:	**acquire the possession or right by paying or promising to pay**
ex:	
admin:	**LR2event "11/12 20:33:02"**
syn:	[root: [0] [cat: **N**, sem: [00]]]
sem:	[[00] **buy**]
lex-rul:	**comprar-V1 "LR2event"**
...	

Figure 3: Partial Entry for the Spanish lexical item *compra* generated automatically.

and adds to the semantics of *comprar* the shade of meaning of possibility.

In this example no forms rejected by the dictionaries were found in the corpora, and therefore there was no reason to generate these new entries. However, the citation forms *supercompra, precompra, precomprado, autocomprar* actually appeared in other corpora, so that entries for them could be generated automatically at run time.

4 The Cost of Lexical Rules

It is clear by now that LRs are most useful in large-scale acquisition. In the process of Spanish acquisition, 20% of all entries were created from scratch by PI-level lexicographers and 80% were generated by LRs and checked by research associates. It should be made equally clear, however, that the use of LRs is not cost-free. Besides the effort of discovering and implementing them, there is also the significant time and effort expenditure on the procedure of semi-automatic checking of the results of the application of LRs to the basic entries, such as those for the verbs.

The shifts and modulations studied in the literature in connection with the LRs and generative lexicon have also been shown to be not problem-free: sometimes the generation processes are blocked–or preempted–for a variety of lexical, semantic and other reasons (see (Ostler and Atkins, 1992)). In fact, the study of blocking processes, their view as systemic rather than just a bunch of exceptions, is by itself an interesting enterprise (see (Briscoe et al., 1995)).

Obviously, similar problems occur in real-life large-scale lexical rules as well. Even the most seemingly regular processes do not typically go through in 100% of all cases. This makes the LR-affected entries not generable fully automatically and this is why each application of an LR to a qualifying phe-

Derived form	POS	Lexical Rule
comprar	v	lr1event
compra	n	lr2event8b
compra	n	lr2theme_of_event9b
comprado	n	lr2reputation_att1a
comprador	n	lr2reputation_att2c
comprador	n	lr2social_role_rel2c
comprado	n	lr2theme_of_event1a
comprado	adj	lr3event_telic1a
comprable	adj	lr3feasibility_att1
compradero	adj	lr3feasibility_att2c
compradizo	adj	lr3feasibility_att3c
comprado	adj	lr3reputation_att1a
comprador	adj	lr3reputation_att2c
comprador	adj	lr3social_role_relc
malcomprar	v	neg_eval_attitude1 lr1event
malcomprado	adj	lr3event_telic1a
subcomprar	v	part_of_relation3 lr1event
subcomprado	adj	lr3event_telic1a
autocomprar	v	agent_beneficiary1b lr1event
autocompra	n	lr2event8b
autocompra	n	lr2theme_of_event9b
autocomprado	adj	lr3event_telic1a
recomprar	v	aspect_iter_semelfact1 lr1event
recompra	n	lr2event8b
recompra	n	lr2theme_of_event9b
recomprado	adj	lr3event_telic1a
supercomprar	v	eval_attitude6 lr1event
supercompra	n	lr2event8b
supercompra	n	lr2theme_of_event9b
supercomprado	adj	lr3event_telic1a
precomprar	v	before_temporal_rel5 lr1event
precompra	n	lr2event8b
precompra	n	lr2theme_of_event9b
precomprado	adj	lr3event_telic1a
descomprar	v	opp_rel2 lr1event
descompra	n	lr2event8b
descompra	n	lr2theme_of_event9b
descomprado	adj	lr3event_telic1a
compraventa	n	lr2p_event8b lr2s_event8b

Figure 4: Morpho-semantic Output.

Derived form	POS	Lexical Rule
comprar	v	lr1event
comprado	n	lr2theme_of_event1a
compra	n	lr2event8b
comprado	n	lr2reputation_att1a
comprador	n	lr2agent_of2c
comprador	n	lr2social_role_rel2c
compra	n	lr2theme_of_event9b
comprable	adj	lr3feasibility_att1
compradero	adj	lr3feasibility_att2c
compradizo	adj	lr3feasibility_att3c
comprado	adj	lr3agent_of1a
comprador	adj	lr3reputation_att2c
comprador	adj	lr3social_role_rel2c
comprado	adj	lr3event_telic1a
recomprar	v	aspect_iter_semelfact1 lr1event
recompra	n	lr2event8b
recompra	n	lr2theme_of_event9b
compraventa	n	lr2p_event8b lr2s_event8b

Figure 5: Dictionary Checking Output.

nomenon must be checked manually in the process of acquisition.

Adjectives provide a good case study for that. The acquisition of adjectives in general (see (Raskin and Nirenburg, 1995)) results in the discovery and application of several large-scope lexical rules, and it appears that no exceptions should be expected. Table 1 illustrates examples of LRs discovered and used in adjective entries.

The first three and the last rule are truly large-scope rules. Out of these, the *-able* rule seems to be the most homogeneous and 'error-proof.' Around 300 English adjectives out of the 6,000 or so, which occur in the intersection of LDOCE and the 1987-89 Wall Street Journal corpora, end in *-able*.

About 87% of all the *-able* adjectives are like *readable*: they mean, basically, something that can be read. In other words, they typically modify the noun which is the theme (or beneficiary, if animate) of the verb from which the adjective is derived:

One can read the book.–The book is readable.

The temptation to mark all the verbs as capable of assuming the suffix *-able* (or *-ible*) and forming adjectives with this type of meaning is strong, but it cannot be done because of various forms of blocking or preemption. Verbs like *kill, relate*, or *necessitate* do not form such adjectives comfortably or at all. Adjectives like *audible* or *legible* do conform to the formula above, but they are derived, as it were, from suppletive verbs, *hear* and *read*, respectively. More distressingly, however, a complete acquisition process for these adjectives uncovers 17 different combinations of semantic roles for the nouns modified by the *-ble* adjectives, involving, besides the "standard" theme or beneficiary roles, the agent, experiencer, location, and even the entire event expressed by the verb. It is true that some of these combinations are extremely rare (e.g. *perishable*), and all together they account for under 40 adjectives. The point remains, however, that each case has to be checked manually (well, semi-automatically, because the same tools that we have developed for acquisition are used in checking), so that the exact meaning of the derived adjective with regard to that of the verb itself is determined. It turns out also that, for a polysemous verb, the adjective does not necessarily inherit all its meanings (e.g., *perishable* again).

5 Conclusion

In this paper, we have discussed several aspects of the discovery, representation, and implementation of LRs, where, we believe, they count, namely, in the actual process of developing a realistic-size, real-life NLP system. Our LRs tend to be large-scope rules, which saves us a lot of time and effort on massive lexical acquisition.

Research reported in this paper has exhibited a finer grain size of description of morphemic semantics by recognizing more meaning components of non-root morphemes than usually acknowledged.

The reported research concentrated on lexical rules for derivational morphology. The same mechanism has been shown, in small-scale experiments, to work for other kinds of lexical regularities, notably cases of regular polysemy (e.g., (Ostler and Atkins, 1992), (Apresjan, 1974)).

Our treatment of transcategoriality allows for a lexicon superentry to contain senses which are not simply enumerated. The set of entries in a superentry can be seen as an hierarchy of a few "original" senses and a number of senses derived from them according to well-defined rules. Thus, the argument between the sense-enumeration and sense-derivation schools in computational lexicography may be shown to be of less importance than suggested by recent literature.

Our lexical rules are quite different from the lexical rules used in lexically-based grammars (such as (GPSG, (Gazdar et al., 1985) or sign-based theories (HPSG, (Pollard and Sag, 1987)), as the latter can rather be viewed as linking rules and often deal with issues such as subcategorization.

The issue of when to apply the lexical rules in a computational environment is relatively new. More studies must be made to determine the most beneficial place of LRs in a computational process.

Finally, it is also clear that each LR comes at a certain human-labor and computational expense, and if the applicability, or "payload," of a rule is limited, its use may not be worth the extra effort. We cannot say at this point that LRs provide any advantages in computation or quality of the deliverables. What

LRs	Applied to	Entry Type 1	Entry Type 2	Examples
Comparative	All scalars	Positive Degree	Comparative Degree	good–better big–bigger
Semantic Role Shifter Family of LR's	Event-Based Adjs	Adj. Entry corresponding to one semantic role of the underlying verb	Adj. entry corresponding to another semantic role of the underlying verb	abusive noticeable
-Able LR	Event-Based Adjs	Verbs taking the -able suffix to form an adj	Adjs formed with the help of -able from these verbs (including "suppletivism")	noticeable vulnerable
Human Organs LR	Size adjs	Adjs denoting general human size	Adjs denoting the corresponding size of all or some external organs	undersized-1-2 buxom-1-2
Size Importance LR	Size adjs	Basic size adjs	Figurative meanings of same adjectives	big-1-2
-Scaled LR	VeryTrueScalars (age, size, price,)	True scalar adjectives	Adj-scale(d)	modest-modest(ly)- -price(d)old -old-age
Negative LR	All adjs	Positive adjs	Corresponding Negative adjectives	noticeable unnoticeable

Table 1: Lexical Rules for Adjectives.

we do know is that, when used justifiably and maintained at a large scope, they facilitate tremendously the costly but unavoidable process of semi-automatic lexical acquisition.

6 Acknowledgements

This work has been supported in part by Department of Defense under contract number MDA-904-92-C-5189. We would like to thank Margarita Gonzales and Jeff Longwell for their help and implementation of the work reported here. We are also grateful to anonymous reviewers and the Mikrokosmos team from CRL.

References

Ju. D. Apresjan 1976 Regular Polysemy *Linguistics* vol 142, pp. 5-32.

B. T. S. Atkins 1991 Building a lexicon:The contribution of lexicography In B. Boguraev (ed.), "Building a Lexicon", Special Issue, *International Journal of Lexicography* 4:3, pp. 167-204.

E. J. Briscoe and A. Copestake 1991 Sense extensions as lexical rules In *Proceedings of the IJCAI Workshop on Computational Approaches to Non-Literal Language.* Sydney, Australia, pp. 12-20.

E. J. Briscoe, Valeria de Paiva, and Ann Copestake (eds.) 1993 *Inheritance, Defaults, and the Lexicon.* Cambridge: Cambridge University Press.

E. J. Briscoe, Ann Copestake, and Alex Lascarides. 1995. Blocking. In P. Saint-Dizier and E.Viegas, *Computational Lexical Semantics.* Cambridge University Press.

Lynn Carlson and Sergei Nirenburg 1990. *World Modeling for NLP.* Center for Machine Translation, Carnegie Mellon University, Tech Report CMU-CMT-90-121.

Ann Copestake and Ted Briscoe 1992 Lexical operations in a unification-based framework. In J. Pustejovsky and S. Bergler (eds), *Lexical Semantics and Knowledge Representation.* Berlin: Springer, pp. 101-119.

D. A. Cruse 1986 *Lexical Semantics* Cambridge: Cambridge University Press.

Bonnie Dorr 1993 *Machine Translation: A View from the Lexicon* Cambridge, MA: M.I.T. Press.

Bonnie Dorr 1995 A lexical-semantic solution to the divergence problem in machine translation. In St-Dizier P. and Viegas E. (eds), *Computational Lexical Semantics*: CUP.

Gerald Gazdar, E. Klein, Geoffrey Pullum and Ivan Sag 1985 *Generalized Phrase Structure Grammar.* Blackwell: Oxford.

Ulrich Heid 1993 Le lexique : quelques problèmes de description et de représentation lexicale pour la traduction automatique. In Bouillon, P. and Clas, A. (eds), *La Traductique*: AUPEL-UREF.

M. Kameyama, R. Ochitani and S. Peters 1991 Resolving Translation Mismatches With Information Flow. Proceedings of *ACL'91*.

Geoffrey Leech 1981 *Semantics*. Cambridge: Cambridge University Press.

Beth Levin 1992 *Towards a Lexical Organization of English Verbs* Chicago: University of Chicago Press.

Igor' Mel'čuk 1979. *Studies in Dependency Syntax.* Ann Arbor, MI: Karoma.

Kavi Mahesh and Sergei Nirenburg 1995 A situated ontology for practical NLP. Proceedings of the Workshop on Basic Ontological Issues in Knowledge Sharing, *International Joint Conference on Artificial Intelligence* (IJCAI-95), Montreal, Canada, August 1995.

Sergei Nirenburg and Lori Levin 1992 Syntax-Driven and Ontology-Driven Lexical Semantics In J. Pustejovsky and S. Bergler (eds), *Lexical Semantics and Knowledge Representation.* Berlin: Springer, pp. 5-20.

Sergei Nirenburg and Victor Raskin 1986 A Metric for Computational Analysis of Meaning: Toward an Applied Theory of Linguistic Semantics *Proceedings of COLING '86.* Bonn, F.R.G.: University of Bonn, pp. 338-340

Sergei Nirenburg, Jaime Carbonell, Masaru Tomita, and Kenneth Goodman 1992 *Machine Translation: A Knowledge-Based Approach.* San Mateo CA: Morgan Kaufmann Publishers.

Boyan Onyshkevysh and Sergei Nirenburg 1995 A Lexicon for Knowledge-based MT *Machine Translation 10: 1-2.*

Nicholas Ostler and B. T. S. Atkins 1992 Predictable meaning shift: Some linguistic properties of lexical implication rules In J. Pustejovsky and S. Bergler (eds), *Lexical Semantics and Knowledge Representation.* Berlin: Springer, pp. 87-100.

C. Pollard and I. Sag. 1987 *An Information-based Approach to Syntax and Semantics: Volume 1 Fundamentals.* CSLI Lecture Notes 13, Stanford CA.

James Pustejovsky 1991 The generative lexicon. *Computational Linguistics* 17:4, pp. 409-441.

James Pustejovsky 1993 Type coercion and lexical selection. In James Pustejovsky (ed.), *Semantics and the Lexicon.* Dordrecht-Boston: Kluwer, pp. 73-94.

James Pustejovsky 1995 *The Generative Lexicon.* Cambridge, MA: MIT Press.

Victor Raskin 1987 What Is There in Linguistic Semantics for Natural Language Processing? In Sergei Nirenburg (ed.), *Proceedings of Natural Language Planning Workshop.* Blue Mountain Lake, N.Y.: RADC, pp. 78-96.

Victor Raskin and Sergei Nirenburg 1995 *Lexical Semantics of Adjectives: A Microtheory of Adjectival Meaning.* MCCS-95-28, CRL, NMSU, Las Cruces, N.M.

Evelyne Viegas and Sergei Nirenburg 1995 Acquisition semi-automatique du lexique. Proceedings of "Quatrièmes Journées scientifiques de Lyon", *Lexicologie Langage Terminologie*, Lyon 95, France.

Evelyne Viegas, Margarita Gonzalez and Jeff Longwell 1996 *Morpho-semantics and Constructive Derivational Morphology: a Transcategorial Approach to Lexical Rules.* Technical Report MCCS-96-295, CRL, NMSU.

Evelyne Viegas and Stephen Beale 1996 Multilinguality and Reversibility in Computational Semantic Lexicons Proceedings of *INLG'96*, Sussex, England.

Integrating Multiple Knowledge Sources to Disambiguate Word Sense: An Exemplar-Based Approach

Hwee Tou Ng
Defence Science Organisation
20 Science Park Drive
Singapore 118230
nhweetou@trantor.dso.gov.sg

Hian Beng Lee
Defence Science Organisation
20 Science Park Drive
Singapore 118230
lhianben@trantor.dso.gov.sg

Abstract

In this paper, we present a new approach for word sense disambiguation (WSD) using an exemplar-based learning algorithm. This approach integrates a diverse set of knowledge sources to disambiguate word sense, including part of speech of neighboring words, morphological form, the unordered set of surrounding words, local collocations, and verb-object syntactic relation. We tested our WSD program, named LEXAS, on both a common data set used in previous work, as well as on a large sense-tagged corpus that we separately constructed. LEXAS achieves a higher accuracy on the common data set, and performs better than the most frequent heuristic on the highly ambiguous words in the large corpus tagged with the refined senses of WORDNET.

1 Introduction

One important problem of Natural Language Processing (NLP) is figuring out what a word means when it is used in a particular context. The different meanings of a word are listed as its various senses in a dictionary. The task of Word Sense Disambiguation (WSD) is to identify the correct sense of a word in context. Improvement in the accuracy of identifying the correct word sense will result in better machine translation systems, information retrieval systems, etc. For example, in machine translation, knowing the correct word sense helps to select the appropriate target words to use in order to translate into a target language.

In this paper, we present a new approach for WSD using an exemplar-based learning algorithm. This approach integrates a diverse set of knowledge sources to disambiguate word sense, including part of speech (POS) of neighboring words, morphological form, the unordered set of surrounding words, local collocations, and verb-object syntactic relation. To evaluate our WSD program, named LEXAS (LEXical Ambiguity-resolving System), we tested it on a common data set involving the noun "interest" used by Bruce and Wiebe (Bruce and Wiebe, 1994). LEXAS achieves a mean accuracy of 87.4% on this data set, which is higher than the accuracy of 78% reported in (Bruce and Wiebe, 1994).

Moreover, to test the scalability of LEXAS, we have acquired a corpus in which 192,800 word occurrences have been manually tagged with senses from WORDNET, which is a public domain lexical database containing about 95,000 word forms and 70,000 lexical concepts (Miller, 1990). These sense tagged word occurrences consist of 191 most frequently occurring and most ambiguous nouns and verbs. When tested on this large data set, LEXAS performs better than the default strategy of picking the most frequent sense. To our knowledge, this is the first time that a WSD program has been tested on such a large scale, and yielding results better than the most frequent heuristic on highly ambiguous words with the refined sense distinctions of WORDNET.

2 Task Description

The input to a WSD program consists of unrestricted, real-world English sentences. In the output, each word occurrence w is tagged with its correct sense (according to the context) in the form of a sense number i, where i corresponds to the i-th sense definition of w as given in some dictionary. The choice of which sense definitions to use (and according to which dictionary) is agreed upon in advance.

For our work, we use the sense definitions as given in WORDNET, which is comparable to a good desktop printed dictionary in its coverage and sense distinction. Since WORDNET only provides sense definitions for content words, (i.e., words in the parts of speech (POS) noun, verb, adjective, and adverb), LEXAS is only concerned with disambiguating the sense of content words. However, almost all existing work in WSD deals only with disambiguating content words too.

LEXAS assumes that each word in an input sentence has been pre-tagged with its correct POS, so that the possible senses to consider for a content word w are only those associated with the particular POS of w in the sentence. For instance, given the sentence "A reduction of principal and interest is one way the problem may be solved.", since the word "interest" appears as a noun in this sentence, LEXAS will only consider the noun senses of "interest" but not its verb senses. That is, LEXAS is only concerned with disambiguating senses of a word in a given POS. Making such an assumption is reasonable since POS taggers that can achieve accuracy of 96% are readily available to assign POS to unrestricted English sentences (Brill, 1992; Cutting et al., 1992).

In addition, sense definitions are only available for root words in a dictionary. These are words that are not morphologically inflected, such as "interest" (as opposed to the plural form "interests"), "fall" (as opposed to the other inflected forms like "fell", "fallen", "falling", "falls"), etc. The sense of a morphologically inflected content word is the sense of its uninflected form. LEXAS follows this convention by first converting each word in an input sentence into its morphological root using the morphological analyzer of WORDNET, before assigning the appropriate word sense to the root form.

3 Algorithm

LEXAS performs WSD by first learning from a training corpus of sentences in which words have been pre-tagged with their correct senses. That is, it uses supervised learning, in particular exemplar-based learning, to achieve WSD. Our approach has been fully implemented in the program LEXAS. Part of the implementation uses PEBLS (Cost and Salzberg, 1993; Rachlin and Salzberg, 1993), a public domain exemplar-based learning system.

LEXAS builds one exemplar-based classifier for each content word w. It operates in two phases: training phase and test phase. In the training phase, LEXAS is given a set S of sentences in the training corpus in which sense-tagged occurrences of w appear. For each training sentence with an occurrence of w, LEXAS extracts the parts of speech (POS) of words surrounding w, the morphological form of w, the words that frequently co-occur with w in the same sentence, and the local collocations containing w. For disambiguating a noun w, the verb which takes the current noun w as the object is also identified. This set of values form the features of an example, with one training sentence contributing one training example.

Subsequently, in the test phase, LEXAS is given new, previously unseen sentences. For a new sentence containing the word w, LEXAS extracts from the new sentence the values for the same set of features, including parts of speech of words surrounding w, the morphological form of w, the frequently co-occurring words surrounding w, the local collocations containing w, and the verb that takes w as an object (for the case when w is a noun). These values form the features of a test example.

This test example is then compared to every training example. The sense of word w in the test example is the sense of w in the closest matching training example, where there is a precise, computational definition of "closest match" as explained later.

3.1 Feature Extraction

The first step of the algorithm is to extract a set F of features such that each sentence containing an occurrence of w will form a training example supplying the necessary values for the set F of features.

Specifically, LEXAS uses the following set of features to form a training example:

$$L_3, L_2, L_1, R_1, R_2, R_3, M, K_1, \ldots, K_m, C_1, \ldots, C_9, V$$

3.1.1 Part of Speech and Morphological Form

The value of feature L_i is the part of speech (POS) of the word i-th position to the left of w. The value of R_i is the POS of the word i-th position to the right of w. Feature M denotes the morphological form of w in the sentence s. For a noun, the value for this feature is either singular or plural; for a verb, the value is one of infinitive (as in the uninflected form of a verb like "fall"), present-third-person-singular (as in "falls"), past (as in "fell"), present-participle (as in "falling") or past-participle (as in "fallen").

3.1.2 Unordered Set of Surrounding Words

$K_1, \ldots, K_m$ are features corresponding to a set of keywords that frequently co-occur with word w in the same sentence. For a sentence s, the value of feature K_i is one if the keyword K_i appears somewhere in sentence s, else the value of K_i is zero.

The set of keywords $K_1, \ldots, K_m$ are determined based on conditional probability. All the word tokens other than the word occurrence w in a sentence s are candidates for consideration as keywords. These tokens are converted to lower case form before being considered as candidates for keywords.

Let $cp(i|k)$ denotes the conditional probability of sense i of w given keyword k, where

$$cp(i|k) = \frac{N_{i,k}}{N_k}$$

N_k is the number of sentences in which keyword k co-occurs with w, and $N_{i,k}$ is the number of sentences in which keyword k co-occurs with w where w has sense i.

For a keyword k to be selected as a feature, it must satisfy the following criteria:

1. $cp(i|k) \geq M_1$ for some sense i, where M_1 is some predefined minimum probability.

2. The keyword k must occur at least M_2 times in some sense i, where M_2 is some predefined minimum value.

3. Select at most M_3 number of keywords for a given sense i if the number of keywords satisfying the first two criteria for a given sense i exceeds M_3. In this case, keywords that co-occur more frequently (in terms of absolute frequency) with sense i of word w are selected over those co-occurring less frequently.

Condition 1 ensures that a selected keyword is indicative of some sense i of w since $cp(i|k)$ is at least some minimum probability M_1. Condition 2 reduces the possibility of selecting a keyword based on spurious occurrence. Condition 3 prefers keywords that co-occur more frequently if there is a large number of eligible keywords.

For example, $M_1 = 0.8$, $M_2 = 5$, $M_3 = 5$ when LEXAS was tested on the common data set reported in Section 4.1.

To illustrate, when disambiguating the noun "interest", some of the selected keywords are: expressed, acquiring, great, attracted, expressions, pursue, best, conflict, served, short, minority, rates, rate, bonds, lower, payments.

3.1.3 Local Collocations

Local collocations are common expressions containing the word to be disambiguated. For our purpose, the term *collocation* does not imply idiomatic usage, just words that are frequently adjacent to the word to be disambiguated. Examples of local collocations of the noun "interest" include "in the interest of", "principal and interest", etc. When a word to be disambiguated occurs as part of a collocation, its sense can be frequently determined very reliably. For example, the collocation "in the interest of" always implies the "advantage, advancement, favor" sense of the noun "interest". Note that the method for extraction of keywords that we described earlier will fail to find the words "in", "the", "of" as keywords, since these words will appear in many different positions in a sentence for many senses of the noun "interest". It is only when these words appear in the exact order "in the interest of" around the noun "interest" that strongly implies the "advantage, advancement, favor" sense.

There are nine features related to collocations in an example. Table 1 lists the nine features and some collocation examples for the noun "interest". For example, the feature with left offset = -2 and right offset = 1 refers to the possible collocations beginning at the word two positions to the left of "interest" and ending at the word one position to the right of "interest". An example of such a collocation is "in the interest of".

The method for extraction of local collocations is similar to that for extraction of keywords. For each of the nine collocation features, LEXAS concatenates the words between the left and right offset positions. Using similar conditional probability criteria for the selection of keywords, collocations that are predictive of a certain sense are selected to form the possible values for a collocation feature.

Left Offset	Right Offset	Collocation Example
-1	-1	accrued interest
1	1	interest rate
-2	-1	principal and interest
-1	1	national interest in
1	2	interest and dividends
-3	-1	sale of an interest
-2	1	in the interest of
-1	2	an interest in a
1	3	interest on the bonds

Table 1: Features for Collocations

3.1.4 Verb-Object Syntactic Relation

LEXAS also makes use of the verb-object syntactic relation as one feature V for the disambiguation of nouns. If a noun to be disambiguated is the head of a noun group, as indicated by its last position in a noun group bracketing, and if the word immediately preceding the opening noun group bracketing is a verb, LEXAS takes such a verb-noun pair to be in a verb-object syntactic relation. Again, using similar conditional probability criteria for the selection of keywords, verbs that are predictive of a certain sense of the noun to be disambiguated are selected to form the possible values for this verb-object feature V.

Since our training and test sentences come with noun group bracketing, determining verb-object relation using the above heuristic can be readily done. In future work, we plan to incorporate more syntactic relations including subject-verb, and adjective-headnoun relations. We also plan to use verb-object and subject-verb relations to disambiguate verb senses.

3.2 Training and Testing

The heart of exemplar-based learning is a measure of the similarity, or distance, between two examples. If the distance between two examples is small, then the two examples are similar. We use the following definition of distance between two symbolic values v_1 and v_2 of a feature f:

$$d(v_1, v_2) = \sum_{i=1}^{n} \left| \frac{C_{1,i}}{C_1} - \frac{C_{2,i}}{C_2} \right|$$

$C_{1,i}$ is the number of training examples with value v_1 for feature f that is classified as sense i in the training corpus, and C_1 is the number of training examples with value v_1 for feature f in any sense. $C_{2,i}$ and C_2 denote similar quantities for value v_2 of feature f. n is the total number of senses for a word w.

This metric for measuring distance is adopted from (Cost and Salzberg, 1993), which in turn is adapted from the value difference metric of the earlier work of (Stanfill and Waltz, 1986). The distance between two examples is the sum of the distances between the values of all the features of the two examples.

During the training phase, the appropriate set of features is extracted based on the method described in Section 3.1. From the training examples formed, the distance between any two values for a feature f is computed based on the above formula.

During the test phase, a test example is compared against *all* the training examples. LEXAS then determines the closest matching training example as the one with the minimum distance to the test example. The sense of w in the test example is the sense of w in this closest matching training example.

If there is a tie among several training examples with the same minimum distance to the test example, LEXAS randomly selects one of these training examples as the closet matching training example in order to break the tie.

4 Evaluation

To evaluate the performance of LEXAS, we conducted two tests, one on a common data set used in (Bruce and Wiebe, 1994), and another on a larger data set that we separately collected.

4.1 Evaluation on a Common Data Set

To our knowledge, very few of the existing work on WSD has been tested and compared on a common data set. This is in contrast to established practice in the machine learning community. This is partly because there are not many common data sets publicly available for testing WSD programs.

One exception is the sense-tagged data set used in (Bruce and Wiebe, 1994), which has been made available in the public domain by Bruce and Wiebe. This data set consists of 2369 sentences each containing an occurrence of the noun "interest" (or its plural form "interests") with its correct sense manually tagged. The noun "interest" occurs in six different senses in this data set. Table 2 shows the distribution of sense tags from the data set that we obtained. Note that the sense definitions used in this data set are those from Longman Dictionary of Contemporary English (LDOCE) (Procter, 1978). This does not pose any problem for LEXAS, since LEXAS only requires that there be a division of senses into different classes, regardless of how the sense classes are defined or numbered.

POS of words are given in the data set, as well as the bracketings of noun groups. These are used to determine the POS of neighboring words and the verb-object syntactic relation to form the features of examples.

LDOCE sense	Frequency	Percent
1: readiness to give attention	361	15%
2: quality of causing attention to be given	11	<1%
3: activity, subject, etc. which one gives time and attention to	67	3%
4: advantage, advancement, or favor	178	8%
5: a share (in a company, business, etc.)	499	21%
6: money paid for the use of money	1253	53%

Table 2: Distribution of Sense Tags

In the results reported in (Bruce and Wiebe, 1994), they used a test set of 600 randomly selected sentences from the 2369 sentences. Unfortunately, in the data set made available in the public domain, there is no indication of which sentences are used as test sentences. As such, we conducted 100 random trials, and in each trial, 600 sentences were randomly selected to form the test set. LEXAS is trained on the remaining 1769 sentences, and then tested on a *separate* test set of sentences in each trial.

Note that in Bruce and Wiebe's test run, the proportion of sentences in each sense in the test set is approximately equal to their proportion in the whole data set. Since we use random selection of test sentences, the proportion of each sense in our test set is also approximately equal to their proportion in the whole data set in our random trials.

The average accuracy of LEXAS over 100 random trials is 87.4%, and the standard deviation is 1.37%. In each of our 100 random trials, the accuracy of LEXAS is always higher than the accuracy of 78% reported in (Bruce and Wiebe, 1994).

Bruce and Wiebe also performed a separate test by using a subset of the "interest" data set with only 4 senses (sense 1, 4, 5, and 6), so as to compare their results with previous work on WSD (Black, 1988; Zernik, 1990; Yarowsky, 1992), which were tested on 4 senses of the noun "interest". However, the work of (Black, 1988; Zernik, 1990; Yarowsky, 1992) were not based on the present set of sentences, so the comparison is only suggestive. We reproduced in Table 3 the results of past work as well as the classification accuracy of LEXAS, which is 89.9% with a standard deviation of 1.09% over 100 random trials.

In summary, when tested on the noun "interest", LEXAS gives higher classification accuracy than previous work on WSD.

In order to evaluate the relative contribution of the knowledge sources, including (1) POS and mor-

WSD research	Accuracy
Black (1988)	72%
Zernik (1990)	70%
Yarowsky (1992)	72%
Bruce & Wiebe (1994)	79%
LEXAS (1996)	89%

Table 3: Comparison with previous results

Knowledge Source	Mean Accuracy	Std Dev
POS & morpho	77.2%	1.44%
surrounding words	62.0%	1.82%
collocations	80.2%	1.55%
verb-object	43.5%	1.79%

Table 4: Relative Contribution of Knowledge Sources

phological form; (2) unordered set of surrounding words; (3) local collocations; and (4) verb to the left (verb-object syntactic relation), we conducted 4 separate runs of 100 random trials each. In each run, we utilized only one knowledge source and compute the average classification accuracy and the standard deviation. The results are given in Table 4.

Local collocation knowledge yields the highest accuracy, followed by POS and morphological form. Surrounding words give lower accuracy, perhaps because in our work, only the current sentence forms the surrounding context, which averages about 20 words. Previous work on using the unordered set of surrounding words have used a much larger window, such as the 100-word window of (Yarowsky, 1992), and the 2-sentence context of (Leacock et al., 1993). Verb-object syntactic relation is the weakest knowledge source.

Our experimental finding, that local collocations are the most predictive, agrees with past observation that humans need a narrow window of only a few words to perform WSD (Choueka and Lusignan, 1985).

The processing speed of LEXAS is satisfactory. Running on an SGI Unix workstation, LEXAS can process about 15 examples per second when tested on the "interest" data set.

4.2 Evaluation on a Large Data Set

Previous research on WSD tend to be tested only on a dozen number of words, where each word frequently has either two or a few senses. To test the scalability of LEXAS, we have gathered a corpus in which 192,800 word occurrences have been manually tagged with senses from WORDNET 1.5. This data set is almost two orders of magnitude larger in size than the above "interest" data set. Manual tagging was done by university undergraduates majoring in Linguistics, and approximately one man-year of efforts were expended in tagging our data set.

These 192,800 word occurrences consist of 121 nouns and 70 verbs which are the most frequently occurring and most ambiguous words of English. The 121 nouns are:

> action activity age air area art board body book business car case center century change child church city class college community company condition cost country course day death development difference door effect effort end example experience face fact family field figure foot force form girl government ground head history home hour house information interest job land law level life light line man material matter member mind moment money month name nation need number order part party picture place plan point policy position power pressure problem process program public purpose question reason result right room school section sense service side society stage state step student study surface system table term thing time town type use value voice water way word work world

The 70 verbs are:

> add appear ask become believe bring build call carry change come consider continue determine develop draw expect fall give go grow happen help hold indicate involve keep know lead leave lie like live look lose mean meet move need open pay raise read receive remember require return rise run see seem send set show sit speak stand start stop strike take talk tell think turn wait walk want work write

For this set of nouns and verbs, the average number of senses per noun is 7.8, while the average number of senses per verb is 12.0. We draw our sentences containing the occurrences of the 191 words listed above from the combined corpus of the 1 million word Brown corpus and the 2.5 million word Wall Street Journal (WSJ) corpus. For every word in the two lists, up to 1,500 sentences each containing an occurrence of the word are extracted from the combined corpus. In all, there are about 113,000 noun occurrences and about 79,800 verb occurrences. This set of 121 nouns accounts for about 20% of all occurrences of nouns that one expects to encounter in any unrestricted English text. Similarly, about 20% of all verb occurrences in any unrestricted text come from the set of 70 verbs chosen.

We estimate that there are 10–20% errors in our sense-tagged data set. To get an idea of how the sense assignments of our data set compare with those provided by WORDNET linguists in SEMCOR, the sense-tagged subset of Brown corpus prepared by Miller et al. (Miller et al., 1994), we compare

Test set	Sense 1	Most Frequent	LEXAS
BC50	40.5%	47.1%	54.0%
WSJ6	44.8%	63.7%	68.6%

Table 5: Evaluation on a Large Data Set

a subset of the occurrences that overlap. Out of 5,317 occurrences that overlap, about 57% of the sense assignments in our data set agree with those in SEMCOR. This should not be too surprising, as it is widely believed that sense tagging using the full set of refined senses found in a large dictionary like WORDNET involve making subtle human judgments (Wilks et al., 1990; Bruce and Wiebe, 1994), such that there are many genuine cases where two humans will not agree fully on the best sense assignments.

We evaluated LEXAS on this larger set of noisy, sense-tagged data. We first set aside two subsets for testing. The first test set, named BC50, consists of 7,119 occurrences of the 191 content words that occur in 50 text files of the Brown corpus. The second test set, named WSJ6, consists of 14,139 occurrences of the 191 content words that occur in 6 text files of the WSJ corpus.

We compared the classification accuracy of LEXAS against the default strategy of picking the most frequent sense. This default strategy has been advocated as the baseline performance level for comparison with WSD programs (Gale et al., 1992). There are two instantiations of this strategy in our current evaluation. Since WORDNET orders its senses such that sense 1 is the most frequent sense, one possibility is to always pick sense 1 as the best sense assignment. This assignment method does not even need to look at the training sentences. We call this method "Sense 1" in Table 5. Another assignment method is to determine the most frequently occurring sense in the training sentences, and to assign this sense to all test sentences. We call this method "Most Frequent" in Table 5. The accuracy of LEXAS on these two test sets is given in Table 5.

Our results indicate that exemplar-based classification of word senses scales up quite well when tested on a large set of words. The classification accuracy of LEXAS is always better than the default strategy of picking the most frequent sense. We believe that our result is significant, especially when the training data is noisy, and the words are highly ambiguous with a large number of refined sense distinctions per word.

The accuracy on Brown corpus test files is lower than that achieved on the Wall Street Journal test files, primarily because the Brown corpus consists of texts from a wide variety of genres, including newspaper reports, newspaper editorial, biblical passages, science and mathematics articles, general fiction, romance story, humor, etc. It is harder to disambiguate words coming from such a wide variety of texts.

5 Related Work

There is now a large body of past work on WSD. Early work on WSD, such as (Kelly and Stone, 1975; Hirst, 1987) used hand-coding of knowledge to perform WSD. The knowledge acquisition process is laborious. In contrast, LEXAS learns from tagged sentences, without human engineering of complex rules.

The recent emphasis on corpus based NLP has resulted in much work on WSD of unconstrained real-world texts. One line of research focuses on the use of the knowledge contained in a machine-readable dictionary to perform WSD, such as (Wilks et al., 1990; Luk, 1995). In contrast, LEXAS uses supervised learning from tagged sentences, which is also the approach taken by most recent work on WSD, including (Bruce and Wiebe, 1994; Miller et al., 1994; Leacock et al., 1993; Yarowsky, 1994; Yarowsky, 1993; Yarowsky, 1992).

The work of (Miller et al., 1994; Leacock et al., 1993; Yarowsky, 1992) used only the unordered set of surrounding words to perform WSD, and they used statistical classifiers, neural networks, or IR-based techniques. The work of (Bruce and Wiebe, 1994) used parts of speech (POS) and morphological form, in addition to surrounding words. However, the POS used are abbreviated POS, and only in a window of ±2 words. No local collocation knowledge is used. A probabilistic classifier is used in (Bruce and Wiebe, 1994).

That local collocation knowledge provides important clues to WSD is pointed out in (Yarowsky, 1993), although it was demonstrated only on performing binary (or very coarse) sense disambiguation. The work of (Yarowsky, 1994) is perhaps the most similar to our present work. However, his work used decision list to perform classification, in which only the single best disambiguating evidence that matched a target context is used. In contrast, we used exemplar-based learning, where the contributions of all features are summed up and taken into account in coming up with a classification. We also include verb-object syntactic relation as a feature, which is not used in (Yarowsky, 1994). Although the work of (Yarowsky, 1994) can be applied to WSD, the results reported in (Yarowsky, 1994) only dealt with accent restoration, which is a much simpler problem. It is unclear how Yarowsky's method will fare on WSD of a common test data set like the one we used, nor has his method been tested on a large data set with highly ambiguous words tagged with the refined senses of WORDNET.

The work of (Miller et al., 1994) is the only prior work we know of which attempted to evaluate WSD on a large data set and using the refined sense distinction of WORDNET. However, their results show no improvement (in fact a slight degradation in performance) when using surrounding words to perform WSD as compared to the most frequent heuristic. They attributed this to insufficient training data in SEMCOR. In contrast, we adopt a different strategy of collecting the training data set. Instead of tagging every word in a running text, as is done in SEMCOR, we only concentrate on the set of 191 most frequently occurring and most ambiguous words, and collected large enough training data for these words only. This strategy yields better results, as indicated by a better performance of LEXAS compared with the most frequent heuristic on this set of words.

Most recently, Yarowsky used an unsupervised learning procedure to perform WSD (Yarowsky, 1995), although this is only tested on disambiguating words into binary, coarse sense distinction. The effectiveness of unsupervised learning on disambiguating words into the refined sense distinction of WORDNET needs to be further investigated. The work of (McRoy, 1992) pointed out that a diverse set of knowledge sources are important to achieve WSD, but no quantitative evaluation was given on the relative importance of each knowledge source. No previous work has reported any such evaluation either. The work of (Cardie, 1993) used a case-based approach that simultaneously learns part of speech, word sense, and concept activation knowledge, although the method is only tested on domain-specific texts with domain-specific word senses.

6 Conclusion

In this paper, we have presented a new approach for WSD using an exemplar based learning algorithm. This approach integrates a diverse set of knowledge sources to disambiguate word sense. When tested on a common data set, our WSD program gives higher classification accuracy than previous work on WSD. When tested on a large, separately collected data set, our program performs better than the default strategy of picking the most frequent sense. To our knowledge, this is the first time that a WSD program has been tested on such a large scale, and yielding results better than the most frequent heuristic on highly ambiguous words with the refined senses of WORDNET.

7 Acknowledgements

We would like to thank: Dr Paul Wu for sharing the Brown Corpus and Wall Street Journal Corpus; Dr Christopher Ting for downloading and installing WORDNET and SEMCOR, and for reformatting the corpora; the 12 undergraduates from the Linguistics Program of the National University of Singapore for preparing the sense-tagged corpus; and Prof K. P. Mohanan for his support of the sense-tagging project.

References

Ezra Black. 1988. An experiment in computational discrimination of English word senses. *IBM Journal of Research and Development*, 32(2):185–194.

Eric Brill. 1992. A simple rule-based part of speech tagger. In *Proceedings of the Third Conference on Applied Natural Language Processing*, pages 152–155.

Rebecca Bruce and Janyce Wiebe. 1994. Word-sense disambiguation using decomposable models. In *Proceedings of the 32nd Annual Meeting of the Association for Computational Linguistics*, Las Cruces, New Mexico.

Claire Cardie. 1993. A case-based approach to knowledge acquisition for domain-specific sentence analysis. In *Proceedings of the Eleventh National Conference on Artificial Intelligence*, pages 798–803, Washington, DC.

Y. Choueka and S. Lusignan. 1985. Disambiguation by short contexts. *Computers and the Humanities*, 19:147–157.

Scott Cost and Steven Salzberg. 1993. A weighted nearest neighbor algorithm for learning with symbolic features. *Machine Learning*, 10(1):57–78.

Doug Cutting, Julian Kupiec, Jan Pedersen, and Penelope Sibun. 1992. A practical part-of-speech tagger. In *Proceedings of the Third Conference on Applied Natural Language Processing*, pages 133–140.

William Gale, Kenneth Ward Church, and David Yarowsky. 1992. Estimating upper and lower bounds on the performance of word-sense disambiguation programs. In *Proceedings of the 30th Annual Meeting of the Association for Computational Linguistics*, Newark, Delaware.

Graeme Hirst. 1987. *Semantic Interpretation and the Resolution of Ambiguity.* Cambridge University Press, Cambridge.

Edward Kelly and Phillip Stone. 1975. *Computer Recognition of English Word Senses.* North-Holland, Amsterdam.

Claudia Leacock, Geoffrey Towell, and Ellen Voorhees. 1993. Corpus-based statistical sense resolution. In *Proceedings of the ARPA Human Language Technology Workshop.*

Alpha K. Luk. 1995. Statistical sense disambiguation with relatively small corpora using dictionary definitions. In *Proceedings of the 33rd Annual Meeting of the Association for Computational Linguistics*, Cambridge, Massachusetts.

Susan W. McRoy 1992. Using multiple knowledge sources for word sense discrimination. *Computational Linguistics*, 18(1):1–30.

George A. Miller, Ed. 1990. WordNet: An on-line lexical database. *International Journal of Lexicography*, 3(4):235–312.

George A. Miller, Martin Chodorow, Shari Landes, Claudia Leacock, and Robert G. Thomas. 1994. Using a semantic concordance for sense identification. In *Proceedings of the ARPA Human Language Technology Workshop*.

Paul Procter et al. 1978. Longman Dictionary of Contemporary English.

John Rachlin and Steven Salzberg. 1993. PEBLS 3.0 User's Guide.

C Stanfill and David Waltz. 1986. Toward memory-based reasoning. *Communications of the ACM*, 29(12):1213–1228.

Yorick Wilks, Dan Fass, Cheng-Ming Guo, James E. McDonald, Tony Plate, and Brian M. Slator. 1990. Providing machine tractable dictionary tools. *Machine Translation*, 5(2):99–154.

David Yarowsky. 1992. Word-sense disambiguation using statistical models of Roget's categories trained on large corpora. In *Proceedings of the Fifteenth International Conference on Computational Linguistics*, pages 454–460, Nantes, France.

David Yarowsky. 1993. One sense per collocation. In *Proceedings of the ARPA Human Language Technology Workshop*.

David Yarowsky. 1994. Decision lists for lexical ambiguity resolution: Application to accent restoration in Spanish and French. In *Proceedings of the 32nd Annual Meeting of the Association for Computational Linguistics*, Las Cruces, New Mexico.

David Yarowsky. 1995. Unsupervised word sense disambiguation rivaling supervised methods. In *Proceedings of the 33rd Annual Meeting of the Association for Computational Linguistics*, Cambridge, Massachusetts.

Uri Zernik. 1990. Tagging word senses in corpus: the needle in the haystack revisited. Technical Report 90CRD198, GE R&D Center.

INVITED TALK

Eye Movements and Spoken Language Comprehension

Michael K. Tanenhaus*
Department of Brain and Cognitive Sciences
University of Rochester
Rochester, NY 14627
mtan@bcs.rochester.edu

Julie C. Sedivy
Department of Linguistics
University of Rochester
Rochester, NY 14627
sedivy@bcs.rochester.edu

Michael J. Spivey-Knowlton
Department of Psychology
Cornell University
Ithaca, NY 14583
mjsk@cornell.edu

Paul D. Allopenna
Department of Brain and Cognitive Sciences
University of Rochester
Rochester, NY 14627
allopen@bcs.rochester.edu

Kathleen M. Eberhard
Department of Psychology
University of Notre Dame
Notre Dame, IN 46556
kathleen.m.eberhard.1@nd.edu

James S. Magnuson
Department of Brain and Cognitive Sciences
University of Rochester
Rochester, NY 14627
magnuson@bcs.rochester.edu

Abstract

We present an overview of recent work in which eye movements are monitored as people follow spoken instructions to move objects or pictures in a visual workspace. Subjects naturally make saccadic eye-movements to objects that are closely time-locked to relevant information in the instruction. Thus the eye-movements provide a window into the rapid mental processes that underlie spoken language comprehension. We review studies of reference resolution, word recognition, and pragmatic effects on syntactic ambiguity resolution. Our studies show that people seek to establish reference with respect to their behavioral goals during the earliest moments of linguistic processing. Moreover, referentially relevant non-linguistic information immediately affects how the linguistic input is initially structured.

Introduction

Many important questions about language comprehension can only be answered by examining processes that are closely time-locked to the linguistic input. These processes take place quite rapidly and they are largely opaque to introspection. As a consequence, psycholinguists have increasingly turned to experimental methods designed to tap real-time language processing. These include a variety of reading time measures as well as paradigms in which subjects monitor the incoming speech for targets or respond to visually presented probes. The hope is that these "on-line" measures can provide information that can be used to inform and evaluate explicit computational models of language processing.

Although on-line measures have provided increasingly fine-grained information about the time-course of language processing, they are also limited in some important respects. Perhaps the most serious limitation is that they cannot be used to study language in natural tasks with real-world referents. This makes it difficult to study how interpretation develops. Moreover, the emphasis on processing "decontextualized" language may be underestimating the importance of interpretive processes in immediate language processing.

Recently, we have been exploring a new paradigm for studying spoken language comprehension. Participants in our experiments follow spoken instructions to touch or manipulate objects in a visual workspace while we monitor their eye-movements using a lightweight camera mounted on a headband. The camera, manufactured by Applied Scientific Laboratories, provides an infrared image of the eye at 60Hz. The center of the pupil and the corneal reflection are tracked to determine the orbit of the eye relative to the head. Accuracy is better than one degree of arc, with virtually unrestricted head and body movements [Ballard, Hayhoe, and Pelz, 1995]. Instructions are spoken into a microphone connected to a Hi-8 VCR. The VCR also records the participant's field of view from a "scene" camera mounted on the headband. The participant's gaze fixation is superimposed on the video image We analyze each frame of the instructions to determine the location and timing of eye movements with respect to critical words in the instruction.

We find that subjects make eye-movements to objects in the visual workspace that are closely time-locked to relevant information in the instruction. Thus the timing and patterns of the eye movements provide a window into comprehension processes as the speech unfolds. Unlike most of the on-line measures that have been used to study spoken language processing in the past, our procedure can be used to examine comprehension during natural tasks with real-world referents [Tanenhaus, M. K., Spivey-Knowlton, M. J., Eberhard, K. M., & Sedivy, J. C., 1996].

In the remainder of this paper, we review some of our recent work using the visual world paradigm. We will focus on three areas: (a) reference resolution; (b) word recognition, and (c) the interaction of referential context and syntactic ambiguity resolution.

Reference Resolution

Evidence for Incremental Interpretation

In order to investigate the time course with which people establish reference we use different displays to manipulate where in an instruction the referent of a definite noun phrase becomes unique. The timing and patterns of the eye-movements clearly show that people establish reference incrementally by continuously evaluating the information in the instruction against the alternatives in the visual workspace. For example, in one experiment [Eberhard, Spivey-Knowlton, Sedivy & Tanenhaus, 1995], participants were told to touch one of four blocks. The blocks varied along three dimensions: marking (plain or starred), color (pink, yellow, blue and red) and shape (square or rectangle). The instructions referred to the block using a definite noun phrase with adjectives (e.g., "Touch the starred yellow square."). The display determined which word in the noun phrase disambiguated the target block with respect to the visual alternatives For example, the earliest point of disambiguation would be after "starred" if only one of the blocks was starred, after "yellow" if only one of the starred blocks was yellow, and after "square" if there were two starred yellow blocks, only one of which was a square (Instructions with definite noun phrases always had a unique referent).

An instruction began with subjects looking at a fixation cross. We then measured the latency from the beginning of the noun phrase until the onset of the eye-movement to the target object. Subjects made eye-movements before touching the target block on about 75% of the trials.

Eye-movement latencies increased monotonically as the point of disambiguation shifted from the marking adjective to the color adjective to the head noun. Moreover, eye-movements were launched within 300 milliseconds of the end of the disambiguating word. It takes about 200 milliseconds from the point that an eye-movement is programmed until when the eye actually begins to move. On average then, participants began programming an eye-movement to the target block once they had heard the disambiguating word and before they had finished hearing the next word in the instruction.

We used the same logic in an experiment with displays containing more objects and syntactically more complex instructions [Eberhard et al, 1995]. Participants were instructed to move miniature playing cards placed on slots on a 5X5 vertical board. Seven cards were displayed on each trial. A trial consisted of a sequence of three instructions. On the instructions of interest, there were two cards of the same suit and denomination in the display. The target card was disambiguated using a restrictive relative clause, e.g. "Put the five of hearts that is below the eight of clubs above the three of diamonds." Figure 1 shows one of the displays for this instruction.

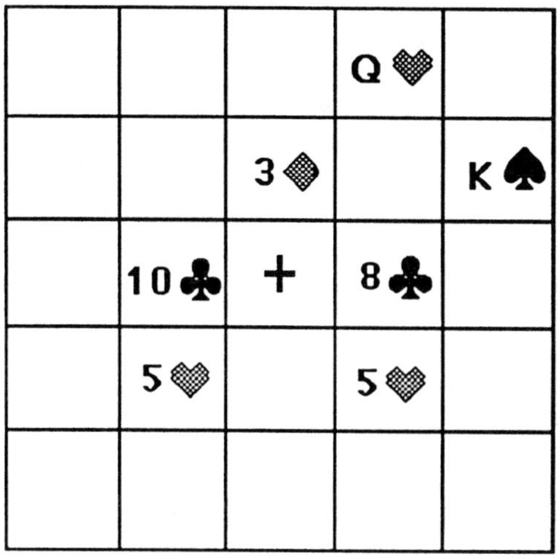

"Put the five of hearts that is below the eight of clubs above the three of diamonds."

Figure 1: Display of cards in which their are two fives of hearts. As each five of heart is below a different numbered card, the above instruction becomes unambiguous at "eight".

The display determined the point of disambiguation in the instruction. For the display in Figure 1, the point of disambiguation occurs after the word "eight" because only one of the fives is below an eight. We also used an early point of disambiguation display in which only one of the potential target cards was immediately below a" "context" card and a late point of disambiguation display in which the denomination of the "context" card disambiguated the target (i.e., one five was below an eight of spades and the other was below and eight of clubs).

Participants always made an eye-movement to the target card before reaching for it. We again found a clear point of disambiguation effect. The mean latency of the eye-movement that preceded the hand movement to the target card (measured from a common point in the instruction) increased monotonically with the point of disambiguation.

In addition, participants made sequences of eye-movements which made it clear that interpretation was taking place continuously. We quantified this by examining the probability that the subject would be looking at (fixating on) particular classes of cards during segments of the instruction. For example, during the noun phrase that introduced the potential targets, "the five of hearts", nearly all of the fixations were on one of the potential target cards.

During the beginning of the relative clause "...that is below the..." , most of the fixations were to one of the context cards (i.e. the card that was above or below a potential target card). Shortly after the disambiguating word, the fixations shifted to the target card.

Contrastive focus

The presence of a circumscribed set of referents in a visual model makes it possible to use eye-movements to examine how presuppositional information associated with intonation is used in on-line comprehension. [Sedivy, Tanenhaus, Spivey-Knowlton, Eberhard & Carlson, 1995] For example, semantic analyses of contrast have converged on a representation of contrastive focus which involves the integration of presupposed and asserted information [e.g., Rooth, 1992; Kratzer, 1991; Krifka, 1991]. Thus a speaker uttering "Computational linguists give good talks" is making an assertion about computational linguists. However, a speaker who says "COMPUTATIONAL linguists give good talks." is both complimenting the community of computational linguists and making a derogatory comparison with a presupposed set of contrasting entities (perhaps the community of non-computationally oriented linguists).

We explored whether contrast sets are computed on-line by asking whether contrastive focus could be used to disambiguate among potential referents, using a variation on the point of disambiguation manipulation described earlier. We used displays with objects that could differ along three dimensions: size (large or small), color (red, blue and yellow), and shape (circles, triangles and squares). Each display contained four objects [see Sedivy et al., 1995 for details].

Consider now the display illustrated in Figure 2 which contains a small yellow triangle, a large blue circle and two red squares, one large and one small. With the instruction "Touch the large red square." the point of disambiguation comes after "red" . After "large" there are still two possible referents: the large red square and the large blue circle. After "red" only the large red square is a possible referent. . However, with the instruction "Touch the LARGE red square", contrastive focus on "large" restricts felicitous reference to objects that have a contrast member differing along the dimension indicated by the contrast (size). In the display in Figure 2, the small red square contrasts with the large red square. However, the display does not contain a contrast element for the large blue circle. Thus, if people use contrastive stress to compute a contrast set on-line, then they should have sufficient information to determine the target object after hearing the size adjective Thus eye-movements to the target object should be faster with contrastive stress. That is, in fact, what we found. Latencies to launch a saccade to the target were faster with contrastive stress than with neutral stress.

However, there is a possible objection to an interpretation invoking contrasts sets. One could argue that stress simply focused participants' attention on the size dimension, allowing them to restrict attention to the large objects. To rule out this alternative, we also included displays with two contrast sets: e.g., two red squares, one large and one small, and two blue circles, one large and one small. With a two contrast display, contrastive focus is still felicitous. However, the point of disambiguation now does not come until after the color adjective for instructions with contrastive stress and with neutral stress. Under these conditions, we found no effect of contrast. The interaction between type of display and stress provides clear evidence that participants were computing contrast sets rapidly enough to select among potential referents.

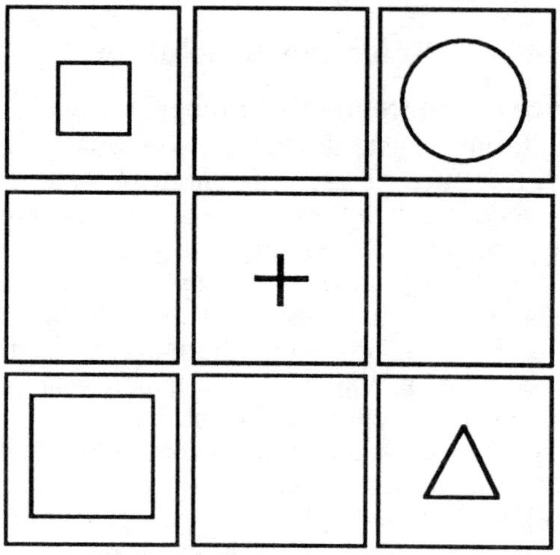

Figure 2: Display with one large and one small red square. The large circle is blue; the small triangle is yellow.

Word Recognition

The time course of spoken word recognition is strongly influenced by both the properties of the word itself (e.g., its frequency) and the set of words to which it is phonetically similar. Recognition of a spoken word occurs shortly after the auditory input uniquely specifies a lexical candidate [Marslen-Wilson, 1987]. For polysyllabic words, this is often prior to the end of the word. For example, the word "elephant" would be recognized shortly after the "phoneme" /f/. Prior to that, the auditory input would be consistent with the beginnings of several words, including "elephant", "elegant", "eloquent" and "elevator".

Most models of spoken word recognition account for these data by proposing that multiple lexical candidates are activated as the speech stream unfolds. Recognition then takes place with respect to the set of competing activated candidates. However, models differ in how the candidate set is defined. In some models, such as Marslen-Wilson's classic Cohort model, competition takes place in a strictly "left-to right" fashion. [Marslen-Wilson, 1987]. Thus the competitor set for "paddle" would contain "padlock", which has the same initial phonemes as "paddle", but would not include a phonetically similar word that did not overlap in its initial phonemes, such as a rhyming word like "saddle". In contrast, activation models such as TRACE [McClelland & Elman, 1986] assume that competition can occur throughout the word and thus rhyming words would also compete for activation.

Our initial experiments used real objects and instructions such as "Pick up the candy". We manipulated whether or not the display contained an object with a name that began with the same phonetic sequence as the target object [Tanenhaus, Spivey-Knowlton, Eberhard & Sedivy, 1995; Spivey-Knowlton, Tanenhaus, Eberhard & Sedivy, 1995]. Examples of objects with overlapping initial phonemes were "candy" and "candle", and "doll" and "dolphin". An eye-movement to the target object typically began shortly after the word ended, indicating that programming of the eye-movement often began before the end of the word. The presence of a competitor increased the latency of eye-movements to the target and induced frequent false launches to the competitor. The timing of these eye-movements indicated that they were programmed during the "ambiguous" segment of the target word. These results demonstrated that the two objects with similar names were, in fact, competing as the target word unfolded. Moreover, they highlight the sensitivity of the eye-movement paradigm.

In ongoing work, we are exploring more fine-grained questions about the time-course of lexical activation. For example, in an experiment in progress [Allopenna, Magnuson & Tanenhaus, 1996], the stimuli are line drawings of objects presented on a computer screen (see Figure 3). On each trial, participants are shown a set of four objects and asked to "pick up" one of the objects with the mouse and move it to a specified location on the grid. The paddle was the target object for the trial shown in Figure 3. The display includes a "cohort" competitor sharing initial phonemes with the target (padlock) a rhyme competitor (saddle) and an unrelated object (castle).

Figure 3: Sample Display for the Instruction: "Pick up the paddle."

Figure 4 shows the probability that the eye is fixating on the target and the cohort competitor as the spoken target word unfolds. Early on in the speech stream, the eye is on the fixation cross, where subjects are told to look at the beginning of the trial. The probability of a fixation to the target word and the cohort competitor then increases. As the target word unfolds, the probability that the eye is fixated on the target increases compared to the cohort competitor. These data replicate our initial experiments and show how eye-movements can be used to trace the time course of spoken word recognition. Our preliminary data also make it clear that rhyme competitors attract fixations, as predicted by activation models.

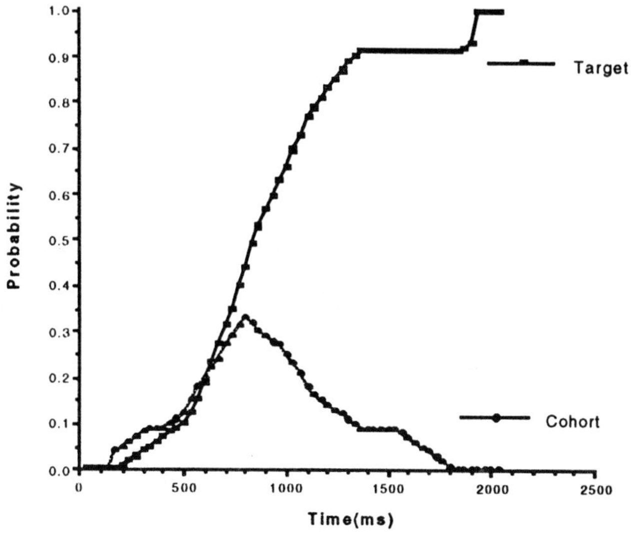

Figure 4: Probabilities of eye-fixations in a competitor trial.

Reference and Syntactic Ambiguity Resolution

There has been an unresolved debate in the language processing community about whether there are initial stages in syntactic processing that are strictly encapsulated from influences of referential and pragmatic context. The strongest evidence for encapsulated processing modules has come from studies using sentences with brief syntactic "attachment" ambiguities in which readers have clear preferences for interpretations, associated with particular syntactic configurations. For example, in the instruction "put the apple on the towel...," people prefer to attach the prepositional phrase "on the towel" to the verb "put", rather than the noun phrase "the apple", thus interpreting it as the argument of the verb (encoding the thematic relation of Goal), rather than as a modifier of the noun.

If the instruction continues "Put the apple on the towel into the box", the initial preference for a verb-phrase attachment is revealed by clear "garden-path" effects when "into" is encountered. Encapsulated models account for this preference in terms of principles such as pursue the simplest attachment first, or initially attach a phrase as an argument rather than as an adjunct. In contrast, constraint-based models attribute these preferences to the strength of multiple interacting constraints, including those provided by discourse context. [For a recent review, see Tanenhaus and Trueswell, 1995]

An influential proposal, most closely associated with Crain and Steedman [1985], is that pragmatically driven expectations about reference are an important source of discourse constraint. For example, a listener hearing "put the apple..." might reasonably assume that there is a single apple and thus expect to be told where to put the apple (the verb-phrase attachment). However, in a context in which there was more than one apple, the listener might expect to be told which of the apples is the intended referent and thus prefer the noun phrase attachment.

Numerous experiments have investigated whether or not the referential context established by a discourse context can modify attachment preferences. These studies typically introduce the context in a short paragraph and examine eye-movements to the disambiguating words in a target sentences containing the temporary ambiguity. While some studies have shown effects of discourse context, others have not. In particular, strong syntactic preferences persist momentarily, even when the referential context introduced by the discourse supports the normally less-preferred attachment. For example, the preference to initially attach a prepositional phrase to a verb requiring a goal argument (e.g., "put") cannot be overridden by linguistic context. These results have been taken as strong evidence for an encapsulated syntactic processing system.

However, typical psycholinguistic experiments may be strongly biased against finding pragmatic effects on syntactic processing. For example, the context may not be immediately accessible because it has to be represented in memory. Moreover, readers may not consider the context to be relevant when the ambiguous region of the sentence is being processed.

We reasoned that a relevant visual context that was available for the listener to interrogate as the linguistic input unfolded might influence initial syntactic analysis even though the same information might not be effective when introduced linguistically.

Sample instructions are illustrated by the examples in (1).

1. a. Put the apple on the towel in the box.
   b. Put the apple that's on the towel in the box.

In sentence (1a), the first prepositional phrase "on the towel", is ambiguous as to whether it modifies the noun phrase ("the apple") thus specifying the location of the object to be picked up, or whether it modifies the verb, thus introducing the goal location. In example (1b) the word "that's" disambiguates the phrase as a modifier, serving as an unambiguous control condition.

These instructions were paired with three types of display contexts. Each context contained four sets of real objects placed on a horizontal board. Sample displays for the instructions presented in (1) are illustrated in Figures 5, 6, and 7 Three of the objects were the same across all of the displays. Each display contained the target object (an apple on a towel) the correct goal, (a box) and an incorrect goal (another towel). In the one referent display (Figure 4) there was only one possible referent for the definite noun phrase "the apple", the apple on the towel. Upon hearing the phrase "the apple", participants can immediately identify the object to be moved because there is only one apple and thus they are likely to assume that "on the towel" is specifying the goal. In the two-referent display (Figure 5), there was a second possible referent (an apple on a napkin). Thus, "the apple", could refer to either of the two apples and the phrase "on the towel" provides modifying information that specifies which apple is the correct referent. Under these conditions a listener seeking to establish reference should interpret the prepositional phrase "on the towel" as providing disambiguating information about the location of the apple. In the three and one display, we added an apple cluster. The uniqueness presupposition associated with the definite noun phrase should bias the listener to assume that the single apple (the apple on the towel) is the intended referent for the theme argument. However, it is more felicitous to use a modifier with this instruction. This display was used to test if even a relatively subtle pragmatic effects will influence syntactic processing

Strikingly different fixation patterns among the visual contexts revealed that the ambiguous phrase "on the towel" was initially interpreted as the goal in the one-referent context but as a modifier in the two-referent contexts and the three-and-one contexts [for details see Spivey-Knowlton et al, 1995; Tanenhaus et al., 1995] In the one-referent context, subjects looked at the incorrect goal (e.g., the irrelevant towel) on 55% of the trials shortly after hearing the ambiguous prepositional phrase, whereas they never looked at the incorrect goal with the unambiguous instruction. In contrast, when the context contained two possible referents, subjects rarely looked at the incorrect goal, and there were no differences between the ambiguous and unambiguous instructions. Similar results obtained for the three-and-one context.

Figures 5 and 6 summarize the most typical sequences of eye-movements and their timing in relation to words in the ambiguous instructions for the one-referent and the two-referent contexts, respectively. In the one-referent context, subjects first looked at the target object (the apple) 500 ms after hearing "apple" then looked at the incorrect goal (the towel) 484 ms after hearing "towel". In contrast, with the unambiguous instruction, the first look to a goal did not occur until 500 ms after the subject heard the word "box".

In the two-referent context, subjects often looked at both apples, reflecting the fact that the referent of "the apple" was temporarily ambiguous. Subjects looked at the incorrect object on 42% of the unambiguous trials and on 61% of the ambiguous trials. In contrast, in the one-referent context, subjects rarely looked at the incorrect object (0% and 6% of the trials for the ambiguous and unambiguous instructions, respectively). In the two-referent context, subjects selected the correct referent as quickly for the ambiguous instruction as for the unambiguous instruction providing additional evidence that the first prepositional phrase was immediately interpreted as a modifier.

The three-and-one context provided additional information. Typical sequences of eye-movements for this context are presented in Figure 7. Participants rarely looked at the apple cluster, making their initial eye-movement to the apple on the towel. The next eye-movement was to the box for both the ambiguous and unambiguous instruction. These data also rule out a possible objection to the results from the two referent condition. One could argue that participants were, in fact, temporarily misparsing the prepositional phrase as the goal. However, this misanalysis might not be reflected in eye-movements to the towel because the eye was already in transit, moving between the two apples. However, in the three-and-one condition, the eye remains on the referent throughout the prepositional phrase. Given the sensitivity of eye-movements to probabilistic information, e.g., false launches to cohort and rhyme competitors, it is difficult to argue that the participants experienced a temporary garden-path that was too brief to influence eye-movements.

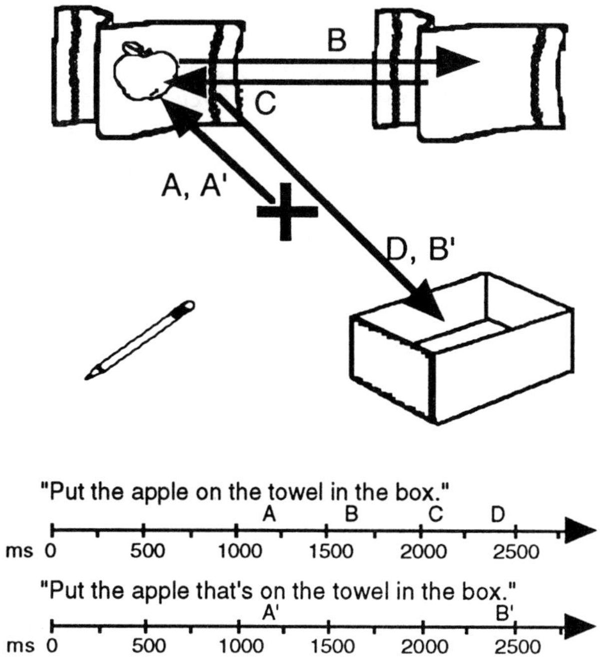

Figure 5: Typical sequence of eye movements in the one-referent context for the ambiguous and unambiguous instructions. Letters on the timeline show when in the instruction each eye movement occurred, as determined by mean latency of that type of eye movement (A' and B' correspond to the unambiguous instruction).

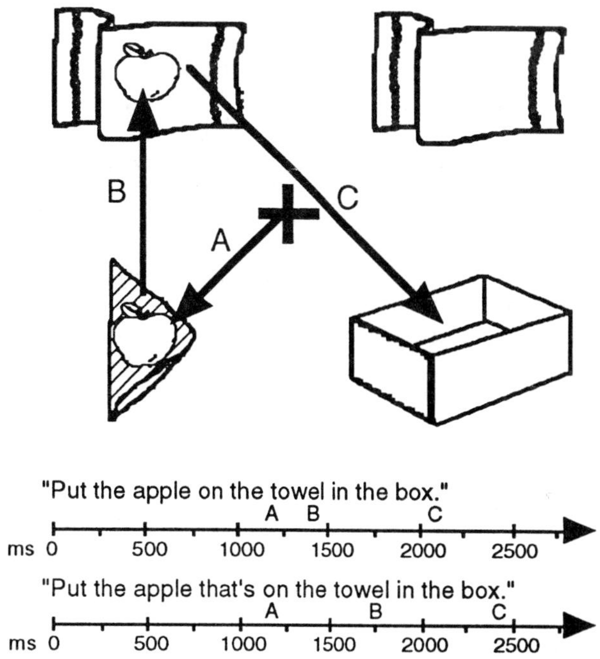

Figure 6: Typical sequence of eye movements in the two-referent context. Note that the sequence and the timing of eye movements, relative to the nouns in the speech stream, did not differ for the ambiguous and unambiguous instructions.

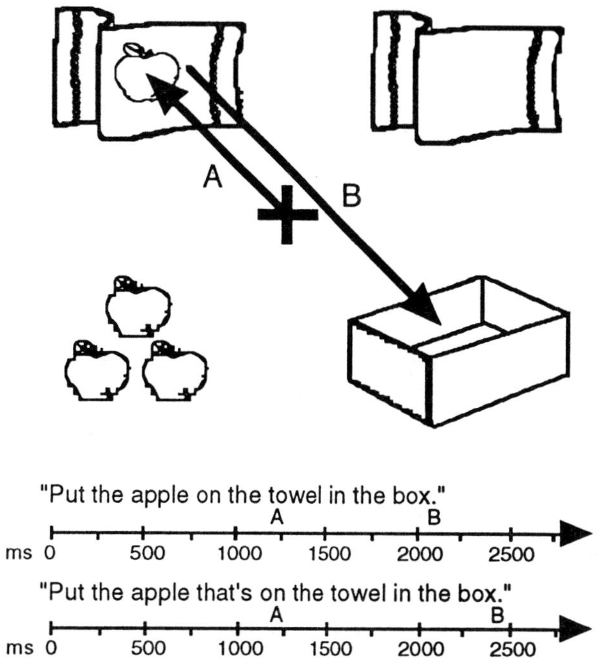

Figure 7: Typical sequence of eye movements in the three-and-one context. Note that the sequence and the timing of eye movements, relative to the nouns in the speech stream, did not differ for the ambiguous and unambiguous instructions.

Conclusion

We have reviewed results establishing that, with well-defined tasks, eye-movements can be used to observe under natural conditions the rapid mental processes that underlie spoken language comprehension. We believe that this paradigm will prove valuable for addressing questions on a full spectrum of topics in spoken language comprehension, ranging from the uptake of acoustic information during word recognition to conversational interactions during cooperative problem solving.

Our results demonstrate that in natural contexts people interpret spoken language continuously, seeking to establish reference with respect to their behavioral goals during the earliest moments of linguistic processing. Thus our results provide strong support for models that support continuous interpretation. Our experiments also show that referentially relevant non-linguistic information immediately affects how the linguistic input is initially structured. Given these results, approaches to language comprehension that emphasize fully encapsulated processing modules are unlikely to prove fruitful. More promising are approaches in which grammatical constraints are integrated into processing systems that coordinate linguistic and non-linguistic information as the linguistic input is processed.

Acknowledgments

* This paper summarizes work that the invited talk by the first author (MKT) was based upon. Supported by NIH resource grant 1-P41-RR09283; NIH HD27206 to MKT; NIH F32DC00210 to PDA, NSF Graduate Research Fellowships to MJS-K and JSM and a Canadian Social Science Research Fellowship to JCS.

References

Allopenna, P. D., Magnuson, J. S., & Tanenhaus, M. K. (1996). Watching spoken language perception: Using eye-movements to track lexical access. *Proceedings of the Eighteenth Annual Conference of the Cognitive Science Society*. Mahwah, NJ: Erlbaum.

Ballard, D., Hayhoe, M. & Pelz, J. (1995). Memory representations in natural tasks. *Journal of Cognitive Neuroscience,* 7, 68-82.

Crain, S. & Steedman, M. (1985). On not being led up the garden path. In Dowty, Kartunnen & Zwicky (eds.), *Natural Language Parsing*. Cambridge, MA: Cambridge U. Press.

Eberhard, K., Spivey-Knowlton, M., Sedivy, J. & Tanenhaus, M. (1995). Eye movements as a window into real-time spoken language comprehension in natural contexts. *Journal of Psycholinguistic Research,* 24, 409-436.

Kratzer, J. (1991). Representation of focus. In A. von Stechow & D. Wunderlich (Eds.), *Semantik: Ein Internationales Hundbuch der Zeitgenossichen Forschung*. Berlin: Walter de Guyter.

Krifka, M. (1991). A compositional semantics for multiple focus constructions. *Proceedings of Semantics and Linguistic Theory (SALT) I*, Cornell Working Papers, 11.

Marslen-Wilson, W. D. (1987). Functional Parallelism in spoken word-recognition. *Cognition* , 25, 71-102.

McClelland, J. L., & Elman, J. L. (1986). The TRACE model of speech perception. *Cognitive Psychology*, 18, 1-86.

Rooth, M. (1992). A theory of focus interpretation, *Natural Language Interpretation*, 1, 75-116.

Sedivy, J., Tanenhaus, M., Spivey-Knowlton, M., Eberhard, K. & Carlson, G. (1995). Using intonationally-marked presuppositional information in on-line language processing: Evidence from eye movements to a visual model. *Proceedings of the 17th Annual Conference of the Cognitive Science Society* (pp.375-380). Hillsdale, NJ: Erlbaum.

Spivey-Knowlton, M., Tanenhaus, M., Eberhard, K. & Sedivy, J. (1995). Eye-movements accompanying language and action in a visual context: Evidence against modularity. *Proceedings of the 17th Annual Conference of the Cognitive Science Society* (pp.25-30). Hillsdale, NJ: Erlbaum.

Tanenhaus, M. K., Spivey-Knowlton, M. J., Eberhard, K. M., & Sedivy, J. C. (1995). Integration of visual and linguistic information in spoken language-comprehension. *Science*, 268, 1632-1634.

Tanenhaus, M. K., Spivey-Knowlton, M. J., Eberhard, K. M., & Sedivy, J. C. (1996). Using eye-movements to study spoken language comprehension: Evidence for visually mediated incremental interpretation. In T Inui & J.L. McClelland (eds.). *Attention and Performance XVI: Information integration in perception and communication.*, 457-478. Cambridge Mass: MIT Press.

Tanenhaus, M. & Trueswell, J. (1995). Sentence comprehension. In J. Miller & P. Eimas (Eds.). *Handbook of Perception and Cognition: Volume 11: Speech, Language and Communication.* Academic Press., 217-262. New York: Academic Press.

A FULLY STATISTICAL APPROACH TO NATURAL LANGUAGE INTERFACES

Scott Miller, David Stallard, Robert Bobrow, Richard Schwartz
BBN Systems and Technologies
70 Fawcett Street
Cambridge, MA 02138

szmiller@bbn.com, stallard@bbn.com, rusty@bbn.com, schwartz@bbn.com

Abstract

We present a natural language interface system which is based entirely on trained statistical models. The system consists of three stages of processing: parsing, semantic interpretation, and discourse. Each of these stages is modeled as a statistical process. The models are fully integrated, resulting in an end-to-end system that maps input utterances into meaning representation frames.

1. Introduction

A recent trend in natural language processing has been toward a greater emphasis on statistical approaches, beginning with the success of statistical part-of-speech tagging programs (Church 1988), and continuing with other work using statistical part-of-speech tagging programs, such as BBN PLUM (Weischedel et al. 1993) and NYU Proteus (Grishman and Sterling 1993). More recently, statistical methods have been applied to domain-specific semantic parsing (Miller et al. 1994), and to the more difficult problem of wide-coverage syntactic parsing (Magerman 1995). Nevertheless, most natural language systems remain primarily rule based, and even systems that do use statistical techniques, such as AT&T Chronus (Levin and Pieraccini 1995), continue to require a significant rule based component. Development of a complete end-to-end statistical understanding system has been the focus of several ongoing research efforts, including (Miller et al. 1995) and (Koppelman et al. 1995). In this paper, we present such a system. The overall structure of our approach is conventional, consisting of a parser, a semantic interpreter, and a discourse module. The implementation and integration of these elements is far less conventional. Within each module, every processing step is assigned a probability value, and very large numbers of alternative theories are pursued in parallel. The individual modules are integrated through an *n*-best paradigm, in which many theories are passed from one stage to the next, together with their associated probability scores. The meaning of a sentence is determined by taking the highest scoring theory from among the *n*-best possibilities produced by the final stage in the model.

Some key advantages to statistical modeling techniques are:

- All knowledge required by the system is acquired through training examples, thereby eliminating the need for hand-written rules. In parsing for example, it is sufficient to provide the system with examples specifying the correct parses for a set of training examples. There is no need to specify an exact set of rules or a detailed procedure for producing such parses.
- All decisions made by the system are graded, and there are principled techniques for estimating the gradations. The system is thus free to pursue unusual theories, while remaining aware of the fact that they are unlikely. In the event that a more likely theory exists, then the more likely theory is selected, but if no more likely interpretation can be found, the unlikely interpretation is accepted.

The focus of this work is primarily to extract sufficient information from each utterance to give an appropriate response to a user's request. A variety of problems regarded as standard in computational linguistics, such as quantification, reference and the like, are thus ignored.

To evaluate our approach, we trained an experimental system using data from the Air Travel Information (ATIS) domain (Bates et al. 1990; Price 1990). The selection of ATIS was motivated by three concerns. First, a large corpus of ATIS sentences already exists and is readily available. Second, ATIS provides an existing evaluation methodology, complete with independent training and test corpora, and scoring programs. Finally, evaluating on a common corpus makes it easy to compare the performance of the system with those based on different approaches.

We have evaluated our system on the same blind test sets used in the ARPA evaluations (Pallett et al. 1995), and present a preliminary result at the conclusion of this paper.

The remainder of the paper is divided into four sections, one describing the overall structure of our models, and one for each of the three major components of parsing, semantic interpretation and discourse.

2. Model Structure

Given a string of input words W and a discourse history H, the task of a statistical language understanding system is to search among the many possible discourse-dependent meanings M_D for the most likely meaning M_0:

$$M_0 = \underset{M_D}{\arg\max}\, P(M_D \mid W, H).$$

Directly modeling $P(M_D \mid W, H)$ is difficult because the gap that the model must span is large. A common approach in non-statistical natural language systems is to bridge this gap by introducing intermediate representations such as parse structure and pre-discourse sentence meaning. Introducing these intermediate levels into the statistical framework gives:

$$M_0 = \underset{M_D}{\arg\max} \sum_{M_S,T} P(M_D \mid W,H,M_S,T)P(M_S,T \mid W,H)$$

where T denotes a semantic parse tree, and M_S denotes pre-discourse sentence meaning. This expression can be simplified by introducing two independence assumptions:

1. Neither the parse tree T, nor the pre-discourse meaning M_S, depends on the discourse history H.
2. The post-discourse meaning M_D does not depend on the words W or the parse structure T, once the pre-discourse meaning M_S is determined.

Under these assumptions,

$$M_0 = \underset{M_D}{\arg\max} \sum_{M_S,T} P(M_D \mid H,M_S)\ P(M_S,T \mid W)\ .$$

Next, the probability $P(M_S,T \mid W)$ can be rewritten using Bayes rule as:

$$P(M_S,T \mid W) = \frac{P(M_S,T)\ P(W \mid M_S,T)}{P(W)},$$

leading to:

$$M_0 = \underset{M_D}{\arg\max} \sum_{M_S,T} P(M_D \mid H,M_S) \frac{P(M_S,T)\ P(W \mid M_S,T)}{P(W)}$$

Now, since $P(W)$ is constant for any given word string, the problem of finding meaning M_D that maximizes

$$\sum_{M_S,T} P(M_D \mid H,M_S) \frac{P(M_S,T)\ P(W \mid M_S,T)}{P(W)}$$

is equivalent to finding M_D that maximizes

$$\sum_{M_S,T} P(M_D \mid H,M_S)\ P(M_S,T)\ P(W \mid M_S,T).$$

Thus,

$$M_0 = \underset{M_D}{\arg\max} \sum_{M_S,T} P(M_D \mid H,M_S)\ P(M_S,T)\ P(W \mid M_S,T).$$

We now introduce a third independence assumption:

3. The probability of words W does not depend on meaning M_S, given that parse T is known.

This assumption is justified because the word tags in our parse representation specify both semantic and syntactic class information. Under this assumption:

$$M_0 = \underset{M_D}{\arg\max} \sum_{M_S,T} P(M_D \mid H,M_S)\ P(M_S,T)\ P(W \mid T)$$

Finally, we assume that most of the probability mass for each discourse-dependent meaning is focused on a single parse tree and on a single pre-discourse meaning. Under this (Viterbi) assumption, the summation operator can be replaced by the maximization operator, yielding:

$$M_0 = \underset{M_D}{\arg\max}\left(\max_{M_S,T}\left(P(M_D \mid H,M_S)\ P(M_S,T)\ P(W \mid T)\right)\right)$$

This expression corresponds to the computation actually performed by our system which is shown in Figure 1.

Processing proceeds in three stages:

1. Word string W arrives at the parsing model. The full space of possible parses T is searched for n-best candidates according to the measure $P(T)\ P(W \mid T)$. These parses, together with their probability scores, are passed to the semantic interpretation model.
2. The constrained space of candidate parses T (received from the parsing model), combined with the full space of possible pre-discourse meanings M_S, is searched for n-best candidates according to the measure $P(M_S,T)\ P(W \mid T)$. These pre-discourse meanings, together with their associated probability scores, are passed to the discourse model.

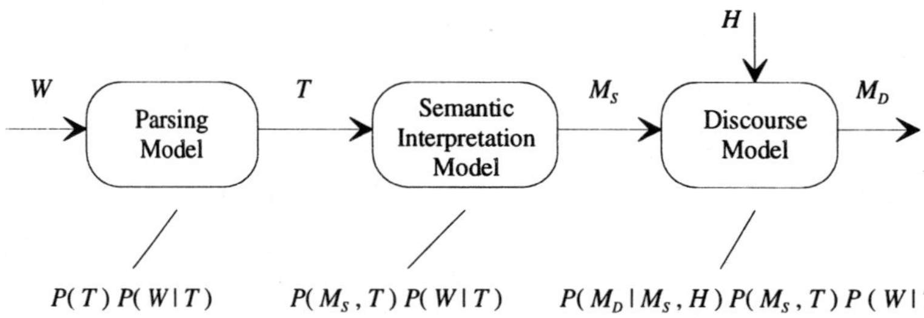

Figure 1: Overview of statistical processing.

3. The constrained space of candidate pre-discourse meanings M_S (received from the semantic interpretation model), combined with the full space of possible post-discourse meanings M_D, is searched for the single candidate that maximizes $P(M_D \mid H, M_S)\ P(M_S, T)\ P(W \mid T)$, conditioned on the current history H. The discourse history is then updated and the post-discourse meaning is returned.

We now proceed to a detailed discussion of each of these three stages, beginning with parsing.

3. Parsing

Our parse representation is essentially syntactic in form, patterned on a simplified head-centered theory of phrase structure. In content, however, the parse trees are as much semantic as syntactic. Specifically, each parse node indicates both a semantic and a syntactic class (excepting a few types that serve purely syntactic functions). Figure 2 shows a sample parse of a typical ATIS sentence. The semantic/syntactic character of this representation offers several advantages:

1. Annotation: Well-founded syntactic principles provide a framework for designing an organized and consistent annotation schema.
2. Decoding: Semantic and syntactic constraints are simultaneously available during the decoding process; the decoder searches for parses that are both syntactically and semantically coherent.
3. Semantic Interpretation: Semantic/syntactic parse trees are immediately useful to the semantic interpretation process: semantic labels identify the basic units of meaning, while syntactic structures help identify relationships between those units.

3.1 Statistical Parsing Model

The parsing model is a probabilistic recursive transition network similar to those described in (Miller et al. 1994) and (Seneff 1992). The probability of a parse tree T given a word string W is rewritten using Bayes rule as:

$$P(T \mid W) = \frac{P(T)P(W \mid T)}{P(W)}.$$

Since $P(W)$ is constant for any given word string, candidate parses can be ranked by considering only the product $P(T)$ $P(W \mid T)$. The probability $P(T)$ is modeled by state transition probabilities in the recursive transition network, and $P(W \mid T)$ is modeled by word transition probabilities.

- State transition probabilities have the form $P(state_n \mid state_{n-1}, state_{up})$. For example, *P(location/pp | arrival/vp-head, arrival/vp)* is the probability of a *location/pp* following an *arrival/vp-head* within an *arrival/vp* constituent.
- Word transition probabilities have the form $P(word_n \mid word_{n-1}, tag)$. For example, P("class" | "first", *class-of-service/npr*) is the probability of the word sequence "first class" given the tag *class-of-service/npr*.

Each parse tree T corresponds directly with a path through the recursive transition network. The probability $P(T)$ $P(W \mid T)$ is simply the product of each transition

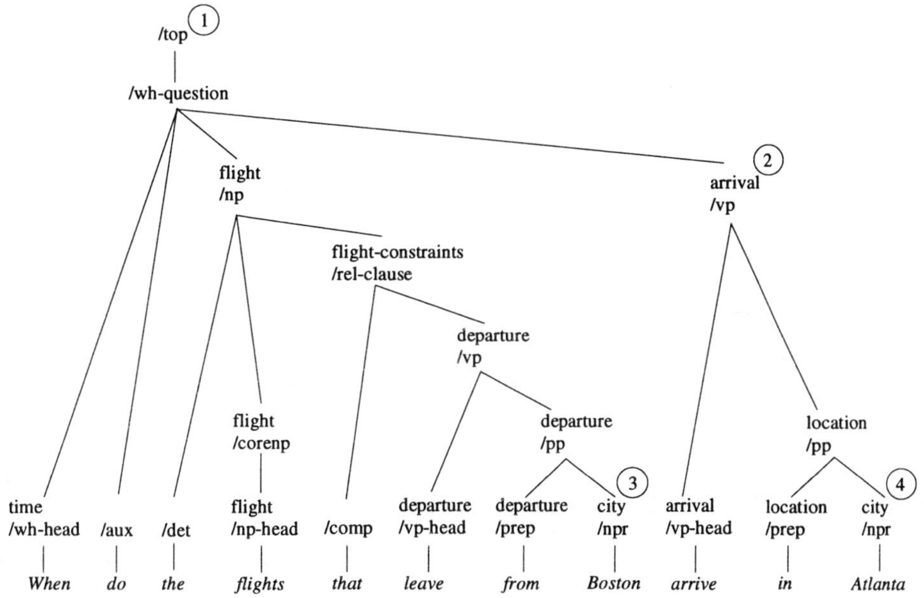

Figure 2: A sample parse tree.

probability along the path corresponding to T.

3.2 Training the Parsing Model

Transition probabilities are estimated directly by observing occurrence and transition frequencies in a training corpus of annotated parse trees. These estimates are then smoothed to overcome sparse data limitations. The semantic/syntactic parse labels, described above, provide a further advantage in terms of smoothing: for cases of undertrained probability estimates, the model backs off to independent syntactic and semantic probabilities as follows:

$$
\begin{aligned}
P_s(sem/syn_n \mid sem/syn_{n-1}, sem/syn_{up}) = {} \\
\lambda(sem/syn_n \mid sem/syn_{n-1}, sem/syn_{up}) \\
\times P(sem/syn_n \mid sem/syn_{n-1}, sem/syn_{up}) \\
+ (1 - \lambda(sem/syn_n \mid sem/syn_{n-1}, sem/syn_{up}) \\
\times P(sem_n \mid sem_{up}) P(syn_n \mid syn_{n-1}, syn_{up})
\end{aligned}
$$

where λ is estimated as in (Placeway et al. 1993). Backing off to independent semantic and syntactic probabilities potentially provides more precise estimates than the usual strategy of backing off directly form bigram to unigram models.

3.3 Searching the Parsing Model

In order to explore the space of possible parses efficiently, the parsing model is searched using a decoder based on an adaptation of the Earley parsing algorithm (Earley 1970). This adaptation, related to that of (Stolcke 1995), involves reformulating the Earley algorithm to work with probabilistic recursive transition networks rather than with deterministic production rules. For details of the decoder, see (Miller 1996).

4. Semantic Interpretation

Both pre-discourse and post-discourse meanings in our current system are represented using a simple frame representation. Figure 3 shows a sample semantic frame corresponding to the parse in Figure 2.

Air-Transportation
Show: (Arrival-Time)
Origin: (City "Boston")
Destination: (City "Atlanta")

Figure 3: A sample semantic frame.

Recall that the semantic interpreter is required to compute $P(M_S,T)\,P(W \mid T)$. The conditional word probability $P(W \mid T)$ has already been computed during the parsing phase and need not be recomputed. The current problem, then, is to compute the prior probability of meaning M_S and parse T occurring together. Our strategy is to embed the instructions for constructing M_S directly into parse T, resulting in an augmented tree structure. For example, the instructions needed to create the frame shown in Figure 3 are:

1. Create an Air-Transportation frame.
2. Fill the Show slot with Arrival-Time.
3. Fill the Origin slot with (City "Boston")
4. Fill the Destination slot with (City "Atlanta")

These instructions are attached to the parse tree at the points indicated by the circled numbers (see

Figure 2). The probability $P(M_S,T)$ is then simply the prior probability of producing the augmented tree structure.

4.1 Statistical Interpretation Model

Meanings M_S are decomposed into two parts: the frame type FT, and the slot fillers S. The frame type is always attached to the topmost node in the augmented parse tree, while the slot filling instructions are attached to nodes lower down in the tree. Except for the topmost node, all parse nodes are required to have some slot filling operation. For nodes that do not directly trigger any slot fill operation, the special operation *null* is attached. The probability $P(M_S, T)$ is then:

$$P(M_S,T) = P(FT,S,T) = P(FT)\;P(T \mid FT)\;P(S \mid FT,T).$$

Obviously, the prior probabilities $P(FT)$ can be obtained directly from the training data. To compute $P(T \mid FT)$, each of the state transitions from the previous parsing model are simply rescored conditioned on the frame type. The new state transition probabilities are:

$$P(state_n \mid state_{n-1}, state_{up}, FT).$$

To compute $P(S \mid FT, T)$, we make the independence assumption that slot filling operations depend only on the frame type, the slot operations already performed, and on the local parse structure around the operation. This local neighborhood consists of the parse node itself, its two left siblings, its two right siblings, and its four immediate ancestors. Further, the syntactic and semantic components of these nodes are considered independently. Under these assumptions, the probability of a slot fill operation is:

$$
\begin{aligned}
P(slot_n \mid FT, S_{n-1}, sem_{n-2}, \ldots, sem_n, \ldots, sem_{n+2}, \\
syn_{n-2}, \ldots, syn_n, \ldots, syn_{n+2}, \\
sem_{up1}, \ldots, sem_{up4}, syn_{up1}, \ldots, syn_{up4})
\end{aligned}
$$

and the probability $P(S \mid FT, T)$ is simply the product of all such slot fill operations in the augmented tree.

4.2 Training the Semantic Interpretation Model

Transition probabilities are estimated from a training corpus of augmented trees. Unlike probabilities in the parsing model, there obviously is not sufficient training data to estimate slot fill probabilities directly. Instead, these probabilities are estimated by statistical decision trees similar to those used in the Spatter parser (Magerman 1995). Unlike more common decision tree classifiers, which simply classify sets of conditions, statistical decision trees give a probability distribution over all possible outcomes. Statistical decision trees are constructed in a two phase process. In the first phase, a decision tree is constructed in the standard fashion using entropy reduction to guide the construction process. This phase is the same as for classifier models, and the distributions at the leaves are often extremely sharp, sometimes consisting of one outcome with probability 1, and all others with probability 0. In the second phase, these distributions are smoothed by mixing together distributions of various nodes in the decision tree. As in (Magerman 1995), mixture weights are determined by deleted interpolation on a separate block of training data.

4.3 Searching the Semantic Interpretation Model

Searching the interpretation model proceeds in two phases. In the first phase, every parse T received from the parsing model is rescored for every possible frame type, computing $P(T \mid FT)$ (our current model includes only a half dozen different types, so this computation is tractable). Each of these theories is combined with the corresponding prior probability $P(FT)$ yielding $P(FT)\ P(T \mid FT)$. The n-best of these theories are then passed to the second phase of the interpretation process. This phase searches the space of slot filling operations using a simple beam search procedure. For each combination of FT and T, the beam search procedure considers all possible combinations of fill operations, while pruning partial theories that fall beneath the threshold imposed by the beam limit. The surviving theories are then combined with the conditional word probabilities $P(W \mid T)$, computed during the parsing model. The final result of these steps is the n-best set of candidate pre-discourse meanings, scored according to the measure $P(M_S,T)\ P(W \mid T)$.

5. Discourse Processing

The discourse module computes the most probable post-discourse meaning of an utterance from its pre-discourse meaning and the discourse history, according to the measure:

$$P(M_D \mid H, M_S)\ P(M_S,T)\ P(W \mid T).$$

Because pronouns can usually be ignored in the ATIS domain, our work does not treat the problem of pronominal reference. Our probability model is instead shaped by the key discourse problem of the ATIS domain, which is the inheritance of constraints from context. This inheritance phenomenon, similar in spirit to one-anaphora, is illustrated by the following dialog::

USER1: I want to fly from Boston to Denver.

SYSTEM1: <displays Boston to Denver flights>

USER2: Which flights are available on Tuesday?

SYSTEM2: <displays Boston to Denver flights for Tuesday>

In USER2, it is obvious from context that the user is asking about flights whose ORIGIN is BOSTON and whose DESTINATION is DENVER, and not all flights between any two cities. Constraints are not always inherited, however. For example, in the following continuation of this dialogue:

USER3: Show me return flights from Denver to Boston,

it is intuitively much less likely that the user means the "on Tuesday" constraint to continue to apply.

The discourse history H simply consists of the list of all post-discourse frame representations for all previous utterances in the current session with the system. These frames are the source of candidate constraints to be inherited. For most utterances, we make the simplifying assumption that we need only look at the last (i.e. most recent) frame in this list, which we call M_P.

5.1 Statistical Discourse Model

The statistical discourse model maps a 23 element input vector X onto a 23 element output vector Y. These vectors have the following interpretations:

- X represents the combination of previous meaning M_P and the pre-discourse meaning M_S.
- Y represents the post-discourse meaning M_D.

Thus,

$$P(M_D \mid H, M_S) = P(Y \mid X).$$

The 23 elements in vectors X and Y correspond to the 23 possible slots in the frame schema. Each element in X can have one of five values, specifying the relationship between the filler of the corresponding slot in M_P and M_S:

INITIAL - slot filled in M_S but not in M_P

TACIT - slot filled in M_P but not in M_S

REITERATE - slot filled in both M_P and M_S; value the same

CHANGE - slot filled in both M_P and M_S; value different

IRRELEVANT - slot not filled in either M_P or M_S

Output vector Y is constructed by directly copying all fields from input vector X except those labeled TACIT. These direct copying operations are assigned probability 1. For fields labeled TACIT, the corresponding field in Y is filled with either INHERITED or NOT-INHERITED. The probability of each of these operations is determined by a statistical decision tree model. The discourse model contains 23 such statistical decision trees, one for each slot position. An ordering is imposed on the set of frame slots, such that inheritance decisions for slots higher in the order are conditioned on the decisions for slots lower in the order.

The probability $P(Y \mid X)$ is then the product of all 23 decision probabilities:

$$P(Y \mid X) = P(y_1 \mid X)\, P(y_2 \mid X, y_1) \ldots P(y_{23} \mid X, y_1, y_2, \ldots, y_{22}) .$$

5.2 Training the Discourse Model

The discourse model is trained from a corpus annotated with both pre-discourse and post-discourse semantic frames. Corresponding pairs of input and output (*X*, *Y*) vectors are computed from these annotations, which are then used to train the 23 statistical decision trees. The training procedure for estimating these decision tree models is similar to that used for training the semantic interpretation model.

5.3 Searching The Discourse Model

Searching the discourse model begins by selecting a meaning frame M_P from the history stack *H*, and combining it with each pre-discourse meaning M_S received from the semantic interpretation model. This process yields a set of candidate input vectors *X*. Then, for each vector *X*, a search process exhaustively constructs and scores all possible output vectors *Y* according to the measure $P(Y \mid X)$ (this computation is feasible because the number of TACIT fields is normally small). These scores are combined with the pre-discourse scores $P(M_S, T)\, P(W \mid T)$, already computed by the semantic interpretation process. This computation yields:

$$P(Y \mid X)\, P(M_S, T)\, P(W \mid T) ,$$

which is equivalent to:

$$P(M_D \mid H, M_S)\, P(M_S, T)\, P(W \mid T) .$$

The highest scoring theory is then selected, and a straightforward computation derives the final meaning frame M_D from output vector *Y*.

6. Experimental Results

We have trained and evaluated the system on a common corpus of utterances collected from naive users in the ATIS domain. In this test, the system was trained on approximately 4000 ATIS 2 and ATIS 3 sentences, and then evaluated on the December 1994 test material (which was held aside as a blind test set). The combined system produced an error rate of 21.6%. Work on the system is ongoing, however, and interested parties are encouraged to contact the authors for more recent results.

7. Conclusion

We have presented a fully trained statistical natural language interface system, with separate models corresponding to the classical processing steps of parsing, semantic interpretation and discourse. Much work remains to be done in order to refine the statistical modeling techniques, and to extend the statistical models to additional linguistic phenomena such as quantification and anaphora resolution.

8. Acknowledgments

We wish to thank Robert Ingria for his effort in supervising the annotation of the training corpus, and for his helpful technical suggestions.

This work was supported by the Advanced Research Projects Agency and monitored by the Office of Naval Research under Contract No. N00014-91-C-0115, and by Ft. Huachuca under Contract Nos. DABT63-94-C-0061 and DABT63-94-C-0063 . The content of the information does not necessarily reflect the position or the policy of the Government and no official endorsement should be inferred.

9. References

Bates, M., Boisen, S., and Makhoul, J. "Developing an Evaluation Methodology for Spoken Language Systems." Speech and Natural Language Workshop, Hidden Valley, Pennsylvania, 102-108.

Church, K. "A Stochastic Parts Program and Noun Phrase Parser for Unrestricted Text." Second Conference on Applied Natural Language Processing, Austin, Texas.

Earley, J. (1970). "An Efficient Context-Free Parsing Algorithm." Communications of the ACM, 6, 451-455.

Grishman, R., and Sterling, J. "Description of the Proteus System as Used for MUC-5." Fifth Message Understanding Conference, Baltimore, Maryland, 181-194.

Koppelman, J., Pietra, S. D., Epstein, M., Roukos, S., and Ward, T. "A statistical approach to language modeling for the ATIS task." Eurospeech 1995, Madrid.

Levin, E., and Pieraccini, R. "CHRONUS: The Next Generation." Spoken Language Systems Technology Workshop, Austin, Texas, 269-271.

Magerman, D. "Statistical Decision Tree Models for Parsing." 33rd Annual Meeting of the Association for Computational Linguistics, Cambridge, Massachusetts, 276-283.

Miller, S. (1996). "Hidden Understanding Models," Northeastern University, Boston, MA.

Miller, S., Bates, M., Bobrow, R., Ingria, R., Makhoul, J., and Schwartz, R. "Recent Progress in Hidden Understanding Models." Spoken Language Systems Technology Workshop, Austin, Texas, 276-280.

Miller, S., Bobrow, R., Ingria, R., and Schwartz, R. "Hidden Understanding Models of Natural Language." 32nd Annual Meeting of the Association for Computational Linguistics, Las Cruces, New Mexico, 25-32.

Pallett, D., Fiscus, J., Fisher, W., Garofolo, J., Lund, B., Martin, A., and Przybocki, M. "1994 Benchmark Tests for the ARPA Spoken Language Program." Spoken Language Systems Technology Workshop, Austin, Texas.

Placeway, P., Schwartz, R., Fung, P., and Nguyen, L. "The Estimation of Powerful Language Models from Small and Large Corpora." IEEE ICASSP, 33-36.

Price, P. "Evaluation of Spoken Language Systems: the ATIS Domain." Speech and Natural Language Workshop, Hidden Valley, Pennsylvania, 91-95.

Seneff, S. (1992). "TINA: A Natural Language System for Spoken Language Applications." Computational Linguistics, 18,1, 61-86.

Stolcke, A. (1995). "An Efficient Probabilistic Context-Free Parsing Algorithm that Computes Prefix Probabilites." Computational Linguistics, 21(2), 165-201.

Weischedel, R., Ayuso, D., Boisen, S., Fox, H., Ingria, R., Matsukawa, T., Papageorgiou, C., MacLaughlin, D., Kitagawa, M., Sakai, T., Abe, J., Hosihi, H., Miyamoto, Y., and Miller, S. "Description of the PLUM System as Used for MUC-5." Fifth Message Understanding Conference, Baltimore, Maryland, 93-107.

A Robust System for Natural Spoken Dialogue

James F. Allen, Bradford W. Miller, Eric K. Ringger, Teresa Sikorski
Dept. of Computer Science
University of Rochester
Rochester, NY 14627
{james, miller, ringger, sikorski}@cs.rochester.edu
http://www.cs.rochester.edu/research/trains/

Abstract

This paper describes a system that leads us to believe in the feasibility of constructing natural spoken dialogue systems in task-oriented domains. It specifically addresses the issue of robust interpretation of speech in the presence of recognition errors. Robustness is achieved by a combination of statistical error post-correction, syntactically- and semantically-driven robust parsing, and extensive use of the dialogue context. We present an evaluation of the system using time-to-completion and the quality of the final solution that suggests that most native speakers of English can use the system successfully with virtually no training.

1. Introduction

While there has been much research on natural dialogue, there have been few working systems because of the difficulties in obtaining robust behavior. Given over twenty years of research in this area, if we can't construct a robust system even in a simple domain then that bodes ill for progress in the field. In particular, without some working systems, we are very limited in how we can evaluate the worth of different models.

The prime goal of the work reported here was to demonstrate that it is feasible to construct robust spoken natural dialogue systems. We were not seeking to develop new theories, but rather to develop techniques to enable existing theories to be applied in practice. We chose a domain and task that was as simple as possible yet couldn't be solved without the collaboration of the human and system. In addition, there were three fundamental requirements:

- the system must run in near real-time;
- the user should need minimal training and not be constrained in what can be said; and
- the dialogue should have a concrete result that can be independently evaluated.

The second constraint means we must handle natural dialogue, namely dialogue as people use it rather than a constrained form of interaction determined by the system (which is often called a dialogue). We can only control the complexity of the dialogue by controlling the complexity of the task. Increasing the task complexity naturally increases the complexity of the dialogue. This paper reports on the first stage of this process, working with a highly simplified domain.

At the start of this experiment in November 1994, we had no idea whether it was possible. While researchers were reporting good accuracy (upwards of 95%) for speech systems in simple question-answering tasks, our domain was considerably different with a much more spontaneous form of interaction.

We also knew that it would not be possible to directly use general models of plan recognition to aid in speech act interpretation (as in Allen & Perrault, 1980, Litman & Allen 1987, Carberry 1990), as these models would not lend themselves to real-time processing. Similarly, it would not be feasible to use general planning models for the system back-end and for planning its responses. We could not, on the other hand, completely abandon the ideas underlying the plan-based approach, as we knew of no other theory that could provide an account for the interactions. Our approach was to try to retain the overall structure of plan-based systems, but to use domain-specific reasoning techniques to provide real-time performance.

Dialogue systems are notoriously hard to evaluate as there is no well-defined "correct answer". So we cannot give end-to-end accuracy measures as is typically done to measure the performance of speech recognition systems and parsing systems. This is especially true when evaluating dialogue robustness, which results from many different sources: correcting speech recognition errors, using semantic knowledge to interpret fragments, and using dialogue strategies to keep the dialogue flowing efficiently despite recognition and interpretation errors.

The approach we take is to use task-based evaluation. We measure how well the system does at helping the user solve the problem. The two most telling measures are time-to-completion and the quality of the final solution. In the evaluation described later in this paper, we show that all our subjects were able to use TRAINS-95 to solve problems with only minimal training. We also evaluated the overall effectiveness of our robust processing techniques by comparing spoken dialogues with keyboard dialogues by the same subjects. Even with a 30% word error rate (including insertion errors), speech turned out to be considerably more efficient than keyboard input in this domain.

2. The Task and Example Session

The domain in TRAINS-95 is simple route planning. The user is given a map on a screen showing cities, connections and the locations of a set of trains (see Figure 1), and a verbal specification of a set of destination cities where trains are needed. The task is to find the most efficient set of routes possible. The route planner used by the system is deliberately weak so that interaction is needed to find good plans. Specifically, the planner cannot find routes longer than four hops without an intermediate city, and when it can generate a route, it randomly selects among the possibilities.

Typically, the examples in papers on dialogue systems are carefully hand-constructed and designed to show off specific system capabilities. Such examples, however, give little feeling for how robust a system is. Much more revealing is how a system responds to unplanned interactions with naive users, and how it deals with the interaction when things start to go wrong. Thus, we won't present any examples in which everything went smoothly. Rather, we present a dialogue that stresses the system's capabilities, better illuminating what works and what areas require further improvement.

The dialogue below was with a non-computer person who had used the system a few times before. In the transcripts, we show the input as it was produced by the speech recognizer in ALL CAPS followed by what was actually said. If the recognition was perfect we just show the speech recognition output. The dialogue contains a significant number of errors and has a 29.5% word error rate. The system display is also shown at key points[1]. In this problem, the engines start at Detroit, Montreal and Albany and the goal is to get trains to Milwaukee, Lexington and Washington.

S: Ok. I think I'm ready to start.

U: OKAY LET'S SEE CONTAIN FROM DETROIT TO WASHINGTON
Okay. Let's take a train from Detroit to Washington.

S: What route would you like to get from Detroit to Washington?

U: LET'S GO VIA TOLEDO AND PITTSBURGH

S: *(displays Figure 2)* The terminal at city Scranton is delaying traffic due to localized heavy winds. The terminal at city Baltimore is delaying traffic due to localized heavy winds. An additional five hours will be needed to travel through them due to decreased visibility.

U: NOW LET'S TAKE THE TRAIN FROM DETROIT TO WASHINGTON D S_X ANY
No. Let's take the train from Detroit to Washington via Cincinnati.

S: *(displays Figure 3)* Okay.

U: OKAY IT THAT'S OKAY NOW
Okay that - that's okay now

S: Pardon Me?

U: UP OKAY NOW LET'S TAKE THE TRAIN FROM MONTREAL TO LEXINGTON
Okay. Now let's take the train from Montreal to Lexington.

[1] We apologize for the figures. The actual system uses color displays. The best way to present examples is by video. A quicktime movie can be found in
http://www.cs.rochester.edu/research/trains/ACL96.

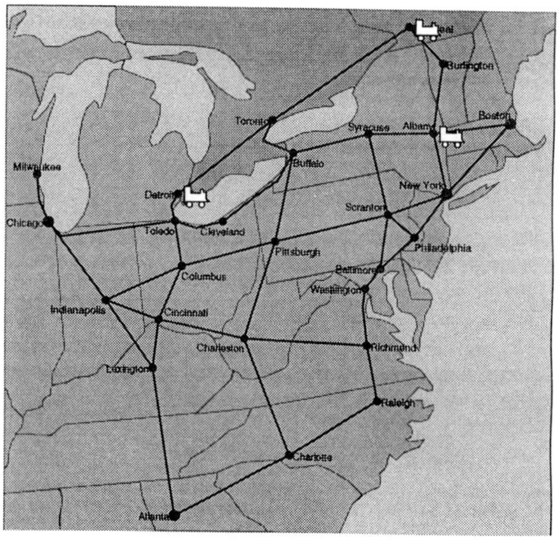

Figure 1: The initial scenario

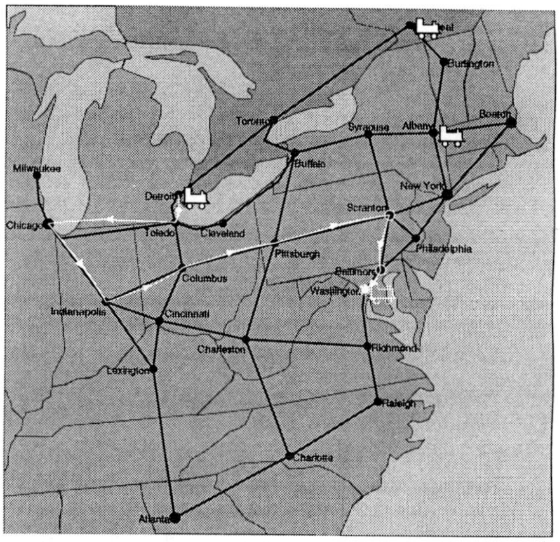

Figure 2: The proposed route

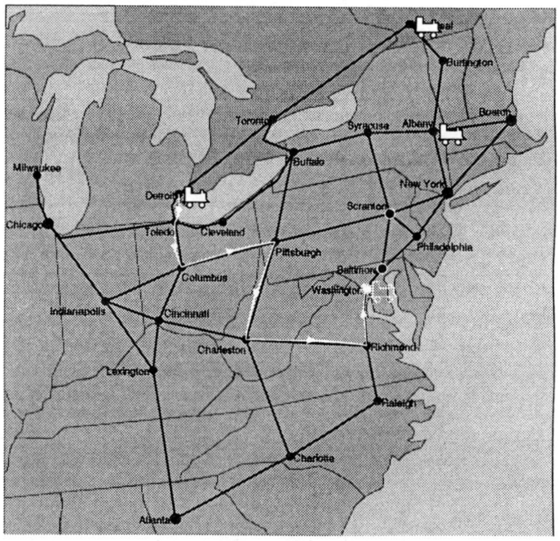

Figure 3: The corrected route

S: I need help choosing a route from Montreal to Lexington.

U: LET'S GO P_M TO TRY
Let's go via Detroit

S: *(displays a route to Detroit but not on to Lexington)* Is this OK?

U: YES NOW LET'S GO TO LEXINGTON

S: Yep.

U: OKAY NOW ADD STATE THE LAST TRAIN AND GO FROM ALBANY TO O_O'S
Okay Now let's take the last train and go from Albany to Milwaukee.

S: No. What city are you trying to have the engine at Montreal arrive at, if I caught your drift. I don't understand where we are sending the engine at Albany to.

U: ME A JET ADD ALBANY NEEDS TO GO TO MILWAUKEE
The engine at Albany needs to go to Milwaukee.

S: Tell me a route to use to get from Albany to Milwaukee, please.

U: I'D GO VIA BUFFALO
Uh - Go via Buffalo.

S: *(displays a route through Toronto and Buffalo)* Yes.

U: GO B_X SYRACUSE AT BUFFALO
Go via Syracuse and Buffalo.

S: *(displays Figure 4)* yeah.

U: THAT'S COULD I CAN
That's good. I'm done.

S: Hey, its the programming.

U: I_NEED DONE
I'm done.

3. The System

The TRAINS-95 system is organized as shown in Figure 5. At the top are the I/O facilities. The speech recognition system is the Sphinx-II system from CMU (Huang et al, 1993). The speech synthesizer is a commercial product: the TRUETALK system from Entropics. The rest of the system was built at Rochester. The display supports a communication language that allows other modules to control the content of the display. It also handles keyboard input. The speech recognition output is passed through the post-processor described in section 4. The parser, described in section 5, accepts input either from the post-processor (for speech) or the display manager (for keyboard), and produces a set of speech act interpretations that are passed to the discourse manager, described in section 6. The discourse manager breaks into a range of subcomponents handling reference, speech act interpretation and planning (the verbal reasoner), and the back-end of the system: the problem solver and domain reasoner. When a speech act is planned for output, it is passed to the generator, which constructs a sentence and passes this to both the speech synthesizer and the display.

The generator is a simple template-based system. It uses templates associated with different speech act forms that are instantiated with descriptions of the particular objects involved. The form of these descriptions is defined for each class of objects in the domain.

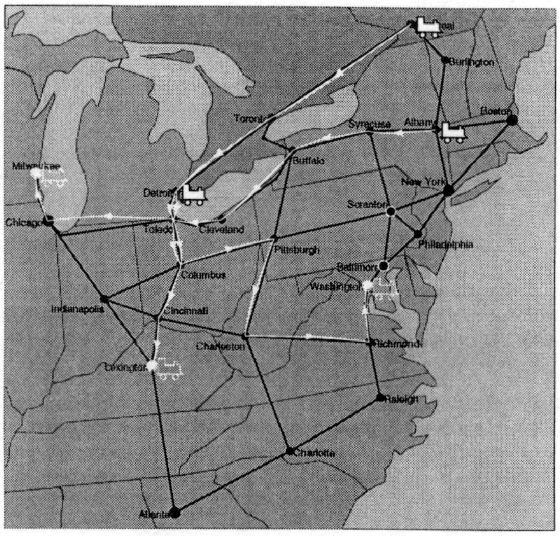

Figure 4: The final routes

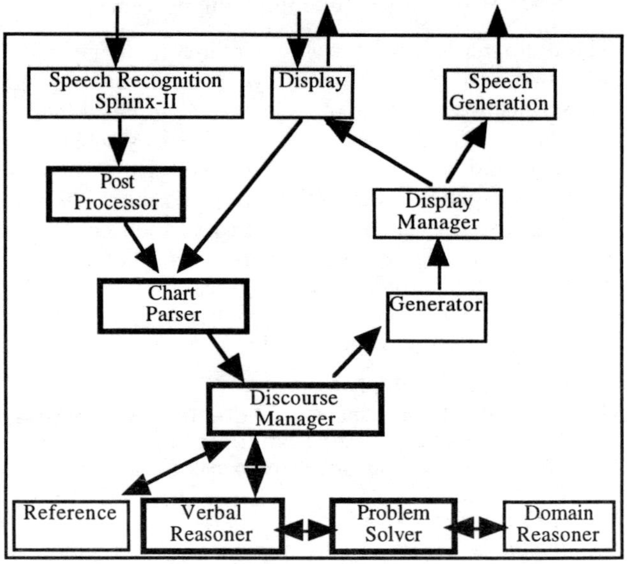

Figure 5 : The TRAINS-95 System Architecture

In order to stress the system in our robustness evaluation, we used the ATIS language model provided from CMU. This system yields an overall word error rate of 30% on TRAINS-95 dialogues, as opposed to a 20% error rate that we can currently obtain by using language models trained on our TRAINS corpus. While this accuracy rate is significantly lower than often reported in the literature, remember that most speech recognition results are reported for read speech, or for constrained dialogue applications such as ATIS. Natural dialogue involves a more spontaneous form of interaction that is much more difficult to interpret.

4. Statistical Error Post-Correction

The following are examples of speech recognition (SR) errors that occurred in the sample dialogue. In each, the words tagged REF indicate what was actually said, while those tagged with HYP indicate what the speech recognition system proposed, and HYP' indicates the output of SPEECHPP, our post-processor. While the corrected transcriptions are not perfect, they are typically a better approximation of the actual utterance. As the first example shows, some recognition errors are simple word-for-word confusions:

HYP: GO B_X SYRACUSE AT BUFFALO
HYP': GO VIA SYRACUSE VIA BUFFALO
REF: GO VIA SYRACUSE AND BUFFALO

In the next example, a single word was replaced by more than one smaller word:

HYP: LET'S GO P_M TO TRY
HYP': LET'S GO P_M TO DETROIT
REF: LET'S GO VIA DETROIT

The post-processor yields fewer errors by effectively refining and tuning the vocabulary used by the speech recognizer. To achieve this, we adapted some techniques from statistical machine translation (such as Brown et al., 1990) in order to model the errors that Sphinx-II makes in our domain. Briefly, the model consists of two parts: a channel model, which accounts for errors made by the SR, and the language model, which accounts for the likelihood of a sequence of words being uttered in the first place.

More precisely, given an observed word sequence ***o*** from the speech recognizer, SPEECHPP finds the most likely original word sequence by finding the sequence ***s*** that maximizes Prob(***o***|***s***) * Prob(***s***), where

- Prob(***s***) is the probability that the user would utter sequence ***s***, and
- Prob(***o***|***s***) is the probability that the SR produces the sequence ***o*** when ***s*** was actually spoken.

For efficiency, it is necessary to estimate these distributions with relatively simple models by making independence assumptions. For Prob(***s***), we train a word-bigram "back-off" language model (Katz, 87) from hand-transcribed dialogues previously collected with the TRAINS-95 system. For P(***o***|***s***), we build a channel model that assumes independent word-for-word substitutions; i.e.,

$$\text{Prob}(\boldsymbol{o} \mid \boldsymbol{s}) = \prod_i \text{Prob}(o_i \mid s_i)$$

The channel model is trained by automatically aligning the hand transcriptions with the output of Sphinx-II on the utterances in the (SPEECHPP) training set and by tabulating the confusions that occurred. We use a Viterbi beam-search to find the ***s*** that maximizes the expression. This technique is widely known so is not described here (see Forney (1973) and Lowerre (1986)).

Having a relatively small number of TRAINS-95 dialogues for training, we wanted to investigate how well the data could be employed in models for both the SR and the SPEECHPP. We ran several experiments to weigh our options. For a baseline, we built a class-based back-off language model for Sphinx-II using only transcriptions of ATIS spoken utterances. Using this model, the performance of Sphinx-II alone on TRAINS-95 data was 58.7%. Note that this figure is lower than our previously mentioned average of 70%, since we were unable to exactly replicate the ATIS model from CMU.

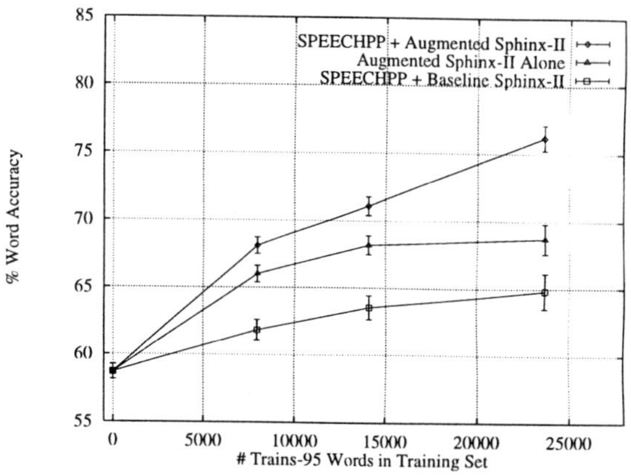

Figure 6: Post-processing Evaluation

First, we used varying amounts of training data exclusively for building models for the SPEECHPP; this scenario would be most relevant if the speech recognizer were a black-box and we did not know how to train its model(s). Second, we used varying amounts of the training data exclusively for augmenting the ATIS data to build language models for Sphinx-II. Third, we combined the methods, using the training data both to extend the language models for Sphinx-II and to then train SPEECHPP on the newly trained SR.

The results of the first experiment are shown by the bottom curve of Figure 6, which indicates the performance of the SPEECHPP with the baseline Sphinx-II. The first point comes from using approx. 25% of the available training data in the SPEECHPP models. The second and third points come from using approx. 50% and 75%, respectively, of the available training data. The curve clearly indicates that the SPEECHPP does a reasonable job of boosting our word recognition rates over baseline Sphinx-II and performance improves with additional training data. We did not train with all of our available data, since the remainder was used for testing to determine the results via repeated leave-one-out cross-validation. The error bars in the figure indicate 95% confidence intervals.

Similarly, the results of the second experiment are shown by the middle curve. The points reflect the performance of Sphinx-II (without SPEECHPP) when using 25%, 50%, and 75% of the available training data in its LM. These results indicate that equivalent amounts of training data can be used with greater impact in the language model of the SR than in the post-processor.

Finally, the outcome of the third experiment is reflected

in the uppermost curve. Each point indicates the performance of the SPEECHPP using a set of models trained on the behavior of Sphinx-II for the corresponding point from the second experiment. The results from this experiment indicate that even if the language model of the SR can be modified, then the post-processor trained on the same new data can still significantly improve word recognition accuracy on a separate test set. Hence, whether the SR's models are tunable or not, the post-processor is in neither case redundant.

Since these experiments were performed, we have enhanced the channel model by relaxing the constraint that replacement errors be aligned on a word-by-word basis. We employ a fertility model (Brown et al, 1990) that indicates how likely each word is to map to multiple words or to a partial word in the SR output. This extension allows us to better handle the second example above, replacing TO TRY with DETROIT. For more details, see Ringger and Allen (1996).

5. Robust Parsing

Given that speech recognition errors are inevitable, robust parsing techniques are essential. We use a pure bottom-up parser (using the system described in (Allen, 1995)) in order to identify the possible constituents at any point in the utterance based on syntactic and semantic restrictions. Every constituent in each grammar rule specifies both a syntactic category and a semantic category, plus other features to encode co-occurance restrictions as found in many grammars. The semantic features encode selectional restrictions, most of which are domain-independent. For example, there is no general rule for PP attachment in the grammar. Rather there are rules for temporal adverbial modification (e.g., *at eight o'clock*), locational modification (e.g., *in Chicago*), and so on.

The end result of parsing is a sequence of speech acts rather than a syntactic analysis. Viewing the output as a sequence of speech acts has significant impact on the form and style of the grammar. It forces an emphasis on encoding semantic and pragmatic features in the grammar. There are, for instance, numerous rules that encode specific conventional speech acts (e.g., *That's good* is a CONFIRM, *Okay* is a CONFIRM/ACKNOWLEDGE, *Let's go to Chicago* is a SUGGEST, and so on). Simply classifying such utterances as sentences would miss the point. Thus the parser computes a set of plausible speech act interpretation based on the surface form, similar to the model described in Hinkelman & Allen (1989).

We use a hierarchy of speech acts that encode different levels of vagueness, including a TELL act that indicates content without an identifiable illocutionary force. This allows us to always have an illocutionary force that can be refined as more of the utterance is processed. The final interpretation of an utterance is the sequence of speech acts that provides the "minimal covering" of the input - i.e., the shortest sequence that accounts for the input. Even if an utterance was completely uninterpretable, the parser would still produce output - a TELL act with no content.

For example, consider an utterance from the sample dialogue that was garbled: OKAY NOW I TAKE THE LAST TRAIN IN GO FROM ALBANY TO IS. The best sequence of speech acts to cover this input consists of three acts:

1. a CONFIRM/ACKNOWLEDGE (OKAY)
2. a TELL, with content to take the last train (NOW I TAKE THE LAST TRAIN)
3. a REQUEST to go from Albany (GO FROM ALBANY)

Note that the *to is* at the end of the utterance is simply ignored as it is uninterpretable. While not present in the output, the presence of unaccounted words will lower the parser's confidence score that it assigns to the interpretation.

The actual utterance was *Okay now let's take the last train and go from Albany to Milwaukee*. Note that while the parser is not able to reconstruct the complete intentions of the user, it has extracted enough to continue the dialogue in a reasonable fashion by invoking a clarification subdialogue. Specifically, it has correctly recognized the confirmation of the previous exchange (act 1), and recognized a request to move a train from Albany (act 3). Act 2 is an incorrect analysis, and results in the system generating a clarification question that the user ends up ignoring. Thus, as far as furthering the dialogue, the system has done reasonably well.

6. Robust Speech Act Processing

The dialogue manager is responsible for interpreting the speech acts in context, formulating responses, and maintaining the system's idea of the state of the discourse. It maintains a discourse state that consists of a goal stack with similarities to the plan stack of Litman & Allen (1987) and the attentional state of Grosz & Sidner (1986). Each element of the stack captures

1. the domain or discourse goal motivating the segment
2. the object focus and history list for the segment
3. information on the status of problem solving activity (e.g., has the goal been achieved yet or not).

A fundamental principle in the design of TRAINS-95 was a decision that, when faced with ambiguity it is better to choose a specific interpretation and run the risk of making a mistake as opposed to generating a clarification subdialogue. Of course, the success of this strategy depends on the system's ability to recognize and interpret subsequent corrections if they arise. Significant effort was made in the system to detect and handle a wide range of corrections, both in the grammar, the discourse processing and the domain reasoning. In later systems, we plan to specifically evaluate the effectiveness of this strategy.

The discourse processing is divided into reference resolution, verbal reasoning, problem solving and domain reasoning.

Reference resolution, other than having the obvious job of identifying the referents of noun phrases, also may reinterpret the parser's assignment of illocutionary force if it has additional information to draw upon. One way we attain robustness is by having overlapping realms of responsibility: one module may be able to do a better job resolving a problem because it has an alternative view of it. On the other hand, it's important to recognize another module's expertise as well. It could be disastrous to combine two speech acts that arise from *I really <garbled> think that's good.* for instance, since the garbled part may include *don't.* Since speech recognition may substitute important words one for the other, it's important to keep in mind that speech acts that have no firm illocutionary force due to grammatical problems may have little to do with what the speaker actually said.

The verbal reasoner is organized as a set of prioritized rules that match patterns in the input speech acts and the discourse state. These rules allow robust processing in the face of partial or ill-formed input as they match at varying levels of specificity, including rules that interpret fragments that have no identified illocutionary force. For instance, one rule would allow a fragment such as *to Avon* to be interpreted as a suggestion to extend a route, or an identification of a new goal. The prioritized rules are used in turn until an acceptable result is obtained.

The problem solver handles all speech acts that appear to be requests to constrain, extend or change the current plan. It is also based on a set of prioritized rules, this time dealing with plan corrections and extensions. These rules match against the speech act, the problem solving state, and the current state of the domain. If fragmentary information is supplied, the problem solver attempts to incorporate the fragment into what it knows about the current state of the plan.

As example of the discourse processing, consider how the system handles the user's first utterance in the dialogue, OKAY LET'S SEND CONTAIN FROM DETROIT TO WASHINGTON. From the parser we get three acts:

1. a CONFIRM/ACKNOWLEDGE (OKAY)
2. a TELL involving mostly uninterpretable words (LET'S SEND CONTAIN)
3. a TELL act that mentions a route (FROM DETROIT TO WASHINGTON)

The discourse manager sets up its initial conversation state and passes the act to reference for identification of particular objects, and then hands the acts to the verbal reasoner. Because there is nothing on the discourse stack, the initial confirm has no effect. (Had there been something on the stack, e.g. a question of a plan, the initial confirm might have been taken as an answer to the question, or a confirm of the plan, respectively). The following empty TELL act is uninterpretable and hence ignored. While it is possible to claim the "send" could be used to indicate the illocutionary force of the following fragment, and that a "container" might even be involved, the fact that the parser separated out the speech act indicates there may have been other fragments lost. The last speech act could be a suggestion of a new goal to move from Detroit to Washington. After checking that there is an engine at Detroit, this interpretation is accepted. The planner is unable to generate a path between these points (since it is greater than four hops). It returns two items:

1. an identification of the speech act as a suggestion of a goal to take a train from Detroit to Washington
2. a signal that it couldn't find a path to satisfy the goal

The discourse context is updated and the verbal reasoner generates a response to clarify the route desired, which is realized in the system's response *What route would you like to get from Detroit to Washington?*

As another example of robust processing, consider an interaction later in the dialogue in which the user's response *no* is misheard as *now:Now let's take the train from Detroit to Washington do S_X Albany* (instead of *No let's take the train from Detroit to Washington via Cincinnati*). Since no explicit rejection is identified due to the recognition error, this utterance looks like a confirm and continuation of the plan. Thus the problem solver is called to extend the path with the currently focused engine (engine1) from Detroit to Washington.

The problem solver realizes that engine1 isn't currently in Detroit, so this can't be a route extension. In addition, there is no other engine at Detroit, so this is not plausible as a focus shift to a different engine. Since engine1 originated in Detroit, it then decides to reinterpret the utterance as a correction. Since the utterance adds no new constraints, but there are the cities that were just mentioned as having delays, it presumes the user is attempting to avoid them, and invokes the domain reasoner to plan a new route avoiding the congested cities. The new path is returned and presented to the user.

While the response does not address the user's intention to go through Cincinnati due to the speech recognition errors, it is a reasonable response to the problem the user is trying to solve. In fact, the user decides to accept the proposed route and forget about going through Cincinnati. In other cases, the user might persevere and continue with another correction such as *No, through Cincinnati.* Robustness arises in the example because the system uses its knowledge of the domain to produce a reasonable response. Note these examples both illustrate the "strong commitment" model. We believe it is easier to correct a poor plan, than having to keep trying to explain a perfect one, particularly in the face of recognition problems. For further detail on the problem solver, see Ferguson et al (1996).

7. Evaluating the System

While examples can be illuminating, they don't address the issue of how well the system works overall. To explore how well the system robustly handles spoken dialogue, we designed an experiment to contrast speech input with keyboard input. The experiment uses the different input media to manipulate the word error rate and the degree of spontaneity. Task performance was evaluated in terms of two metrics: the amount of time taken to arrive at a solution and the quality of the solution. Solution quality for our domain is determined by the amount of time needed to travel the routes.

Sixteen subjects for the experiment were recruited from undergraduate computer science courses. None of the subjects had ever used the system before. The procedure was as follows:

- The subject viewed an online tutorial lasting 2.4 minutes.
- The subject was then allowed a few minutes to practice both speech and keyboard input.
- All subjects were given identical sets of 5 tasks to perform, in the same order. Half of the subjects were asked to use speech first, keyboard second, speech third and keyboard fourth. The other half used keyboard first and then alternated. All subjects were given a choice of whether to use speech or keyboard input to accomplish the final task.
- After performing the final task, the subject completed a questionnaire.

An analysis of the experiment results shows that the plans generated when speech input was used are of similar quality to those generated when keyboard input was used. However, the time needed to develop plans was significantly lower when speech input was used.

Overall, problems were solved using speech in 68% of the time needed to solve them using the keyboard. Figure 7 shows the task completion time results, and Figure 8 gives the solution quality results, each broken out by task.

Of the 16 subjects, 12 selected speech as the input medium for the final task and 4 selected keyboard input. Three of the four selecting keyboard input had actually experienced better or similar performance using keyboard input during the first four tasks. The fourth subject indicated on his questionnaire that he believed he could solve the problem more quickly using the keyboard; however, that subject had solved the two tasks using speech input 19% faster than the two tasks he solved using keyboard input.

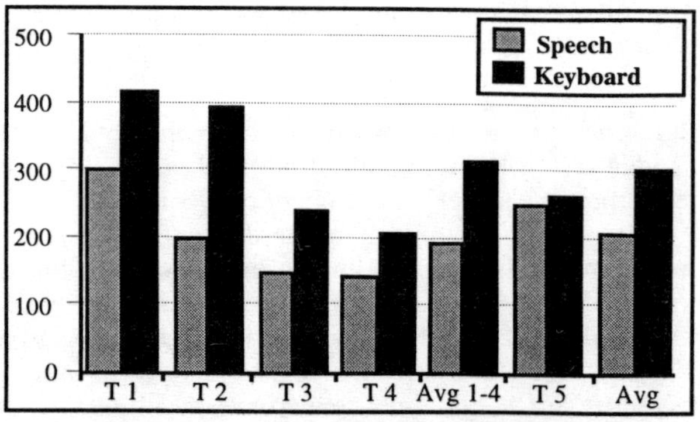

Figure 7: Time to Completion by Task

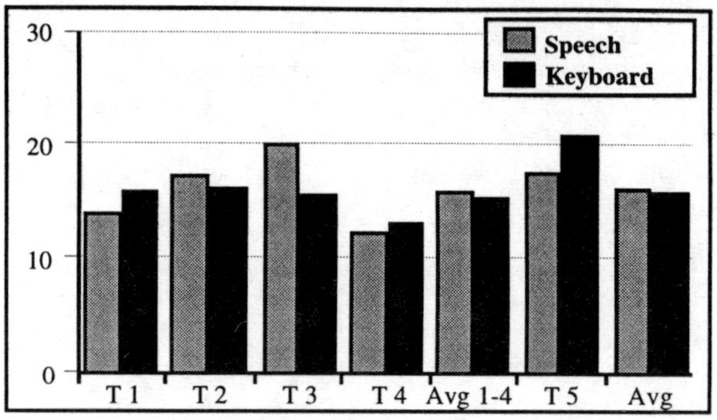

Figure 8 : Length of Solution by Task

Of the 80 tasks attempted, there were 7 in which the stated goals were not met. In each unsuccessful attempt, the subject was using speech input. There was no particular task that was troublesome and no particular subject that had difficulty. Seven different subjects had a task where the goals were not met, and each of the five tasks was left unaccomplished at least once.

A review of the transcripts for the unsuccessful attempts revealed that in three cases, the subject misinterpreted the system's actions, and ended the dialogue believing the goals were met. Each of the other four unsuccessful attempts resulted from a common sequence of events: after the system proposed an inefficient route, word recognition errors caused the system to misinterpret rejection of the proposed route as acceptance. The subsequent subdialogues intended to improve the route were interpreted to be extensions to the route, causing the route to "overshoot" the intended destination.

This suggests that, while our robustness techniques were effective on average, the errors do create a higher variance in the effectiveness of the interaction. These problems reveal a need for better handling of corrections, especially as resumptions of previous topics. More details on the evaluation can be found in (Sikorski & Allen, forthcoming).

8. Discussion

There are few systems that attempt to handle unconstrained natural dialogue. In most current speech systems, the interaction is driven by a template filling mechanism (e.g., the ATIS systems (ARPA, 1995), BeRP (Jurafsky et al, 1994), Pegasus (Seneff *et al*, 1995)). Some of these systems support system-initiated questions to elicit missing information in the template, but that is the extent of the mixed initiative interaction. Specifically, there is no need for goal management because the goal is fixed throughout the dialogue. In addition, there is little support for clarification and correction subdialogues. The Duke system (Smith and Hipp, 1994) uses a more general model based on a reasoning system, but allows only a limited vocabulary and grammar and requires extensive training to use.

Our approach here is clearly bottom-up. We have attempted to build a fully functional system in the simplest domain possible and focused on the problems that most significantly degraded overall performance. This leaves us open to the criticism that we are not using the most sophisticated models available. For instance, consider our generation strategy. Template-based generation is clearly inadequate for many generation tasks. In fact, when starting the project we thought generation would be a major problem. However, the problems we expected have not arisen. While we could clearly improve the output of the system even in this small domain, the current generator does not appear to drag the system's performance down. We approached other problems similarly. We tried the simplest approaches first and then only generalized those algorithms whose inadequacies clearly degrade the performance of the system.

Likewise, we view the evaluation as only a very preliminary first step. While our evaluation appears similar to HCI experiments on whether speech or keyboard is a more effective interface in general (cf. Oviatt and Cohen, 1991), this comparison was not our goal. Rather, we used the modality switch as a way of manipulating the error rate and the degree of spontaneity. While keyboard performance is not perfect because of typos (we had a 5% word error rate on keyboard), it is considerably less error prone than speech. All we conclude from this experiment is that our robust processing techniques are sufficiently good that speech is a viable interface in such tasks even with high word error rates. In fact, it appears to be more efficient in this application than keyboard. In contrast to the results of Rudnicky (1993), who found users preferred speech even when less efficient, our subjects generally preferred the most efficient modality for them (which in a majority of cases was speech).

Despite the limitations of the current evaluation, we are encouraged by this first step. It seems obvious to us that progress in dialogue systems is intimately tied to finding suitable evaluation measures. And task-based evaluation seems one of the most promising candidates. It measures the impact of proposed techniques directly rather than indirectly with an abstract accuracy figure.

Another area where we are open to criticism is that we used algorithms specific to the domain in order to produce effective intention recognition, disambiguation, and domain planning. Thus, the success of the system may be a result of the domain and say little about the plan-based approach to dialogue. To be honest, with the current system, it is hard to defend ourselves against this. This is is a first step in what we see as a long ongoing process. To look at it another way: if we couldn't build a successful system by employing whatever means available, then there is little hope for finding more effective general solutions.

We are addressing this problem in our current research: we are developing a domain-independent plan reasoning "shell" that manages the plan recognition, evaluation and construction around which the dialogue system is structured. This shell provides the abstract model of problem solving upon which the dialogue manager is built. It is then instantiated by domain specific reasoning algorithms to perform the actual searches, constraint checking and intention recognition for a specific application. The structure of the model remains constant across domains, but the actual details of constructing plans remain domain specific.

Our next iteration of this process, TRAINS-96, involves adding complexity to the dialogues by increasing the complexity of the task. Specifically, we are adding distances and travel times between cities, several new modes of transportation (trucks and planes) with associated costs, and simple cargoes to be transported and possibly transferred between different vehicles. The expanded domain will require a much more sophisticated ability to answer questions, to display complex information concisely, and will stress our abilities to track plans and identify focus shifts.

While there are clearly many places in which our current system requires further work, it does set a new standard for spoken dialogue systems. More importantly, it allows us to address new research issues in a much more systematic way, supported by empirical evaluation.

Acknowledgements

This work was supported in part by ONR/ARPA grants N0004-92-J-1512 and N00014-95-1-1088, and NSF grant IRI-9503312. Many thanks to Alex Rudnicky, Ronald Rosenfeld and Sunil Issar at CMU for providing the Sphinx-II system and related tools. This work would not have been possible without the efforts of George Ferguson on the TRAINS system infrastructure and model of problem solving.

References

J. F. Allen. 1995. *Natural Language Understanding, 2nd Edition*, Benjamin-Cummings, Redwood City, CA.

J. F. Allen, G. Ferguson, B. Miller, and E. Ringger. 1995. Spoken dialogue and interactive planning. In *Proc.* ARPA SLST Workshop, Morgan Kaufmann

J. F. Allen and C. R. Perrault. 1980. Analyzing intention in utterances, *Artificial Intelligence* 15(3):143-178

ARPA, 1995. Proceedings of the Spoken Language Systems Technology Workshop, Jan. 1995. Distributed by Morgan Kaufmann.

P. F. Brown, J. Cocke, S. A. Della Pietra, V. J. Della Pietra, F. Jelinek, J. D. Lafferty, R. L. Mercer and P. S. Roossin. 1990. A Statistical Approach to Machine Translation. *Computational Linguistics* 16(2):79--85.

S. Carberry. 1990. *Plan Recognition in Natural Language Dialogue*, MIT Press, Cambridge, MA.

P. R. Cohen and C. R. Perrault. 1979. Elements of a plan-based theory of speech acts, *Cognitive Science* 3

G. M. Ferguson, J. F. Allen and B. W. Miller, 1996. TRAINS-95: Towards a Mixed-Initiative Planning Assistant, to appear in *Proc. Third Conference on Artificial Intelligent Planning Systems (AIPS-96)*.

G. E. Forney, Jr. 1973. The Viterbi Algorithm. Proc. of IEEE 61:266--278.

B. Grosz and C. Sidner. 1986. Attention, intention and the structure of discourse. *Computational Linguistics* 12(3).

E. Hinkelman and J. F. Allen. 1989.Two Constraints on Speech Act Ambiguity, Proc. ACL.

X. D. Huang, F. Alleva, H. W. Hon, M. Y. Hwang, K. F. Lee, and R. Rosenfeld. 1993. The Sphinx-II Speech Recognition System. *Computer, Speech and Language*

D. Jurafsky, C. Wooters, G. Tajchman, J. Segal, A. Stolcke, E. Fosler and N. Morgan. 1994. The Berkeley Restaurant Project, *Proc. ICSLP-94*.

S. M. Katz. 1987. Estimation of Probabilities from Sparse Data for the Language Model Component of a Speech Recognizer. In *IEEE Transactions on Acoustics, Speech, and Signal Processing*. IEEE. pp. 400-401.

D. Litman and J. F. Allen. 1987. A plan recognition model for subdialogues in conversation. *Cognitive Science* 11(2): 163-200

B, Lowerre and R. Reddy. 1986. The Harpy Speech Understanding System. Reprinted in Waibel and Lee, 1990: 576-586.

S. L. Oviatt and P.R. Cohen. 1991. The contributing influence of speech and interaction on human discourse patterns. In J.W. Sullivan and S.W. Tyler (eds), *Intelligent User Interfaces*. Addison-Wesley, NY, NY.

E. K. Ringger and J. F. Allen. 1996. A Fertility Channel Model for Post-Correction of Continuous Speech Recognition. To appear in *Proc. 1996 ICSLP*, IEEE, October, 1996.

A. Rudnicky. 1993. Mode Preference in a Simple Data-Retrieval Task, *Proc. of ARPA Workshop on Human Language Technology*, Dist. by Morgan Kaufmann.

S. Seneff, V. Zue, J. Polifroni, C. Pao, L. Hetherington, D. Goddeau, and J. Glass. 1995. The Preliminary Development of a Displayless PEGASUS System. *Proc.* SLST Workshop, Jan. 1995. Morgan Kaufmann

R. Smith and R. D. Hipp. 1994. *Spoken Natural Language Dialog Systems: A Practical Approach*, Oxford University Press.

A. Waibel and K. F. Lee, editors. 1990. *Readings in Speech Recognition*. Morgan Kaufmann, CA.

Appendix A: Transcript of post-processor repairs in the dialogue.

HYP: OKAY LET'S SEE CONTAIN FROM DETROIT TO WASHINGTON
HYP': OKAY LET'S SEND CONTAIN FROM DETROIT TO WASHINGTON
REF: OKAY LET'S TAKE THE TRAIN FROM DETROIT TO WASHINGTON

HYP: LET'S GO VIA TOLEDO AND PITTSBURGH
HYP': LET'S GO VIA TOLEDO AND PITTSBURGH
REF: LET'S GO VIA TOLEDO AND PITTSBURGH

HYP: NOW LET'S TAKE THE TRAIN FROM DETROIT TO WASHINGTON D S_X ANY
HYP': NOW LET'S TAKE THE TRAIN FROM DETROIT TO WASHINGTON DO S_X ALBANY)
REF: NO LET'S TAKE THE TRAIN FROM DETROIT TO WASHINGTON VIA CINCINNATI

HYP: OKAY IT THAT'S OKAY NOW
HYP': OKAY IT THAT'S OKAY NOW
REF: OKAY THAT- THAT'S OKAY NOW

HYP: UP OKAY NOW LET'S TAKE THE TRAIN FROM MONTREAL TO LEXINGTON
HYP': UP OKAY NOW LET'S TAKE THE TRAIN FROM MONTREAL TO LEXINGTON
REF: OKAY NOW LET'S TAKE THE TRAIN FROM MONTREAL TO LEXINGTON

HYP: LET'S GO P_M TO TRY
HYP': LET'S GO P_M TO DETROIT
REF: LET'S GO VIA DETROIT

HYP: YES NOW LET'S GO TO LEXINGTON
HYP': YES NOW LET'S GO TO LEXINGTON
REF: YES NOW LET'S GO TO LEXINGTON

HYP: OKAY NOW ADD STATE THE LAST TRAIN AND GO FROM ALBANY TO O_O'S
HYP': OKAY NOW I TAKE THE LAST TRAIN IN GO FROM ALBANY TO IS
REF: OKAY NOW LET'S TAKE THE LAST TRAIN AND GO FROM ALBANY TO MILWAUKEE

HYP: ME A JET ADD ALBANY NEEDS TO GO TO MILWAUKEE
HYP': ME THE JET AT ALBANY INSTEAD TO GO TO MILWAUKEE
REF: THE ENGINE AT ALBANY NEEDS TO GO TO MILWAUKEE

HYP: I'D GO VIA BUFFALO
HYP': UH GO VIA BUFFALO
REF: UH GO VIA BUFFALO

HYP: GO B_X SYRACUSE AT BUFFALO
HYP': GO VIA SYRACUSE VIA BUFFALO
REF: GO VIA SYRACUSE AND BUFFALO

HYP: THAT'S COULD I CAN
HYP': THAT'S GREAT UH CAN
REF: THAT'S GOOD I'M DONE

HYP: I_NEED DONE
HYP': I'M DONE
REF: I'M DONE

Combining Trigram-based and Feature-based Methods for Context-Sensitive Spelling Correction

Andrew R. Golding and **Yves Schabes**
Mitsubishi Electric Research Laboratories
201 Broadway
Cambridge, MA 02139
{golding, schabes}@merl.com

Abstract

This paper addresses the problem of correcting spelling errors that result in valid, though unintended words (such as *peace* and *piece*, or *quiet* and *quite*) and also the problem of correcting particular word usage errors (such as *amount* and *number*, or *among* and *between*). Such corrections require contextual information and are not handled by conventional spelling programs such as Unix *spell*. First, we introduce a method called *Trigrams* that uses part-of-speech trigrams to encode the context. This method uses a small number of parameters compared to previous methods based on word trigrams. However, it is effectively unable to distinguish among words that have the same part of speech. For this case, an alternative feature-based method called *Bayes* performs better; but Bayes is less effective than Trigrams when the distinction among words depends on syntactic constraints. A hybrid method called *Tribayes* is then introduced that combines the best of the previous two methods. The improvement in performance of Tribayes over its components is verified experimentally. Tribayes is also compared with the grammar checker in Microsoft Word, and is found to have substantially higher performance.

1 Introduction

Spelling correction has become a very common technology and is often not perceived as a problem where progress can be made. However, conventional spelling checkers, such as Unix *spell*, are concerned only with spelling errors that result in words that cannot be found in a word list of a given language. One analysis has shown that up to 15% of spelling errors that result from elementary typographical errors (character insertion, deletion, or transposition) yield another valid word in the language (Peterson, 1986). These errors remain undetected by traditional spelling checkers. In addition to typographical errors, words that can be easily confused with each other (for instance, the homophones *peace* and *piece*) also remain undetected. Recent studies of actual observed spelling errors have estimated that overall, errors resulting in valid words account for anywhere from 25% to over 50% of the errors, depending on the application (Kukich, 1992).

We will use the term *context-sensitive spelling correction* to refer to the task of fixing spelling errors that result in valid words, such as:

(1) * Can I have a *peace* of cake?

where *peace* was typed when *piece* was intended. The task will be cast as one of lexical disambiguation: we are given a predefined collection of *confusion sets*, such as {*peace*, *piece*}, {*than*, *then*}, etc., which circumscribe the space of spelling errors to look for. A confusion set means that each word in the set could mistakenly be typed when another word in the set was intended. The task is to predict, given an occurrence of a word in one of the confusion sets, which word in the set was actually intended.

Previous work on context-sensitive spelling correction and related lexical disambiguation tasks has its limitations. Word-trigram methods (Mays, Damerau, and Mercer, 1991) require an extremely large body of text to train the word-trigram model; even with extensive training sets, the problem of sparse data is often acute. In addition, huge word-trigram tables need to be available at run time. Moreover, word trigrams are ineffective at capturing long-distance properties such as discourse topic and tense.

Feature-based approaches, such as Bayesian classifiers (Gale, Church, and Yarowsky, 1993), decision lists (Yarowsky, 1994), and Bayesian hybrids (Golding, 1995), have had varying degrees of success for the problem of context-sensitive spelling correction. However, we report experiments that show that these methods are of limited effectiveness for cases such as {*their*, *there*, *they're*} and {*than*, *then*}, where the predominant distinction to be made among the words is syntactic.

Confusion set	Train	Test	Most freq.	Base
their, there, they're	3265	850	their	56.8
than, then	2096	514	than	63.4
its, it's	1364	366	its	91.3
your, you're	750	187	your	89.3
begin, being	559	146	being	93.2
passed, past	307	74	past	68.9
quiet, quite	264	66	quite	83.3
weather, whether	239	61	whether	86.9
accept, except	173	50	except	70.0
lead, led	173	49	led	46.9
cite, sight, site	115	34	sight	64.7
principal, principle	147	34	principle	58.8
raise, rise	98	39	rise	64.1
affect, effect	178	49	effect	91.8
peace, piece	203	50	peace	44.0
country, county	268	62	country	91.9
amount, number	460	123	number	71.5
among, between	764	186	between	71.5

Table 1: Performance of the baseline method for 18 confusion sets. "Train" and "Test" give the number of occurrences of any word in the confusion set in the training and test corpora. "Most freq." is the word in the confusion set that occurred most often in the training corpus. "Base" is the percentage of correct predictions of the baseline system on the test corpus.

In this paper, we first introduce a method called *Trigrams* that uses part-of-speech trigrams to encode the context. This method greatly reduces the number of parameters compared to known methods, which are based on *word* trigrams. This method also has the advantage that training can be done once and for all, and quite manageably, for all confusion sets; new confusion sets can be added later without any additional training. This feature makes Trigrams a very easily expandable system.

Empirical evaluation of the trigram method demonstrates that it performs well when the words to be discriminated have different parts of speech, but poorly when they have the same part of speech. In the latter case, it is reduced to simply guessing whichever word in the confusion set is the most common representative of its part-of-speech class.

We consider an alternative method, *Bayes*, a Bayesian hybrid method (Golding, 1995), for the case where the words have the same part of speech. We confirm experimentally that Bayes and Trigrams have complementary performance, Trigrams being better when the words in the confusion set have different parts of speech, and Bayes being better when they have the same part of speech. We introduce a hybrid method, *Tribayes*, that exploits this complementarity by invoking each method when it is strongest. Tribayes achieves the best accuracy of the methods under consideration in all situations.

To evaluate the performance of Tribayes with respect to an external standard, we compare it to the grammar checker in Microsoft Word. Tribayes is found to have substantially higher performance.

This paper is organized as follows: first we present the methodology used in the experiments. We then discuss the methods mentioned above, interleaved with experimental results. The comparison with Microsoft Word is then presented. The final section concludes.

2 Methodology

Each method will be described in terms of its operation on a single confusion set $C = \{w_1, \ldots, w_n\}$; that is, we will say how the method disambiguates occurrences of words w_1 through w_n. The methods handle multiple confusion sets by applying the same technique to each confusion set independently.

Each method involves a training phase and a test phase. We trained each method on 80% (randomly selected) of the Brown corpus (Kučera and Francis, 1967) and tested it on the remaining 20%. All methods were run on a collection of 18 confusion sets, which were largely taken from the list of "Words Commonly Confused" in the back of Random House (Flexner, 1983). The confusion sets were selected on the basis of being frequently-occurring in Brown, and representing a variety of types of errors, including homophone confusions (e.g., {*peace*, *piece*}) and grammatical mistakes (e.g., {*among*, *between*}). A few confusion sets not in Random House were added, representing typographical errors (e.g., {*begin*, *being*}). The confusion sets appear in Table 1.

3 Baseline

As an indicator of the difficulty of the task, we compared each of the methods to the method which ignores the context in which the word occurred, and just guesses based on the priors.

Table 1 shows the performance of the baseline method for the 18 confusion sets.

4 Trigrams

Mays, Damerau, and Mercer (1991) proposed a word-trigram method for context-sensitive spelling correction based on the noisy channel model. Since this method is based on word trigrams, it requires an enormous training corpus to fit all of these parameters accurately; in addition, at run time it requires extensive system resources to store and manipulate the resulting huge word-trigram table.

In contrast, the method proposed here uses part-of-speech trigrams. Given a target occurrence of a word to correct, it substitutes in turn each word in the confusion set into the sentence. For each substitution, it calculates the probability of the resulting sentence. It selects as its answer the word that gives the highest probability.

More precisely, assume that the word w_k occurs in a sentence $W = w_1 \ldots w_k \ldots w_n$, and that w'_k is a word we are considering substituting for it, yielding sentence W'. Word w'_k is then preferred over w_k iff $P(W') > P(W)$, where $P(W)$ and $P(W')$ are the probabilities of sentences W and W' respectively.[1] We calculate $P(W)$ using the tag sequence of W as an intermediate quantity, and summing, over all possible tag sequences, the probability of the sentence with that tagging; that is:

$$P(W) = \sum_T P(W, T)$$

where T is a tag sequence for sentence W.

The above probabilities are estimated as is traditionally done in trigram-based part-of-speech tagging (Church, 1988; DeRose, 1988):

$$\begin{aligned} P(W,T) &= P(W|T)P(T) & (1) \\ &= \prod_i P(w_i|t_i) \prod_i P(t_i|t_{i-2}t_{i-1}) & (2) \end{aligned}$$

where $T = t_1 \ldots t_n$, and $P(t_i|t_{i-2}t_{i-1})$ is the probability of seeing a part-of-speech tag t_i given the two preceding part-of-speech tags t_{i-2} and t_{i-1}. Equations 1 and 2 will also be used to tag sentences W and W' with their most likely part-of-speech sequences. This will allow us to determine the tag that would be assigned to each word in the confusion set when substituted into the target sentence.

Table 2 gives the results of the trigram method (as well as the Bayesian method of the next section) for the 18 confusion sets.[2] The results are broken down into two cases: "Different tags" and "Same tags". A target occurrence is put in the latter iff all words in the confusion set would have the same tag when substituted into the target sentence. In the "Different tags" condition, Trigrams generally does well, outscoring Bayes for all but 3 confusion sets — and in each of these cases, making no more than 3 errors more than Bayes.

In the "Same tags" condition, however, Trigrams performs only as well as Baseline. This follows from Equations 1 and 2: when comparing $P(W)$ and $P(W')$, the dominant term corresponds to the most likely tagging; and in this term, if the target word w_k and its substitute w'_k have the same tag t, then the comparison amounts to comparing $P(w_k|t)$ and $P(w'_k|t)$. In other words, the decision reduces to which of the two words, w_k and w'_k, is the more common representative of part-of-speech class t.[3]

5 Bayes

The previous section showed that the part-of-speech trigram method works well when the words in the confusion set have different parts of speech, but essentially cannot distinguish among the words if they have the same part of speech. In this case, a more effective approach is to learn *features* that characterize the different contexts in which each word tends to occur. A number of feature-based methods have been proposed, including Bayesian classifiers (Gale, Church, and Yarowsky, 1993), decision lists (Yarowsky, 1994), Bayesian hybrids (Golding, 1995), and, more recently, a method based on the Winnow multiplicative weight-updating algorithm (Golding and Roth, 1996). We adopt the Bayesian hybrid method, which we will call *Bayes*, having experimented with each of the methods and found Bayes to be among the best-performing for the task at hand. This method has been described elsewhere (Golding, 1995) and so will only be briefly reviewed here; however, the version used here uses an improved smoothing technique, which is mentioned briefly below.

---

[1]To enable fair comparisons between sequences of different length (as when considering *maybe* and *may be*), we actually compare the per-word geometric mean of the sentence probabilities. Otherwise, the shorter sequence will usually be preferred, as shorter sequences tend to have higher probabilities than longer ones.

[2]In the experiments reported here, the trigram method was run using the tag inventory derived from the Brown corpus, except that a handful of common function words were tagged as themselves, namely: *except*, *than*, *then*, *to*, *too*, and *whether*.

[3]In a few cases, however, Trigrams does not get exactly the same score as Baseline. This can happen when the words in the confusion set have more than one tag in common; e.g., for {*affect*, *effect*}, the words can both be nouns or verbs. Trigrams may then choose differently when the words are tagged as nouns versus verbs, whereas Baseline makes the same choice in all cases.

Confusion set	Different tags				Same tags			
	Break-down	System scores			Break-down	System scores		
		Base	T	B		Base	T	B
their, there, they're	100	56.8	97.6	94.4	0	—	—	—
than, then	100	63.4	94.9	93.2	0	—	—	—
its, it's	100	91.3	98.1	95.9	0	—	—	—
your, you're	100	89.3	98.9	89.8	0	—	—	—
begin, being	100	93.2	97.3	91.8	0	—	—	—
passed, past	100	68.9	95.9	89.2	0	—	—	—
quiet, quite	100	83.3	95.5	89.4	0	—	—	—
weather, whether	100	86.9	93.4	96.7	0	—	—	—
accept, except	100	70.0	82.0	88.0	0	—	—	—
lead, led	100	46.9	83.7	79.6	0	—	—	—
cite, sight, site	100	64.7	70.6	73.5	0	—	—	—
principal, principle	29	0.0	100.0	70.0	71	83.3	83.3	91.7
raise, rise	8	100.0	100.0	100.0	92	61.1	61.1	72.2
affect, effect	6	100.0	100.0	66.7	94	91.3	93.5	97.8
peace, piece	2	0.0	100.0	100.0	98	44.9	42.9	89.8
country, county	0	—	—	—	100	91.9	91.9	85.5
amount, number	0	—	—	—	100	71.5	73.2	82.9
among, between	0	—	—	—	100	71.5	71.5	75.3

Table 2: Performance of the component methods, Baseline (Base), Trigrams (T), and Bayes (B). System scores are given as percentages of correct predictions. The results are broken down by whether or not all words in the confusion set would have the same tagging when substituted into the target sentence. The "Breakdown" columns show the percentage of examples that fall under each condition.

Bayes uses two types of features: context words and collocations. Context-word features test for the presence of a particular word within $\pm k$ words of the target word; collocations test for a pattern of up to ℓ contiguous words and/or part-of-speech tags around the target word. Examples for the confusion set {*dairy*, *diary*} include:

(2) *milk* within ± 10 words
(3) *in* POSS-DET __

where (2) is a context-word feature that tends to imply *dairy*, while (3) is a collocation implying *diary*. Feature (3) includes the tag POSS-DET for possessive determiners (*his*, *her*, etc.), and matches, for example, the sequence *in his*[4] in:

(4) He made an entry in his *diary*.

Bayes learns these features from a training corpus of correct text. Each time a word in the confusion set occurs in the corpus, Bayes proposes every feature that matches the context — one context-word feature for every distinct word within $\pm k$ words of the target word, and one collocation for every way of expressing a pattern of up to ℓ contiguous elements. After working through the whole training corpus, Bayes collects and returns the set of features proposed. Pruning criteria may be applied at this point to eliminate features that are based on insufficient data, or that are ineffective at discriminating among the words in the confusion set.

At run time, Bayes uses the features learned during training to correct the spelling of target words. Let $\mathcal{F}$ be the set of features that match a particular target occurrence. Suppose for a moment that we were applying a *naive* Bayesian approach. We would then calculate the probability that each word w_i in the confusion set is the correct identity of the target word, given that we have observed features $\mathcal{F}$, using Bayes' rule with the independence assumption:

$$P(w_i|\mathcal{F}) = \left(\prod_{f \in \mathcal{F}} P(f|w_i) \right) \frac{P(w_i)}{P(\mathcal{F})}$$

where each probability on the right-hand side is calculated by a maximum-likelihood estimate (MLE) over the training set. We would then pick as our answer the w_i with the highest $P(w_i|\mathcal{F})$. The method presented here differs from the naive approach in two respects: first, it does not assume independence among features, but rather has heuristics for detecting strong dependencies, and resolving them by deleting features until it is left with a reduced set $\mathcal{F}'$

[4] A tag is taken to match a word in the sentence iff the tag is a member of the word's set of possible part-of-speech tags. Tag sets are used, rather than actual tags, because it is in general impossible to tag the sentence uniquely at spelling-correction time, as the identity of the target word has not yet been established.

of (relatively) independent features, which are then used in place of $\mathcal{F}$ in the formula above. Second, to estimate the $P(f|w_i)$ terms, rather than using a simple MLE, it performs *smoothing* by interpolating between the MLE of $P(f|w_i)$ and the MLE of the unigram probability, $P(f)$. These enhancements greatly improve the performance of Bayes over the naive Bayesian approach.

The results of Bayes are shown in Table 2.[5] Generally speaking, Bayes does worse than Trigrams when the words in the confusion set have different parts of speech. The reason is that, in such cases, the predominant distinction to be made among the words is *syntactic*; and the trigram method, which brings to bear part-of-speech knowledge for the whole sentence, is better equipped to make this distinction than Bayes, which only tests up to two syntactic elements in its collocations. Moreover, Bayes' use of context-word features is arguably misguided here, as context words pick up differences in topic and tense, which are irrelevant here, and in fact tend to degrade performance by detecting spurious differences. In a few cases, such as {*begin*, *being*}, this effect is enough to drive Bayes slightly below Baseline.[6]

For the condition where the words have the same part of speech, Table 2 shows that Bayes almost always does better than Trigrams. This is because, as discussed above, Trigrams is essentially acting like Baseline in this condition. Bayes, on the other hand, learns features that allow it to discriminate among the particular words at issue, regardless of their part of speech. The one exception is {*country*, *county*}, for which Bayes scores somewhat below Baseline. This is another case in which context words actually hurt Bayes, as running it without context words again improved its performance to the Baseline level.

6 Tribayes

The previous sections demonstrated the complementarity between Trigrams and Bayes: Trigrams works best when the words in the confusion set do not all have the same part of speech, while Bayes works best when they do. This complementarity leads directly to a hybrid method, *Tribayes*, that gets the best of each. It applies Trigrams first; in the process, it ascertains whether all the words in the confusion set would have the same tag when substituted into the target sentence. If they do not, it accepts the answer provided by Trigrams; if they do, it applies Bayes.

Two points about the application of Bayes in the hybrid method: first, Bayes is now being asked to distinguish among words only when they have the same part of speech. It should be trained accordingly — that is, only on examples where the words have the same part of speech. The Bayes component of the hybrid will therefore be trained on a subset of the examples that would be used for training the stand-alone version of Bayes.

The second point about Bayes is that, like Trigrams, it sometimes makes uninformed decisions — decisions based only on the priors. For Bayes, this happens when none of its features matches the target occurrence. Since, for now, we do not have a good "third-string" algorithm to call when both Trigrams and Bayes fall by the wayside, we content ourselves with the guess made by Bayes in such situations.

Table 3 shows the performance of Tribayes compared to its components. In the "Different tags" condition, Tribayes invokes Trigrams, and thus scores identically. In the "Same tags" condition, Tribayes invokes Bayes. It does not necessarily score the same, however, because, as mentioned above, it is trained on a subset of the examples that stand-alone Bayes is trained on. This can lead to higher or lower performance — higher because the training examples are more homogeneous (representing only cases where the words have the same part of speech); lower because there may not be enough training examples to learn from. Both effects show up in Table 3.

Table 4 summarizes the overall performance of all methods discussed. It can be seen that Trigrams and Bayes each have their strong points. Tribayes, however, achieves the maximum of their scores, by and large, the exceptions being due to cases where one method or the other had an unexpectedly low score (discussed in Sections 4 and 5). The confusion set {*raise*, *rise*} demonstrates (albeit modestly) the ability of the hybrid to outscore *both* of its components, by putting together the performance of the better component for both conditions.

7 Comparison with Microsoft Word

The previous section evaluated the performance of Tribayes with respect to its components, and showed that it got the best of both. In this section, we calibrate this overall performance by comparing Tribayes with Microsoft Word (version 7.0), a widely used word-processing system whose grammar checker represents the state of the art in commercial context-sensitive spelling correction.

Unfortunately we cannot evaluate Word using "prediction accuracy" (as we did above), as we do not always have access to the system's predictions — sometimes it *suppresses* its predictions in an effort to filter out the bad ones. Instead, in this section

[5] For the experiments reported here, Bayes was configured as follows: k (the half-width of the window of context words) was set to 10; ℓ (the maximum length of a collocation) was set to 2; feature strength was measured using the reliability metric; pruning of collocations at training time was enabled; and pruning of context words was minimal — context words were pruned only if they had fewer than 2 occurrences or non-occurrences.

[6] We confirmed this by running Bayes without context words (i.e., with collocations only). Its performance was then always at or above Baseline.

Confusion set	Different tags			Same tags		
	Break-down	System scores		Break-down	System scores	
		T	TB		B	TB
their, there, they're	100	97.6	97.6	0	—	—
than, then	100	94.9	94.9	0	—	—
its, it's	100	98.1	98.1	0	—	—
your, you're	100	98.9	98.9	0	—	—
begin, being	100	97.3	97.3	0	—	—
passed, past	100	95.9	95.9	0	—	—
quiet, quite	100	95.5	95.5	0	—	—
weather, whether	100	93.4	93.4	0	—	—
accept, except	100	82.0	82.0	0	—	—
lead, led	100	83.7	83.7	0	—	—
cite, sight, site	100	70.6	70.6	0	—	—
principal, principle	29	100.0	100.0	71	91.7	83.3
raise, rise	8	100.0	100.0	92	72.2	75.0
affect, effect	6	100.0	100.0	94	97.8	95.7
peace, piece	2	100.0	100.0	98	89.8	89.8
country, county	0	—	—	100	85.5	85.5
amount, number	0	—	—	100	82.9	82.9
among, between	0	—	—	100	75.3	75.3

Table 3: Performance of the hybrid method, Tribayes (TB), as compared with Trigrams (T) and Bayes (B). System scores are given as percentages of correct predictions. The results are broken down by whether or not all words in the confusion set would have the same tagging when substituted into the target sentence. The "Breakdown" columns give the percentage of examples under each condition.

Confusion set	System scores			
	Base	T	B	TB
their, there, they're	56.8	97.6	94.4	97.6
than, then	63.4	94.9	93.2	94.9
its, it's	91.3	98.1	95.9	98.1
your, you're	89.3	98.9	89.8	98.9
begin, being	93.2	97.3	91.8	97.3
passed, past	68.9	95.9	89.2	95.9
quiet, quite	83.3	95.5	89.4	95.5
weather, whether	86.9	93.4	96.7	93.4
accept, except	70.0	82.0	88.0	82.0
lead, led	46.9	83.7	79.6	83.7
cite, sight, site	64.7	70.6	73.5	70.6
principal, principle	58.8	88.2	85.3	88.2
raise, rise	64.1	64.1	74.4	76.9
affect, effect	91.8	93.9	95.9	95.9
peace, piece	44.0	44.0	90.0	90.0
country, county	91.9	91.9	85.5	85.5
amount, number	71.5	73.2	82.9	82.9
among, between	71.5	71.5	75.3	75.3

Table 4: Overall performance of all methods: Baseline (Base), Trigrams (T), Bayes (B), and Tribayes (TB). System scores are given as percentages of correct predictions.

we will use two parameters to evaluate system performance: system accuracy when tested on *correct* usages of words, and system accuracy on *incorrect* usages. Together, these two parameters give a complete picture of system performance: the score on correct usages measures the system's rate of false negative errors (changing a right word to a wrong one), while the score on incorrect usages measures false positives (failing to change a wrong word to a right one). We will not attempt to combine these two parameters into a single measure of system "goodness", as the appropriate combination varies for different users, depending on the user's typing accuracy and tolerance of false negatives and positives.

The test sets for the correct condition are the same ones used earlier, based on 20% of the Brown corpus. The test sets for the incorrect condition were generated by corrupting the correct test sets; in particular, each correct occurrence of a word in the confusion set was replaced, in turn, with each other word in the confusion set, yielding $n-1$ incorrect occurrences for each correct occurrence (where n is the size of the confusion set). We will also refer to the incorrect condition as the *corrupted* condition.

To run Microsoft Word on a particular test set, we started by disabling error checking for all error types except those needed for the confusion set at issue. This was done to avoid confounding effects. For {*their*, *there*, *they're*}, for instance, we enabled "word usage" errors (which include substitutions of *their* for *there*, etc.), but we disabled "contractions" (which include replacing *they're* with *they are*). We then invoked the grammar checker, accepting every suggestion offered. Sometimes errors were pointed out but no correction given; in such cases, we skipped over the error. Sometimes the suggestions led to an infinite loop, as with the sentence:

(5) Be sure it's out when you leave.

where the system alternately suggested replacing *it's* with *its* and vice versa. In such cases, we accepted the first suggestion, and then moved on.

Unlike Word, Tribayes, as presented above, is purely a predictive system, and never suppresses its suggestions. This is somewhat of a handicap in the comparison, as Word can achieve higher scores in the correct condition by suppressing its weaker suggestions (albeit at the cost of lowering its scores in the corrupted condition). To put Tribayes on an equal footing, we added a postprocessing step in which it uses *thresholds* to decide whether to suppress its suggestions. A suggestion is allowed to go through iff the ratio of the probability of the word being suggested to the probability of the word that appeared originally in the sentence is above a threshold. The probability associated with each word is the per-word sentence probability in the case of Trigrams, or the conditional probability $P(w_i|\mathcal{F})$ in the case of Bayes. The thresholds are set in a preprocessing phase based on the training set (80% of Brown, in our case). A single tunable parameter controls how steeply the thresholds are set; for the study here, this parameter was set to the middle of its useful range, providing a fairly neutral balance between reducing false negatives and increasing false positives.

The results of Word and Tribayes for the 18 confusion sets appear in Table 5. Six of the confusion sets (marked with asterisks in the table) are not handled by Word; Word's scores in these cases are 100% for the correct condition and 0% for the corrupted condition, which are the scores one gets by never making a suggestion. The opposite behavior — *always* suggesting a different word — would result in scores of 0% and 100% (for a confusion set of size 2). Although this behavior is never observed in its extreme form, it is a good approximation of Word's behavior in a few cases, such as {*principal*, *principle*}, where it scores 12% and 94%. In general, Word achieves a high score in either the correct or the corrupted condition, but not both at once.

Tribayes compares quite favorably with Word in this experiment. In both the correct and corrupted conditions, Tribayes' scores are mostly higher (often by a wide margin) or the same as Word's; in the cases where they are lower in one condition, they are almost always considerably higher in the other. The one exception is {*raise*, *rise*}, where Tribayes and Word score about the same in both conditions.

8 Conclusion

Spelling errors that result in valid, though unintended words, have been found to be very common in the production of text. Such errors were thought to be too difficult to handle and remain undetected in conventional spelling checkers. This paper introduced Trigrams, a part-of-speech trigram-based method, that improved on previous trigram methods, which were word-based, by greatly reducing the number of parameters. The method was supplemented by Bayes, a method that uses context features to discriminate among the words in the confusion set. Trigrams and Bayes were shown to have complementary strengths. A hybrid method, Tribayes, was then introduced to exploit this complementarity by applying Trigrams when the words in the confusion set do not have the same part of speech, and Bayes when they do. Tribayes thereby gets the best of both methods, as was confirmed experimentally. Tribayes was also compared with the grammar checker in Microsoft Word, and was found to have substantially higher performance.

Tribayes is being used as part of a grammar-checking system we are currently developing. We are presently working on elaborating the system's threshold model; scaling up the number of confusion sets that can be handled efficiently; and acquiring confusion sets (or confusion matrices) automatically.

Confusion set	Tribayes		Microsoft Word	
	Correct	Corrupted	Correct	Corrupted
their, there, they're	99.4	87.6	98.8	59.8
than, then	97.9	85.8	100.0	22.2
its, it's	99.5	92.1	96.2	73.0
your, you're	98.9	98.4	98.9	79.1
begin, being	100.0	84.2	100.0 *	0.0 *
passed, past	100.0	92.4	37.8	86.5
quiet, quite	100.0	72.7	100.0 *	0.0 *
weather, whether	100.0	65.6	100.0 *	0.0 *
accept, except	90.0	70.0	74.0	36.0
lead, led	87.8	81.6	100.0 *	0.0 *
cite, sight, site	100.0	35.3	17.6	66.2
principal, principle	94.1	73.5	11.8	94.1
raise, rise	92.3	48.7	92.3	51.3
affect, effect	98.0	93.9	100.0	77.6
peace, piece	96.0	74.0	36.0	88.0
country, county	90.3	80.6	100.0 *	0.0 *
amount, number	91.9	68.3	100.0 *	0.0 *
among, between	88.7	54.8	97.8	0.0

Table 5: Comparison of Tribayes with Microsoft Word. System scores are given for two test sets, one containing correct usages, and the other containing incorrect (corrupted) usages. Scores are given as percentages of correct answers. Asterisks mark confusion sets that are not handled by Microsoft Word.

References

Church, Kenneth Ward. 1988. A stochastic parts program and noun phrase parser for unrestricted text. In *Second Conference on Applied Natural Language Processing*, pages 136–143, Austin, TX.

DeRose, S.J. 1988. Grammatical category disambiguation by statistical optimization. *Computational Linguistics*, 14:31–39.

Flexner, S. B., editor. 1983. *Random House Unabridged Dictionary*. Random House, New York. Second edition.

Gale, William A., Kenneth W. Church, and David Yarowsky. 1993. A method for disambiguating word senses in a large corpus. *Computers and the Humanities*, 26:415–439.

Golding, Andrew R. and Dan Roth. 1996. Applying Winnow to context-sensitive spelling correction. In Lorenza Saitta, editor, *Machine Learning: Proceedings of the 13th International Conference*, Bari, Italy. To appear.

Golding, Andrew R. 1995. A Bayesian hybrid method for context-sensitive spelling correction. In *Proceedings of the Third Workshop on Very Large Corpora*, pages 39–53, Boston, MA.

Kukich, Karen. 1992. Techniques for automatically correcting words in text. *ACM Computing Surveys*, 24(4):377–439, December.

Kučera, H. and W. N. Francis. 1967. *Computational Analysis of Present-Day American English*. Brown University Press, Providence, RI.

Mays, Eric, Fred J. Damerau, and Robert L. Mercer. 1991. Context based spelling correction. *Information Processing and Management*, 27(5):517–522.

Peterson, James L. 1986. A note on undetected typing errors. *Communications of the ACM*, 29(7):633–637, July.

Yarowsky, David. 1994. Decision lists for lexical ambiguity resolution: Application to accent restoration in Spanish and French. In *Proceedings of the 32nd Annual Meeting of the Association for Computational Linguistics*, pages 88–95, Las Cruces, NM.

Efficient Normal-Form Parsing for Combinatory Categorial Grammar*

Jason Eisner
Dept. of Computer and Information Science
University of Pennsylvania
200 S. 33rd St., Philadelphia, PA 19104-6389, USA
jeisner@linc.cis.upenn.edu

Abstract

Under categorial grammars that have powerful rules like composition, a simple n-word sentence can have exponentially many parses. Generating all parses is inefficient and obscures whatever true semantic ambiguities are in the input. This paper addresses the problem for a fairly general form of Combinatory Categorial Grammar, by means of an efficient, correct, and easy to implement normal-form parsing technique. The parser is proved to find *exactly one* parse in each semantic equivalence class of allowable parses; that is, spurious ambiguity (as carefully defined) is shown to be both safely and completely eliminated.

1 Introduction

Combinatory Categorial Grammar (Steedman, 1990), like other "flexible" categorial grammars, suffers from *spurious ambiguity* (Wittenburg, 1986). The non-standard constituents that are so crucial to CCG's analyses in (1), and in its account of intonational focus (Prevost & Steedman, 1994), remain available even in simpler sentences. This renders (2) syntactically ambiguous.

(1) a. **Coordination:** [[John likes]$_{S/NP}$, and [Mary pretends to like]$_{S/NP}$], the big galoot in the corner.
b. **Extraction:** Everybody at this party [whom [John likes]$_{S/NP}$] is a big galoot.

(2) a. John [likes Mary]$_{S\backslash NP}$.
b. [John likes]$_{S/NP}$ Mary.

The practical problem of "extra" parses in (2) becomes exponentially worse for longer strings, which can have up to a Catalan number of parses. An exhaustive parser serves up 252 CCG parses of (3), which must be sifted through, at considerable cost, in order to identify the two distinct meanings for further processing.[1]

(3) the galoot in the corner
NP/N N (N\N)/NP NP/N N
that I said Mary
(N\N)/(S/NP) S/(S\NP) (S\NP)/S S/(S\NP)
pretends to
$(S\backslash NP)/(S_{inf}\backslash NP)$ $(S_{inf}\backslash NP)/(S_{stem}\backslash NP)$
like
$(S_{stem}\backslash NP)/NP$

This paper presents a simple and flexible CCG parsing technique that prevents any such explosion of redundant CCG derivations. In particular, it is proved in §4.2 that the method constructs *exactly one* syntactic structure per semantic reading—e.g., just two parses for (3). All other parses are suppressed by simple normal-form constraints that are enforced throughout the parsing process. This approach works because CCG's spurious ambiguities arise (as is shown) in only a small set of circumstances. Although similar work has been attempted in the past, with varying degrees of success (Karttunen, 1986; Wittenburg, 1986; Pareschi & Steedman, 1987; Bouma, 1989; Hepple & Morrill, 1989; König, 1989; Vijay-Shanker & Weir, 1990; Hepple, 1990; Moortgat, 1990; Hendriks, 1993; Niv, 1994), this appears to be the first full normal-form result for a categorial formalism having more than context-free power.

2 Definitions and Related Work

CCG may be regarded as a generalization of context-free grammar (CFG)—one where a grammar has infinitely many nonterminals and phrase-structure rules. In addition to the familiar *atomic* nonterminal categories (typically S for sentences, N for

*This material is based upon work supported under a National Science Foundation Graduate Fellowship. I have been grateful for the advice of Aravind Joshi, Nobo Komagata, Seth Kulick, Michael Niv, Mark Steedman, and three anonymous reviewers.

[1] Namely, Mary pretends to like the galoot in 168 parses and the corner in 84. One might try a statistical approach to ambiguity resolution, discarding the low-probability parses, but it is unclear how to model and train any probabilities when no single parse can be taken as the standard of correctness.

nouns, NP for noun phrases, etc.), CCG allows infinitely many *slashed* categories. If x and y are categories, then x/y (respectively $x\backslash y$) is the category of an incomplete x that is missing a y at its right (respectively left). Thus verb phrases are analyzed as subjectless sentences S\NP, while "John likes" is an objectless sentence or S/NP. A complex category like ((S\NP)\(S\NP))/N may be written as S\NP\(S\NP)/N, under a convention that slashes are left-associative.

The results herein apply to the TAG-equivalent CCG formalization given in (Joshi et al., 1991).[2] In this variety of CCG, every (non-lexical) phrase-structure rule is an instance of one of the following binary-rule templates (where $n \geq 0$):

(4) Forward generalized composition >Bn:
$$x/y \quad y\,|_n z_n \cdots |_2 z_2\,|_1 z_1 \;\rightarrow\; x\,|_n z_n \cdots |_2 z_2\,|_1 z_1$$
Backward generalized composition <Bn:
$$y\,|_n z_n \cdots |_2 z_2\,|_1 z_1 \quad x\backslash y \;\rightarrow\; x\,|_n z_n \cdots |_2 z_2\,|_1 z_1$$

Instances with $n = 0$ are called *application* rules, and instances with $n \geq 1$ are called *composition* rules. In a given rule, $x, y, z_1 \ldots z_n$ would be instantiated as categories like NP, S/NP, or S\NP\(S\NP)/N. Each of $|_1$ through $|_n$ would be instantiated as either / or \.

A fixed CCG grammar need not include every phrase-structure rule matching these templates. Indeed, (Joshi et al., 1991) place certain restrictions on the rule set of a CCG grammar, including a requirement that the rule degree n is bounded over the set. The results of the present paper apply to such restricted grammars and also more generally, to any CCG-style grammar with a *decidable* rule set.

Even as restricted by (Joshi et al., 1991), CCGs have the "mildly context-sensitive" expressive power of Tree Adjoining Grammars (TAGs). Most work on spurious ambiguity has focused on categorial formalisms with substantially less power. (Hepple, 1990) and (Hendriks, 1993), the most rigorous pieces of work, each establish a normal form for the syntactic calculus of (Lambek, 1958), which is weakly context-free. (König, 1989; Moortgat, 1990) have also studied the Lambek calculus case. (Hepple & Morrill, 1989), who introduced the idea of normal-form parsing, consider only a small CCG fragment that lacks backward or order-changing composition; (Niv, 1994) extends this result but does not show completeness. (Wittenburg, 1987) assumes a CCG fragment lacking order-changing or higher-order composition; furthermore, his revision of the combinators creates new, conjoinable constituents that conventional CCG rejects. (Bouma, 1989) proposes to replace composition with a new combinator, but the resulting product-grammar scheme assigns different types to "John likes" and "Mary pretends to like," thus losing the ability to conjoin such constituents or subcategorize for them as a class. (Pareschi & Steedman, 1987) do tackle the CCG case, but (Hepple, 1987) shows their algorithm to be incomplete.

3 Overview of the Parsing Strategy

As is well known, general CFG parsing methods can be applied directly to CCG. Any sort of chart parser or non-deterministic shift-reduce parser will do. Such a parser repeatedly decides whether two adjacent constituents, such as S/NP and NP/N, should be combined into a larger constituent such as S/N. The role of the grammar is to state which combinations are allowed. The key to efficiency, we will see, is for the parser to be less permissive than the grammar—for it to say "no, redundant" in some cases where the grammar says "yes, grammatical."

(5) shows the constituents that untrammeled CCG will find in the course of parsing "John likes Mary." The spurious ambiguity problem is not that the grammar allows (5c), but that the grammar allows both (5f) and (5g)—distinct parses of the *same* string, with the *same* meaning.

(5) a. $[\text{John}]_{S/(S\backslash NP)}$
b. $[\text{likes}]_{(S\backslash NP)/NP}$
c. $[\text{John likes}]_{S/NP}$
d. $[\text{Mary}]_{NP}$
e. $[\text{likes Mary}]_{S\backslash NP}$
f. $[[\text{John likes}]\ \text{Mary}]_{S}$ ⟵ *to be disallowed*
g. $[\text{John}\ [\text{likes Mary}]]_{S}$

The proposal is to construct all constituents shown in (5) except for (5f). If we slightly constrain the use of the grammar rules, the parser will still produce (5c) and (5d)—constituents that are indispensable in contexts like (1)—while refusing to *combine* those constituents into (5f). The relevant rule S/NP NP → S will actually be blocked when it attempts to construct (5f). Although rule-blocking may eliminate an analysis of the sentence, as it does here, a semantically equivalent analysis such as (5g) will always be derivable along some other route.

In general, our goal is to discover exactly one analysis for each <substring, meaning> pair. By practicing "birth control" for each bottom-up generation of constituents in this way, we avoid a population explosion of parsing options. "John likes Mary" has only one reading semantically, so just one of its analyses (5f)–(5g) is discovered while parsing (6). Only that analysis, and not the other, is allowed to continue on and be built into the final parse of (6).

(6) that galoot in the corner that thinks $[\text{John likes Mary}]_S$

For a chart parser, where each chart cell stores the analyses of some substring, this strategy says that

[2] This formalization sweeps any type-raising into the lexicon, as has been proposed on linguistic grounds (Dowty, 1988; Steedman, 1991, and others). It also treats conjunction lexically, by giving "and" the generalized category $x\backslash x/x$ and barring it from composition.

all analyses in a cell are to be semantically distinct. (Karttunen, 1986) suggests enforcing that property directly—by comparing each new analysis semantically with existing analyses in the cell, and refusing to add it if redundant—but (Hepple & Morrill, 1989) observe briefly that this is inefficient for large charts.[3] The following sections show how to obtain effectively the same result without doing any semantic interpretation or comparison at all.

4 A Normal Form for "Pure" CCG

It is convenient to begin with a special case. Suppose the CCG grammar includes not some but *all* instances of the binary rule templates in (4). (As always, a separate lexicon specifies the possible categories of each word.) If we group a sentence's parses into semantic equivalence classes, it always turns out that exactly one parse in each class satisfies the following simple declarative constraints:

(7) a. No constituent produced by >Bn, any $n \geq 1$, ever serves as the primary (left) argument to >Bn', any $n' \geq 0$.
b. No constituent produced by <Bn, any $n \geq 1$, ever serves as the primary (right) argument to <Bn', any $n' \geq 0$.

The notation here is from (4). More colloquially, (7) says that the output of rightward (leftward) composition may not compose or apply over anything to *its* right (left). A parse tree or subtree that satisfies (7) is said to be in *normal form* (NF).

As an example, consider the effect of these restrictions on the simple sentence "John likes Mary." Ignoring the tags -OT, -FC, and -BC for the moment, (8a) is a normal-form parse. Its competitor (8b) is not, nor is any larger tree containing (8b). But non-standard constituents are allowed when necessary: (8c) *is* in normal form (cf. (1)).

(8)
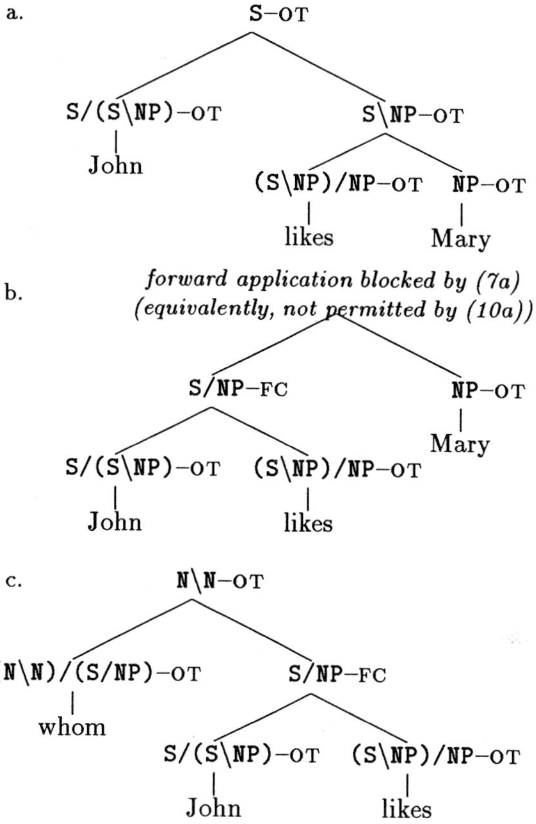

It is not hard to see that (7a) eliminates all but right-branching parses of "forward chains" like A/B B/C C or A/B/C C/D D/E/F/G G/H, and that (7b) eliminates all but left-branching parses of "backward chains." (Thus every functor will get its arguments, if possible, before it becomes an argument itself.) But it is hardly obvious that (7) eliminates *all* of CCG's spurious ambiguity. One might worry about unexpected interactions involving crossing composition rules like A/B B\C → A\C. Significantly, it turns out that (7) really does suffice; the proof is in §4.2.

It is trivial to modify any sort of CCG parser to find only the normal-form parses. No semantics is necessary; simply block any rule use that would violate (7). In general, detecting violations will not hurt performance by more than a constant factor. Indeed, one might implement (7) by modifying CCG's phrase-structure grammar. Each ordinary CCG category is split into three categories that bear the respective tags from (9). The 24 templates schematized in (10) replace the two templates of (4). Any CFG-style method can still parse the resulting spuriosity-free grammar, with tagged parses as in (8). In particular, the polynomial-time, polynomial-space CCG chart parser of (Vijay-Shanker & Weir, 1993) can be trivially adapted to respect the constraints by tagging chart entries.

---

[3]How inefficient? (i) has exponentially many semantically *distinct* parses: $n = 10$ yields 82,756,612 parses in $\binom{20}{10} = 48{,}620$ equivalence classes. Karttunen's method must therefore add 48,620 representative parses to the appropriate chart cell, first comparing each one against all the previously added parses—of which there are 48,620/2 on average—to ensure it is not semantically redundant. (Additional comparisons are needed to reject parses other than the lucky 48,620.) Adding a parse can therefore take exponential time.

(i) $\overbrace{\ldots\ \texttt{S/S}\ \texttt{S/S}\ \texttt{S/S}}^{n}\ \texttt{S}\ \overbrace{\texttt{S\textbackslash S}\ \texttt{S\textbackslash S}\ \texttt{S\textbackslash S}\ \ldots}^{n}$

Structure sharing does not appear to help: parses that are grouped in a parse forest have only their syntactic category in common, not their meaning. Karttunen's approach must tease such parses apart and compare their various meanings individually against each new candidate. By contrast, the method proposed below is purely syntactic—just like any "ordinary" parser—so it never needs to unpack a subforest, and can run in polynomial time.

(9) –FC output of >Bn, some $n \geq 1$ (a forward composition rule)
–BC output of <Bn, some $n \geq 1$ (a backward composition rule)
–OT output of >B0 or <B0 (an application rule), or lexical item

(10) a. Forward application >B0: $\left\{\begin{array}{l} x/y\text{–BC} \\ x/y\text{–OT} \end{array}\right\} \left\{\begin{array}{l} y\text{–FC} \\ y\text{–BC} \\ y\text{–OT} \end{array}\right\} \rightarrow x\text{–OT}$

b. Backward application <B0: $\left\{\begin{array}{l} y\text{–FC} \\ y\text{–BC} \\ y\text{–OT} \end{array}\right\} \left\{\begin{array}{l} x\backslash y\text{–FC} \\ x\backslash y\text{–OT} \end{array}\right\} \rightarrow x\text{–OT}$

c. Fwd. composition >Bn ($n \geq 1$): $\left\{\begin{array}{l} x/y\text{–BC} \\ x/y\text{–OT} \end{array}\right\} \left\{\begin{array}{l} y\,|_n z_n \cdots |_2 z_2\,|_1 z_1\text{–FC} \\ y\,|_n z_n \cdots |_2 z_2\,|_1 z_1\text{–BC} \\ y\,|_n z_n \cdots |_2 z_2\,|_1 z_1\text{–OT} \end{array}\right\} \rightarrow x\,|_n z_n \cdots |_2 z_2\,|_1 z_1\text{–FC}$

d. Bwd. composition <Bn ($n \geq 1$): $\left\{\begin{array}{l} y\,|_n z_n \cdots |_2 z_2\,|_1 z_1\text{–FC} \\ y\,|_n z_n \cdots |_2 z_2\,|_1 z_1\text{–BC} \\ y\,|_n z_n \cdots |_2 z_2\,|_1 z_1\text{–OT} \end{array}\right\} \left\{\begin{array}{l} x\backslash y\text{–FC} \\ x\backslash y\text{–OT} \end{array}\right\} \rightarrow x\,|_n z_n \cdots |_2 z_2\,|_1 z_1\text{–BC}$

(11) a. Syn/sem for >Bn ($n \geq 0$):

$$\begin{array}{ccccc} x/y & & y\,|_n z_n \cdots |_2 z_2\,|_1 z_1 & \rightarrow & x\,|_n z_n \cdots |_2 z_2\,|_1 z_1 \\ \Updownarrow & & \Updownarrow & & \Updownarrow \\ f & & g & & \lambda c_1 \lambda c_2 \ldots \lambda c_n . f(g(c_1)(c_2)\cdots(c_n)) \end{array}$$

b. Syn/sem for <Bn ($n \geq 0$):

$$\begin{array}{ccccc} y\,|_n z_n \cdots |_2 z_2\,|_1 z_1 & & x\backslash y & \rightarrow & x\,|_n z_n \cdots |_2 z_2\,|_1 z_1 \\ \Updownarrow & & \Updownarrow & & \Updownarrow \\ g & & f & & \lambda c_1 \lambda c_2 \ldots \lambda c_n . f(g(c_1)(c_2)\cdots(c_n)) \end{array}$$

(12)

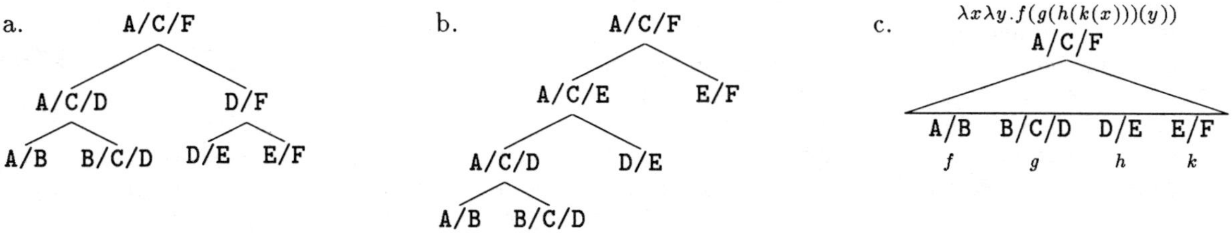

It is interesting to note a rough resemblance between the tagged version of CCG in (10) and the tagged Lambek calculus **L***, which (Hendriks, 1993) developed to eliminate spurious ambiguity from the Lambek calculus **L**. Although differences between CCG and **L** mean that the details are quite different, each system works by marking the output of certain rules, to prevent such output from serving as input to certain other rules.

4.1 Semantic equivalence

We wish to establish that each semantic equivalence class contains exactly one NF parse. But what does "semantically equivalent" mean? Let us adopt a standard model-theoretic view.

For each leaf (i.e., lexeme) of a given syntax tree, the lexicon specifies a *lexical interpretation* from the model. CCG then provides a *derived interpretation* in the model for the complete tree. The standard CCG theory builds the semantics compositionally, guided by the syntax, according to (11). We may therefore regard a syntax tree as a static "recipe" for combining word meanings into a phrase meaning.

One might choose to say that two parses are semantically equivalent iff they derive the same phrase meaning. However, such a definition would make spurious ambiguity sensitive to the fine-grained semantics of the lexicon. Are the two analyses of `VP/VP VP VP\VP` semantically equivalent? If the lexemes involved are "softly knock twice," then yes, as softly(twice(knock)) and twice(softly(knock)) arguably denote a common function in the semantic model. Yet for "intentionally knock twice" this is not the case: these adverbs do not commute, and the semantics are distinct.

It would be difficult to make such subtle distinctions rapidly. Let us instead use a narrower, "intensional" definition of spurious ambiguity. The trees in (12a–b) will be considered equivalent because they specify the same "recipe," shown in (12c). No matter what lexical interpretations f, g, h, k are fed into the leaves A/B, B/C/D, D/E, E/F, both the trees end up with the same derived interpretation, namely a model element that can be determined from f, g, h, k by calculating $\lambda x \lambda y . f(g(h(k(x)))(y))$.

By contrast, the two readings of "softly knock

twice" are considered to be distinct, since the parses specify different recipes. That is, given a suitably free choice of meanings for the words, the two parses can be made to pick out two different VP-type functions in the model. The parser is therefore conservative and keeps both parses.[4]

4.2 Normal-form parsing is safe & complete

The motivation for producing only NF parses (as defined by (7)) lies in the following existence and uniqueness theorems for CCG.

Theorem 1 *Assuming "pure CCG," where all possible rules are in the grammar, any parse tree α is semantically equivalent to some NF parse tree $NF(\alpha)$.*

(This says the NF parser is *safe* for pure CCG: we will not lose any readings by generating just normal forms.)

Theorem 2 *Given distinct NF trees $\alpha \neq \alpha'$ (on the same sequence of leaves). Then α and α' are not semantically equivalent.*

(This says that the NF parser is *complete*: generating only normal forms eliminates *all* spurious ambiguity.)

Detailed proofs of these theorems are available on the cmp-lg archive, but can only be sketched here. Theorem 1 is proved by a constructive induction on the order of α, given below and illustrated in (13):

- For α a leaf, put $NF(\alpha) = \alpha$.
- ($<R, \beta, \gamma>$ denotes the parse tree formed by combining subtrees β, γ via rule R.)
  If $\alpha = <R, \beta, \gamma>$, then take $NF(\alpha) = <R, NF(\beta), NF(\gamma)>$, which exists by inductive hypothesis, unless this is not an NF tree. In the latter case, WLOG, R is a forward rule and $NF(\beta) = <Q, \beta_1, \beta_2>$ for some forward composition rule Q. Pure CCG turns out to provide forward rules S and T such that $\alpha' = <S, \beta_1, NF(<T, \beta_2, \gamma>)>$ is a constituent and is semantically equivalent to α. Moreover, since β_1 serves as the primary subtree of the NF tree $NF(\beta)$, β_1 cannot be the output of forward composition, and is NF besides. Therefore α' is NF: take $NF(\alpha) = \alpha'$.

(13) If $NF(\beta)$ not output of fwd. composition,

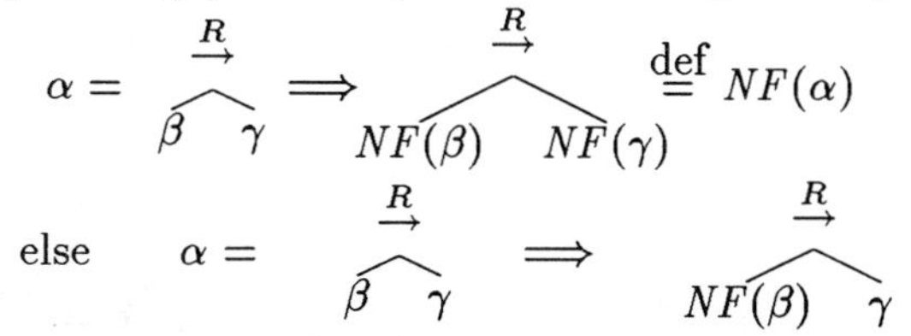

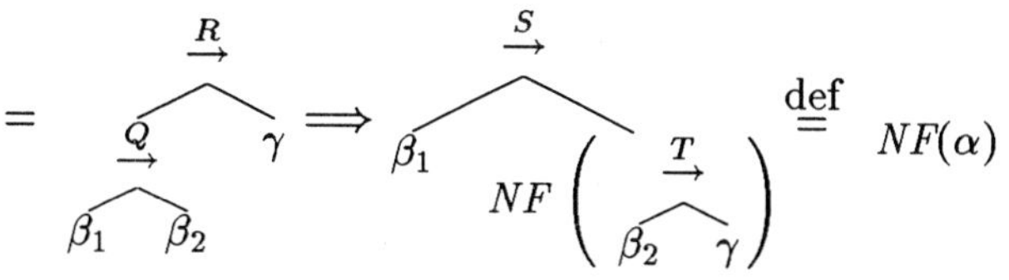

This construction resembles a well-known normal-form reduction procedure that (Hepple & Morrill, 1989) propose (without proving completeness) for a small fragment of CCG.

The proof of theorem 2 (completeness) is longer and more subtle. First it shows, by a simple induction, that since α and α' disagree they must disagree in at least one of these ways:

(a) There are trees β, γ and rules $R \neq R'$ such that $<R, \beta, \gamma>$ is a subtree of α and $<R', \beta, \gamma>$ is a subtree of α'. (For example, S/S S\S may form a constituent by either <B1x or >B1x.)

(b) There is a tree γ that appears as a subtree of both α and α', but combines to the left in one case and to the right in the other.

Either condition, the proof shows, leads to different "immediate scope" relations in the full trees α and α' (in the sense in which f takes immediate scope over g in $f(g(x))$ but not in $f(h(g(x)))$ or $g(f(x))$). Condition (a) is straightforward. Condition (b) splits into a case where γ serves as a secondary argument inside both α and α', and a case where it is a primary argument in α or α'. The latter case requires consideration of γ's ancestors; the NF properties crucially rule out counterexamples here.

The notion of scope is relevant because semantic interpretations for CCG constituents can be written as restricted lambda terms, in such a way that constituents having distinct terms must have different interpretations in the model (for suitable interpretations of the words, as in §4.1). Theorem 2 is proved by showing that the terms for α and α' differ somewhere, so correspond to different semantic recipes.

Similar theorems for the Lambek calculus were previously shown by (Hepple, 1990; Hendriks, 1993). The present proofs for CCG establish a result that has long been suspected: the spurious ambiguity problem is not actually very widespread in CCG. Theorem 2 says *all* cases of spurious ambiguity can be eliminated through the construction given in theorem 1. But that construction merely ensures a right-branching structure for "forward constituent chains" (such as A/B B/C C or A/B/C C/D D/E/F/G G/H), and a left-branching structure for backward constituent chains. So these familiar chains are the *only* source of spurious ambiguity in CCG.

5 Extending the Approach to "Restricted" CCG

The "pure" CCG of §4 is a fiction. Real CCG grammars can and do choose a subset of the possible rules.

[4](Hepple & Morrill, 1989; Hepple, 1990; Hendriks, 1993) appear to share this view of semantic equivalence. Unlike (Karttunen, 1986), they try to eliminate only parses whose denotations (or at least λ-terms) are systematically equivalent, not parses that happen to have the same denotation through an accident of the lexicon.

For instance, to rule out (14), the (crossing) backward rule N/N N\N → N/N must be omitted from English grammar.

(14) [the$_{NP/N}$ [[big$_{N/N}$ [that likes John]$_{N\backslash N}$]$_{N/N}$ galoot$_N$]$_N$]$_{NP}$

If some rules are removed from a "pure" CCG grammar, some parses will become unavailable. Theorem 2 remains true ($\leq$ 1 NF per reading). Whether theorem 1 ($\geq$ 1 NF per reading) remains true depends on what set of rules is removed. For most linguistically reasonable choices, the proof of theorem 1 *will* go through,[5] so that the normal-form parser of §4 remains safe. But imagine removing only the rule B/C C → B: this leaves the string A/B B/C C with a left-branching parse that has no (legal) NF equivalent.

In the sort of restricted grammar where theorem 1 does *not* obtain, can we still find one (possibly non-NF) parse per equivalence class? Yes: a different kind of efficient parser can be built for this case.

Since the new parser must be able to generate a non-NF parse when no equivalent NF parse is available, its method of controlling spurious ambiguity cannot be to enforce the constraints (7). The old parser refused to build non-NF constituents; the new parser will refuse to build constituents that are semantically equivalent to already-built constituents.

This idea originates with (Karttunen, 1986). However, we can take advantage of the core result of this paper, theorems 1 and 2, to do Karttunen's redundancy check in $O(1)$ time—no worse than the normal-form parser's check for -FC and -BC tags. (Karttunen's version takes worst-case exponential time for each redundancy check: see footnote §3.)

The insight is that theorems 1 and 2 establish a one-to-one map between semantic equivalence classes and normal forms of the pure (unrestricted) CCG:

(15) Two parses α, α' of the pure CCG are semantically equivalent iff they have the *same* normal form: $NF(\alpha) = NF(\alpha')$.

The *NF* function is defined recursively by §4.2's proof of theorem 1; semantic equivalence is also defined independently of the grammar. So (15) is meaningful and true even if α, α' are produced by a restricted CCG. The tree $NF(\alpha)$ may not be a legal *parse* under the restricted grammar. However, it is still a perfectly good data structure that can be maintained outside the parse chart, to serve as a magnet for α's semantic class. The proof of theorem 1 (see (13)) actually shows how to construct $NF(\alpha)$ in $O(1)$ time from the values of *NF* on smaller constituents. Hence, an appropriate parser can compute and cache the NF of each parse in $O(1)$ time as it is added to the chart. It can detect redundant parses by noting (via an $O(1)$ array lookup) that their NFs have been previously computed.

Figure (1) gives an efficient CKY-style algorithm based on this insight. (Parsing strategies besides CKY would also work, in particular (Vijay-Shanker & Weir, 1993).) The management of cached NFs in steps 9, 12, and especially 16 ensures that duplicate NFs never enter the *oldNFs* array: thus any alternative copy of $\alpha.nf$ has the same array coordinates used for $\alpha.nf$ itself, because it was built from identical subtrees.

The function PreferableTo(σ, τ) (step 15) provides flexibility about *which* parse represents its class. PreferableTo may be defined at whim to choose the parse discovered first, the more left-branching parse, or the parse with fewer non-standard constituents. Alternatively, PreferableTo may call an intonation or discourse module to pick the parse that better reflects the topic-focus division of the sentence. (A variant algorithm ignores PreferableTo and constructs one parse forest per reading. Each forest can later be unpacked into individual equivalent parse trees, if desired.)

(Vijay-Shanker & Weir, 1990) also give a method for removing "one well-known source" of spurious ambiguity from restricted CCGs; §4.2 above shows that this is in fact the only source. However, their method relies on the grammaticality of certain intermediate forms, and so can fail if the CCG rules can be *arbitrarily* restricted. In addition, their method is less efficient than the present one: it considers parses in pairs, not singly, and does not remove any parse until the entire parse forest has been built.

6 Extensions to the CCG Formalism

In addition to the **B***n* ("generalized composition") rules given in §2, which give CCG power equivalent to TAG, rules based on the **S** ("substitution") and **T** ("type-raising") combinators can be linguistically useful. **S** provides another rule template, used in the analysis of parasitic gaps (Steedman, 1987; Szabolcsi, 1989):

(16) a. >S: $x/y\,|_1 z \quad y\,|_1 z \quad \rightarrow \quad x\,|_1 z$

$$\Updownarrow \qquad \Updownarrow \qquad\qquad \Updownarrow$$

$$f \qquad g \qquad\qquad \lambda z.f(z)(g(z))$$

b. <S: $y\,|_1 z \quad x\backslash y\,|_1 z \quad \rightarrow \quad x\,|_1 z$

Although **S** interacts with **B***n* to produce another source of spurious ambiguity, illustrated in (17), the additional ambiguity is not hard to remove. It can be shown that when the restriction (18) is used together with (7), the system again finds exactly one

[5] For the proof to work, the rules S and T must be available in the restricted grammar, given that R and Q are. This is usually true: since (7) favors standard constituents and prefers application to composition, most grammars will not block the NF derivation while allowing a non-NF one. (On the other hand, the NF parse of A/B B/C C/D/E uses >B2 twice, while the non-NF parse gets by with >B2 and >B1.)

```
for i := 1 to n
  C[i − 1, i] := LexCats(word[i])                (* word i stretches from point i − 1 to point i *)
for width := 2 to n
  for start := 0 to n − width
    end := start + width
    for mid := start + 1 to end − 1
      for each parse tree α = <R, β, γ> that could be formed by combining some
      β ∈ C[start, mid] with some γ ∈ C[mid, end] by a rule R of the (restricted) grammar
        α.nf := NF(α)        (* can be computed in constant time using the .nf fields of β, γ, and
                                other constituents already in C. Subtrees are also NF trees. *)
        existingNF := oldNFs[α.nf.rule, α.nf.leftchild.seqno, α.nf.rightchild.seqno]
        if undefined(existingNF)                                    (* the first parse with this NF *)
          α.nf.seqno := (counter := counter + 1)       (* number the new NF & add it to oldNFs *)
          oldNFs[α.nf.rule, α.nf.leftchild.seqno, α.nf.rightchild.seqno] := α.nf
          add α to C[start, end]
          α.nf.currparse := α
        elsif PreferableTo(α, existingNF.currparse)                 (* replace reigning parse? *)
          α.nf := existingNF                              (* use cached copy of NF, not new one *)
          remove α.nf.currparse from C[start, end]
          add α to C[start, end]
          α.nf.currparse := α
return(all parses from C[0, n] having root category S)
```

Figure 1: Canonicalizing CCG parser that handles arbitrary restrictions on the rule set. (In practice, a simpler normal-form parser will suffice for most grammars.)

parse from every equivalence class.

(17) a.

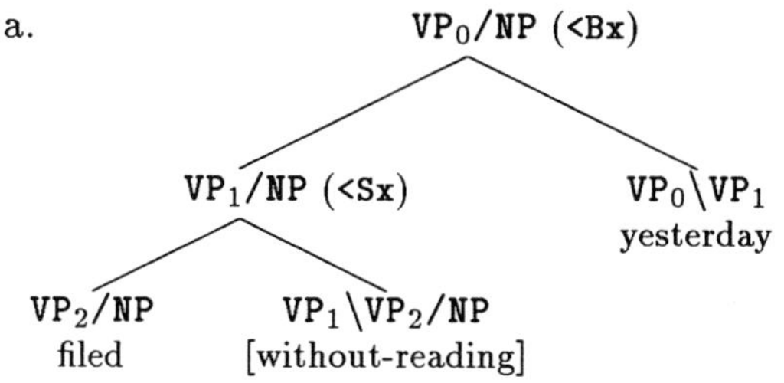

b.

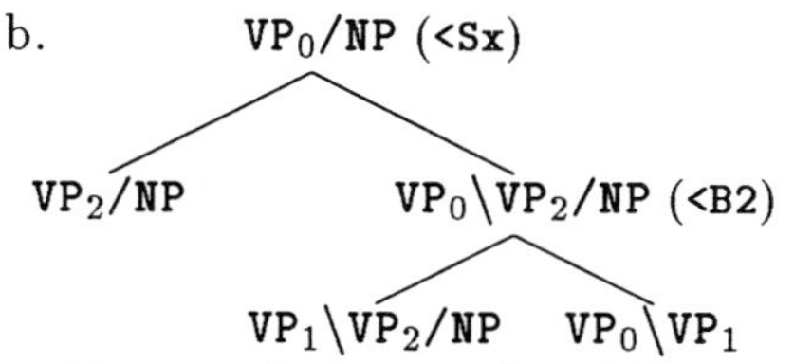

(18) a. No constituent produced by >Bn, any $n \geq 2$, ever serves as the primary (left) argument to >S.

b. No constituent produced by <Bn, any $n \geq 2$, ever serves as the primary (right) argument to <S.

Type-raising presents a greater problem. Various new spurious ambiguities arise if it is permitted freely in the grammar. In principle one could proceed without grammatical type-raising: (Dowty, 1988; Steedman, 1991) have argued on linguistic grounds that type-raising should be treated as a mere lexical redundancy property. That is, whenever the lexicon contains an entry of a certain category X, with semantics x, it also contains one with (say) category T/(T\X) and interpretation $\lambda p.p(x)$. As one might expect, this move only sweeps the problem under the rug. If type-raising is lexical, then the definitions of this paper do not recognize (19) as a spurious ambiguity, because the two parses are now, technically speaking, analyses of different sentences. Nor do they recognize the redundancy in (20), because—just as for the example "softly knock twice" in §4.1—it is contingent on a kind of lexical coincidence, namely that a type-raised subject commutes with a (generically) type-raised object. Such ambiguities are left to future work.

(19) $[\text{John}_{\text{NP}}\ \text{left}_{\text{S}\backslash\text{NP}}]_{\text{S}}$ vs. $[\text{John}_{\text{S}/(\text{S}\backslash\text{NP})}\ \text{left}_{\text{S}\backslash\text{NP}}]_{\text{S}}$

(20) $[\text{S}/(\text{S}\backslash\text{NP}_{\text{S}})\ [\text{S}\backslash\text{NP}_{\text{S}}/\text{NP}_{\text{O}}/\text{NP}_{\text{I}}\ \text{T}\backslash(\text{T}/\text{NP}_{\text{O}})]]_{\text{S}/\text{S}_{\text{I}}}$
vs. $[\text{S}/(\text{S}\backslash\text{NP}_{\text{S}})\ \text{S}\backslash\text{NP}_{\text{S}}/\text{NP}_{\text{O}}/\text{NP}_{\text{I}}]\ \text{T}\backslash(\text{T}/\text{NP}_{\text{O}})]_{\text{S}/\text{S}_{\text{I}}}$

7 Conclusions

The main contribution of this work has been formal: to establish a normal form for parses of "pure" Combinatory Categorial Grammar. Given a sentence, every reading that is available to the grammar has exactly one normal-form parse, no matter how many parses it has *in toto*.

A result worth remembering is that, although TAG-equivalent CCG allows free interaction among forward, backward, and crossed composition rules of any degree, two simple constraints serve to eliminate all spurious ambiguity. It turns out that all spurious ambiguity arises from associative "chains" such as A/B B/C C or A/B/C C/D D/E\F/G G/H. (Wittenburg, 1987; Hepple & Morrill, 1989) anticipate this result, at least for some fragments of CCG, but leave the proof to future work.

These normal-form results for pure CCG lead directly to useful parsers for real, restricted CCG grammars. Two parsing algorithms have been presented for practical use. One algorithm finds only normal forms; this simply and safely eliminates spurious ambiguity under *most* real CCG grammars. The other, more complex algorithm solves the spurious ambiguity problem for *any* CCG grammar, by using normal forms as an efficient tool for grouping semantically equivalent parses. Both algorithms are safe, complete, and efficient.

In closing, it should be repeated that the results provided are for the TAG-equivalent **B***n* (generalized composition) formalism of (Joshi et al., 1991), optionally extended with the **S** (substitution) rules of (Szabolcsi, 1989). The technique eliminates all spurious ambiguities resulting from the interaction of these rules. Future work should continue by eliminating the spurious ambiguities that arise from grammatical or lexical type-raising.

References

Gosse Bouma. 1989. Efficient processing of flexible categorial grammar. In *Proceedings of the Fourth Conference of the European Chapter of the Association for Computational Linguistics*, 19–26, University of Manchester, April.

David Dowty. 1988. Type raising, functional composition, and non-constituent conjunction. In R. Oehrle, E. Bach and D. Wheeler, editors, *Categorial Grammars and Natural Language Structures.* Reidel.

Mark Hepple. 1987. Methods for parsing combinatory categorial grammar and the spurious ambiguity problem. Unpublished M.Sc. thesis, Centre for Cognitive Science, University of Edinburgh.

Mark Hepple. 1990. *The Grammar and Processing of Order and Dependency: A Categorial Approach.* Ph.D. thesis, University of Edinburgh.

Mark Hepple and Glyn Morrill. 1989. Parsing and derivational equivalence. In *Proceedings of the Fourth Conference of the European Chapter of the Association for Computational Linguistics*, 10–18, University of Manchester, April.

Herman Hendriks. 1993. *Studied Flexibility: Categories and Types in Syntax and Semantics.* Ph.D. thesis, Institute for Logic, Language, and Computation, University of Amsterdam.

Aravind Joshi, K. Vijay-Shanker, and David Weir. 1991. The convergence of mildly context-sensitive grammar formalisms. In *Foundational Issues in Natural Language Processing*, MIT Press.

Lauri Karttunen. 1986. Radical lexicalism. Report No. CSLI-86-68, CSLI, Stanford University.

E. König. 1989. Parsing as natural deduction. In *Proceedings of the 27th Annual Meeting of the Association for Computational Linguistics*, Vancouver.

J. Lambek. 1958. The mathematics of sentence structure. *American Mathematical Monthly* 65:154–169.

Michael Moortgat. 1990. Unambiguous proof representations for the Lambek Calculus. In *Proceedings of the Seventh Amsterdam Colloquium.*

Michael Niv. 1994. A psycholinguistically motivated parser for CCG. In *Proceedings of the 32nd Annual Meeting of the Association for Computational Linguistics*, Las Cruces, NM, June.

Remo Pareschi and Mark Steedman. A lazy way to chart parse with combinatory grammars. In *Proceedings of the 25th Annual Meeting of the Association for Computational Linguistics*, Stanford University, July.

Scott Prevost and Mark Steedman. 1994. Specifying intonation from context for speech synthesis. *Speech Communication*, 15:139-153.

Mark Steedman. 1990. Gapping as constituent coordination. *Linguistics and Philosophy*, 13:207–264.

Mark Steedman. 1991. Structure and intonation. *Language*, 67:260–296.

Mark Steedman. 1987. Combinatory grammars and parasitic gaps. *Natural Language and Linguistic Theory*, 5:403–439.

Anna Szabolcsi. 1989. Bound variables in syntax: Are there any? In R. Bartsch, J. van Benthem, and P. van Emde Boas (eds.), *Semantics and Contextual Expression*, 295–318. Foris, Dordrecht.

K. Vijay-Shanker and David Weir. 1990. Polynomial time parsing of combinatory categorial grammars. In *Proceedings of the 28th Annual Meeting of the Association for Computational Linguistics.*

K. Vijay-Shanker and David Weir. 1993. Parsing some constrained grammar formalisms. *Computational Linguistics*, 19(4):591–636.

K. Vijay-Shanker and David Weir. 1994. The equivalence of four extensions of context-free grammars. *Mathematical Systems Theory*, 27:511–546.

Kent Wittenburg. 1986. *Natural Language Parsing with Combinatory Categorial Grammar in a Graph-Unification-Based Formalism.* Ph.D. thesis, University of Texas.

Kent Wittenburg. 1987. Predictive combinators: A method for efficient parsing of Combinatory Categorial Grammars. In *Proceedings of the 25th Annual Meeting of the Association for Computational Linguistics*, Stanford University, July.

Another Facet of LIG Parsing

Pierre Boullier
INRIA-Rocquencourt
BP 105
78153 Le Chesnay Cedex, France
Pierre.Boullier@inria.fr

Abstract

In this paper[1] we present a new parsing algorithm for linear indexed grammars (LIGs) in the same spirit as the one described in (Vijay-Shanker and Weir, 1993) for tree adjoining grammars. For a LIG L and an input string x of length n, we build a non ambiguous context-free grammar whose sentences are all (and exclusively) valid derivation sequences in L which lead to x. We show that this grammar can be built in $\mathcal{O}(n^6)$ time and that individual parses can be extracted in linear time with the size of the extracted parse tree. Though this $\mathcal{O}(n^6)$ upper bound does not improve over previous results, the average case behaves much better. Moreover, practical parsing times can be decreased by some statically performed computations.

1 Introduction

The class of mildly context-sensitive languages can be described by several equivalent grammar types. Among these types we can notably cite tree adjoining grammars (TAGs) and linear indexed grammars (LIGs). In (Vijay-Shanker and Weir, 1994) TAGs are transformed into equivalent LIGs. Though context-sensitive linguistic phenomena seem to be more naturally expressed in TAG formalism, from a computational point of view, many authors think that LIGs play a central role and therefore the understanding of LIGs and LIG parsing is of importance. For example, quoted from (Schabes and Shieber, 1994) "The LIG version of TAG can be used for recognition and parsing. Because the LIG formalism is based on augmented rewriting, the parsing algorithms can be much simpler to understand and easier to modify, and no loss of generality is incurred". In (Vijay-Shanker and Weir, 1993) LIGs are used to express the derivations of a sentence in TAGs. In (Vijay-Shanker, Weir and Rambow, 1995) the approach used for parsing a new formalism, the D-Tree Grammars (DTG), is to translate a DTG into a Linear Prioritized Multiset Grammar which is similar to a LIG but uses multisets in place of stacks.

LIGs can be seen as usual context-free grammars (CFGs) upon which constraints are imposed. These constraints are expressed by stacks of symbols associated with non-terminals. We study parsing of LIGs, our goal being to define a structure that verifies the LIG constraints and codes all (and exclusively) parse trees deriving sentences.

Since derivations in LIGs are constrained CF derivations, we can think of a scheme where the CF derivations for a given input are expressed by a shared forest from which individual parse trees which do not satisfied the LIG constraints are erased. Unhappily this view is too simplistic, since the erasing of individual trees whose parts can be shared with other valid trees can only be performed after some unfolding (unsharing) that can produced a forest whose size is exponential or even unbounded.

In (Vijay-Shanker and Weir, 1993), the context-freeness of adjunction in TAGs is captured by giving a CFG to represent the set of all possible derivation sequences. In this paper we study a new parsing scheme for LIGs based upon similar principles and which, on the other side, emphasizes as (Lang, 1991) and (Lang, 1994), the use of grammars (shared forest) to represent parse trees and is an extension of our previous work (Boullier, 1995).

This previous paper describes a recognition algorithm for LIGs, but not a parser. For a LIG and an input string, all valid parse trees are actually coded into the CF shared parse forest used by this recognizer, but, on some parse trees of this forest, the

[1]See (Boullier, 1996) for an extended version.

checking of the LIG constraints can possibly failed. At first sight, there are two conceivable ways to extend this recognizer into a parser:

1. only "good" trees are kept;

2. the LIG constraints are [re-]checked while the extraction of valid trees is performed.

As explained above, the first solution can produce an unbounded number of trees. The second solution is also uncomfortable since it necessitates the reevaluation on each tree of the LIG conditions and, doing so, we move away from the usual idea that individual parse trees can be extracted by a simple walk through a structure.

In this paper, we advocate a third way which will use (see section 4), the same basic material as the one used in (Boullier, 1995). For a given LIG L and an input string x, we exhibit a non ambiguous CFG whose sentences are all possible valid derivation sequences in L which lead to x. We show that this CFG can be constructed in $\mathcal{O}(n^6)$ time and that individual parses can be extracted in time linear with the size of the extracted tree.

2 Derivation Grammar and CF Parse Forest

In a CFG $G = (V_N, V_T, P, S)$, the *derives* relation $\underset{G}{\Rightarrow}$ is the set $\{(\sigma B \sigma', \sigma\beta\sigma') \mid B \rightarrow \beta \in P \wedge V = V_N \cup V_T \wedge \sigma, \sigma' \in V^*\}$. A *derivation* is a sequence of strings in V^* s.t. the relation derives holds between any two consecutive strings. In a *rightmost* derivation, at each step, the rightmost non-terminal say B is replaced by the right-hand side (RHS) of a B-production. Equivalently if $\sigma_0 \overset{r_1}{\underset{G}{\Rightarrow}} \ldots \overset{r_n}{\underset{G}{\Rightarrow}} \sigma_n$ is a rightmost derivation where the relation symbol is overlined by the production used at each step, we say that $r_1 \ldots r_n$ is a rightmost σ_0/σ_n-derivation.

For a CFG G, the set of its rightmost S/x-derivations, where $x \in \mathcal{L}(G)$, can itself be defined by a grammar.

Definition 1 *Let* $G = (V_N, V_T, P, S)$ *be a CFG, its rightmost derivation grammar is the CFG* $D = (V_N, P, P^D, S)$ *where* $P^D = \{A_0 \rightarrow A_1 \ldots A_q r \mid r = A_0 \rightarrow w_0 A_1 w_1 \ldots w_{q-1} A_q w_q \in P \wedge w_i \in V_T^* \wedge A_j \in V_N\}$

¿From the natural bijection between P and P^D, we can easily prove that

$$\mathcal{L}(D) = \{r_n \ldots r_1 \mid r_1 \ldots r_n \text{ is a rightmost } S/x\text{-derivation in } G\}$$

This shows that the rightmost derivation language of a CFG is also CF. We will show in section 4 that a similar result holds for LIGs.

Following (Lang, 1994), CF parsing is the intersection of a CFG and a finite-state automaton (FSA) which models the input string x[2]. The result of this intersection is a CFG $G^x = (V_N^x, V_T^x, P^x, [S]_0^n)$ called a *shared parse forest* which is a specialization of the initial CFG $G = (V_N, V_T, P, S)$ to x. Each production $r_i^j \in P^x$, is the production $r_i \in P$ up to some non-terminal renaming. The non-terminal symbols in V_N^x are triples denoted $[A]_p^q$ where $A \in V_N$, and p and q are states. When such a non-terminal is productive, $[A]_p^q \underset{G^x}{\overset{+}{\Rightarrow}} w$, we have $q \in \delta(p, w)$.

If we build the rightmost derivation grammar associated with a shared parse forest, and we remove all its useless symbols, we get a reduced CFG say D^x. The CF recognition problem for (G, x) is equivalent to the existence of an $[S]_0^n$-production in D^x. Moreover, each rightmost S/x-derivation in G is (the reverse of) a sentence in $\mathcal{L}(D^x)$. However, this result is not very interesting since individual parse trees can be as easily extracted directly from the parse forest. This is due to the fact that in the CF case, a tree that is derived (a parse tree) contains all the information about its derivation (the sequence of rewritings used) and therefore there is no need to distinguish between these two notions. Though this is not always the case with non CF formalisms, we will see in the next sections that a similar approach, when applied to LIGs, leads to a shared parse forest which is a LIG while it is possible to define a derivation grammar which is CF.

3 Linear Indexed Grammars

An indexed grammar is a CFG in which stack of symbols are associated with non-terminals. LIGs are a restricted form of indexed grammars in which the dependence between stacks is such that at most one stack in the RHS of a production is related with the stack in its LHS. Other non-terminals are associated with independant stacks of bounded size.

Following (Vijay-Shanker and Weir, 1994)

Definition 2 $L = (V_N, V_T, V_I, P_L, S)$ *denotes a LIG where* V_N, V_T, V_I *and* P_L *are respectively finite sets of non-terminals, terminals, stack symbols and productions, and* S *is the start symbol.*

In the sequel we will only consider a restricted

[2] if $x = a_1 \ldots a_n$, the states can be the integers $0 \ldots n$, 0 is the initial state, n the unique final state, and the transition function δ is s.t. $i \in \delta(i-1, a_i)$ and $i \in \delta(i, \varepsilon)$.

form of LIGs with productions of the form

$$P_L = \{A() \to w\} \cup \{A(..\alpha) \to \Gamma_1 B(..\alpha')\Gamma_2\}$$

where $A, B \in V_N$, $w \in V_T^* \wedge 0 \leq |w| \leq 2$, $\alpha\alpha' \in V_I^* \wedge 0 \leq |\alpha\alpha'| \leq 1$ and $\Gamma_1\Gamma_2 \in V_T \cup \{\varepsilon\} \cup \{C() \mid C \in V_N\}$.

An element like $A(..\alpha)$ is a *primary constituent* while $C()$ is a *secondary constituent*. The stack schema $(..\alpha)$ of a primary constituent matches all the stacks whose prefix (bottom) part is left unspecified and whose suffix (top) part is α; the stack of a secondary constituent is always empty.

Such a form has been chosen both for complexity reasons and to decrease the number of cases we have to deal with. However, it is easy to see that this form of LIG constitutes a normal form.

We use $r()$ to denote a production in P_L, where the parentheses remind us that we are in a LIG!

The *CF-backbone* of a LIG is the underlying CFG in which each production is a LIG production where the stack part of each constituent has been deleted, leaving only the non-terminal part. We will only consider LIGs such there is a bijection between its production set and the production set of its CF-backbone[3].

We call *object* the pair denoted $A(\alpha)$ where A is a non-terminal and (α) a stack of symbols. Let $V_O = \{A(\alpha) \mid A \in V_N \wedge \alpha \in V_I^*\}$ be the set of objects. We define on $(V_O \cup V_T)^*$ the binary relation *derives* denoted $\underset{L}{\Rightarrow}$ (the relation symbol is sometimes overlined by a production):

$$\Gamma_1' A(\alpha''\alpha)\Gamma_2' \overset{A(..\alpha)\to\Gamma_1 B(..\alpha')\Gamma_2}{\underset{L}{\Rightarrow}} \Gamma_1'\Gamma_1 B(\alpha''\alpha')\Gamma_2\Gamma_2'$$

$$\Gamma_1' A()\Gamma_2' \overset{A()\to w}{\underset{L}{\Rightarrow}} \Gamma_1' w \Gamma_2'$$

In the first above element we say that the object $B(\alpha''\alpha')$ is the *distinguished child* of $A(\alpha''\alpha)$, and if $\Gamma_1\Gamma_2 = C()$, $C()$ is the *secondary object*. A *derivation* $\Gamma_1, \ldots, \Gamma_i, \Gamma_{i+1}, \ldots, \Gamma_l$ is a sequence of strings where the relation derives holds between any two consecutive strings

The language defined by a LIG L is the set:

$$\mathcal{L}(L) = \{x \mid S() \overset{+}{\underset{L}{\Rightarrow}} x \wedge x \in V_T^*\}$$

As in the CF case we can talk of rightmost derivations when the rightmost object is derived at each step. Of course, many other derivation strategies may be thought of. For our parsing algorithm, we need such a particular derives relation. Assume that at one step an object derives both a distinguished child and a secondary object. Our particular derivation strategy is such that this distinguished child will always be derived after the secondary object (and its descendants), whether this secondary object lays to its left or to its right. This derives relation is denoted $\underset{\ell,L}{\Rightarrow}$ and is called *linear*[4].

A *spine* is the sequence of objects $A_1(\alpha_1) \ldots A_i(\alpha_i)\ A_{i+1}(\alpha_{i+1}) \ldots A_p(\alpha_p)$ if, there is a derivation in which each object $A_{i+1}(\alpha_{i+1})$ is the distinguished child of $A_i(\alpha_i)$ (and therefore the *distinguished descendant* of $A_j(\alpha_j), 1 \leq j \leq i$).

4 Linear Derivation Grammar

For a given LIG L, consider a linear $S()/x$-derivation

$$S() \overset{r_n()}{\underset{\ell,L}{\Rightarrow}} \cdots \overset{r_i()}{\underset{\ell,L}{\Rightarrow}} \cdots \overset{r_1()}{\underset{\ell,L}{\Rightarrow}} x$$

The sequence of productions $r_1() \ldots r_i() \ldots r_n()$ (considered in reverse order) is a string in P_L^*. The purpose of this section is to define the set of such strings as the language defined by some CFG.

Associated with a LIG $L = (V_N, V_T, V_I, P_L, S)$, we first define a bunch of binary relations which are borrowed from (Boullier, 1995)

$$\underset{1}{\diamond} = \{(A,B) \mid A(..) \to \Gamma_1 B(..)\Gamma_2 \in P_L\}$$

$$\overset{\gamma}{\underset{1}{\prec}} = \{(A,B) \mid A(..) \to \Gamma_1 B(..\gamma)\Gamma_2 \in P_L\}$$

$$\overset{\gamma}{\underset{1}{\succ}} = \{(A,B) \mid A(..\gamma) \to \Gamma_1 B(..)\Gamma_2 \in P_L\}$$

$$\underset{+}{\diamond} = \{(A_1,A_p) \mid A_1() \overset{+}{\underset{L}{\Rightarrow}} \Gamma_1 A_p()\Gamma_2 \text{ and } A_p() \text{ is a distinguished descendant of } A_1()\}$$

The *1-level* relations simply indicate, for each production, which operation can be apply to the stack associated with the LHS non-terminal to get the stack associated with its distinguished child; $\underset{1}{\diamond}$ indicates equality, $\overset{\gamma}{\underset{1}{\prec}}$ the pushing of γ, and $\overset{\gamma}{\underset{1}{\succ}}$ the popping of γ.

If we look at the evolution of a stack along a spine $A_1(\alpha_1) \ldots A_i(\alpha_i) A_{i+1}(\alpha_{i+1}) \ldots A_p(\alpha_p)$, between any two objects one of the following holds: $\alpha_i = \alpha_{i+1}$, $\alpha_i\gamma = \alpha_{i+1}$, or $\alpha_i = \alpha_{i+1}\gamma$.

The $\underset{+}{\diamond}$ relation select pairs of non-terminals (A_1, A_p) s.t. $\alpha_1 = \alpha_p = \varepsilon$ along non trivial spines.

[3] r_p and $r_p()$ with the same index p designate associated productions.

[4] linear reminds us that we are in a LIG and relies upon a linear (total) order over object occurrences in a derivation. See (Boullier, 1996) for a more formal definition.

If the relations $\overset{\gamma}{\underset{+}{\succ}}$ and $\approx$ are defined as $\overset{\gamma}{\underset{+}{\succ}} = \overset{\gamma}{\underset{1}{\succ}} \cup \underset{+}{\diamond}\overset{\gamma}{\underset{1}{\succ}}$ and $\approx = \bigcup_{\gamma \in V_I} \overset{\gamma}{\underset{1}{\prec}}\overset{\gamma}{\underset{+}{\succ}}$, we can see that the following identity holds

Property 1

$$\underset{+}{\diamond} \quad = \quad \underset{1}{\diamond} \cup \approx \cup \underset{1}{\diamond}\underset{+}{\diamond} \cup \approx \underset{+}{\diamond}$$

In (Boullier, 1995) we can found an algorithm[5] which computes the $\underset{+}{\diamond}$, $\overset{\gamma}{\underset{+}{\succ}}$ and $\approx$ relations as the composition of $\underset{1}{\diamond}$, $\overset{\gamma}{\underset{1}{\prec}}$ and $\overset{\gamma}{\underset{1}{\succ}}$ in $\mathcal{O}(|V_N|^3)$ time.

Definition 3 *For a LIG* $L = (V_N, V_T, V_I, P_L, S)$, *we call linear derivation grammar (LDG) the CFG* D_L *(or* D *when* L *is understood)* $D = (V_N^D, V_T^D, P^D, S^D)$ *where*

- $V_N^D = \{[A] \mid A \in V_N\} \cup \{[A\rho B] \mid A, B \in V_N \wedge \rho \in \mathcal{R}\}$, *and* $\mathcal{R}$ *is the set of relations* $\{\overset{\gamma}{\underset{1}{\prec}}, \underset{1}{\diamond}, \overset{\gamma}{\underset{1}{\succ}}, \underset{+}{\diamond}, \approx, \overset{\gamma}{\underset{+}{\succ}}\}$[6]
- $V_T^D = P_L$
- $S^D = [S]$
- *Below,* $[\Gamma_1\Gamma_2]$ *denotes either the non-terminal symbol* $[X]$ *when* $\Gamma_1\Gamma_2 = X()$ *or the empty string* ε *when* $\Gamma_1\Gamma_2 \in V_T^*$. P^D *is defined as being*

$$\begin{aligned}
&\{[A] \to r() \mid r() = A() \to w \in P_L\} && (1)\\
&\cup\{[A] \to r()[A \underset{+}{\diamond} B] \mid \\
&\qquad r() = B() \to w \in P_L\} && (2)\\
&\cup\{[A \underset{+}{\diamond} C] \to [\Gamma_1\Gamma_2]r() \mid \\
&\qquad r() = A(..) \to \Gamma_1 C(..)\Gamma_2 \in P_L\} && (3)\\
&\cup\{[A \underset{+}{\diamond} C] \to [A \approx C]\} && (4)\\
&\cup\{[A \underset{+}{\diamond} C] \to [B \underset{+}{\diamond} C][\Gamma_1\Gamma_2]r() \mid \\
&\qquad r() = A(..) \to \Gamma_1 B(..)\Gamma_2 \in P_L\} && (5)\\
&\cup\{[A \underset{+}{\diamond} C] \to [B \underset{+}{\diamond} C][A \approx B]\} && (6)\\
&\cup\{[A \approx C] \to [B \overset{\gamma}{\underset{+}{\succ}} C][\Gamma_1\Gamma_2]r() \mid \\
&\qquad r() = A(..) \to \Gamma_1 B(..\gamma)\Gamma_2 \in P_L\} && (7)\\
&\cup\{[A \overset{\gamma}{\underset{+}{\succ}} C] \to [\Gamma_1\Gamma_2]r() \mid \\
&\qquad r() = A(..\gamma) \to \Gamma_1 C(..)\Gamma_2 \in P_L\} && (8)\\
&\cup\{[A \overset{\gamma}{\underset{+}{\succ}} C] \to [\Gamma_1\Gamma_2]r()[A \underset{+}{\diamond} B] \mid \\
&\qquad r() = B(..\gamma) \to \Gamma_1 C(..)\Gamma_2 \in P_L\} && (9)
\end{aligned}$$

[5]Though in the referred paper, these relations are defined on constituents, the algorithm also applies to non-terminals.

[6]In fact we will only use *valid* non-terminals $[A\rho B]$ for which the relation ρ holds between A and B.

The productions in P^D define all the ways linear derivations can be composed from linear sub-derivations. This compositions rely on one side upon property 1 (recall that the productions in P_L, must be produced in reverse order) and, on the other side, upon the order in which secondary spines (the $\Gamma_1\Gamma_2$-spines) are processed to get the linear derivation order.

In (Boullier, 1996), we prove that LDGs are not ambiguous (in fact they are SLR(1)) and define

$$\begin{aligned}\mathcal{L}(D) \quad = \quad & \{r_1() \ldots r_n() \mid S() \overset{r_n()}{\underset{\ell,L}{\Rightarrow}} \ldots \overset{r_1()}{\underset{\ell,L}{\Rightarrow}} x \\ & \wedge x \in \mathcal{L}(L)\}\end{aligned}$$

If, by some classical algorithm, we remove from D all its useless symbols, we get a reduced CFG say $D' = (V_N^{D'}, V_T^{D'}, P^{D'}, S^{D'})$. In this grammar, all its terminal symbols, which are productions in L, are useful. By the way, the construction of D' solve the emptiness problem for LIGs: L specify the empty set iff the set $V_T^{D'}$ is empty[7].

5 LIG parsing

Given a LIG $L = (V_N, V_T, V_I, P_L, S)$ we want to find all the syntactic structures associated with an input string $x \in V_T^*$. In section 2 we used a CFG (the shared parse forest) for representing all parses in a CFG. In this section we will see how to build a CFG which represents all parses in a LIG.

In (Boullier, 1995) we give a recognizer for LIGs with the following scheme: in a first phase a general CF parsing algorithm, working on the CF-backbone builds a shared parse forest for a given input string x. In a second phase, the LIG conditions are checked on this forest. This checking can result in some subtree (production) deletions, namely the ones for which there is no valid symbol stack evaluation. If the resulting grammar is not empty, then x is a sentence. However, in the general case, this resulting grammar is not a shared parse forest for the initial LIG in the sense that the computation of stack of symbols along spines are not guaranteed to be consistent. Such invalid spines are not deleted during the check of the LIG conditions because they could be

[7]In (Vijay-Shanker and Weir, 1993) the emptiness problem for LIGs is solved by constructing an FSA.

composed of sub-spines which are themselves parts of other valid spines. One way to solve this problem is to unfold the shared parse forest and to extract individual parse trees. A parse tree is then kept iff the LIG conditions are valid on that tree. But such a method is not practical since the number of parse trees can be unbounded when the CF-backbone is cyclic. Even for non cyclic grammars, the number of parse trees can be exponential in the size of the input. Moreover, it is problematic that a worst case polynomial size structure could be reached by some sharing compatible both with the syntactic and the "semantic" features.

However, we know that derivations in TAGs are context-free (see (Vijay-Shanker, 1987)) and (Vijay-Shanker and Weir, 1993) exhibits a CFG which represents all possible derivation sequences in a TAG. We will show that the analogous holds for LIGs and leads to an $\mathcal{O}(n^6)$ time parsing algorithm.

Definition 4 *Let $L = (V_N, V_T, V_I, P_L, S)$ be a LIG, $G = (V_N, V_T, P_G, S)$ its CF-backbone, x a string in $\mathcal{L}(G)$, and $G^x = (V_N^x, V_T^x, P_G^x, S^x)$ its shared parse forest for x. We define the LIGed forest for x as being the LIG $L^x = (V_N^x, V_T^x, V_I, P_L^x, S^x)$ s.t. G^x is its CF-backbone and its productions are the productions of P_G^x in which the corresponding stack-schemas of L have been added. For example $r_p^q() = [A]_i^k(..\alpha) \to [B]_i^j(..\alpha')[C]_j^k() \in P_L^x$ iff $r_p^q = [A]_i^k \to [B]_i^j[C]_j^k \in P_G^x \wedge r_p = A \to BC \in G \wedge r_p() = A(..\alpha) \to B(..\alpha')C() \in L$.*

Between a LIG L and its LIGed forest L^x for x, we have:

$$x \in \mathcal{L}(L) \iff x \in \mathcal{L}(L^x)$$

If we follow(Lang, 1994), the previous definition which produces a LIGed forest from any L and x is a (LIG) parser[8]: given a LIG L and a string x, we have constructed a new LIG L^x for the intersection $\mathcal{L}(L) \cap \{x\}$, which is the shared forest for all parses of the sentences in the intersection. However, we wish to go one step further since the parsing (or even recognition) problem for LIGs cannot be trivially extracted from the LIGed forests.

Our vision for the parsing of a string x with a LIG L can be summarized in few lines. Let G be the CF-backbone of L, we first build G^x the CFG shared parse forest by any classical general CF parsing algorithm and then L^x its LIGed forest. Afterwards, we build the reduced LDG D_{L^x} associated with L^x as shown in section 4.

[8] Of course, instead of x, we can consider any FSA.

The recognition problem for (L, x) (i.e. is x an element of $\mathcal{L}(L)$) is equivalent to the non-emptiness of the production set of D_{L^x}.

Moreover, each linear $S()/x$-derivation in L is (the reverse of) a string in $\mathcal{L}(D_{L^x})$[9]. So the extraction of individual parses in a LIG is merely reduced to the derivation of strings in a CFG.

An important issue is about the complexity, in time and space, of D_{L^x}. Let n be the length of the input string x. Since G is in binary form we know that the shared parse forest G^x can be build in $\mathcal{O}(n^3)$ time and the number of its productions is also in $\mathcal{O}(n^3)$. Moreover, the cardinality of V_N^x is $\mathcal{O}(n^2)$ and, for any given non-terminal, say $[A]_p^q$, there are at most $\mathcal{O}(n)$ $[A]_p^q$-productions. Of course, these complexities extend to the LIGed forest L^x.

We now look at the LDG complexity when the input LIG is a LIGed forest. In fact, we mainly have to check two forms of productions (see definition 3). The first form is production (6) ($[A \underset{+}{\diamond} C] \to [B \underset{+}{\diamond} C][A \approx B]$), where three different non-terminals in V_N are implied (i.e. A, B and C), so the number of productions of that form is cubic in the number of non-terminals and therefore is $\mathcal{O}(n^6)$.

In the second form (productions (5), (7) and (9)), exemplified by $[A \approx C] \to [B \overset{\gamma}{\underset{+}{\succ}} C][\Gamma_1\Gamma_2]r()$, there are four non-terminals in V_N (i.e. A, B, C, and X if $\Gamma_1\Gamma_2 = X()$) and a production $r()$ (the number of relation symbols $\overset{\gamma}{\underset{+}{\succ}}$ is a constant), therefore, the number of such productions seems to be of fourth degree in the number of non-terminals and linear in the number of productions. However, these variables are not independant. For a given A, the number of triples $(B, X, r())$ is the number of A-productions hence $\mathcal{O}(n)$. So, at the end, the number of productions of that form is $\mathcal{O}(n^5)$.

We can easily check that the other form of productions have a lesser degree.

Therefore, the number of productions is dominated by the first form and the size (and in fact the construction time) of this grammar is $\mathcal{O}(n^6)$.

This (once again) shows that the recognition and parsing problem for a LIG can be solved in $\mathcal{O}(n^6)$ time.

For a LDG $D = (V_N^D, V_T^D, P^D, S^D)$, we note that for any given non-terminal $A \in V_N^D$ and string $\sigma \in \mathcal{L}(A)$ with $|\sigma| \geq 2$, a single production $A \to X_1X_2$ or $A \to X_1X_2X_3$ in P^D is needed to "cut" σ into two or three non-empty pieces σ_1, σ_2, and σ_3, such that

[9] In fact, the terminal symbols in D_{L^x} are productions in L^x (say $R_p^q()$), which trivially can be mapped to productions in L (here $r_p()$).

$X_i \overset{*}{\underset{D}{\Rightarrow}} \sigma_i$, except when the production form number (4) is used. In such a case, this cutting needs two productions (namely (4) and (7)). This shows that the cutting out of any string of length l, into elementary pieces of length 1, is performed in using $\mathcal{O}(l)$ productions. Therefore, the extraction of a linear $S()/x$-derivation in L is performed in time linear with the length of that derivation. If we assume that the CF-backbone G is non cyclic, the extraction of a parse is linear in n. Moreover, during an extraction, since D_{L^x} is not ambiguous, at some place, the choice of another A-production will result in a different linear derivation.

Of course, practical generations of LDGs must improve over a blind application of definition 3. One way is to consider a top-down strategy: the X-productions in a LDG are generated iff X is the start symbol or occurs in the RHS of an already generated production. The examples in section 6 are produced this way.

If the number of ambiguities in the initial LIG is bounded, the size of D_{L^x}, for a given input string x of length n, is linear in n.

The size and the time needed to compute D_{L^x} are closely related to the actual sizes of the $\underset{+}{\diamond}$, $\overset{\gamma}{\underset{+}{\succ}}$ and $\approx$ relations. As pointed out in (Boullier, 1995), their $\mathcal{O}(n^4)$ maximum sizes seem to be seldom reached in practice. This means that the average parsing time is much better than this $\mathcal{O}(n^6)$ worst case.

Moreover, our parsing schema allow to avoid some useless computations. Assume that the symbol $[A \underset{+}{\diamond} B]$ is useless in the LDG D_L associated with the initial LIG L, we know that any non-terminal s.t. $[[A]_i^j \underset{+}{\diamond} [B]_k^l]$ is also useless in D_{L^x}. Therefore, the static computation of a reduced LDG for the initial LIG L (and the corresponding $\underset{+}{\diamond}$, $\overset{\gamma}{\underset{+}{\succ}}$ and $\approx$ relations) can be used to direct the parsing process and decrease the parsing time (see section 6).

6 Two Examples

6.1 First Example

In this section, we illustrate our algorithm with a LIG $L = (\{S, T\}, \{a, b, c\}, \{\gamma_a, \gamma_b, \gamma_c\}, P_L, S)$ where P_L contains the following productions:

$$
\begin{array}{ll}
r_1() = S(..) \to S(..\gamma_a)a & r_2() = S(..) \to S(..\gamma_b)b \\
r_3() = S(..) \to S(..\gamma_c)c & r_4() = S(..) \to T(..) \\
r_5() = T(..\gamma_a) \to aT(..) & r_6() = T(..\gamma_b) \to bT(..) \\
r_7() = T(..\gamma_c) \to cT(..) & r_8() = T() \to c
\end{array}
$$

It is easy to see that its CF-backbone G, whose production set P_G is:

$$
\begin{array}{llll}
S \to Sa & S \to Sb & S \to Sc & S \to T \\
T \to aT & T \to bT & T \to cT & T \to c
\end{array}
$$

defines the language $\mathcal{L}(G) = \{wcw' \mid w, w' \in \{a, b, c\}^*\}$. We remark that the stacks of symbols in L constrain the string w' to be equal to w and therefore the language $\mathcal{L}(L)$ is $\{wcw \mid w \in \{a, b, c\}^*\}$.

We note that in L the key part is played by the middle c, introduced by production $r_8()$, and that this grammar is non ambiguous, while in G the symbol c, introduced by the last production $T \to c$, is only a separator between w and w' and that this grammar is ambiguous (any occurrence of c may be this separator).

The computation of the relations gives:

$$
\begin{array}{ccccccc}
 & & & & \underset{1}{\diamond} & = & \{(S,T)\} \\
\overset{\gamma_a}{\underset{1}{\prec}} & = & \overset{\gamma_b}{\underset{1}{\prec}} & = & \overset{\gamma_c}{\underset{1}{\prec}} & = & \{(S,S)\} \\
\overset{\gamma_a}{\underset{1}{\succ}} & = & \overset{\gamma_b}{\underset{1}{\succ}} & = & \overset{\gamma_c}{\underset{1}{\succ}} & = & \{(T,T)\} \\
 & & & & \underset{+}{\diamond} & = & \{(S,T)\} \\
 & & & & \approx & = & \{(S,T)\} \\
\overset{\gamma_a}{\underset{+}{\succ}} & = & \overset{\gamma_b}{\underset{+}{\succ}} & = & \overset{\gamma_c}{\underset{+}{\succ}} & = & \{(T,T),(S,T)\}
\end{array}
$$

The production set P^D of the LDG D associated with L is:

$$
\begin{array}{lcll}
[S] & \to & r_8()[S \underset{+}{\diamond} T] & (2) \\
[S \underset{+}{\diamond} T] & \to & r_4() & (3) \\
[S \underset{+}{\diamond} T] & \to & [S \approx T] & (4) \\
[S \approx T] & \to & [S \overset{\gamma_a}{\underset{+}{\succ}} T]r_1() & (7) \\
[S \approx T] & \to & [S \overset{\gamma_b}{\underset{+}{\succ}} T]r_2() & (7) \\
[S \approx T] & \to & [S \overset{\gamma_c}{\underset{+}{\succ}} T]r_3() & (7) \\
[S \overset{\gamma_a}{\underset{+}{\succ}} T] & \to & r_5()[S \underset{+}{\diamond} T] & (9) \\
[S \overset{\gamma_b}{\underset{+}{\succ}} T] & \to & r_6()[S \underset{+}{\diamond} T] & (9) \\
[S \overset{\gamma_c}{\underset{+}{\succ}} T] & \to & r_7()[S \underset{+}{\diamond} T] & (9)
\end{array}
$$

The numbers (i) refer to definition 3. We can easily checked that this grammar is reduced.

Let $x = ccc$ be an input string. Since x is an element of $\mathcal{L}(G)$, its shared parse forest G^x is not empty. Its production set P_G^x is:

$$
\begin{array}{ll}
r_3^1 = [S]_0^3 \to [S]_0^2 c & r_4^2 = [S]_0^3 \to [T]_0^3 \\
r_3^3 = [S]_0^2 \to [S]_0^1 c & r_4^4 = [S]_0^2 \to [T]_0^2 \\
r_4^5 = [S]_0^1 \to [T]_0^1 & r_7^6 = [T]_0^3 \to c[T]_1^3 \\
r_7^7 = [T]_1^3 \to c[T]_2^3 & r_8^8 = [T]_2^3 \to c \\
r_7^9 = [T]_0^2 \to c[T]_1^2 & r_8^{10} = [T]_1^2 \to c \\
r_8^{11} = [T]_0^1 \to c &
\end{array}
$$

We can observe that this shared parse forest denotes in fact three different parse trees. Each one corresponding to a different cutting out of $x = wcw'$ (i.e. $w = \varepsilon$ and $w' = cc$, or $w = c$ and $w' = c$, or $w = cc$ and $w' = \varepsilon$).

The corresponding LIGed forest whose start symbol is $S^x = [S]_0^3$ and production set P_L^x is:

$$
\begin{array}{lcll}
r_3^1() & = & [S]_0^3(..) & \to [S]_0^2(..\gamma_c)c \\
r_4^2() & = & [S]_0^3(..) & \to [T]_0^3(..) \\
r_3^3() & = & [S]_0^2(..) & \to [S]_0^1(..\gamma_c)c \\
r_4^4() & = & [S]_0^2(..) & \to [T]_0^2(..) \\
r_4^5() & = & [S]_0^1(..) & \to [T]_0^1(..) \\
r_7^6() & = & [T]_0^3(..\gamma_c) & \to c[T]_1^3(..) \\
r_7^7() & = & [T]_1^3(..\gamma_c) & \to c[T]_2^3(..) \\
r_8^8() & = & [T]_2^3() & \to c \\
r_7^9() & = & [T]_0^2(..\gamma_c) & \to c[T]_1^2(..) \\
r_8^{10}() & = & [T]_1^2() & \to c \\
r_8^{11}() & = & [T]_0^1() & \to c
\end{array}
$$

For this LIGed forest the relations are:

$$
\begin{array}{lcl}
\underset{1}{\diamond} & = & \{([S]_0^3, [T]_0^3), ([S]_0^2, [T]_0^2), ([S]_0^1, [T]_0^1)\} \\
\overset{\gamma_c}{\underset{1}{\prec}} & = & \{([S]_0^3, [S]_0^2), ([S]_0^2, [S]_0^1)\} \\
\overset{\gamma_c}{\underset{1}{\succ}} & = & \{([T]_0^3, [T]_1^3), ([T]_1^3, [T]_2^3), ([T]_0^2, [T]_1^2)\} \\
\approx & = & \{([S]_0^3, [T]_1^2)\} \\
\underset{+}{\diamond} & = & \underset{1}{\diamond} \cup \approx \\
\overset{\gamma_c}{\underset{+}{\succ}} & = & \overset{\gamma_c}{\underset{1}{\succ}} \cup \{([S]_0^3, [T]_1^3), ([S]_0^2, [T]_1^2)\}
\end{array}
$$

The start symbol of the LDG associated with the LIGed forest L^x is $[[S]_0^3]$. If we assume that an A-production is generated iff it is an $[[S]_0^3]$-production or A occurs in an already generated production, we get:

$$
\begin{array}{lcll}
[[S]_0^3] & \to & r_8^{10}()[[S]_0^3 \underset{+}{\diamond} [T]_1^2] & (2) \\
[[S]_0^3 \underset{+}{\diamond} [T]_1^2] & \to & [[S]_0^3 \approx [T]_1^2] & (4) \\
[[S]_0^3 \approx [T]_1^2] & \to & [[S]_0^2 \overset{\gamma_c}{\underset{+}{\succ}} [T]_1^2]r_3^1() & (7) \\
[[S]_0^2 \overset{\gamma_c}{\underset{+}{\succ}} [T]_1^2] & \to & r_7^9()[[S]_0^2 \underset{+}{\diamond} [T]_0^2] & (9) \\
[[S]_0^2 \underset{+}{\diamond} [T]_0^2] & \to & r_4^4() & (3)
\end{array}
$$

This CFG is reduced. Since its production set is non empty, we have $ccc \in \mathcal{L}(L)$. Its language is $\{r_8^{10}()r_7^9()r_4^4()r_3^1()\}$ which shows that the only linear derivation in L is $S() \overset{r_3()}{\underset{\ell,L}{\Rightarrow}} S(\gamma_c)c \overset{r_4()}{\underset{\ell,L}{\Rightarrow}} T(\gamma_c)c \overset{r_7()}{\underset{\ell,L}{\Rightarrow}} cT()c \overset{r_8()}{\underset{\ell,L}{\Rightarrow}} ccc$.

In computing the relations for the initial LIG L, we remark that though $T \overset{\gamma_a}{\underset{+}{\succ}} T$, $T \overset{\gamma_b}{\underset{+}{\succ}} T$, and $T \overset{\gamma_c}{\underset{+}{\succ}} T$, the non-terminals $[T \overset{\gamma_a}{\underset{+}{\succ}} T]$, $[T \overset{\gamma_b}{\underset{+}{\succ}} T]$, and $[T \overset{\gamma_c}{\underset{+}{\succ}} T]$ are not used in P^D. This means that for any LIGed forest L^x, the elements of the form $([T]_p^q, [T]_{p'}^{q'})$ do not need to be computed in the $\overset{\gamma_a}{\underset{+}{\succ}}$, $\overset{\gamma_b}{\underset{+}{\succ}}$, and $\overset{\gamma_c}{\underset{+}{\succ}}$ relations since they will never produce a useful non-terminal. In this example, the subset $\overset{\gamma_c}{\underset{1}{\succ}}$ of $\overset{\gamma_c}{\underset{+}{\succ}}$ is useless.

The next example shows the handling of a cyclic grammar.

6.2 Second Example

The following LIG L, where A is the start symbol:

$$
\begin{array}{ll}
r_1() = A(..) \to A(..\gamma_a) & r_2() = A(..) \to B(..) \\
r_3() = B(..\gamma_a) \to B(..) & r_4() = B() \to a
\end{array}
$$

is cyclic (we have $A \overset{+}{\Rightarrow} A$ and $B \overset{+}{\Rightarrow} B$ in its CF-backbone), and the stack schemas in production $r_1()$ indicate that an unbounded number of push γ_a actions can take place, while production $r_3()$ indicates an unbounded number of pops. Its CF-backbone is unbounded ambiguous though its language contains the single string a.

The computation of the relations gives:

$$
\begin{array}{lcl}
\underset{1}{\diamond} & = & \{(A, B)\} \\
\overset{\gamma_a}{\underset{1}{\prec}} & = & \{(A, A)\} \\
\overset{\gamma_a}{\underset{1}{\succ}} & = & \{(B, B)\} \\
\underset{+}{\diamond} & = & \{(A, B)\} \\
\approx & = & \{(A, B)\} \\
\overset{\gamma_a}{\underset{+}{\succ}} & = & \{(A, B), (B, B)\}
\end{array}
$$

The start symbol of the LDG associated with L is $[A]$ and its productions set P^D is:

$$
\begin{array}{lcll}
[A] & \to & r_4()[A \underset{+}{\diamond} B] & (2) \\
[A \underset{+}{\diamond} B] & \to & r_2() & (3) \\
[A \underset{+}{\diamond} B] & \to & [A \approx B] & (4) \\
[A \approx B] & \to & [A \overset{\gamma_a}{\underset{+}{\succ}} B]r_1() & (7) \\
[A \overset{\gamma_a}{\underset{+}{\succ}} B] & \to & r_3()[A \underset{+}{\diamond} B] & (9)
\end{array}
$$

We can easily checked that this grammar is reduced.

We want to parse the input string $x = a$ (i.e. find all the linear $S()/a$-derivations).

Its LIGed forest, whose start symbol is $[A]_0^1$ is:

$$\begin{array}{lcll} r_1^1() & = & [A]_0^1(..) & \rightarrow & [A]_0^1(..\gamma_a) \\ r_2^2() & = & [A]_0^1(..) & \rightarrow & [B]_0^1(..) \\ r_3^3() & = & [B]_0^1(..\gamma_a) & \rightarrow & [B]_0^1(..) \\ r_4^4() & = & [B]_0^1() & \rightarrow & a \end{array}$$

For this LIGed forest L^x, the relations are:

$$\begin{array}{lcl} \underset{1}{\diamond} & = & \{([A]_0^1, [B]_0^1)\} \\ \overset{\gamma_a}{\underset{1}{\prec}} & = & \{([A]_0^1, [A]_0^1)\} \\ \overset{\gamma_a}{\underset{1}{\succ}} & = & \{([B]_0^1, [B]_0^1)\} \\ \approx & = & \{([A]_0^1, [B]_0^1)\} \\ \underset{+}{\diamond} & = & \{([A]_0^1, [B]_0^1)\} \\ \overset{\gamma_a}{\underset{+}{\succ}} & = & \{([A]_0^1, [B]_0^1), ([B]_0^1, [B]_0^1)\} \end{array}$$

The start symbol of the LDG associated with L^x is $[[A]_0^1]$. If we assume that an A-production is generated iff it is an $[[A]_0^1]$-production or A occurs in an already generated production, its production set is:

$$\begin{array}{lcll} [[A]_0^1] & \rightarrow & r_4^4()[[A]_0^1 \underset{+}{\diamond} [B]_0^1] & (2) \\ [[A]_0^1 \underset{+}{\diamond} [B]_0^1] & \rightarrow & r_2^2() & (3) \\ [[A]_0^1 \underset{+}{\diamond} [B]_0^1] & \rightarrow & [[A]_0^1 \approx [B]_0^1] & (4) \\ [[A]_0^1 \approx [B]_0^1] & \rightarrow & [[A]_0^1 \overset{\gamma_a}{\underset{+}{\succ}} [B]_0^1]r_1^1() & (7) \\ [[A]_0^1 \overset{\gamma_a}{\underset{+}{\succ}} [B]_0^1] & \rightarrow & r_3^3()[[A]_0^1 \underset{+}{\diamond} [B]_0^1] & (9) \end{array}$$

This CFG is reduced. Since its production set is non empty, we have $a \in \mathcal{L}(L)$. Its language is $\{r_4^4()\{r_3^3()\}^k r_2^2()\{r_1^1()\}^k \mid 0 \leq k\}$ which shows that the only valid linear derivations w.r.t. L must contain an identical number k of productions which push γ_a (i.e. the production $r_1()$) and productions which pop γ_a (i.e. the production $r_3()$).

As in the previous example, we can see that the element $[B]_0^1 \overset{\gamma_a}{\underset{+}{\succ}} [B]_0^1$ is useless.

7 Conclusion

We have shown that the parses of a LIG can be represented by a non ambiguous CFG. This representation captures the fact that the values of a stack of symbols is well parenthesized. When a symbol γ is pushed on a stack at a given index at some place, this very symbol must be popped some place else, and we know that such (recursive) pairing is the essence of context-freeness.

In this approach, the number of productions and the construction time of this CFG is at worst $\mathcal{O}(n^6)$, though much better results occur in practical situations. Moreover, static computations on the initial LIG may decrease this practical complexity in avoiding useless computations. Each sentence in this CFG is a derivation of the given input string by the LIG, and is extracted in linear time.

References

Pierre Boullier. 1995. Yet another $\mathcal{O}(n^6)$ recognition algorithm for mildly context-sensitive languages. In *Proceedings of the fourth international workshop on parsing technologies (IWPT'95)*, Prague and Karlovy Vary, Czech Republic, pages 34–47. See also *Research Report No 2730* at `http://www.inria.fr/RRRT/RR-2730.html`, INRIA-Rocquencourt, France, Nov. 1995, 22 pages.

Pierre Boullier. 1996. Another Facet of LIG Parsing (extended version). In *Research Report No 2858* at `http://www.inria.fr/RRRT/RR-2858.html`, INRIA-Rocquencourt, France, Apr. 1996, 22 pages.

Bernard Lang. 1991. Towards a uniform formal framework for parsing. In *Current Issues in Parsing Technology*, edited by M. Tomita, Kluwer Academic Publishers, pages 153–171.

Bernard Lang. 1994. Recognition can be harder than parsing. In *Computational Intelligence*, Vol. 10, No. 4, pages 486–494.

Yves Schabes, Stuart M. Shieber. 1994. An Alternative Conception of Tree-Adjoining Derivation. In *ACL Computational Linguistics*, Vol. 20, No. 1, pages 91–124.

K. Vijay-Shanker. 1987. A study of tree adjoining grammars. *PhD thesis*, University of Pennsylvania.

K. Vijay-Shanker, David J. Weir. 1993. The Used of Shared Forests in Tree Adjoining Grammar Parsing. In *Proceedings of the 6th Conference of the European Chapter of the Association for Computational Linguistics (EACL'93)*, Utrecht, The Netherlands, pages 384–393.

K. Vijay-Shanker, David J. Weir. 1994. Parsing some constrained grammar formalisms. In *ACL Computational Linguistics*, Vol. 19, No. 4, pages 591–636.

K. Vijay-Shanker, David J. Weir, Owen Rambow. 1995. Parsing D-Tree Grammars. In *Proceedings of the fourth international workshop on parsing technologies (IWPT'95)*, Prague and Karlovy Vary, Czech Republic, pages 252–259.

Parsing for Semidirectional Lambek Grammar is NP-Complete

Jochen Dörre

Institut für maschinelle Sprachverarbeitung
University of Stuttgart

Abstract

We study the computational complexity of the parsing problem of a variant of Lambek Categorial Grammar that we call *semidirectional*. In semidirectional Lambek calculus SDL there is an additional nondirectional abstraction rule allowing the formula abstracted over to appear anywhere in the premise sequent's left-hand side, thus permitting non-peripheral extraction. SDL grammars are able to generate each context-free language and more than that. We show that the parsing problem for semidirectional Lambek Grammar is NP-complete by a reduction of the 3-Partition problem.

Key words: computational complexity, Lambek Categorial Grammar

1 Introduction

Categorial Grammar (CG) and in particular Lambek Categorial Grammar (LCG) have their well-known benefits for the formal treatment of natural language syntax and semantics. The most outstanding of these benefits is probably the fact that the specific way, how the complete grammar is encoded, namely in terms of 'combinatory potentials' of its words, gives us at the same time recipes for the construction of meanings, once the words have been combined with others to form larger linguistic entities. Although both frameworks are equivalent in weak generative capacity — both derive exactly the context-free languages —, LCG is superior to CG in that it can cope in a natural way with extraction and unbounded dependency phenomena. For instance, no special category assignments need to be stipulated to handle a relative clause containing a trace, because it is analyzed, via hypothetical reasoning, like a traceless clause with the trace being the hypothesis to be discharged when combined with the relative pronoun.

Figure 1 illustrates this proof-logical behaviour. Notice that this natural-deduction-style proof in the type logic corresponds very closely to the phrase-structure tree one would like to adopt in an analysis with traces. We thus can derive `Bill misses` ϵ as an s from the hypothesis that there is a "phantom" np in the place of the trace. Discharging the hypothesis, indicated by index 1, results in `Bill misses` being analyzed as an s/np from zero hypotheses. Observe, however, that such a bottom-up synthesis of a new unsaturated type is only required, if that type is to be consumed (as the antecedent of an implication) by another type. Otherwise there would be a simpler proof without this abstraction. In our example the relative pronoun has such a complex type triggering an extraction.

A drawback of the pure Lambek Calculus L is that it only allows for so-called 'peripheral extraction', i.e., in our example the trace should better be initial or final in the relative clause.

This inflexibility of Lambek Calculus is one of the reasons why many researchers study richer systems today. For instance, the recent work by Moortgat (Moortgat 94) gives a systematic in-depth study of mixed Lambek systems, which integrate the systems L, NL, NLP, and LP. These ingredient systems are obtained by varying the Lambek calculus along two dimensions: adding the permutation rule (P) and/or dropping the assumption that the type combinator (which forms the sequences the systems talk about) is associative (N for *non-associative*).

Taken for themselves these variants of L are of little use in linguistic descriptions. But in Moortgat's mixed system all the different resource management modes of the different systems are left intact in the combination and can be exploited in different parts of the grammar. The relative pronoun `which` would, for instance, receive category $(np\backslash np)/(np \multimap s)$ with $\multimap$ being implication in LP,[1] i.e., it requires

[1] The Lambek calculus with permutation LP is also called the "nondirectional Lambek calculus" (Benthem 88). In it the leftward and rightward implication

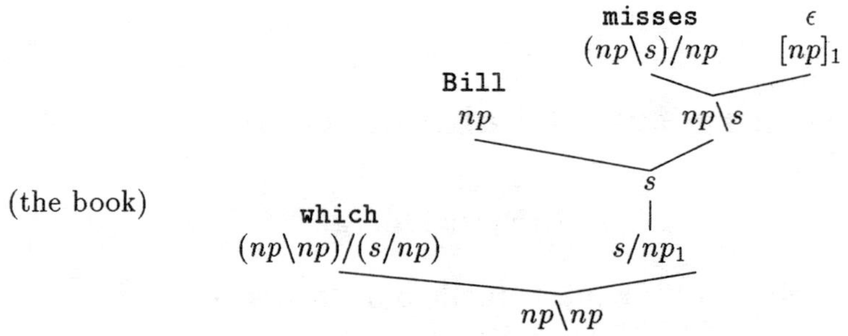

Figure 1: Extraction as resource-conscious hypothetical reasoning

as an argument "an s lacking an np somewhere".[2].

The present paper studies the computational complexity of a variant of the Lambek Calculus that lies between L and LP, the Semidirectional Lambek Calculus SDL.[3] Since LP derivability is known to be NP-complete, it is interesting to study restrictions on the use of the LP operator $\multimap$. A restriction that leaves its proposed linguistic applications intact is to admit a type $B \multimap A$ only as the argument type in functional applications, but never as the functor. Stated prove-theoretically for Gentzen-style systems, this amounts to disallowing the left rule for $\multimap$. Surprisingly, the resulting system SDL can be stated without the need for structural rules, i.e., as a monolithic system with just one structural connective, because the ability of the abstracted-over formula to permute can be directly encoded in the right rule for $\multimap$. [4]

Note that our purpose for studying SDL is not that it might be in any sense better suited for a theory of grammar (except perhaps, because of its simplicity), but rather, because it exhibits a core of logical behaviour that any richer system also needs to include, at least if it should allow for non-peripheral extraction. The sources of complexity uncovered here are thus a forteriori present in all these richer systems as well.

collapse.

[2]Morrill (Morrill 94) achieves the same effect with a permutation modality Δ applied to the np gap: $(s/\Delta np)$

[3]This name was coined by Esther König-Baumer, who employs a variant of this calculus in her LexGram system (König 95) for practical grammar development.

[4]It should be pointed out that the resource management in this calculus is very closely related to the handling and interaction of local valency and unbounded dependencies in HPSG. The latter being handled with set-valued features SLASH, QUE and REL essentially emulates the permutation potential of abstracted categories in semidirectional Lambek Grammar. A more detailed analysis of the relation between HPSG and SDL is given in (König 95).

2 Semidirectional Lambek Grammar

2.1 Lambek calculus

The semidirectional Lambek calculus (henceforth SDL) is a variant of J. Lambek's original (Lambek 58) calculus of syntactic types. We start by defining the Lambek calculus and extend it to obtain SDL.

Formulae (also called "syntactic types") are built from a set of propositional variables (or "primitive types") $\mathcal{B} = \{b_1, b_2, \ldots\}$ and the three binary connectives $\bullet$, $\backslash$, $/$, called *product, left implication*, and *right implication*. We use generally capital letters A, B, C, ... to denote formulae and capitals towards the end of the alphabet T, U, V, ... to denote sequences of formulae. The concatenation of sequences U and V is denoted by (U, V).

The (usual) formal framework of these logics is a Gentzen-style sequent calculus. Sequents are pairs (U, A), written as $U \Rightarrow A$, where A is a type and U is a sequence of types.[5] The claim embodied by sequent $U \Rightarrow A$ can be read as "formula A is derivable from the structured database U". Figure 2 shows Lambek's original calculus L.

First of all, since we don't need products to obtain our results and since they only complicate matters, we eliminate products from consideration in the sequel.

In Semidirectional Lambek Calculus we add as additional connective the LP implication $\multimap$, but equip it only with a right rule.

$$\frac{U, B, V \Rightarrow A}{T \Rightarrow B \multimap A} (\multimap R) \text{ if } T = (U, V) \text{ nonempty.}$$

[5]In contrast to Linear Logic (Girard 87) the order of types in U is essential, since the structural rule of permutation is not assumed to hold. Moreover, the fact that only a single formula may appear on the right of $\Rightarrow$, make the Lambek calculus an intuitionistic fragment of the multiplicative fragment of non-commutative propositional Linear Logic.

$$\frac{}{b \Rightarrow b}\ (Ax)$$

$$\frac{T \Rightarrow B \quad U, A, V \Rightarrow C}{U, A/B, T, V \Rightarrow C}\ (/L) \qquad \frac{U, B \Rightarrow A}{U \Rightarrow A/B}\ (/R) \text{ if } U \text{ nonempty}$$

$$\frac{T \Rightarrow B \quad U, A, V \Rightarrow C}{U, T, B\backslash A, V \Rightarrow C}\ (\backslash L) \qquad \frac{B, U \Rightarrow A}{U \Rightarrow B\backslash A}\ (\backslash R) \text{ if } U \text{ nonempty}$$

$$\frac{U, A, B, V \Rightarrow C}{U, A \bullet B, V \Rightarrow C}\ (\bullet L) \qquad \frac{U \Rightarrow A \quad V \Rightarrow B}{U, V \Rightarrow A \bullet B}\ (\bullet R)$$

$$\frac{T \Rightarrow A \quad U, A, V \Rightarrow C}{U, T, V \Rightarrow C}\ (Cut)$$

Figure 2: Lambek calculus L

Let us define the polarity of a subformula of a sequent $A_1, \ldots, A_n \Rightarrow A$ as follows: A has positive polarity, each of A_i have negative polarity and if B/C or $C\backslash B$ has polarity p, then B also has polarity p and C has the opposite polarity of p in the sequent.

A consequence of only allowing the $(\multimap R)$ rule, which is easily proved by induction, is that in any derivable sequent $\multimap$ may only appear in positive polarity. Hence, $\multimap$ may not occur in the (cut) formula A of a (Cut) application and any subformula $B \multimap A$ which occurs somewhere in the prove must also occur in the final sequent. When we assume the final sequent's RHS to be primitive (or $\multimap$-less), then the $(\multimap R)$ rule will be used exactly once for each (positively) occuring $\multimap$-subformula. In other words, $(\multimap R)$ may only do what it is supposed to do: extraction, and we can directly read off the category assignment which extractions there will be.

We can show Cut Elimination for this calculus by a straight-forward adaptation of the Cut elimination proof for L. We omit the proof for reasons of space.

Proposition 1 (Cut Elimination) *Each SDL-derivable sequent has a cut-free proof.*

The cut-free system enjoys, as usual for Lambek-like logics, the *Subformula Property*: in any proof only subformulae of the goal sequent may appear.

In our considerations below we will make heavy use of the well-known count invariant for Lambek systems (Benthem 88), which is an expression of the resource-consciousness of these logics. Define $\#_b(A)$ (*the b-count of A*), a function counting positive and negative occurrences of primitive type b in an arbitrary type A, to be

$$\#_b(A) = \begin{cases} 1 & \text{if } A = b \\ 0 & \text{if } A \text{ primitive and } A \neq b \\ \#_b(B) - \#_b(C) & \text{if } A = B/C \text{ or } A = C\backslash B \\ & \quad \text{or } A = C \multimap B \\ \#_b(B) + \#_b(C) & \text{if } A = B \bullet C \end{cases}$$

The invariant now states that for any primitive b, the b-count of the RHS and the LHS of any derivable sequent are the same. By noticing that this invariant is true for (Ax) and is preserved by the rules, we immediately can state:

Proposition 2 (Count Invariant) *If* $\vdash_{\mathsf{SDL}} U \Rightarrow A$, *then* $\#_b(U) = \#_b(A)$ *for any* $b \in \mathcal{B}$.

Let us in parallel to SDL consider the fragment of it in which $(/R)$ and $(\backslash R)$ are disallowed. We call this fragment SDL$^-$. Remarkable about this fragment is that any positive occurrence of an implication must be $\multimap$ and any negative one must be $/$ or $\backslash$.

2.2 Lambek Grammar

Definition 3 *We define a* Lambek grammar *to be a quadruple* $\langle \Sigma, \mathcal{F}, b_S, l \rangle$ *consisting of the finite alphabet of terminals* Σ, *the set* $\mathcal{F}$ *of all Lambek formulae generated from some set of propositional variables which includes the distinguished variable* s, *and the lexical map* $l : \Sigma \to 2^{\mathcal{F}}$ *which maps each terminal to a finite subset of* $\mathcal{F}$.

We extend the lexical map l to nonempty strings of terminals by setting $l(w_1 w_2 \ldots w_n) := l(w_1) \times l(w_2) \times \ldots \times l(w_n)$ for $w_1 w_2 \ldots w_n \in \Sigma^+$.

The *language generated by a Lambek grammar* $G = \langle \Sigma, \mathcal{F}, b_S, l \rangle$ is defined as the set of all strings $w_1 w_2 \ldots w_n \in \Sigma^+$ for which there exists a sequence

$$\vdots$$

$$\dfrac{x \Rightarrow x \qquad \dfrac{B_1^n,\, B_2,\, C_1^n,\, C_2,\, c^{n+1},\, b^{n+1} \Rightarrow y\ (\star)}{B_1^n,\, B_2,\, C_1^n,\, C_2,\, c^n,\, b^n \Rightarrow c \multimap (b \multimap y)}\,2{\times}(\multimap R)}{A_2,\, B_1^n,\, B_2,\, C_1^n,\, C_2,\, c^n,\, b^n \Rightarrow x}\,(/L)$$

$$\vdots$$

$$\dfrac{x \Rightarrow x \qquad \dfrac{A_1^{n-1},\, A_2,\, B_1^n,\, B_2,\, C_1^n,\, C_2,\, c,\, b \Rightarrow x}{A_1^{n-1},\, A_2,\, B_1^n,\, B_2,\, C_1^n,\, C_2 \Rightarrow c \multimap (b \multimap x)}\,2{\times}(\multimap R)}{A_1^n,\, A_2,\, B_1^n,\, B_2,\, C_1^n,\, C_2 \Rightarrow x}\,(/L)$$

Figure 3: Proof of $A_1^n, A_2, B_1^n, B_2, C_1^n, C_2 \Rightarrow x$

of types $U \in l(w_1 w_2 \ldots w_n)$ and $\vdash_{\mathsf{L}} U \Rightarrow b_S$. We denote this language by $L(G)$.

An *SDL-grammar* is defined exactly like a Lambek grammar, except that $\vdash_{\mathsf{SDL}}$ replaces $\vdash_{\mathsf{L}}$.

Given a grammar G and a string $w = w_1 w_2 \ldots w_n$, the *parsing (or recognition) problem* asks the question, whether w is in $L(G)$.

It is not immediately obvious, how the generative capacity of SDL-grammars relate to Lambek grammars or nondirectional Lambek grammars (based on calculus LP). Whereas Lambek grammars generate exactly the context-free languages (modulo the missing empty word) (Pentus 93), the latter generate all permutation closures of context-free languages (Benthem 88). This excludes many context-free or even regular languages, but includes some context-sensitive ones, e.g., the permutation closure of $a^n b^n c^n$.

Concerning SDL, it is straightforward to show that all context-free languages can be generated by SDL-grammars.

Proposition 4 *Every context-free language is generated by some SDL-grammar.*

Proof. We can use a the standard transformation of an arbitrary cfr. grammar $G = \langle N, T, P, S\rangle$ to a categorial grammar G'. Since $\multimap$ does not appear in G' each SDL-proof of a lexical assignment must be also an L-proof, i.e. exactly the same strings are judged grammatical by SDL as are judged by L. □

Note that since the $\{(Ax), (/L), (\backslash L)\}$ subset of L already accounts for the cfr. languages, this observation extends to SDL^-.

Moreover, some languages which are not context-free can also be generated.

Example. Consider the following grammar G for the language $a^n b^n c^n$. We use primitive types $\mathcal{B} = \{b, c, x, y, z\}$ and define the lexical map for $\Sigma = \{a, b, c\}$ as follows:

$$\begin{aligned} l(a) &:= \{\, \underbrace{x/(c \multimap (b \multimap x))}_{=A_1},\ \underbrace{x/(c \multimap (b \multimap y))}_{=A_2} \,\} \\ l(b) &:= \{\, \underbrace{(y/b)/y}_{=B_1},\ \underbrace{(y/b)/z}_{=B_2} \,\} \\ l(c) &:= \{\, \underbrace{(z/c)/z}_{=C_1},\ \underbrace{z/c}_{=C_2} \,\}. \end{aligned}$$

The distinguished primitive type is x. To simplify the argumentation, we abbreviate types as indicated above.

Now, observe that a sequent $U \Rightarrow x$, where U is the image of some string over Σ, only then may have balanced primitive counts, if U contains exactly one occurrence of each of A_2, B_2 and C_2 (accounting for the one supernumerary x and balanced y and z counts) and for some number $n \geq 0$, n occurrences of each of A_1, B_1, and C_1 (because, resource-oriented speaking, each B_i and C_i "consume" a b and c, resp., and each A_i "provides" a pair b, c). Hence, only strings containing the same number of a's, b's and c's may be produced. Furthermore, due to the Subformula Property we know that in a cut-free proof of $U \Rightarrow x$, the main formula in abstractions (right rules) may only be either $c \multimap (b \multimap X)$ or $b \multimap X$, where $X \in \{x, y\}$, since all other implication types have primitive antecedents. Hence, the LHS of any sequent in the proof must be a subsequence of U, with some additional b types and c types interspersed. But then it is easy to show that U can only be of the form

$$A_1^n,\, A_2,\, B_1^n,\, B_2,\, C_1^n,\, C_2,$$

since any / connective in U needs to be introduced via $(/L)$.

It remains to be shown, that there is actually a proof for such a sequent. It is given in Figure 3.

The sequent marked with $\star$ is easily seen to be derivable without abstractions.

A remarkable point about SDL's ability to cover this language is that neither L nor LP can generate it. Hence, this example substantiates the claim made in

(Moortgat 94) that the inferential capacity of mixed Lambek systems may be greater than the sum of its component parts. Moreover, the attentive reader will have noticed that our encoding also extends to languages having more groups of n symbols, i.e., to languages of the form $a_1^n a_2^n \ldots a_k^n$.

Finally, we note in passing that for this grammar the rules $(/R)$ and $(\backslash R)$ are irrelevant, i.e. that it is at the same time an SDL^- grammar.

3 NP-Completeness of the Parsing Problem

We show that the Parsing Problem for SDL-grammars is NP-complete by a reduction of the 3-Partition Problem to it.[6] This well-known NP-complete problem is cited in (GareyJohnson 79) as follows.

Instance:	Set $\mathcal{A}$ of $3m$ elements, a bound $N \in Z^+$, and a size $s(a) \in Z^+$ for each $a \in \mathcal{A}$ such that $\frac{N}{4} < s(a) < \frac{N}{2}$ and $\sum_{a \in \mathcal{A}} s(a) = mN$.
Question:	Can $\mathcal{A}$ be partitioned into m disjoint sets $\mathcal{A}_1, \mathcal{A}_2, \ldots, \mathcal{A}_m$ such that, for $1 \leq i \leq m$, $\sum_{a \in \mathcal{A}_i} s(a) = N$ (note that each $\mathcal{A}_i$ must therefore contain exactly 3 elements from $\mathcal{A}$)?
Comment:	NP-complete in the strong sense.

Here is our reduction. Let $\Gamma = \langle \mathcal{A}, m, N, s \rangle$ be a given 3-Partition instance. For notational convenience we abbreviate $(\ldots((A/B_1)/B_2)/\ldots)/B_n$ by $A/B_n \bullet \ldots \bullet B_2 \bullet B_1$ and similarly $B_n \multimap (\ldots(B_1 \multimap A)\ldots)$ by $B_n \bullet \ldots \bullet B_2 \bullet B_1 \multimap A$, but note that this is just an abbreviation in the product-free fragment. Moreover the notation A^k stands for

$$\underbrace{A \bullet A \bullet \ldots \bullet A}_{k \text{ times}}$$

We then define the SDL-grammar $G_\Gamma = \langle \Sigma, \mathcal{F}, b_S, l \rangle$ as follows:

$\Sigma := \{v, w_1, \ldots, w_{3m}\}$
$\mathcal{F} :=$ *all formulae over primitive types*
$\quad \mathcal{B} = \{a, d\} \cup \bigcup_{i=1}^{m} \{b_i, c_i\}$
$b_S := a$
$l(v) := a/(b_1^3 \bullet b_2^3 \bullet \ldots \bullet b_m^3 \bullet c_1^N \bullet c_2^N \bullet \ldots \bullet c_m^N \multimap d)$
for $1 \leq i \leq 3m-1$:
$l(w_i) := \bigcup_{1 \leq j \leq m} d/d \bullet b_j \bullet c_j^{s(a_i)}$
$l(w_{3m}) := \bigcup_{1 \leq j \leq m} d/b_j \bullet c_j^{s(a_{3m})}$

[6]A similar reduction has been used in (LincolnWinkler 94) to show that derivability in the multiplicative fragment of propositional Linear Logic with only the connectives $\multimap$ and $\otimes$ (equivalently Lambek calculus with permutation LP) is NP-complete.

The word we are interested in is $v\, w_1\, w_2 \ldots w_{3m}$. We do not care about other words that might be generated by G_Γ. Our claim now is that a given 3-Partition problem Γ is solvable **if and only if** $v\, w_1 \ldots w_{3m}$ is in $L(G_\Gamma)$. We consider each direction in turn.

Lemma 5 (Soundness) *If a 3-Partition problem $\Gamma = \langle \mathcal{A}, m, N, s \rangle$ has a solution, then $v\, w_1 \ldots w_{3m}$ is in $L(G_\Gamma)$.*

Proof. We have to show, when given a solution to Γ, how to choose a type sequence $U \in l(vw_1 \ldots w_{3m})$ and construct an SDL proof for $U \Rightarrow a$. Suppose $\mathcal{A} = \{a_1, a_2, \ldots, a_{3m}\}$. From a given solution (set of triples) $\mathcal{A}_1, \mathcal{A}_2, \ldots, \mathcal{A}_m$ we can compute in polynomial time a mapping k that sends the index of an element to the index of its solution triple, i.e., $k(i) = j$ iff $a_i \in \mathcal{A}_j$. To obtain the required sequence U, we simply choose for the w_i terminals the type $d/d \bullet b_{k(i)} \bullet c_{k(i)}^{s(a_i)}$ (resp. $d/b_{k(3m)} \bullet c_{k(3m)}^{s(a_{3m})}$ for w_{3m}). Hence the complete sequent to solve is:

$$
\begin{array}{ll}
 & a/(b_1^3 \bullet b_2^3 \bullet \ldots \bullet b_m^3 \bullet c_1^N \bullet c_2^N \bullet \ldots \bullet c_m^N \multimap d) \\
 & d/d \bullet b_{k(1)} \bullet c_{k(1)}^{s(a_1)} \\
 & \vdots \\
(*) & d/d \bullet b_{k(3m-1)} \bullet c_{k(3m-1)}^{s(a_{3m-1})} \\
 & d/b_{k(3m)} \bullet c_{k(3m)}^{s(a_{3m})} \\
 & \Rightarrow \\
 & a
\end{array}
$$

Let $a/B_0, B_1, \ldots B_{3m} \Rightarrow a$ be a shorthand for $(*)$, and let X stand for the sequence of primitive types

$$b_{k(3m)}, c_{k(3m)}^{s(a_{3m})}, b_{k(3m-1)}, c_{k(3m-1)}^{s(a_{3m-1})}, \ldots b_{k(1)}, c_{k(1)}^{s(a_1)}.$$

Using rule $(/L)$ only, we can obviously prove $B_1, \ldots B_{3m}, X \Rightarrow d$. Now, applying $(\multimap R)$ $3m+Nm$ times we can obtain $B_1, \ldots B_{3m} \Rightarrow B_0$, since there are in total, for each i, 3 b_i and N c_i in X. As final step we have

$$\frac{B_1, \ldots B_{3m} \Rightarrow B_0 \quad a \Rightarrow a}{a/B_0, B_1, \ldots B_{3m} \Rightarrow a} (/L)$$

which completes the proof. □

Lemma 6 (Completeness) *Let $\Gamma = \langle \mathcal{A}, m, N, s \rangle$ be an arbitrary 3-Partition problem and G_Γ the corresponding SDL-grammar as defined above. Then Γ has a solution, if $v\, w_1 \ldots w_{3m}$ is in $L(G_\Gamma)$.*

Proof. Let $v\, w_1 \ldots w_{3m} \in L(G_\Gamma)$ and

$$a/(b_1^3 \bullet \ldots \bullet b_m^3 \bullet c_1^N \bullet \ldots \bullet c_m^N \multimap d), B_1, \ldots B_{3m} \Rightarrow a$$

be a witnessing derivable sequent, i.e., for $1 \leq i \leq 3m$, $B_i \in l(w_i)$. Now, since the counts of this sequent must be balanced, the sequence $B_1, \ldots B_{3m}$

must contain for each $1 \leq j \leq m$ exactly 3 b_j and exactly N c_j as subformulae. Therefore we can read off the solution to Γ from this sequent by including in $\mathcal{A}_j$ (for $1 \leq j \leq m$) those three a_i for which B_i has an occurrence of b_j, say these are $a_{j(1)}$, $a_{j(2)}$ and $a_{j(3)}$. We verify, again via balancedness of the primitive counts, that $s(a_{j(1)}) + s(a_{j(2)}) + s(a_{j(3)}) = N$ holds, because these are the numbers of positive and negative occurrences of c_j in the sequent. This completes the proof. □

The reduction above proves NP-hardness of the parsing problem. We need strong NP-completeness of 3-Partition here, since our reduction uses a unary encoding. Moreover, the parsing problem also lies within NP, since for a given grammar G proofs are linearly bound by the length of the string and hence, we can simply guess a proof and check it in polynomial time. Therefore we can state the following:

Theorem 7 *The parsing problem for* SDL *is NP-complete.*

Finally, we observe that for this reduction the rules $(/R)$ and $(\backslash R)$ are again irrelevant and that we can extend this result to SDL^-.

4 Conclusion

We have defined a variant of Lambek's original calculus of types that allows abstracted-over categories to freely permute. Grammars based on SDL can generate any context-free language and more than that. The parsing problem for SDL, however, we have shown to be NP-complete. This result indicates that efficient parsing for grammars that allow for large numbers of unbounded dependencies from within one node may be problematic, even in the categorial framework. Note that the fact, that this problematic case doesn't show up in the correct analysis of normal NL sentences, doesn't mean that a parser wouldn't have to try it, unless some arbitrary bound to that number is assumed. For practical grammar engineering one can devise the motto *avoid accumulation of unbounded dependencies by whatever means.*

On the theoretical side we think that this result for SDL is also of some importance, since SDL exhibits a core of logical behaviour that any (Lambek-based) logic must have which accounts for non-peripheral extraction by some form of permutation. And hence, this result increases our understanding of the necessary computational properties of such richer systems. To our knowledge the question, whether the Lambek calculus itself or its associated parsing problem are NP-hard, are still open.

References

J. van Benthem. The Lambek Calculus. In R. T. O. et al. (Ed.), *Categorial Grammars and Natural Language Structures*, pp. 35–68. Reidel, 1988.

M. R. Garey and D. S. Johnson. *Computers and Intractability—A Guide to the Theory of NP-Completeness.* Freeman, San Francisco, Cal., 1979.

J.-Y. Girard. Linear Logic. *Theoretical Computer Science*, 50(1):1–102, 1987.

E. König. LexGram - a practical categorial grammar formalism. In *Proceedings of the Workshop on Computational Logic for Natural Language Processing. A Joint COMPULOGNET/ELSNET/EAGLES Workshop*, Edinburgh, Scotland, April 1995.

J. Lambek. The Mathematics of Sentence Structure. *American Mathematical Monthly*, 65(3):154–170, 1958.

P. Lincoln and T. Winkler. Constant-Only Multiplicative Linear Logic is NP-Complete. *Theoretical Computer Science*, 135(1):155–169, Dec. 1994.

M. Moortgat. Residuation in Mixed Lambek Systems. In M. Moortgat (Ed.), *Lambek Calculus. Multimodal and Polymorphic Extensions, DYANA-2 deliverable R1.1.B.* ESPRIT, Basic Research Project 6852, Sept. 1994.

G. Morrill. *Type Logical Grammar: Categorial Logic of Signs.* Kluwer, 1994.

M. Pentus. Lambek grammars are context free. In *Proceedings of Logic in Computer Science*, Montreal, 1993.

Computing Optimal Descriptions for Optimality Theory Grammars with Context-Free Position Structures

Bruce Tesar
The Rutgers Center for Cognitive Science /
The Linguistics Department
Rutgers University
Piscataway, NJ 08855 USA
tesar@ruccs.rutgers.edu

Abstract

This paper describes an algorithm for computing optimal structural descriptions for Optimality Theory grammars with context-free position structures. This algorithm extends Tesar's dynamic programming approach (Tesar, 1994) (Tesar, 1995a) to computing optimal structural descriptions from regular to context-free structures. The generalization to context-free structures creates several complications, all of which are overcome without compromising the core dynamic programming approach. The resulting algorithm has a time complexity cubic in the length of the input, and is applicable to grammars with universal constraints that exhibit context-free locality.

1 Computing Optimal Descriptions in Optimality Theory

In Optimality Theory (Prince and Smolensky, 1993), grammaticality is defined in terms of optimization. For any given linguistic input, the grammatical structural description of that input is the description, selected from a set of candidate descriptions for that input, that best satisfies a ranked set of universal constraints. The universal constraints often conflict: satisfying one constraint may only be possible at the expense of violating another one. These conflicts are resolved by ranking the universal constraints in a strict dominance hierarchy: one violation of a given constraint is strictly worse than any number of violations of a lower-ranked constraint. When comparing two descriptions, the one which better satisfies the ranked constraints has higher Harmony. Cross-linguistic variation is accounted for by differences in the ranking of the same constraints.

The term *linguistic input* should here be understood as something like an underlying form. In phonology, an input might be a string of segmental material; in syntax, it might be a verb's argument structure, along with the arguments. For expositional purposes, this paper will assume linguistic inputs to be ordered strings of segments. A candidate structural description for an input is a full linguistic description containing that input, and indicating what the (pronounced) surface realization is. An important property of Optimality Theory (OT) grammars is that they do not accept or reject inputs; every possible input is assigned a description by the grammar.

The formal definition of Optimality Theory posits a function, *Gen*, which maps an input to a large (often infinite) set of candidate structural descriptions, all of which are evaluated in parallel by the universal constraints. An OT grammar does not itself specify an algorithm, it simply assigns a grammatical structural description to each input. However, one can ask the computational question of whether efficient algorithms exist to compute the description assigned to a linguistic input by a grammar.

The most apparent computational challenge is posed by the allowance of *faithfulness* violations: the surface form of a structural description may not be identical with the input. Structural positions not filled with input segments constitute overparsing (epenthesis). Input segments not parsed into structural positions do not appear in the surface pronunciation, and constitute underparsing (deletion). To the extent that underparsing and overparsing are avoided, the description is said to be faithful to the input. Crucial to Optimality Theory are faithfulness constraints, which are violated by underparsing and overparsing. The faithfulness constraints ensure that a grammar will only tolerate deviations of the surface form from the input form which are necessary to satisfy structural constraints dominating the faithfulness constraints.

Computing an optimal description means considering a space of candidate descriptions that include structures with a variety of faithfulness violations, and evaluating those candidates with respect to a ranking in which structural and faithfulness constraints may be interleaved. This is parsing in the generic sense: a structural description is being assigned to an input. It is, however, distinct from what is traditionally thought of as parsing in computational linguistics. Traditional parsing attempts to construct a grammatical description with a surface form matching the given input string exactly; if a description cannot be fit exactly, the input string is rejected as ungrammatical. Traditional parsing can be thought of as enforcing faithfulness absolutely, with no faithfulness violations are allowed. Partly for this reason, traditional parsing is usually understood as mapping a surface form to a description. In the computation of optimal descriptions considered here, a candidate that is fully faithful to the input may be tossed aside by the grammar in favor of a less faithful description better satisfying other (dominant) constraints. Computing an optimal description in Optimality Theory is more naturally thought of as mapping an underlying form to a description, perhaps as part of the process of language production.

Tesar (Tesar, 1994) (Tesar, 1995a) has developed algorithms for computing optimal descriptions, based upon dynamic programming. The details laid out in (Tesar, 1995a) focused on the case where the set of structures underlying the *Gen* function are formally regular. In this paper, Tesar's basic approach is adopted, and extended to grammars with a *Gen* function employing fully context-free structures. Using such context-free structures introduces some complications not apparent with the regular case. This paper demonstrates that the complications can be dealt with, and that the dynamic programming case may be fully extended to grammars with context-free structures.

2 Context-Free Position Structure Grammars

Tesar (Tesar, 1995a) formalizes *Gen* as a set of matchings between an ordered string of input segments and the terminals of each of a set of position structures. The set of possible position structures is defined by a formal grammar, the *position structure grammar.* A position structure has as terminals structural positions. In a valid structural description, each structural position may be filled with at most one input segment, and each input segment may be parsed into at most one position. The linear order of the input must be preserved in all candidate structural descriptions.

This paper considers Optimality Theory grammars where the position structure grammar is context-free; that is, the space of position structures can be described by a formal context-free grammar. As an illustration, consider the grammar in Examples 1 and 2 (this illustration is not intended to represent any plausible natural language theory, but does use the "peak/margin" terminology sometimes employed in syllable theories). The set of inputs is $\{C,V\}^+$. The candidate descriptions of an input consist of a sequence of pieces, each of which has a peak (p) surrounded by one or more pairs of margin positions (m). These structures exhibit prototypical context-free behavior, in that margin positions to the left of a peak are balanced with margin positions to the right. 'e' is the empty string, and 'S' the start symbol.

Example 1 *The Position Structure Grammar*

S	⇒	F | e
F	⇒	Y | YF
Y	⇒	P | MFM
M	⇒	m
P	⇒	p

Example 2 *The Constraints*

-(m/V)	Do not parse V into a margin position
-(p/C)	Do not parse C into a peak position
PARSE	Input segments must be parsed
FILL^m	A margin position must be filled
FILL^p	A peak position must be filled

The first two constraints are structural, and mandate that V not be parsed into a margin position, and that C not be parsed into a peak position. The other three constraints are faithfulness constraints. The two structural constraints are satisfied by descriptions with each V in a peak position surrounded by matched C's in margin positions: CCVCC, V, CVCCCVCC, etc. If the input string permits such an analysis, it will be given this completely faithful description, with no resulting constraint violations (ensuring that it will be optimal with respect to any ranking).

Consider the constraint hierarchy in Example 3.

Example 3 *A Constraint Hierarchy*

$$\{\text{-(m/V), -(p/C), PARSE}\} \gg \{\text{FILL}^p\} \gg \{\text{FILL}^m\}$$

This ranking ensures that in optimal descriptions, a V will only be parsed as a peak, while a C will only be parsed as a margin. Further, all input segments will be parsed, and unfilled positions will be included only as necessary to produce a sequence of balanced structures. For example, the input /VC/ receives the description[1] shown in Example 4.

Example 4 *The Optimal Description for /VC/*

$$\text{S(F(Y(M(}\mathcal{C}\text{),P(V),M(C))))}$$

The surface string for this description is $\mathcal{C}$VC: the first $\mathcal{C}$ was "epenthesized" to balance with the one following the peak V. This candidate is optimal because it only violates FILL^m, the lowest-ranked constraint.

Tesar identifies locality as a sufficient condition on the universal constraints for the success of his

[1] In this paper, tree structures will be denoted with parentheses: a parent node X with child nodes Y and Z is denoted X(Y,Z).

approach. For formally regular position structure grammars, he defines a local constraint as one which can be evaluated strictly on the basis of two consecutive positions (and any input segments filling those positions) in the linear position structure. That idea can be extended to the context-free case as follows. A local constraint is one which can be evaluated strictly on the basis of the information contained within a local region. A local region of a description is either of the following:

- a non-terminal and the child non-terminals that it immediately dominates;
- a non-terminal which dominates a terminal symbol (position), along with the terminal and the input segment (if present) filling the terminal position.

It is important to keep clear the role of the position structure grammar. It does not define the set of grammatical structures, it defines the space of candidate structures. Thus, the computation of descriptions addressed in this paper should be distinguished from robust, or error-correcting, parsing (Anderson and Backhouse, 1981, for example). There, the input string is mapped to the grammatical structure that is 'closest'; if the input completely matches a structure generated by the grammar, that structure is automatically selected. In the OT case presented here, the full grammar is the entire OT system, of which the position structure grammar is only a part. Error-correcting parsing uses optimization only with respect to the faithfulness of pre-defined grammatical structures to the input. OT uses optimization to define grammaticality.

3 The Dynamic Programming Table

The Dynamic Programming (DP) Table is here a three-dimensional, pyramid-shaped data structure. It resembles the tables used for context-free chart parsing (Kay, 1980) and maximum likelihood computation for stochastic context-free grammars (Lari and Young, 1990) (Charniak, 1993). Each cell of the table contains a partial description (a part of a structural description), and the Harmony of that partial description. A partial description is much like an edge in chart parsing, covering a contiguous substring of the input. A cell is identified by three indices, and denoted with square brackets (e.g., [X,a,c]). The first index identifying the cell (X) indicates the cell category of the cell. The other two indices (a and c) indicate the contiguous substring of the input string covered by the partial description contained in the cell (input segments i_a through i_c).

In chart parsing, the set of cell categories is precisely the set of non-terminals in the grammar, and thus a cell contains a subtree with a root non-terminal corresponding to the cell category, and with leaves that constitute precisely the input substring covered by the cell. In the algorithm presented here, the set of cell categories are the non-terminals of the position structure grammar, along with a category for each left-aligned substring of the right hand side of each position grammar rule. Example 5 gives the set of cell categories for the position structure grammar in Example 1.

Example 5 *The Set of Cell Categories*

S, F, Y, M, P, MF

The last category in Example 5, MF, comes from the rule Y ⇒ MFM of Example 1, which has more than two non-terminals on the right hand side. Each such category corresponds to an incomplete edge in normal chart parsing; having a table cell for each such category eliminates the need for a separate data structure containing edges. The cell [MF,a,c] may contain an ordered pair of subtrees, the first with root M covering input [a,b], and the second with root F covering input [b+1,c].

The DP Table is perhaps best envisioned as a set of layers, one for each category. A layer is a set of all cells in the table indexed by a particular cell category.

Example 6 *A Layer of the Dynamic Programming Table for Category M (input i_1-i_3)*

[M,1,3]		
[M,1,2]	[M,2,3]	
[M,1,1]	[M,2,2]	[M,3,3]
i_1	i_2	i_3

For each substring length, there is a collection of rows, one for each category, which will collectively be referred to as a *level*. The first level contains the cells which only cover one input segment; the number of cells in this level will be the number of input segments multiplied by the number of cell categories. Level two contains cells which cover input substrings of length two, and so on. The top level contains one cell for each category. One other useful partition of the DP table is into blocks. A block is a set of all cells covering a particular input subsequence. A block has one cell for each cell category.

A cell of the DP Table is filled by comparing the results of several operations, each of which try to fill a cell. The operation producing the partial description with the highest Harmony actually fills the cell. The operations themselves are discussed in Section 4.

The algorithm presented in Section 6 fills the table cells level by level: first, all the cells covering only one input segment are filled, then the cells covering two consecutive segments are filled, and so forth. When the table has been completely filled, cell [S,1,J] will contain the optimal description of the input, and its Harmony. The table may also be filled in a more left-to-right manner, bottom-up, in the spirit of CKY. First, the cells covering only segment i_1, and then i_2, are filled. Then, the cells covering the first two segments are filled, using the entries in the cells covering each of i_1 and i_2. The cells of the next diagonal are then filled.

4 The Operations Set

The Operations Set contains the operations used to fill DP Table cells. The algorithm proceeds by considering all of the operations that could be used to fill a cell, and selecting the one generating the partial description with the highest Harmony to actually fill the cell. There are three main types of operations, corresponding to underparsing, parsing, and overparsing actions. These actions are analogous to the three primitive actions of sequence comparison (Sankoff and Kruskal, 1983): deletion, correspondence, and insertion.

The discussion that follows makes the assumption that the right hand side of every production is either a string of non-terminals or a single terminal. Each parsing operation generates a new element of structure, and so is associated with a position structure grammar production. The first type of parsing operation involves productions which generate a single terminal (e.g., P⇒p). Because we are assuming that an input segment may only be parsed into at most one position, and that a position may have at most one input segment parsed into it, this parsing operation may only fill a cell which covers exactly one input segment. in our example, cell [P,1,1] could be filled by an operation parsing i_1 into a p position, giving the partial description P(p filled with i_1).

The other kinds of parsing operations are matched to position grammar productions in which a parent non-terminal generates child non-terminals. One of these kinds of operations fills the cell for a category by combining cell entries for two factor categories, in order, so that the substrings covered by each of them combine (concatenatively, with no overlap) to form the input substring covered by the cell being filled. For rule Y ⇒ MFM, there will be an operation of this type combining entries in [M,a,b] and [F,b+1,c], creating the concatenated structure[2] [M,a,b]+[F,b+1,c], to fill [MF,a,c]. The final type of parsing operation fills a cell for a category which is a single non-terminal on the left hand side of a production, by combining two entries which jointly form the entire right hand side of the production. This operation would combining entries in [MF,a,c] and [M,c+1,d], creating the structure Y([MF,a,c],[M,c+1,d]), to fill [Y,a,d]. Each of these operations involves filling a cell for a target category by using the entries in the cells for two factor categories.

The resulting Harmony of the partial description created by a parsing operation will be the combination of the marks assessed each of the partial descriptions for the factor categories, plus any additional marks incurred as a result of the structure added by the production itself. This is true because the constraints must be local: any new constraint violations are determinable on the basis of the cell category of the factor partial descriptions, and not any other internal details of those partial descriptions.

All possible ways in which the factor categories, taken in order, may combine to cover the substring, must be considered. Because the factor categories must be contiguous and in order, this amounts to considering each of the ways in which the substring can be split into two pieces. This is reflected in the parsing operation descriptions given in Section 6.2.

Underparsing operations are not matched with position grammar productions. A DP Table cell which covers only one input segment may be filled by an underparsing operation which marks the input segment as underparsed. In general, any partial description covering any substring of the input may be extended to cover an adjacent input segment by adding that additional segment marked as underparsed. Thus, a cell covering a given substring of length greater than one may be filled in two mirror-image ways via underparsing: by taking a partial description which covers all but the leftmost input segment and adding that segment as underparsed, and by taking a partial description which covers all but the rightmost input segment and adding that segment as underparsed.

Overparsing operations are discussed in Section 5.

5 The Overparsing Operations

Overparsing operations consume no input; they only add new unfilled structure. Thus, a block of cells (the set of cells each covering the same input substring) is interdependent with respect to overparsing operations, meaning that an overparsing operation trying to fill one cell in the block is adding structure to a partial description from a different cell in the same block. The first consequence of this is that the overparsing operations must be considered after the underparsing and parsing operations for that block. Otherwise, the cells would be empty, and the overparsing operations would have nothing to add on to.

The second consequence is that overparsing operations may need to be considered more than once, because the result of one overparsing operation (if it fills a cell) could be the source for another overparsing operation. Thus, more than one pass through the overparsing operations for a block may be necessary. In the description of the algorithm given in Section 6.3, each Repeat-Until loop considers the overparsing operations for a block of cells. The number of loop iterations is the number of passes through the overparsing operations for the block. The loop iterations stop when none of the overparsing operations

[2]This partial description is not a single tree, but an ordered pair of trees. In general, such concatenated structures will be ordered lists of trees.

is able to fill a cell (each proposed partial description is less harmonic than the partial description already in the cell).

In principle, an unbounded number of overparsing operations could apply, and in fact descriptions with arbitrary numbers of unfilled positions are contained in the output space of *Gen* (as formally defined). The algorithm does not have to explicitly consider arbitrary amounts of overparsing, however. A necessary property of the faithfulness constraints, given constraint locality, is that a partial description cannot have overparsed structures repeatedly added to it until the resulting partial description falls into the same cell category as the original prior to overparsing, and be more Harmonic. Such a sequence of overparsing operations can be considered a *overparsing cycle*. Thus, the faithfulness constraints must ban overparsing cycles. This is not solely a computational requirement, but is necessary for the grammar to be well-defined: overparsing cycles must be harmonically suboptimal, otherwise arbitrary amounts of overparsing will be permitted in optimal descriptions. In particular, the constraints should prevent overparsing from adding an entire overparsed non-terminal more than once to the same partial description while passing through the overparsing operations. In Example 2, the constraints FILL^m and FILL^p effectively ban overparsing cycles: no matter where these constraints are ranked, a description containing an overparsing cycle will be less harmonic (due to additional FILL violations) than the same description with the cycle removed.

Given that the universal constraints meet this criterion, the overparsing operations may be repeatedly considered for a given level until none of them increase the Harmony of the entries in any of the cells. Because each overparsing operation maps a partial description in one cell category to one for another cell category, a partial description cannot undergo more consecutive overparsing operations than there are cell categories without repeating at least one cell category, thereby creating a cycle. Thus, the number of cell categories places a constant bound on the number of passes made through the overparsing operations for a block.

A single non-terminal may dominate an entire subtree in which none of the syllable positions at the leaves of the tree are filled. Thus, the optimal "unfilled structure" for each non-terminal, and in fact each cell category, must be determined, for use by the overparsing operations. The optimal overparsing structure for category X is denoted with [X,0], and such an entity is referred to as a *base overparsing structure*. A set of such structures must be computed, one for each category, before filling input-dependent DP table cells. Because these values are not dependent upon the input, base overparsing structures may be computed and stored in advance. Computing them is just like computing other cell entries, except that only overparsing operations are considered. First, consider (once) the overparsing operations for each non-terminal X which has a production rule permitting it to dominate a terminal x: each tries to set [X,0] to contain the corresponding partial description with the terminal x left unfilled. Next consider the other overparsing operations for each cell, choosing the most Harmonic of those operations' partial descriptions and the prior value of [X,0].

6 The Dynamic Programming Algorithm

6.1 Notation

maxH{} returns the argument with maximum Harmony
$\langle i_a \rangle$ denotes input segment i_a underparsed
X^t is a non-terminal
x^t is a terminal
+ denotes concatenation

6.2 The Operations

Underparsing Operations for [X^t,a,a]:
  create $\langle i_a \rangle$+[X^t,0]

Underparsing Operations for [X^t,a,c]:
  create $\langle i_a \rangle$+[X^t,a+1,c]
  create [X^t,a,c-1]+$\langle i_a \rangle$

Parsing operations for [X^t,a,a]:
  for each production $X^t \Rightarrow x^k$
    create X^t(x^k filled with i_a)

Parsing operations for [X^t,a,c],
where c>a and all X are cell categories:
  for each production $X^t \Rightarrow X^k X^m$
    for b = a+1 to c-1
      create X^t([X^k,a,b],[X^m,b+1,c])
  for each production $X^u \Rightarrow X^k X^m X^n$...
  where $X^t = X^k X^m$:
    for b=a+1 to c-1
      create [X^k,a,b]+[X^m,b+1,c]

Overparsing operations for [X^t,0]:
  for each production $X^t \Rightarrow x^k$
    create X^t(x^k unfilled)
  for each production $X^t \Rightarrow X^k X^m$
    create X^t([X^k,0],[X^m,0])
  for each production $X^u \Rightarrow X^k X^m X^n$...
  where $X^t = X^k X^m$:
    create [X^k,0]+[X^m,0]

Overparsing operations for [X^t,a,a]:
  same as for [X^t,a,c]

Overparsing operations for [X^t,a,c]:
  for each production $X^t \Rightarrow X^k$
    create X^t([X^k,a,c])

```
for each production X^t ⇒ X^k X^m
  create X^t([X^k,0],[X^m,a,c])
  create X^t([X^k,a,c],[X^m,0])
for each production X^u ⇒ X^k X^m X^n...
where X^t = X^k X^m:
  create [X^k,a,c]+[X^m,0]
  create [X^k,0]+[X^m,a,c]
```

6.3 The Main Algorithm

```
/* create the base overparsing structures */

Repeat
  For each X^t, Set [X^t,0] to
  maxH{[X^t,0], overparsing ops for [X^t,0]}
Until no [X^t,0] has changed during a pass

/* fill the cells covering only a single segment */

For a = 1 to J
  For each X^t, Set [X^t,a,a] to
  maxH{underparsing ops for [X^t,a,a]}
  For each X^t, Set [X^t,a,a] to
  maxH{[X^t,a,a], parsing ops for [X^t,a,a]}
  Repeat
    For each X^t, Set [X^t,a,a] to
    maxH{[X^t,a,a], overparsing ops for [X^t,a,a]}
  Until no [X^t,a,a] has changed during a pass

/* fill the rest of the cells */

For d=1 to (J-1)
  For a=1 to (J-d)
    For each X^t, Set [X^t,a,a+d] to
    maxH{underparsing ops for [X^t,a,a+d]}
    For each X^t, Set [X^t,a,a+d]
    maxH{[X^t,a,a+d], parsing ops for [X^t,a,a+d]}
    Repeat
      For each X^t,
        Set [X^t,a,a+d] to
        maxH{[X^t,a,a+d],
          overparsing ops for [X^t,a,a+d]}
    Until no [X^t,a,a+d] has changed during a pass
Return [S,1,J] as the optimal description
```

6.4 Complexity

Each block of cells for an input subsequence is processed in time linear in the length of the subsequence. This is a consequence of the fact that in general parsing operations filling such a cell must consider all ways of dividing the input subsequence into two pieces. The number of overparsing passes through the block is bounded from above by the number of cell categories, due to the fact that overparsing cycles are suboptimal. Thus, the number of passes is bounded by a constant, for any fixed position structure grammar. The number of such blocks is the number of distinct, contiguous input subsequences (equivalently, the number of cells in a layer), which is on the order of the square of the length of the input. If N is the length of the input, the algorithm has computational complexity $O(N^3)$.

7 Discussion

7.1 Locality

That locality helps processing should be no great surprise to computationalists; the computational significance of locality is widely appreciated. Further, locality is often considered a desirable property of principles in linguistics, independent of computational concerns. Nevertheless, locality is a sufficient but not necessary restriction for the applicability of this algorithm. The locality restriction is really a special case of a more general sufficient condition. The general condition is a kind of "Markov" property. This property requires that, for any substring of the input for which partial descriptions are constructed, the set of possible partial descriptions for that substring may be partitioned into a finite set of classes, such that the consequences in terms of constraint violations for the addition of structure to a partial description may be determined entirely by the identity of the class to which that partial description belongs. The special case of strict locality is easy to understand with respect to context-free structures, because it states that the only information needed about a subtree to relate it to the rest of the tree is the identity of the root non-terminal, so that the (necessarily finite) set of non-terminals provides the relevant set of classes.

7.2 Underparsing and Derivational Redundancy

The treatment of the underparsing operations given above creates the opportunity for the same partial description to be arrived at through several different paths. For example, suppose the input is $i_a...i_b i_c i_d...i_e$, and there is a constituent in [X,a,b] and a constituent [Y,d,e]. Further suppose the input segment i_c is to be marked underparsed, so that the final description [S,a,e] contains [X,a,b] $\langle i_c \rangle$ [Y,d,e]. That description could be arrived at either by combining [X,a,b] and $\langle i_c \rangle$ to fill [X,a,c], and then combine [X,a,c] and [Y,d,e], or it could be arrived at by combining $\langle i_c \rangle$ and [Y,d,e] to fill [Y,c,e], and then combine [X,a,b] and [Y,c,e]. The potential confusion stems from the fact that an underparsed segment is part of the description, but is not a proper constituent of the tree.

This problem can be avoided in several ways. An obvious one is to only permit underparsings to be added to partial descriptions on the right side. One exception would then have to be made to permit input segments prior to any parsed input segments to be underparsed (i.e., if the first input segment is underparsed, it has to be attached to the left side of some constituent because it is to the left of everything in the description).

8 Conclusions

The results presented here demonstrate that the basic cubic time complexity results for processing context-free structures are preserved when Optimality Theory grammars are used. If *Gen* can be specified as matching input segments to structures generated by a context-free position structure grammar, and the constraints are local with respect to those structures, then the algorithm presented here may be applied directly to compute optimal descriptions.

9 Acknowledgments

I would like to thank Paul Smolensky for his valuable contributions and support. I would also like to thank David Haussler, Clayton Lewis, Mark Liberman, Jim Martin, and Alan Prince for useful discussions, and three anonymous reviewers for helpful comments. This work was supported in part by an NSF Graduate Fellowship to the author, and NSF grant IRI-9213894 to Paul Smolensky and Geraldine Legendre.

References

S. O. Anderson and R. C. Backhouse. 1981. Locally least-cost error recovery in Earley's algorithm. *ACM Transactions on Programming Languages and Systems* 3: 318-347.

Eugene Charniak. 1993. *Statistical language learning*. Cambridge, MA: MIT Press.

Martin Kay. 1980. Algorithmic schemata and data structures in syntactic processing. CSL-80-12, October 1980.

K. Lari and S. J. Young. 1990. The estimation of stochastic context-free grammars using the inside-outside algorithm. *Computer Speech and Language* 4: 35-36.

Harry R. Lewis and Christos H. Papadimitriou. 1981. *Elements of the theory of computation*. Englewood Cliffs, New Jersey: Prentice-Hall, Inc.

Alan Prince and Paul Smolensky. 1993. *Optimality Theory: Constraint interaction in generative grammar*. Technical Report CU-CS-696-93, Department of Computer Science, University of Colorado at Boulder, and Technical Report TR-2, Rutgers Center for Cognitive Science, Rutgers University, New Brunswick, NJ. March. To appear in the Linguistic Inquiry Monograph Series, Cambridge, MA: MIT Press.

David Sankoff and Joseph Kruskal. 1983. *Time warps, string edits, and macromolecules: The theory and practice of sequence comparison*. Reading, MA: Addison-Wesley.

Bruce Tesar. 1994. Parsing in Optimality Theory: A dynamic programming approach. Technical Report CU-CS-714-94, April 1994. Department of Computer Science, University of Colorado, Boulder.

Bruce Tesar. 1995a. Computing optimal forms in Optimality Theory: Basic syllabification. Technical Report CU-CS-763-95, February 1995. Department of Computer Science, University of Colorado, Boulder.

Bruce Tesar. 1995b. Computational Optimality Theory. Unpublished Ph.D. Dissertation. Department of Computer Science, University of Colorado, Boulder. June 1995.

A.J. Viterbi. 1967. Error bounds for convolution codes and an asymptotically optimal decoding algorithm. *IEEE Trans. on Information Theory* 13:260-269.

Directed Replacement

Lauri Karttunen
Rank Xerox Research Centre Grenoble
6, chemin de Maupertuis
F-38240 MEYLAN, FRANCE
lauri.karttunen@xerox.fr

Abstract

This paper introduces to the finite-state calculus a family of directed replace operators. In contrast to the simple replace expression, `UPPER -> LOWER`, defined in Karttunen (1995), the new directed version, `UPPER @-> LOWER`, yields an unambiguous transducer if the lower language consists of a single string. It transduces the input string from left to right, making only the longest possible replacement at each point.

A new type of replacement expression, `UPPER @-> PREFIX ... SUFFIX`, yields a transducer that inserts text around strings that are instances of `UPPER`. The symbol ... denotes the matching part of the input which itself remains unchanged. `PREFIX` and `SUFFIX` are regular expressions describing the insertions.

Expressions of the type `UPPER @-> PREFIX ... SUFFIX` may be used to compose a deterministic parser for a "local grammar" in the sense of Gross (1989). Other useful applications of directed replacement include tokenization and filtering of text streams.

1 Introduction

Transducers compiled from simple replace expressions `UPPER -> LOWER` (Karttunen 1995, Kempe and Karttunen 1996) are generally nondeterministic in the sense that they may yield multiple results even if the lower language consists of a single string. For example, let us consider the transducer in Figure 1, representing `a b | b | b a | a b a -> x`.[1]

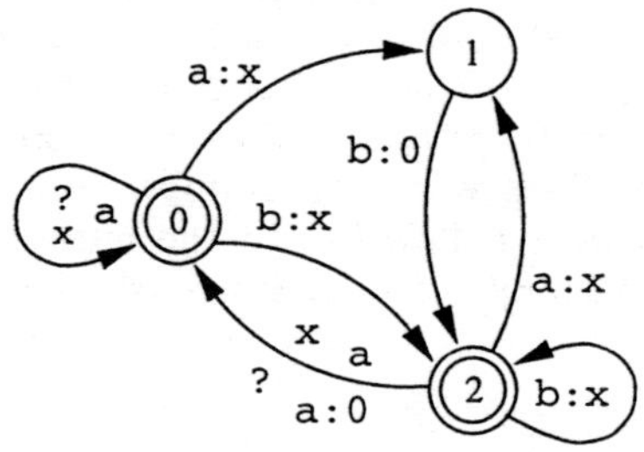

Figure 1: `a b | b | b a | a b a -> x` . The four paths with "aba" on the upper side are: <0 `a` 0 `b:x` 2 `a` 0>, <0 `a` 0 `b:x` 2 `a:0` 0>, <0 `a:x` 1 `b:0` 2 `a` 0>, and <0 `a:x` 1 `b:0` 2 `a:0` 0>.

The application of this transducer to the input "aba" produces four alternate results, "axa", "ax", "xa", and "x", as shown in Figure 1, since there are four paths in the network that contain "aba" on the upper side with different strings on the lower side.

This nondeterminism arises in two ways. First of all, a replacement can start at any point. Thus we get different results for the "aba" depending on whether we start at the beginning of the string or in the middle at the "b". Secondly, there may be alternative replacements with the same starting point. In the beginning of "aba", we can replace either "ab" or "aba". Starting in the middle, we can replace either "b" or "ba". The underlining in Figure 2 shows

```
a b a     a b a     a b a     a b a
  -       ---         ---     -----

a x a     a x         x a       x
```

Figure 2: Four factorizations of "aba".

the four alternate factorizations of the input string, that is, the four alternate ways to partition the string "aba" with respect to the upper language of the replacement expression. The corresponding paths in the transducer are listed in Figure 1.

For many applications, it is useful to define an-

[1] The regular expression formalism and other notational conventions used in the paper are explained in the Appendix at the end.

other version of replacement that produces a unique outcome whenever the lower language of the relation consists of a single string. To limit the number of alternative results to one in such cases, we must impose a unique factorization on every input.

The desired effect can be obtained by constraining the directionality and the length of the replacement. Directionality means that the replacement sites in the input string are selected starting from the left or from the right, not allowing any overlaps. The length constraint forces us always to choose the longest or the shortest replacement whenever there are multiple candidate strings starting at a given location. We use the term **directed replacement** to describe a replacement relation that is constrained by directionality and length of match. (See the end of Section 2 for a discussion about the choice of the term.)

With these two kinds of constraints we can define four types of directed replacement, listed in Figure 3.

	longest match	shortest match
left-to-right	@->	@>
right-to-left	->@	>@

Figure 3: Directed replacement operators

For reasons of space, we discuss here only the left-to-right, longest-match version. The other cases are similar.

The effect of the directionality and length constraints is that some possible replacements are ignored. For example, `a b | b | b a | a b a @-> x` maps "aba" uniquely into "x", Figure 4.

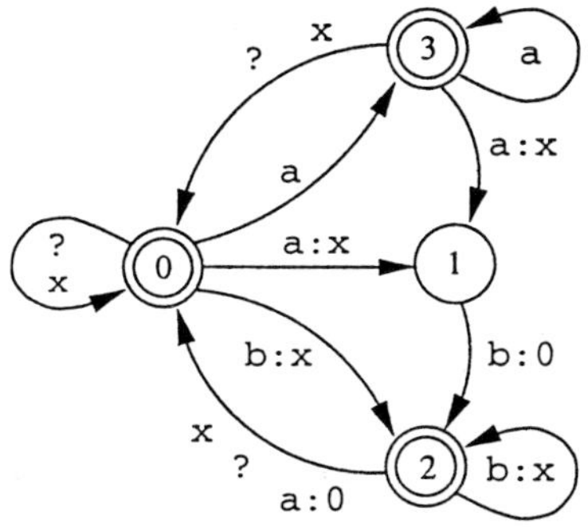

Figure 4: `a b | b | b a | a b a @-> x`. The single path with "aba" on the upper side is: <0 `a:x` 1 `b:0` 2 `a:0` 0>.

Because we must start from the left and have to choose the longest match, "aba" must be replaced, ignoring the possible replacements for "b", "ba", and "ab". The `@->` operator allows only the last factorization of "aba" in Figure 2.

Left-to-right, longest-match replacement can be thought of as a procedure that rewrites an input string sequentially from left to right. It copies the input until it finds an instance of `UPPER`. At that point it selects the longest matching substring, which is rewritten as `LOWER`, and proceeds from the end of that substring without considering any other alternatives. Figure 5 illustrates the idea.

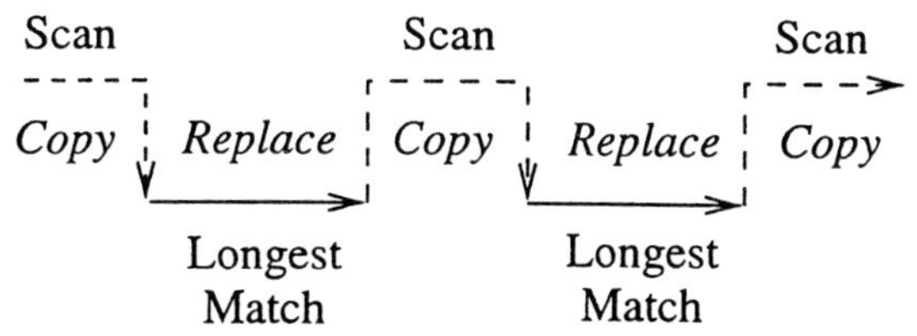

Figure 5: Left-to-right, longest-match replacement

It is not obvious at the outset that the operation can in fact be encoded as a finite-state transducer for arbitrary regular patterns. Although a unique substring is selected for replacement at each point, in general the transduction is not unambiguous because `LOWER` is not required to be a single string; it can be any regular language.

The idea of treating phonological rewrite rules in this way was the starting point of Kaplan and Kay (1994). Their notion of obligatory rewrite rule incorporates a directionality constraint. They observe (p. 358), however, that this constraint does not by itself guarantee a single output. Kaplan and Kay suggest that additional restrictions, such as longest-match, could be imposed to further constrain rule application.[2] We consider this issue in more detail.

The crucial observation is that the two constraints, left-to-right and longest-match, force a unique factorization on the input string thus making the transduction unambiguous if the `LOWER` language consists of a single string. In effect, the input string is unambiguously **parsed** with respect to the `UPPER` language. This property turns out to be important for a number of applications. Thus it is useful to provide a replacement operator that implements these constraints directly.

The definition of the `UPPER @-> LOWER` relation is presented in the next section. Section 3 introduces a novel type of replace expression for constructing transducers that unambiguously recognize and mark

[2]The tentative formulation of the longest-match constraint in (Kaplan and Kay, 1994, p. 358) is too weak. It does not cover all the cases.

instances of a regular language without actually replacing them. Section 4 identifies some useful applications of the new replacement expressions.

2 Directed Replacement

We define directed replacement by means of a composition of regular relations. As in Kaplan and Kay (1994), Karttunen (1995), and other previous works on related topics, the intermediate levels of the composition introduce auxiliary symbols to express and enforce constraints on the replacement relation. Figure 6 shows the component relations and how they are composed with the input.

```
Input string
    .o.
Initial match
    .o.
Left-to-right constraint
    .o.
Longest-match constraint
    .o.
Replacement
```

Figure 6: Composition of directed replacement

If the four relations on the bottom of Figure 6 are composed in advance, as our compiler does, the application of the replacement to an input string takes place in one step without any intervening levels and with no auxiliary symbols. But it helps to understand the logic to see where the auxiliary marks would be in the hypothetical intermediate results.

Let us consider the case of `a b | b | b a | a b a @-> x` applying to the string "aba" and see in detail how the mapping implemented by the transducer in Figure 4 is composed from the four component relations. We use three auxiliary symbols, caret (^), left bracket (<) and right bracket (>), assuming here that they do not occur in any input. The first step, shown in Figure 7, composes the input string with a transducer that inserts a caret, in the beginning of every substring that belongs to the upper language.

```
 a  b a
^a ^b a
```

Figure 7: Initial match. Each caret marks the beginning of a substring that matches "ab", "b", "ba", or "aba".

Note that only one ^ is inserted even if there are several candidate strings starting at the same location.

In the left-to-right step, we enclose in angle brackets all the substrings starting at a location marked by a caret that are instances of the upper language. The initial caret is replaced by a <, and a closing > is inserted to mark the end of the match. We permit carets to appear freely while matching. No carets are permitted outside the matched substrings and the ignored internal carets are eliminated. In this case, there are four possible outcomes, shown in Figure 8, but only two of them are allowed under the constraint that there can be no carets outside the brackets.

```
              ALLOWED

^ a ^ b   a       ^ a ^ b   a
< a   b > a       < a   b   a >

            NOT ALLOWED

^ a   ^ b   a     ^ a ^ b   a
^ a   < b > a     ^ a < b   a >
```

Figure 8: Left-to-right constraint. *No caret outside a bracketed region.*

In effect, no starting location for a replacement can be skipped over except in the context of another replacement starting further left in the input string. (Roche and Schabes (1995) introduce a similar technique for imposing the left-to-right order on the transduction.) Note that the four alternatives in Figure 8 represent the four factorizations in Figure 2.

The longest-match constraint is the identity relation on a certain set of strings. It forbids any replacement that starts at the same location as another, longer replacement. In the case at hand, it means that the internal > is disallowed in the context `< a b > a`. Because "aba" is in the upper language, there is a longer, and therefore preferred, `< a b a >` alternative at the same starting location, Figure 9.

```
   ALLOWED          NOT ALLOWED

< a   b   a >       < a   b > a
```

Figure 9: Longest match constraint. *No upper language string with an initial < and a nonfinal > in the middle.*

In the final replacement step, the bracketed regions of the input string, in the case at hand, just `< a b a >` , are replaced by the strings of the lower language, yielding "x" as the result for our example.

Note that longest match constraint ignores any internal brackets. For example, the bracketing < a

> < a > is not allowed if the upper language contains "aa" as well as "a". Similarly, the left-to-right constraint ignores any internal carets.

As the first step towards a formal definition of `UPPER @-> LOWER` it is useful to make the notion of "ignoring internal brackets" more precise. Figure 10 contains the auxiliary definitions. For the details of the formalism (briefly explained in the Appendix), please consult Karttunen (1995), Kempe and Karttunen (1996).[3]

```
UPPER'  = UPPER/[%^] - [?* %^]
UPPER'' = UPPER/[%<|%>] - [?* [%<|%>]]
```

Figure 10: Versions of `UPPER` that freely allow nonfinal diacritics.

The precise definition of the `UPPER @-> LOWER` relation is given in Figure 11. It is a composition of many auxiliary relations. We label the major components in accordance with the outline in Figure 6. The formulation of the longest-match constraint is based on a suggestion by Ronald M. Kaplan (p.c.).

Initial match

```
        ~$[ %^ | %< | %> ]
                .o.
      [. .] -> %^ || _ UPPER
                .o.
```

Left to right

```
  [~$[%^] [%^:%< UPPER' 0:%>]]* ~$[%^]
                .o.
             %^ -> []
                .o.
```

Longest match

```
      ~$[%< [UPPER'' & $[%>]]]
                .o.
```

Replacement

```
       %< ~$[%>] %> -> LOWER  ;
```

Figure 11: Definition of `UPPER @-> LOWER`

The logic of `@->` replacement could be encoded in many other ways, for example, by using the three pairs of auxiliary brackets, <i, >i, <c, >c, and <a, >a, introduced in Kaplan and Kay (1994). We take here a more minimalist approach. One reason is that we prefer to think of the simple unconditional (uncontexted) replacement as the basic case, as in Karttunen (1995). Without the additional complexities introduced by contexts, the directionality and length-of-match constraints can be encoded with fewer diacritics. (We believe that the conditional case can also be handled in a simpler way than in Kaplan and Kay (1994).) The number of auxiliary markers is an important consideration for some of the applications discussed below.

In a phonological or morphological rewrite rule, the center part of the rule is typically very small: a modification, deletion or insertion of a single segment. On the other hand, in our text processing applications, the upper language may involve a large network representing, for example, a lexicon of multiword tokens. Practical experience shows that the presence of many auxiliary diacritics makes it difficult or impossible to compute the left-to-right and longest-match constraints in such cases. The size of intermediate states of the computation becomes a critical issue, while it is irrelevant for simple phonological rules. We will return to this issue in the discussion of tokenizing transducers in Section 4.

The transducers derived from the definition in Figure 11 have the property that they unambiguously parse the input string into a sequence of substrings that are either copied to the output unchanged or replaced by some other strings. However they do not fall neatly into any standard class of transducers discussed in the literature (Eilenberg 1974, Schützenberger 1977, Berstel 1979). If the `LOWER` language consists of a single string, then the relation encoded by the transducer is in Berstel's terms a **rational function**, and the network is an **unambigous** transducer, even though it may contain states with outgoing transitions to two or more destinations for the same input symbol. An unambiguous transducer may also be **sequentiable**, in which case it can be turned into an equivalent **sequential** transducer (Mohri, 1994), which can in turn be minimized. A transducer is sequential just in case there are no states with more than one transition for the same input symbol. Roche and Schabes (1995) call such transducers **deterministic**.

Our replacement transducers in general are not unambiguous because we allow `LOWER` to be any regular language. It may well turn out that, in all cases that are of practical interest, the lower language is in fact a singleton, or at least some finite set, but it is not so by definition. Even if the replacement transducer is unambiguous, it may well be unsequentiable if `UPPER` is an infinite language. For example, the simple transducer for `a+ b @-> x` in Figure 12 cannot be sequentialized. It has to replace any string of "a"s by "x" or copy it to the output unchanged depending on whether the string eventually terminates at "b". It is obviously impossible for any finite-state

[3] `UPPER'` is the same language as `UPPER` except that carets may appear freely in all nonfinal positions. Similarly, `UPPER''` accepts any nonfinal brackets.

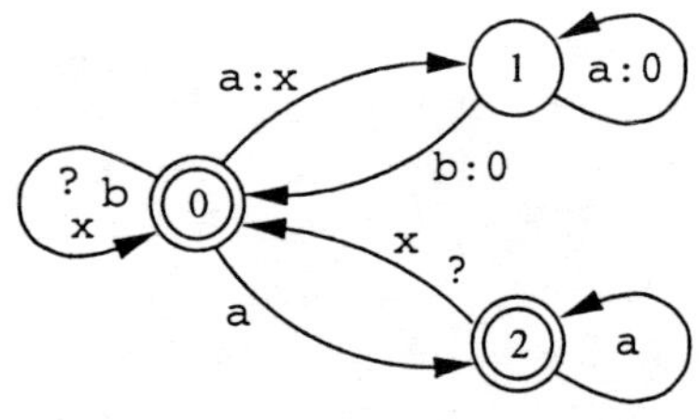

Figure 12: `a+ b @-> x`. This transducer is unambiguous but cannot be sequentialized.

device to accumulate an unbounded amount of delayed output. On the other hand, the transducer in Figure 4 is sequentiable because there the choice between `a` and `a:x` just depends on the next input symbol.

Because none of the classical terms fits exactly, we have chosen a novel term, **directed transduction**, to describe a relation induced by the definition in Figure 11. It is meant to suggest that the mapping from the input into the output strings is guided by the directionality and length-of-match constraints. Depending on the characteristics of the `UPPER` and `LOWER` languages, the resulting transducers may be unambiguous and even sequential, but that is not guaranteed in the general case.

3 Insertion

The effect of the left-to-right and longest-match constraint is to factor any input string uniquely with respect to the upper language of the replace expression, to parse it into a sequence of substrings that either belong or do not belong to the language. Instead of replacing the instances of the upper language in the input by other strings, we can also take advantage of the unique factorization in other ways. For example, we may insert a string before and after each substring that is an instance of the language in question simply to mark it as such.

To implement this idea, we introduce the special symbol ... on the right-hand side of the replacement expression to mark the place around which the insertions are to be made. Thus we allow replacement expressions of the form `UPPER @-> PREFIX ... SUFFIX`. The corresponding transducer locates the instances of `UPPER` in the input string under the left-to-right, longest-match regimen just described. But instead of replacing the matched strings, the transducer just copies them, inserting the specified prefix and suffix. For the sake of generality, we allow `PREFIX` and `SUFFIX` to denote any regular language.

The definition of `UPPER @-> PREFIX ... SUFFIX` is just as in Figure 11 except that the Replacement expression is replaced by the Insertion formula in Figure 13, a simple parallel replacement of the two auxiliary brackets that mark the selected regions. Because the placement of < and > is strictly controlled, they do not occur anywhere else.

Insertion

```
%< -> PREFIX, %> -> SUFFIX ;
```

Figure 13: Insertion expression in the definition of `UPPER @-> PREFIX ... SUFFIX`.

With the ... expressions we can construct transducers that mark maximal instances of a regular language. For example, let us assume that noun phrases consist of an optional determiner, `(d)`, any number of adjectives, `a*`, and one or more nouns, `n+`. The expression `(d) a* n+ @-> %[ ... %]` compiles into a transducer that inserts brackets around maximal instances of the noun phrase pattern. For example, it maps `"dannvaan"` into `"[dann]v[aan]"`, as shown in Figure 14.

```
      d a n n   v   a a n
      -------       -----
    [ d a n n ] v [ a a n ]
```

Figure 14: Application of `(d) a* n+ @-> %[...%]` to `"dannvaan"`

Although the input string `"dannvaan"` contains many other instances of the noun phrase pattern, `"n"`, `"an"`, `"nn"`, etc., the left-to-right and longest-match constraints pick out just the two maximal ones. The transducer is displayed in Figure 15. Note that `?` here matches symbols, such as `v`, that are not included in the alphabet of the network.

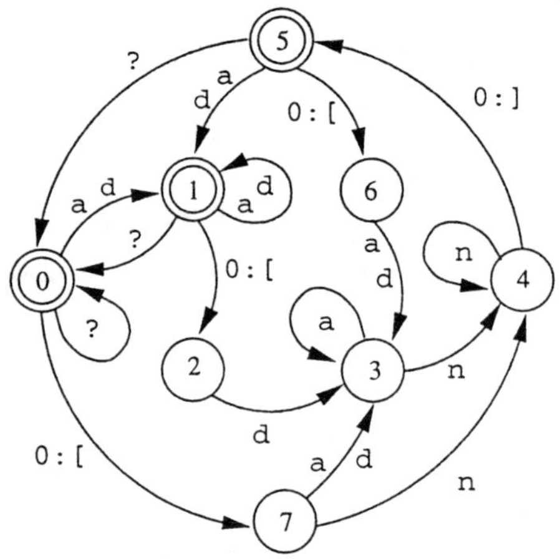

Figure 15: `(d) a* n+ @-> %[...%]`. The one path with "dannvaan" on the upper side is: <0 0:[7 d 3 a 3 n 4 n 4 0:] 5 v 0 0:[7 a 3 a 3 n 4 0:] 5>.

4 Applications

The directed replacement operators have many useful applications. We describe some of them. Although the same results could often be achieved by using lex and yacc, sed, awk, perl, and other Unix utilities, there is an advantage in using finite-state transducers for these tasks because they can then be smoothly integrated with other finite-state processes, such as morphological analysis by lexical transducers (Karttunen et al 1992, Karttunen 1994) and rule-based part-of-speech disambiguation (Chanod and Tapanainen 1995, Roche and Schabes 1995).

4.1 Tokenization

A tokenizer is a device that segments an input string into a sequence of tokens. The insertion of end-of-token marks can be accomplished by a finite-state transducer that is compiled from tokenization rules. The tokenization rules may be of several types. For example, `[WHITE_SPACE+ @-> SPACE]` is a normalizing transducer that reduces any sequence of tabs, spaces, and newlines to a single space. `[LETTER+ @-> ... END_OF_TOKEN]` inserts a special mark, e.g. a newline, at the end of a letter sequence.

Although a space generally counts as a token boundary, it can also be part of a multiword token, as in expressions like "at least", "head over heels", "in spite of", etc. Thus the rule that introduces the `END_OF_TOKEN` symbol needs to combine the `LETTER+` pattern with a list of multiword tokens which may include spaces, periods and other delimiters.

Figure 16 outlines the construction of a simple tokenizing transducer for English.

```
WHITE%_SPACE+ @-> SPACE
         .o.
[ LETTER+ |
  a t %  l e a s t |
  h e a d %  o v e r %  h e e l s |
  i n %  s p i t e %  o f ]
 @-> ... END%_OF%_TOKEN
         .o.
SPACE -> [] || .#. | END%_OF%_TOKEN _ ;
```

Figure 16: A simple tokenizer

The tokenizer in Figure 16 is composed of three transducers. The first reduces strings of whitespace characters to a single space. The second transducer inserts an `END_OF_TOKEN` mark after simple words and the, listed multiword expressions. The third removes the spaces that are not part of some multiword token. The percent sign here means that the following blank is to be taken literally, that is, parsed as a symbol.

Without the left-to-right, longest-match constraints, the tokenizing transducer would not produce deterministic output. Note that it must introduce an `END_OF_TOKEN` mark after a sequence of letters just in case the word is not part of some longer multiword token. This problem is complicated by the fact that the list of multiword tokens may contain overlapping expressions. A tokenizer for French, for example, needs to recognize "de plus" (moreover), "en plus" (more), "en plus de" (in addition to), and "de plus en plus" (more and more) as single tokens. Thus there is a token boundary after "de plus" in *de plus on ne le fait plus* (moreover one doesn't do it anymore) but not in *on le fait de plus en plus* (one does it more and more) where "de plus en plus" is a single token.

If the list of multiword tokens contains hundreds of expressions, it may require a lot of time and space to compile the tokenizer even if the final result is not too large. The number of auxiliary symbols used to encode the constraints has a critical effect on the efficiency of that computation. We first observed this phenomenon in the course of building a tokenizer for the British National Corpus according to the specifications of the BNC Users Guide (Leech, 1995), which lists around 300 multiword tokens and 260 foreign phrases. With the current definition of the directed replacement we have now been able to compute similar tokenizers for several other languages (French, Spanish, Italian, Portuguese, Dutch, German).

4.2 Filtering

Some text processing applications involve a preliminary stage in which the input stream is divided into regions that are passed on to the calling process and regions that are ignored. For example, in processing an SGML-coded document, we may wish to delete all the material that appears or does not appear in a region bounded by certain SGML tags, say <A> and </A>.

Both types of filters can easily be constructed using the directed replace operator. A negative filter that deletes all the material between the two SGML codes, including the codes themselves, is expressed as in Figure 17.

```
"<A>" ~$["<A>"|"</A>"] "</A>" @-> [] ;
```

Figure 17: A negative filter

A positive filter that excludes everything else can be expressed as in Figure 18.

```
~$"</A>" "<A>" @-> "<A>"
          .o.
"</A>" ~$"<A>" @-> "</A>" ;
```

Figure 18: A positive filter

The positive filter is composed of two transducers. The first reduces to <A> any string that ends with it and does not contain the </A> tag. The second transducer does a similar transduction on strings that begin with </A>. Figure 12 illustrates the effect of the positive filter.

```
<B>one</B><A>two</A><C>three</C><A>four</A>
-------------   ----------------
     <A>       two        </A>        <A>four</A>
```

Figure 19: Application of a positive filter

The idea of filtering by finite-state transduction of course does not depend on SGML codes. It can be applied to texts where the interesting and uninteresting regions are defined by any kind of regular pattern.

4.3 Marking

As we observed in section 3, by using the ... symbol on the lower side of the replacement expression, we can construct transducers that mark instances of a regular language without changing the text in any other way. Such transducers have a wide range of applications. They can be used to locate all kinds of expressions that can be described by a regular pattern, such as proper names, dates, addresses, social security and phone numbers, and the like. Such a marking transducer can be viewed as a deterministic parser for a "local grammar" in the sense of Gross (1989), Roche (1993), Silberztein (1993) and others.

By composing two or more marking transducers, we can also construct a single transducer that builds nested syntactic structures, up to any desired depth. To make the construction simpler, we can start by defining auxiliary symbols for the basic regular patterns. For example, we may define NP as [(d) a* n+]. With that abbreviatory convention, a composition of a simple NP and VP spotter can be defined as in Figure 20.

```
NP @-> %[NP ... %]
       .o.
v %[NP NP %]  @-> %[VP ... %] ;
```

Figure 20: Composition of an NP and a VP spotter

Figure 21 shows the effect of applying this composite transducer to the string "dannvaan".

```
    d a n n       v     a a n
    -------       -     -----
[NP d a n n ] [VP v [NP a a n ] ]
```

Figure 21: Application of an NP-VP parser

By means of this simple "bottom-up" technique, it is possible to compile finite-state transducers that approximate a context-free parser up to a chosen depth of embedding. Of course, the left-to-right, longest-match regimen implies that some possible analyses are ignored. To produce all possible parses, we may introduce the ... notation to the simple replace expressions in Karttunen (1995).

5 Extensions

The definition of the left-to-right, longest-match replacement can easily be modified for the three other directed replace operators mentioned in Figure 3. Another extension, already implemented, is a directed version of parallel replacement (Kempe and Karttunen 1996), which allows any number of replacements to be done simultaneously without interfering with each other. Figure 22 is an example of a directed parallel replacement. It yields a transducer that maps a string of "a"s into a single "b" and a string of "b"s into a single "a".

```
a+ @-> b, b+ @-> a ;
```

Figure 22: Directed, parallel replacement

The definition of directed parallel replacement requires no additions to the techniques already presented. In the near future we also plan to allow directional and length-of-match constraints in the more complicated case of conditional context-constrained replacement.

6 Acknowledgements

I would like to thank Ronald M. Kaplan, Martin Kay, André Kempe, John Maxwell, and Annie Zaenen for helpful discussions at the beginning of the project, as well as Paula Newman and Kenneth R. Beesley for editorial advice on the first draft of the paper. The work on tokenizers and phrasal analyzers by Anne Schiller and Gregory Grefenstette revealed the need for a more efficient implementation of the idea. The final version of the paper has benefited from detailed comments by Ronald M. Kaplan and two anonymous reviewers, who convinced me to discard the ill-chosen original title ("Deterministic Replacement") in favor of the present one.

7 Appendix: Notational conventions

The regular expression formalism used in this paper is essentially the same as in Kaplan and Kay (1994), in Karttunen (1995), and in Kempe and Karttunen (1996). Upper-case strings, such as `UPPER`, represent regular languages, and lower-case letters, such as `x`, represent symbols. We recognize two types of symbols: unary symbols (`a`, `b`, `c`, etc) and symbol pairs (`a:x`, `b:0`, etc.).

A symbol pair `a:x` may be thought of as the crossproduct of `a` and `x`, the minimal relation consisting of `a` (the upper symbol) and `x` (the lower symbol). To make the notation less cumbersome, we systematically ignore the distinction between the language `A` and the identity relation that maps every string of `A` into itself. Consequently, we also write `a:a` as just `a`.

Three special symbols are used in regular expressions: `0` (zero) represents the empty string (often denoted by ϵ); `?` stands for any symbol in the known alphabet and its extensions; in replacement expressions, `.#.` marks the start (left context) or the end (right context) of a string. The percent sign, `%`, is used as an escape character. It allows letters that have a special meaning in the calculus to be used as ordinary symbols. Thus `%[` denotes the literal square bracket as opposed to `[`, which has a special meaning as a grouping symbol; %0 is the ordinary zero symbol.

The following simple expressions appear freqently in the formulas: `[]` the empty string language, `?*` the universal ("sigma star") language.

The regular expression operators used in the paper are: `*` zero or more (Kleene star), `+` one or more (Kleene plus), `~` not (complement), `$` contains, `/` ignore, `|` or (union), `&` and (intersection), `-` minus (relative complement), `.x.` crossproduct, `.o.` composition, `->` simple replace.

In the transducer diagrams (Figures 1, 4, etc.), the nonfinal states are represented by single circles, final states by double circles. State 0 is the initial state. The symbol `?` represents any symbols that are not explicitly present in the network. Transitions that differ only with respect to the label are collapsed into a single multiply labelled arc.

References

Jean Berstel. 1979. *Transductions and Context-Free Languages.* B.G. Teubner, Stuttgart, Germany.

Jean-Pierre Chanod and Pasi Tapanainen. 1995. Tagging French—comparing a statistical and a constraint-based model. In *The Proceedings of the Seventh Conference of the European Chapter of the Association for Computational Linguistics,* Dublin, Ireland.

Samuel Eilenberg. 1974. *Automata, Languages, and Machines.* Academic Press.

Maurice Gross. 1989. The Use of Finite Automata in the Lexical Representation of Natural Language. In *Lecture Notes in Computer Science,* pages 34–50, Springer-Verlag, Berlin, Germany.

Ronald M. Kaplan and Martin Kay. 1994. Regular Models of Phonological Rule Systems. *Computational Linguistics,* 20:3, pages 331–378.

Lauri Karttunen, Kimmo Koskenniemi, and Ronald M. Kaplan. 1987. A Compiler for Two-level Phonological Rules. In *Report No. CSLI-87-108. Center for the Study of Language and Information,* Stanford University. Palo Alto, California.

Lauri Karttunen. 1994. Constructing Lexical Transducers. In *The Proceedings of the Fifteenth International Conference on Computational Linguistics. Coling 94,* I, pages 406–411, Kyoto, Japan.

Lauri Karttunen. 1995. The Replace Operator. In *The Proceedings of the 33rd Annual Meeting of the Association for Computational Linguistics. ACL-94,* pages 16–23, Boston, Massachusetts.

André Kempe and Lauri Karttunen. 1996. Parallel Replacement in the Finite-State Calculus. In *The Proceedings of the Sixteenth International Conference on Computational Linguistics. Coling 96.* Copenhagen, Denmark.

Geoffrey Leech. 1995. *User's Guide to the British National Corpus.* Lancaster University.

Mehryar Mohri. 1994. *On Some Applications of Finite-State Automata Theory to Natural Language Processing.* Technical Report 94-22. L'Institute Gaspard Monge. Université de Marne-la-Vallée. Noisy Le Grand.

Emmanuel Roche. 1993. *Analyse syntaxique transformationelle du français par transducteurs et lexique-grammaire.* Doctoral dissertation, Université Paris 7.

Emmanuel Roche and Yves Schabes. 1995. Deterministic Part-of-Speech Tagging. *Computational Linguistics,* 21:2, pages 227–53.

Marcel Paul Schützenberger. 1977. Sur une variante des fonctions sequentielles. *Theoretical Computer Science,* 4, pages 47–57.

Max Silberztein. 1993. *Dictionnaires Electroniques et Analyse Lexicale du Français—Le Système INTEX,* Masson, Paris, France.

Synchronous Models of Language

Owen Rambow
CoGenTex, Inc.
840 Hanshaw Road, Suite 11
Ithaca, NY 14850-1589
owen@cogentex.com

Giorgio Satta
Dipartimento di Elettronica ed Informatica
Università di Padova
via Gradenigo, 6/A
I-35131 Padova, Italy
satta@dei.unipd.it

Abstract

In synchronous rewriting, the productions of two rewriting systems are paired and applied synchronously in the derivation of a pair of strings. We present a new synchronous rewriting system and argue that it can handle certain phenomena that are not covered by existing synchronous systems. We also prove some interesting formal/computational properties of our system.

1 Introduction

Much of theoretical linguistics can be formulated in a very natural manner as stating correspondences (translations) between layers of representation; for example, related interface layers LF and PF in GB and Minimalism (Chomsky, 1993), semantic and syntactic information in HPSG (Pollard and Sag, 1994), or the different structures such as c-structure and f-structure in LFG (Bresnan and Kaplan, 1982). Similarly, many problems in natural language processing, in particular parsing and generation, can be expressed as transductions, which are calculations of such correspondences. There is therefore a great need for formal models of corresponding levels of representation, and for corresponding algorithms for transduction.

Several different transduction systems have been used in the past by the computational and theoretical linguistics communities. These systems have been borrowed from translation theory, a subfield of formal language theory, or have been originally (and sometimes redundantly) developed. *Finite state transducers* (for an overview, see, e.g., (Aho and Ullman, 1972)) provide translations between regular languages. These devices have been popular in computational morphology and computational phonology since the early eighties (Koskenniemi, 1983; Kaplan and Kay, 1994), and more recently in parsing as well (see, e.g., (Gross, 1989; Pereira, 1991; Roche, 1993)). *Pushdown transducers* and *syntax directed translation schemata* (SDTS) (Aho and Ullman, 1969) translate between context-free languages and are therefore more powerful than finite state transducers. Pushdown transducers are a standard model for parsing, and have also been used (usually implicitly) in speech understanding. Recently, variants of SDTS have been proposed as models for simultaneously bracketing parallel corpora (Wu, 1995). Synchronization of tree adjoining grammars (TAGs) (Shieber and Schabes, 1990; Shieber, 1994) are even more powerful than the previous formalisms, and have been applied in machine translation (Abeillé, Schabes, and Joshi, 1990; Egedi and Palmer, 1994; Harbusch and Poller, 1994; Prigent, 1994), natural language generation (Shieber and Schabes, 1991), and theoretical syntax (Abeillé, 1994). The common underlying idea in all of these formalisms is to combine two generative devices through a pairing of their productions (or, in the case of the corresponding automata, of their transitions) in such a way that right-hand side nonterminal symbols in the paired productions are *linked*. The processes of derivation proceed synchronously in the two devices by applying the paired grammar rules only to linked nonterminals introduced previously in the derivation. The fact that the above systems all reflect the same translation technique has not always been recognized in the computational linguistics literature. Following (Shieber and Schabes, 1990) we will refer to the general approach as *synchronous rewriting*. While synchronous systems are becoming more and more popular, surprisingly little is known about the formal characteristics of these systems (with the exception of the finite-state devices).

In this paper, we argue that existing synchronous systems cannot handle, in a computationally attractive way, a standard problem in syntax/semantics translation, namely quantifier scoping. We propose a new system that provides a synchronization between two unordered vector grammars with dominance links (UVG-DL) (Rambow, 1994). The type of synchronization is closely based on a previously proposed model, which we will call "local" synchronization. We argue that this synchronous system can deal with quantifier scoping in the desired way. The proposed system has the *weak language preservation property*, that is, the defined synchronization mechanism does not alter the weak generative capacity of the formalism being synchronized. Furthermore, the *tree-to-forest translation* problem for our system can be solved in polynomial time; that is, given a derivation tree obtained according to one of the synchronized grammars, we can construct the forest of all the translated derivation trees in the other grammar, using a polynomial amount of time.

The structure of this paper is as follows. In Section 2, we introduce quantifier raising and review two types of synchronization and mention some new formal results. We introduce our new synchronous system in Section 3, and present our formal results and outline the proof techniques in Section 4.

2 Types of Synchronization

2.1 Quantifier Raising

We start by presenting an example which is based on transfer between a syntactic representation and a "semantic" representation of the scoping of quantified NPs. It is generally assumed that in English (and many other languages), quantified arguments of a verb can (in appropriate contexts) take scope in any possible order, and that this generalization extends to cases of embedded clauses (May, 1985).[1] For example, sentence (1) can have four possible interpretations (of the six possible orderings of the quantifiers, two pairs are logically equivalent), two of which are shown in (2).

(1) Every man thinks some official said some Norwegian arrived

(2) a. $\forall x$, x a man, $\exists y$, y an official, $\exists z$, z a Norwegian, x thinks y said z arrived

b. $\exists z$, z a Norwegian, $\exists y$, y an official, $\forall x$, x a man, x thinks y said z arrived

[1]We explicitly exclude from our analysis cases of quantified NPs embedded in NPs, and do not, of course, propose to develop a serious linguistic theory of quantifier scoping.

We give a simplified syntactic representation for (1) in Figure 1, and a simplified semantic representation for (2b) in Figure 2.

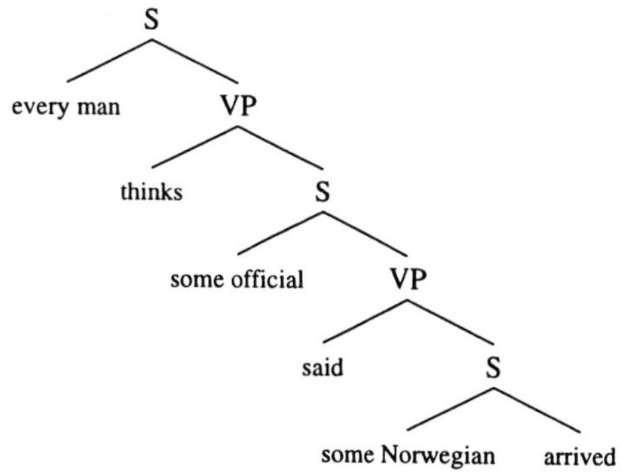

Figure 1: Syntactic representation for (1)

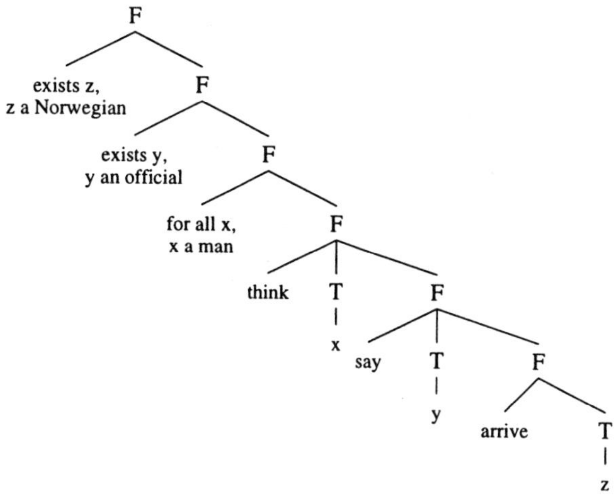

Figure 2: Semantic representation for (2b)

2.2 Non-Local Synchronization

We will first discuss a type of synchronization proposed by (Shieber and Schabes, 1990), based on TAG. We will refer to this system as *non-local synchronous TAG* (nlSynchTAG). The synchronization is non-local in the sense that once links are introduced during a derivation by a synchronized pair of grammar rules, they need not continue to impinge on the nodes that introduced them: the links may be reassigned to a newly introduced nonterminal when an original node is rewritten. We will refer to this mechanism as *link inheritance*. To illustrate, we will give as an example an analysis of the quantifier-raising example introduced above, extending in a natural manner an example given by Shieber and Schabes.

The elementary structures are shown in Figure 3 (we only give one NP — the others are similar). The nominal arguments in the syntax are associated with

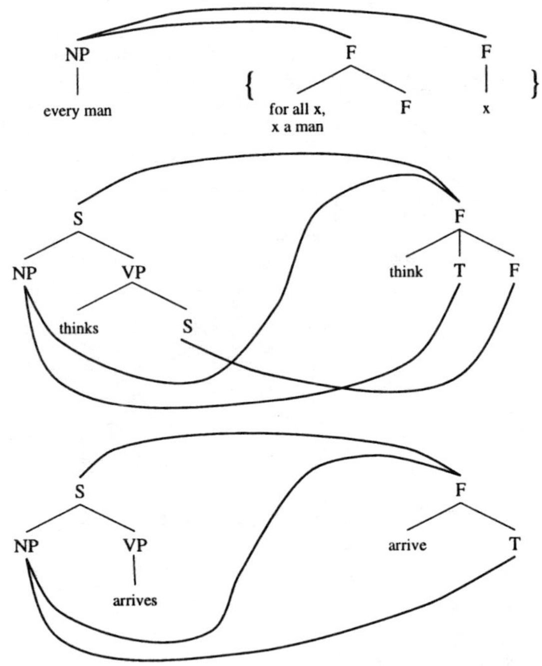

Figure 3: Elementary structures in nlSynchTAG

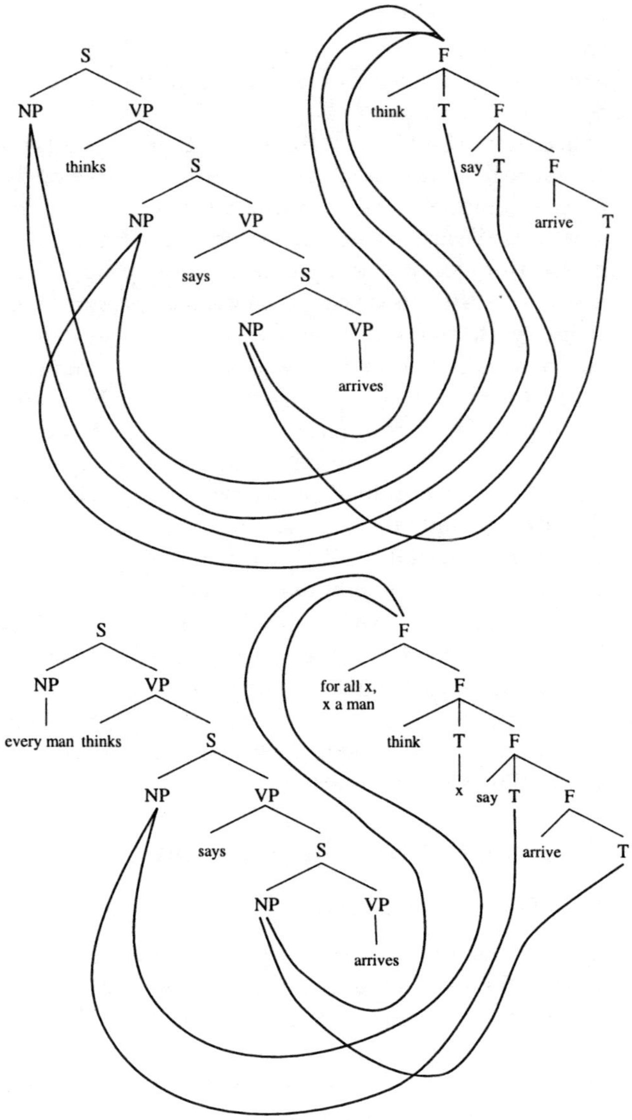

Figure 4: Non-local derivation in nlSynchTAG

pairs of trees in the semantics, and are linked to two nodes, the quantifier and the variable. The derivation proceeds as illustrated in Figure 4, finally yielding the two structures in Figure 1 and Figure 2. Note that some of the links originating with the NP nodes are inherited during the derivation. By changing the order in which we add the nominal arguments at the end of the derivation, we can obtain all quantifier scopes in the semantics.

The problem with non-local synchronization is that the weak language preservation property does not hold. (Shieber, 1994) shows that not all nlSynchTAG left-projection languages can be generated by TAGs. As a new result, in (Rambow and Satta, 1996) we show that the recognition of some fixed left-projection languages of a nlSynchTAG is NP-complete. Our reduction crucially relies on link inheritance. This makes nlSynchTAG unattractive for applications in theoretical or computational linguistics.

2.3 Local Synchronous Systems

In contrast with non-local synchronization, in local synchronization there is no inheritance of synchronization links. This is enforced by requiring that the links establish a bijection between nonterminals in the two synchronously derived sentential forms, that is, each nonterminal must be involved in exactly one link. In this way, once a nonterminal is rewritten through the application of a pair of rules to two linked nonterminals, no additional link remains to be transferred to the newly introduced nonterminals. As a consequence of this, the derivation structures in the left and right grammars are always isomorphic (up to ordering and labeling of nodes).

The canonical example of local synchronization is SDTS (Aho and Ullman, 1969), in which two context-free grammars are synchronized. We give an example of an SDTS and a derivation in Figure 5. The links are indicated as boxed numbers to the right of the nonterminal to which they apply. (Shieber, 1994) defines the tree-rewriting version of SDTS, which we will call *synchronous TAG* (SynchTAG), and argues that SynchTAG does not have the formal problems of nlSynchTAG (though

Grammar:

S$\boxed{1}$ → NP$\boxed{2}$ *likes* NP$\boxed{3}$ S$\boxed{1}$ → NP$\boxed{3}$ *plaît à* NP$\boxed{2}$
NP$\boxed{4}$ → *John*   NP$\boxed{4}$ → *Jean*
NP$\boxed{5}$ → *the white* N$\boxed{6}$ NP$\boxed{5}$ → *la* N$\boxed{6}$ *blanche*
N$\boxed{7}$ → *house*   N$\boxed{7}$ → *maison*

Derivation:

(S$\boxed{0}$, S$\boxed{0}$)
⟹(NP$\boxed{2}$ *likes* NP$\boxed{3}$, NP$\boxed{3}$ *plaît à* NP$\boxed{2}$)
⟹(NP$\boxed{2}$ *likes the white* N$\boxed{6}$, *la* N$\boxed{6}$ *blanche plaît à* NP$\boxed{2}$)
$\stackrel{*}{\Longrightarrow}$ (*John likes the white house, la maison blanche plaît à Jean*)

Figure 5: Sample SDTS and derivation

(Shieber, 1994) studies the translation problem making the unappealing assumption that each tree in the input grammar is associated with only one output grammar tree).

However, SynchTAG cannot derive all possible scope orderings, because of the locality restriction. This can be shown by adapting the proof technique in (Becker, Rambow, and Niv, 1992). In the following section, we will present a synchronous system which has local synchronization's formal advantages, but handles the scoping data.

3 Extended Local Synchronization

In this section, we propose a new synchronous system, which is based on local synchronization of unordered vector grammars with dominance links (UVG-DL) (Rambow, 1994). The presentations will be informal for reasons of space; we refer to (Rambow and Satta, 1996) for details. In UVG-DL, several context-free string rewriting rules are grouped into sets, called *vectors*. In a derivation, all or no rules from a given instance of a vector must be used. Put differently, all productions from a given vector must be used the same number of times. They can be applied in any order and need not be applied simultaneously or one right after the other. In addition, UVG-DL has *dominance links*. An occurrence of a nonterminal A in the right-hand side of a rule p can be linked to the left-hand nonterminal of another rule p' in the same vector. This dominance link will act as a constraint on derivations: if p is used in a derivation, then p' must be used subsequently in the subderivation that starts with the occurrence of A introduced by p. A UVG-DL is *lexicalized* iff at least one production in every vector contains a terminal symbol. Henceforth, all UVG-DLs mentioned in this paper will implicitly be assumed to be lexicalized. The derivation structure of a UVG-DL is just the derivation structure of the same derivation in the underlying context-free grammar (the CFG obtained by forming the union of all vectors). We give an example of a UVG-DL in Figure 6, in which the dotted lines represent the dominance links. A sample derivation is in Figure 7.

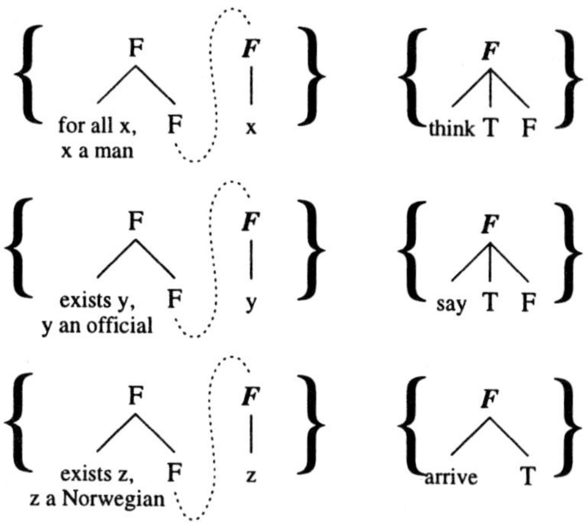

Figure 6: A UVG-DL for deriving semantic representations such as (2)

Our proposal for the synchronization of two UVG-DL uses the notion of locality in synchronization, but with respect to entire vectors, not individual productions in these vectors. This approach, as we will see, gives us both the desired empirical coverage and acceptable computational and formal results. We suppose that in each vector v of a UVG-DL there is exactly one privileged element, which we call the *synchronous production* of v. All other elements of v are referred to as *asynchronous productions*. In Figures 6 and 7, the synchronous productions are designated by a bold-italic left-hand side symbol. Furthermore, in the right-hand side of each asynchronous production of v we identify a single nonterminal nonterminal, called the *heir*.

In a *synchronous UVG-DL* (SynchUVG-DL), vectors from one UVG-DL are synchronized with vectors from another UVG-DL. Two vectors are synchronized by specifying a bijective synchronization mapping (as in local synchronization) between the non-heir right-hand side occurrences of nonterminals in the productions of the two vectors. A nonterminal on which a synchronization link impinges is referred to as a *synchronous nonterminal*. A sample SynchUVG-DL grammar is shown in Figure 9.

Informally speaking, during a SynchUVG-DL derivation, the two synchronous productions in a pair of synchronized vectors must be applied at the same time and must rewrite linked occurrences of nonterminals previously introduced. The asynchronous productions of the two synchronized grammars are not subject to the synchronization requirement, and they can be applied at any time and independently of the other grammar (but of course subject to the grammar-specific dominance links). Any synchronous links that impinge on a nonterminal rewritten by an asynchronous production are transferred to the heir of the asynchronous production. A production may introduce a synchronous nonterminal whose counterpart in the other grammar has not yet been introduced. In this case, the link remains "pending". Thus, while in SynchUVG-DL there is link inheritance as in non-local synchronization, link inheritance is only possible with those productions that themselves are not subject to the synchronization requirement.

The locality of the synchronization becomes clear when we consider a new tree structure which we introduce here, called the *vector derivation tree.* Consider two synchronized UVG-DLderivations in a SynchUVG-DL. The vector derivation tree for either component derivation is obtained as follows. Each instance of a vector used in the derivation is represented as a single node (which we label with that vector's lexeme). A node representing a vector v_1 is immediately dominated by the node representing the vector v_2 which introduced the synchronization link that the synchronous production of v_1 rewrites. Unlike the standard derivation tree for UVG-DL, the vector derivation tree clearly shows how the vectors (rather than the component rules of the vectors) were combined during the derivation. The vector derivation tree for the derivation in Figure 7 is shown in Figure 8.

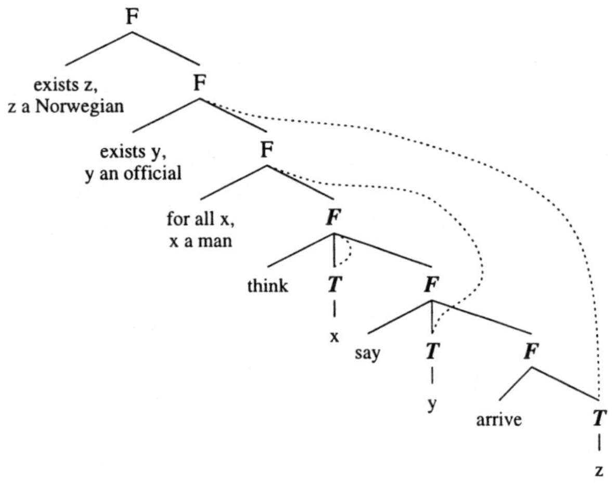

Figure 7: Derivation of (2b) in a UVG-DL

It should be clear that the vector derivation trees for two synchronized derivations are isomorphic, reflecting the fact that our definition of SynchUVG-DL is local with respect to vectors (though not with respect to productions, since the derivation trees of two synchronized UVG-DL derivations need not be isomorphic). The vector derivation tree can be seen as representing an "outline" for the derivation. Such a view is attractive from a linguistic perspective: if each vector represents a lexeme and its projection (where the synchronous production is the basis of the lexical projection that the vector represents), then the vector derivation tree is in fact the dependency tree of the sentence (representing direct relations between lexemes such as grammatical function). In this respect, the vector derivation tree of UVG-DL is like the derivation tree of tree adjoining grammar and of D-tree grammars (DTG) (Rambow, Vijay-Shanker, and Weir, 1995), which is not surprising, since all three formalisms share the same extended domain of locality. Furthermore, the vector derivation tree of SynchUVG-DL shares with the the derivation tree of DTG the property that it reflects linguistic dependency uniformly; however, while the definition of DTG was motivated precisely from considerations of dependency, the vector derivation tree is merely a by-product of our definition of SynchUVG-DL, which was motivated from the desire to have a computationally tractable model of synchronization more powerful than SynchTAG.[2]

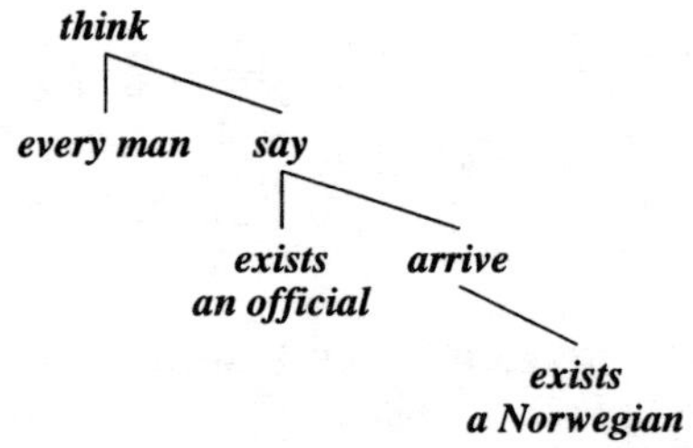

Figure 8: Vector derivation tree for derivation of (2b)

We briefly discuss a sample derivation. We start with the two start symbols, which are linked. We then apply an asynchronous production from the semantic grammar. In Figure 10 (top) we see how the link is inherited by the heir nonterminal of the applied production. This step is repeated with two more asynchronous productions, yielding Figure 10 (bottom). We now apply productions for the bodies of the clauses, but stop short before the two synchronous productions for the *arrive* clause, yielding Figure 11. We see the asynchronous production of the syntactic *arrive* vector has not only inherited the link to its heir nonterminal, but has introduced a link

[2]We do not discuss modifiers in this paper for lack of space.

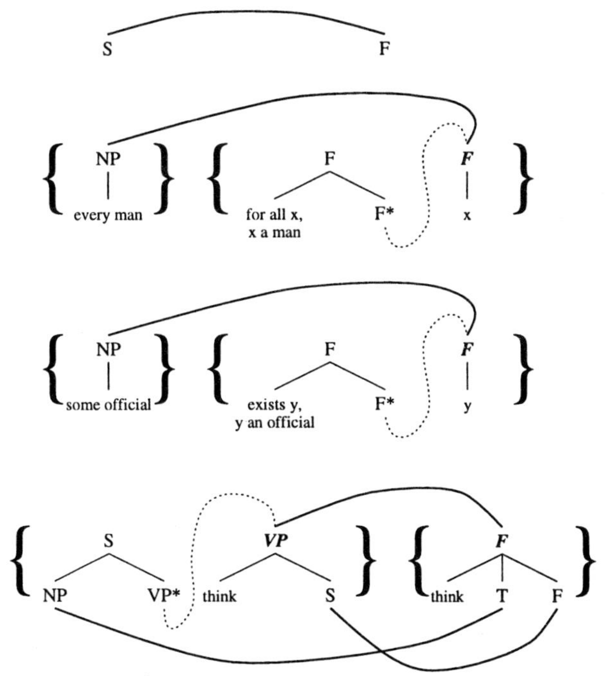

Figure 9: SynchUVG-DL grammar for quantifier scope disambiguation

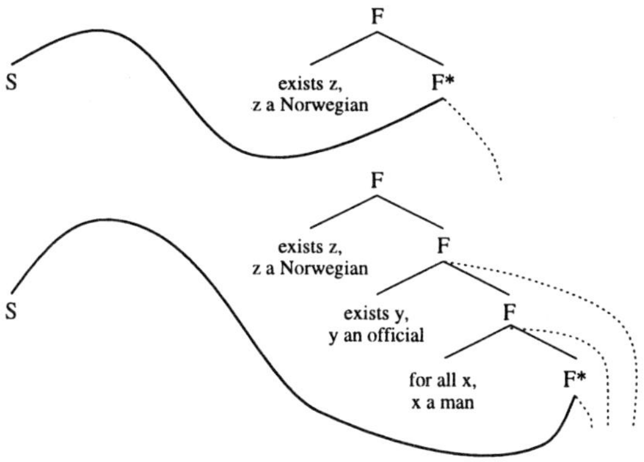

Figure 10: SynchUVG-DL derivation, steps 1 and 2

of its own. Since the semantic end of the link has not been introduced yet, the links remains "pending" until that time. We then finish the derivation to obtain the two trees in Figure 1 and Figure 2, with no synchronization or dominance links left.

4 Formal results

Theorem 1 SynchUVG-DL *has the language preservation property.*

Proof (outline). Let G_s be a SynchUVG-DL, G' and G'' its left and right UVG-DL components, respectively. We construct a UVG-DL G generating the left-projection language of G_s. G uses all the

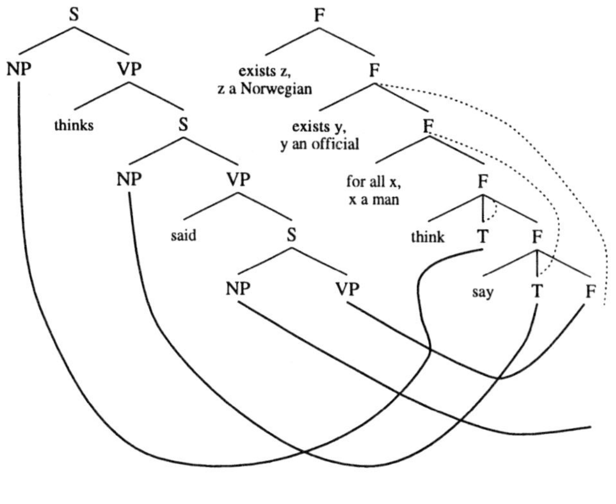

Figure 11: SynchUVG-DL derivation, step 3

nonterminal symbols of G' and G'', and some compound nonterminals of the form $[A, B]$, A and B nonterminals of G' and G'', respectively. G simulates G_s derivations by intermixing symbols of G' and symbols of G'', and without generating any of the terminal symbols of G''. Most important, each pair of linked nonterminals generated by G_s is represented by G using a compound symbol. This enforces the requirement of simultaneous application of synchronous productions to linked nonterminals.

Each vector v of G is constructed from a pair of synchronous vectors (v', v'') of G_s as follows. First, all instances of nonterminals in v'' are replaced by ε. Furthermore, for any instance B of a right-hand side nonterminal of v'' linked to a right-hand side nonterminal A of v', B is replaced by ε and A by $[A, B]$. Then the two synchronous productions in v' and v'' are composed into a single production in v, by composing the two left-hand sides in a compound symbol and by concatenating the two right-hand sides. Finally, to simulate link inheritance in derivations of G_s, each asynchronous production in v' and v'' is transferred to v, either without any change, or by composing with some nonterminal C both its left-hand side and the heir nonterminal in its right-hand side. Note that there are finitely many choices for the last step, and each choice gives a different vector in G, simulating the application of v' and v'' to a set of (occurrences of) nonterminals in a particular link configuration in a sentential form of G_s. ■

We now introduce a representation for sets of derivation trees in a UVG-DL G. A *parse tree* in G is an ordered tree representing a derivation in G and encoding at each node the production p used to start the corresponding subderivation and the multiset of productions f used in that subderivation. A *parse forest* in G is a directed acyclic graph which is ordered and bipartite. (We use ideas originally developed in (Lang, 1991) for the context-free case.) Nodes of the graph are of two different types, called *and-nodes* and *or-nodes*, respectively, and each directed arc connects nodes of different types. A parse forest in G represents a set T of parse trees in G if the following holds. When starting at a root node and walking through the graph, if we follow exactly one of the outgoing arcs at each or-node, and all of the outgoing arcs at each and-node, we obtain a tree in T modulo the removal of the or-nodes. Furthermore, every tree in T can be obtained in this way.

Lemma 2 *Let G be a* UVG-DL *and let $q \geq 1$ be a natural number. The parse forest representing the set of all parse trees in G with no more than q vectors can be constructed in an amount of time bounded by a polynomial function of q.* ∎

Let G_s be a SynchUVG-DL, G' and G'' its left and right UVG-DL components, respectively. For a parse tree τ in G', we denote as $T(\tau)$ the set of all parse trees in G'' that are synchronous with τ according to G_s. The *parse-to-forest translation* problem for G_s takes as input a parse tree τ in G' and gives as output a parse forest representation for $T(\tau)$. If G_s is lexicalized, such a parse forest has size bounded by a polynomial function of $|\tau|$, despite the fact that the size of $T(\tau)$ can be exponentially larger than the size of τ. In fact, we have a stronger result.

Theorem 3 *The parse-to-forest translation problem for a lexicalized* SynchUVG-DL *can be computed in polynomial time.*

Proof (outline). Let G_s be a SynchUVG-DL with G' and G'' its left and right UVG-DL components, respectively. Let τ be a parse tree in G' and π be the parse forest representing $T(\tau)$. The construction of π consists of two stages.

In the first stage, we construct the vector derivation tree γ associated with τ. Let q be the number of nodes of γ. We also construct a parse forest π_q representing the set of all parse trees in G'' with no more than q vectors. This stage takes polynomial time in the size of τ, since γ can be constructed from τ in linear time and π_q can be constructed as in Lemma 2.

In the second stage, we remove from π_q all the parse trees not in π. This completes the construction, since the set of parse trees represented by π is included in the set of parse trees represented by π_q. Let n_r and Γ be the root node and the set of all nodes of γ, respectively. For $n \in \Gamma$, $out(n)$ denotes the set of all children of n. We call *family* the set $\{n_r\}$ and any nonempty subset of $out(n)$, $n \in \Gamma$. The main idea is to associate a set of families $\mathcal{F}_n$ to each node n of π_q, such that the following condition is satisfied. A family F belongs to $\mathcal{F}_n$ if and only if at least one subderivation in G'' represented at n induces a forest of vector derivation trees whose root nodes are all and only the nodes in F. Each $\mathcal{F}_n$ can easily be computed visiting π_q in a bottom-up fashion. Crucially, we "block" a node of π_q if we fail in the construction of $\mathcal{F}_n$. We claim that each set $\mathcal{F}_n$ has size bounded by the number of nodes in γ. This can be shown using the fact that all derivation trees represented at a node of π_q employ the same multiset of productions of G''. From the above claim, it follows that π_q can be processed in time polynomial in the size of τ. Finally, we obtain π simply by removing from π_q all nodes that have been blocked. ∎

5 Conclusion

We have presented SynchUVG-DL, a synchronous system which has restricted formal power, is computationally tractable, and which handles the quantifier-raising data. In addition, SynchUVG-DL can be used for modeling the syntax of languages with syntactic constructions which have been argued to be beyond the formal power of TAG, such as scrambling in German and many other languages (Rambow, 1994) or *wh*-movement in Kashmiri (Rambow, Vijay-Shanker, and Weir, 1995). SynchUVG-DL can be used to synchronize a syntactic grammar for these languages either with a semantic grammar, or with the syntactic grammar of another language for machine translation applications. However, SynchUVG-DL cannot handle the list of cases listed in (Shieber, 1994). These pose a problem for SynchUVG-DL for the same reason that they pose a problem for other local synchronous systems: the (syntactic) dependency structures represented by the two derivations are different. These cases remain an open research issue.

Acknowledgments

Parts of the present research were done while Rambow was supported by the North Atlantic Treaty Organization under a Grant awarded in 1993, while at TALANA, Université Paris 7, and while Satta was visiting the Center for Language and Speech Processing, Johns Hopkins University, Baltimore, MD.

References

Abeillé, Anne. 1994. Syntax or semantics? Handling nonlocal dependencies with MCTAGs or

Synchronous TAGs. *Computational Intelligence*, 10(4):471–485.

Abeillé, Anne, Yves Schabes, and Aravind Joshi. 1990. Using lexicalized TAGs for machine translation. In *Proceedings of the 13th International Conference on Computational Linguistics (COLING'90)*, Helsinki. COLING-90.

Aho, A. V. and J. D. Ullman. 1969. Syntax directed translations and the pushdown assembler. *J. Comput. Syst. Sci.*, 3(1):37–56.

Aho, A. V. and J. D. Ullman. 1972. *The Theory of Parsing, Translation, and Compiling.* Prentice Hall, Englewood Cliffs, NJ.

Becker, Tilman, Owen Rambow, and Michael Niv. 1992. The derivational generative power, or, scrambling is beyond LCFRS. Technical Report IRCS-92-38, Institute for Research in Cognitive Science, University of Pennsylvania.

Bresnan, J. and R. Kaplan. 1982. Lexical-functional grammar: A formal system for grammatical representation. In J. Bresnan, editor, *The Mental Representation of Grammatical Relations.* MIT Press.

Chomsky, Noam. 1993. A minimalist program for linguistic theory. In Kenneth Hale and Samuel J. Keyser, editors, *The View from Building 20.* MIT Press, Cambridge, Mass., pages 1–52.

Egedi, Dana and Martha Palmer. 1994. Constraining lexical selection across languages using TAG. In *3e Colloque International sur les Grammaires d'Arbres Adjoints (TAG+3)*, Rapport Technique TALANA-RT-94-01. Université Paris 7.

Gross, Maurice. 1989. The use of Finite-State Automata in the lexical representation of natural language. In M. Gross and D. Perrin, editors, *Electronic Dictionaries and Automata in Computational Linguistics.* Springer.

Harbusch, Karin and Peter Poller. 1994. Structural rewriting with synchronous rewriting systems. In *3e Colloque International sur les Grammaires d'Arbres Adjoints (TAG+3)*, Rapport Technique TALANA-RT-94-01. Université Paris 7.

Kaplan, Ronald M. and Martin Kay. 1994. Regular models of phonological rule systems. *Computational Linguistics*, 20(3):331–378.

Koskenniemi, Kimmo. 1983. Two-level morphology: A general computational model for word-form recognition and production. Technical Report 11, Department of General Linguistics, University of Helsinki.

Lang, B. 1991. Towards a uniform formal framework for parsing. In M. Tomita, editor, *Current Issues in Parsing technology.* Kluwer Academic Publishers, chapter 11, pages 153–171.

May, Robert. 1985. *Logical Form: Its structure and Derivation.* MIT Press, Cambridge, Mass.

Pereira, Fernando. 1991. Finite-state approximation of phrase structure grammars. In *29th Meeting of the Association for Computational Linguistics (ACL'91)*, Berkeley, California. ACL.

Pollard, Carl and Ivan Sag. 1994. *Head-Driven Phrase Structure Grammar.* University of Chicago Press, Chicago.

Prigent, Gilles. 1994. Synchronous tags and machine translation. In *3e Colloque International sur les Grammaires d'Arbres Adjoints (TAG+3)*, Rapport Technique TALANA-RT-94-01. Université Paris 7.

Rambow, Owen. 1994. Multiset-valued linear index grammars. In *32nd Meeting of the Association for Computational Linguistics (ACL'94).* ACL.

Rambow, Owen and Giorgio Satta. 1996. Synchronous models of language. Manuscript under preparation.

Rambow, Owen, K. Vijay-Shanker, and David Weir. 1995. D-Tree Grammars. In *33rd Meeting of the Association for Computational Linguistics (ACL'95).* ACL.

Roche, Emmanuel. 1993. *Analyse syntaxique transformationelle du français par transducteur et lexique-grammaire.* Ph.D. thesis, Université Raris 7, Paris, France.

Shieber, Stuart and Yves Schabes. 1990. Synchronous tree adjoining grammars. In *Proceedings of the 13th International Conference on Computational Linguistics*, Helsinki.

Shieber, Stuart and Yves Schabes. 1991. Generation and synchronous tree adjoining grammars. *Computational Intelligence*, 4(7):220–228.

Shieber, Stuart B. 1994. Restricting the weak generative capacity of Synchronous Tree Adjoining Grammar. *Computational Intelligence*, 10(4):371–385.

Wu, Dekai. 1995. An algorithm for simultaneously bracketing parallel texts by aligning words. In *33rd Meeting of the Association for Computational Linguistics (ACL'95).* ACL.

Coordination as a Direct Process

Augusta Mela
LIPN-CNRS URA 1507
Université de Paris XIII
93 430 Villetaneuse FRANCE
am@ura1507.univ-paris13.fr

Christophe Fouqueré
LIPN-CNRS URA 1507
Université de Paris XIII
93 430 Villetaneuse FRANCE
cf@ura1507.univ-paris13.fr

Abstract

We propose a treatment of coordination based on the concepts of functor, argument and subcategorization. Its formalization comprises two parts which are conceptually independent. On one hand, we have extended the feature structure unification to disjunctive and set values in order to check the compatibility and the satisfiability of subcategorization requirements by structured complements. On the other hand, we have considered the conjunction *et (and)* as the head of the coordinate structure, so that coordinate structures stem simply from the subcategorization specifications of *et* and the general schemata of a head saturation. Both parts have been encoded within HPSG using the same resource that is the subcategorization and its principle which we have just extended.

1 Introduction

Coordination has always been a centre of academic interest, be it in linguistic theory or in computational linguistics. The problem is that the assumption according to only the constituents of the same category (1) may be conjoined is false; indeed, coordinations of different categories (2)-(3) and of more than one constituent (4)-(5) should not be dismissed though being marginal in written texts and must be accounted for[1].

[1] This research has been done for the French coordination *et (and)*.

(1) Jean danse la valse et le tango
(Jean dances the waltz and the tango.)

(2) Je sais son âge et qu'elle est venue ici.
(I know her age and that she came here.)

(3) Un livre intéressant et que j'aurai du plaisir à lire.
(An interesting book and which I will enjoy to read.)

(4) Je demande à Pierre son vélo et à Marie sa canne à pêche.
(I ask Peter for his bike and Mary for her fishing rod.)

(5) Pierre vend un vélo et donne une canne à pêche à Marie.
(Peter sells a bike and gives a fishing rod to Mary.)

We claim here that the "local combinatory potential" of lexical heads, encoded in the subcategorization feature, explains the previous linguistic facts: conjuncts may be of different categories as well as of more than one constituent, they just have to satisfy the subcategorization constraints.

We focus here on the coordination of syntagmatic categories (as opposite of lexical categories). More precisely, we account for cases of non constituent coordination (4), of Right Node Raising (5) but not for cases of Gapping.

Our approach which is independent of any framework, is easily and precisely encoded in the formalism of Head Driven Phrase Structure Grammar (HPSG) (Pollard and Sag, 1994), which is based on the notion of head and makes available the feature sharing mechanism we need. The paper is organized as follows. Section 2 gives a brief description of basic data and discusses some constraints and available structures. Section 3 summarizes previous approaches and section 4 is devoted to our approach. The french coordination with *et* serves throughout the paper as an example.

2 A brief description of Basic Data and Constraints

The classical typology of coordination, i.e. coordination of constituents (1) and of non-constituents, hides some regularity of the phenomenon as it focuses on concepts of constituent and syntactic category.

A coordination of constituents is interpreted as one phrase without any gap. The constituents may be of the same category (1) as well as of different categories (2)-(3). However, this last case is constrained as examplified hereafter[2].

(2) Je sais son âge et qu'elle est venue ici.
(I know her age and that she came here.)
(2a) Je sais son âge et son adresse.
(I know her age and her address.)
(2b) Je sais qu'elle a 30 ans et qu'elle est venue ici.
(I know that she is 30 and that she came here.)
(2c) *Je sais à Marie et qu'elle est venue ici.
*(I know to Marie and that she came here.)
(2d) Je demande l'addition et que quelqu'un paie.
(I ask for the bill and for someone to pay.)
(2e) *Je rends l'addition et que quelqu'un paie.
*(I give back the bill and someone to pay.)

In these examples, the coordinate structure acts as the argument of the verb. This verb must subcategorize for each constituent of the coordination and this is not the case in example (2c)-(2e). Note that modelizing coordination of different categories as the unification (i.e. underspecification) of the different categories would lead to accept the six examples or wrongly reject (2d) according to the descriptions used[3].

Coordination of more than one constituent are often classified as Conjunction Reduction (4), Gapping (1a-1b) and Right Node Raising (5) (Hudson, 1976).

(1a) Jean danse la valse et Pierre, le tango.
(Jean dances the waltz and Pierre the tango.)
(1b) Hier, Jean a dansé la valse et aujourd'hui, le tango.
(Yesterday, Jean danced the waltz and today, the tango.)

In the case of Gapping structures, the subject (1a) and/or an extracted element (1b) is present in the two sides. The only allowed coordinated structure is *[Jean danse la valse] et [Pierre le tango]* for (1a) and *[Hier, Jean a dansé la valse] et [aujourd'hui, le tango]* for (1b) as wh-sentences on other parts (*[la valse] et [Pierre]* or *[la valse] et [Pierre le tango]*) are impossible.

A contrario, in the case of Conjunction Reductions, wh-sentences as well as cliticization are allowed referring to what follows the verb (as for coordination of constituents) and treating the arguments simultaneously on the two parts of the coordination:

(4a) Je sais à qui demander un vélo et une canne à pêche.
(I know who I ask for a bike and for a fishing rod.)
(4b) Je sais à qui les demander.
(I know who I ask for them.)
(4c) Je leur demande un vélo et une canne à pêche.
(I ask them for a bike and for a fishing rod.)
(4d) Je les leur demande.
(I ask them for them.)

Let us remark that a comma is inserted between *à Marie* and *sa canne à pêche* in case of extraction before *et* as in (1b), indicating the two sentences have not necessarily to be analyzed in the same way:

(4e) Je demande à Pierre son vélo et à Marie sa canne à pêche.
(I ask Peter for his bike and Marie for her fishing rod.)
(4f) A Pierre, je demande son vélo et à Marie, sa canne à pêche.
(Peter, I ask for a bike and Marie, for a fishing rod.)

Two structures are available in case of Conjunction Reductions. One structure corresponds to a coordination of sentences with a gap of the verb after *et*, the other one consists in taking the coordinate parallel sequence of constituents as only one structure. The previous facts argue for the second possibility (see also section 3 for criticism of deletion approach).

Last, note that gapping the verb is less compatible with head-driven mechanisms (and the comma in (4f) could be such a head mark, see (BEF, 1996) for an analysis of Gapping coordinations). It seems then that the structure needed for Conjunction Reduction is some generalization of the standard structure used for coordination of constituents. Our proposal is then focused on this extension. We do not care of Gapping cases as their linguistic properties seem to be different.

It remains to integrate Right-Node Raising and to extend these cases to more complicated ones. Section 4 includes examples of such cases and shows that our proposal can manage them adequately.

3 Previous Approaches

There exists a classical way to eschew the question "what can be coordinated ?" if one assumes a deletion analysis. Indeed, according to this approach (Chomsky, 1957; Banfield, 1981), only coordination of sentences are basic and other syntagmatic coordinations should be considered as coordinations of reduced sentences, the reduction being performed by deleting repeated elements. This approach comes up

[2] The star * marks ungrammatical sentences.
[3] Apart from *ad hoc* modelizations.

against insurmountable obstacles, chiefly with the problem of applying transformation in reverse, in the analysis process (Schachter, 1973).

A direct approach has been proposed at once by Sag & al. (Sag et al., 1985) within the framework of Generalized Phrase Structure Grammar (GPSG), by (Pollard and Sag, 1994) within HPSG, and (Bresnan, 1986) within Lexical Functional Grammar (LFG). These approaches have tried to account for coordination of different categories in reducing the constraint from requiring the same category for conjuncts to a weaker constraint of category compatibility. Whatever the nature of subcategorization information may be, syntactical in GPSG, hybrid in HPSG, functional in LFG, two categories are compatible if they subsume a "common denominator", in this case a common partial structure.

Technically, the compatibility is checked by computing a "generalization" of categories and imposing the generalization comprises all features expected in the given context. For example, the context in (6), that is, the verb *être (to be)*, expects a predicative argument and both categories NP and AP are just predicative categories.

(6) Il est le père de Marie et fier de l'être.
(He is Mary's father and proud of it.)

However, this solution cannot be applied generally because all coordinations have not such "natural" intersection (see (2)). So we claim that we have nothing else to do but explicitly enumerate, within the head subcategorization feature, all the structures allowed as complement.

4 Our Approach

Our proposition involves three stages. We begin by formulating constraints on coordinate structures, then we define how to build the coordinate structures and we end by specifying how the previous constraints filter through such coordinate structures.

4.1 Constraints on coordinate structures

In order to precisely formulate the constraints on coordinate structures, we distinguish the role of functor and that of argument, where functor categories are those that bear unsatisfied subcategorization requirements, as it is the case in Categorial Grammars (Dowty, 1988). Lexical heads (1) are functors in relation to the arguments they select and, by composition, any expression that contains an unsaturated functor is a functor (5)-(7).

(7) Il prétend détester et refuse ces beaux spots lumineux.
(He claims to hate and refuses these beautiful spotlights.)

Arguments are the complements selected by the head[4]. An argument may often be realized by different categories. For example, the argument required by *savoir (to know)* may be a NP or a Completive: we say that the requirement is disjunctive and we represent the different alternatives within subcategorization feature disjunctive values. An argument specification is then a disjunction of categories. When the lexical head requires several complements (*to ask somebody something*), the requirement is said multiple or n-requirement. To the extent that disjunction only appears in argument specifications, a n-requirement is a multi-set of simple requirements. The choice of set (or more precisely multiset) rather than list value for the feature SUBCAT allows us to account for *Je demande à Pierre son vélo* as well as *Je demande son vélo à Pierre.* Gunji (Gunji, 1987) makes the same choice. However our criterion can be formalized in a theory whose order of arguments obeys to an obliqueness hierarchy.

Requirement inheritance. A functor may compose with another functor or with arguments. In functor-arguments composition, the resulting expression inherits the unsatisfied requirement from the functor when it is not empty. For example, in (5), both conjuncts inherit the unsatisfied requirement from their heads. Likewise the functor composition inherits a requirement from the unsatisfied functor[5]. In (7), *prétend détester* inherits the unsatisfied requirement of *détester*, i.e. the requirement of an object.

Adjuncts. To account for the continuum which exists from strictly subcategorized complements to adjuncts, we adopt the hypothesis suggested by (Miller, 1991) according to which adjuncts could be accorded the same status as arguments by integrating them into the subcategorization requirement through an optional lexical rule. That would enable us to account for coordination of adjuncts of different categories (3) as well as coordination of more than one constituent with adjuncts (10)-(11) below. Note that we may still have a special feature ADJUNCT in order to distinguish adjuncts from other complements if necessary. Note also that these lexical rules can be interpreted statically as well as dynamically. In the first case, the extended lexicon is pre-computed and requires no runtime application.

[4]In this paper, we restrict arguments to complements. In our HPSG encoding, they are treated in the SUBCAT feature. In a Borsley-like manner, we suppose a special feature for the subject. However, our approach can be generalized to subjects.

[5]In functor composition, functors cannot be both unsaturated: ** Il promet de manger à sa mère des bananes.(* he promises to eat his mother bananas.)*, cf. the Incomplete Constituent Constraint (Pollard and Sag, 1994).

Satisfiability conditions of requirements. We observe here that a coordination of different categories may appear as head complement when the head requirement is disjunctive and a coordination of more than one constituent appears when such a requirement is multiple. Last, functors may conjoin when their subcategorization requirements are compatible. These observations are synthesized in one coordination criterion.

The first observation is summarized in (C1) and illustrated in (2').

> (C1) A subcategorization 1-requirement is satisfied either by one of the disjuncts or by a coordination of disjuncts.

(2') Je sais son âge /qu'elle est venue ici / son âge et qu'elle est venue ici.
(I know her age /that she came here / her age and that she came here.)

The second one is illustrated below, where subcategorization n-requirements are satisfied either by:

- a series of n complements which satisfy respectively the n requirements
  (8) Je demande à Pierre son vélo et sa canne à pêche.
  (I ask Peter for his bike and for his fishing rod.)
- a coordination of a series of this kind
  (9) Je demande à Pierre son vélo et à Marie d'où elle vient.
  (I ask Peter for his bike and Mary where she comes from.)
- a coordination may concern sub-series of arguments
  (10) Pierre a acheté un livre à Marie et un disque à Pierre pour 100F.
  (Peter has bought a book for Mary and a CD for Peter for 20$.)
- or sequences of more than one constituent with adjuncts (11)
  (11) J'ai vu Pierre hier et Marie lundi.
  (I have seen Peter yesterday and Mary monday.)
- or adjuncts of different categories (3).
  (3) Un livre intéressant et que j'aurai du plaisir à lire.
  (An interesting book and which I will enjoy to read.)

All these situations are summarized in (C2):

> (C2) A subcategorization n-requirement is satisfied by m arguments, $0 < m \leq n$, either by a sequence of m arguments such that each argument satisfies one and only one element of the requirement or by a coordination of such sequences. The result has a $n - m$ requirement.

Note that (C1) and (C2) should be computed simultaneously in order to account for structures as (9). The notion of partial saturation in (C2) allows us to account for coordination of sub-series of arguments as in (10).

Functors coordination and compatibility of requirements. Functors may be simple (1), composed (7), of different structures (12) or partially saturated (13)-(5).

(12) Je pense offrir et que je recevrai des cadeaux.
(I think to offer and that I will receive gifts.)

(13) Je pense recevoir de Jean et offrir à Pierre du caviar de Russie.
(I expect to receive from John and offer to Peter Russian caviar.)

In all cases, when they are conjoined, they share their arguments: there must therefore exist at least one possibility of satisfying them simultaneously. In this case, the unification of their subcategorization requirements succeeds and they are said to be compatible and the two functors may be conjoined. This unification has to account for disjunctive values.

Coordination criterion : satisfying and imposing requirements. As an entity can be both functor and argument (12)-(13) our coordination criterion (necessary condition) is the following one: the conjuncts must satisfy the same simple or multiple subcategorization requirement and impose compatible subcategorization requirements.

4.2 Computing the subcategorization requirements compatibility

We have now to define an extension of the usual unification $\sqcup$ of structures in order to compute the subcategorization requirements compatibility. This extension is an internal operation over the subcategorization requirements which accounts for disjunctive and set values. $\mathcal{U}$ is the unification of argument specifications defined from $\sqcup$, $\mathcal{U}^+$ is its extension to n-requirements.

- **Unification of two argument specifications α and β.**
  Let us have $\alpha = \bigvee_{k=1...p} s_k, \beta = \bigvee_{l=1...q} t_l$, with categories s_k, t_l, then
  $\alpha \mathcal{U} \beta = \bigvee_{k,l} s_k \sqcup t_l$ for k, l s.t. $s_k \sqcup t_l$ exists
  undefined if $s_k \sqcup t_l$ does not exist, $\forall k, l$
- **Unification of two n-requirements Φ and Ψ.** $\Phi = \{\alpha_i / i \in [1, n]\}$ and $\Psi = \{\beta_i / i \in [1, n]\}$ be 2 n-requirements, where α_i and β_i are argument specifications, the extended unification $\mathcal{U}^+$ of Φ and Ψ is defined if there exists a permutation p on $[1, n]$ such that $\alpha_i \mathcal{U} \beta_{p[i]}$ exists $\forall i \in [1, n]$. In this case $\Phi \mathcal{U}^+ \Psi = \{\alpha_i \mathcal{U} \beta_{p[i]} / i \in [1, n]\}$ else $\Phi \mathcal{U}^+ \Psi$ is undefined.

Two n-requirements are compatible iff their unification $\mathcal{U}^+$ succeeds.

We consider that conjoined functors should have the same valence[6]. Note that the unification of two n-requirements is ambiguous because we may have several permutations which lead to success.

4.3 How coordinate structures are built

Until now we have just defined constraints on the coordinate structures but we did not mention how these structures are built. We want that a coordinate structure inherits features from its conjuncts without necessarily failing in case of conflicting values. The generalization method (Sag et al., 1985) has this objective but overgenerates because the conflicting values are ignored. In contrast, the use of composite categories (Cooper, 1991) keeps conflicting values within the connective "$\wedge$". Intuitively, if *son âge (her age)* is a NP and *qu'elle est venue ici (that she came here)* is a Completive, *son âge et qu'elle est venue ici (her age and that she came here)* is a conjunctive composite category NP$\wedge$Compl.

The structuring of categories : composite and tuple of categories. We propose to extend the operation $\wedge$ to complex categories and to use a new connective $< \ldots >$ in order to define tuple of categories. With these two connectives, a total structuring of categories is possible and all the coordinate structures may have a status. For example, the underlined expression in (14) will be represented by the structured category: $\left\langle PP, \begin{bmatrix} NP\wedge Compl \\ Subcat\ PP \end{bmatrix} \right\rangle$.

(14) Je recommande à Pierre la lecture et qu'il s'inspire de la Bible.
(I recommend to Peter the lecture and that he inspires himself of the Bible.)

The extension to complex categories is not uniform. Coordinate structure features are not necessarily composites or tuples of corresponding features from each conjunct. In fact, features which are allowed to have conflicting values will be compounded, whereas other features as SUBCAT must unify. This structuring is encoded later within the definition of the lexical entry of *et*.

Lexicalization of the coordination rule. We consider, as in (Paritong, 1992), the conjunction *et* as the head of the coordinate structure. Consequently, coordinate structures no longer have to be postulated in the grammar by a special rule of coordination: they stem simply from the general schemata of the head saturation and the subcategorization specifications of the conjunction. For sake of simplicity, only binary coordination is treated here. (Paritong, 1992) accounts for multiple coordination as a binary structure where the comma has a similar function as a lexical conjunction. With that one restriction, the HPSG-like lexical entry of *et* can be:

$$\begin{bmatrix} Phon\ \backslash et\backslash \\ Synsem\ <[1],\ldots,[M]>\wedge<[1'],\ldots,[M']>|Cat= \\ \quad \begin{bmatrix} Part\ <C_1,\ldots,C_M>\wedge<C'_1,\ldots,C'_M> \\ Subcat \left\{ \begin{array}{l} [1]\begin{bmatrix} Part\ C_1 \\ Subcat\ \{\} \end{bmatrix},\ldots,[M]\begin{bmatrix} Part\ C_M \\ Subcat\ \Phi_M \end{bmatrix}, \\ [1']\begin{bmatrix} Part\ C'_1 \\ Subcat\ \{\} \end{bmatrix},\ldots,[M']\begin{bmatrix} Part\ C'_M \\ Subcat\ \Phi'_M \end{bmatrix}, \\ \Phi_M \mathcal{U}^+ \Phi'_M \end{array} \right\} \end{bmatrix} \end{bmatrix}$$

The following LP-constraint on the lexical entry of *et* ensures the correct order of conjunction and conjuncts:

$$[i] < conj < [i'], \text{ where } i \in [1, M], i' \in [1', M'].$$

This LP-constraint is the minimum required to distinguish the two parts of the coordinate structure. However, the functor this coordinate structure (partially-)saturates may impose its own LP-constraint (e.g. an obliqueness hierarchy). In such a case, this LP-constraint has to be satisfied simultaneously by the two sets $\{[1],\ldots,[M]\}$ and $\{[1'],\ldots,[M']\}$.

To represent the inheritance of the complements, here $\Phi_M \mathcal{U}^+ \Phi'_M$, we use a mechanism of argument composition inspired by (Hinrichs and Nakazawa, 1994): the conjunction *et* takes as complements the two conjuncts $< C_1,\ldots,C_M >$ and $< C'_1,\ldots,C'_M >$ which may remain unsaturated for their complements Φ_M and Φ'_M, and the set $\Phi_M \mathcal{U}^+ \Phi'_M$. The coordination of m-tuples, as well as the coordination of simple conjuncts ($M = 1$) stems from the saturation of the conjunction *et*. As noted in 4.1., only the last element of the tuple C_M (or C'_M) can be unsaturated and be the source of inheritance. Example of resulting HPSG-like analysis is given in figure 1 for the underlined phrase in (15).

(15) Jean conseille à son père d'acheter et à sa mère d'utiliser un lave-vaisselle.
(Jean advises his father to buy and his mother to use a dish washer.)

4.4 How the constraints apply on coordinate structures

We have now to define how arguments satisfy disjunctive and set requirements. Intuitively, if α_i is a (possibly disjunctive) argument specification, an argument (possibly composite) satisfies α_i iff each element of the composite category matches one disjunct of α_i. Then, if Φ is a n-requirement, a tuple (or a coordination of tuples) of categories (possibly composite) satisfies Φ iff each element of the tuple (for each tuple) satisfies one and only one argument specification of Φ. More formally:

[6]This condition will forbid the conjunction of e.g. verbs with SUBCAT lists of different lengths, but which would have a unification under the alternative interpretation, thus avoiding sentences like **John bought and gave the book to Mary,* (Miller, 1991).

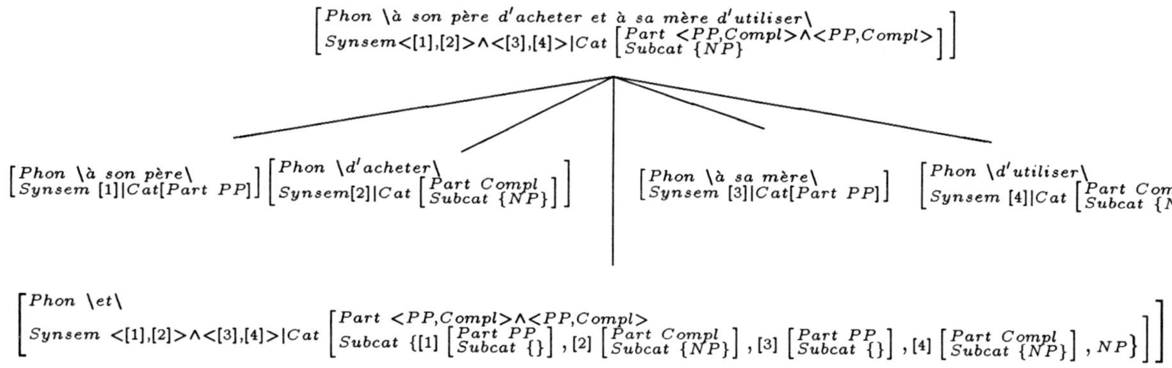

Figure 1: Analysis of *à son père d'acheter et à sa mère d'utiliser*

i) let $\alpha = S^1 \vee \ldots \vee S^p$ be an argument specification, and $C = \bigwedge_{r=1\ldots z} C_r$ be a composite category, then

> C satisfies α iff for each element of the composite category C, there exists one disjunct of α that matches it (iff $\forall r \in [1,z], \exists l \in [1,p] / C_r \cup S^l$ exists).

ii) let Φ be a n-requirement s.t.:

$$\Phi = \{\underbrace{S_1^1 \vee \ldots \vee S_1^{p_1}}_{\alpha_1}, \ldots, \underbrace{S_n^1 \vee \ldots \vee S_n^{p_n}}_{\alpha_n}\}$$

and Σ be a coordination of p tuples (if $p > 1$) or one tuple (if $p = 1$) of composite categories C_i^k s.t.:

$\Sigma = < C_1^1, \ldots, C_n^1 > \wedge \ldots \wedge < C_1^p, \ldots, C_n^p >$

$C_i^k = \bigwedge_{r=1\ldots z_i^k} C_{i,r}^k$

then

> Σ satisfies Φ iff each specification α_i has one and only one realization in each tuple of Σ (iff $\forall k \in [1,p], \exists$ a permutation π_k on $[1,n] / \forall i \in [1,n]$ $C_{\pi_k[i]}^k$ satisfies α_i).

Note that these requirement satisfiability conditions allows us to account for examples such as (9).

4.5 A Coding in HPSG

We extend here the functor saturation schemata to the coordination case, within the framework of Head Driven Phrase Structure Grammar (Pollard and Sag, 1994).

A subcategorization **n-requirement** is satisfied by **m arguments**, $m \leq n$, either by a sequence of m arguments (m-tuple) or by a coordination of m-tuples. The result has a $n - m$ requirement.

Saturation schemata[7]

- **partial** ($\Psi \neq \{\}$) or total ($\Psi = \{\}$) of saturated complements ($\Psi' = \{\}$)
- **total** ($\Psi = \{\}$) of complements, the last being partially ($\Psi' \neq \{\}$) or totally saturated ($\Psi' = \{\}$)

$$\begin{bmatrix} Synsem|Cat[Subcat \;\; \Psi \cup \Psi'] \\ Branches = \\ \quad \begin{bmatrix} B-Head|Synsem|Cat[Subcat \;\; \Phi \cup \Psi] \\ B-Comp = \Sigma[Subcat \;\; \Psi'] \end{bmatrix} \end{bmatrix}$$

where Σ satisfies Φ and:

- $\Phi = \{< S_1^1 \vee \ldots \vee S_1^{p_1} >, \ldots, < S_m^1 \vee \ldots \vee S_m^{p_m} >\}$ m-requirement, Ψ $n - m$ requirement
- $\Sigma = < C_1^1, \ldots, C_m^1 > \wedge \ldots \wedge < C_1^q, \ldots, C_m^q >$ coordination of q m-tuples (if $q > 1$) or one m- tuple (if $q = 1$) of composite Synsem $C_i^k = \bigwedge_{r=1\ldots z_i^k} C_{i,r}^k$
- Ψ or Ψ' must be empty

Example of resulting analysis is given in figure 2 for the underlined phrase in (15):

(15) Jean conseille à son père d'acheter et à sa mère d'utiliser un lave-vaisselle.
(Jean advises his father to buy and his mother to use a dish washer.)

Note that within a theory as HPSG which integrates syntactic and semantic information in a single representation, a whole range of lexically determined dependencies, e.g. case assignment, government (of particular prepositions) and role assignment, are modeled at the same time via subcategorization because the value of subcategorization feature is a complex of syntactic and semantic information.

[7] $\Phi \cup \Psi$ is the set-union of Φ and Ψ

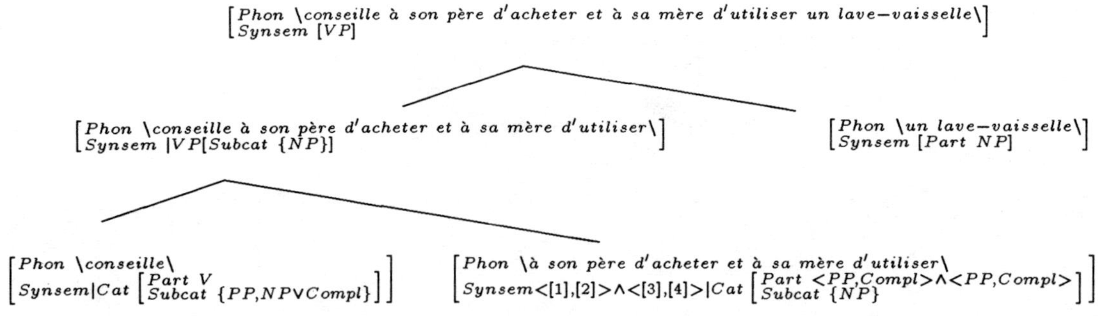

Figure 2: Analysis of *conseille à son père d'acheter et à sa mère d'utiliser un lave-vaisselle*

5 Conclusion

This approach based on concept of functor, argument and subcategorization allows us to account for many coordination data. Its formalization comprises two parts which are conceptually independent. On one hand, we have extended the feature structure unification to disjunctive and set values in order to check the compatibility and the satisfiability of subcategorization requirements by structured complements. On the other hand, we have considered the conjunction *et* as the head of the coordinate structure, so that coordinate structures stem simply from the subcategorization specifications of *et* and a general schemata of the head saturation. Both parts have been encoded within HPSG using the same resource that is the subcategorization and its principle which we have just extended.

It remains to know in which extent our approach can be used for other linguistic phenomena with symetrical sequences of more than one constituent (comparative constructions, alternative constructions):

(16) Paul donne autant <u>de couteaux aux filles</u> que <u>de pièces aux garçons</u>.
(Paul gives as much knives to the girls as coins to the boys.)

References

Banfield, A. 1981. Stylistic deletion in coordinate structures. *Linguistics Analysis*, 7(1):1–32.

Bouchard, L., Emirkanian, L., Fouqueré, C. 1996. La coordination à trouée : étude et analyse en GPSG et HPSG. In submission.

Bresnan, J., Kaplan, R., Peterson, P. 1986. Coordination and the Flow of Information Through Phrase Structure. *Ms., CSLI, Stanford University.*

Chomsky, N. 1957. *Structures syntaxiques.* Seuil.

Cooper, R. P. 1991. Coordination in unification-based grammars. In *Proceedings of the ACL*, pages 167–172.

Dowty, D. 1988. Type raising, functional composition, and non-constituent conjunction. In *Categorial Grammars and Natural Language Structures.* Richard T. Oehrle et al., pages 153–197.

Gunji, T. 1987. *Japanese Phrase Structure Grammar.* Dordrecht, Reidel.

Hinrichs, E. and T. Nakazawa. 1994. Linearizing AUXs in German Verbal Complexes. In *German in Head-Driven Phrase Structure Grammar.* J. Nerbonne, K. Netter and C. Pollard, pages 11–37, CSLI Publications.

Hudson, R. 1976. Conjunction reduction, gapping and right-node raising. *Language*, 52(3):535–562.

Miller, P. 1991. *Clitics and Constituents in Phrase Structure Grammar.* Ph.D. thesis, Université libre de Bruxelles, Faculté de Philosophie et Lettres en Institut de Recherches en Intelligence Artificielle (IRIDIA).

Paritong, M. 1992. Constituent coordination in HPSG. In *KONVENS 92*, pages 228–237. Springer Verlag.

Pollard, C. and I. A. Sag. 1994. *Head-Driven Phrase Structure Grammar.* CSLI.

Sag, I., G. Gazdar, T. Wasow, and S. Weisler. 1985. Coordination and how to distinguish categories. *Natural Language and Linguistic theory*, (3):117–171.

Schachter, P. 1973. Conjunction. In *The Major structures of English.* Holt, Rinehart and Winston, chapter 6.

Steedman, M. 1990. Gapping as constituent coordination. *Linguistics and Philosophy*, (13):207–263.

High-Performance Bilingual Text Alignment Using Statistical and Dictionary Information

Masahiko Haruno Takefumi Yamazaki
NTT Communication Science Labs.
1-2356 Take Yokosuka-Shi
Kanagawa 238-03, Japan
haruno@nttkb.ntt.jp yamazaki@nttkb.ntt.jp

Abstract

This paper describes an accurate and robust text alignment system for structurally different languages. Among structurally different languages such as Japanese and English, there is a limitation on the amount of word correspondences that can be statistically acquired. The proposed method makes use of two kinds of word correspondences in aligning bilingual texts. One is a bilingual dictionary of general use. The other is the word correspondences that are statistically acquired in the alignment process. Our method gradually determines sentence pairs (anchors) that correspond to each other by relaxing parameters. The method, by combining two kinds of word correspondences, achieves adequate word correspondences for complete alignment. As a result, texts of various length and of various genres in structurally different languages can be aligned with high precision. Experimental results show our system outperforms conventional methods for various kinds of Japanese-English texts.

1 Introduction

Corpus-based approaches based on bilingual texts are promising for various applications(i.e., lexical knowledge extraction (Kupiec, 1993; Matsumoto et al., 1993; Smadja et al., 1996; Dagan and Church, 1994; Kumano and Hirakawa, 1994; Haruno et al., 1996), machine translation (Brown and others, 1993; Sato and Nagao, 1990; Kaji et al., 1992) and information retrieval (Sato, 1992)). Most of these works assume voluminous aligned corpora.

Many methods have been proposed to align bilingual corpora. One of the major approaches is based on the statistics of simple features such as sentence length in words (Brown and others, 1991) or in characters (Gale and Church, 1993). These techniques are widely used because they can be implemented in an efficient and simple way through dynamic programing. However, their main targets are rigid translations that are almost literal translations. In addition, the texts being aligned were structurally similar European languages (i.e., English-French, English-German).

The simple-feature based approaches don't work in flexible translations for structurally different languages such as Japanese and English, mainly for the following two reasons. One is the difference in the character types of the two languages. Japanese has three types of characters (Hiragana, Katakana, and Kanji), each of which has different amounts of information. In contrast, English has only one type of characters. The other is the grammatical and rhetorical difference of the two languages. First, the systems of functional (closed) words are quite different from language to language. Japanese has a quite different system of closed words, which greatly influence the length of simple features. Second, due to rhetorical difference, the number of multiple match (i.e., 1-2, 1-3, 2-1 and so on) is more than that among European languages. Thus, it is impossible in general to apply the simple-feature based methods to Japanese-English translations.

One alternative alignment method is the lexicon-based approach that makes use of the word-correspondence knowledge of the two languages. (Church, 1993) employed n-grams shared by two languages. His method is also effective for Japanese-English computer manuals both containing lots of the same alphabetic technical terms. However, the method cannot be applied to general translations in structurally different languages. (Kay and Roscheisen, 1993) proposed a relaxation method to iteratively align bilingual texts using the word correspondences acquired during the alignment process. Although the method works well among European languages, the method does not work in aligning structurally different languages. In Japanese-English translations, the method does not capture enough word correspondences to permit alignment. As a result, it can align only some of the two texts. This is mainly because the syntax and rhetoric are greatly differ in the two languages even in literal translations. The number of confident word correspondences of words is not enough for complete alignment. Thus, the problem cannot be addressed as long as the method relies only on statistics. Other methods in the lexicon-based approach embed lexical knowledge into stochastic models (Wu, 1994; Chen, 1993), but these methods were tested using rigid translations.

To tackle the problem, we describe in this paper a text alignment system that uses both statistics and bilingual dictionaries at the same time. Bilingual dictionaries are now widely available on-line due to advances in CD-ROM technologies. For example, English-Spanish, English-French, English-German, English-Japanese, Japanese-French, Japanese-Chinese and other dictionaries are now commercially available. It is reasonable to make use of these dictionaries in bilingual text alignment. The pros and cons of statistics and online dictionaries are discussed below. They show that statistics and on-line dictionaries are complementary in terms of bilingual text alignment.

Statistics Merit Statistics is robust in the sense that it can extract context-dependent usage of words and that it works well even if word segmentation[1] is not correct.

Statistics Demerit The amount of word correspondences acquired by statistics is not enough for complete alignment.

Dictionaries Merit They can contain the information about words that appear only once in the corpus.

Dictionaries Demerit They cannot capture context-dependent keywords in the corpus and are weak against incorrect word segmentation. Entries in the dictionaries differ from author to author and are not always the same as those in the corpus.

Our system iteratively aligns sentences by using statistical and on-line dictionary word correspondences. The characteristics of the system are as follows.

- The system performs well and is robust for various lengths (especially short) and various genres of texts.
- The system is very economical because it assumes only online-dictionaries of general use and doesn't require the labor-intensive construction of domain-specific dictionaries.
- The system is extendable by registering statistically acquired word correspondences into user dictionaries.

[1]In Japanese, there are no explicit delimiters between words. The first task for alignment is , therefore, to divide the text stream into words.

We will treat hereafter Japanese-English translations although the proposed method is language independent.

The construction of the paper is as follows. First, Section 2 offers an overview of our alignment system. Section 3 describes the entire alignment algorithm in detail. Section 4 reports experimental results for various kinds of Japanese-English texts including newspaper editorials, scientific papers and critiques on economics. The evaluation is performed from two points of view: precision-recall of alignment and word correspondences acquired during alignment. Section 5 concerns related works and Section 6 concludes the paper.

2 System Overview

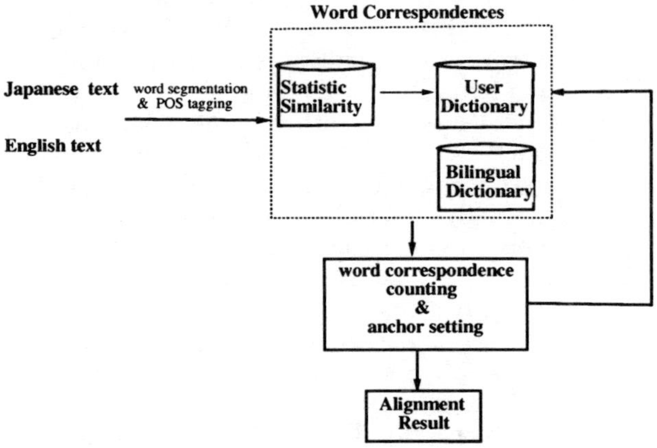

Figure 1: Overview of the Alignment System

Figure 1 overviews our alignment system. The input to the system is a pair of Japanese and English texts, one the translation of the other. First, sentence boundaries are found in both texts using finite state transducers. The texts are then part-of-speech (POS) tagged and separated into original form words[2]. Original forms of English words are determined by 80 rules using the POS information. From the word sequences, we extract only nouns, adjectives, adverbs verbs and unknown words (only in Japanese) because Japanese and English closed words are different and impede text alignment. These pre-processing operation can be easily implemented with regular expressions.

[2]We use in this phase the JUMAN morphological analyzing system (Kurohashi et al., 1994) for tagging Japanese texts and Brill's transformation-based tagger (Brill, 1992; Brill, 1994) for tagging English texts (JUMAN: ftp://ftp.aist-nara.ac.jp/pub/nlp/tools/juman/ Bril: ftp://ftp.cs.jhu.edu/pub/brill). We would like to thank all people concerned for providing us with the tools.

The initial state of the algorithm is a set of already known anchors (sentence pairs). These are determined by article boundaries, section boundaries and paragraph boundaries. In the most general case, initial anchors are only the first and final sentence pairs of both texts as depicted in Figure 2. Possible sentence correspondences are determined from the anchors. Intuitively, the number of possible correspondences for a sentence is small near anchors, while large between the anchors. In this phase, the most important point is that each set of possible sentence correspondences should include the correct correspondence.

The main task of the system is to find anchors from the possible sentence correspondences by using two kinds of word correspondences: statistical word correspondences and word correspondences as held in a bilingual dictionary[3]. By using both correspondences, the sentence pair whose correspondences exceeds a pre-defined threshold is judged as an anchor. These newly found anchors make word correspondences more precise in the subsequent session. By repeating this anchor setting process with threshold reduction, sentence correspondences are gradually determined from confident pairs to non-confident pairs. The gradualism of the algorithm makes it robust because anchor-setting errors in the last stage of the algorithm have little effect on overall performance. The output of the algorithm is the alignment result (a sequence of anchors) and word correspondences as by-products.

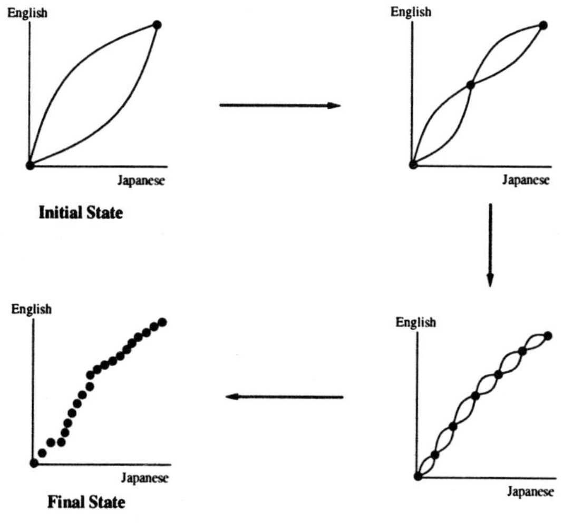

Figure 2: Alignment Process

[3]Adding to the bilingual dictionary of general use, users can reuse their own dictionaries created in previous sessions.

3 Algorithms

3.1 Statistics Used

In this section, we describe the statistics used to decide word correspondences. From many similarity metrics applicable to the task, we choose mutual information and *t-score* because the relaxation of parameters can be controlled in a sophisticated manner. Mutual information represents the similarity on the occurrence distribution and *t-score* represents the confidence of the similarity. These two parameters permit more effective relaxation than the single parameter used in conventional methods(Kay and Roscheisen, 1993).

Our basic data structure is the alignable sentence matrix (ASM) and the anchor matrix (AM). ASM represents possible sentence correspondences and consists of ones and zeros. A one in ASM indicates the intersection of the column and row constitutes a possible sentence correspondence. On the contrary, AM is introduced to represent how a sentence pair is supported by word correspondences. The *i-j* Element of AM indicates how many times the corresponding words appear in the *i-j* sentence pair. As alignment proceeds, the number of ones in ASM reduces, while the elements of AM increase.

Let p_i be a sentence set comprising the ith Japanese sentence and its possible English correspondences as depicted in Figure 3. For example, p_2 is the set comprising $Jsentence_2$, $Esentence_2$ and $Esentence_3$, which means $Jsentence_2$ has the possibility of aligning with $Esentence_2$ or $Esentence_3$. The p_is can be directly derived from ASM.

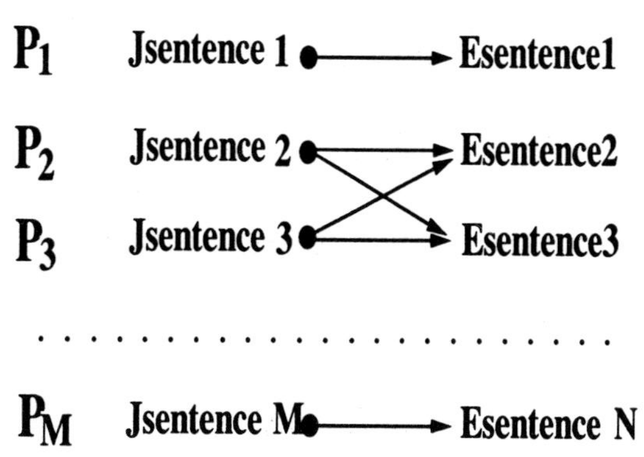

Figure 3: Possible Sentence Correspondences

We introduce the contingency matrix (Fung and Church, 1994) to evaluate the similarity of word occurrences. Consider the contingency matrix shown Table 1, between Japanese word w_{jpn} and English word w_{eng}. The contingency matrix shows: (a) the number of p_is in which both w_{jpn} and w_{eng} were found, (b) the number of p_is in which just w_{eng} was found, (c) the number of p_is in which just w_{jpn} was found, (d) the number of p_is in which neither word was found. Note here that p_is overlap each other and w_{eng} may be double counted in the contingency matrix. We count each w_{eng} only once, even if it occurs more than twice in p_is.

	w_{jpn}	
w_{eng}	a	b
	c	d

Table 1: Contingency Matrix

If w_{jpn} and w_{eng} are good translations of one another, a should be large, and b and c should be small. In contrast, if the two are not good translations of each other, a should be small, and b and c should be large. To make this argument more precise, we introduce mutual information:

$$\log \frac{prob(w_{jpn}, w_{eng})}{prob(w_{jpn})prob(w_{eng})}$$

The probabilities are:

$$prob(w_{jpn}) = \frac{a+c}{a+b+c+d} = \frac{a+c}{M}$$

$$prob(w_{eng}) = \frac{a+b}{a+b+c+d} = \frac{a+b}{M}$$

$$prob(w_{jpn}, w_{eng}) = \frac{a}{a+b+c+d} = \frac{a}{M}$$

Unfortunately, mutual information is not reliable when the number of occurrences is small. Many words occur just once which weakens the statistics approach. In order to avoid this, we employ *t-score*, defined below, where M is the number of Japanese sentences. Insignificant mutual information values are filtered out by thresholding *t-score*. For example, *t-scores* above 1.65 are significant at the $p > 0.95$ confidence level.

$$t \approx \frac{prob(w_{jpn}, w_{eng}) - prob(w_{jpn})prob(w_{eng})}{\sqrt{\frac{1}{M} prob(w_{jpn}, w_{eng})}}$$

3.2 Basic Alignment Algorithm

Our basic algorithm is an iterative adjustment of the Anchor Matrix (AM) using the Alignable Sentence Matrix (ASM). Given an ASM, mutual information and *t-score* are computed for all word pairs in possible sentence correspondences. A word combination exceeding a predefined threshold is judged as a word correspondence. In order to find new anchors, we combine these statistical word correspondences with the word correspondences in a bilingual dictionary. Each element of AM, which represents a sentence pair, is updated by adding the number of word correspondences in the sentence pair. A sentence pair containing more than a predefined number of corresponding words is determined to be a new anchor. The detailed algorithm is as follows.

3.2.1 Constructing Initial ASM

This step constructs the initial ASM. If the texts contain M and N sentences respectively, the ASM is an $M \times N$ matrix. First, we decide a set of anchors using article boundaries, section boundaries and so on. In the most general case, initial anchors are the first and last sentences of both texts as depicted in Figure 2. Next, possible sentence correspondences are generated. Intuitively, true correspondences are close to the diagonal linking the two anchors. We construct the initial ASM using such a function that pairs sentences near the middle of the two anchors with as many as $O(\sqrt[2]{L})$ (L is the number of sentences existing between two anchors) sentences in the other text because the maximum deviation can be stochastically modeled as $O(\sqrt[2]{L})$ (Kay and Roscheisen, 1993). The initial ASM has little effect on the alignment performance so long as it contains all correct sentence correspondences.

3.2.2 Constructing AM

This step constructs an AM when given an ASM and a bilingual dictionary. Let t_{high}, t_{low}, I_{high} and I_{low} be two thresholds for *t-score* and two thresholds for mutual information, respectively. Let ANC be the minimal number of corresponding words for a sentence pair to be judged as an anchor.

First, mutual information and *t-score* are computed for all word pairs appearing in a possible sentence correspondence in ASM. We use hereafter the word correspondences whose mutual information exceeds I_{low} and whose *t-score* exceeds t_{low}. For all possible sentence correspondences $Jsentence_i$ and $Esentence_j$ (any pair in ASM), the following operations are applied in order.

1. If the following three conditions hold, add 3 to the *i-j* element of AM. (1) $Jsentence_i$ and $Esentence_j$ contain a bilingual dictionary word correspondence (w_{jpn} and w_{eng}). (2) w_{eng} does not occur in any other English sentence that is a possible translation of $Jsentence_i$. (3) $Jsentence_i$ and $Esentence_j$ do not cross any sentence pair that has more than ANC word correspondences.
2. If the following three conditions hold, add 3 to the *i-j* element of AM. (1) $Jsentence_i$ and $Esentence_j$ contain a stochastic word correspondence (w_{jpn} and w_{eng}) that has mutual information I_{high} and whose *t-score* exceeds t_{high}. (2) w_{eng} does not occur in any other English sentence that is a possible translation of $Jsentence_i$. (3) $Jsentence_i$ and $Esentence_j$ do not cross any sentence pair that has more than ANC word correspondences.
3. If the following three conditions hold, add 1 to the *i-j* element of AM. (1) $Jsentence_i$ and $Esentence_j$ contain a stochastic word correspondence (w_{jpn} and w_{eng}) that has mutual

information I_{low} and whose *t-score* exceeds t_{low}. (2) w_{eng} does not occur in any other English sentence that is a possible translation of $Jsentence_i$. (3) $Jsentence_i$ and $Esentence_j$ does not cross any sentence pair that has more than ANC word correspondences.

The first operation deals with word correspondences in the bilingual dictionary. The second operation deals with stochastic word correspondences which are highly confident and in many cases involve domain specific keywords. These word correspondences are given the value of 3. The third operation is introduced because the number of highly confident corresponding words are too small to align all sentences. Although word correspondences acquired by this step are sometimes false translations of each other, they play a crucial role mainly in the final iterations phase. They are given one point.

3.2.3 Adjusting ASM

This step adjusts ASM using the AM constructed by the above operations. The sentence pairs that have at least ANC word correspondences are determined to be new anchors. By using the new set of anchors, a new ASM is constructed using the same method as used for initial ASM construction.

Our algorithm implements a kind of relaxation by gradually reducing t_{low}, I_{low} and ANC, which enables us to find confident sentence correspondences first. As a result, our method is more robust than dynamic programing techniques against the shortage of word-correspondence knowledge.

4 Experimental Results

In this section, we report the result of experiments on aligning sentences in bilingual texts and on statistically acquired word correspondences. The texts for the experiment varied in length and genres as summarized in Table 2. Texts 1 and 2 are editorials taken from 'Yomiuri Shinbun' and its English version 'Daily Yomiuri'. This data was distributed electrically via a WWW server[4]. The first two texts clarify the systems's performance on shorter texts. Text 3 is an essay on economics taken from a quarterly publication of The International House of Japan. Text 4 is a scientific survey on brain science taken from 'Scientific American' and its Japanese version 'Nikkei Science'[5]. **Jpn** and **Eng** in Table2 represent the number of sentences in the Japanese and English texts respectively. The remaining table entries show categories of matches by manual alignment and indicate the difficulty of the task.

Our evaluation focuses on much smaller texts than those used in other study(Brown and others, 1993; Gale and Church, 1993; Wu, 1994; Fung, 1995; Kay and Roscheisen, 1993) because our main targets are well-separated articles. However, our method will work on larger and noisy sets too, by using word anchors rather than using sentence boundaries as segment boundaries. In such a case, the method constructing initial ASM needs to be modified.

We briefly report here the computation time of our method. Let us consider Text 4 as an example. After 15 seconds for full preprocessing, the first iteration took 25 seconds with $t_{low} = 1.55$ and $I_{low} = 1.8$. The rest of the algorithm took 20 seconds in all. This experiment was performed on a SPARC Station 20 Model HS21. From the result, we may safely say that our method can be applied to voluminous corpora.

4.1 Sentence Alignment

Table 3 shows the performance on sentence alignments for the texts in Table 2. **Combined**, **Statistics** and **Dictionary** represent the methods using both statistics and dictionary, only statistics and only dictionary, respectively. Both **Combined** and **Dictionary** use a CD-ROM version of a Japanese-English dictionary containing 40 thousands entries. **Statistics** repeats the iteration by using statistical corresponding words only. This is identical to Kay's method (Kay and Roscheisen, 1993) except for the statistics used. **Dictionary** performs the iteration of the algorithm by using corresponding words of the bilingual dictionary. This delineates the coverage of the dictionary. The parameter setting used for each method was the optimum as determined by empirical tests.

In Table 3, PRECISION delineates how many of the aligned pairs are correct and RECALL delineates how many of the manual alignments we included in systems output. Unlike conventional sentence-chunk based evaluations, our result is measured on the sentence-sentence basis. Let us consider a 3-1 matching. Although conventional evaluations can make only one error from the chunk, three errors may arise by our evaluation. Note that our evaluation is more strict than the conventional one, especially for difficult texts, because they contain more complex matches.

For Text 1 and Text 2, both the combined method and the dictionary method perform much better than the statistical method. This is obviously because statistics cannot capture word-correspondences in the case of short texts.

Text 3 is easy to align in terms of both the complexity of the alignment and the vocabularies used. All methods performed well on this text.

For Text 4, **Combined** and **Statistics** perform

[4] The Yomiuri data can be obtained from www.yomiuri.co.jp. We would like to thank Yomiuri Shinbun Co. for permitting us to use the data.

[5] We obtained the data from paper version of the magazine by using OCR. We would like to thank Nikkei Science Co. for permitting us to use the data.

No.	Text Name	Jpn	Eng	1-1	1-2	2-1	3-1
1	*Root out guns at all costs*	26	28	24	2	0	0
2	*Economy facing last hurdle*	36	41	25	7	2	0
3	*Pacific Asia in the Post-Cold-War World*	134	124	114	0	10	0
4	*Visualizing the Mind*	225	214	186	6	15	1

Table 2: Test Texts

	Combined		Statistics		Dictionary	
Text	PRECISION	RECALL	PRECISION	RECALL	PRECISION	RECALL
1	96.4%	96.3%	65.0%	48.5%	89.3%	88.9%
2	95.3%	93.1%	61.3%	49.6%	87.2%	75.1%
3	96.5%	97.1%	87.3%	85.1%	86.3%	88.2%
4	91.6%	93.8%	82.2%	79.3%	74.3%	63.8%

Table 3: Result of Sentence Alignment

much better than **Dictionary**. The reason for this is that Text 4 concerns brain science and the bilingual dictionaries of general use did not contain domain specific keywords. On the other hand, the combined and statistical methods well capture the keywords as described in the next section. Note here that **Combined** performs better than **Statistics** in the case of longer texts, too. There is clearly a limitation in the amount of word correspondences that can be captured by statistics. In summary, the performance of **Combined** is better than either **Statistics** or **Dictionary** for all texts, regardless of text length and the domain.

4.2 Word Correspondence

In this section, we will demonstrate how well the proposed method captured domain specific word correspondences by using Text 4 as an example. Table 4 shows the word correspondences that have high mutual information. These are typical keywords concerning the non-invasive approach to human brain analysis. For example, NMR, MEG, PET, CT, MRI and functional MRI are devices for measuring brain activity from outside the head. These technical terms are the subjects of the text and are essential for alignment. However, none of them have their own entry in the bilingual dictionary, which would strongly obstruct the dictionary method.

It is interesting to note that the correct Japanese translation of 'MEG' is '脳磁図'. The Japanese morphological analyzer we used does not contain an entry for '脳磁図' and split it into a sequence of three characters '脳','磁' and '図'. Our system skillfully combined '磁' and '図' with 'MEG', as a result of statistical acquisition. These word correspondences greatly improved the performance for Text 4. Thus, the statistical method well captures the domain specific keywords that are not included in general-use bilingual dictionaries. The dictionary method would yield false alignments if statistically acquired word correspondences were not used.

Although these word correspondences are very effective for sentence alignment task, they are unsatisfactory when regarded as a bilingual dictionary. For example, 'ファンクショナルＭＲＩ' in Japanese is the translation of 'functional MRI'. In Table 4, the correspondence of these compound nouns was captured only in their constituent level. (Haruno et al., 1996) proposes an efficient n-gram based method to extract bilingual collocations from sentence aligned bilingual corpora.

5 Related Work

Sentence alignment between Japanese and English was first explored by Sato and Murao (Murao, 1991). They found (character or word) length-based approaches were not appropriate due to the structural difference of the two languages. They devised a dynamic programming method based on the number of corresponding words in a hand-crafted bilingual dictionary. Although some results were promising, the method's performance strongly depended on the domain of the texts and the dictionary entries. (Utsuro et al., 1994) introduced a statistical post-processing step to tackle the problem. He first applied Sato's method and extracted statistical word correspondences from the result of the first path. Sato's method was then reiterated using both the acquired word correspondences and the hand-crafted dictionary. His method involves the following two problems. First, unless the hand-crafted dictionary contains domain specific key words, the first path yields false alignment, which in turn leads to false statistical correspondences. Because it is impossible in general to cover key words in all domains, it is inevitable that statistics and hand-crafted bilingual dictionaries must be used at the same time.

Japanese	English	Mutual Information
記録	recording	3.58
リアルタイム	real	3.51
ニューロン	neuron	3.51
フィルム	film	3.51
グルコース	glucose	3.51
増加	increase	3.51
磁	MEG	3.51
解像度	resolution	3.43
電気	electrical	3.43
グループ	group	3.39
電気	recording	3.39
記録	electrical	3.39
言う	generate	3.33
提供	provide	3.33
図	MEG	3.33
言う	noun	3.17
NMR	NMR	3.17
ファンクショナル	functional	3.17
機器	equipment	3.17
臓器	organ	3.15
注射	compound	3.10
水	water	3.10
標識	radioactive	3.10
ＰＥＴ	PET	3.10
解像度	spatial	3.10
そのようだ	such	3.10
代謝	metabolism	3.06
言う	verb	3.04
科学者	scientist	2.95
同位	water	2.95
体	water	2.95
地図	mapping	2.92
時間	take	2.92
大学	university	2.92
思考	thought	2.90
化合物	compound	2.82
標識	label	2.82
言う	task	2.82
オートラジオ	radioactivity	2.77
視覚	visual	2.77
聴覚	noun	2.77
信号	signal	2.77
言う	present	2.72
リアルタイム	time	2.69
タスク	damage	2.69
オートラジオ	autoradiography	2.67
能力	ability	2.63
ＣＴ	CT	2.63
• • •	• • •	• • •
聴覚	auditory	2.15
心	mental	2.05
ＭＲＩ	MRI	1.8

Table 4: Statistically Acquired Keywords

The proposed method involves iterative alignment which simultaneously uses both statistics and a bilingual dictionary.

Second, their score function is not reliable especially when the number of corresponding words contained in corresponding sentences is small. Their method selects a matching type (such as 1-1, 1-2 and 2-1) according to the number of word correspondences per contents word. However, in many cases, there are a few word translations in a set of corresponding sentences. Thus, it is essential to decide sentence alignment on the sentence-sentence basis. Our iterative approach decides sentence alignment level by level by counting the word correspondences between a Japanese and an English sentence.

(Fung and Church, 1994; Fung, 1995) proposed methods to find Chinese-English word correspondences without aligning parallel texts. Their motivation is that structurally different languages such as Chinese-English and Japanese-English are difficult to align in general. Their methods bypassed aligning sentences and directly acquired word correspondences. Although their approaches are robust for noisy corpora and do not require any information source, aligned sentences are necessary for higher level applications such as well-grained translation template acquisition (Matsumoto et al., 1993; Smadja et al., 1996; Haruno et al., 1996) and example-based translation (Sato and Nagao, 1990). Our method performs accurate alignment for such use by combining the detailed word correspondences: statistically acquired word correspondences and those from a bilingual dictionary of general use.

(Church, 1993) proposed char_align that makes use of n-grams shared by two languages. This kind of matching techniques will be helpful in our dictionary-based approach in the following situation: Entries of a bilingual dictionary do not completely match the word in the corpus but partially do. By using the matching technique, we can make the most of the information compiled in bilingual dictionaries.

6 Conclusion

We have described a text alignment method for structurally different languages. Our iterative method uses two kinds of word correspondences at the same time: word correspondences acquired by statistics and those of a bilingual dictionary. By combining these two types of word correspondences, the method covers both domain specific keywords not included in the dictionary and the infrequent words not detected by statistics. As a result, our method outperforms conventional methods for texts of different lengths and different domains.

Acknowledgement

We would like to thank Pascale Fung and Takehito Utsuro for helpful comments and discussions.

References

Eric Brill. 1992. A simple rule-based part of speech tagger. In *Proc. Third Conference on Apolied Natural Language Processing*, pages 152–155.

Eric Brill. 1994. Some advances in transformation-based part of speech tagging. In *Proc. 12th AAAI*, pages 722–727.

P F Brown et al. 1991. Aligning sentences in parallel corpora. In *the 29th Annual Meeting of ACL*, pages 169–176.

P F Brown et al. 1993. The mathematics of statistical machine translation. *Computational Linguistics*, 19(2):263–311, June.

S F Chen. 1993. Aligning sentences in bilingual corpora using lexical information. In *the 31st Annual Meeting of ACL*, pages 9–16.

K W Church. 1993. Char_align: A program for aligning parallel texts at the character level. In *the 31st Annual Meeting of ACL*, pages 1–8.

Ido Dagan and Ken Church. 1994. *Termight:* identifying and translating technical terminology. In *Proc. Fourth Conference on Apolied Natural Language Processing*, pages 34–40.

Pascale Fung and K W Church. 1994. K-vec: A new approach for aligning parallel texts. In *Proc. 15th COLING*, pages 1096–1102.

Pascale Fung. 1995. A pattern matching method for finding noun and proper nouns translations from noisy parallel corpora. In *Proc. 33rd ACL*, pages 236–243.

W A Gale and K W Church. 1993. A program for aligning sentences in bilingual corpora. *Computational Linguistics*, 19(1):75–102, March.

Masahiko Haruno, Satoru Ikehara, and Takefumi Yamazaki. 1996. Learning Bilingual Collocations by Word-Level Sorting,. In *Proc. 16th COLING.*

Hiroyuki Kaji, Yuuko Kida, and Yasutsugu Morimoto. 1992. Learning translation templates from bilingaul text. In *Proc. 14th COLING*, pages 672–678.

Martin Kay and Martin Roscheisen. 1993. Text-translation alignment. *Computational Linguistics*, 19(1):121–142, March.

Akira Kumano and Hideki Hirakawa. 1994. Building an MT dictionary from parallel texts based on linguisitic and statistical information. In *Proc. 15th COLING*, pages 76–81.

Julian Kupiec. 1993. An algorithm for finding noun phrase correspondences in bilingual corpora. In *the 31st Annual Meeting of ACL*, pages 17–22.

Sadao Kurohashi, Toshihisa Nakamura, Yuji Matsumoto, and Makoto Nagao. 1994. Improvements of Japanese morphological analyzer juman. In *Proc. International Workshop on Sharable Natural Language Resources*, pages 22–28.

Yuji Matsumoto, Hiroyuki Ishimoto, and Takehito Utsuro. 1993. Structural matching of parallel texts. In *the 31st Annual Meeting of ACL*, pages 23–30.

H. Murao. 1991. Studies on bilingual text alignment. Bachelor Thesis, Kyoto University (in Japanese).

Satoshi Sato and Makoto Nagao. 1990. Toward memory-based translation. In *Proc. 13th COLING*, pages 247–252.

Satoshi Sato. 1992. CTM: an example-based translation aid system. In *Proc. 14th COLING*, pages 1259–1263.

Frank Smadja, Kathleen McKeown, and Vasileios Hatzivassiloglou. 1996. Translating collocations for bilingual lexicons: A statistical approach. *Computational Linguistics*, 22(1):1–38, March.

Takehito Utsuro, Hiroshi Ikeda Masaya Yamane, Yuji Matsumoto, and Makoto Nagao. 1994. Bilingual text matching using bilingual dictionary and statistics. In *Proc. 15th COLING*, pages 1076–1082.

Dekai Wu. 1994. Aligning a parallel English-Chinese corpus statistically with lexical criteria. In *the 32nd Annual Meeting of ACL*, pages 80–87.

An Iterative Algorithm to Build Chinese Language Models

Xiaoqiang Luo
Center for Language
and Speech Processing
The Johns Hopkins University
3400 N. Charles St.
Baltimore, MD21218, USA
xiao@jhu.edu

Salim Roukos
IBM T. J. Watson Research Center
Yorktown Heights, NY 10598, USA
roukos@watson.ibm.com

Abstract

We present an iterative procedure to build a Chinese language model (LM). We segment Chinese text into words based on a word-based Chinese language model. However, the construction of a Chinese LM itself requires word boundaries. To get out of the chicken-and-egg problem, we propose an iterative procedure that alternates two operations: segmenting text into words and building an LM. Starting with an initial segmented corpus and an LM based upon it, we use a Viterbi-liek algorithm to segment another set of data. Then, we build an LM based on the second set and use the resulting LM to segment again the first corpus. The alternating procedure provides a self-organized way for the segmenter to detect automatically unseen words and correct segmentation errors. Our preliminary experiment shows that the alternating procedure not only improves the accuracy of our segmentation, but discovers unseen words surprisingly well. The resulting word-based LM has a perplexity of 188 for a general Chinese corpus.

1 Introduction

In statistical speech recognition(Bahl et al., 1983), it is necessary to build a language model(LM) for assigning probabilities to hypothesized sentences. The LM is usually built by collecting statistics of words over a large set of text data. While doing so is straightforward for English, it is not trivial to collect statistics for Chinese words since word boundaries are not marked in written Chinese text. Chinese is a morphosyllabic language (DeFrancis, 1984) in that almost all Chinese characters represent a single syllable and most Chinese characters are also morphemes. Since a word can be multi-syllabic, it is generally non-trivial to segment a Chinese sentence into words(Wu and Tseng, 1993). Since segmentation is a fundamental problem in Chinese information processing, there is a large literature to deal with the problem. Recent work includes (Sproat et al., 1994) and (Wang et al., 1992). In this paper, we adopt a statistical approach to segment Chinese text based on an LM because of its autonomous nature and its capability to handle unseen words.

As far as speech recognition is concerned, what is needed is a model to assign a probability to a string of characters. One may argue that we could bypass the segmentation problem by building a character-based LM. However, we have a strong belief that a word-based LM would be better than a character-based[1] one. In addition to speech recognition, the use of word based models would have value in information retrieval and other language processing applications.

If word boundaries are given, all established techniques can be exploited to construct an LM (Jelinek et al., 1992) just as is done for English. Therefore, segmentation is a key issue in building the Chinese LM. In this paper, we propose a segmentation algorithm based on an LM. Since building an LM itself needs word boundaries, this is a chicken-and-egg problem. To get out of this, we propose an iterative procedure that alternates between the segmentation of Chinese text and the construction of the LM. Our preliminary experiments show that the iterative procedure is able to improve the segmentation accuracy and more importantly, it can detect unseen words automatically.

In section 2, the Viterbi-like segmentation algorithm based on a LM is described. Then in section section:iter-proc we discuss the alternating procedure of segmentation and building Chinese LMs. We test the segmentation algorithm and the alternating procedure and the results are reported in sec-

[1] A character-based trigram model has a perplexity of 46 per character or 46^2 per word (a Chinese word has an average length of 2 characters), while a word-based trigram model has a perplexity 188 on the same set of data. While the comparison would be fairer using a 5-gram character model, that the word model would have a lower perplexity as long as the coverage is high.

tion 4. Finally, the work is summarized in section 5.

2 segmentation based on LM

In this section, we assume there is a word-based Chinese LM at our disposal so that we are able to compute the probability of a sentence (with word boundaries). We use a Viterbi-like segmentation algorithm based on the LM to segment texts.

Denote a sentence S by $C_1C_2\cdots C_{n-1}C_n$, where each C_i ($1 \le i \le n$) is a Chinese character. To segment a sentence into words is to group these characters into words, i.e.

$$\begin{aligned} S &= C_1C_2\cdots C_{n-1}C_n && (1)\\ &= (C_1\cdots C_{x_1})(C_{x_1+1}\cdots C_{x_2}) && (2)\\ &\quad \cdots(C_{x_{m-1}+1}\cdots C_{x_m}) && (3)\\ &= w_1w_2\cdots w_m && (4)\end{aligned}$$

where x_k is the index of the last character in k^{th} word w_k, i,e $w_k = C_{x_{k-1}+1}\cdots C_{x_k}(k = 1, 2, \cdots, m)$, and of course, $x_0 = 0, x_m = n$.

Note that a segmentation of the sentence S can be uniquely represented by an integer sequence $x_1, \cdots, x_m$, so we will denote a segmentation by its corresponding integer sequence thereafter. Let

$$G(S) = \{(x_1\cdots x_m) : 1 \le x_1 \le \cdots \le x_m, m \le n\} \quad (5)$$

be the set of all possible segmentations of sentence S. Suppose a word-based LM is given, then for a segmentation $g(S) = (x_1\cdots x_m) \in G(S)$, we can assign a score to $g(S)$ by

$$\begin{aligned} L(g(S)) &= \log P_g(w_1\cdots w_m) && (6)\\ &= \sum_{i=1}^{m} \log P_g(w_i|h_i) && (7)\end{aligned}$$

where $w_j = C_{x_{j-1}+1}\cdots C_{x_j}(j = 1, 2, \cdots, m)$, and h_i is understood as the history words $w_1\cdots w_{i-1}$. In this paper the trigram model(Jelinek et al., 1992) is used and therefore $h_i = w_{i-2}w_{i-1}$

Among all possible segmentations, we pick the one g^* with the highest score as our result. That is,

$$\begin{aligned} g^* &= arg \max_{g\in G(S)} L(g(S)) && (8)\\ &= arg \max_{g\in G(S)} \log P_g(w_1\cdots w_m) && (9)\end{aligned}$$

Note the score depends on segmentation g and this is emphasized by the subscript in (9). The optimal segmentation g^* can be obtained by dynamic programming. With a slight abuse of notation, let $L(k)$ be the max accumulated score for the first k characters. $L(k)$ is defined for $k = 1, 2, \cdots, n$ with $L(1) = 0$ and $L(g^*) = L(n)$. Given $\{L(i) : 1 \le i \le k - 1\}$, $L(k)$ can be computed recursively as follows:

$$L(k) = \max_{1\le i\le k-1} [L(i) + \log P(C_{i+1}\cdots C_k|h_i)] \quad (10)$$

where h_i is the history words ended with the ith character C_i. At the end of the recursion, we need to trace back to find the segmentation points. Therefore, it's necessary to record the segmentation points in (10).

Let $p(k)$ be the index of the last character in the preceding word. Then

$$p(k) = arg \max_{1\le i\le k-1} [L(i) + \log P(C_{i+1}\cdots C_k|h_i)] \quad (11)$$

that is, $C_{p(k)+1}\cdots C_k$ comprises the last word of the optimal segmentation up to the kth character.

A typical example of a six-character sentence is shown in table 1. Since $p(6) = 4$, we know the last word in the optimal segmentation is C_5C_6. Since $p(4) = 3$, the second last word is C_4. So on and so forth. The optimal segmentation for this sentence is $(C_1)(C_2C_3)(C_4)(C_5C_6)$.

Table 1: A segmentation example

chars	C_1	C_2	C_3	C_4	C_5	C_6
k	1	2	3	4	5	6
p(k)	0	1	1	3	3	4

The searches in (10) and (11) are in general time-consuming. Since long words are very rare in Chinese(94% words are with three or less characters (Wu and Tseng, 1993)), it won't hurt at all to limit the search space in (10) and (11) by putting an upper bound(say, 10) to the length of the exploring word, i.e, impose the constraint $i \ge max1, k - d$ in (10) and (11), where d is the upper bound of Chinese word length. This will speed the dynamic programming significantly for long sentences.

It is worth of pointing out that the algorithm in (10) and (11) could pick an unseen word(i.e, a word not included in the vocabulary on which the LM is built on) in the optimal segmentation provided LM assigns proper probabilities to unseen words. This is the beauty of the algorithm that it is able to handle unseen words automatically.

3 Iterative procedure to build LM

In the previous section, we assumed there exists a Chinese word LM at our disposal. However, this is not true in reality. In this section, we discuss an iterative procedure that builds LM and automatically appends the unseen words to the current vocabulary.

The procedure first splits the data into two parts, set T_1 and T_2. We start from an initial segmentation of the set T_1. This can be done, for instance, by a simple greedy algorithm described in (Sproat et al., 1994). With the segmented T_1, we construct a LM_i on it. Then we segment the set T_2 by using the LM_i and the algorithm described in section 2. At the same time, we keep a counter for each unseen word in optimal segmentations and increment the counter whenever its associated word appears in an optimal segmentation. This gives us a measure to tell whether an unseen word is an accidental character string or a real word not included in our vocabulary. The higher a counter is, the more likely it is a word. After segmenting the set T_2, we add to our vocabulary all unseen words with its counter greater than a threshold c. Then we use the augmented vocabulary and construct another LM_{i+1} using the segmented T_2. The pattern is clear now: LM_{i+1} is used to segment the set T_1 again and the vocabulary is further augmented.

To be more precise, the procedure can be written in pseudo code as follows.

Step 0: Initially segment the set T_1.
Construct an LM LM_0 with an initial vocabulary V_0.
set i=1.

Step 1: Let j=i mod 2;
For each sentence S in the set T_j, do

1.1 segment it using LM_{i-1}.

1.2 for each unseen word in the optimal segmentation, increment its counter by the number of times it appears in the optimal segmentation.

Step 2: Let A=the set of unseen words with counter greater than c.
set $V_i = V_{i-1} \cup A$.
Construct another LM_i using the segmented set T_j and the vocabulary V_i.

Step 3: i=i+1 and goto step 1.

Unseen words, most of which are proper nouns, pose a serious problem to Chinese text segmentation. In (Sproat et al., 1994) a class based model was proposed to identify personal names. In (Wang et al., 1992), a title driven method was used to identify personal names. The iterative procedure proposed here provides a self-organized way to detect unseen words, including proper nouns. The advantage is that it needs little human intervention. The procedure provides a chance for us to correct segmenting errors.

4 Experiments and Evaluation

4.1 Segmentation Accuracy

Our first attempt is to see how accurate the segmentation algorithm proposed in section 2 is. To this end, we split the whole data set [2] into two parts, half for building LMs and half reserved for testing. The trigram model used in this experiment is the standard deleted interpolation model described in (Jelinek et al., 1992) with a vocabulary of 20K words.

Since we lack an objective criterion to measure the accuracy of a segmentation system, we ask three native speakers to segment manually 100 sentences picked randomly from the test set and compare them with segmentations by machine. The result is summed in table 2, where ORG stands for the original segmentation, P1, P2 and P3 for three human subjects, and TRI and UNI stand for the segmentations generated by trigram LM and unigram LM respectively. The number reported here is the arithmetic average of recall and precision, as was used in (Sproat et al., 1994), i.e., $1/2(\frac{n_c}{n_1} + \frac{n_c}{n_2})$, where n_c is the number of common words in both segmentations, n_1 and n_2 are the number of words in each of the segmentations.

Table 2: Segmentation Accuracy

	ORG	P1	P2	P3	TRI	UNI
ORG					94.2	91.2
P1	85.9				85.3	87.4
P2	79.1	90.9			80.1	82.2
P3	87.4	85.7	82.2		85.6	85.7

We can make a few remarks about the result in table 2. First of all, it is interesting to note that the agreement of segmentations among human subjects is roughly at the same level of that between human subjects and machine. This confirms what reported in (Sproat et al., 1994). The major disagreement for human subjects comes from compound words, phrases and suffices. Since we don't give any specific instructions to human subjects, one of them tends to group consistently phrases as words because he was implicitly using semantics as his segmentation criterion. For example, he segments the sentence [3] `dao4 jia1 li2 chi1 dun4 fan4`(see table 3) as two words `dao4 jia1 li2(go home)` and `chi1 dun4 fan4(have a meal)` because the two "words" are clearly two semantic units. The other two subjects and machine segment it as `dao4 / jia1 li2/ chi1/ dun4 / fan4`.

Chinese has very limited morphology (Spencer, 1991) in that most grammatical concepts are conveyed by separate words and not by morphological processes. The limited morphology includes some ending morphemes to represent tenses of verbs, and this is another source of disagreement. For example, for the partial sentence `zuo4 wan2 le`, where `le` functions as labeling the verb `zuo4 wan2` as "perfect" tense, some subjects tend to segment it as two words `zuo4 wan2/ le` while the other treat it as one single word.

Second, the agreement of each of the subjects with either the original, trigram, or unigram segmentation is quite high (see columns 2, 6, and 7 in Table 2) and appears to be specific to the subject.

[2]The corpus has about 5 million characters and is coarsely pre-segmented.

[3]Here we use Pin Yin followed by its tone to represent a character.

Third, it seems puzzling that the trigram LM agrees with the original segmentation better than a unigram model, but gives a worse result when compared with manual segmentations. However, since the LMs are trained using the presegmented data, the trigram model tends to keep the original segmentation because it takes the preceding two words into account while the unigram model is less restricted to deviate from the original segmentation. In other words, if trained with "cleanly" segmented data, a trigram model is more likely to produce a better segmentation since it tends to preserve the nature of training data.

4.2 Experiment of the iterative procedure

In addition to the 5 million characters of segmented text, we had unsegmented data from various sources reaching about 13 million characters. We applied our iterative algorithm to that corpus.

Table 4 shows the figure of merit of the resulting segmentation of the 100 sentence test set described earlier. After one iteration, the agreement with the original segmentation decreased by 3 percentage points, while the agreement with the human segmentation increased by less than one percentage point. We ran our computation intensive procedure for one iteration only. The results indicate that the impact on segmentation accuracy would be small. However, the new unsegmented corpus is a good source of automatically discovered words. A 20 examples picked randomly from about 1500 unseen words are shown in Table 5. 16 of them are reasonably good words and are listed with their translated meanings. The problematic words are marked with "?".

4.3 Perplexity of the language model

After each segmentation, an interpolated trigram model is built, and an independent test set with 2.5 million characters is segmented and then used to measure the quality of the model. We got a perplexity 188 for a vocabulary of 80K words, and the alternating procedure has little impact on the perplexity. This can be explained by the fact that the change of segmentation is very little (which is reflected in table reftab:accuracy-iter) and the addition of unseen words(1.5K) to the vocabulary is also too little to affect the overall perplexity. The merit of the alternating procedure is probably its ability to detect unseen words.

5 Conclusion

In this paper, we present an iterative procedure to build Chinese language model(LM). We segment Chinese text into words based on a word-based Chinese language model. However, the construction of a Chinese LM itself requires word boundaries. To get out of the chicken-egg problem, we propose an iterative procedure that alternates two operations: segmenting text into words and building an LM. Starting with an initial segmented corpus and an LM based upon it, we use Viterbi-like algorithm to segment another set of data. Then we build an LM based on the second set and use the LM to segment again the first corpus. The alternating procedure provides a self-organized way for the segmenter to detect automatically unseen words and correct segmentation errors. Our preliminary experiment shows that the alternating procedure not only improves the accuracy of our segmentation, but discovers unseen words surprisingly well. We get a perplexity 188 for a general Chinese corpus with 2.5 million characters [4].

6 Acknowledgment

The first author would like to thank various members of the Human Language technologies Department at the IBM T.J Watson center for their encouragement and helpful advice. Special thanks go to Dr. Martin Franz for providing continuous help in using the IBM language model tools. The authors would also thank the comments and insight of two anonymous reviewers which help improve the final draft.

References

Richard Sproat, Chilin Shih, William Gale and Nancy Chang. 1994. A stochastic finite-state word segmentation algorithm for Chinese. In *Proceedings of ACL'94* , pages 66–73

Zimin Wu and Gwyneth Tseng 1993. Chinese Text Segmentation for Text Retrieval: Achievements and Problems *Journal of the American Society for Information Science*, 44(9):532–542.

John DeFrancis. 1984. The Chinese Language. University of Hawaii Press, Honolulu.

Frederick Jelinek, Robert L. Mercer and Salim Roukos. 1992. Principles of Lexical Language Modeling for Speech recognition. In *Advances in Speech Signal Processing*, pages 651–699, edited by S. Furui and M. M. Sondhi. Marcel Dekker Inc., 1992

L.R Bahl, Fred Jelinek and R.L. Mercer. 1983. A Maximum Likelihood Approach to Continuous Speech Recognition. In *IEEE Transactions on Pattern Analysis and Machine Intelligence*, 1983,5(2):179–190

Liang-Jyh Wang, Wei-Chuan Li, and Chao-Huang Chang. 1992. Recognizing unregistered names for mandarin word identification. In *Proceedings of COLING-92*, pages 1239–1243. COLING

[4] Unfortunately, we could not find a report of Chinese perplexity for comparison in the published literature concerning Mandarin speech recognition

Andrew Spencer. 1992. Morphological theory : an introduction to word structure in generative grammar pages 38–39. Oxford, UK ; Cambridge, Mass., USA. Basil Blackwell, 1991.

Table 3: Segmentation of phrases

Chinese	dao4	jia1 li2	chi1	dun4	fan4
Meaning	go	home	eat	a	meal

Table 4: Segmentation of accuracy after one iteration

	TR0	TR1
ORG	.920	.890
P1	.863	.877
P2	.817	.832
P3	.850	.849

Table 5: Examples of unseen words

PinYin	Meaning
kui2 er2	last name of former US vice president
he2 shi4 lu4 yin1 dai4	cassette of audio tape
shou2 dao3	(abbr)pretect (the) island
ren4 zhong4	first name or part of a phrase
ji4 jian3	(abbr) discipline monitoring
zi4 hai4	?
shuang1 bao3	double guarantee
ji4 dong1	(abbr) Eastern He Bei province
zi3 jiao1	purple glue
xiao1 long2 shi2	personal name
li4 bo4 hai3	?
du4 shan1	?
shang1 ban4	(abbr) commercial oriented
liu6 hai4	six (types of) harms
sa4 he4 le4	translated name
kuai4 xun4	fast news
cheng4 jing3	train cop
huang2 du2	yellow poison
ba3 lian2	?
he2 dao3	a (biological) jargon

Pattern-Based Context-Free Grammars for Machine Translation

Koichi Takeda
Tokyo Research Laboratory, IBM Research
1623-14 Shimotsuruma, Yamato, Kanagawa 242, Japan
Phone: 81-462-73-4569, 81-462-73-7413 (FAX)
takeda@trl.vnet.ibm.com

Abstract

This paper proposes the use of "pattern-based" context-free grammars as a basis for building machine translation (MT) systems, which are now being adopted as personal tools by a broad range of users in the cyberspace society. We discuss major requirements for such tools, including easy customization for diverse domains, the efficiency of the translation algorithm, and scalability (incremental improvement in translation quality through user interaction), and describe how our approach meets these requirements.

1 Introduction

With the explosive growth of the World-Wide Web (WWW) as information source, it has become routine for Internet users to access textual data written in foreign languages. In Japan, for example, a dozen or so inexpensive MT tools have recently been put on the market to help PC users understand English text in WWW home pages. The MT techniques employed in the tools, however, are fairly conventional. For reasons of affordability, their designers appear to have made no attempt to tackle the well-known problems in MT, such as how to ensure the learnability of correct translations and facilitate customization. As a result, users are forced to see the same kinds of translation errors over and over again, except they in cases where they involve merely adding a missing word or compound to a user dictionary, or specifying one of several word-to-word translations as a correct choice.

There are several alternative approaches that might eventually liberate us from this limitation on the usability of MT systems:

Unification-based grammar formalisms and lexical-semantics formalisms (see LFG (Kaplan and Bresnan, 1982), HPSG (Pollard and Sag, 1987), and Generative Lexicon (Pustejovsky, 1991), for example) have been proposed to facilitate computationally precise description of natural-language syntax and semantics. It is possible that, with the descriptive power of these grammars and lexicons, individual usages of words and phrases may be defined specifically enough to give correct translations. Practical implementation of MT systems based on these formalisms, on the other hand, would not be possible without much more efficient parsing and disambiguation algorithms for these formalisms and a method for building a lexicon that is easy even for novices to use.

Corpus-based or example-based MT (Sato and Nagao, 1990; Sumita and Iida, 1991) and statistical MT (Brown et al., 1993) systems provide the easiest customizability, since users have only to supply a collection of source and target sentence pairs (a bilingual corpus). Two open questions, however, have yet to be satisfactorily answered before we can confidently build commercial MT systems based on these approaches:

- Can the system be used for various domains without showing severe degradation of translation accuracy?
- What is the minimum number of examples (or training data) required to achieve reasonable MT quality for a new domain?

TAG-based MT (Abeillé, Schabes, and Joshi, 1990)[1] and pattern-based translation (Maruyama, 1993) share many important properties for successful implementation in practical MT systems, namely:

- The existence of a polynomial-time parsing algorithm
- A capability for describing a larger *domain of locality* (Schabes, Abeillé, and Joshi, 1988)
- *Synchronization* (Shieber and Schabes, 1990) of the source and target language structures

Readers should note, however, that the pars-

[1]See LTAG (Schabes, Abeillé, and Joshi, 1988) (Lexicalized TAG) and STAG (Shieber and Schabes, 1990) (Synchronized TAG) for each member of the TAG (Tree Adjoining Grammar) family.

ing algorithm for TAGs has $O(|G|n^6)^2$ worst case time complexity (Vijay-Shanker, 1987), and that the "patterns" in Maruyama's approach are merely context-free grammar (CFG) rules. Thus, it has been a challenge to find a framework in which we can enjoy both a grammar formalism with better descriptive power than CFG and more efficient parsing/generation algorithms than those of TAGs.[3]

In this paper, we will show that there exists a class of "pattern-based" grammars that is weakly equivalent to CFG (thus allowing the CFG parsing algorithms to be used for our grammars), but that it facilitates description of the domain of locality. Furthermore, we will show that our framework can be extended to incorporate example-based MT and a powerful learning mechanism.

2 Pattern-Based Context-Free Grammars

Pattern-based context-free grammars (PCFG) consists of a set of translation *patterns*. A pattern is a pair of CFG rules, and zero or more *syntactic head* and *link* constraints for nonterminal symbols. For example, the English-French translation pattern[4]

NP:1 miss:V:2 NP:3 → S:2
S:2 ← NP:3 manquer:V:2 *à* NP:1

essentially describes a *synchronized*[5] pair consisting of a left-hand-side English CFG rule (called a *source* rule)

NP V NP → S

and a French CFG rule (called a *target* rule)

S ← NP V *à* NP

accompanied by the following constraints.

1. **Head constraints:** The nonterminal symbol V in the source rule must have the verb *miss* as a syntactic head. The symbol V in the target rule must have the verb *manquer* as a syntactic head. The head of symbol S in the source (target) rule is identical to the head of symbol V in the source (target) rule as they are co-indexed.
2. **Link constraints:** Nonterminal symbols in source and target CFG rules are *linked* if they are given the same index ":*i*". Linked nonterminal must be derived from a sequence of synchronized pairs. Thus, the first NP (NP:1) in the source rule corresponds to the second NP (NP:1) in the target rule, the Vs in both rules correspond to each other, and the second NP (NP:3) in the source rule corresponds to the first NP (NP:3) in the target rule.

The source and target rules are called *CFG skeleton* of the pattern. The notion of a syntactic head is similar to that used in unification grammars, although the heads in our patterns are simply encoded as character strings rather than as complex feature structures. A head is typically introduced[6] in preterminal rules such as

leave → V V ← partir

where two verbs, "leave" and "partir," are associated with the heads of the nonterminal symbol V. This is equivalently expressed as

leave:1 → V:1 V:1 ← partir:1

which is physically implemented as an entry of an English-French lexicon.

A set T of translation patterns is said to *accept* an input *s* iff there is a derivation sequence Q for *s* using the source CFG skeletons of T, and every head constraint associated with the CFG skeletons in Q is satisfied. Similarly, T is said to *translate s* iff there is a synchronized derivation sequence Q for *s* such that T accepts *s*, and every head and link constraint associated with the source and target CFG skeletons in Q is satisfied. The derivation Q then produces a translation *t* as the resulting sequence of terminal symbols included in the target CFG skeletons in Q. Translation of an input string *s* essentially consists of the following three steps:

1. Parsing *s* by using the source CFG skeletons
2. Propagating link constraints from source to target CFG skeletons to build a target CFG derivation sequence
3. Generating *t* from the target CFG derivation sequence

The third step is a trivial procedure when the target CFG derivation is obtained.

Theorem 1 *Let T be a PCFG. Then, there exists a CFG G_T such that for two languages $L(T)$ and $L(G_T)$ accepted by T and G_T, respectively, $L(T) = L(G_T)$ holds. That is, T accepts a sentence s iff G_T accepts s.*

Proof: We can construct a CFG G_T as follows:

1. G_T has the same set of terminal symbols as T.

[2]Where $|G|$ stands for the size of grammar G, and n is the length of an input string.

[3]Lexicalized CFG, or Tree Insertion Grammar (TIG) (Schabes and Waters, 1995), has been recently introduced to achieve such efficiency and lexicalization.

[4]and its inflectional variants — we will discuss inflections and agreement issues later.

[5]The meaning of the word "synchronized" here is exactly the same as in STAG (Shieber and Schabes, 1990). See also bilingual signs (Tsujii and Fujita, 1991) for a discussion of the importance of combining the appropriate domain of locality and synchronization.

[6]A nonterminal symbol X in a source or target CFG rule $X \rightarrow X_1 \cdots X_k$ can only be constrained to have one of the heads in the RHS $X_1 \cdots X_k$. Thus, *monotonicity* of head constraints holds throughout the parsing process.

2. For each nonterminal symbol X in T, G_T includes a set of nonterminal symbols $\{X_w | w$ is either a terminal symbol in T or a special symbol $\epsilon\}$.

3. For each preterminal rule

   X:i $\rightarrow w_1$:1 w_2:2 ... w_k:k $(1 \leq i \leq k)$,

   G_T includes[7]

   $Xw_i \rightarrow w_1\ w_2\ \ldots\ w_k\ (1 \leq i \leq k)$.

   If X is not co-indexed with any of w_i, G_T includes

   $X_\epsilon \rightarrow w_1\ w_2\ \ldots\ w_k$.

4. For each source CFG rule with head constraints $(h_1, h_2, \ldots, h_k)$ and indexes $(i_1, i_2, \ldots, i_k)$,

   Y:$i_j \rightarrow h_1$:X_1:i_1 ... h_k:X_k:i_k $(1 \leq j \leq k)$,

   G_T includes

   $Yh_j \rightarrow Xh_1\ Xh_2\ \ldots\ Xh_k$.

   If Y is not co-indexed with any of its children, we have

   $Y_\epsilon \rightarrow Xh_1\ Xh_2\ \ldots\ Xh_k$.

   If X_j has no head constraint in the above rule, G_T includes a set of $(N+1)$ rules, where Xh_j above is replaced with X_w for every terminal symbol w and X_ϵ (Yh_j will also be replaced if it is co-indexed with X_j).[8]

Now, $L(T) \subseteq L(G_T)$ is obvious, since G_T can simulate the derivation sequence in T with corresponding rules in G_T. $L(G_T) \subseteq L(T)$ can be proven, with mathematical induction, from the fact that every valid derivation sequence of G_T satisfies head constraints of corresponding rules in T.

□

Proposition 1 *Let a CFG G be a set of source CFG skeletons in T. Then, $L(T) \subseteq L(G)$.*

Since a valid derivation sequence in T is always a valid derivation sequence in G, the proof is immediate. Similarly, we have

Proposition 2 *Let a CFG H be a subset of source CFG skeletons in T such that a source CFG skeleton k is in H iff k has no head constraints associated with it. Then, $L(H) \subseteq L(T)$.*

[7]Head constraints are trivially satisfied or violated in preterminal rules. Hence, we assume, without loss of generality, that no head constraint is given in preterminal rules. We also assume that "$X \rightarrow w$" implies "X:1 $\rightarrow w$:1".

[8]Therefore, a single rule in T can be mapped to as many as $(N+1)^k$ rules in G_T, where N is the number of terminal symbols in T. G_T could be exponentially larger than T.

Two CFGs G and H define the range of CFL L(T). These two CFGs can be used to measure the "default" translation quality, since idioms and collocational phrases are typically translated by patterns with head constraints.

Theorem 2 *Let a CFG G be a set of source CFG skeletons in T. Then, $L(T) \subset L(G)$ is undecidable.*

Proof: The decision problem, $L(T) \subset L(G)$, of two CFLs such that $L(T) \subseteq L(G)$ is solvable iff $L(T) = L(G)$ is solvable. This includes a known undecidable problem, $L(T) = \Sigma^*$?, since we can choose a grammar U with $L(U) = \Sigma^*$, nullify the entire set of rules in U by defining T to be a vacuous set $\{S$:1 $\rightarrow a$:S_b:1, S_b:1 $\rightarrow$ b:S_U:1$\}$ ∪ U (S_U and S are start symbols in U and T, respectively), and, finally, let T further include an arbitrary CFG F. $L(G) = \Sigma^*$ is obvious, since G has $\{S \rightarrow S_b,\ S_b \rightarrow S_U\} \cup$ U. Now, we have $L(G) = L(T)$ iff $L(F) = \Sigma^*$.

□

Theorem 2 shows that the syntactic coverage of T is, in general, only computable by T itself, even though T is merely a CFL. This may pose a serious problem when a grammar writer wishes to know if there is a specific expression that is only acceptable by using at least one pattern with head constraints, for which the answer is "no" iff L(G) = L(T). One way to trivialize this problem is to let T include a pattern with a pair of pure CFG rules for every pattern with head constraints, which guarantees that L(H) = L(T) = L(G). In this case, we know that the coverage of "default" patterns is always identical to L(T).

Although our "patterns" have no more theoretical descriptive power than CFG, they can provide considerably better descriptions of the domain of locality than ordinary CFG rules. For example,

be:V:1 year:NP:2 old → VP:1
VP:1 ← avoir:V:1 an:NP:2

can handle such NP pairs as "one year" and "un an," and "more than two years" and "plus que deux ans," which would have to be covered by a large number of plain CFG rules. TAGs, on the other hand, are known to be "mildly context-sensitive" grammars, and they can capture a broader range of syntactic dependencies, such as cross-serial dependencies. The computational complexity of parsing for TAGs, however, is $O(|G|n^6)$, which is far greater than that of CFG parsing. Moreover, defining a new STAG rule is not as easy for the users as just adding an entry into a dictionary, because each STAG rule has to be specified as a pair of tree structures. Our patterns, on the other hand, concentrate on specifying linear ordering of source and target constituents, and can be written by the users as easily as[9]

[9]By sacrificing linguistic accuracy for the description of syntactic structures.

to leave * = de quitter *
to be year:* old = d'avoir an:*

Here, the wildcard "*" stands for an NP by default. The preposition "to" and "de" are used to specify that the patterns are for VP pairs, and "to be" is used to show that the phrase is the BE-verb and its complement. A wildcard can be constrained with a head, as in "house:*" and "maison:*". The internal representations of these patterns are as follows:

leave:V:1 NP:2 → VP:1
VP:1 ← quitter:V:1 NP:2

be:V:1 year:NP:2 old → VP:1
VP:1 ← avoir:V:1 an:NP:2

These patterns can be associated with an explicit nonterminal symbol such as "V:*" or "ADJP:*" in addition to head constraints (e.g., "leave:V:*"). By defining a few such notations, these patterns can be successfully converted into the formal representations defined in this section. Many of the divergences (Dorr, 1993) in source and target language expressions are fairly collocational, and can be appropriately handled by using our patterns. Note the simplicity that results from using a notation in which users only have to specify the surface ordering of words and phrases. More powerful grammar formalisms would generally require either a structural description or complex feature structures.

3 The Translation Algorithm

The parsing algorithm for translation patterns can be any of known CFG parsing algorithms including CKY and Earley algorithms[10] At this stage, head and link constraints are ignored. It is easy to show that the number of target charts for a single source chart increases exponentially if we build target charts simultaneously with source charts. For example, the two patterns

A:1 B:2 → B:2 B:2 ← A:1 B:2, and
A:1 B:2 → B:2 A:1 ← B:2 A:1

will generate the following 2^n synchronized pairs of charts for the sequence of (n+1) nonterminal symbols $AAA \ldots AB$, for which no effective packing of the target charts is possible.

(A (A ... (A B))) with (A (A ... (A B)))
(A (A ... (A B))) with ((A ... (A B)) A)
...
(A (A ... (A B))) with (((B A) A) ... A)

Our strategy is thus to find a candidate set of source charts in polynomial time. We therefore apply heuristic measurements to identify the most promising patterns for generating translations. In this sense, the entire translation algorithm is not guaranteed to run in polynomial time. Practically, a timeout mechanism and a process for recovery from unsuccessful translation (e.g., applying the idea of fitted parse (Jensen and Heidorn, 1983) to target CFG rules) should be incorporated into the translation algorithm.

Some restrictions on patterns must be imposed to avoid infinitely many ambiguities and arbitrarily long translations. The following patterns are therefore not allowed:

1. $A \rightarrow X\ Y \leftarrow B$
2. $A \rightarrow X\ Y \leftarrow C_1 \ldots B \ldots C_k$

if there is a cycle of synchronized derivation such that

$A \rightarrow X \ldots \rightarrow A$ and
B (or $C_1 \ldots B \ldots C_k$) $\rightarrow Y \ldots \rightarrow B$,

where A, B, X, and Y are nonterminal symbols with or without head and link constraints, and C's are either terminal or nonterminal symbols.

The basic strategy for choosing a candidate derivation sequence from ambiguous parses is as follows.[11] A simplified view of the Earley algorithm (Earley, 1970) consists of three major components, *predict(i), complete(i),* and *scan(i),* which are called at each position $i = 0, 1, \ldots, n$ in an input string I $= s_1 s_2 \ldots s_n$. Predict(i) returns a set of currently applicable CFG rules at position i. Complete(i) combines inactive charts ending at i with active charts that look for the inactive charts at position i to produce a new collection of active and inactive charts. Scan(i) tries to combine inactive charts with the symbol s_{i+1} at position i. Complete(n) gives the set of possible parses for the input I.

Now, for every inactive chart associated with a nonterminal symbol X for a span of ⟨i,j⟩ ($1 \le i, j \le n$), there exists a set P of patterns with the source CFG skeleton, $\ldots \rightarrow X$. We can define the following ordering of patterns in P; this gives patterns with which we can use head and link constraints for building target charts and translations. These candidate patterns can be arranged and associated with the chart in the complete() procedure.

1. Prefer a pattern p with a source CFG skeleton $X \rightarrow X_1 \cdots X_k$ over any other pattern q with the same source CFG skeleton $X \rightarrow X_1 \cdots X_k$, such that p has a head constraint $h{:}X_i$ if q has $h{:}X_i$ ($i = 1, \ldots, k$). The pattern p is said to be *more specific* than q. For example, p =

[10]Our prototype implementation was based on the Earley algorithm, since this does not require lexicalization of CFG rules.

[11]This strategy is similar to that of transfer-driven MT (TDMT) (Furuse and Iida, 1994). TDMT, however, is based on a combination of declarative/procedural knowledge sources for MT, and no clear computational properties have been investigated.

"leave:V:1 house:NP → VP:1" is preferred to q = "leave:V:1 NP → VP:1".

2. Prefer a pattern p with a source CFG skeleton to any pattern q that has fewer terminal symbols in the source CFG skeleton than p. For example, prefer "take:V:1 a walk" to "take:V:1 NP" if these patterns give the VP charts with the same span.
3. Prefer a pattern p which does not violate any head constraint over those which violate a head constraint.
4. Prefer the shortest derivation sequence for each input substring. A pattern for a larger domain of locality tends to give a shorter derivation sequence.

These preferences can be expressed as numeric values (*cost*) for patterns.[12] Thus, our strategy favors *lexicalized* (or head constrained) and *collocational* patterns, which is exactly what we are going to achieve with pattern-based MT. Selection of patterns in the derivation sequence accompanies the construction of a target chart. Link constraints are propagated from source to target derivation trees. This is basically a bottom-up procedure.

Since the number M of distinct pairs ⟨X,w⟩, for a nonterminal symbol X and a subsequence w of input string s, is bounded by Kn^2, we can compute the *m-best choice* of pattern candidates for every inactive chart in time $O(|T|Kn^3)$ as claimed by Maruyama (Maruyama, 1993), and Schabes and Waters (Schabes and Waters, 1995). Here, K is the number of distinct nonterminal symbols in T, and n is the size of the input string. Note that the head constraints associated with the source CFG rules can be incorporated in the parsing algorithm, since the number of triples ⟨X,w,h⟩, where h is a head of X, is bounded by Kn^3. We can modify the predict(), complete(), and scan() procedures to run in $O(|T|Kn^4)$ while checking the source head constraints. Construction of the target charts, if possible, on the basis of the m best candidate patterns for each source chart takes $O(Kn^2m)$ time. Here, m can be larger than 2^n if we generate every possible translation.

The reader should note critical differences between lexicalized grammar rules (in the sense of LTAG and TIG) and translation patterns when they are used for MT.

Firstly, a pattern is not necessarily lexicalized. An economical way of organizing translation patterns is to include non-lexicalized patterns as "default" translation rules.

[12]A similar preference can be defined for the target part of each pattern, but we found many counter-examples, where the number of nonterminal symbols shows no specificity of the patterns, in the target part of English-to-Japanese translation patterns. Therefore, only the head constraint violation in the target part is accounted for in our prototype.

Secondly, lexicalization might increase the size of STAG grammars (in particular, compositional grammar rules such as ADJP NP → NP) considerably when a large number of phrasal variations (adjectives, verbs in present participle form, various numeric expressions, and so on) multiplied by the number of their translations, are associated with the ADJP part. The notion of structure sharing (Vijay-Shanker and Schabes, 1992) may have to be extended from lexical to phrasal structures, as well as from monolingual to bilingual structures.

Thirdly, a translation pattern can omit the tree structure of a collocation, and leave it as just a sequence of terminal symbols. The simplicity of this helps users to add patterns easily, although precise description of syntactic dependencies is lost.

4 Features and Agreements

Translation patterns can be enhanced with unification and feature structures to give patterns additional power for describing gender, number, agreement, and so on. Since the descriptive power of unification-based grammars is considerably greater than that of CFG (Berwick, 1982), feature structures have to be restricted to maintain the efficiency of parsing and generation algorithms. Shieber and Schabes briefly discuss the issue (Shieber and Schabes, 1990). We can also extend translation patterns as follows:

> Each nonterminal node in a pattern can be associated with a fixed-length *vector* of *binary features*.

This will enable us to specify such syntactic dependencies as agreement and subcategorization in patterns. Unification of binary features, however, is much simpler: unification of a feature-value pair succeeds only when the pair is either ⟨0,0⟩ or ⟨1,1⟩. Since the feature vector has a fixed length, unification of two feature vectors is performed in a constant time. For example, the patterns[13]

V:1:+TRANS NP:2 → VP:1 VP:1 ← V:1:+TRANS NP:2
V:1:+INTRANS → VP:1 VP:1 ← V:1:+INTRANS

are unifiable with transitive and intransitive verbs, respectively. We can also distinguish *local* and *head* features, as postulated in HPSG. Simplified version of verb subcategorization is then encoded as

VP:1:+TRANS-OBJ NP:2 → VP:1:+OBJ
VP:1:+OBJ ← VP:1:+TRANS-OBJ NP:2

where "-OBJ" is a local feature for head VPs in LHSs, while "+OBJ" is a local feature for VPs in

[13]Again, these patterns can be mapped to a weakly equivalent set of CFG rules. See GPSG (Gazdar, Pullum, and Sag, 1985) for more details.

the RHSs. Unification of a local feature with +OBJ succeeds since it is not *bound*.

Agreement on subjects (nominative NPs) and finite-form verbs (VPs, excluding the BE verb) is disjunctively specified as

```
NP:1:+NOMI+3RD+SG VP:2:+FIN+3SG
NP:1:+NOMI+3RD+PL VP:2:+FIN-3SG
NP:1:+NOMI-3RD    VP:2:+FIN-3SG
NP:1:+NOMI        VP:2:+FIN+PAST
```

which is collectively expressed as

```
NP:1:*AGRS VP:2:*AGRV
```

Here, *AGRS and *AGRV are a pair of *aggregate* unification specifiers that succeeds only when one of the above combinations of the feature values is unifiable.

Another way to extend our grammar formalism is to associate weights with patterns. It is then possible to rank the matching patterns according to a linear ordering of the weights rather than the pairwise partial ordering of patterns described in the previous section. In our prototype system, each pattern has its original weight, and according to the preference measurement described in the previous section, a penalty is added to the weight to give the effective weight of the pattern in a particular context. Patterns with the least weight are to be chosen as the most preferred patterns.

Numeric weights for patterns are extremely useful as means of assigning higher priorities uniformly to user-defined patterns. Statistical training of patterns can also be incorporated to calculate such weights systematically (Fujisaki et al., 1989).

Figure 1 shows a sample translation of the input "He knows me well," using the following patterns.

NP:1:*AGRS VP:1:*AGRS → S:1
S:1 ← NP:1:*AGRS VP:1:*AGRS ... (a)

VP:1 ADVP:2 → VP:1
VP:1 ← VP:1 ADVP:2 ... (b)

know:VP:1:+OBJ well → VP:1
VP:1 ← connaitre:VP:1:+OBJ bien ... (c)

V:1 NP:2 → VP:1:+OBJ
VP:1:+OBJ ← V:1 NP:2:-PRO ... (d)

V:1 NP:2 → VP:1:+OBJ
VP:1:+OBJ ← NP:2:+PRO V:1 ... (e)

To simplify the example, let us assume that we have the following preterminal rules:

he → NP:+PRO+NOMI+3RD+SG
NP:+PRO+NOMI+3RD+SG ← il ... (f)

me → NP:+PRO+CAUS+SG-3RD
NP:+PRO+CAUS+SG-3RD ← me ... (g)

knows → V:+FIN+3SG
V:+FIN+3SG ← sait ... (h)
knows → V:+FIN+3SG
V:+FIN+3SG ← connait ... (i)

```
Input: He knows me well
Phase 1: Source Analysis
[0 1] He    ---> (f) NP
   (active arc [0 1] (a) NP.VP)
[1 2] knows ---> (h) V, (i) V
   (active arcs [1 2] (d) V.NP,
                [1 2] (e) V.NP)
[2 3] me    ---> (g) NP
   (inactive arcs [1 3] (d) V NP,
                  [1 3] (e) V NP)
[1 3] knows me ---> (d), (e) VP
   (inactive arc [0 3] (a) NP VP,
    active arcs [1 3] (b) VP.well,
                [1 3] (c) VP.ADVP)
[0 3] He knows me ---> (a) S
[3 4] well   ---> (j) ADVP, (k) ADVP
   (inactive arcs [1 4] (b) VP ADVP,
                  [1 4] (c) VP ADVP)
[1 4] knows me well ---> (b), (c) VP
   (inactive arc [0 4] (a) NP VP)
[0 4] He knows me well ---> (a) S
Phase 2: Constraint Checking
[0 1] He    ---> (f) NP
[1 2] knows ---> (i) V, (j) V
[2 3] me    ---> (g) NP
[1 3] knows me ---> (e) VP
   (pattern (d) fails)
[0 3] He knows me ---> (a) S
[3 4] well   ---> (i) ADVP, (j) ADVP
[1 4] knows me well ---> (b), (c) VP
   (preference ordering (c), (b))
[0 4] He knows me well ---> (a) S
Phase 3: Target Generation
[0 4] He knows me well ---> (a) S
[0 1] He     ---> il
[1 4] knows me well ---> (c) VP
      well   ---> bien
[1 3] knows me ---> (e) VP
[1 2] knows  ---> connait
      (h) violates a head constraint
[2 3] me     ---> me
Translation: il me connait bien
```

Figure 1: Sample Translation

well → ADVP ADVP ← bien ... (j)
well → ADVP ADVP ← beaucoup ... (k)

In the above example, the Earley-based algorithm with source CFG rules is used in Phase 1. In Phase 2, head and link constraints are examined, and unification of feature structures is performed by using the charts obtained in Phase 1. Candidate patterns are ordered by their weights and preferences. Finally, in Phase 3, the target charts are built to generate translations based on the selected patterns.

5 Integration of Bilingual Corpora

Integration of translation patterns with translation examples, or *bilingual corpora*, is the most important extension of our framework. There is no discrete line between patterns and bilingual corpora. Rather, we can view them together as a uniform set of translation pairs with varying degrees of lexicalization. Sentence pairs in the corpora, however, should not be just added as patterns, since they are often redundant, and such additions contribute to neither acquisition nor refinement of non-sentential patterns.

Therefore, we have been testing the integration method with the following steps. Let T be a set of translation patterns, B be a bilingual corpus, and ⟨s,t⟩ be a pair of source and target sentences.

1. [**Correct Translation**] If T can translate s into t, do nothing.
2. [**Competitive Situation**] If T can translate s into t' ($t \neq t'$), do the following:
   (a) [**Lexicalization**] If there is a paired derivation sequence Q of ⟨s,t⟩ in T, create a new pattern p' for a pattern p used in Q such that every nonterminal symbol X in p with no head constraint is associated with h:X in q, where the head h is instantiated in X of p. Add p' to T if it is not already there. Repeat the addition of such patterns, and assign low weights to them until the refined sequence Q becomes the most likely translation of s. For example, add

      leave:VP:1:+OBJ
      considerably:ADVP:2 → VP:1
      VP:1 ← laisser:VP:1:+OBJ considérablement:ADVP:2

   if the existing VP ADVP pattern does not give a correct translation.
   (b) [**Addition of New Patterns**] If there is no such paired derivation sequence, add specific patterns, if possible, for idioms and collocations that are missing in T, or add the pair ⟨s,t⟩ to T as a translation pattern. For example, add

      leave:VP:1:+OBJ behind → VP:1
      VP:1 ← laisser:VP:1:+OBJ

   if the phrase "leave it behind" is not correctly translated.
3. [**Translation Failure**] If T cannot translate s at all, add the pair ⟨s,t⟩ to T as a translation pattern.

The grammar acquisition scheme described above has not yet been automated, but has been manually simulated for a set of 770 English-Japanese simple sentence pairs designed for use in MT system evaluation, which is available from JEIDA (the Japan Electronic Industry Development Association) ((the Japan Electronic Industry Development Association), 1995), including:

#100: Any question will be welcomed.
#200: He kept calm in the face of great danger.
#300: He is what is called "the man in the news".
#400: Japan registered a trade deficit of $101 million, reflecting the country's economic sluggishness, according to government figures.
#500: I also went to the beach 2 weeks earlier.

At an early stage of grammar acquisition, [**Addition of New Patterns**] was primarily used to enrich the set T of patterns, and many sentences were unambiguously and correctly translated. At a later stage, however, JEIDA sentences usually gave several translations, and [**Lexicalization**] with careful assignment of weights was the most critical task. Although these sentences are intended to test a system's ability to translate one basic linguistic phenomenon in each simple sentence, the result was strong evidence for our claim. Over 90% of JEIDA sentences were correctly translated. Among the failures were:

#95: I see some stamps on the desk .
#171: He is for the suggestion, but I'm against it.
#244: She made him an excellent wife.
#660: He painted the walls and the floor white.

Some (prepositional and sentential) attachment ambiguities needs to be resolved on the basis of semantic information, and scoping of coordinated structures would have to be determined by using not only collocational patterns but also some measures of balance and similarities among constituents.

6 Conclusions and Future Work

Some assumptions about patterns should be reexamined when we extend the definition of patterns. The notion of head constraints may have to be extended into one of a set membership constraint if we need to handle coordinated structures (Kaplan and Maxwell III, 1988). Some light-verb phrases cannot be correctly translated without "exchanging" several feature values between the verb and its object. A similar problem has been found in be-verb phrases.

Grammar acquisition and corpus integration are fundamental issues, but automation of these processes (Watanabe, 1993) is still not complete. Development of an efficient translation algorithm, not just an efficient parsing algorithm, will make a significant contribution to research on synchronized grammars, including STAGs and our PCFGs.

Acknowledgments

Hideo Watanabe designed and implemented a prototype MT system for pattern-based CFGs, while Shiho Ogino developed a Japanese generator of the prototype. Their technical discussions and suggestions greatly helped me shape the idea of pattern-based CFGs. I would also like to thank Taijiro Tsutsumi, Masayuki Morohashi, Hiroshi Nomiyama, Tetsuya Nasukawa, and Naohiko Uramoto for their valuable comments. Michael McDonald, as usual, helped me write the final version.

References

Abeillé, A., Y. Schabes, and A. K. Joshi. 1990. "Using Lexicalized Tags for Machine Translation". In *Proc. of the 13th International Conference on Computational Linguistics*, volume 3, pages 1–6, Aug.

Berwick, R. C. 1982. "Computational Complexity and Lexical-Functional Grammar". *American Journal of Computational Linguistics*, pages 97–109, July-Dec.

Brown, P. F., S. A. Della Pietra, V. J. Della Pietra, and R. L. Mercer. 1993. "The Mathematics of Statistical Machine Translation: Parametric Estimation". *Computational Linguistics*, 19(2):263–311, June.

Dorr, B. J. 1993. *"Machine Translation: A View from the Lexicon"*. The MIT Press, Cambridge, Mass.

Earley, J. 1970. "An Efficient Context-free Parsing Algorithm". *Communications of the ACM*, 6(8):94–102, February.

Fujisaki, T., F. Jelinek, J. Cocke, E. Black, and T. Nishino. 1989. "A Probabilistic Parsing Method for Sentence Disambiguation". In *Proc. of the International Workshop on Parsing Technologies*, pages 85–94, Pittsburgh, Aug.

Furuse, O. and H. Iida. 1994. "Cooperation between Transfer and Analysis in Example-Based Framework". In *Proc. of the 15th International Conference on Computational Linguistics*, pages 645–651, Aug.

Gazdar, G., G. K. Pullum, and I. A. Sag. 1985. *"Generalized Phrase Structure Grammar"*. Harvard University Press, Cambridge, Mass.

Jensen, K. and G. E. Heidorn. 1983. "The Fitted Parse: 100% Parsing Capability in a Syntactic Grammar of English". In *Proc. of the 1st Conference on Applied NLP*, pages 93–98.

Kaplan, R. and J. Bresnan. 1982. "Lexical-Functional Grammar: A Formal System for Generalized Grammatical Representation". In J. Bresnan, editor, *"Mental Representation of Grammatical Relations"*. MIT Press, Cambridge, Mass., pages 173–281.

Kaplan, R. M. and J. T. Maxwell III. 1988. "Constituent Coordination in Lexical-Functional Grammar". In *Proc. of the 12th International Conference on Computational Linguistics*, pages 303–305, Aug.

Maruyama, H. 1993. "Pattern-Based Translation: Context-Free Transducer and Its Applications to Practical NLP". In *Proc. of Natural Language Pacific Rim Symposium (NLPRS' 93)*, pages 232–237, Dec.

Pollard, C. and I. A. Sag. 1987. *"An Information-Based Syntax and Semantics, Vol.1 Fundamentals"*. CSLI Lecture Notes, Number 13.

Pustejovsky, J. 1991. "The Generative Lexicon". *Computational Linguistics*, 17(4):409–441, December.

Sato, S. and M. Nagao. 1990. "Toward Memory-based Translation". In *Proc. of the 13th International Conference on Computational Linguistics*, pages 247–252, Helsinki, Aug.

Schabes, Y., A. Abeillé, and A. K. Joshi. 1988. "Parsing Algorithm with 'lexicalized' grammars: Application to tree adjoining grammars". In *Proc. of the 12th International Conference on Computational Linguistics*, pages 578–583, Aug.

Schabes, Y. and R. C. Waters. 1995. "Tree Insertion Grammar: A Cubic-Time, Parsable Formalism that Lexicalizes Context-Free Grammar without Changing the Trees Produced". *Computational Linguistics*, 21(4):479–513, Dec.

Shieber, S. M. and Y. Schabes. 1990. "Synchronous Tree-Adjoining Grammars". In *Proc. of the 13th International Conference on Computational Linguistics*, pages 253–258, August.

Sumita, E. and H. Iida. 1991. "Experiments and Prospects of Example-Based Machine Translation". In *Proc. of the 29th Annual Meeting of the Association for Computational Linguistics*, pages 185–192, Berkeley, June.

JEIDA (the Japan Electronic Industry Development Association). 1995. *"Evaluation Standards for Machine Translation Systems (in Japanese)"*. 95-COMP-17, Tokyo.

Tsujii, J. and K. Fujita. 1991. "Lexical Transfer based on Bilingual Signs". In *Proc. of the 5th European ACL Conference.*

Vijay-Shanker, K. 1987. *"A Study of Tree Adjoining Grammars"*. Ph.D. thesis, Department of Computer and Information Science, University of Pennsylvania.

Vijay-Shanker, K. and Y. Schabes. 1992. "Structure Sharing in Lexicalized Tree-Adjoining Grammars". In *Proc. of the 14th International Conference on Computational Linguistics*, pages 205–211, Aug.

Watanabe, H. 1993. "A Method for Extracting Translation Patterns from Translation Examples". In *Proc. of 5th Intl. Conf. on Theoretical and Methodological Issues in Machine Translation of Natural Languages*, pages 292–301, July.

A Polynomial-Time Algorithm for Statistical Machine Translation

Dekai Wu
HKUST
Department of Computer Science
University of Science and Technology
Clear Water Bay, Hong Kong
dekai@cs.ust.hk

Abstract

We introduce a polynomial-time algorithm for statistical machine translation. This algorithm can be used in place of the expensive, slow best-first search strategies in current statistical translation architectures. The approach employs the stochastic bracketing transduction grammar (SBTG) model we recently introduced to replace earlier word alignment channel models, while retaining a bigram language model. The new algorithm in our experience yields major speed improvement with no significant loss of accuracy.

1 Motivation

The statistical translation model introduced by IBM (Brown et al., 1990) views translation as a noisy channel process. Assume, as we do throughout this paper, that the input language is Chinese and the task is to translate into English. The underlying generative model, shown in Figure 1, contains a stochastic English sentence generator whose output is "corrupted" by the translation channel to produce Chinese sentences. In the IBM system, the language model employs simple n-grams, while the translation model employs several sets of parameters as discussed below. Estimation of the parameters has been described elsewhere (Brown et al., 1993).

Translation is performed in the reverse direction from generation, as usual for recognition under generative models. For each Chinese sentence $\mathbf{c}$ that is to be translated, the system must attempt to find the English sentence $\mathbf{e}*$ such that:

$$(1)\qquad \mathbf{e}* = \operatorname*{argmax}_{\mathbf{e}} \Pr(\mathbf{e}|\mathbf{c})$$

$$(2)\qquad \quad = \operatorname*{argmax}_{\mathbf{e}} \Pr(\mathbf{c}|\mathbf{e}) \Pr(\mathbf{e})$$

In the IBM model, the search for the optimal $\mathbf{e}*$ is performed using a best-first heuristic "stack search" similar to A* methods.

One of the primary obstacles to making the statistical translation approach practical is slow speed of translation, as performed in A* fashion. This price is paid for the robustness that is obtained by using very flexible language and translation models. The language model allows sentences of arbitrary order and the translation model allows arbitrary word-order permutation. The models employ no structural constraints, relying instead on probability parameters to assign low probabilities to implausible sentences. This exhaustive space, together with massive number of parameters, permits greater modeling accuracy.

But while accuracy is enhanced, translation efficiency suffers due to the lack of structure in the hypothesis space. The translation channel is characterized by two sets of parameters: translation and alignment probabilities.[1] The translation probabilities describe lexical substitution, while alignment probabilities describe word-order permutation. The key problem is that the formulation of alignment probabilities $a(i|j, V, T)$ permits the Chinese word in position j of a length-T sentence to map to any position i of a length-V English sentence. So V^T alignments are possible, yielding an exponential space with correspondingly slow search times.

Note there are no explicit linguistic grammars in the IBM channel model. Useful methods do exist for incorporating constraints fed in from other preprocessing modules, and some of these modules do employ linguistic grammars. For instance, we previously reported a method for improving search times in channel translation models that exploits bracketing information (Wu and Ng, 1995). If any brackets for the Chinese sentence can be supplied as additional input information, produced for example by a preprocessing stage, a modified version of the A*-based algorithm can follow the brackets to guide the search heuristically. This strategy appears to produces moderate improvements in search speed and slightly better translations.

Such linguistic-preprocessing techniques could

[1] Various models have been constructed by the IBM team (Brown et al., 1993). This description corresponds to one of the simplest ones, "Model 2"; search costs for the more complex models are correspondingly higher.

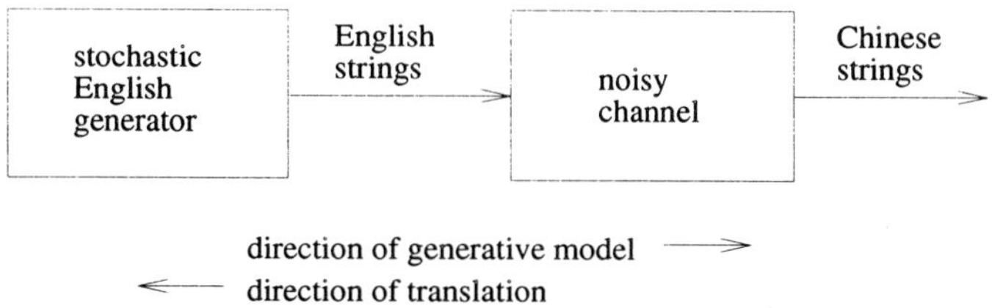

Figure 1: Channel translation model.

also be used with the new model described below, but the issue is independent of our focus here. In this paper we address the underlying assumptions of core channel model itself which does not directly use linguistic structure.

A slightly different model is employed for a word alignment application by Dagan *et al.* (Dagan, Church, and Gale, 1993). Instead of alignment probabilities, offset probabilities $o(k)$ are employed, where k is essentially the positional distance between the English words aligned to two adjacent Chinese words:

$$(3) \qquad k = i - (\mathbf{A}(j_{prev}) + (j - j_{prev})N)$$

where j_{prev} is the position of the immediately preceding Chinese word and N is a constant that normalizes for average sentence lengths in different languages. The motivation is that words that are close to each other in the Chinese sentence should tend to be close in the English sentence as well. The size of the parameter set is greatly reduced from the $|i| \times |j| \times |T| \times |V|$ parameters of the alignment probabilities, down to a small set of $|k|$ parameters. However, the search space remains the same.

The A*-style stack-decoding approach is in some ways a carryover from the speech recognition architectures that inspired the channel translation model. It has proven highly effective for speech recognition in both accuracy and speed, where the search space contains no order variation since the acoustic and text streams can be assumed to be linearly aligned. But in contrast, for translation models the stack search alone does not adequately compensate for the combinatorially more complex space that results from permitting arbitrary order variations. Indeed, the stack-decoding approach remains impractically slow for translation, and has not achieved the same kind of speed as for speech recognition.

The model we describe in this paper, like Dagan *et al.*'s model, encourages related words to stay together, and reduces the number of parameters used to describe word-order variation. But more importantly, it makes structural assumptions that eliminate large portions of the space of alignments, based on linguistic motivatations. This greatly reduces the search space and makes possible a polynomial-time optimization algorithm.

2 ITG and BTG Overview

The new translation model is based on the recently introduced *bilingual language modeling* approach. Specifically, the model employs a *bracketing transduction grammar* or BTG (Wu, 1995a), which is a special case of *inversion transduction grammars* or ITGs (Wu, 1995c; Wu, 1995c; Wu, 1995b; Wu, 1995d). These formalisms were originally developed for the purpose of parallel corpus annotation, with applications for bracketing, alignment, and segmentation. This paper finds they are also useful for the translation system itself. In this section we summarize the main properties of BTGs and ITGs.

An ITG consists of context-free productions where terminal symbols come in *couples*, for example x/y, where x is a Chinese word and y is an English translation of x.[2] Any parse tree thus generates two strings, one on the Chinese stream and one on the English stream. Thus, the tree:

(1) [我/I [[拿了/took [一/a 本/ϵ 書/book]$_{\mathrm{NP}}$]$_{\mathrm{VP}}$ [給/for 你/you]$_{\mathrm{PP}}$]$_{\mathrm{VP}}$]$_{\mathrm{S}}$

produces, for example, the mutual translations:

(2) a. [我 [[拿了 [一本書]$_{\mathrm{NP}}$]$_{\mathrm{VP}}$ [給你]$_{\mathrm{PP}}$]$_{\mathrm{VP}}$]$_{\mathrm{S}}$
[Wǒ [[ná le [yī běn shū]$_{\mathrm{NP}}$]$_{\mathrm{VP}}$ [géi nǐ]$_{\mathrm{PP}}$]$_{\mathrm{VP}}$]$_{\mathrm{S}}$

b. [I [[took [a book]$_{\mathrm{NP}}$]$_{\mathrm{VP}}$ [for you]$_{\mathrm{PP}}$]$_{\mathrm{VP}}$]$_{\mathrm{S}}$

An additional mechanism accommodates a conservative degree of word-order variation between the two languages. With each production of the grammar is associated either a *straight* orientation or an *inverted* orientation, respectively denoted as follows:

$$\begin{array}{lcl} \mathrm{VP} & \rightarrow & [\mathrm{VP\ PP}] \\ \mathrm{VP} & \rightarrow & \langle \mathrm{VP\ PP} \rangle \end{array}$$

In the case of a production with straight orientation, the right-hand-side symbols are visited left-to-right for both the Chinese and English streams. But for a production with inverted orientation, the

[2] Readers of the papers cited above should note that we have switched the roles of English and Chinese here, which helps simplify the presentation of the new translation algorithm.

f	BTG	all matchings	ratio
0	1	1	1.000
1	1	1	1.000
2	2	2	1.000
3	6	6	1.000
4	22	24	0.917
5	90	120	0.750
6	394	720	0.547
7	1806	5040	0.358
8	8558	40320	0.212
9	41586	362880	0.115
10	206098	3628800	0.057
11	1037718	39916800	0.026
12	5293446	479001600	0.011
13	27297738	6227020800	0.004
14	142078746	87178291200	0.002
15	745387038	1307674368000	0.001
16	3937603038	20922789888000	0.000

Figure 2: Number of legal word alignments between sentences of length f, with and without the BTG restriction.

right-hand-side symbols are visited left-to-right for Chinese and right-to-left for English. Thus, the tree:

(3) [我/I ⟨[給/for 你/you]$_{PP}$ [拿了/took [一/a 本/ϵ 書/book]$_{NP}$]$_{VP}$ ⟩$_{VP}$]$_{S}$

produces translations with different word order:

(4) a. [我 [[給你]$_{PP}$ [拿了 [一本書]$_{NP}$]$_{VP}$]$_{VP}$]$_{S}$
b. [I [[took [a book]$_{NP}$]$_{VP}$ [for you]$_{PP}$]$_{VP}$]$_{S}$

In the special case of BTGs which are employed in the model presented below, there is only one undifferentiated nonterminal category (aside from the start symbol). Designating this category A, this means all non-lexical productions are of one of these two forms:

$$A \rightarrow [A\,A \cdots A]$$
$$A \rightarrow \langle A\,A \cdots A \rangle$$

The degree of word-order flexibility is the critical point. BTGs make a favorable trade-off between efficiency and expressiveness: constraints are strong enough to allow algorithms to operate efficiently, but without so much loss of expressiveness as to hinder useful translation. We summarize here; details are given elsewhere (Wu, 1995b).

With regard to efficiency, Figure 2 demonstrates the kind of reduction that BTGs obtain in the space of possible alignments. The number of possible alignments, compared against the unrestricted case where any English word may align to any Chinese position, drops off dramatically for strings longer than four words. (This table makes the simplification of counting only 1-1 matchings and is merely representative.)

With regard to expressiveness, we believe that almost all variation in the order of arguments in a syntactic frame can be accommodated.[3] Syntactic frames generally contain four or fewer subconstituents. Figure 2 shows that for the case of four subconstituents, BTGs permit 22 out of the 24 possible alignments. The only prohibited arrangements are "inside-out" transformations (Wu, 1995b), which we have been unable to find any examples of in our corpus. Moreover, extremely distorted alignments can be handled by BTGs (Wu, 1995c), without resorting to the unrestricted-alignment model.

The translation expressiveness of BTGs is by no means perfect. They are nonetheless proving very useful in applications and are substantially more feasible than previous models. In our previous corpus analysis applications, any expressiveness limitations were easily tolerable since degradation was graceful. In the present translation application, any expressiveness limitation simply means that certain translations are not considered.

For the remainder of the paper, we take advantage of a convenient normal-form theorem (Wu, 1995a) that allows us to assume without loss of generality that the BTG only contains the binary-branching form for the non-lexical productions.[4]

3 BTG-Based Search for the Original Models

A first approach to improving the translation search is to limit the allowed word alignment patterns to those permitted by a BTG. In this case, Equation (2) is kept as the objective function and the translation channel can be parameterized similarly to Dagan *et al.* (Dagan, Church, and Gale, 1993). The effect of the BTG restriction is just to constrain the *shapes* of the word-order distortions. A BTG rather than ITG is used since, as we discussed earlier, pure channel translation models operate without explicit grammars, providing no constituent categories around which a more sophisticated ITG could be structured. But the structural constraints of the BTG can improve search efficiency, even without differentiated constituent categories. Just as in the baseline system, we rely on the language and translation models to take up the slack in place of an explicit grammar. In this approach, an $O(T^7)$ algorithm similar to the one described later can be constructed to replace A* search.

[3] Note that these points are not directed at free word-order languages. But in such languages, explicit morphological inflections make role identification and translation easier.

[4] But see the conclusion for a caveat.

However we do not feel it is worth preserving offset (or alignment or distortion) parameters simply for the sake of preserving the original translation channel model. These parameterizations were only intended to crudely model word-order variation. Instead, the BTG itself can be used directly to probabilistically rank alternative alignments, as described next.

4 Replacing the Channel Model with a SBTG

The second possibility is to use a stochastic bracketing transduction grammar (SBTG) in the channel model, replacing the translation model altogether. In a SBTG, a probability is associated with each production. Thus for the normal-form BTG, we have: The translation lexicon is encoded in productions of

$$
\begin{array}{llll}
A & \overset{a^{[]}}{\rightarrow} & [A\,A] & \\
A & \overset{a^{\langle\rangle}}{\rightarrow} & \langle A\,A\rangle & \\
A & \overset{b(x,y)}{\rightarrow} & x/y & \text{for all } x,y \text{ lexical translations} \\
A & \overset{b(x,\epsilon)}{\rightarrow} & x/\epsilon & \text{for all } x \text{ Chinese vocabulary} \\
A & \overset{b(\epsilon,y)}{\rightarrow} & \epsilon/y & \text{for all } y \text{ English vocabulary}
\end{array}
$$

the third kind. The latter two kinds of productions allow words of either Chinese or English to go unmatched.

The SBTG assigns a probability $\Pr(\mathbf{c},\mathbf{e},\mathbf{q})$ to all generable trees $\mathbf{q}$ and sentence-pairs. In principle it can be used as the translation channel model by normalizing with $\Pr(\mathbf{e})$ and integrating out $\Pr(\mathbf{q})$ to give $\Pr(\mathbf{c}|\mathbf{e})$ in Equation (2). In practice, a strong language model makes this unnecessary, so we can instead optimize the simpler Viterbi approximation

$$(4) \qquad \mathbf{e}* \;=\; \underset{\mathbf{e}}{\operatorname{argmax}} \Pr(\mathbf{c},\mathbf{e},\mathbf{q}) \Pr(\mathbf{e})$$

To complete the picture we add a bigram model $g_{e_{j-1}e_j} = g(e_j|e_{j-1})$ for the English language model $\Pr(\mathbf{e})$.

Offset, alignment, or distortion parameters are entirely eliminated. A large part of the implicit function of such parameters—to prevent alignments where too many frame arguments become separated—is rendered unnecessary by the BTG's structural constraints, which prohibit many such configurations altogether. Another part of the parameters' purpose is subsumed by the SBTG's probabilities $a^{[]}$ and $a^{\langle\rangle}$, which can be set to prefer straight or inverted orientation depending on the language pair. As in the original models, the language model heavily influences the remaining ordering decisions.

Matters are complicated by the presence of the bigram model in the objective function (which word-alignment models, as opposed to translation models, do not need to deal with). As in our word-alignment model, the translation algorithm optimizes Equation (4) via dynamic programming, similar to chart parsing (Earley, 1970) but with a probabilistic objective function as for HMMs (Viterbi, 1967). But unlike the word-alignment model, to accommodate the bigram model we introduce indexes in the recurrence not only on subtrees over the source Chinese string, but also on the delimiting words of the target English substrings.

Another feature of the algorithm is that segmentation of the Chinese input sentence is performed in parallel with the translation search. Conventional architectures for Chinese NLP generally attempt to identify word boundaries as a preprocessing stage.[5] Whenever the segmentation preprocessor prematurely commits to an inappropriate segmentation, difficulties are created for later stages. This problem is particularly acute for translation, since the decision as to whether to regard a sequence as a single unit depends on whether its components can be translated compositionally. This in turn often depends on what the target language is. In other words, the Chinese cannot be appropriately segmented except with respect to the target language of translation—a *task-driven* definition of correct segmentation.

The algorithm is given below. A few remarks about the notation used: $\mathbf{c}_{s..t}$ denotes the subsequence of Chinese tokens $\mathbf{c}_{s+1}, \mathbf{c}_{s+2}, \ldots, \mathbf{c}_t$. We use $E(s..t)$ to denote the set of English words that are translations the Chinese word created by taking all tokens in $\mathbf{c}_{s..t}$ together. $E(s,t)$ denotes the set of English words that are translations of any of the Chinese words anywhere within $\mathbf{c}_{s..t}$. Note also that we assume the explicit sentence-start and sentence-end tokens $\mathbf{c}_0 =$ <s> and $\mathbf{c}_{T+1} =$ </s>, which makes the algorithm description more parsimonious. Finally, the argmax operator is generalized to vector notation to accomodate multiple indices.

1. Initialization

$$\delta^0_{stYY}(i) \;=\; b_i(\mathbf{c}_{s..t}/Y), \qquad \begin{array}{c} 0 \le s < t \le T \\ Y \in E(s..t) \end{array}$$

2. Recursion For all s,t,y,z such that $\left\{\begin{array}{l} -1 \le s < t \le T+1 \\ y \in E(s,t) \\ z \in E(s,t) \end{array}\right.$

$$\delta_{styz} \;=\; \max[\delta^{[]}_{styz}, \delta^{\langle\rangle}_{styz}, \delta^0_{styz}]$$

$$\theta_{styz} \;=\; \left\{\begin{array}{ll} [] & \text{if } \delta^{[]}_{styz} > \delta^{\langle\rangle}_{styz} \text{ and } \delta^{[]}_{styz} > \delta^0_{styz} \\ \langle\rangle & \text{if } \delta^{\langle\rangle}_{styz} > \delta^{[]}_{styz} \text{ and } \delta^{\langle\rangle}_{styz} > \delta^0_{styz} \\ 0 & \text{otherwise} \end{array}\right.$$

[5] Written Chinese contains no spaces to delimit words; any spaces in the earlier examples are artifacts of the parse tree brackets.

Category	Original A*	Bracket A*	BTG-Channel
Correct	67.5	69.8	68.2
Incorrect	32.5	30.2	31.8

Figure 3: Translation accuracy (percentage correct).

where

$$\delta_{styz}^{[]} = \max_{\substack{s<S<t \\ Y\in E(s,S) \\ Z\in E(S,t)}} a^{[]}\, \delta_{sSyY}\, \delta_{StZz}\, g_{YZ}$$

$$\begin{bmatrix} \sigma_{styz}^{[]} \\ \psi_{styz}^{[]} \\ \omega_{styz}^{[]} \end{bmatrix} = \operatorname*{argmax}_{\substack{s<S<t \\ Y\in E(s,S) \\ Z\in E(S,t)}} a^{[]}\, \delta_{sSyY}\, \delta_{StZz}\, g_{YZ}$$

$$\delta_{styz}^{\langle\rangle} = \max_{\substack{s<S<t \\ Y\in E(S,t) \\ Z\in E(s,S)}} a^{\langle\rangle}\, \delta_{sSZz}\, \delta_{StyY}\, g_{YZ}$$

$$\begin{bmatrix} \sigma_{styz}^{\langle\rangle} \\ \psi_{styz}^{\langle\rangle} \\ \omega_{styz}^{\langle\rangle} \end{bmatrix} = \operatorname*{argmax}_{\substack{s<S<t \\ Y\in E(S,t) \\ Z\in E(s,S)}} a^{\langle\rangle}\, \delta_{sSZz}(j)\, \delta_{StyY}(k)\, g_{YZ}$$

3. Reconstruction Initialize by setting the root of the parse tree to $q_0 = (-1, T-1, \text{<s>}, \text{</s>})$. The remaining descendants in the optimal parse tree are then given recursively for any $q = (s, t, y, z)$ by:

$$\text{LEFT}(q) = \begin{cases} \text{NIL} & \text{if } t-s \leq 1 \\ (s, \sigma_q^{[]}, y, \psi_q^{[]}) & \text{if } \theta_q = [] \\ (s, \sigma_q^{\langle\rangle}, \omega_q^{\langle\rangle}, z) & \text{if } \theta_q = \langle\rangle \\ \text{NIL} & \text{otherwise} \end{cases}$$

$$\text{RIGHT}(q) = \begin{cases} \text{NIL} & \text{if } t-s \leq 1 \\ (\sigma_q^{[]}, t, \omega_q^{[]}, z) & \text{if } \theta_q = [] \\ (\sigma_q^{\langle\rangle}, t, y, \psi_q^{\langle\rangle}) & \text{if } \theta_q = \langle\rangle \\ \text{NIL} & \text{otherwise} \end{cases}$$

Assume the number of translations per word is bounded by some constant. Then the maximum size of $E(s,t)$ is proportional to $t - s$. The asymptotic time complexity for the translation algorithm is thus bounded by $O(T^7)$. Note that in practice, actual performance is improved by the sparseness of the translation matrix.

An interesting connection has been suggested to direct parsing for ID/LP grammars (Shieber, 1984), in which word-order variations would be accommodated by the parser, and related ideas for generation of free word-order languages in the TAG framework (Joshi, 1987). Our work differs from the ID/LP work in several important respects. First, we are not merely parsing, but translating with a bigram language model. Also, of course, we are dealing with a probabilistic optimization problem. But perhaps most importantly, our goal is to constrain as tightly as possible the space of possible transduction relationships between two languages with fixed word-order, making no other language-specific assumptions; we are thus driven to seek a kind of language-universal property. In contrast, the ID/LP work was directed at parsing a single language with free word-order. As a consequence, it would be necessary to enumerate a specific set of linear-precedence (LP) relations for the language, and moreover the immediate-dominance (ID) productions would typically be more complex than binary-branching. This significantly increases time complexity, compared to our BTG model. Although it is not mentioned in their paper, the time complexity for ID/LP parsing rises exponentially with the length of production right-hand-sides, due to the number of permutations. ITGs avoid this with their restriction to inversions, rather than permutations, and BTGs further minimize the grammar size. We have also confirmed empirically that our models would not be feasible under general permutations.

5 Results

The algorithm above was tested in the SILC translation system. The translation lexicon was largely constructed by training on the HKUST English-Chinese Parallel Bilingual Corpus, which consists of governmental transcripts. The corpus was sentence-aligned statistically (Wu, 1994); Chinese words and collocations were extracted (Fung and Wu, 1994; Wu and Fung, 1994); then translation pairs were learned via an EM procedure (Wu and Xia, 1995). The resulting English vocabulary is approximately 6,500 words and the Chinese vocabulary is approximately 5,500 words, with a many-to-many translation mapping averaging 2.25 Chinese translations per English word. Due to the unsupervised training, the translation lexicon contains noise and is only at about 86% percent weighted precision.

With regard to accuracy, we merely wish to demonstrate that for statistical MT, accuracy is not significantly compromised by substituting our efficient optimization algorithm. It is not our purpose here to argue that accuracy can be increased with our model. No morphological processing has been used to correct the output, and until now we have only been testing with a bigram model trained on extremely limited samples. A coarse evaluation of

Input:	香港的安定繁榮是我們生活方式的支柱。
	(Xiāng gǎng de ān dìng fān róng shì wǒ mén shēng huó fāng shì de zhī zhù.)
Output:	*Hong Kong's stabilize boom is us life styles's pillar.*
Corpus:	Our prosperity and stability underpin our way of life.
Input:	本港的經濟前景與中國, 特別是廣東省的經濟前景息息相關。
	(Běn gǎng de jīng jì qían jǐng yǔ zhōng guó, tè bié shì guǎng dōng shěng de jīng jì qián jǐng xī xī xiāng guān.)
Output:	*Hong Kong's economic foreground with China, particular Guangdong province's economic foreground vitally interrelated.*
Corpus:	Our economic future is inextricably bound up with China, and with Guangdong Province in particular.
Input:	我完全支持他的意見。
	(Wǒ wán quán zhī chí tā de yì jiàn.)
Output:	*I absolutely uphold his views.*
Corpus:	I fully support his views.
Input:	這些安排可加強我們日後維持金融穩定的能力。
	(Zhè xiē ān pái kě jiā qiáng wǒ mén rì hòu wéi chí jīn róng wěn dìng de néng lì.)
Output:	*These arrangements can enforce us future kept financial stabilization's competency.*
Corpus:	These arrangements will enhance our ability to maintain monetary stability in the years to come.
Input:	不過, 我現在可以肯定的說, 我們將會提供為達到各項主要目標所需的經費。
	(Bù guò, wǒ xiàn zài kě yǐ kěn dìng de shuō, wǒ mén jiāng huì tí gōng wèi dá dào gè xiàng zhǔ yào mù biāo suǒ xū de jīng fèi.)
Output:	*However, I now can certainty's say, will provide for us attain various dominant goal necessary's current expenditure.*
Corpus:	The consultation process is continuing but I can confirm now that the necessary funds will be made available to meet the key targets.

Figure 4: Example translation outputs.

translation accuracy was performed on a random sample drawn from Chinese sentences of fewer than 20 words from the parallel corpus, the results of which are shown in Figure 3. We have judged only whether the correct meaning (as determined by the corresponding English sentence in the parallel corpus) is conveyed by the translation, paying particular attention to word order, but otherwise ignoring morphological and function word choices. For comparison, the accuracies from the A*-based systems are also shown. There is no significant difference in the accuracy. Some examples of the output are shown in Figure 4.

On the other hand, the new algorithm has indeed proven to be much faster. At present we are unable to use direct measurement to compare the speed of the systems meaningfully, because of vast implementational differences between the systems. However, the order-of-magnitude improvements are immediately apparent. In the earlier system, translation of single sentences required on the order of hours (Sun Sparc 10 workstations). In contrast the new algorithm generally takes less than one minute—usually substantially less—with no special optimization of the code.

6 Conclusion

We have introduced a new algorithm for the runtime optimization step in statistical machine translation systems, whose polynomial-time complexity addresses one of the primary obstacles to practicality facing statistical MT. The underlying model for the algorithm is a combination of the stochastic BTG and bigram models. The improvement in speed does not appear to impair accuracy significantly.

We have implemented a version that accepts ITGs rather than BTGs, and plan to experiment with more heavily structured models. However, it is important to note that the search complexity rises exponentially rather than polynomially with the size of the grammar, just as for context-free parsing (Barton, Berwick, and Ristad, 1987). This is not relevant to the BTG-based model we have described since its grammar size is fixed; in fact the BTG's minimal grammar size has been an important advantage over more linguistically-motivated ITG-based models.

We have also implemented a generalized version that accepts arbitrary grammars not restricted to normal form, with two motivations. The pragmatic benefit is that structured grammars become easier to write, and more concise. The expressiveness benefit is that a wider family of probability distributions can be written. As stated earlier, the normal form theorem guarantees that the same set of shapes will be explored by our search algorithm, regardless of whether a binary-branching BTG or an arbitrary BTG is used. But it may sometimes be useful to place probabilities on n-ary productions that vary with n in a way that cannot be expressed by composing binary productions; for example one might wish to encourage longer straight productions. The generalized version permits such strategies.

Currently we are evaluating robustness extensions of the algorithm that permit words suggested by the language model to be inserted in the output sentence, which the original A* algorithms permitted.

Acknowledgements

Thanks to an anonymous referee for valuable comments, and to the SILC group members: Xuanyin Xia, Eva Wai-Man Fong, Cindy Ng, Hong-sing Wong, and Daniel Ka-Leung Chan. Many thanks also to Kathleen McKeown and her group for discussion, support, and assistance.

References

Barton, G. Edward, Robert C. Berwick, and Eric Sven Ristad. 1987. *Computational Complexity and Natural Language.* MIT Press, Cambridge, MA.

Brown, Peter F., John Cocke, Stephen A. DellaPietra, Vincent J. DellaPietra, Frederick Jelinek, John D. Lafferty, Robert L. Mercer, and Paul S. Roossin. 1990. A statistical approach to machine translation. *Computational Linguistics*, 16(2):29–85.

Brown, Peter F., Stephen A. DellaPietra, Vincent J. DellaPietra, and Robert L. Mercer. 1993. The mathematics of statistical machine translation: Parameter estimation. *Computational Linguistics*, 19(2):263–311.

Dagan, Ido, Kenneth W. Church, and William A. Gale. 1993. Robust bilingual word alignment for machine aided translation. In *Proceedings of the Workshop on Very Large Corpora*, pages 1–8, Columbus, OH, June.

Earley, Jay. 1970. An efficient context-free parsing algorithm. *Communications of the Association for Computing Machinery*, 13(2):94–102.

Fung, Pascale and Dekai Wu. 1994. Statistical augmentation of a Chinese machine-readable dictionary. In *Proceedings of the Second Annual Workshop on Very Large Corpora*, pages 69–85, Kyoto, August.

Joshi, Aravind K. 1987. Word-order variation in natural language generation. In *Proceedings of AAAI-87, Sixth National Conference on Artificial Intelligence*, pages 550–555.

Shieber, Stuart M. 1984. Direct parsing of ID/LP grammars. *Linguistics and Philosophy*, 7:135–154.

Viterbi, Andrew J. 1967. Error bounds for convolutional codes and an asymptotically optimal decoding algorithm. *IEEE Transactions on Information Theory*, 13:260–269.

Wu, Dekai. 1994. Aligning a parallel English-Chinese corpus statistically with lexical criteria. In *Proceedings of the 32nd Annual Conference of the Association for Computational Linguistics*, pages 80–87, Las Cruces, New Mexico, June.

Wu, Dekai. 1995a. An algorithm for simultaneously bracketing parallel texts by aligning words. In *Proceedings of the 33rd Annual Conference of the Association for Computational Linguistics*, pages 244–251, Cambridge, Massachusetts, June.

Wu, Dekai. 1995b. Grammarless extraction of phrasal translation examples from parallel texts. In *TMI-95, Proceedings of the Sixth International Conference on Theoretical and Methodological Issues in Machine Translation*, volume 2, pages 354–372, Leuven, Belgium, July.

Wu, Dekai. 1995c. Stochastic inversion transduction grammars, with application to segmentation, bracketing, and alignment of parallel corpora. In *Proceedings of IJCAI-95, Fourteenth International Joint Conference on Artificial Intelligence*, pages 1328–1334, Montreal, August.

Wu, Dekai. 1995d. Trainable coarse bilingual grammars for parallel text bracketing. In *Proceedings of the Third Annual Workshop on Very Large Corpora*, pages 69–81, Cambridge, Massachusetts, June.

Wu, Dekai and Pascale Fung. 1994. Improving Chinese tokenization with linguistic filters on statistical lexical acquisition. In *Proceedings of the Fourth Conference on Applied Natural Language Processing*, pages 180–181, Stuttgart, October.

Wu, Dekai and Cindy Ng. 1995. Using brackets to improve search for statistical machine translation. In *PACLIC-10, Pacific Asia Conference on Language, Information and Computation*, pages 195–204, Hong Kong, December.

Wu, Dekai and Xuanyin Xia. 1995. Large-scale automatic extraction of an English-Chinese lexicon. *Machine Translation*, 9(3–4):285–313.

ṢEMḤE: A Generalised Two-Level System

George Anton Kiraz*
Computer Laboratory
University of Cambridge (St John's College)
Email: George.Kiraz@cl.cam.ac.uk
URL: http://www.cl.cam.ac.uk/users/gk105

Abstract

This paper presents a generalised two-level implementation which can handle linear and non-linear morphological operations. An algorithm for the interpretation of multi-tape two-level rules is described. In addition, a number of issues which arise when developing non-linear grammars are discussed with examples from Syriac.

1 Introduction

The introduction of two-level morphology (Koskenniemi, 1983) and subsequent developments has made implementing computational-morphology models a feasible task. Yet, two-level formalisms fell short from providing elegant means for the description of non-linear operations such as infixation, circumfixation and root-and-pattern morphology.[1] As a result, two-level implementations – e.g. (Antworth, 1990; Karttunen, 1983; Karttunen and Beesley, 1992; Ritchie et al., 1992) – have always been biased towards linear morphology.

The past decade has seen a number of proposals for handling non-linear morphology;[2] however, none (apart from Beesley's work) seem to have been implemented over large descriptions, nor have they provided means by which the grammarian can develop non-linear descriptions using higher level notation.

To test the validity of one's proposal or formalism, minimally a medium-scale description is a desideratum. SemHe[3] fulfils this requirement. It is a generalised multi-tape two-level system which is being used in developing non-linear grammars.

This paper (1) presents the algorithms behind SemHe; (2) discusses the issues involved in compiling non-linear descriptions; and (3) proposes extension/solutions to make writing non-linear rules easier and more elegant. The paper assumes knowledge of multi-tape two-level morphology (Kay, 1987; Kiraz, 1994c).

2 Linguistic Descriptions

The linguist provides SemHe with three pieces of data: a lexicon, two-level rules and word formation grammar. All entries take the form of Prolog terms.[4] (Identifiers starting with an uppercase letter denote variables, otherwise they are instantiated symbols.) A lexical entry is described by the term

$$\texttt{synword}(\langle morpheme\rangle, \langle category\rangle).$$

Categories are of the form

$$\langle category\_symbol\rangle : [\langle feature\_attr_1 = value_1\rangle, \ldots, \langle feature\_attr_n = value_n\rangle]$$

a notational variant of the PATR-II category formalism (Shieber, 1986).

* Supported by a Benefactor Studentship from St John's College. This research was done under the supervision of Dr Stephen G. Pulman. Thanks to the anonymous reviewers for their comments. All mistakes remain mine.

[1] Although it is possible to express some classes of non-linear rules using standard two-level formalisms by means of *ad hoc* diacritics, e.g., infixation in (Antworth, 1990, p. 156), there are no means for expressing other classes as root-and-pattern phenomena.

[2] (Kay, 1987), (Kataja and Koskenniemi, 1988), (Beesley et al., 1989), (Lavie et al., 1990), (Beesley, 1990), (Beesley, 1991), (Kornai, 1991), (Wiebe, 1992), (Pulman and Hepple, 1993), (Narayanan and Hashem, 1993), and (Bird and Ellison, 1994). See (Kiraz, 1996) for a review.

[3] The name SemHe (Syriac *ṣemḥê* 'rays') is not an acronym, but the title of a grammatical treatise written by the Syriac polymath (*inter alia* mathematician and grammarian) Bar 'Eḇrōyô (1225-1286), viz. *kṯōḇô ḏṣemḥê* 'The Book of Rays'.

[4] We describe here the terms which are relevant to this paper. For a full description, see (Kiraz, 1996).

```
tl_alphabet(0, [k,t,b,a,e]).                                                        % surface alphabet
tl_alphabet(1, [c1,c2,c3,v,♭]). tl_alphabet(2, [k,t,b,♭]). tl_alphabet(3, [a,e,♭]). % lexical alphabets
tl_set(radical, [k,t,b]). tl_set(vowel, [a,e]). tl_set(c1c3, [c1,c3]).              % variable sets
tl_rule(R1, [[],[],[]], [[♭],[♭],[♭]], [[],[],[]], =>, [], [], [],
        [], [[],[],[]]).
tl_rule(R2, [[],[],[]], [[P],[C],[]], [[],[],[]], =>, [], [C], [],
        [c1c3(P),radical(C)], [[],[],[]]).
tl_rule(R3, [[],[],[]], [[v],[],[V]], [[],[],[]], =>, [], [V], [],
        [vowel(V)], [[],[],[]]).
tl_rule(R4, [[],[],[]], [[v],[],[V]], [[c2,v],[],[]], <=>, [], [], [],
        [vowel(V)], [[],[],[]]).
tl_rule(R5, [[],[],[]], [[c2],[C],[]], [[],[],[]], <=>, [], [C], [],
        [radical(C)], [[], [root:[measure=p'al]], []]).
tl_rule(R6, [[],[],[]], [[c2],[C],[]], [[],[],[]], <=>, [], [C,C], [],
        [radical(C)], [[], [root:[measure=pa''el]], []]).
```

Listing 1

A two-level rule is described using a syntactic variant of the formalism described by (Ruessink, 1989; Pulman and Hepple, 1993), including the extensions by (Kiraz, 1994c),

$$\texttt{tl\_rule}(\langle id\rangle, \langle LLC\rangle, \langle Lex\rangle, \langle RLC\rangle, \langle Op\rangle, \langle LSC\rangle, \langle Surf\rangle, \langle RSC\rangle, \langle variables\rangle, \langle features\rangle).$$

The arguments are: (1) a rule identifier, *id*; (2) the left-lexical-context, *LLC*, the lexical center, *Lex*, and the right-lexical-context, *RLC*, each in the form of a list-of-lists, where the *i*th list represents the *i*th lexical tape; (3) an operator, => for optional rules or <=> for obligatory rules; (4) the left-surface-context, *LSC*, the surface center, *Surf*, and the right-surface-context, *RSC*, each in the form of a list; (5) a list of the *variables* used in the lexical and surface expressions, each member in the form of a predicate indicating the set identifier (see *infra*) and an argument indicating the variable in question; and (6) a set of *features* (i.e. category forms) in the form of a list-of-lists, where the *i*th item must unify with the feature-structure of the morpheme affected by the rule on the *i*th lexical tape.

A lexical string maps to a surface string iff (1) they can be partitioned into pairs of lexical-surface subsequences, where each pair is licenced by a rule, and (2) no partition violates an obligatory rule.

Alphabet declarations take the form `tl_alphabet(`⟨*tape*⟩, ⟨*symbol_list*⟩`)`, and variable sets are described by the predicate `tl_set(`⟨*id*⟩, ⟨*symbol_list*⟩`)`. Word formation rules take the form of unification-based CFG rules, `synrule(`⟨*identifier*⟩, ⟨*mother*⟩, [⟨*daughter*$_1$⟩, ..., ⟨*daughter*$_n$⟩]`)`.

The following example illustrates the derivation of Syriac /ktab/[5] 'he wrote' (in the simple *p'al* measure)[6] from the pattern morpheme {cvcvc} 'verbal pattern', root {ktb} 'notion of writing', and vocalism {a}. The three morphemes produce the underlying form */katab/, which surfaces as /ktab/ since short vowels in open unstressed syllables are deleted. The process is illustrated in (1).[7]

(1) 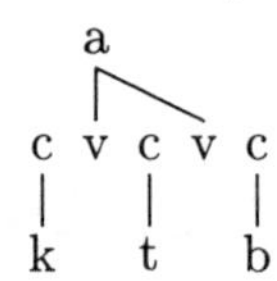

= */katab/ ⟹ /ktab/

The *pa"el* measure of the same verb, viz. /katteb/, is derived by the gemination of the middle consonant (i.e. t) and applying the appropriate vocalism {ae}.

The two-level grammar (Listing 1) assumes three lexical tapes. Uninstantiated contexts are denoted by an empty list. R1 is the morpheme boundary (= ♭) rule. R2 and R3 sanction stem consonants and vowels, respectively. R4 is the obligatory vowel deletion rule. R5 and R6 map the second radical, [t], for *p'al* and *pa"el* forms, respectively. In this example, the lexicon contains the entries in (2).[8]

(2) synword($c_1vc_2vc_3$, `pattern` : []).
synword(`ktb`, `root` : [`measure` = `M`]).
synword(`aa`, `vocalism` : [`measure` = `p'al`]).
synword(`ae`, `vocalism` : [`measure` = `pa"el`]).

Note that the value of 'measure' in the root entry is

[5]Spirantization is ignored here; for a discussion on Syriac spirantization, see (Kiraz, 1995).

[6]Syriac verbs are classified under various measures (forms). The basic ones are: *p'al, pa"el* and *'af'el.*

[7]This analysis is along the lines of (McCarthy, 1981) – based on autosegmental phonology (Goldsmith, 1976).

[8]Spreading is ignored here; for a discussion, see (Kiraz, 1994c).

uninstantiated; it is determined from the feature values in R5, R6 and/or the word grammar (see *infra*, §4.3).

3 Implementation

There are two current methods for implementing two-level rules (both implemented in `SemHe`): (1) compiling rules into finite-state automata (multi-tape transducers in our case), and (2) interpreting rules directly. The former provides better performance, while the latter facilitates the debugging of grammars (by tracing and by providing debugging utilities along the lines of (Carter, 1995)). Additionally, the interpreter facilitates the incremental compilation of rules by simply allowing the user to toggle rules on and off.

The compilation of the above formalism into automata is described by (Grimley-Evans et al., 1996). The following is a description of the interpreter.

3.1 Internal Representation

The word grammar is compiled into a shift-reduce parser. In addition, a first-and-follow algorithm, based on (Aho and Ullman, 1977), is applied to compute the feasible follow categories for each category type. The set of feasible follow categories, *NextCats*, of a particular category *Cat* is returned by the predicate FOLLOW(+*Cat*, −*NextCats*). Additionally, FOLLOW(`bos`, *NextCats*) returns the set of category symbols at the beginning of strings, and `eos` $\in$ *NextCats* indicates that *Cat* may occur at the end of strings.

The lexical component is implemented as character tries (Knuth, 1973), one per tape. Given a list of lexical strings, *Lex*, and a list of lexical pointers, *LexPtrs*, the predicate

$$\text{LEXICAL-TRANSITIONS}(+Lex,\ +LexPtrs,\ -NewLexPtrs,\ -LexCats)$$

succeeds iff there are transitions on *Lex* from *LexPtrs*; it returns *NewLexPtrs*, and the categories, *LexCats*, at the end of morphemes, if any.

Two-level predicates are converted into an internal representation: (1) every left-context expression is reversed and appended to an uninstantiated tail; (2) every right-context expression is appended to an uninstantiated tail; and (3) each rule is assigned a 6-bit 'precedence value' where every bit represents one of the six lexical and surface expressions. If an expression is *not* an empty list (i.e. context is specified), the relevant bit is set. In analysis, surface expressions are assigned the most significant bits, while lexical expressions are assigned the least significant ones. In generation, the opposite state of affairs holds. Rules are then reasserted in the order of their precedence value. This ensures that rules which contain the most specified expressions are tested first resulting in better performance.

3.2 The Interpreter Algorithm

The algorithms presented below are given in terms of prolog-like non-deterministic operations. A clause is satisfied iff all the conditions under it are satisfied. The predicates are depicted top-down in (3). (`SemHe` makes use of an earlier implementation by (Pulman and Hepple, 1993).)

(3)

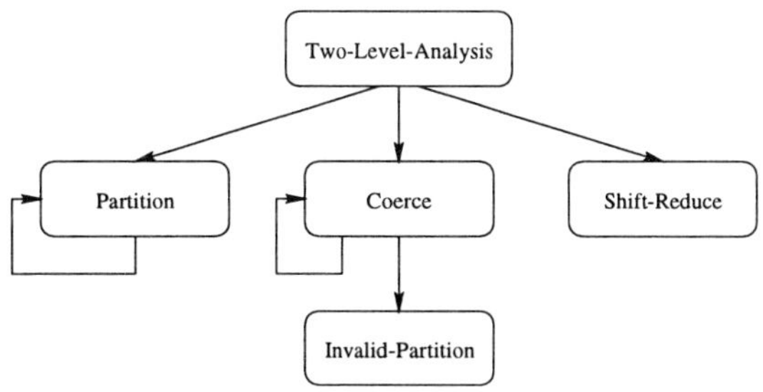

In order to minimise accumulator-passing arguments, we assume the following initially-empty stacks: *ParseStack* accumulates the category structures of the morphemes identified, and *FeatureStack* maintains the rule features encountered so far. ('+' indicates concatenation.)

PARTITION partitions a two-level analysis into sequences of lexical-surface pairs, each licenced by a rule. The base case of the predicate is given in Listing 2,[9] and the recursive case in Listing 3.

The recursive COERCE predicate ensures that no partition is violated by an obligatory rule. It takes three arguments: *Result* is the output of PARTITION (usually reversed by the calling predicate, hence, COERCE deals with the last partition first), *PrevCats* is a register which keeps track of the last morpheme category encountered, and *Partition* returns selected elements from *Result*. The base case of the predicate is simply COERCE(`[]`, `_`, `[]`) – i.e., no more partitions. The recursive case is shown in Listing 4. *CurrentCats* keeps track of the category of the morpheme which occures in the current partition. The invalidity of a partition is determined by INVALID-PARTITION (Listing 5).

TWO-LEVEL-ANALYSIS (Listing 6) is the main predicate. It takes a surface string or lexical string(s) and returns a list of partitions and a

[9]For efficiency, variables appearing in left-context and centre expressions are evaluated after LEXICAL-TRANSITIONS since they will be fully instantiated then; only right-contexts are evaluated after the recursion.

```
PARTITION(SurfDone, SurfToDo, LexDone, LexToDo, LexPtrs, NextCats, Result)
SurfToDo = [] &                       % surface string exhausted
LexToDo = [[],[],···,[]] &            % all lexical strings exhausted
LexPtrs = [rt,rt,···,rt] &            % all lexical pointers are at the root node
eos ∈ NextCats &                      % end-of-string
Result = [].                          % output: no more results
```

Listing 2

```
PARTITION(SurfDone, SurfToDo, LexDone, LexToDo, LexPtrs, NextCats,
          [ResultHead | ResultTail])
there is tl_rule(Id, LLC, Lex, RLC, Op, LSC, Surf, RSC, Variables, Features) such that
    (Op = (=> or <=>), LexDone = LLC, SurfDone = LSC,
    SurfToDo = Surf + RSC and LexToDo = Lex + RLC) &
LEXICAL-TRANSITIONS(Lex, LexPtrs, NewLexPtrs, LexCats) &
push Features onto FeatureStack &                 % keep track of rule features
if LexCats ≠ nil then                             % found a morpheme boundary?
    while FeatureStack is not empty               % unify rule and lexical features
        unify LexCats with (pop FeatureStack) &
    push LexCats onto ParseStack &                % update the parse stack
    if LexCats ∈ NextCats then                    % get next category
        FOLLOW(LexCats, NewNextCats)
end if &
ResultHead = Id/SurfDone/Surf/RSC/
             LexDone/Lex/RLC/LexCats &
NewSurfDone = SurfDone + reverse Surf &           % make new arguments ...
NewSurfToDo = RSC &                               % ... and recurse
NewLexDone = LexDone + reverse Lex &
NewLexToDo = RLC &
PARTITION(NewSurfDone, NewSurfToDo,
          NewLexDone, NewLexToDo,
          NewLexPtrs, NewNextCats, ResultTail) &
for all SetId(Var) ∈ Variables                    % check variables
    there is tl_set(SetId, Set) such that Var ∈ Set.
```

Listing 3

```
COERCE([Id/LSC/Surf/RSC/LLC/Lex/RLC/LexCats | ResultTail], PrevCats,
       [Id/Surf/Lex | PartitionTail])
if LexCats ≠ nil then
    CurrentCats = LexCats
else
    CurrentCats = PrevCats &
not INVALID-PARTITION(LSC, Surf, RSC, LLC, Lex, RLC, CurrentCats) &
COERCE(ResultTail, CurrentCats, PartitionTail).
```

Listing 4

```
INVALID-PARTITION(LSC, Surf, RSC, LLC, Lex, RLC, Cats)
there is tl_rule(Id, LLC, Lex, RLC, <=>, LSC, NotSurf, RSC, Variables, Features) such that
    NotSurf ≠ Surf &
for all SetId(Var) ∈ Variables          % check variables
    there is tl_set(SetId, Set) such that Var ∈ Set &
unify Cats with Features &
fail.
```

Listing 5

TWO-LEVEL-ANALYSIS(?*Surf*, ?*Lex*, -*Partition*, -*Parse*)
FOLLOW(bos, *NextCats*) &
PARTITION([], *Surf*, [[],[],⋯,[]], *Lex*, [rt,rt,⋯,rt], *NextCats*, *Result*) &
COERCE(**reverse** *Result*, nil, *Partition*) &
SHIFT-REDUCE(*ParseStack*, *Parse*).

Listing 6

morphosyntactic parse tree. To analyse a surface form, one calls TWO-LEVEL-ANALYSIS(+*Surf*, −*Lex*, −*Partition*, −*Parse*). To generate a surface form, one calls TWO-LEVEL-ANALYSIS(−*Surf*, +*Lex*, −*Partition*, −*Parse*).

4 Developing Non-Linear Grammars

When developing Semitic grammars, one comes across various issues and problems which normally do not arise with linear grammars. Some can be solved by known methods or 'tricks'; others require extensions in order to make developing grammars easier and more elegant. This section discuss issues which normally do not arise when compiling linear grammars.

4.1 Linearity vs. Non-Linearity

In Semitic languages, non-linearity occurs only in stems. Hence, lexical descriptions of stems make use of three lexical tapes (pattern, root & vocalism), while those of prefixes and suffixes use the first lexical tape. This requires duplicating rules when stating lexical constraints. Consider rule R4 (Listing 1). It allows the deletion of the first stem vowel by the virtue of *RLC* (even if c_2 was not indexed); hence /katab/ → /ktab/. Now consider adding the suffix {eh} 'him/it': /katab/+{eh} → /katbeh/, where the second stem vowel is deleted since deletion applies right-to-left; however, *RLC* can only cope with stem vowels. Rule R7 (Listing 7) is required. One might suggest placing constraints on surface expressions instead. However, doing so causes surface expressions to be dependent on other rules.

Additionally, *Lex* in R4 and R7 deletes stem vowels. Consider adding the prefix {wa} 'and': {wa} + /katab/ + {eh} → /wkatbeh/, where the prefix vowel is also deleted. To cope with this, two additional rules like R4 and R7 are required, but with *Lex* = [[V],[],[]].

We resolve this by allowing the user to write expansion rules of the from

expand(⟨*symbol*⟩, ⟨*expansion*⟩, ⟨*variables*⟩).

In our example, the expansion rules in (4) are needed.

(4) expand(C, [[C],[],[]], [radical(C)]).
expand(C, [[c],[C],[]], [radical(C)]).
expand(V, [[V],[],[]], [vowel(V)]).
expand(V, [[v],[],[V]], [vowel(V)]).

The linguist can then rewrite R4 as R8 (Listing 7), and expand it with the command expand(R8). This produces four rules of the form of R4, but with the following expressions for *Lex* and *RLC*:[10]

Lex	*RLC*
[[V1],[],[]]	[[C,V2],[],[]]
[[V1],[],[]]	[[c,v],[C],[V2]]
[[v],[],[V1]]	[[C,V2],[],[]]
[[v],[],[V1]]	[[c,v],[C],[V2]]

4.2 Vocalisation

Orthographically, Semitic texts are written without short vowels. It was suggested by (Beesley et al., 1989, et. seq.) and (Kiraz, 1994c) to allow short vowels to be optionally deleted. This, however, puts a constraint on the grammar: no surface expression can contain a vowel, lest the vowel is optionally deleted.

We assume full vocalisation in writing rules. A second set of rules can allow the deletion of vowels. The whole grammar can be taken as the composition of the two grammars: e.g. {cvcvc},{ktb},{aa} → /ktab/ → [ktab, ktb].

4.3 Morphosyntactic Issues

Finite-state models of two-level morphology implement morphotactics in two ways: using 'continuation patterns/classes' (Koskenniemi, 1983; Antworth, 1990; Karttunen, 1993) or unification-based grammars (Bear, 1986; Ritchie et al., 1992). The former fails to provide elegant morphosyntactic parsing for Semitic languages, as will be illustrated in this section.

4.3.1 Stems and $\overline{X}$-Theory

A pattern, a root and a vocalism do not alway produce a free stem which can stand on its own. In Syriac, for example, some verbal forms are bound: they require a **stem morpheme** which indicates the measure in question, e.g. the prefix {ʔa} for *af'el*

[10] Note, however, that the **expand** command does not insert ♭ randomly in context expressions.

```
tl_rule(R7, [[],[],[]], [[v],[],[V]], [[c3,♭,e],[],[]], <=>, [], [], [],
        [vowel(V)], [[],[],[]]).
tl_rule(R8, [], [V1], [C,V2], <=>, [], [], [],
        [vowel(V1),vowel(V2),radical(C)], [[],[],[]]).
```

Listing 7

```
synrule(rule1, stem:[X̄=-2,measure=M,measure=p'al|pa''el],
               [pattern:[], root:[measure=M,measure=p'al|pa''el],
                vocalism:[measure=M,measure=p'al|pa''el]]).
synrule(rule2, stem:[X̄=-2,measure=M],
               [stem_affix:[measure=M],
                pattern:[], root:[measure=M], vocalism:[measure=M]]).
synrule(rule3, stem:[X̄=-1,measure=M,mood=act],
               [stem:[bar=-2,measure=M,mood=act]]).
synrule(rule4, stem:[X̄=-1,measure=M,mood=pass],
               [reflexive:[], stem:[X̄=-2,measure=M,mood=pass]]).
synrule(rule5, stem:[X̄=0,measure=M,mood=MD,npg=s&3&m],
               [stem:[X̄=-1,measure=M,mood=MD]]).
synrule(rule6, stem:[X̄=0,measure=M,mood=MD,npg=NPG],
               [stem:[X̄=-1,measure=M,mood=MD], vim:[type=suff,circum=no,npg=NPG]]).
synrule(rule7, stem:[X̄=0,measure=M,mood=MD,npg=NPG],
               [vim:[type=pref,circum=no,npg=NPG], stem:[X̄=-1,measure=M,mood=MD]]).
synrule(rule8, stem:[X̄=0,measure=M,mood=MD,npg=NPG],
               [vim:[type=pref,circum=yes,npg=NPG], stem:[X̄=-1,measure=M,mood=MD],
                vim:[type=suff,circum=yes,npg=NPG]]).
```

Listing 8

stems. Additionally, passive forms are marked by the **reflexive morpheme** {ʔet}, while active forms are not marked at all.

This structure of stems can be handled hierarchically using $\overline{X}$-theory. A stem whose stem morpheme is known is assigned $\overline{X}$=-2 (Rules 1-2 in Listing 8). Rules which indicate mood can apply only to stems whose measure has been identified (i.e. they have $\overline{X}$=-2). The resulting stems are assigned $\overline{X}$=-1 (Rules 3-4 in Listing 8). The parsing of Syriac /ʔetkteb/ (from {ʔet}+/kateb/ after the deletion of /a/ by R4) appears in (5).[11]

(5)

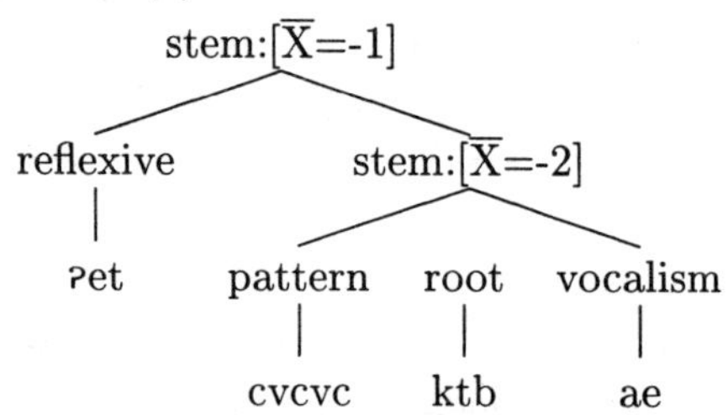

Now free stems which may stand on their own can be assigned $\overline{X}$=0. However, some stems require verbal inflectional markers.

4.3.2 Verbal Inflectional Markers

With respect to verbal inflexional markers (VIMs), there are various types of Semitic verbs: those which do not require a VIM (e.g. sing. 3rd masc.), and those which require a VIM in the form of a prefix (e.g. perfect), suffix (e.g. some imperfect forms), or circumfix (e.g. other imperfect forms).

Each VIM is lexically marked *inter alia* with two features: 'type' which states whether it is a prefix or a suffix, and 'circum' which denotes whether it is a circumfix. Rules 5-8 (Listing 8) handle this.

The parsing of Syriac /netkatbun/ (from {ne}+{ʔet}+/katab/+{un}) appears in (6).

(6)

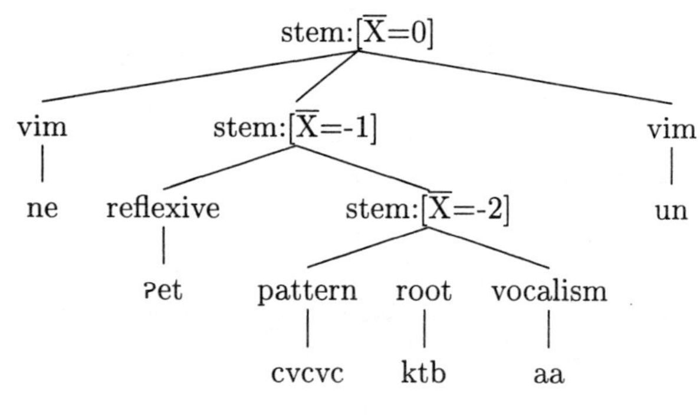

[11]In the remaining examples, it is assumed that the lexicon and two-level rules are expanded to cater for the new material.

Verb Class	Inflections Analysed	1st Analysis (sec/word)	Subsequent Analysis (sec/word)	Mean (sec/word)
Strong	78	5.053	0.028	2.539
Initial *nūn*	52	6.756	0.048	3.404
Initial *ālaph*	57	4.379	0.077	2.228
Middle *ālaph*	67	5.107	0.061	2.584
Overall mean	63.5	5.324	0.054	**2.689**

Table 1

(Beesley et al., 1989) handle this problem by finding a logical expression for the prefix and suffix portions of circumfix morphemes, and use unification to generate only the correct forms – see (Sproat, 1992, p. 158). This approach, however, cannot be used here since, unlike Arabic, not all Syriac VIMs are in the form of circumfixes.

4.3.3 Interfacing with a Syntactic Parser

A Semitic 'word' (string separated by word boundary) may in fact be a clause or a sentence. Therefore, a morphosyntactic parsing of a 'word' may be a (partial) syntactic parsing of a sentence in the form of a (partial) tree. The output of a morphological analyser can be structured in a manner suitable for syntactic processing. Using tree-adjoining grammars (Joshi, 1985) might be a possibility.

5 Performance

To test the integrity, robustness and performance of the implementation, a two-level grammar of the most frequent words in the Syriac New Testament was compiled based on the data in (Kiraz, 1994b). The grammar covers most classes of verbal and nominal forms, in addition to prepositions, proper nouns and words of Greek origin. A wider coverage would involve enlarging the lexicon (currently there are 165 entries) and might triple the number of two-level rules (currently there are *c.* 50 rules).

Table 1 provides the results of analysing verbal classes. The test for each class represents analysing most of its inflexions. The test was executed on a Sparc ELC computer.

By constructing a corpus which consists only of the most frequent words, one can estimate the performance of analysing the corpus as follows,

$$P = \frac{5.324n + \sum_{i=1}^{n} 0.054(f_i - 1)}{\sum_{i=1}^{n} f_i} \text{ sec/word}$$

where n is the number of distinct words in the corpus and f_i is the frequency of occurrence of the ith word. The SEDRA database (Kiraz, 1994a) provides such data. All occurrences of the 100 most frequent lexemes in their various inflections (a total of 72,240 occurrences) can be analysed at the rate of 16.35 words/sec. (Performance will be less if additional rules are added for larger coverage.)

The results may not seem satisfactory when compared with other prolog implementations of the same formalism (cf. 50 words/sec, in (Carter, 1995)). One should, however, keep in mind the complexity of Syriac morphology. In addition to morphological non-linearity, phonological conditional changes – consonantal and vocalic – occur in all stems, and it is not unusual to have more than five such changes per word. Once developed, a grammar is usually compiled into automata which provides better performance.

6 Conclusion

This paper has presented a computational morphology system which is adequate for handling non-linear grammars. We are currently expanding the grammar to cover the whole of New Testament Syriac. One of our future goals is to optimise the prolog implementation for speedy processing and to add debugging facilities along the lines of (Carter, 1995).

For useful results, a Semitic morphological analyser needs to interact with a syntactic parser in order to resolve ambiguities. Most non-vocalised strings give more than one solution, and some inflectional forms are homographs even if fully vocalised (e.g. in Syriac imperfect verbs: sing. 3rd masc. = plural 1st common, and sing. 3rd fem. = sing. 2nd masc.). We mentioned earlier the possibility of using TAGs.

References

Aho, A. and Ullman, J. (1977). *Principles of Compiler Design.* Addison-Wesley.

Antworth, E. (1990). *PC-KIMMO: A two-Level Processor for Morphological Analysis.* Occasional Publications in Academic Computing 16. Summer Institute of Linguistics, Dallas.

Bear, J. (1986). A morphological recognizer with syntactic and phonological rules. In *COLING-86*, pages 272–6.

Beesley, K. (1990). Finite-state description of Arabic morphology. In *Proceedings of the Second Cambridge Conference: Bilingual Computing in Arabic and English.*

Beesley, K. (1991). Computer analysis of Arabic morphology. In Comrie, B. and Eid, M., editors, *Perspectives on Arabic Linguistics III: Papers from the Third Annual Symposium on Arabic Linguistics.* Benjamins, Amsterdam.

Beesley, K., Buckwalter, T., and Newton, S. (1989). Two-level finite-state analysis of Arabic morphology. In *Proceedings of the Seminar on Bilingual Computing in Arabic and English.* The Literary and Linguistic Computing Centre, Cambridge.

Bird, S. and Ellison, T. (1994). One-level phonology. *Computational Linguistics*, 20(1):55–90.

Carter, D. (1995). Rapid development of morphological descriptions for full language processing systems. In *EACL-95*, pages 202–9.

Goldsmith, J. (1976). *Autosegmental Phonology.* PhD thesis, MIT. Published as *Autosegmental and Metrical Phonology*, Oxford 1990.

Grimley-Evans, E., Kiraz, G., and Pulman, S. (1996). Compiling a partition-based two-level formalism. In *COLING-96.* Forthcoming.

Joshi, A. (1985). Tree-adjoining grammars: How much context sensitivity is required to provide reasonable structural descriptions. In Dowty, D., Karttunen, L., and Zwicky, A., editors, *Natural Language Parsing.* Cambridge University Press.

Karttunen, L. (1983). Kimmo: A general morphological processor. *Texas Linguistic Forum*, 22:165–86.

Karttunen, L. (1993). Finite-state lexicon compiler. Technical report, Palo Alto Research Center, Xerox Corporation.

Karttunen, L. and Beesley, K. (1992). Two-level rule compiler. Technical report, Palo Alto Research Center, Xerox Corporation.

Kataja, L. and Koskenniemi, K. (1988). Finite state description of Semitic morphology. In *COLING-88*, volume 1, pages 313–15.

Kay, M. (1987). Nonconcatenative finite-state morphology. In *EACL-87*, pages 2–10.

Kiraz, G. (1994a). Automatic concordance generation of Syriac texts. In Lavenant, R., editor, *VI Symposium Syriacum 1992*, Orientalia Christiana Analecta 247, pages 461–75. Pontificio Institutum Studiorum Orientalium.

Kiraz, G. (1994b). *Lexical Tools to the Syriac New Testament.* JSOT Manuals 7. Sheffield Academic Press.

Kiraz, G. (1994c). Multi-tape two-level morphology: a case study in Semitic non-linear morphology. In *COLING-94*, volume 1, pages 180–6.

Kiraz, G. (1995). *Introduction to Syriac Spirantization.* Bar Hebraeus Verlag, The Netherlands.

Kiraz, G. (1996). *Computational Approach to Non-Linear Morphology.* PhD thesis, University of Cambridge.

Knuth, D. (1973). *The Art of Computer Programming*, volume 3. Addison-Wesley.

Kornai, A. (1991). *Formal Phonology.* PhD thesis, Stanford University.

Koskenniemi, K. (1983). *Two-Level Morphology.* PhD thesis, University of Helsinki.

Lavie, A., Itai, A., and Ornan, U. (1990). On the applicability of two level morphology to the inflection of Hebrew verbs. In Choueka, Y., editor, *Literary and Linguistic Computing 1988: Proceedings of the 15th International Conference*, pages 246–60.

McCarthy, J. (1981). A prosodic theory of nonconcatenative morphology. *Linguistic Inquiry*, 12(3):373–418.

Narayanan, A. and Hashem, L. (1993). On abstract finite-state morphology. In *EACL-93*, pages 297–304.

Pulman, S. and Hepple, M. (1993). A feature-based formalism for two-level phonology: a description and implementation. *Computer Speech and Language*, 7:333–58.

Ritchie, G., Black, A., Russell, G., and Pulman, S. (1992). *Computational Morphology: Practical Mechanisms for the English Lexicon.* MIT Press, Cambridge Mass.

Ruessink, H. (1989). Two level formalisms. Technical Report 5, Utrecht Working Papers in NLP.

Shieber, S. (1986). *An Introduction to Unification-Based Approaches to Grammar.* CSLI Lecture Notes Number 4. Center for the Study of Language and Information, Stanford.

Sproat, R. (1992). *Morphology and Computation.* MIT Press, Cambridge Mass.

Wiebe, B. (1992). Modelling autosegmental phonology with multi-tape finite state transducers. Master's thesis, Simon Fraser University.

INVITED TALK

Head Automata and Bilingual Tiling: Translation with Minimal Representations

Hiyan Alshawi
AT&T Research
600 Mountain Avenue, Murray Hill, NJ 07974, USA
hiyan@research.att.com

Abstract

We present a language model consisting of a collection of costed bidirectional finite state automata associated with the head words of phrases. The model is suitable for incremental application of lexical associations in a dynamic programming search for optimal dependency tree derivations. We also present a model and algorithm for machine translation involving optimal "tiling" of a dependency tree with entries of a costed bilingual lexicon. Experimental results are reported comparing methods for assigning cost functions to these models. We conclude with a discussion of the adequacy of annotated linguistic strings as representations for machine translation.

1 Introduction

Until the advent of statistical methods in the mainstream of natural language processing, syntactic and semantic representations were becoming progressively more complex. This trend is now reversing itself, in part because statistical methods reduce the burden of detailed modeling required by constraint-based grammars, and in part because statistical models for converting natural language into complex syntactic or semantic representations is not well understood at present. At the same time, lexically centered views of language have continued to increase in popularity. We can see this in lexicalized grammatical theories, head-driven parsing and generation, and statistical disambiguation based on lexical associations.

These themes — simple representations, statistical modeling, and lexicalism — form the basis for the models and algorithms described in the bulk of this paper. The primary purpose is to build effective mechanisms for machine translation, the oldest and still the most commonplace application of non-superficial natural language processing. A secondary motivation is to test the extent to which a non-trivial language processing task can be carried out without complex semantic representations.

In Section 2 we present reversible mono-lingual models consisting of collections of simple automata associated with the heads of phrases. These *head automata* are applied by an algorithm with admissible incremental pruning based on semantic association costs, providing a practical solution to the problem of combinatoric disambiguation (Church and Patil 1982). The model is intended to combine the lexical sensitivity of N-gram models (Jelinek et al. 1992) and the structural properties of statistical context free grammars (Booth 1969) without the computational overhead of statistical lexicalized tree-adjoining grammars (Schabes 1992, Resnik 1992).

For translation, we use a model for mapping dependency graphs written by the source language head automata. This model is coded entirely as a bilingual lexicon, with associated cost parameters. The transfer algorithm described in Section 4 searches for the lowest cost 'tiling' of the target dependency graph with entries from the bilingual lexicon. Dynamic programming is again used to make exhaustive search tractable, avoiding the combinatoric explosion of shake-and-bake translation (Whitelock 1992, Brew 1992).

In Section 5 we present a general framework for associating costs with the solutions of search processes, pointing out some benefits of cost functions other than log likelihood, including an error-minimization cost function for unsupervised training of the parameters in our translation application. Section 6 briefly describes an English-Chinese translator employing the models and algorithms. We also present experimental results comparing the performance of different cost assignment methods.

Finally, we return to the more general discussion of representations for machine translation and other natural language processing tasks, arguing the case for simple representations close to natural language itself.

2 Head Automata Language Models

2.1 Lexical and Dependency Parameters

Head automata mono-lingual language models consist of a *lexicon*, in which each entry is a pair $\langle w, m \rangle$ of a word w from a vocabulary V and a head automaton m (defined below), and a *parameter table* giving an assignment of costs to events in a generative process involving the automata.

We first describe the model in terms of the familiar paradigm of a generative statistical model, presenting the parameters as conditional probabilities. This gives us a stochastic version of dependency grammar (Hudson 1984).

Each derivation in the generative statistical model produces an *ordered dependency tree*, that is, a tree in which nodes dominate ordered sequences of left and right subtrees and in which the nodes have labels taken from the vocabulary V and the arcs have labels taken from a set R of relation symbols. When a node with label w immediately dominates a node with label w' via an arc with label r, we say that w' is an *r-dependent* of the *head* w. The interpretation of this directed arc is that relation r holds between particular instances of w and w'. (A word may have several or no r-dependents for a particular relation r.) A recursive left-parent-right traversal of the nodes of an ordered dependency tree for a derivation yields the word string for the derivation.

A head automaton m of a lexical entry $\langle w, m\rangle$ defines possible ordered local trees immediately dominated by w in derivations. Model parameters for head automata, together with dependency parameters and lexical parameters, give a probability distribution for derivations.

A *dependency parameter*

$$P(\downarrow, w'|w, r')$$

is the probability, given a head w with a dependent arc with label r', that w' is the r'-dependent for this arc.

A *lexical parameter*

$$P(m, q|r, \downarrow, w)$$

is the probability that a local tree immediately dominated by an r-dependent w is derived by starting in state q of some automaton m in a lexical entry $\langle w, m\rangle$. The model also includes lexical parameters

$$P(w, m, q|\triangleright)$$

for the probability that w is the head word for an entire derivation initiated from state q of automaton m.

2.2 Head Automata

A head automaton is a weighted finite state machine that writes (or accepts) a pair of sequences of relation symbols from R:

$$(\langle r_1 \cdots r_k\rangle, \langle r_{k+1} \cdots r_n\rangle).$$

These correspond to the relations between a head word and the sequences of dependent phrases to its left and right (see Figure 1). The machine consists of a finite set $q_0, \cdots, q_s$ of states and an *action table* specifying the finite cost (non-zero probability) actions the automaton can undergo.

There are three types of action for an automaton m: left transitions, right transitions, and stop actions. These actions, together with associated probabilistic model parameters, are as follows.

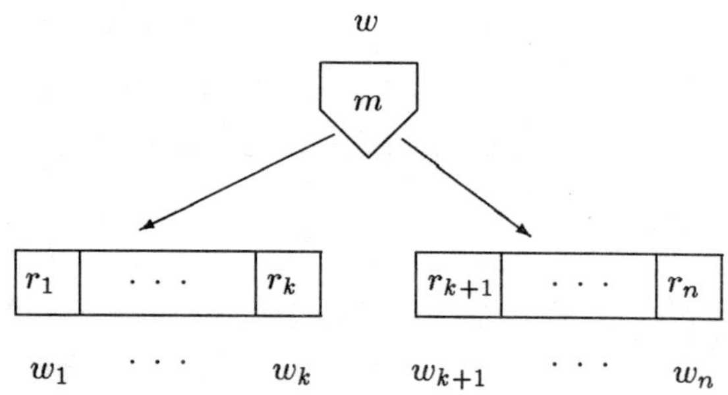

Figure 1: Head automaton m scans left and right sequences of relations r_i for dependents w_i of w.

- Left transition: if in state q_{i-1}, m can write a symbol r onto the right end of the current left sequence and enter state q_i with probability $P(\leftarrow, q_i, r|q_{i-1}, m)$.
- Right transition: if in state q_{i-1}, m can write a symbol r onto the left end of the current right sequence and enter state q_i with probability $P(\rightarrow, q_i, r|q_{i-1}, m)$.
- Stop: if in state q, m can stop with probability $P(\square|q, m)$, at which point the sequences are considered complete.

For a consistent probabilistic model, the probabilities of all transitions and stop actions from a state q must sum to unity. Any state of a head automaton can be an initial state, the probability of a particular initial state in a derivation being specified by lexical parameters. A derivation of a pair of symbol sequence thus corresponds to the selection of an initial state, a sequence of zero or more transitions (writing the symbols) and a stop action. The probability, given an initial state q, that automaton m will a generate a pair of sequences, i.e.

$$P(\langle r_1 \cdots r_k\rangle, \langle r_{k+1} \cdots r_n\rangle|m, q)$$

is the product of the probabilities of the actions taken to generate the sequences. The case of zero transitions will yield empty sequences, corresponding to a leaf node of the dependency tree.

From a linguistic perspective, head automata allow for a compact, graded, notion of lexical subcategorization (Gazdar et al. 1985) and the linear order of a head and its dependent phrases. Lexical parameters can control the saturation of a lexical item (for example a verb that is both transitive and intransitive) by starting the same automaton in different states. Head automata can also be used to code a grammar in which states of an automaton for word w corresponds to X-bar levels (Jackendoff 1977) for phrases headed by w.

Head automata are formally more powerful than finite state automata that accept regular languages in the following sense. Each head automaton defines a formal language with alphabet R whose strings are the concatenation of the left and right sequence pairs written by the automaton. The class of languages defined in this way clearly includes all regular languages, since strings of a regular language can be generated, for example, by a head automaton that only writes a left sequence. Head automata can also accept some non-regular languages requiring coordination of the left and right sequences, for example the language $a^n b^n$ (requiring two states), and the language of palindromes over a finite alphabet.

2.3 Derivation Probability

Let the probability of generating an ordered dependency subtree D headed by an r-dependent word w be $P(D|w,r)$. The recursive process of generating this subtree proceeds as follows:

1. Select an initial state q of an automaton m for w with lexical probability $P(m, q|r, \downarrow, w)$.

2. Run the automaton m_0 with initial state q to generate a pair of relation sequences with probability $P(\langle r_1 \cdots r_k \rangle, \langle r_{k+1} \cdots r_n \rangle | m, q)$.

3. For each relation r_i in these sequences, select a dependent word w_i with dependency probability $P(\downarrow, w_i | w, r_i)$.

4. For each dependent w_i, recursively generate a subtree with probability $P(D_i | w_i, r_i)$.

We can now express the probability $P(D_0)$ for an entire ordered dependency tree derivation D_0 headed by a word w_0 as

$$
\begin{aligned}
P(D_0) = & \\
& P(w_0, m_0, q_0 | \rhd) \\
& P(\langle r_1 \cdots r_k \rangle, \langle r_{k+1} \cdots r_n \rangle | m_0, q_0) \\
& \textstyle\prod_{1 \le i \le n} P(\downarrow, w_i | w_0, r_i) P(D_i | w_i, r_i).
\end{aligned}
$$

In the translation application we search for the highest probability derivation (or more generally, the N-highest probability derivations). For other purposes, the probability of strings may be of more interest. The probability of a string according to the model is the sum of the probabilities of derivations of ordered dependency trees yielding the string.

In practice, the number of parameters in a head automaton language model is dominated by the dependency parameters, that is, $O(|V|^2|R|)$ parameters. This puts the size of the model somewhere in between 2-gram and 3-gram model. The similarly motivated link grammar model (Lafferty, Sleator and Temperley 1992) has $O(|V|^3)$ parameters. Unlike simple N-gram models, head automata models yield an interesting distribution of sentence lengths. For example, the average sentence length for Monte-Carlo generation with our probabilistic head automata model for ATIS was 10.6 words (the average was 9.7 words for the corpus it was trained on).

3 Analysis and Generation

3.1 Analysis

Head automaton models admit efficient lexically driven analysis (parsing) algorithms in which partial analyses are costed incrementally as they are constructed. Put in terms of the traditional parsing issues in natural language understanding, "semantic" associations coded as dependency parameters are applied at each parsing step allowing semantically suboptimal analyses to be eliminated, so the analysis with the best semantic score can be identified without scoring an exponential number of syntactic parses. Since the model is lexical, linguistic constructions headed by lexical items not present in the input are not involved in the search the way they are with typical top-down or predictive parsing strategies.

We will sketch an algorithm for finding the lowest cost ordered dependency tree derivation for an input string in polynomial time in the length of the string. In our experimental system we use a more general version of the algorithm to allow input in the form of word lattices.

The algorithm is a bottom-up tabular parser (Younger 1967, Early 1970) in which constituents are constructed "head-outwards" (Kay 1989, Sata and Stock 1989). Since we are analyzing bottom-up with generative model automata, the algorithm 'runs' the automata backwards. Edges in the parsing lattice (or "chart") are tuples representing partial or complete phrases headed by a word w from position i to position j in the string:

$$\langle w, t, i, j, m, q, c \rangle.$$

Here m is the head automaton for w in this derivation; the automaton is in state q; t is the dependency tree constructed so far, and c is the cost of the partial derivation. We will use the notation $C(x|y)$ for the cost of a model event with probability $P(x|y)$; the assignment of costs to events is discussed in Section 5.

Initialization: For each word w in the input between positions i and j, the lattice is initialized with phrases

$$\langle w, \{\}, i, j, m, q_f, c_f \rangle$$

for any lexical entry $\langle w, m \rangle$ and any final state q_f of the automaton m in the entry. A final state is one for which the stop action cost $c_f = C(\square | q_f, m)$ is finite.

Transitions: Phrases are combined bottom-up to form progressively larger phrases. There are two types of combination corresponding to left and right transitions of the automaton for the word acting as the head in the combination. We will specify left combination; right combination is the mirror image of left combination. If the lattice contains two phrases abutting at position k in the string:

$$\langle w_1, t_1, i, k, m_1, q_1, c_1\rangle$$
$$\langle w_2, t_2, k, j, m_2, q_2, c_2\rangle,$$

and the parameter table contains the following finite costs parameters (a left r-transition of m_2, a lexical parameter for w_1, and an r-dependency parameter):

$$c_3 = C(\leftarrow, q_2, r|q_2', m_2)$$
$$c_4 = C(m_1, q_1|r, \downarrow, w_1)$$
$$c_5 = C(\downarrow, w_1|w_2, r),$$

then build a new phrase headed by w_2 with a tree t_2' formed by adding t_1 to t_2 as an r-dependent of w_2:

$$\langle w_2, t_2', i, j, m_2, q_2', c_1 + c_2 + c_3 + c_4 + c_5\rangle.$$

When no more combinations are possible, for each phrase spanning the entire input we add the appropriate start of derivation cost to these phrases and select the one with the lowest total cost.

Pruning: The dynamic programming condition for pruning suboptimal partial analyses is as follows. Whenever there are two phrases

$$p = \langle w, t, i, j, m, q, c\rangle$$
$$p' = \langle w, t', i, j, m, q, c'\rangle,$$

and c' is greater than c, then we can remove p' because for any derivation involving p' that spans the entire string, there will be a lower cost derivation involving p. This pruning condition is effective at curbing a combinatorial explosion arising from, for example, prepositional phrase attachment ambiguities (coded in the alternative trees t and t').

The worst case asymptotic time complexity of the analysis algorithm is $O(\min(n^2, |V|^2)n^3)$, where n is the length of an input string and $|V|$ is the size of the vocabulary. This limit can be derived in a similar way to cubic time tabular recognition algorithms for context free grammars (Younger 1967) with the grammar related term being replaced by the term $\min(n^2, |V|^2)$ since the words of the input sentence also act as categories in the head automata model. In this context "recognition" refers to checking that the input string can be generated from the grammar. Note that our algorithm is for analysis (in the sense of finding the best derivation) which, in general, is a higher time complexity problem than recognition.

3.2 Generation

By generation here we mean determining the lowest cost linear surface ordering for the dependents of each word in an *unordered* dependency structure resulting from the transfer mapping described in Section 4. In general, the output of transfer is a dependency graph and the task of the generator involves a search for a backbone dependency tree for the graph, if necessary by adding dependency edges to join up unconnected components of the graph. For each graph component, the main steps of the search process, described non-deterministically, are

1. Select a node with word label w having a finite start of derivation cost $C(w, m, q|\triangleright)$.
2. Execute a path through the head automaton m starting at state q and ending at state q' with a finite stop action cost $C(\square|q', m)$. When making a transition with relation r_i in the path, select a graph edge with label r_i from w to some previously unvisited node w_i with finite dependency cost $C(\downarrow, w_i|w, r_i)$. Include the cost of the transition (e.g. $C(\rightarrow, q_i, r_i|q_{i-1}, m)$) in the running total for this derivation.
3. For each dependent node w_i, select a lexical entry with cost $C(m_i, q_i|r_i, \downarrow, w_i)$, and recursively apply the machine m_i from state q_i as in step 2.
4. Perform a left-parent-right traversal of the nodes of the resulting dependency tree, yielding a target string.

The target string resulting from the lowest cost tree that includes all nodes in the graph is selected as the translation target string. The independence assumptions implicit in head automata models mean that we can select lowest cost orderings of local dependency trees, below a given relation r, independently in the search for the lowest cost derivation.

When the generator is used as part of the translation system, the dependency parameter costs are not, in fact, applied by the generator. Instead, because these parameters are independent of surface order, they are applied earlier by the transfer component, influencing the choice of structure passed to the generator.

4 Transfer Maps

4.1 Transfer Model Bilingual Lexicon

The transfer model defines possible mappings, with associated costs, of dependency trees with source-language word node labels into ones with target-language word labels. Unlike the head automata monolingual models, the transfer model operates with unordered dependency trees, that is, it treats the dependents of a word as an unordered bag. The model is general enough to cover the common translation problems discussed in the literature (e.g. Lindop and Tsujii 1991 and Dorr 1994) including many-to-many word mapping, argument switching, and head switching.

A transfer model consists of a bilingual lexicon and a transfer parameter table. The model uses *dependency tree fragments*, which are the same as unordered dependency trees except that some nodes may not have word labels. In the *bilingual lexicon*, an entry for a source word w_i (see top portion of Figure 2) has the form

$$\langle w_i, H_i, n_i, G_i, f_i\rangle$$

where H_i is a source language tree fragment, n_i (the *primary node*) is a distinguished node of H_i with label w_i, G_i is a target tree fragment, and f_i is a *mapping function*, i.e. a (possibly partial) function from the nodes of H_i to the nodes of G_i.

The *transfer parameter table* specifies costs for the application of transfer entries. In a context-independent model, each entry has a single cost parameter. In context-dependent transfer models, the cost function takes into account the identities of the labels of the arcs and nodes dominating w_i in the source graph. (Context dependence is discussed further in Section 5.) The set of transfer parameters may also include costs for the *null transfer entries* for w_i, for use in derivations in which w_i is translated by the entry for another word v. For example, the entry for v might be for translating an idiom involving w_i as a modifier.

Each entry in the bilingual lexicon specifies a way of mapping part of a dependency tree, specifically that part "matching" (as explained below) the source fragment of the entry, into part of a target graph, as indicated by the target fragment. Entry mapping functions specify how the set of target fragments for deriving a translation are to be combined: whenever an entry is applied, a global node-mapping function is extended to include the entry mapping function.

4.2 Matching, Tiling, and Derivation

Transfer mapping takes a source dependency tree S from analysis and produces a minimum cost derivation of a target graph T and a (possibly partial) function f from source nodes to target nodes. In fact, the transfer model is applicable to certain types of source dependency graphs that are more general than trees, although the version of the head automata model described here only produces trees.

We will say that a tree fragment H *matches* an unordered dependency tree S if there is a function g (a *matching function*) from the nodes of H to the nodes of S such that

- g is a total one-one function;
- if a node n of H has a label, and that label is word w, then the word label for $g(n)$ is also w;
- for every arc in H with label r from node n_1 to node n_2, there is an arc with label r from $g(n_1)$ to $g(n_2)$.

Unlike first order unification, this definition of matching is not commutative and is not deterministic in that there may be multiple matching functions for applying a bilingual entry to an input source tree. A particular match of an entry against a dependency tree can be represented by the matching function g, a set of arcs A in S, and the (possibly context dependent) cost c of applying the entry.

A *tiling* of a source graph with respect to a transfer model is a set of entry matches

$$\{\langle E_1, g_1, A_1, c_1\rangle, \cdots, \langle E_k, g_k, A_k, c_k\rangle\}$$

which is such that

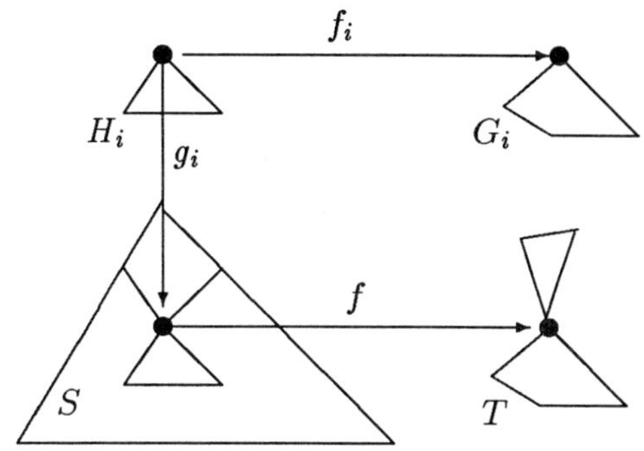

Figure 2: Transfer matching and mapping functions

- k is the number of nodes in the source tree S.
- Each E_i, $1 \leq i \leq k$, is a bilingual entry $\langle w_i, H_i, n_i, G_i, f_i\rangle$ matching S with function g_i (see Figure 2) and arcs A_i.
- For primary nodes n_i and n_j of two distinct entries E_i and E_j, $g_i(n_i)$ and $g_j(n_j)$ are distinct.
- The sets of edges A_i form a partition of the edges of S.
- The images $g_i(L_i)$ form a partition of the nodes of S, where L_i is the set of *labeled* source nodes in the source fragment H_i of E_i.
- c_i is the cost of the match specified by the parameter table.

A tiling of S yields a costed derivation of a target dependency graph T as follows:

- The cost of the derivation is the sum of the costs c_i for each match in the tiling.
- The nodes and arcs of T are composed of the nodes and arcs of the target fragments G_i for the entries E_i.
- Let f_i and f_j be the mapping functions for entries E_i and E_j. For any node n of S for which target nodes $f_i(g_i^{-1}(n))$ and $f_j(g_i^{-1}(n))$ are defined, these two nodes are identified as a single node $f(n)$ in T.

The merging of target fragment nodes in the last condition has the effect of joining the target fragments in a consistent fashion. The node mapping function f for the entire tree thus has a different role from the alignment function in the IBM statistical translation model (Brown et al. 1990, 1993); the role of the latter includes the linear ordering of words in the target string. In our approach, target word order is handled exclusively by the target monolingual model.

4.3 Transfer Algorithm

The main transfer search is preceded by a bilingual lexicon matching phase. This leads to greater efficiency as it avoids repeating matching operations during the search phase, and it allows a static analysis of the matching entries and source tree to identify subtrees for which the search phase can safely prune out suboptimal partial translations.

Transfer Configurations In order to apply target language model relation costs incrementally, we need to distinguish between complete and incomplete arcs: an arc is complete if both its nodes have labels, otherwise it is incomplete. The output of the lexicon matching phrase, and the partial derivations manipulated by the search phase are both in the form of *transfer configurations*

$$\langle S, R, T, P, f, c, I \rangle$$

where S is the set of source nodes and arcs consumed so far in the derivation, R the remaining source nodes and arcs, f the mapping function built so far, T the set of nodes and complete arcs of the target graph, P the set of incomplete target arcs, c the partial derivation cost, and I a set of source nodes for which entries have yet to be applied.

Lexical matching phase The algorithm for lexical matching has a similar control structure to standard unification algorithms, except that it can result in multiple matches. We omit the details. The lexicon matching phase returns, for each source node i, a set of *runtime entries.* There is one runtime entry for each successful match and possibly a null entry for the node if the word label for i is included in successful matches for other entries. Runtime entries are transfer configurations of the form

$$\langle H_i, \phi, G_i, P_i, f_i, c_i, \{i\} \rangle$$

in which H_i is the source fragment for the entry with each node replaced by its image under the applicable matching function; G_i the target fragment for the entry, except for the incomplete arcs P_i of this fragment; f_i the composition of mapping function for the entry with the inverse of the matching function; c_i the cost of applying the entry in the context of its match with the source graph plus the cost in the target model of the arcs in G_i.

Transfer Search Before the transfer search proper, the resulting runtime entries together with the source graph are analyzed to determine *decomposition nodes.* A decomposition node n is a source tree node for which it is safe to prune suboptimal translations of the subtree dominated by n. Specifically, it is checked that n is the root node of all source fragments H_n of runtime entries in which both n *and* its node label are included, and that $f_n(n)$ is not dominated by (i.e. not reachable via directed arcs from) another node in the target graph G_n of such entries.

Transfer search maintains a set M of active runtime entries. Initially, this is the set of runtime entries resulting from the lexicon matching phase. Overall search control is as follows:

1. Determine the set of decomposition nodes.
2. Sort the decomposition nodes into a list D such that if n_1 dominates n_2 in S then n_2 precedes n_1 in D.
3. If D is empty, apply the subtree transfer search (given below) to S, return the lowest cost solution, and stop.
4. Remove the first decomposition node n from D and apply the subtree transfer search to the subtree S' dominated by n, to yield solutions $\langle S', \phi, T', \phi, f', c', \phi \rangle$.
5. Partition these solutions into subsets with the same word label for the node $f'(n)$, and select the solution with lowest cost c' from each subset.
6. Remove from M the set of runtime entries for nodes in S'.
7. For each selected subtree solution, add to M a new runtime entry $\langle S', \phi, T', f', c', \{n\} \rangle$.
8. Repeat from step 3.

The subtree transfer search maintains a queue Q of configurations corresponding to partial derivations for translating the subtree. Control follows a standard non-deterministic search paradigm:

1. Initialize Q to contain a single configuration $\langle \phi, R_0, \phi, \phi, \phi, 0, I_0 \rangle$ with the input subtree R_0 and the set of nodes I_0 in R_0.
2. If Q is empty, return the lowest cost solution found and stop.
3. Remove a configuration $\langle S, R, T, P, f, c, I \rangle$ from the queue.
4. If R is empty, add the configuration to the set of subtree solutions.
5. Select a node i from I.
6. For each runtime entry $\langle H_i, \phi, G_i, P_i, f_i, c_i, \{i\} \rangle$ for i, if H_i is a subgraph of R, add to Q a configuration $\langle S \cup H_i, R - H_i, T \cup G_i \cup G', P \cup P_i - G', f \cup f_i, c + c_i + c_{G'}, I - \{i\} \rangle$, where G' is the set of newly completed arcs (those in $P \cup P_i$ with both node labels in $T \cup G_i \cup P \cup P_i$) and $c_{G'}$ is the cost of the arcs G' in the target language model.
7. For any source node n for which $f(n)$ and $f_i(n)$ are both defined, merge these two target nodes.
8. Repeat from step 2.

Keeping the arcs P separate in the configuration allows efficient incremental application of target dependency costs $c_{G'}$ during the search, so these costs are taken into account in the pruning step of the overall search control. This way we can keep the benefits of monolingual/bilingual modularity (Isabelle and Macklovitch 1986) without the computational overhead of transfer-and-filter (Alshawi et al. 1992).

It is possible to apply the subtree search directly to the whole graph starting with the initial runtime entries from lexical matching. However, this would result in an exponential search, specifically a search tree with a branching factor of the order of the number of matching entries per input word. Fortunately, long sentences typically have several decomposition nodes, such as the heads of noun phrases, so the search as described is factored into manageable components.

5 Cost Functions

5.1 Costed Search Processes

The head automata model and transfer model were originally conceived as probabilistic models. In order to take advantage of more of the information available in our training data, we experimented with cost functions that make use of incorrect translations as negative examples and also to treat the correctness of a translation hypothesis as a matter of degree.

To experiment with different models, we implemented a general mechanism for associating costs to solutions of a search process. Here, a search process is conceptualized as a non-deterministic computation that takes a single input string, undergoes a sequence of state transitions in a non-deterministic fashion, then outputs a solution string. Process states are distinct from, but may include, head automaton states.

A cost function for a search process is a real valued function defined on a pair of equivalence classes of process states. The first element of the pair, a *context* c, is an equivalence class of states before transitions. The second element, an *event* e, is an equivalence class of states after transitions. (The equivalence relations for contexts and events may be different.) We refer to an event-context pair as a *choice*, for which we use the notation

$$(e|c)$$

borrowed from the special case of conditional probabilities. The cost of a derivation of a solution by the process is taken to be the sum of costs of choices involved in the derivation.

We represent events and contexts by finite sequences of symbols (typically words or relation symbols in the translation application). We write

$$C(a_1 \cdots a_n | b_1 \cdots b_k)$$

for the cost of the event represented by $\langle a_1 \cdots a_n \rangle$ in the context represented by $\langle b_1 \cdots b_k \rangle$.

"Backed off" costs can be computed by averaging over larger equivalence classes (represented by shorter sequences in which positions are eliminated systematically). A similar smoothing technique has been applied to the specific case of prepositional phrase attachment by Collins and Brooks (1995). We have used backed off costs in the translation application for the various cost functions described below. Although this resulted in some improvement in testing, so far the improvement has not been statistically significant.

5.2 Model Cost Functions

Taken together, the events, contexts, and cost function constitute a *process cost model*, or simply a *model*. The cost function specifies the *model parameters*; the other components are the *model structure*.

We have experimented with a number of model types, including the following.

Probabilistic model: In this model we assume a probability distribution on the possible events for a context, that is,

$$\sum_e P(e|c) = 1.$$

The cost parameters of the model are defined as:

$$C(e|c) = -\ln(P(e|c)).$$

Given a set of solutions from executions of a process, let $n^+(e|c)$ be the number of times choice $(e|c)$ was taken leading to acceptable solutions (e.g. correct translations) and $n^+(c)$ be the number of times context c was encountered for these solutions. We can then estimate the probabilistic model costs with

$$C(e|c) \approx \ln(n^+(c)) - \ln(n^+(e|c)).$$

Discriminative model: The costs in this model are likelihood ratios comparing positive and negative solutions, for example correct and incorrect translations. (See Dunning 1993 on the application of likelihood ratios in computational linguistics.) Let $n^-(e|c)$ be the count for choice $(e|c)$ leading to negative solutions. The cost function for the discriminative model is estimated as

$$C(e|c) \approx \ln(n^-(e|c)) - \ln(n^+(e|c)).$$

Mean distance model: In the mean distance model, we make use of some measure of goodness of a solution t_s for some input s by comparing it against an ideal solution $\hat{t}_s$ for s with a distance metric h:

$$h(t_s, \hat{t}_s) \mapsto d$$

in which d is a non-negative real number. A parameter for choice $(e|c)$ in the distance model

$$C(e|c) = E_h(e|c)$$

is the mean value of $h(t_s, \hat{t}_s)$ for solutions t_s produced by derivations including the choice $(e|c)$.

Normalized distance model: The mean distance model does not use the constraint that a particular choice faced by a process is always a choice between events with the same context. It is also somewhat sensitive to peculiarities of the distance function h. With the same assumptions we made for the mean distance model, let

$$E_h(c)$$

be the average of $h(t_s, \hat{t}_s)$ for solutions derived from sequences of choices including the context c. The cost parameter for $(e|c)$ in the normalized distance model is

$$C(e|c) = \frac{E_h(e|c)}{E_h(c)},$$

that is, the ratio of the expected distance for derivations involving the choice and the expected distance for all derivations involving the context for that choice.

Reflexive Training If we have a manually translated corpus, we can apply the mean and normalized distance models to translation by taking the ideal solution $\hat{t}_s$ for translating a source string s to be the manual translation for s. In the absence of good metrics for comparing translations, we employ a heuristic string distance metric to compare word selection and word order in t_s and $\hat{t}_s$.

In order to train the model parameters without a manually translated corpus, we use a "reflexive" training method (similar in spirit to the "wake-sleep" algorithm, Hinton et al. 1995). In this method, our search process translates a source sentence s to t_s in the target language and then translates t_s back to a source language sentence s'. The original sentence s can then act as the ideal solution of the overall process. For this training method to be effective, we need a reasonably good initial model, i.e. one for which the distance $h(s, s')$ is inversely correlated with the probability that t_s is a good translation of s.

6 Experimental System

We have built an experimental translation system using the monolingual and translation models described in this paper. The system translates sentences in the ATIS domain (Hirschman et al. 1993) between English and Mandarin Chinese. The translator is in fact a subsystem of a speech translation prototype, though the experiments we describe here are for transcribed spoken utterances. (We informally refer to the transcribed utterances as sentences.) The average time taken for translation of sentences (of unrestricted length) from the ATIS corpus was around 1.7 seconds with approximately 0.4 seconds being taken by the analysis algorithm and 0.7 seconds by the transfer algorithm.

English and Chinese lexicons of around 1200 and 1000 words respectively were constructed. Altogether, the entries in these lexicons made reference to around 200 structurally distinct head automata. The transfer lexicon contained around 3500 paired graph fragments, most of which were used in both transfer directions. With this model structure, we tried a number of methods for assigning cost functions. The nature of the training methods and their corresponding cost functions meant that different amounts of training data could be used, as discussed further below.

The methods make use of a supervised training set and an unsupervised training set, both sets being chosen at random from the 20,000 or so ATIS sentences available to us. The supervised training set comprised around 1950 sentences. A subcollection of 1150 of these sentences were translated by the system, and the resulting translations manually classified as 'good' (800 translations) or 'bad' (350 translations). The remaining 800 supervised training set sentences were hand-tagged for prepositional attachment points. (Prepositional phrase attachment is a major cause of ambiguity in the ATIS corpus, and moreover can affect English-Chinese translation, see Chen and Chen 1992.) The attachment information was used to generate additional negative and positive counts for dependency choices. The unsupervised training set consisted of approximately 13,000 sentences; it was used for automatic training (as described under 'Reflexive Training' above) by translating the sentences into Chinese and back to English.

A. *Qualitative Baseline:* In this model, all choices were assigned the same cost except for irregular events (such as unknown words or partial analyses) which were all assigned a high penalty cost. This model gives an indication of performance based solely on model structure.

B. *Probabilistic:* Counts for choices leading to good translations for sentences of the supervised training corpus, together with counts from the manually assigned attachment points, were used to compute negated log probability costs.

C. *Discriminative:* The positive counts as in the probabilistic method, together with corresponding negative counts from bad translations or incorrect attachment choices, were used to compute log likelihood ratio costs.

D. *Normalized Distance:* In this fully automatic method, normalized distance costs were computed from reflexive translation of the sentences in the unsupervised training corpus. The translation runs were carried out with parameters from method A.

E. *Bootstrapped Normalized Distance:* The same as method D except that the system used to carry out the reflexive translation was running with parameters from method C.

Table 1 shows the results of evaluating the performance of these models for translating 200 unrestricted length ATIS sentences into Chinese. This was a previously unseen test set not included in any of the training sets. Two measures of translation acceptability are shown, as judged by a Chinese speaker. (In separate experiments, we verified that the judgments of this speaker were near the average of five Chinese speakers). The first measure, "meaning and grammar", gives the percentage of sentence translations judged to preserve meaning without the introduction of grammatical errors. For the second measure, "meaning preservation", grammatical errors were allowed if they did not interfere with meaning (in the sense of misleading the hearer). In the table, we have grouped together methods A and D for

Table 1: Translation performance of different cost assignment methods

Method	Meaning and Grammar (%)	Meaning Preservation (%)
A	29	71
D	37	71
B	46	82
C	52	83
E	54	83

which the parameters were derived without human supervision effort, and methods B, C, and E which depended on the same amount of human supervision effort. This means that side by side comparison of these methods has practical relevance, even though the methods exploited different amounts of data. In the case of E, the supervision effort was used only as an oracle during training, not directly in the cost computations.

We can see from Table 1 that the choice of method affected translation quality (meaning and grammar) more than it affected preservation of meaning. A possible explanation is that the model structure was adequate for most lexical choice decisions because of the relatively low degree of polysemy in the ATIS corpus. For the stricter measure, the differences were statistically significant, according to the sign test at the 5% significance level, for the following comparisons: C and E each outperformed B and D, and B and D each outperformed A.

7 Language Processing and Semantic Representations

The translation system we have described employs only simple representations of sentences and phrases. Apart from the words themselves, the only symbols used are the dependency relations R. In our experimental system, these relation symbols are themselves natural language words, although this is not a necessary property of our models. Information coded explicitly in sentence representations by word senses and feature constraints in our previous work (Alshawi 1992) is implicit in the models used to derive the dependency trees and translations. In particular, dependency parameters and context-dependent transfer parameters give rise to an implicit, graded notion of word sense.

For language-centered applications like translation or summarization, for which we have a large body of examples of the desired behavior, we can think of the task in terms of the formal problem of modeling a relation between strings based on examples of that relation. By taking this viewpoint, we seem to be ignoring the intuition that most interesting natural language processing tasks (translation, summarization, interfaces) are semantic in nature. It is therefore tempting to conclude that an adequate treatment of these tasks requires the manipulation of artificial semantic representation languages with well-understood formal denotations. While the intuition seems reasonable, the conclusion might be too strong in that it rules out the possibility that natural language itself is adequate for manipulating semantic denotations. After all, this is the primary function of natural language.

The main justification for artificial semantic representation languages is that they are unambiguous by design. This may not be as critical, or useful, as it might first appear. While it is true that natural language is ambiguous and under-specified out of context, this uncertainty is greatly reduced by context to the point where further resolution (e.g. full scoping) is irrelevant to the task, or even the intended meaning. The fact that translation is insensitive to many ambiguities motivated the use of unresolved quasi-logical form for transfer (Alshawi et al. 1992).

To the extent that contextual resolution is necessary, context may be provided by the state of the language processor rather than complex semantic representations. Local context may include the state of local processing components (such as our head automata) for capturing grammatical constraints, or the identity of other words in a phrase for capturing sense distinctions. For larger scale context, I have argued elsewhere (Alshawi 1987) that memory activation patterns resulting from the process of carrying out an understanding task can act as global context without explicit representations of discourse. Under this view, the challenge is how to exploit context in performing a task rather than how to map natural language phrases to expressions of a formalism for coding meaning independently of context or intended use.

There is now greater understanding of the formal semantics of under-specified and ambiguous representations. In Alshawi 1996, I provide a denotational semantics for a simple under-specified language and argue for extending this treatment to a formal semantics of natural language strings as expressions of an under-specified representation. In this paradigm, ordered dependency trees can be viewed as natural language strings annotated so that some of the implicit relations are more explicit. A milder form of this kind of annotation is a bracketed natural language string. We are not advocating an approach in which linguistic structure is ignored (as it is in the IBM translator described by Brown et al. 1990), but rather one in which the syntactic and semantic structure of a string is implicit in the way it is processed by an interpreter.

One important advantage of using representations that are close to natural language itself is that it reduces the degrees of freedom in specifying language and task models, making these models easier to acquire automatically. With these considerations in mind, we have started to experiment with a version of the translator described here with even simpler representations and for which the model structure, not just the parameters, can be acquired automatically.

Acknowledgments

The work on cost functions and training methods was carried out jointly with Adam Buchsbaum who also customized the English model to ATIS and integrated the translator into our speech translation prototype. Jishen He constructed the Chinese ATIS language model and bilingual lexicon and identified many problems with early versions of the transfer component. I am also grateful for advice and help from Don Hindle, Fernando Pereira, Chi-Lin Shih, Richard Sproat, and Bin Wu.

References

Alshawi, H. 1987. *Memory and Context for Language Interpretation.* Cambridge University Press, Cambridge, England.

Alshawi, H. 1996. "Underspecified First Order Logics". In *Semantic Ambiguity and Underspecification,* edited by K. van Deemter and S. Peters, CSLI Publications, Stanford, California.

Alshawi, H. 1992. *The Core Language Engine.* MIT Press, Cambridge, Massachusetts.

Alshawi, H., D. Carter, B. Gamback and M. Rayner. 1992. "Swedish-English QLF Translation". In H. Alshawi (ed.) *The Core Language Engine.* MIT Press, Cambridge, Massachusetts.

Booth, T. 1969. "Probabilistic Representation of Formal Languages". *Tenth Annual IEEE Symposium on Switching and Automata Theory.*

Brew, C. 1992. "Letting the Cat out of the Bag: Generation for Shake-and-Bake MT". Proceedings of COLING92, the International Conference on Computational Linguistics, Nantes, France.

Brown, P., J. Cocke, S. Della Pietra, V. Della Pietra, F. Jelinek, J. Lafferty, R. Mercer and P. Rossin. 1990. "A Statistical Approach to Machine Translation". *Computational Linguistics* 16:79–85.

Brown, P.F., S.A. Della Pietra, V.J. Della Pietra, and R.L. Mercer. 1993. "The Mathematics of Statistical Machine Translation: Parameter Estimation". *Computational Linguistics* 19:263–312.

Chen, K.H. and H. H. Chen. 1992. "Attachment and Transfer of Prepositional Phrases with Constraint Propagation". *Computer Processing of Chinese and Oriental Languages,* Vol. 6, No. 2, 123–142.

Church K. and R. Patil. 1982. "Coping with Syntactic Ambiguity or How to Put the Block in the Box on the Table". *Computational Linguistics* 8:139–149.

Collins, M. and J. Brooks. 1995. "Prepositional Phrase Attachment through a Backed-Off Model." *Proceedings of the Third Workshop on Very Large Corpora,* Cambridge, Massachusetts, ACL, 27–38.

Dorr, B.J. 1994. "Machine Translation Divergences: A Formal Description and Proposed Solution". *Computational Linguistics* 20:597–634.

Dunning, T. 1993. "Accurate Methods for Statistics of Surprise and Coincidence." *Computational Linguistics.* 19:61–74.

Early, J. 1970. "An Efficient Context-Free Parsing Algorithm". *Communications of the ACM* 14: 453–60.

Gazdar, G., E. Klein, G.K. Pullum, and I.A.Sag. 1985. *Generalised Phrase Structure Grammar.* Blackwell, Oxford.

Hinton, G.E., P. Dayan, B.J. Frey and R.M. Neal. 1995. "The 'Wake-Sleep' Algorithm for Unsupervised Neural Networks". *Science* 268:1158–1161.

Hudson, R.A. 1984. *Word Grammar.* Blackwell, Oxford.

Hirschman, L., M. Bates, D. Dahl, W. Fisher, J. Garofolo, D. Pallett, K. Hunicke-Smith, P. Price, A. Rudnicky, and E. Tzoukermann. 1993. "Multi-Site Data Collection and Evaluation in Spoken Language Understanding". In *Proceedings of the Human Language Technology Workshop,* Morgan Kaufmann, San Francisco, 19–24.

Isabelle, P. and E. Macklovitch. 1986. "Transfer and MT Modularity", *Eleventh International Conference on Computational Linguistics,* Bonn, Germany, 115–117.

Jackendoff, R.S. 1977. *X-bar Syntax: A Study of Phrase Structure.* MIT Press, Cambridge, Massachusetts.

Jelinek, F., R.L. Mercer and S. Roukos. 1992. "Principles of Lexical Language Modeling for Speech Recognition". In S. Furui and M.M. Sondhi (eds.), *Advances in Speech Signal Processing,* Marcel Dekker, New York.

Lafferty, J., D. Sleator and D. Temperley. 1992. "Grammatical Trigrams: A Probabilistic Model of Link Grammar". In *Proceedings of the 1992 AAAI Fall Symposium on Probabilistic Approaches to Natural Language,* 89-97.

Kay, M. 1989. "Head Driven Parsing". In *Proceedings of the Workshop on Parsing Technologies,* Pittsburg, 1989.

Lindop, J. and J. Tsujii. 1991. "Complex Transfer in MT: A Survey of Examples". Technical Report 91/5, Centre for Computational Linguistics, UMIST, Manchester, UK.

Resnik, P. 1992. "Probabilistic Tree-Adjoining Grammar as a Framework for Statistical Natural Language Processing". In *Proceedings of COLING-92,* Nantes, France, 418-424.

Sata, G. and O. Stock. 1989. "Head-Driven Bidirectional Parsing". In *Proceedings of the Workshop on Parsing Technologies,* Pittsburg, 1989.

Schabes, Y. 1992. "Stochastic Lexicalized Tree-Adjoining Grammars". In *Proceedings of COLING-92,* Nantes, France, 426-432.

Whitelock, P.J. 1992. "Shake-and-Bake Translation". Proceedings of COLING92, the International Conference on Computational Linguistics, Nantes, France.

Younger, D. 1967. Recognition and Parsing of Context-Free Languages in Time n^3. *Information and Control,* 10, 189–208.

Parsing Algorithms and Metrics

Joshua Goodman
Harvard University
33 Oxford St.
Cambridge, MA 02138
goodman@das.harvard.edu

Abstract

Many different metrics exist for evaluating parsing results, including Viterbi, Crossing Brackets Rate, Zero Crossing Brackets Rate, and several others. However, most parsing algorithms, including the Viterbi algorithm, attempt to optimize the same metric, namely the probability of getting the correct labelled tree. By choosing a parsing algorithm appropriate for the evaluation metric, better performance can be achieved. We present two new algorithms: the "Labelled Recall Algorithm," which maximizes the expected Labelled Recall Rate, and the "Bracketed Recall Algorithm," which maximizes the Bracketed Recall Rate. Experimental results are given, showing that the two new algorithms have improved performance over the Viterbi algorithm on many criteria, especially the ones that they optimize.

1 Introduction

In corpus-based approaches to parsing, one is given a treebank (a collection of text annotated with the "correct" parse tree) and attempts to find algorithms that, given unlabelled text from the treebank, produce as similar a parse as possible to the one in the treebank.

Various methods can be used for finding these parses. Some of the most common involve inducing Probabilistic Context-Free Grammars (PCFGs), and then parsing with an algorithm such as the Labelled Tree (Viterbi) Algorithm, which maximizes the probability that the output of the parser (the "guessed" tree) is the one that the PCFG produced. This implicitly assumes that the induced PCFG does a good job modeling the corpus.

There are many different ways to evaluate these parses. The most common include the Labelled Tree Rate (also called the Viterbi Criterion or Exact Match Rate), Consistent Brackets Recall Rate (also called the Crossing Brackets Rate), Consistent Brackets Tree Rate (also called the Zero Crossing Brackets Rate), and Precision and Recall. Despite the variety of evaluation metrics, nearly all researchers use algorithms that maximize performance on the Labelled Tree Rate, even in domains where they are evaluating using other criteria.

We propose that by creating algorithms that optimize the evaluation criterion, rather than some related criterion, improved performance can be achieved.

In Section 2, we define most of the evaluation metrics used in this paper and discuss previous approaches. Then, in Section 3, we discuss the Labelled Recall Algorithm, a new algorithm that maximizes performance on the Labelled Recall Rate. In Section 4, we discuss another new algorithm, the Bracketed Recall Algorithm, that maximizes performance on the Bracketed Recall Rate (closely related to the Consistent Brackets Recall Rate). Finally, we give experimental results in Section 5 using these two algorithms in appropriate domains, and compare them to the Labelled Tree (Viterbi) Algorithm, showing that each algorithm generally works best when evaluated on the criterion that it optimizes.

2 Evaluation Metrics

In this section, we first define basic terms and symbols. Next, we define the different metrics used in evaluation. Finally, we discuss the relationship of these metrics to parsing algorithms.

2.1 Basic Definitions

Let w_a denote word a of the sentence under consideration. Let w_a^b denote $w_a w_{a+1} ... w_{b-1} w_b$; in particular let w_1^n denote the entire sequence of terminals (words) in the sentence under consideration.

In this paper we assume all guessed parse trees are binary branching. Let a parse tree T be defined as a set of triples (s, t, X)—where s denotes the position of the first symbol in a constituent, t denotes the position of the last symbol, and X represents a terminal or nonterminal symbol—meeting the following three requirements:

- The sentence was generated by the start symbol, S. Formally, $(1, n, S) \in T$.
- Every word in the sentence is in the parse tree. Formally, for every s between 1 and n the triple $(s, s, w_s) \in T$.
- The tree is binary branching and consistent. Formally, for every (s, t, X) in T, $s \neq t$, there is exactly one r, Y, and Z such that $s \leq r < t$ and $(s, r, Y) \in T$ and $(r + 1, t, Z) \in T$.

Let T_C denote the "correct" parse (the one in the treebank) and let T_G denote the "guessed" parse (the one output by the parsing algorithm). Let N_G denote $|T_G|$, the number of nonterminals in the guessed parse tree, and let N_C denote $|T_C|$, the number of nonterminals in the correct parse tree.

2.2 Evaluation Metrics

There are various levels of strictness for determining whether a constituent (element of T_G) is "correct." The strictest of these is Labelled Match. A constituent $(s, t, X) \in T_G$ is correct according to Labelled Match if and only if $(s, t, X) \in T_C$. In other words, a constituent in the guessed parse tree is correct if and only if it occurs in the correct parse tree.

The next level of strictness is Bracketed Match. Bracketed match is like labelled match, except that the nonterminal label is ignored. Formally, a constituent $(s, t, X) \in T_G$ is correct according to Bracketed Match if and only if there exists a Y such that $(s, t, Y) \in T_C$.

The least strict level is Consistent Brackets (also called Crossing Brackets). Consistent Brackets is like Bracketed Match in that the label is ignored. It is even less strict in that the observed (s, t, X) need not be in T_C—it must simply not be ruled out by any $(q, r, Y) \in T_C$. A particular triple (q, r, Y) rules out (s, t, X) if there is no way that (s, t, X) and (q, r, Y) could both be in the same parse tree. In particular, if the interval (s, t) crosses the interval (q, r), then (s, t, X) is ruled out and counted as an error. Formally, we say that (s, t) crosses (q, r) if and only if $s < q \leq t < r$ or $q < s \leq r < t$.

If T_C is binary branching, then Consistent Brackets and Bracketed Match are identical. The following symbols denote the number of constituents that match according to each of these criteria.

$L = |T_C \cap T_G|$: the number of constituents in T_G that are correct according to Labelled Match.

$B = |\{(s, t, X) : (s, t, X) \in T_G$ and for some $Y\ (s, t, Y) \in T_C\}|$: the number of constituents in T_G that are correct according to Bracketed Match.

$C = |\{(s, t, X) \in T_G :$ there is no $(v, w, Y) \in T_C$ crossing $(s, t)\}|$: the number of constituents in T_G correct according to Consistent Brackets.

Following are the definitions of the six metrics used in this paper for evaluating binary branching trees:

(1) *Labelled Recall Rate* = L/N_C.

(2) *Labelled Tree Rate* = 1 if $L = N_C$. It is also called the Viterbi Criterion.

(3) *Bracketed Recall Rate* = B/N_C.

(4) *Bracketed Tree Rate* = 1 if $B = N_C$.

(5) *Consistent Brackets Recall Rate* = C/N_G. It is often called the Crossing Brackets Rate. In the case where the parses are binary branching, this criterion is the same as the Bracketed Recall Rate.

(6) *Consistent Brackets Tree Rate* = 1 if $C = N_G$. This metric is closely related to the Bracketed Tree Rate. In the case where the parses are binary branching, the two metrics are the same. This criterion is also called the Zero Crossing Brackets Rate.

The preceding six metrics each correspond to cells in the following table:

	Recall	Tree
Consistent Brackets	C/N_G	1 if $C = N_G$
Brackets	B/N_C	1 if $B = N_C$
Labels	L/N_C	1 if $L = N_C$

2.3 Maximizing Metrics

Despite this long list of possible metrics, there is only one metric most parsing algorithms attempt to maximize, namely the Labelled Tree Rate. That is, most parsing algorithms assume that the test corpus was generated by the model, and then attempt to evaluate the following expression, where E denotes the expected value operator:

$$T_G = \arg\max_T E(\ 1 \text{ if } L = N_C) \tag{1}$$

This is true of the Labelled Tree Algorithm and stochastic versions of Earley's Algorithm (Stolcke, 1993), and variations such as those used in Picky parsing (Magerman and Weir, 1992). Even in probabilistic models not closely related to PCFGs, such as Spatter parsing (Magerman, 1994), expression (1) is still computed. One notable exception is Brill's Transformation-Based Error Driven system (Brill, 1993), which induces a set of transformations designed to maximize the Consistent Brackets Recall Rate. However, Brill's system is not probabilistic. Intuitively, if one were to match the parsing algorithm to the evaluation criterion, better performance should be achieved.

Ideally, one might try to directly maximize the most commonly used evaluation criteria, such as Consistent Brackets Recall (Crossing Brackets)

Rate. Unfortunately, this criterion is relatively difficult to maximize, since it is time-consuming to compute the probability that a particular constituent crosses some constituent in the correct parse. On the other hand, the Bracketed Recall and Bracketed Tree Rates are easier to handle, since computing the probability that a bracket matches one in the correct parse is inexpensive. It is plausible that algorithms which optimize these closely related criteria will do well on the analogous Consistent Brackets criteria.

2.4 Which Metrics to Use

When building an actual system, one should use the metric most appropriate for the problem. For instance, if one were creating a database query system, such as an ATIS system, then the Labelled Tree (Viterbi) metric would be most appropriate. A single error in the syntactic representation of a query will likely result in an error in the semantic representation, and therefore in an incorrect database query, leading to an incorrect result. For instance, if the user request "Find me all flights on Tuesday" is misparsed with the prepositional phrase attached to the verb, then the system might wait until Tuesday before responding: a single error leads to completely incorrect behavior. Thus, the Labelled Tree criterion is appropriate.

On the other hand, consider a machine assisted translation system, in which the system provides translations, and then a fluent human manually edits them. Imagine that the system is given the foreign language equivalent of "His credentials are nothing which should be laughed at," and makes the single mistake of attaching the relative clause at the sentential level, translating the sentence as "His credentials are nothing, which should make you laugh." While the human translator must make some changes, he certainly needs to do less editing than he would if the sentence were completely misparsed. The more errors there are, the more editing the human translator needs to do. Thus, a criterion such as the Labelled Recall criterion is appropriate for this task, where the number of incorrect constituents correlates to application performance.

3 Labelled Recall Parsing

Consider writing a parser for a domain such as machine assisted translation. One could use the Labelled Tree Algorithm, which would maximize the expected number of exactly correct parses. However, since the number of correct constituents is a better measure of application performance for this domain than the number of correct trees, perhaps one should use an algorithm which maximizes the Labelled Recall criterion, rather than the Labelled Tree criterion.

The Labelled Recall Algorithm finds that tree T_G which has the highest expected value for the Labelled Recall Rate, L/N_C (where L is the number of correct labelled constituents, and N_C is the number of nodes in the correct parse). This can be written as follows:

$$T_G = \arg\max_T E(L/N_C) \qquad (2)$$

It is not immediately obvious that the maximization of expression (2) is in fact different from the maximization of expression (1), but a simple example illustrates the difference. The following grammar generates four trees with equal probability:

$$\begin{array}{rcll} \text{S} & \rightarrow & \text{A C} & 0.25 \\ \text{S} & \rightarrow & \text{A D} & 0.25 \\ \text{S} & \rightarrow & \text{E B} & 0.25 \\ \text{S} & \rightarrow & \text{F B} & 0.25 \\ \text{A, B, C, D, E, F} & \rightarrow & \text{x x} & 1.0 \end{array} \qquad (3)$$

The four trees are

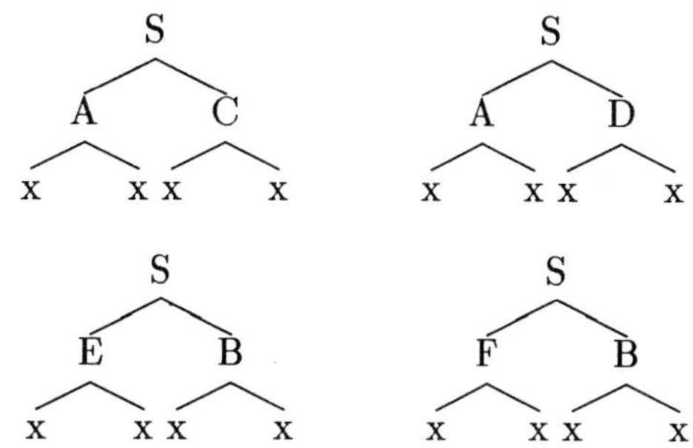

For the first tree, the probabilities of being correct are S: 100%; A:50%; and C: 25%. Similar counting holds for the other three. Thus, the expected value of L for any of these trees is 1.75.

On the other hand, the optimal Labelled Recall parse is

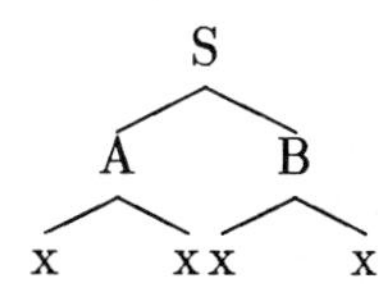

This tree has 0 probability according to the grammar, and thus is non-optimal according to the Labelled Tree Rate criterion. However, for this tree the probabilities of each node being correct are S: 100%; A: 50%; and B: 50%. The expected value of L is 2.0, the highest of any tree. This tree therefore optimizes the Labelled Recall Rate.

3.1 Algorithm

We now derive an algorithm for finding the parse that maximizes the expected Labelled Recall Rate. We do this by expanding expression (2) out into a probabilistic form, converting this into a recursive equation, and finally creating an equivalent dynamic programming algorithm.

We begin by rewriting expression (2), expanding out the expected value operator, and removing the

$\frac{1}{N_C}$, which is the same for all T_G, and so plays no role in the maximization.

$$T_G = \arg\max_T \sum_{T_C} P(T_C \mid w_1^n)\ |T \cap T_C| \qquad (4)$$

This can be further expanded to

$$T_G = \arg\max_T \sum_{T_C} P(T_C \mid w_1^n) \sum_{(s,t,X) \in T} 1 \text{ if } (s,t,X) \in T_C \qquad (5)$$

Now, given a PCFG with start symbol S, the following equality holds:

$$P(S \overset{*}{\Rightarrow} w_1^{s-1} X w_{t+1}^n \mid w_1^n) = \sum_{T_C} P(T_C \mid w_1^n)(\ 1 \text{ if } (s,t,X) \in T_C) \qquad (6)$$

By rearranging the summation in expression (5) and then substituting this equality, we get

$$T_G = \arg\max_T \sum_{(s,t,X) \in T} P(S \overset{*}{\Rightarrow} w_1^{s-1} X w_{t+1}^n \mid w_1^n) \qquad (7)$$

At this point, it is useful to introduce the Inside and Outside probabilities, due to Baker (1979), and explained by Lari and Young (1990). The Inside probability is defined as $e(s,t,X) = P(X \overset{*}{\Rightarrow} w_s^t)$ and the Outside probability is $f(s,t,X) = P(S \overset{*}{\Rightarrow} w_1^{s-1} X w_{t+1}^n)$. Note that while Baker and others have used these probabilites for inducing grammars, here they are used only for parsing.

Let us define a new function, $g(s,t,X)$.

$$\begin{aligned} g(s,t,X) &= P(S \overset{*}{\Rightarrow} w_1^{s-1} X w_{t+1}^n \mid w_1^n) \\ &= \frac{P(S \overset{*}{\Rightarrow} w_1^{s-1} X w_{t+1}^n) P(X \overset{*}{\Rightarrow} w_s^t)}{P(S \overset{*}{\Rightarrow} w_1^n)} \\ &= f(s,t,X) \times e(s,t,X)/e(1,n,S) \end{aligned}$$

Now, the definition of a Labelled Recall Parse can be rewritten as

$$T_G = \arg\max_T \sum_{(s,t,X) \in T} g(s,t,X) \qquad (8)$$

Given the matrix $g(s,t,X)$, it is a simple matter of dynamic programming to determine the parse that maximizes the Labelled Recall criterion. Define

$$\text{MAXC}(s,t) = \max_X g(s,t,X) + \max_{r \mid s \leq r < t} (\text{MAXC}(s,r) + \text{MAXC}(r+1,t))$$

```
for length := 2 to n
   for s := 1 to n-length+1
      t := s + length - 1;
      loop over nonterminals X
         let max_g:=maximum of g(s,t,X)
      loop over r such that s <= r < t
         let best_split:=
            max of maxc[s,r] + maxc[r+1,t]
      maxc[s, t] := max_g + best_split;
```

Figure 1: Labelled Recall Algorithm

It is clear that $\text{MAXC}(1,n)$ contains the score of the best parse according to the Labelled Recall criterion. This equation can be converted into the dynamic programming algorithm shown in Figure 1.

For a grammar with r rules and k nonterminals, the run time of this algorithm is $O(n^3 + kn^2)$ since there are two layers of outer loops, each with run time at most n, and an inner loop, over nonterminals and n. However, this is dominated by the computation of the Inside and Outside probabilities, which takes time $O(rn^3)$.

By modifying the algorithm slightly to record the actual split used at each node, we can recover the best parse. The entry `maxc[1, n]` contains the expected number of correct constituents, given the model.

4 Bracketed Recall Parsing

The Labelled Recall Algorithm maximizes the expected number of correct labelled constituents. However, many commonly used evaluation metrics, such as the Consistent Brackets Recall Rate, ignore labels. Similarly, some grammar induction algorithms, such as those used by Pereira and Schabes (1992) do not produce meaningful labels. In particular, the Pereira and Schabes method induces a grammar from the brackets in the treebank, ignoring the labels. While the induced grammar has labels, they are not related to those in the treebank. Thus, although the Labelled Recall Algorithm could be used in these domains, perhaps maximizing a criterion that is more closely tied to the domain will produce better results. Ideally, we would maximize the Consistent Brackets Recall Rate directly. However, since it is time-consuming to deal with Consistent Brackets, we instead use the closely related Bracketed Recall Rate.

For the Bracketed Recall Algorithm, we find the parse that maximizes the expected Bracketed Recall Rate, B/N_C. (Remember that B is the number of brackets that are correct, and N_C is the number of constituents in the correct parse.)

$$T_G = \arg\max_T E(B/N_C) \qquad (9)$$

Following a derivation similar to that used for the Labelled Recall Algorithm, we can rewrite equation (9) as

$$T_G = \arg\max_T \sum_{(s,t)\in T} \sum_X P(S \stackrel{*}{\Rightarrow} w_1^{s-1} X w_{t+1}^n \mid w_1^n) \tag{10}$$

The algorithm for Bracketed Recall parsing is extremely similar to that for Labelled Recall parsing. The only required change is that we sum over the symbols X to calculate **max_g**, rather than maximize over them.

5 Experimental Results

We describe two experiments for testing these algorithms. The first uses a grammar without meaningful nonterminal symbols, and compares the Bracketed Recall Algorithm to the traditional Labelled Tree (Viterbi) Algorithm. The second uses a grammar with meaningful nonterminal symbols and performs a three-way comparison between the Labelled Recall, Bracketed Recall, and Labelled Tree Algorithms. These experiments show that use of an algorithm matched appropriately to the evaluation criterion can lead to as much as a 10% reduction in error rate.

In both experiments the grammars could not parse some sentences, 0.5% and 9%, respectively. The unparsable data were assigned a right branching structure with their rightmost element attached high. Since all three algorithms fail on the same sentences, all algorithms were affected equally.

5.1 Experiment with Grammar Induced by Pereira and Schabes Method

The experiment of Pereira and Schabes (1992) was duplicated. In that experiment, a grammar was trained from a bracketed form of the TI section of the ATIS corpus[1] using a modified form of the Inside-Outside Algorithm. Pereira and Schabes then used the Labelled Tree Algorithm to select the best parse for sentences in held out test data. The experiment was repeated here, except that both the Labelled Tree and Labelled Recall Algorithm were run for each sentence. In contrast to previous research, we repeated the experiment ten times, with different training set, test set, and initial conditions each time.

Table 1 shows the results of running this experiment, giving the minimum, maximum, mean, and standard deviation for three criteria, Consistent Brackets Recall, Consistent Brackets Tree, and Bracketed Recall. We also display these statistics for the paired differences between the algorithms. The only statistically significant difference is that for Consistent Brackets Recall Rate, which was significant to the 2% significance level (paired t-test). Thus, use of the Bracketed Recall Algorithm leads to a 10% reduction in error rate.

[1]For our experiments the corpus was slightly cleaned up. A diff file for "ed" between the original ATIS data and the cleaned-up version is available from ftp://ftp.das.harvard.edu/pub/goodman/atis-ed/ ti_tb.par-ed and ti_tb.pos-ed. The number of changes made was small, less than 0.2%

Criteria	Min	Max	Mean	SDev
Labelled Tree Algorithm				
Cons Brack Rec	86.06	93.27	90.13	2.57
Cons Brack Tree	51.14	77.27	63.98	7.96
Brack Rec	71.38	81.88	75.87	3.18
Bracketed Recall Algorithm				
Cons Brack Rec	88.02	94.34	91.14	2.22
Cons Brack Tree	53.41	76.14	63.64	7.82
Brack Rec	72.15	80.69	76.03	3.14
Differences				
Cons Brack Rec	-1.55	2.45	1.01	1.07
Cons Brack Tree	-3.41	3.41	-0.34	2.34
Brack Rec	-1.34	2.02	0.17	1.20

Table 1: Percentages Correct for Labelled Tree versus Bracketed Recall for Pereira and Schabes

In addition, the performance of the Bracketed Recall Algorithm was also qualitatively more appealing. Figure 2 shows typical results. Notice that the Bracketed Recall Algorithm's Consistent Brackets Rate (versus iteration) is smoother and more nearly monotonic than the Labelled Tree Algorithm's. The Bracketed Recall Algorithm also gets off to a much faster start, and is generally (although not always) above the Labelled Tree level. For the Labelled Tree Rate, the two are usually very comparable.

5.2 Experiment with Grammar Induced by Counting

The replication of the Pereira and Schabes experiment was useful for testing the Bracketed Recall Algorithm. However, since that experiment induces a grammar with nonterminals not comparable to those in the training, a different experiment is needed to evaluate the Labelled Recall Algorithm, one in which the nonterminals in the induced grammar are the same as the nonterminals in the test set.

5.2.1 Grammar Induction by Counting

For this experiment, a very simple grammar was induced by counting, using a portion of the Penn Tree Bank, version 0.5. In particular, the trees were first made binary branching by removing epsilon productions, collapsing singleton productions, and converting n-ary productions ($n > 2$) as in figure 3. The resulting trees were treated as the "Correct" trees in the evaluation. Only trees with forty or fewer symbols were used in this experiment.

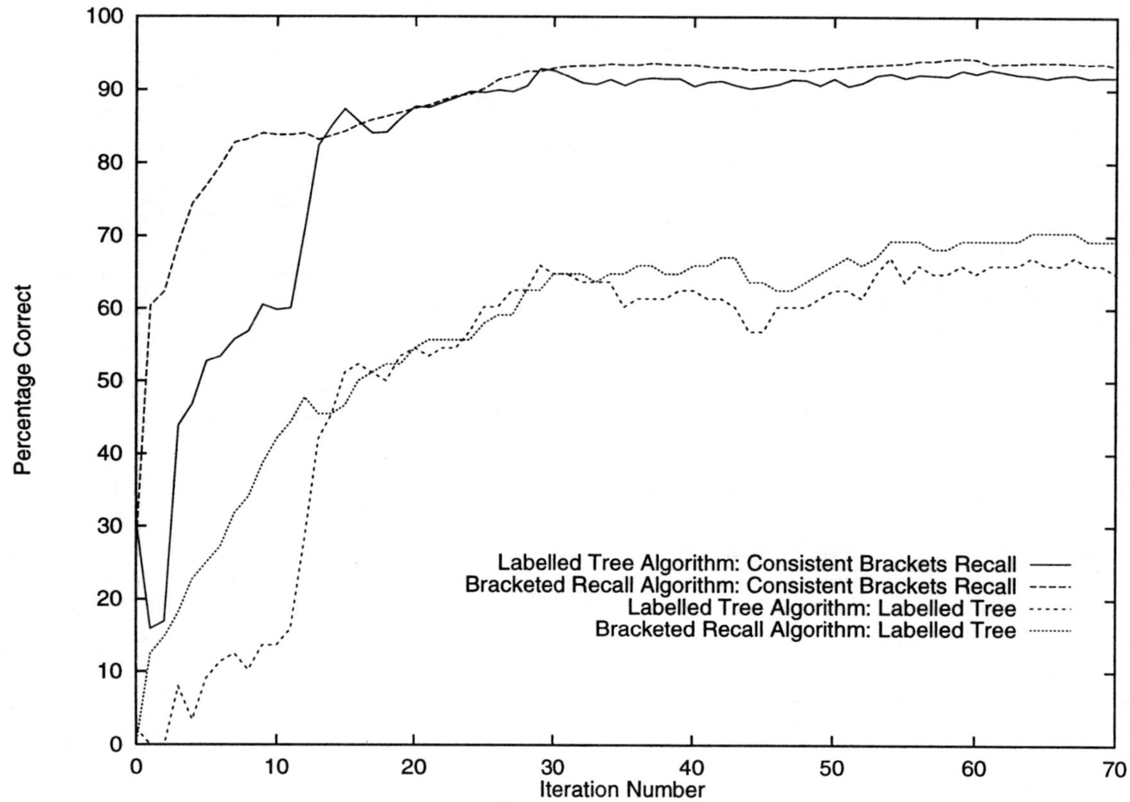

Figure 2: Labelled Tree versus Bracketed Recall in Pereira and Schabes Grammar

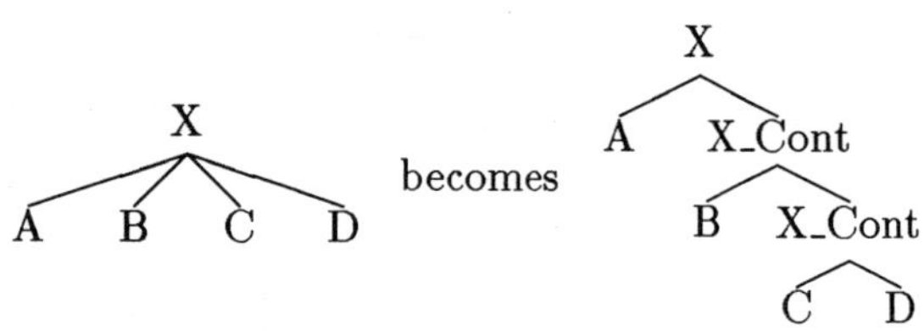

Figure 3: Conversion of Productions to Binary Branching

A grammar was then induced in a straightforward way from these trees, simply by giving one count for each observed production. No smoothing was done. There were 1805 sentences and 38610 nonterminals in the test data.

5.2.2 Results

Table 2 shows the results of running all three algorithms, evaluating against five criteria. Notice that for each algorithm, for the criterion that it optimizes it is the best algorithm. That is, the Labelled Tree Algorithm is the best for the Labelled Tree Rate, the Labelled Recall Algorithm is the best for the Labelled Recall Rate, and the Bracketed Recall Algorithm is the best for the Bracketed Recall Rate.

	Recall	Tree
Brackets	Bracketed Recall	(NP-Complete)
Labels	Labelled Recall	Labelled Tree

Table 3: Metrics and Corresponding Algorithms

6 Conclusions and Future Work

Matching parsing algorithms to evaluation criteria is a powerful technique that can be used to improve performance. In particular, the Labelled Recall Algorithm can improve performance versus the Labelled Tree Algorithm on the Consistent Brackets, Labelled Recall, and Bracketed Recall criteria. Similarly, the Bracketed Recall Algorithm improves performance (versus Labelled Tree) on Consistent Brackets and Bracketed Recall criteria. Thus, these algorithms improve performance not only on the measures that they were designed for, but also on related criteria.

Furthermore, in some cases these techniques can make parsing fast when it was previously impractical. We have used the technique outlined in this paper in other work (Goodman, 1996) to efficiently parse the DOP model; in that model, the only previously known algorithm which summed over all the

	Criterion				
Algorithm	Label Tree	Label Recall	Brack Recall	Cons Brack Recall	Cons Brack Tree
Label Tree	*4.54%*	48.60%	60.98%	66.35%	12.07%
Label Recall	3.71%	*49.66%*	61.34%	68.39%	11.63%
Bracket Recall	0.11%	4.51%	*61.63%*	68.17%	11.19%

Table 2: Grammar Induced by Counting: Three Algorithms Evaluated on Five Criteria

possible derivations was a slow Monte Carlo algorithm (Bod, 1993). However, by maximizing the Labelled Recall criterion, rather than the Labelled Tree criterion, it was possible to use a much simpler algorithm, a variation on the Labelled Recall Algorithm. Using this technique, along with other optimizations, we achieved a 500 times speedup.

In future work we will show the surprising result that the last element of Table 3, maximizing the Bracketed Tree criterion, equivalent to maximizing performance on Consistent Brackets Tree (Zero Crossing Brackets) Rate in the binary branching case, is NP-complete. Furthermore, we will show that the two algorithms presented, the Labelled Recall Algorithm and the Bracketed Recall Algorithm, are both special cases of a more general algorithm, the General Recall Algorithm. Finally, we hope to extend this work to the n-ary branching case.

7 Acknowledgements

I would like to acknowledge support from National Science Foundation Grant IRI-9350192, National Science Foundation infrastructure grant CDA 94-01024, and a National Science Foundation Graduate Student Fellowship. I would also like to thank Stanley Chen, Andrew Kehler, Lillian Lee, and Stuart Shieber for helpful discussions, and comments on earlier drafts, and the anonymous reviewers for their comments.

References

Baker, J.K. 1979. Trainable grammars for speech recognition. In *Proceedings of the Spring Conference of the Acoustical Society of America*, pages 547–550, Boston, MA, June.

Bod, Rens. 1993. Using an annotated corpus as a stochastic grammar. In *Proceedings of the Sixth Conference of the European Chapter of the ACL*, pages 37–44.

Brill, Eric. 1993. *A Corpus-Based Approach to Language Learning*. Ph.D. thesis, University of Pennsylvania.

Goodman, Joshua. 1996. Efficient algorithms for parsing the DOP model. In *Proceedings of the Conference on Empirical Methods in Natural Language Processing*. To appear.

Lari, K. and S.J. Young. 1990. The estimation of stochastic context-free grammars using the inside-outside algorithm. *Computer Speech and Language*, 4:35–56.

Magerman, David. 1994. *Natural Language Parsing as Statistical Pattern Recognition*. Ph.D. thesis, Stanford University University, February.

Magerman, D.M. and C. Weir. 1992. Efficiency, robustness, and accuracy in picky chart parsing. In *Proceedings of the Association for Computational Linguistics*.

Pereira, Fernando and Yves Schabes. 1992. Inside-Outside reestimation from partially bracketed corpora. In *Proceedings of the 30th Annual Meeting of the ACL*, pages 128–135, Newark, Delaware.

Stolcke, Andreas. 1993. An efficient probabilistic context-free parsing algorithm that computes prefix probabilities. Technical Report TR-93-065, International Computer Science Institute, Berkeley, CA.

A New Statistical Parser Based on Bigram Lexical Dependencies

Michael John Collins*
Dept. of Computer and Information Science
University of Pennsylvania
Philadelphia, PA, 19104, U.S.A.
mcollins@gradient.cis.upenn.edu

Abstract

This paper describes a new statistical parser which is based on probabilities of dependencies between head-words in the parse tree. Standard bigram probability estimation techniques are extended to calculate probabilities of dependencies between pairs of words. Tests using Wall Street Journal data show that the method performs at least as well as SPATTER (Magerman 95; Jelinek et al. 94), which has the best published results for a statistical parser on this task. The simplicity of the approach means the model trains on 40,000 sentences in under 15 minutes. With a beam search strategy parsing speed can be improved to over 200 sentences a minute with negligible loss in accuracy.

1 Introduction

Lexical information has been shown to be crucial for many parsing decisions, such as prepositional-phrase attachment (for example (Hindle and Rooth 93)). However, early approaches to probabilistic parsing (Pereira and Schabes 92; Magerman and Marcus 91; Briscoe and Carroll 93) conditioned probabilities on non-terminal labels and part of speech tags alone. The SPATTER parser (Magerman 95; Jelinek et al. 94) does use lexical information, and recovers labeled constituents in Wall Street Journal text with above 84% accuracy – as far as we know the best published results on this task.

This paper describes a new parser which is much simpler than SPATTER, yet performs at least as well when trained and tested on the same Wall Street Journal data. The method uses lexical information directly by modeling head-modifier[1] relations between pairs of words. In this way it is similar to Link grammars (Lafferty et al. 92), and dependency grammars in general.

2 The Statistical Model

The aim of a parser is to take a tagged sentence as input (for example Figure 1(a)) and produce a phrase-structure tree as output (Figure 1(b)). A statistical approach to this problem consists of two components. First, the *statistical model* assigns a probability to every candidate parse tree for a sentence. Formally, given a sentence S and a tree T, the model estimates the conditional probability $P(T|S)$. The most likely parse under the model is then:

$$T_{best} = argmax_T P(T|S) \quad (1)$$

Second, the *parser* is a method for finding T_{best}. This section describes the statistical model, while section 3 describes the parser.

The key to the statistical model is that any tree such as Figure 1(b) can be represented as a set of **baseNPs**[2] and a set of **dependencies** as in Figure 1(c). We call the set of baseNPs B, and the set of dependencies D; Figure 1(d) shows B and D for this example. For the purposes of our model, $T = (B, D)$, and:

$$P(T|S) = P(B, D|S) = P(B|S) \times P(D|S, B) \quad (2)$$

S is the sentence with words tagged for part of speech. That is, $S =< (w_1, t_1), (w_2, t_2)...(w_n, t_n) >$. For POS tagging we use a maximum-entropy tagger described in (Ratnaparkhi 96). The tagger performs at around 97% accuracy on Wall Street Journal Text, and is trained on the first 40,000 sentences of the Penn Treebank (Marcus et al. 93).

Given S and B, the **reduced sentence** $\bar{S}$ is defined as the subsequence of S which is formed by removing punctuation and reducing all baseNPs to their head-word alone.

*This research was supported by ARPA Grant N6600194-C6043.

[1] By 'modifier' we mean the linguistic notion of either an argument or adjunct.

[2] A baseNP or 'minimal' NP is a non-recursive NP, i.e. none of its child constituents are NPs. The term was first used in (Ramshaw and Marcus 95).

(a)

John/NNP Smith/NNP, the/DT president/NN of/IN IBM/NNP, announced/VBD his/PRP$ resignation/NN yesterday/NN .

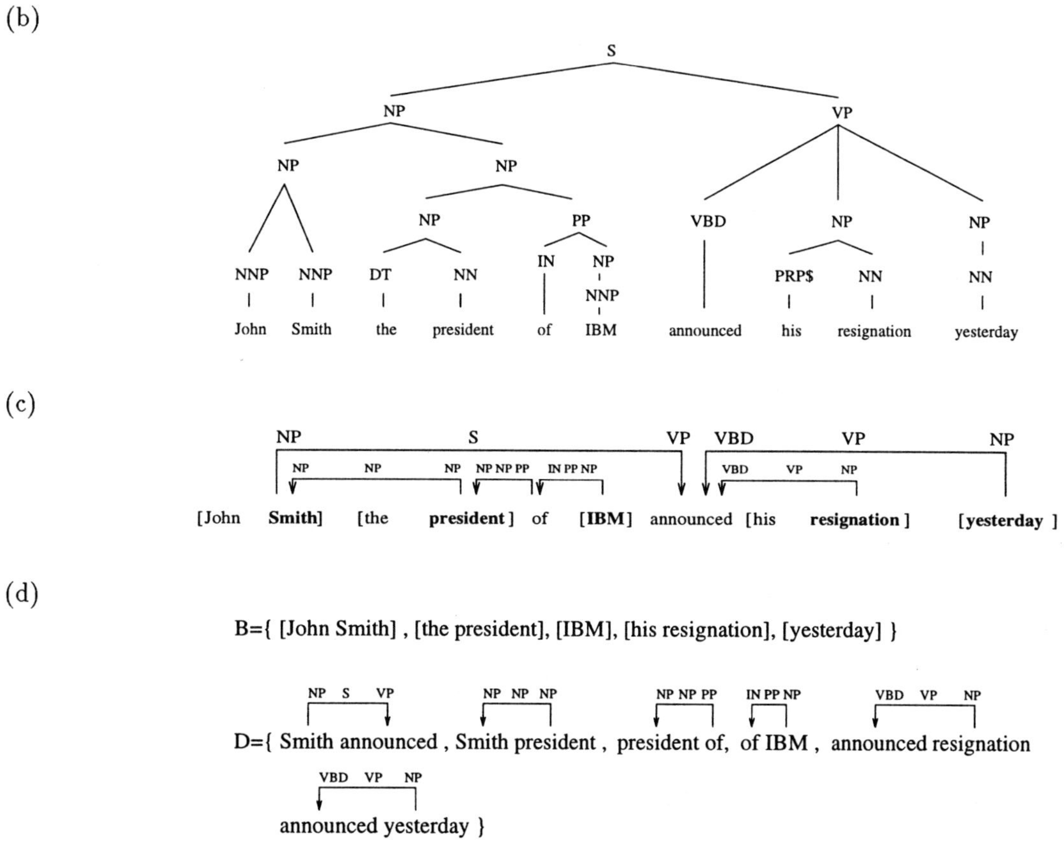

Figure 1: An overview of the representation used by the model. **(a)** The tagged sentence; **(b)** A candidate parse-tree (the correct one); **(c)** A dependency representation of (b). Square brackets enclose baseNPs (heads of baseNPs are marked in bold). Arrows show modifier → head dependencies. Section 2.1 describes how arrows are labeled with non-terminal triples from the parse-tree. Non-head words within baseNPs are excluded from the dependency structure; **(d)** B, the set of baseNPs, and D, the set of dependencies, are extracted from (c).

Thus the reduced sentence is an array of word/tag pairs, $\bar{S} =< \langle \bar{w}_1, \bar{t}_1 \rangle, \langle \bar{w}_2, \bar{t}_2 \rangle ... \langle \bar{w}_m, \bar{t}_m \rangle >$, where $m \leq n$. For example for Figure 1(a)

Example 1 $\bar{S} =$

$$< \langle Smith, NNP \rangle, \langle president, NN \rangle, \langle of, IN \rangle, \langle IBM, NNP \rangle, \langle announced, VBD \rangle, \langle resignation, NN \rangle, \langle yesterday, NN \rangle >$$

Sections 2.1 to 2.4 describe the dependency model. Section 2.5 then describes the baseNP model, which uses bigram tagging techniques similar to (Ramshaw and Marcus 95; Church 88).

2.1 The Mapping from Trees to Sets of Dependencies

The dependency model is limited to relationships between words in **reduced** sentences such as Example 1. The mapping from trees to dependency structures is central to the dependency model. It is defined in two steps:

1. For each constituent $P \rightarrow < C_1 ... C_n >$ in the parse tree a simple set of rules[3] identifies which of the children C_i is the 'head-child' of P. For example, `NN` would be identified as the head-child of `NP` → `<DET JJ JJ NN>`, `VP` would be identified as the head-child of `S` → `<NP VP>`. Head-words propagate up through the tree, each parent receiving its head-word from its head-child. For example, in `S` → `<NP VP>`, `S` gets its head-word, *announced*,

[3] The rules are essentially the same as in (Magerman 95; Jelinek et al. 94). These rules are also used to find the head-word of baseNPs, enabling the mapping from S and B to $\bar{S}$.

from its head-child, the **VP**.

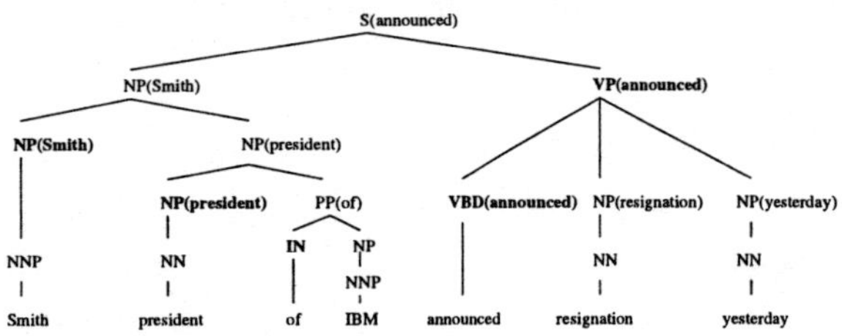

Figure 2: Parse tree for the reduced sentence in Example 1. The head-**child** of each constituent is shown in bold. The head-**word** for each constituent is shown in parentheses.

2. Head-modifier relationships are now extracted from the tree in Figure 2. Figure 3 illustrates how each constituent contributes a set of dependency relationships. **VBD** is identified as the head-child of **VP** → <**VBD NP NP**>. The head-words of the two NPs, *resignation* and *yesterday*, both modify the head-word of the **VBD**, *announced*. Dependencies are labeled by the modifier non-terminal, **NP** in both of these cases, the parent non-terminal, **VP**, and finally the head-child non-terminal, **VBD**. The triple of non-terminals at the start, middle and end of the arrow specify the nature of the dependency relationship – <**NP,S,VP**> represents a subject-verb dependency, <**PP,NP,NP**> denotes prepositional phrase modification of an **NP**, and so on[4].

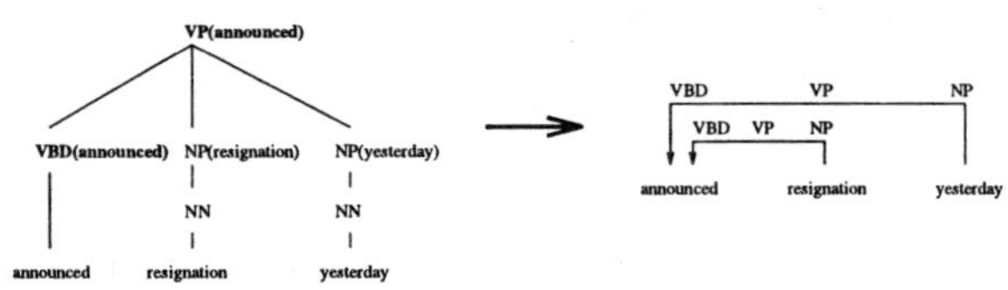

Figure 3: Each constituent with n children (in this case $n = 3$) contributes $n - 1$ dependencies.

Each word in the reduced sentence, with the exception of the sentential head 'announced', modifies exactly one other word. We use the notation

$$AF(j) = (h_j, R_j) \tag{3}$$

to state that the jth word in the reduced sentence is a modifier to the h_jth word, with relationship R_j[5]. AF stands for 'arrow from'. R_j is the triple of labels at the start, middle and end of the arrow. For example, $\bar{w}_1$ = *Smith* in this sentence, and $\bar{w}_5$ = *announced*, so $AF(1) = (5, \texttt{<NP,S,VP>})$.

D is now defined as the m-tuple of dependencies: $D = \{(AF(1), AF(2)...AF(m)\}$. The model assumes that the dependencies are independent, so that:

$$P(D|S,B) = \prod_{j=1}^{m} P(AF(j)|S,B) \tag{4}$$

2.2 Calculating Dependency Probabilities

This section describes the way $P(AF(j)|S,B)$ is estimated. The same sentence is very unlikely to appear both in training and test data, so we need to back-off from the entire sentence context. We believe that lexical information is crucial to attachment decisions, so it is natural to condition on the words and tags. Let $\mathcal{V}$ be the vocabulary of all words seen in training data, $\mathcal{T}$ be the set of all part-of-speech tags, and $\mathcal{TRAIN}$ be the training set, a set of reduced sentences. We define the following functions:

• $C(\langle a,b\rangle, \langle c,d\rangle)$ for $a, c \in \mathcal{V}$, and $b, d \in \mathcal{T}$ is the number of times $\langle a,b\rangle$ and $\langle c,d\rangle$ are seen in the same reduced sentence in training data.[6] Formally,

$$C(\langle a,b\rangle, \langle c,d\rangle) = \sum_{\substack{\bar{S} \in \mathcal{TRAIN} \\ k,l=1..|\bar{S}|,\ l\neq k}} h\left(\bar{S}[k] = \langle a,b\rangle, \bar{S}[l] = \langle c,d\rangle\right) \tag{5}$$

where $h(x)$ is an indicator function which is 1 if x is true, 0 if x is false.

• $C(R, \langle a,b\rangle, \langle c,d\rangle)$ is the number of times $\langle a,b\rangle$ and $\langle c,d\rangle$ are seen in the same reduced sentence in training data, and $\langle a,b\rangle$ modifies $\langle c,d\rangle$ with relationship R. Formally,

$$C(R, \langle a,b\rangle, \langle c,d\rangle) = \sum_{\substack{\bar{S} \in \mathcal{TRAIN} \\ k,l=1..|\bar{S}|,\ l\neq k}} h(\bar{S}[k] = \langle a,b\rangle, \bar{S}[l] = \langle c,d\rangle, AF(k) = (l,R)) \tag{6}$$

• $F(R\,|\,\langle a,b\rangle, \langle c,d\rangle)$ is the probability that $\langle a,b\rangle$ modifies $\langle c,d\rangle$ with relationship R, given that $\langle a,b\rangle$ and $\langle c,d\rangle$ appear in the same reduced sentence. The maximum-likelihood estimate of $F(R\,|\,\langle a,b\rangle, \langle c,d\rangle)$ is:

$$\hat{F}(R\,|\,\langle a,b\rangle, \langle c,d\rangle) = \frac{C(R, \langle a,b\rangle, \langle c,d\rangle)}{C(\langle a,b\rangle, \langle c,d\rangle)} \tag{7}$$

We can now make the following approximation:

$$P(AF(j) = (h_j, R_j)\,|\,S,B) \approx \frac{\hat{F}(R_j\,|\,\langle \bar{w}_j, \bar{t}_j\rangle, \langle \bar{w}_{h_j}, \bar{t}_{h_j}\rangle)}{\sum_{k=1..m, k\neq j, p\in\mathcal{P}} \hat{F}(p\,|\,\langle \bar{w}_j, \bar{t}_j\rangle, \langle \bar{w}_k, \bar{t}_k\rangle)} \tag{8}$$

[4]The triple can also be viewed as representing a semantic predicate-argument relationship, with the three elements being the type of the argument, result and functor respectively. This is particularly apparent in Categorial Grammar formalisms (Wood 93), which make an explicit link between dependencies and functional application.

[5]For the head-word of the entire sentence $h_j = 0$, with R_j=<Label of the root of the parse tree >. So in this case, $AF(5) = (0, < S >)$.

[6]Note that we count multiple co-occurrences in a single sentence, e.g. if $\bar{S} = (< a,b >, < c,d >, < c,d >)$ then $C(< a,b >, < c,d >) = C(< c,d >, < a,b >) = 2$.

where $\mathcal{P}$ is the set of all triples of non-terminals. The denominator is a normalising factor which ensures that

$$\sum_{k=1..m, k \neq j, p \epsilon \mathcal{P}} P(AF(j) = (k,p) \mid S, B) = 1$$

From (4) and (8):

$$P(D|S,B) \approx \tag{9}$$

$$\prod_{j=1}^{m} \frac{\hat{F}(R_j \mid \langle \bar{w}_j, \bar{t}_j \rangle, \langle \bar{w}_{h_j}, \bar{t}_{h_j} \rangle)}{\sum_{k=1..m, k \neq j, p \epsilon \mathcal{P}} \hat{F}(p \mid \langle \bar{w}_j, \bar{t}_j \rangle, \langle \bar{w}_k, \bar{t}_k \rangle)}$$

The denominator of (9) is constant, so maximising $P(D|S,B)$ over D for fixed S, B is equivalent to maximising the product of the numerators, $\mathcal{N}(D|S,B)$. (This considerably simplifies the parsing process):

$$\mathcal{N}(D|S,B) = \prod_{j=1}^{m} \hat{F}(R_j \mid \langle \bar{w}_j, \bar{t}_j \rangle, \langle \bar{w}_{h_j}, \bar{t}_{h_j} \rangle) \tag{10}$$

2.3 The Distance Measure

An estimate based on the identities of the two tokens alone is problematic. Additional context, in particular the relative order of the two words and the distance between them, will also strongly influence the likelihood of one word modifying the other. For example consider the relationship between 'sales' and the three tokens of 'of':

Example 2 *Shaw, based in Dalton, Ga., has annual* **sales of** *about \$ 1.18 billion, and has economies* **of** *scale and lower raw-material costs that are expected to boost the profitability* **of** *Armstrong 's brands, sold under the Armstrong and Evans-Black names .*

In this sentence 'sales' and 'of' co-occur three times. The parse tree in training data indicates a relationship in only one of these cases, so this sentence would contribute an estimate of $\frac{1}{3}$ that the two words are related. This seems unreasonably low given that 'sales of' is a strong collocation. The latter two instances of 'of' are so distant from 'sales' that it is unlikely that there will be a dependency.

This suggests that distance is a crucial variable when deciding whether two words are related. It is included in the model by defining an extra 'distance' variable, Δ, and extending C, F and $\hat{F}$ to include this variable. For example, $C(\langle a,b \rangle, \langle c,d \rangle, \Delta)$ is the number of times $\langle a,b \rangle$ and $\langle c,d \rangle$ appear in the same sentence at a distance Δ apart. (11) is then maximised instead of (10):

$$\mathcal{N}(D|S,B) = \prod_{j=1}^{m} \hat{F}(R_j \mid \langle \bar{w}_j, \bar{t}_j \rangle, \langle \bar{w}_{h_j}, \bar{t}_{h_j} \rangle, \Delta_{j,h_j}) \tag{11}$$

A simple example of Δ_{j,h_j} would be $\Delta_{j,h_j} = h_j - j$. However, other features of a sentence, such as punctuation, are also useful when deciding if two words are related. We have developed a heuristic 'distance' measure which takes several such features into account The current distance measure Δ_{j,h_j} is the combination of 6 features, or questions (we motivate the choice of these questions qualitatively – section 4 gives quantitative results showing their merit):

Question 1 Does the h_jth word precede or follow the jth word? English is a language with strong word order, so the order of the two words in surface text will clearly affect their dependency statistics.

Question 2 Are the h_jth word and the jth word adjacent? English is largely right-branching and head-initial, which leads to a large proportion of dependencies being between adjacent words [7]. Table 1 shows just how local most dependencies are.

Distance	1	≤ 2	≤ 5	≤ 10
Percentage	74.2	86.3	95.6	99.0

Table 1: Percentage of dependencies vs. distance between the head words involved. These figures count baseNPs as a single word, and are taken from WSJ training data.

Number of verbs	0	<=1	<=2
Percentage	94.1	98.1	99.3

Table 2: Percentage of dependencies vs. number of verbs between the head words involved.

Question 3 Is there a verb between the h_jth word and the jth word? Conditioning on the exact distance between two words by making $\Delta_{j,h_j} = h_j - j$ leads to severe sparse data problems. But Table 1 shows the need to make finer distance distinctions than just whether two words are adjacent. Consider the prepositions 'to', 'in' and 'of' in the following sentence:

Example 3 *Oil stocks* **escaped** *the brunt of Friday 's selling and several were able to post gains , including Chevron , which* **rose** *5/8* **to** *66 3/8* **in** *Big Board composite trading* **of** *2.4 million shares .*

The prepositions' main candidates for attachment would appear to be the previous verb, 'rose', and the baseNP heads between each preposition and this verb. They are less likely to modify a more distant verb such as 'escaped'. Question 3 allows the parser to prefer modification of the most recent verb – effectively another, weaker preference for right-branching structures. Table 2 shows that 94% of dependencies do not cross a verb, giving empirical evidence that question 3 is useful.

[7] For example in '(John (likes (to (go (to (University (of Pennsylvania)))))))' all dependencies are between adjacent words.

Questions 4, 5 and 6

- Are there 0, 1, 2, or more than 2 'commas' between the h_jth word and the jth word? (All symbols tagged as a ',' or ':' are considered to be 'commas').
- Is there a 'comma' immediately following the first of the h_jth word and the jth word?
- Is there a 'comma' immediately preceding the second of the h_jth word and the jth word?

People find that punctuation is extremely useful for identifying phrase structure, and the parser described here also relies on it heavily. Commas are not considered to be words or modifiers in the dependency model – but they do give strong indications about the parse structure. Questions 4, 5 and 6 allow the parser to use this information.

2.4 Sparse Data

The maximum likelihood estimator in (7) is likely to be plagued by sparse data problems – $C(\langle \bar{w}_j, \bar{t}_j \rangle, \langle \bar{w}_{h_j}, \bar{t}_{h_j} \rangle, \Delta_{j,h_j})$ may be too low to give a reliable estimate, or worse still it may be zero leaving the estimate undefined. (Collins 95) describes how a backed-off estimation strategy is used for making prepositional phrase attachment decisions. The idea is to back-off to estimates based on less context. In this case, less context means looking at the POS tags rather than the specific words.

There are four estimates, E_1, E_2, E_3 and E_4, based respectively on: 1) both words and both tags; 2) $\bar{w}_j$ and the two POS tags; 3) $\bar{w}_{h_j}$ and the two POS tags; 4) the two POS tags alone.

$$E_1 = \frac{\eta_1}{\delta_1} \quad E_2 = \frac{\eta_2}{\delta_2} \quad E_3 = \frac{\eta_3}{\delta_3} \quad E_4 = \frac{\eta_4}{\delta_4} \tag{12}$$

where[8]

$$\begin{aligned}
\delta_1 &= C(\langle \bar{w}_j, \bar{t}_j \rangle, \langle \bar{w}_{h_j}, \bar{t}_{h_j} \rangle, \Delta_{j,h_j}) \\
\delta_2 &= C(\langle \bar{w}_j, \bar{t}_j \rangle, \langle \bar{t}_{h_j} \rangle, \Delta_{j,h_j}) \\
\delta_3 &= C(\langle \bar{t}_j \rangle, \langle \bar{w}_{h_j}, \bar{t}_{h_j} \rangle, \Delta_{j,h_j}) \\
\delta_4 &= C(\langle \bar{t}_j \rangle, \langle \bar{t}_{h_j} \rangle, \Delta_{j,h_j}) \\
\eta_1 &= C(R_j, \langle \bar{w}_j, \bar{t}_j \rangle, \langle \bar{w}_{h_j}, \bar{t}_{h_j} \rangle, \Delta_{j,h_j}) \\
\eta_2 &= C(R_j, \langle \bar{w}_j, \bar{t}_j \rangle, \langle \bar{t}_{h_j} \rangle, \Delta_{j,h_j}) \\
\eta_3 &= C(R_j, \langle \bar{t}_j \rangle, \langle \bar{w}_{h_j}, \bar{t}_{h_j} \rangle, \Delta_{j,h_j}) \\
\eta_4 &= C(R_j, \langle \bar{t}_j \rangle, \langle \bar{t}_{h_j} \rangle, \Delta_{j,h_j})
\end{aligned} \tag{13}$$

8

$$C(\langle \bar{w}_j, \bar{t}_j \rangle, \langle \bar{t}_{h_j} \rangle, \Delta_{j,h_j}) = \sum_{x \in \mathcal{V}} C(\langle \bar{w}_j, \bar{t}_j \rangle, \langle x, \bar{t}_{h_j} \rangle, \Delta_{j,h_j})$$

$$C(\langle \bar{t}_j \rangle, \langle \bar{t}_{h_j} \rangle, \Delta_{j,h_j}) = \sum_{x \in \mathcal{V}} \sum_{y \in \mathcal{V}} C(\langle x, \bar{t}_j \rangle, \langle y, \bar{t}_{h_j} \rangle, \Delta_{j,h_j})$$

where $\mathcal{V}$ is the set of all words seen in training data: the other definitions of C follow similarly.

Estimates 2 and 3 compete – for a given pair of words in test data both estimates may exist and they are equally 'specific' to the test case example. (Collins 95) suggests the following way of combining them, which favours the estimate appearing more often in training data:

$$E_{23} = \frac{\eta_2 + \eta_3}{\delta_2 + \delta_3} \tag{14}$$

This gives three estimates: E_1, E_{23} and E_4, a similar situation to trigram language modeling for speech recognition (Jelinek 90), where there are trigram, bigram and unigram estimates. (Jelinek 90) describes a deleted interpolation method which combines these estimates to give a 'smooth' estimate, and the model uses a variation of this idea:

If E_1 exists, i.e. $\delta_1 > 0$

$$\hat{F}(R_j \mid \langle \bar{w}_j, \bar{t}_j \rangle, \langle \bar{w}_{h_j}, \bar{t}_{h_j} \rangle, \Delta_{j,h_j}) = \lambda_1 \times E_1 + (1 - \lambda_1) \times E_{23} \tag{15}$$

Else If E_{23} exists, i.e. $\delta_2 + \delta_3 > 0$

$$\hat{F}(R_j \mid \langle \bar{w}_j, \bar{t}_j \rangle, \langle \bar{w}_{h_j}, \bar{t}_{h_j} \rangle, \Delta_{j,h_j}) = \lambda_2 \times E_{23} + (1 - \lambda_2) \times E_4 \tag{16}$$

Else

$$\hat{F}(R_j \mid \langle \bar{w}_j, \bar{t}_j \rangle, \langle \bar{w}_{h_j}, \bar{t}_{h_j} \rangle, \Delta_{j,h_j}) = E_4 \tag{17}$$

(Jelinek 90) describes how to find λ values in (15) and (16) which maximise the likelihood of held-out data. We have taken a simpler approach, namely:

$$\begin{aligned}
\lambda_1 &= \frac{\delta_1}{\delta_1 + 1} \\
\lambda_2 &= \frac{\delta_2 + \delta_3}{\delta_2 + \delta_3 + 1}
\end{aligned} \tag{18}$$

These λ values have the desired property of increasing as the denominator of the more 'specific' estimator increases. We think that a proper implementation of deleted interpolation is likely to improve results, although basing estimates on co-occurrence counts alone has the advantage of reduced training times.

2.5 The BaseNP Model

The overall model would be simpler if we could do without the baseNP model and frame everything in terms of dependencies. However the baseNP model is needed for two reasons. First, while adjacency between words is a good indicator of whether there is some relationship between them, this indicator is made substantially stronger if baseNPs are reduced to a single word. Second, it means that words internal to baseNPs are not included in the co-occurrence counts in training data. Otherwise, in a phrase like 'The Securities and Exchange Commission closed yesterday', pre-modifying nouns like 'Securities' and 'Exchange' would be included in co-occurrence counts, when in practice there is no way that they can modify words outside their baseNP.

The baseNP model can be viewed as tagging the gaps between words with $S(tart)$, $C(ontinue)$, $E(nd)$, $B(etween)$ or $N(ull)$ symbols, respectively meaning that the gap is at the start of a $BaseNP$, continues a $BaseNP$, is at the end of a $BaseNP$, is between two adjacent $baseNPs$, or is between two words which are both not in $BaseNPs$. We call the gap before the ith word G_i (a sentence with n words has $n-1$ gaps). For example,

[John Smith] [the president] of [IBM] has announced [his resignation] [yesterday] ⇒
John **C** Smith **B** the **C** president **E** of **S** IBM **E** has **N** announced **S** his **C** resignation **B** yesterday

The baseNP model considers the words directly to the left and right of each gap, and whether there is a comma between the two words (we write $c_i = 1$ if there is a comma, $c_i = 0$ otherwise). Probability estimates are based on counts of consecutive pairs of words in **unreduced** training data sentences, where baseNP boundaries define whether gaps fall into the S, C, E, B or N categories. The probability of a baseNP sequence in an unreduced sentence S is then:

$$\prod_{i=2 \ldots n} \hat{P}(G_i \mid w_{i-1}, t_{i-1}, w_i, t_i, c_i) \qquad (19)$$

The estimation method is analogous to that described in the sparse data section of this paper. The method is similar to that described in (Ramshaw and Marcus 95; Church 88), where baseNP detection is also framed as a tagging problem.

2.6 Summary of the Model

The probability of a parse tree T, given a sentence S, is:

$$P(T|S) = P(B, D|S) = P(B|S) \times P(D|S, B)$$

The denominator in Equation (9) is not actually constant for different baseNP sequences, but we make this approximation for the sake of efficiency and simplicity. In practice this is a good approximation because most baseNP boundaries are very well defined, so parses which have high enough $P(B|S)$ to be among the highest scoring parses for a sentence tend to have identical or very similar baseNPs. Parses are ranked by the following quantity[9]:

$$\hat{P}(B|S) \times \mathcal{N}(D|S, B) \qquad (20)$$

Equations (19) and (11) define $\hat{P}(B|S)$ and $\mathcal{N}(D|S, B)$. The parser finds the tree which maximises (20) subject to the hard constraint that dependencies cannot cross.

[9]In fact we also model the set of unary productions, U, in the tree, which are of the form $P \rightarrow < C_1 >$. This introduces an additional term, $\hat{P}(U|B, S)$, into (20).

2.7 Some Further Improvements to the Model

This section describes two modifications which improve the model's performance.

- In addition to conditioning on whether dependencies cross commas, a single constraint concerning punctuation is introduced. If for any constituent `Z` in the chart `Z → <.. X Y ..>` two of its children `X` and `Y` are separated by a comma, then the last word in `Y` must be directly followed by a comma, or must be the last word in the sentence. In training data 96% of commas follow this rule. The rule also has the benefit of improving efficiency by reducing the number of constituents in the chart.
- The model we have described thus far takes the single best sequence of tags from the tagger, and it is clear that there is potential for better integration of the tagger and parser. We have tried two modifications. First, the current estimation methods treat occurrences of the same word with different POS tags as effectively distinct types. Tags can be ignored when lexical information is available by defining

$$C(a, c) = \sum_{b, d \epsilon \mathcal{T}} C(\langle a, b \rangle, \langle c, d \rangle) \qquad (21)$$

where $\mathcal{T}$ is the set of all tags. Hence $C(a, c)$ is the number of times that the words a and c occur in the same sentence, ignoring their tags. The other definitions in (13) are similarly redefined, with POS tags only being used when backing off from lexical information. This makes the parser less sensitive to tagging errors.

Second, for each word w_i the tagger can provide the distribution of tag probabilities $P(t_i|S)$ (given the previous two words are tagged as in the best overall sequence of tags) rather than just the first best tag. The score for a parse in equation (20) then has an additional term, $\prod_{i=1}^{n} P(t_i|S)$, the product of probabilities of the tags which it contains.

Ideally we would like to integrate POS tagging into the parsing model rather than treating it as a separate stage. This is an area for future research.

3 The Parsing Algorithm

The parsing algorithm is a simple bottom-up chart parser. There is no grammar as such, although in practice any dependency with a triple of non-terminals which has not been seen in training data will get zero probability. Thus the parser searches through the space of all trees with non-terminal triples seen in training data. Probabilities of baseNPs in the chart are calculated using (19), while probabilities for other constituents are derived from the dependencies and baseNPs that they contain. A dynamic programming algorithm is used: if two proposed constituents span the same set of words, have the same label, head, and distance from

MODEL	$\leq$ 40 Words (2245 sentences)					$\leq$ 100 Words (2416 sentences)				
	LR	LP	CBs	0 CBs	$\leq$ 2 CBs	LR	LP	CBs	0 CBs	$\leq$ 2 CBs
(1)	84.9%	84.9%	1.32	57.2%	80.8%	84.3%	84.3%	1.53	54.7%	77.8%
(2)	85.4%	85.5%	1.21	58.4%	82.4%	84.8%	84.8%	1.41	55.9%	79.4%
(3)	85.5%	85.7%	1.19	59.5%	82.6%	85.0%	85.1%	1.39	56.8%	79.6%
(4)	85.8%	86.3%	1.14	59.9%	83.6%	85.3%	85.7%	1.32	57.2%	80.8%
SPATTER	84.6%	84.9%	1.26	56.6%	81.4%	84.0%	84.3%	1.46	54.0%	78.8%

Table 3: Results on Section 23 of the WSJ Treebank. **(1)** is the basic model; **(2)** is the basic model with the punctuation rule described in section 2.7; **(3)** is model (2) with POS tags ignored when lexical information is present; **(4)** is model (3) with probability distributions from the POS tagger. **LR/LP** = labeled recall/precision. **CBs** is the average number of crossing brackets per sentence. **0 CBs, $\leq$ 2 CBs** are the percentage of sentences with 0 or $\leq$ 2 crossing brackets respectively.

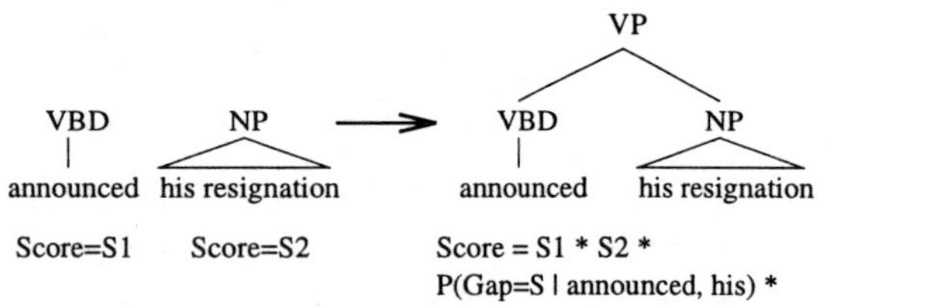

Figure 4: Diagram showing how two constituents join to form a new constituent. Each operation gives two new probability terms: one for the baseNP gap tag between the two constituents, and the other for the dependency between the head words of the two constituents.

Distance Measure	Lexical Information	LR	LP	CBs
Yes	Yes	85.0%	85.1%	1.39
Yes	No	76.1%	76.6%	2.26
No	Yes	80.9%	83.6%	1.51

Table 4: The contribution of various components of the model. The results are for all sentences of $\leq$ 100 words in section 23 using model (3). For 'no lexical information' all estimates are based on POS tags alone. For 'no distance measure' the distance measure is Question 1 alone (i.e. whether $\bar{w}_j$ precedes or follows $\bar{w}_{h_j}$).

the head to the left and right end of the constituent, then the lower probability constituent can be safely discarded. Figure 4 shows how constituents in the chart combine in a bottom-up manner.

4 Results

The parser was trained on sections 02 - 21 of the Wall Street Journal portion of the Penn Treebank (Marcus et al. 93) (approximately 40,000 sentences), and tested on section 23 (2,416 sentences). For comparison SPATTER (Magerman 95; Jelinek et al. 94) was also tested on section 23. We use the PARSEVAL measures (Black et al. 91) to compare performance:

Labeled Precision $= \frac{number\ of\ correct\ constituents\ in\ proposed\ parse}{number\ of\ constituents\ in\ proposed\ parse}$

Labeled Recall $= \frac{number\ of\ correct\ constituents\ in\ proposed\ parse}{number\ of\ constituents\ in\ treebank\ parse}$

Crossing Brackets = number of constituents which violate constituent boundaries with a constituent in the treebank parse.

For a constituent to be 'correct' it must span the same set of words (ignoring punctuation, i.e. all tokens tagged as commas, colons or quotes) and have the same label[10] as a constituent in the treebank parse. Four configurations of the parser were tested: **(1)** The basic model; **(2)** The basic model with the punctuation rule described in section 2.7; **(3)** Model (2) with tags ignored when lexical information is present, as described in 2.7; and **(4)** Model (3) also using the full probability distributions for POS tags. We should emphasise that test data outside of section 23 was used for all development of the model, avoiding the danger of implicit training on section 23. Table 3 shows the results of the tests. Table 4 shows results which indicate how different parts of the system contribute to performance.

4.1 Performance Issues

All tests were made on a Sun SPARCServer 1000E, using 100% of a 60Mhz SuperSPARC processor. The parser uses around 180 megabytes of memory, and training on 40,000 sentences (essentially extracting the co-occurrence counts from the corpus) takes under 15 minutes. Loading the hash table of bigram counts into memory takes approximately 8 minutes.

Two strategies are employed to improve parsing efficiency. First, a constant probability threshold is used while building the chart – any constituents with lower probability than this threshold are discarded. If a parse is found, it must be the highest ranked parse by the model (as all constituents discarded have lower probabilities than this parse and could

[10] SPATTER collapses ADVP and PRT to the same label, for comparison we also removed this distinction when calculating scores.

not, therefore, be part of a higher probability parse). If no parse is found, the threshold is lowered and parsing is attempted again. The process continues until a parse is found.

Second, a beam search strategy is used. For each span of words in the sentence the probability, P_h, of the highest probability constituent is recorded. All other constituents spanning the same words must have probability greater than $\frac{P_h}{\beta}$ for some constant beam size β – constituents which fall out of this beam are discarded. The method risks introducing search-errors, but in practice efficiency can be greatly improved with virtually no loss of accuracy. Table 5 shows the trade-off between speed and accuracy as the beam is narrowed.

Beam Size β	Speed Sentences/minute	LR	LP	CBs
1000	118	84.9%	85.1%	1.39
150	166	84.8%	85.1%	1.38
20	217	84.7%	85.0%	1.40
3	261	84.1%	84.5%	1.44
1.5	283	83.7%	84.1%	1.48
1.2	289	83.5%	83.9%	1.50

Table 5: The trade-off between speed and accuracy as the beam-size is varied. Model (3) was used for this test on all sentences $\leq$ 100 words in section 23.

5 Conclusions and Future Work

We have shown that a simple statistical model based on dependencies between words can parse Wall Street Journal news text with high accuracy. The method is equally applicable to tree or dependency representations of syntactic structures.

There are many possibilities for improvement, which is encouraging. More sophisticated estimation techniques such as deleted interpolation should be tried. Estimates based on relaxing the distance measure could also be used for smoothing – at present we only back-off on words. The distance measure could be extended to capture more context, such as other words or tags in the sentence. Finally, the model makes no account of valency.

Acknowledgements

I would like to thank Mitch Marcus, Jason Eisner, Dan Melamed and Adwait Ratnaparkhi for many useful discussions, and for comments on earlier versions of this paper. I would also like to thank David Magerman for his help with testing SPATTER.

References

E. Black et al. 1991. A Procedure for Quantitatively Comparing the Syntactic Coverage of English Grammars. *Proceedings of the February 1991 DARPA Speech and Natural Language Workshop.*

T. Briscoe and J. Carroll. 1993. Generalized LR Parsing of Natural Language (Corpora) with Unification-Based Grammars. *Computational Linguistics*, 19(1):25-60.

K. Church. 1988. A Stochastic Parts Program and Noun Phrase Parser for Unrestricted Text. *Second Conference on Applied Natural Language Processing, ACL.*

M. Collins and J. Brooks. 1995. Prepositional Phrase Attachment through a Backed-off Model. *Proceedings of the Third Workshop on Very Large Corpora*, pages 27-38.

D. Hindle and M. Rooth. 1993. Structural Ambiguity and Lexical Relations. *Computational Linguistics*, 19(1):103-120.

F. Jelinek. 1990. Self-organized Language Modeling for Speech Recognition. In *Readings in Speech Recognition.* Edited by Waibel and Lee. Morgan Kaufmann Publishers.

F. Jelinek, J. Lafferty, D. Magerman, R. Mercer, A. Ratnaparkhi, S. Roukos. 1994. Decision Tree Parsing using a Hidden Derivation Model. *Proceedings of the 1994 Human Language Technology Workshop*, pages 272-277.

J. Lafferty, D. Sleator and, D. Temperley. 1992. Grammatical Trigrams: A Probabilistic Model of Link Grammar. *Proceedings of the 1992 AAAI Fall Symposium on Probabilistic Approaches to Natural Language.*

D. Magerman. 1995. Statistical Decision-Tree Models for Parsing. *Proceedings of the 33rd Annual Meeting of the Association for Computational Linguistics*, pages 276-283.

D. Magerman and M. Marcus. 1991. Pearl: A Probabilistic Chart Parser. *Proceedings of the 1991 European ACL Conference*, Berlin, Germany.

M. Marcus, B. Santorini and M. Marcinkiewicz. 1993. Building a Large Annotated Corpus of English: the Penn Treebank. *Computational Linguistics*, 19(2):313-330.

F. Pereira and Y. Schabes. 1992. Inside-Outside Reestimation from Partially Bracketed Corpora. *Proceedings of the 30th Annual Meeting of the Association for Computational Linguistics*, pages 128-135.

L. Ramshaw and M. Marcus. 1995. Text Chunking using Transformation-Based Learning. *Proceedings of the Third Workshop on Very Large Corpora*, pages 82-94.

A. Ratnaparkhi. 1996. A Maximum Entropy Model for Part-Of-Speech Tagging. *Conference on Empirical Methods in Natural Language Processing*, May 1996.

M. M. Wood. 1993. *Categorial Grammars*, Routledge.

Two Sources of Control over the Generation of Software Instructions*

Anthony Hartley
Language Centre
University of Brighton, Falmer
Brighton BN1 9PH, UK
afh@itri.bton.ac.uk

Cécile Paris†
Information Technology Research Institute
University of Brighton, Lewes Road
Brighton BN2 4AT, UK
clp@itri.brighton.ac.uk

1 Introduction

Our work addresses the generation of software manuals in French and English, starting from a semantic model of the task to be documented (Paris et al., 1995). Our prime concern is to be able to exercise control over the mapping from the task model to the generated text. We set out to establish whether the task model alone is sufficient to control the linguistic output of a text generation system, or whether additional control is required. In this event, an obvious source to explore is the communicative purpose of the author, which is not necessarily constant throughout a manual. Indeed, in a typical software manual, it is possible to distinguish at least three sections, each with a different purpose: a tutorial containing exercises for new users, a series of step-by-step instructions for the major tasks to be accomplished, and a ready-reference summary of the commands.

We need, therefore, to characterise the linguistic expressions of the different elements of the task model, and to establish whether these expressions are sensitive or not to their context, that is, the functional section in which they appear. This paper presents the results of an analysis we conducted to this end on a corpus of software instructions in French.

2 Methodology

The methodology we employed is similar to that endorsed by (Biber, 1995). It is summarised as follows:

1. Collect the texts and note their situational characteristics. We consider two such characteristics: task structure and communicative purpose.
2. Identify the range of linguistic features to be included in the analysis;
3. Code the corpus in terms of the selected features;
4. Compute the frequency count of each linguistic feature;
5. Identify co-occurrences between linguistic features and the situational characteristics under consideration.

We first carried out a classical sublanguage analysis on our corpus as a whole, without differentiating between any of the situational characteristics (Hartley and Paris, 1995). This initial description was necessary to give us a clear statement of the linguistic potential required of our text generator, to which we could relate any restrictions on language imposed by situational variables. Thus we can account for language restrictions by appealing to general discourse principles, in keeping with the recommendations of (Kittredge, 1995) and (Biber, 1995) for the definition of sublanguages.

We then correlated task elements with grammatical features. Finally, where linguistic realisation was under-determined by task structure alone, we established whether the communicative purpose provided more discriminating control over the linguistic resources available.

3 Linguistic Framework: Systemic Functional Linguistics

Our analysis was carried out within the framework of Systemic-Functional Linguistics (SFL) (Halliday, 1978; Halliday, 1985) which views language as a resource for the creation of meaning. SFL stratifies meaning into context and language. The strata of the linguistic resources are organised into networks of choices, each choice resulting in a different meaning *realised* (i.e., expressed) by appropriate structures. The emphasis is on *paradigmatic* choices, as opposed to *syntagmatic* structures. Choices made in

* This work is partially supported by the Engineering and Physical Sciences Research Council (EPSRC) Grant J19221, by BC/DAAD ARC Project 293, by the Commission of the European Union Grant LRE-62009, and by the Office of Naval Research Grant N00014-96-1-0465.

† Starting this fall, Dr. Paris' address will be CSIRO, Division of Information Technology, Sydney Laboratory, Building E6B, Macquarie University Campus, North Ryde, Sydney, NSW 2113, Australia.

each stratum constrain the choices available in the stratum beneath. Context thus constrains language.

This framework was chosen for several reasons. First, the organisation of linguistic resources according to this principle is well-suited to natural language generation, where the starting point is necessarily a communicative goal, and the task is to find the most appropriate expression for the intended meaning (Matthiessen and Bateman, 1991). Second, a functional perspective offers an advantage for multilingual text generation, because of its ability to achieve a level of linguistic description which holds across languages more effectively than do structurally-based accounts. The approach has been shown capable of supporting the sharing of linguistic resources between languages as structurally distinct as English and Japanese (Bateman et al., 1991a; Bateman et al., 1991b). It is therefore reasonable to expect that at least the same degree of commonality of description is achievable between English and French within this framework. Finally, KPML (Bateman, 1994), the tactical generator we employ, is based on SFL, and it is thus appropriate for us to characterise the corpus in terms immediately applicable to our generator.

4 Coding features

Our lexico-grammatical coding was done using the networks and features of the Nigel grammar (Halliday, 1985). We focused on four main concerns, guided by previous work on instructional texts, e.g., (Lehrberger, 1986; Plum et al., 1990; Ghadessy, 1993; Kosseim and Lapalme, 1994).

- *Relations between processes*: to determine whether textual cohesion was achieved through conjunctives or through relations implicit in the task structure elements. Among the features considered were clause dependency and conjunction type.
- *Agency*: to see whether the actor performing or enabling a particular action is clearly identified, and whether the reader is explicitly addressed. We coded here for features such as voice and agent types.
- *Mood, modality and polarity*: to find out the extent to which actions are presented to the reader as being desirable, possible, mandatory, or prohibited. We coded for both true and implicit negatives, and for both personal and impersonal expressions of modality.
- *Process types*: to see how the domain is construed in terms of actions on the part of the user and the software. We coded for sub-categories of material, mental, verbal and relational processes.

5 The Corpus

The analysis was conducted on the French version of the Macintosh MacWrite manual (Kaehler, 1983). The manual is derived from an English source by a process of *adaptive translation* (Sager, 1993), i.e., one which localises the text to the expectations of the target readership. The fact that the translation is adaptive rather than literal gives us confidence in using this manual for our analysis.[1] Furthermore, we know that Macintosh documentation undergoes thorough local quality control. It certainly conforms to the principles of good documentation established by current research on technical documentation and on the needs of end-users, e.g., (Carroll, 1994; Hammond, 1994), in that it supplies clear and concise information for the task at hand. Finally, we have been assured by French users of the software that they consider this particular manual to be well written and to bear no unnatural trace of its origins.

Technical manuals within a specific domain constitute a sublanguage, e.g., (Kittredge, 1982; Sager et al., 1980). An important defining property of a sublanguage is that of closure, both lexical and syntactic. Lexical closure has been demonstrated by, for example, (Kittredge, 1987), who shows that after as few as the first 2000 words of a sublanguage text, the number of new word types increases little if at all. Other work, e.g., (Biber, 1988; Biber, 1989) and (Grishman and Kittredge, 1986) illustrates the property of syntactic closure, which means that generally available constructions just do not occur in this or that sublanguage. In the light of these results, we considered a corpus of 15000 words to be adequate for our purposes, at least for an initial analysis.

The MacWrite manual is organised into three chapters, corresponding to the three different sections identified earlier: a tutorial, a series of step-by-step instructions for the major word-processing tasks, and a ready-reference summary of the commands. We omitted the tutorial because the generation of such text is not our concern, retaining the other two chapters which provide the user with generic instructions for performing relevant tasks, and descriptions of the commands available within MacWrite. The overlap in information between the two chapters offers opportunities to observe differences in the linguistic expressions of the same task structure elements in different contexts.

[1] We would have preferred to use a manual which originated in French to exclude all possibility of interference from a source language, but this proved impossible. Surprisingly, it appears that large French companies often have their documents authored in English by francophones and subsequently translated into French. One large French software house that we contacted does author its documentation in French, but had registered considerable customer dissatisfaction with its quality. We decided, therefore, that their material would be unsuitable for our purposes.

Goals: La sélection
Gloss: Selection

Pour sélectionner un mot, (faites un double-clic sur le mot)
Gloss: To select a word, (do a double-click on the word)

Functions: (Fermer –) Cet article permet de fermer une fenêtre activée
Gloss: (Close –) This command enables you to close the active window

Constraints: Si vous donnez à votre document le titre d'un document déjà existant, (une zone de dialogue apparaît)
Gloss: If you give your document the title of an existing document, (a dialog box appears)

Results: (Choisissez Coller dans le menu Edition –) Une copie du contenu du presse-papiers apparaît
Gloss: (Choose Paste from the Edit menu –) A copy of the content of the clipboard appears

Substeps: Fermez la fenêtre Rechercher
Gloss: Close the Find window

Ensuite, on ouvre le document de destination
Gloss: Next, one opens the target document

Figure 1: Examples of task element expressions

6 Task Structure

Task structure is constituted by five types of task elements, which we define below. We used the notion of task structure element both as a contextual feature for the analysis and to determine the segmentation of the text into units. Each unit is taken to be the expression of a single task element.

Our definition of the task elements is based on the concepts and relations commonly chosen to represent a task structure (a goal and its associated plan), e.g., (Fikes and Nilsson, 1971; Sacerdoti, 1977), and on related research, e.g., (Kosseim and Lapalme, 1994). Our generator produces instructions from an underlying semantic knowledge base which uses this representation (Paris et al., 1995). To generate an instruction for performing a task is to chose some task elements to be expressed and linearise them so that they form a coherent set for a given goal the user might have. We distinguish the following elements, and provide examples of them in Figure 1:[2]

goals: actions that users will adopt as goals and which motivate the use of a plan.

functions: actions that represent the functionality of an interface object (such as a menu item). A function is closely related to a goal, in that it is also an action that the user may want to perform. However, the function is accessed through the interface object, and not through a plan.

constraints and preconditions: states which must hold before a plan can be employed successfully. The domain model distinguishes constraints (states which cannot be achieved through planning) and preconditions (states which can be achieved through planning). We do not make this distinction in the linguistic analysis and regroup these related task structure elements under one label. We decided to proceed in this way to determine at first how constraints in general are expressed. Moreover, it is not always clear *from the text* which type of constraint is expressed. Drawing too fine distinctions in the corpus analysis at this point, in the absence of a test for assigning a unit to one of these constraint types, would have rendered the results of the analysis more subjective and thus less reliable.

results: states which arise as planned or unplanned effects of carrying out a plan. While it might be important to separate planned and unplanned effects in the underlying representation, we again abstract over them in the lexicogrammatical coding.

[2]The text in parentheses in the Figure is part of the linguistic context of the task element rather than the element itself.

sub-steps: actions which contribute to the execution of the plan. If the sub-steps are not primitive, they can themselves be achieved through other plans.

7 The Coding Procedure

No tools exist to automate a functional analysis of text, which makes coding a large body of text a time-consuming task. We first performed a detailed coding of units of texts on approximately 25% of the corpus, or about 400 units,[3] using the WAG coder (O'Donnell, 1995), a tool designed to facilitate a functional analysis.

We then used a public-domain concordance program, MonoConc (Barlow, 1994), to verify the representativeness of the results. We enumerated the realisations of those features that the first analysis had shown as marked, and produced KWIC[4] listings for each set of realisations. We found that the second analysis corroborated the results of the first, consistent with the nature of sublanguages.

8 Distribution of Grammatical Features over Task Structure and Communicative Purpose

We examined the correlations between lexico-grammatical realisations and task elements and communicative purpose. The results are best expressed using tables generated by WAG: given any system, WAG splits the codings into a number of sets, one for each feature in that system. Percentages and means are computed, and the sets are compared statistically, using the standard T-test. WAG displays the results with an indicator of how statistically significant a value is compared to the combined means in the other sets. The counts were all done using the local mean, that is, the feature count is divided by the total number of codings which select that feature's system. Full definitions of the features can be found in (Halliday, 1985; Bateman et al., 1990).

In some cases, the type of task element is on its own sufficient to determine, or at least strongly constrain, its linguistic realisation. The limited space available here allows us to provide only a small number of examples, shown in Figure 2. We see that the use of modals is excluded in the expression of function, result and constraint, whereas goal and substep do admit modals. As far as the polarity system is concerned, negation is effectively ruled out for function, goal and substep. Finally, with respect to the mood system, only substep can be realised through imperatives.

In other cases, however, we observe a diversity of realisations. We highlight here three cases: modality in goal, polarity in constraint, and mood in substep. In such cases, we must appeal to another source of control over the apparently available choices. We have looked to the construct of *genre* (Martin, 1992) to provide this additional control, on two grounds: (1) since genres are distinguished by their communicative purposes, we can view each of the functional sections already identified as a distinct genre; (2) genre is presented as controlling text structure and realisation. In Martin's view, genre is defined as a staged, goal-oriented social process realised through register, the context of situation, which in turn is realised in language to achieve the goals of a text. Genre is responsible for the selection of a text structure in terms of task elements. As part of the realisation process, generic choices preselect a register associated with particular elements of text structure, which in turn preselect lexico-grammatical features. The coding of our text in terms genre and task elements thus allows us to establish the role played by genre in the realisations of the task elements. It will also allow us to determine the text structures appropriate in each genre, a study we are currently undertaking. This is consistent with other accounts of text structure for text generation in technical domains, e.g., (McKeown, 1985; Paris, 1993; Kittredge et al., 1991).

For those cases where the realisation remains under-determined by the task element type, we conducted a finer-grained analysis, by overlaying a genre partition on the undifferentiated data. We distinguished earlier two genres with which we are concerned: ready-reference and step-by-step. In the manual analysed, we recognised two more specific communicative purposes in the step-by-step section: to enable the reader to perform a task, and to increase the reader's knowledge about the task, the way to achieve it, or the properties of the system as a whole. Because of their distinct communicative purposes, we again feel justified in calling these genres. We label them respectively *procedure* and *elaboration*. The intention that the reader should recognise the differences in function of each section is underscored by the use of distinctive typographical devices, such as fonts and lay-out.[5]

The first step at this stage of the analysis was to establish whether there was an effective overlap in task elements among the three genres under consideration. The results of this step is shown in Figure 3. Sub-step and goal are found in all three genres, while constraint, result and function occur in both ready-reference and elaboration but are absent from procedure.

The next step was to undertake a comparative

[3] The authors followed guidelines for identifying task element units which had yielded consistent results when used by students coding other corpora.

[4] Key Word In Context

[5] See (Hartley and Paris, 1995) for examples extracted from the manuals.

Modal-System	Function	Result	Constraint	Goal	Substep
modal	0%	1%	0%	24%	16%
non-modal	100%	99%	100%	76%	84%
polarity					
positive	100%	90%	68%	97%	97%
negative	0%	10%	32%	3%	3%
mood-system					
declarative	100%	100%	100%	100%	24%
imperative	0%	0%	0%	0%	76%

Figure 2: Selective realisations of task elements

	Ready-Reference	Procedure	Elaboration
Sub-step	37%	77%	42%
Goal	11%	23%	14%
Constraint	10%	0%	14%
Result	23%	0%	27%
Function	11%	0%	3%

Figure 3: Distribution of task structure elements over genres

analysis of the lexico-grammatical features found in the three genres. This analysis indicated that the language employed in these different sections of the text varies greatly. We summarise here the two genres that are strongly contrasted: procedure and ready-reference. Elaboration shares features with both of these.

procedure: The top-level goal of the user is expressed as a nominalisation. Actions to be achieved by the reader are almost exclusively realised by imperatives, directly addressing the reader. These actions are mostly material directed actions, and there are no causatives. Few modals are employed, and, when they are, it is to express obligation impersonally. The polarity of processes is always positive. Procedure employs mostly independent clauses, and, when clause complexes are used, the conjunctions are mostly purpose (linking a user goal and an action) and alternative (linking two user actions or two goals).

ready-reference: In this genre, all task elements are always realised through clauses. The declarative mood predominates, with few imperatives addressing the reader. Virtually all the causatives occur here. On the dimension of modality, the emphasis is on personal possibility, rather than obligation, and on inclination. We find in this genre most of the verbal processes, entirely absent from procedure. Ready-reference is more weighted than procedure towards dependent clauses, and is particularly marked by the presence of temporal conjunctions.

The analysis so far demonstrates that genre, like task structure, provides some measure of control over the linguistic resources but that neither of these alone is sufficient to drive a generation system. The final step was therefore to look at the realisations of the task elements differentiated by genre, in cases where the realisation was not strongly determined by the task element.

We refer the reader back to Figure 2, and the under-constrained cases of modality in goal, polarity in constraint, and mood in substep. Figure 4 shows the realisations the task element goal with respect to the modal system, which brings into sharp relief the absence of modality from procedure. Figure 5 presents the realisations by genre of the polarity system for constraint. We observe that only positive polarity occurs in ready-reference. Finally, we note from Figure 6 that the realisation of substeps is heavily loaded in favour of imperatives in procedure.

These figures show that genre does indeed provide useful additional control over the expression of task elements, which can be exploited by a text generation system. Neither task structure nor genre alone is sufficient to provide this control, but, taken together, they offer a real prospect of adequate control over the output of a text generator.

	Procedure	Ready-Reference	Elaboration
Non-modal	100.0%	75.0%	72.6%
Modal	0.0%	25.0%	28.4%

Figure 4: Genre-related differences in the modal system for goal

	Ready-Reference	Elaboration
Negative	0.0%	41.7%
Positive	100%	58.3%

Figure 5: Genre-related differences in the polarity system for constraint

	Procedure	Ready-Reference	Elaboration
Imperative	97.3%	44.4%	77.6%
Declarative	2.7%	55.6%	22.4%

Figure 6: Genre-related differences in the mood system for substep

9 Related Work

The results from our linguistic analysis are consistent with other research on sublanguages in the instructions domain, in both French and English, e.g., (Kosseim and Lapalme, 1994; Paris and Scott, 1994). Our analysis goes beyond previous work by identifying within the discourse context the means for exercising explicit control over a text generator.

An interesting difference with respect to previous descriptions is the use of the true (or direct) imperative to express an action in the procedure genre, as results from (Paris and Scott, 1994) seem to indicate that the infinitive-form of the imperative is preferred in French. These results, however, were obtained from a corpus of instructions mostly for domestic appliances as opposed to software manuals. Furthermore the use of the infinitive-form in instructions in general as observed by (Kocourek, 1982) is declining, as some of the conventions already common in English technical writing are being adopted by French technical writers, e.g., (Timbal-Duclaux, 1990).

We also note that the patterns of realisations uncovered in our analysis follow the principle of good technical writing practice known as the *minimalist approach*, e.g., (Carroll, 1994; Hammond, 1994). Moreover, we observe that our corpus does not exhibit shortcomings identified in a Systemic Functional analysis of English software manuals (Plum et al., 1990), such as a high incidence of agentless passive and a failure to distinguish the function of informing from that of instructing.

Other work has focused on the cross-linguistic realisations of two specific semantic relations (*generation* and *enablement*) (Delin et al., 1994; Delin et al., 1996), in a more general corpus of instructions for household appliances. Our work focuses on the single application domain of software instructions. However, it takes into consideration the whole task structure and looks at the realisation of semantic elements as found in the knowledge base, instead of two semantic relations not explicitly present in the underlying semantic model.

10 Conclusion

In this paper we have shown how genre and task structure provide two essential sources of control over the text generation process. Genre does so by constraining the selection of the task elements and the range of their expressions. These elements, which are the procedural representation of the user's tasks, constitute a layer of control which mediates between genre and text, but which, without genre, cannot control the grammar adequately.

The work presented here is informing the development of our text generator by specifying the necessary coverage of the French grammar to be implemented, the required discourse structures, and the mechanisms needed to control them. We continue to explore further situational and contextual factors which might allow a system to fully control its available linguistic resources.

References

Michael Barlow. 1994. *A Guide to MonoConc.* Athelston, Houston, TX.

John A. Bateman, Robert T. Kasper, Johanna D. Moore, and Richard Whitney. 1990. A general organization of knowledge for natural language processing: The Penman Upper Model. Technical report, USC/ISI, March.

John A. Bateman, Christian M.I.M. Matthiessen, Keizo Nanri, and Licheng Zeng. 1991a. The re-use of linguistic resources across languages in multilingual generation components. In *Proceedings of the 1991 International Joint Conference on Artificial Intelligence, Volume 2, Sydney, Australia*, pages 966 – 971. Morgan Kaufmann Publishers.

John A. Bateman, Christian M.I.M. Matthiessen, Keizo Nanri, and Licheng Zeng. 1991b. Multilingual text generation: an architecture based on functional typology. In *International Conference on Current Issues in Computational Linguistics*, Penang, Malaysia.

John A. Bateman. 1994. KPML: The KOMET-Penman (Multilingual) Development Environment. Technical report, Institut für Integrierte Publikations- und Informationssysteme (IPSI), GMD, Darmstadt, September. Release 0.6.

Douglas Biber. 1988. *Variation Across Speech and Writing*. Cambridge University Press, Cambridge UK.

Douglas Biber. 1989. A typology of English texts. *Linguistics*, 27:3–43.

Douglas Biber. 1995. *Dimensions of Register Variation: A Cross-linguistic comparison*. Cambridge University Press, Cambridge UK.

John Carroll. 1994. Techniques for minimalist documentation and user interface design. In *Quality of Technical Documentation*, pages 67–75. Rodopi, Amsterdam.

Judy Delin, Anthony Hartley, Cécile Paris, Donia Scott, and Keith Vander Linden. 1994. Expressing procedural relationships in multilingual instructions. In *Proceedings of the Seventh International Workshop on Natural Language Generation*, Kennebunkport, MN, 21–24 June 1994, pages 61–70.

Judy Delin, Donia Scott, and Anthony Hartley. 1996. Language-specific mappings from semantics to syntax. In *Proceedings of the 16th International Conference on Computational Linguistics (COLING-96)*, Copenhagen, Denmark, August.

R. E. Fikes and Nils Nilsson. 1971. STRIPS: a new approach to the application of theorem proving to problem solving. *Artificial Intelligence*, 2:189–208.

Mohsen Ghadessy, editor. 1993. *Register Analysis: Theory and Practice*. Frances Pinter, London.

Ralph Grishman and Richard Kittredge, editors. 1986. *Analyzing Language in Restricted Domains*. Lawrence Erlbaum Associates, Hillsdale, New Jersey.

Michael A. K. Halliday. 1978. *Language as a Social Semiotic: The Social Interpretation of Language and Meaning*. Edward Arnold, London.

Michael A. K. Halliday. 1985. *An Introduction to Functional Grammar*. Edward Arnold, London.

Nick Hammond. 1994. Less is More: The Minimalist Approach. Usability Now! A Guide to Usability. Published by the Open University and the Department of Trade and Industry.

Anthony Hartley and Cécile Paris. 1995. French corpus analysis and grammatical description. Technical Report Project IED/4/1/5827, ITRI, November.

Carol Kaehler. 1983. *Macintosh MacWrite*. Apple Seedrin, Les Ulis, France.

Richard Kittredge, Tanya Korelsky, and Owen Rambow. 1991. On the Need for Domain Communication Knowledge. *Computational Intelligence*, 7(4):305–314, November.

Richard Kittredge. 1982. Variation and Homogeneity of Sublanguages. In Richard Kittredge and J. Lehrberger, editors, *Sublanguage: Studies of language in restricted semantic domains*, pages 107–137. de Gruyter, Berlin and New York.

Richard Kittredge. 1987. The significance of sublanguage for automatic translation. In Sergei Nirenburg, editor, *Machine Translation: Theoretical and methodological issues*, pages 59–67. Cambridge University Press, London.

Richard Kittredge. 1995. Efficiency vs. Generality in Interlingual Design: Some Linguistic Considerations. In *the Working notes of the IJCAI-95 Workshop on Multilingual Text Generation*, August 20–21, Montréal, Canada.

Rostislav Kocourek. 1982. *La langue française de la technique et de la science*. Brandstetter Verlag, Wiesbaden, Germany.

Leila Kosseim and Guy Lapalme. 1994. Content and rhetorical status selection in instructional texts. In *Proceedings of the Seventh International Workshop on Natural Language Generation*, Kennebunkport, MN, 21–24 June 1994, pages 53–60.

John Lehrberger. 1986. Sublanguage Analysis. In Ralph Grishman and Richard Kittredge, editors, *Analyzing Language in Restricted Domains*, pages 19–38. Lawrence Erlbaum Associates, Hillsdale, New Jersey.

James R. Martin. 1992. *English text: systems and structure*. Benjamins, Amsterdam.

Christian M.I.M. Matthiessen and John A. Bateman. 1991. *Text generation and systemic-functional linguistics: experiences from English and Japanese*. Frances Pinter Publishers and St. Martin's Press, London and New York.

Kathleen R. McKeown. 1985. *Text Generation.* Cambridge University Press, New York.

Michael O'Donnell. 1995. From Corpus to Codings: Semi-Automating the Acquisition of Linguistic Features. Proceedings of the AAAI Spring Symposium on Empirical Methods in Discourse Interpretation and Generation, Stanford University, California, March 27 - 29, March.

Cécile Paris and Donia Scott. 1994. Stylistic variation in multilingual instructions. In *Proceedings of the Seventh International Workshop on Natural Language Generation,* Kennebunkport, MN, 21–24 June 1994, pages 45 – 52.

Cécile Paris, Keith Vander Linden, Markus Fischer, Anthony Hartley, Lyn Pemberton, Richard Power, and Donia Scott. 1995. A support tool for writing multilingual instructions. In *Proceedings of the Fourteenth International Joint Conference on Artificial Intelligence,* August 20–25, Montréal, Canada, pages 1398–1404.

Cécile L. Paris. 1993. *User Modelling in Text Generation.* Frances Pinter, London.

Guenter A. Plum, Christian M.I.M. Matthiessen, Michael A.K. Halliday, and Natalie Shea. 1990. The Electronic Discourse Analyzer Project: Report on Textual Analysis of FJ Manuals. Technical report, Fujitsu Australia Limited, Documentation Engineering Division. EDA Project Deliverables; Output 7.

Earl D. Sacerdoti. 1977. *A Structure for Plans and Behavior.* Elsevier, New York.

Juan C. Sager, David Dungworth, and Peter F. McDonald. 1980. *English Special Languages.* Brandstetter Verlag, Wiesbaden, Germany.

Juan C. Sager. 1993. *Language Engineering and Translation: Consequences of Automation.* John Benjamins Publishing Company, Amsterdam.

Louis Timbal-Duclaux. 1990. *La communication écrite scientifique et technique.* ESF, Paris, France.

Chart Generation

Martin Kay
Stanford University and
Xerox Palo Alto Research Center
kay@parc.xerox.com

Abstract

Charts constitute a natural uniform architecture for parsing and generation provided string position is replaced by a notion more appropriate to logical forms and that measures are taken to curtail generation paths containing semantically incomplete phrases.

1 Charts

Shieber (1988) showed that parsing charts can be also used in generation and raised the question, which we take up again here, of whether they constitute a natural uniform architecture for parsing and generation. In particular, we will be interested in the extent to which they bring to the generation process advantages comparable to those that make them attractive in parsing.

Chart parsing is not a well defined notion. The usual conception of it involves at least four related ideas:

Inactive edges. In context-free grammar, all phrases of a given category that cover a given part of the string are equivalent for the purposes of constructing larger phrases. Efficiency comes from collecting equivalent sets of phrases into (inactive) *edges* and constructing edges from edges rather than phrases from phrases.

Active edges. New phrases of whatever size can be built by considering existing edges pair-wise if provision is made for partial phrases. Partial phrases are collected into edges that are said to be *active* because they can be thought of as actively seeking material to complete them.

The algorithm schema. Newly created edges are placed on an *agenda*. Edges are moved from the agenda to the *chart* one by one until none remains to be moved. When an edge is moved, all interactions between it and edges already in the chart are considered and any new edges that they give rise to are added to the agenda.

Indexing. The positions in the string at which phrases begin and end can be used to index edges so that the algorithm schema need consider interactions only between adjacent pairs.

Chart parsing is attractive for the analysis of natural languages, as opposed to programming languages, for the way in which it treats ambiguity. Regardless of the number of alternative structures for a particular string that a given phrase participates in, it will be constructed once and only once. Although the number of structures of a string can grow exponentially with the length of the string, the number of edges that needs to be constructed grows only with the square of the string length and the whole parsing process can be accomplished in cubic time.

Innumerable variants of the basic chart parsing scheme are possible. For example, if there were languages with truly free word order, we might attempt to characterize them by rules like those of context-free grammar, but with a somewhat different interpretation. Instead of replacing nonterminal symbols in a derivation with strings from the right-hand side of corresponding rules, we would remove the nonterminal symbol and insert the symbols from the right-hand side of the rule at arbitrary places in the string.

A chart parser for languages with free word order would be a minor variant of the standard one. An edge would take the form X_v, where v is a vector with a bit for every word in the string and showing which of those words the edge covers. There is no longer any notion of adjacency so that there would be no indexing by string position. Interesting interactions occur between pairs of edges whose bit vectors have empty intersections, indicating that they cover disjoint sets of words. There can now be as many edges as bit-vectors and, not surprisingly, the computational complexity of the parsing process increases accordingly.

2 Generation

A parser is a transducer from strings to structures or logical forms. A generator, for our purposes, is the inverse. One way to think of it, therefore, is as a parser of structures or logical forms that delivers analyses in the form of strings. This view has the apparent disadvantage of putting insignificant differences in the syntax of a logical forms, such as the relative order of the arguments to symmetric operators, on the same footing as more significant facts about them. We know that it will not generally be possible to reduce logical expressions to a canonical form but this does not mean that we should expect our generator to be compromised, or even greatly delayed, by trivial distinctions. Considerations of this kind were, in part, responsible for the recent resurgence of interest in "flat" representations of logical form (Copestake *et al.*,1996) and for the representations used for transfer in Shake-and-Bake translation (Whitelock, 1992). They have made semantic formalisms like those now usually associated with Davison (Davidson, 1980, Parsons, 1990) attractive in artificial intelligence for many years (Hobbs 1985, Kay, 1970). Operationally, the attraction is that the notations can be analyzed largely as free word-order languages in the manner outlined above. Consider the expression (1)

(1) r: run(r), past(r), fast(r), arg1(r, j), name(j, John)

which we will take as a representation of the logical form of the sentences *John ran fast* and *John ran quickly*. It consists of a distinguished index (*r*) and a list of predicates whose relative order is immaterial. The distinguished index identifies this as a sentence that makes a claim about a running event. "John" is the name of the entity that stands in the 'arg1' relation to the running which took place in the past and which was fast. Nothing turns on these details which will differ with differing ontologies, logics, and views of semantic structure. What concerns us here is a procedure for generating a sentence from a structure of this general kind.

Assume that the lexicon contains entries like those in (2) in which the italicized arguments to the semantic predicates are variables.

(2)

Words	Cat	Semantics
John	np(*x*)	*x*: name(*x*, John)
ran	vp(*x*, *y*)	*x*: run(*x*), arg1(*x*, *y*), past(*x*)
fast	adv(*x*)	*x*: fast(*x*)
quickly	adv(*x*)	*x*: fast(*x*)

A *prima facie* argument for the utility of these particular words for expressing (1) can be made simply by noting that, *modulo* appropriate instantiation of the variables, the semantics of each of these words subsumes (1).

3 The Algorithm Schema

The entries in (2), with their variables suitably instantiated, become the initial entries of an agenda and we begin to move them to the chart in accordance with the algorithm schema, say in the order given.

The variables in the 'Cat' and 'Semantics' columns of (2) provide the essential link between syntax and semantics. The predicates that represent the semantics of a phrase will simply be the union of those representing the constituents. The rules that sanction a phrase (e.g. (3) below) show which variables from the two parts are to be identified.

When the entry for *John* is moved, no interactions are possible because the chart is empty. When *run* is moved, the sequence *John ran* is considered as a possible phrase on the basis of rule (3).

(3) s(*x*) → np(*y*), vp(*x*, *y*).

With appropriate replacements for variables, this maps onto the subset (4) of the original semantic specification in (1).

(4) r: run(r), past(r), arg1(r, j), name(j, John)

Furthermore it is a complete sentence. However, it does not count as an output to the generation process as a whole because it subsumes some but not all of (1). It therefore simply becomes a new edge on the agenda.

The string *ran fast* constitutes a verb phrase by virtue of rule (5) giving the semantics (6), and the phrase *ran quickly* with the same semantics is put on the agenda when the *quickly* edge is move to the chart.

(5) vp(*x*) → vp(*x*) adv(*x*)

(6) r: run(r), past(r), fast(r), arg1(r, *y*)

The agenda now contains the entries in (7).

(7)

Words	Cat	Semantics
John ran	s(r)	r: run(r), past(r), arg1(r, j), name(j, John)
ran fast	vp(r, j)	r: run(r), past(r), fast(r), arg1(r, j)
ran quickly	vp(r, j)	r: run(r), past(r), fast(r), arg1(r, j)

Assuming that adverbs modify verb phrases and not sentences, there will be no interactions when the *John ran* edge is moved to the chart.

When the edge for *ran fast* is moved, the possibility arises of creating the phrase *ran fast quickly* as well as *ran fast fast*. Both are rejected, however, on the grounds that they would involve using a predicate from the original semantic specification more than once. This would be similar to allowing a given word to be covered by overlapping phrases in free word-order parsing. We proposed eliminating this by means of a bit vector and the same technique applies here. The fruitful interactions that occur here are between *ran fast* and *ran quickly* on the one hand, and *John* on the other. Both give sentences whose semantics subsumes the entire input.

Several things are noteworthy about the process just outlined.

1. Nothing turns on the fact that it uses a primitive version of event semantics. A scheme in which the indices were handles referring to subexpressions in any variety of flat semantics could have been treated in the same way. Indeed, more conventional formalisms with richly recursive syntax could be converted to this form on the fly.
2. Because all our rules are binary, we make no use of active edges.
3. While it fits the conception of chart parsing given at the beginning of this paper, our generator does not involve string positions centrally in the chart representation. In this respect, it differs from the proposal of Shieber (1988) which starts with all word edges leaving and entering a single vertex. But there is essentially no information in such a representation. Neither the chart nor any other special data structure is required to capture the fact that a new phrase may be constructible out of any given pair, and in either order, if they meet certain syntactic and semantic criteria.
4. Interactions must be considered explicitly between new edges and all edges currently in the chart, because no indexing is used to identify the existing edges that could interact with a given new one.
5. The process is exponential in the worst case because, if a sentence contains a word with k modifiers, then a version it will be generated with each of the 2^k subsets of those modifiers, all but one of them being rejected when it is finally discovered that their semantics does not subsume the entire input. If the relative orders of the modifiers are unconstrained, matters only get worse.

Points 4 and 5 are serious flaws in our scheme for which we shall describe remedies. Point 2 will have some importance for us because it will turn out that the indexing scheme we propose will require the use of distinct active and inactive edges, even when the rules are all binary. We take up the complexity issue first, and then turn to how the efficiency of the generation chart might be enhanced through indexing.

4 Internal and External Indices

The exponential factor in the computational complexity of our generation algorithm is apparent in an example like (8).

(8) Newspaper reports said the tall young Polish athlete ran fast

The same set of predicates that generate this sentence clearly also generate the same sentence with deletion of all subsets of the words *tall*, *young*, and *Polish* for a total of 8 strings. Each is generated in its entirety, though finally rejected because it fails to account for all of the semantic material. The words *newspaper* and *fast* can also be deleted independently giving a grand total of 32 strings.

We concentrate on the phrase *tall young Polish athlete* which we assumed would be combined with the verb phrase *ran fast* by the rule (3). The distinguished index of the noun phrase, call it p, is identified with the variable *y* in the rule, but this variable is not associated with the syntactic category, s, on the left-hand side of the rule. The grammar has access to indices only through the variables that annotate grammatical categories in its rules, so that rules that incorporate this sentence into larger phrases can have no further access to the index p. We therefore say that p is *internal* to the sentence *the tall young Polish athlete ran fast*.

The index p would, of course, also be internal to the sentences *the young Polish athlete ran fast*, *the tall Polish athlete ran fast*, etc. However, in these cases, the semantic material remaining to be expressed contains predicates that refer to this internal index, say 'tall(p)', and 'young(p)'. While the lexicon may have words to express these predicates, the grammar has no way of associating their referents with the above noun phrases because the variables corresponding to those referents are internal. We conclude that, as a matter of principle, no edge should be constructed if the result of doing so would be to make internal an index occurring in part of the input semantics that the new phrase does not subsume. In other words, the semantics of a phrase must contain all predicates from the input specification that refer to any indices internal to it. This strategy does not prevent the generation of an exponential number of variants of phrases containing modifiers. It limits proliferation of the ill effects, however, by allowing only the maximal one to be incorporated in larger phrases. In other words, if the final result has phrases with *m* and *n* modifiers respectively, then 2^n versions of the first and 2^m of the second will be created, but only one of each set will be incorporated into larger phrases and no factor of $2^{(n+m)}$ will be introduced into the cost of the process.

5 Indexing

String positions provide a natural way to index the strings input to the parsing process for the simple reason that there are as many of them as there are words but, for there to be any possibility of interaction between a pair of edges, they must come together at just one index. These are the natural points of articulation in the domain of strings. They cannot fill this role in generation because they are not natural properties of the semantic expressions that are the input to the process. The corresponding natural points of articulation in flat semantic structures are the entities that we have already been referring to as *indices*.

In the modified version of the procedure, whenever a new inactive edge is created with label B(*b* ...), then for all rules of the form in (9), an active edge is also created with label A(...)/C(*c* ...).

(9) A(...) → B(*b* ...) C(*c* ...)

This represents a phrase of category A that requires a phrase of category C on the right for its completion. In these labels, *b* and *c* are (variables representing) the first, or *distinguished* indices associated with B and C. By analogy with parsing charts, an inactive edge labeled B(*b* ...) can be thought of as *incident from* vertex *b*, which means simply that it is efficiently accessible through the index *b*. An active edge A(...)/C(*c* ...) should be thought of as incident from, or accessible through, the index *c*. The key property of this scheme is that active and inactive edges interact by virtue of indices that they share and, by letting vertices correspond to indices, we collect together sets of edges that could interact.

We illustrate the modified procedure with the sentence (10) whose semantics we will take to be (11), the grammar rules (12)-(14), and the lexical entries in (15).

(10) The dog saw the cat.

(11) dog(d), def(d), saw(s), past(s), cat(c), def(c), arg1(s, d), arg2(s, c).

(12) s(*x*) → np(*y*) vp(*x*, *y*)

(13) vp(*x*, *y*) → v(*x*, *y*, *z*) np(*z*)

(14) np(*x*) → det(*x*) n(*x*)

(15)

Words	Cat	Semantics
cat	n(*x*)	*x*: cat(*x*)
saw	v(*x*, *y*, *z*)	*x*: see(*x*), past(*x*), arg1(*x*, *y*), arg2(*x*,*z*)
dog	n(*x*)	*x*: dog(*x*)
the	det(*x*)	*x*: def(*x*)

The procedure will be reminiscent of left-corner parsing. Arguments have been made in favor of a head-driven strategy which would, however, have been marginally more complex (e.g. in Kay (1989), Shieber, *et el.* (1989)) and the differences are, in any case, not germane to our current concerns.

The initial agenda, including active edges, and collecting edges by the vertices that they are incident from, is given in (16).

The grammar is consulted only for the purpose of creating active edges and all interactions in the chart are between active and inactive pairs of edges incident from the same vertex.

(16)

Vert	Words	Cat	Semantics
d	the	det(d)	d: def(d)
	the	np(d)/n(d)	d: def(d)
	dog	n(d)	d: dog(d)
s	saw	v(s, d, c)	s: see(s), past(s), arg1(s, d), arg2(s, c)
c	saw	vp(s, d)/np(c)	r: see(s), past(s), arg1(r, j)
	the	det(c)	c: def(c)
	the	np(c)/n(c)	c: def(c)
	cat	n(c)	c: dog(c)

(17)

Vert	Words	Cat	Semantics
d	the dog	np(d)	d: dog(d), def(d)
	saw the cat	vp(s, d)/np(d)	s: see(s), past(s), arg1(s, d), arg2(s, c), cat(c), def(c)
c	the cat	np(c)	c: cat(c), def(c)
s	saw the cat	vp(s, d)	s: see(s), past(s), arg1(s, d), arg2(s, c), cat(c), def(c)

Among the edges in (16), there are two interactions, one at vertices c and d. They cause the first and third edges in (17) to be added to the agenda. The first interacts with the active edge originally introduced by the verb "saw" producing the fourth entry in (17). The label on this edge matches the first item on the right-hand side of rule (12) and the active edge that we show in the second entry is also introduced. The final interaction is between the first and second edges in (17) which give rise to the edge in (18).

This procedure confirms perfectly to the standard algorithm schema for chart parsing, especially in the version that makes predictions immediately following the recognition of the first constituent of a phrase, that is, in the version that is essentially a caching left-corner parser.

(18)

Vert	Words	Cat	Semantics
s	The dog saw the cat	s(s)	dog(d), def(d), see(s), past(s),arg1(s, d), arg2(s, c), cat(c), def(c).

6 Acknowledgments

Whatever there may be of value in this paper owes much to the interest, encouragement, and tolerance of my colleagues Marc Dymetman, Ronald Kaplan, John Maxwell, and Hadar Shem Tov. I am also indebted to the anonymous reviewers of this paper.

References

Copestake, A., Dan Flickinger, Robert Malouf, and Susanne Riehemann, and Ivan Sag (1996). Translation Using Minimal Recursion Semantics. *Proceedings of The Sixth International Conference on Theoretical and Methodological Issues in Machine Translation*, Leuven (in press).

Davidson, D. (1980). *Essays on Actions and Events. Oxford*: The Clarendon Press.

Hobbs, J. R. (1985). Ontological Promiscuity. *23rd Annual Meeting of the Association for Computational Linguistics*, Chicago, ACL.

Kay, M. (1970). From Semantics to Syntax. *Progress in Linguistics*. Bierwisch Manfred, and K. E. Heidolf. The Hague, Mouton: 114-126.

Kay, M. (1989). Head-driven Parsing. *Proceedings of Workshop on Parsing Technologies*, Pittsburgh, PA.

Parsons, T. (1990). *Events in the Semantics of English*. Cambridge, Mass.: MIT Press.

Shieber, S. (1988). A Uniform Architecture for Parsing and Generation. *COLING-88*, Budapest, John von Neumann Society for Computing Sciences.

Shieber, S. M. *et al.* (1989). A Semantic-Head-Driven Generation Algorithm for Unification Based Formalisms. *27th Annual Meeting of the Association for Computational Linguistics*, Vancouver. B.C.

Whitelock, P. (1992). Shake and-Bake Translation. *COLING-92*, Nantes.

Evaluating the Portability of Revision Rules for Incremental Summary Generation

Jacques Robin
http://www.di.ufpe.br/~jr
jr@di.ufpe.br
Departamento de Informática, Universidade Federal de Pernambuco
Caixa Postal 7851, Cidade Universitária
Recife, PE 50732-970 Brazil

Abstract

This paper presents a quantitative evaluation of the portability to the stock market domain of the revision rule hierarchy used by the system STREAK to incrementally generate newswire sports summaries. The evaluation consists of searching a test corpus of stock market reports for sentence pairs whose (semantic and syntactic) structures respectively match the triggering condition and application result of each revision rule. The results show that at least 59% of all rule classes are fully portable, with at least another 7% partially portable.

1 Introduction

The project STREAK[1] focuses on the specific issues involved in generating short, newswire style, natural language texts that *summarize* vast amount of input tabular data in their historical context. A series of previous publications presented complementary aspects of this project: motivating corpus analysis in (Robin and McKeown, 1993), new revision-based text generation model in (Robin, 1993), system implementation and rule base in (Robin, 1994a) and empirical evaluation of the *robustness* and *scalability* of this new model as compared to the traditional single pass pipeline model in (Robin and McKeown, 1995). The present paper completes this series by describing a second, empirical, corpus-based evaluation, this time quantifying the *portability* to another domain (the stock market) of the revision rule hierarchy acquired in the sports domain and implemented in STREAK. The goal of this paper is twofold: (1) assessing the generality of this particular rule hierarchy and (2) providing a general, semi-automatic methodology for evaluating the portability of semantic and syntactic knowledge structures used for natural language generation. The results reveal that at least 59% of the revision rule hierarchy abstracted from the sports domain could also be used to incrementally generate the complex sentences observed in a corpus of stock market reports.

I start by providing the context of the evaluation with a brief overview of STREAK's revision-based generation model, followed by some details about the empirical acquisition of its revision rules from corpus data. I then present the methodology of this evaluation, followed by a discussion of its quantitative results. Finally, I compare this evaluation with other empirical evaluations in text generation and conclude by discussing future directions.

2 An overview of STREAK

The project STREAK was initially motivated by analyzing a corpus of newswire summaries written by professional sportswriters[2]. This analysis revealed four characteristics of summaries that challenge the capabilities of previous text generators: concise linguistic forms, complex sentences, optional and background facts opportunistically slipped as modifiers of obligatory facts and high paraphrasing power. By greatly increasing the number of content planning and linguistic realization options that the generator must consider, as well as the mutual constraints among them, these characteristics make generating summaries in a single pass impractical.

The example run given in Fig. 1 illustrates how STREAK overcomes these difficulties. It first generates a simple draft sentence that contains only the obligatory facts to include in any game report (location, date, game result and key player statistic). It then applies a series of revision rules[3], each one

[1]Surface Text Reviser Expressing Additional Knowledge.

[2]This 800,000 word corpus covers a whole NBA (National Basketball Association) season.

[3]In Fig. 1, the rule used is indicated above each re-

1. **Initial draft (basic sentence pattern):**
"Dallas, TX – Charles Barkley *scored* 42 points Sunday as the Phoenix Suns defeated the Dallas Mavericks 123-97."

2. **Adjunctization of Created into Instrument:**
"Dallas, TX – Charles Barkley **tied a season high with** 42 points Sunday as the Phoenix Suns defeated the Dallas Mavericks 123-97."

3. **Coordinative Conjoin of Clause:**
"Dallas, TX – Charles Barkley tied a season high with 42 points **and Danny Ainge** added **21** Sunday as the Phoenix Suns defeated the Dallas Mavericks 123-97."

4. **Absorb of Clause in Clause as Result with Agent Control:**
"Dallas, TX – Charles Barkley tied a season high with 42 points and **Danny Ainge came off the bench** to add 21 Sunday as the Phoenix Suns defeated the Dallas Mavericks 123-97."

5. **Nominalization with Ordinal Adjoin:**
"Dallas, TX – Charles Barkley tied a season high with 42 points and Danny Ainge came off the bench to add 21 Sunday as the Phoenix Suns **handed** the Dallas Mavericks **their 13th straight home** defeat 123-97."

6. **Adjoin of Classifier to NP:**
"Dallas, TX – Charles Barkley tied a season high with 42 points and Danny Ainge came off the bench to add 21 Sunday as the Phoenix Suns handed the Dallas Mavericks their **league worst** 13th straight home defeat 123-97."

Figure 1: Complex sentence generation through incremental revisions in STREAK

opportunistically adding a new fact[4] that either:

- Complements an already included fact (*e.g.*, revision of sentence 2 into 3).
- Justifies its relevance by providing its historical background (*e.g.*, revision of sentence 1 into 2).

Some of these revisions are *non-monotonic*, rewording[5] a draft fact to more concisely accommodate the additional fact (*e.g.*, revision of sentence 1 into 2). Popping additional facts from a priority stack, STREAK stops revising when the summary sentence reaches linguistic complexity limits empirically observed in the corpus (*e.g.*, 50 word long or parse tree of depth 10).

vised sentence.

[4]Highlighted in bold in Fig. 1.

[5]In Fig. 1, words that get deleted are italicized and words that get modified are underlined.

Charles Barkley scored 42 points. Those 42 points equal his best scoring performance of the season. Danny Ainge is a teammate of Barkley. They play for the Phoenix Suns. Ainge is a reserve player. Yet he scored 21 points. The high scoring performances by Barkley and Ainge helped the Suns defeat the Dallas Mavericks. The Mavericks played on their homecourt in Texas. They had already lost their 12 previous games there. No other team in the league has lost so many games in a row at home. The final score was 123-97. The game was played Sunday.

Figure 2: Paragraph of simple sentences paraphrasing a single complex sentence

While STREAK generates only single sentences, those complex sentences convey as much information as whole paragraphs made of simple sentences, only far more fluently and concisely. This is illustrated by the 12 sentence paragraph[6] of Fig. 2, which paraphrases sentence 6 of Fig. 1. Because they express facts essentially independently of one another, such multi-sentence paragraphs are much easier to generate than the complex single sentences generated by STREAK.

3 Acquiring revision rules from corpus data

The rules driving the revision process in STREAK were acquired by reverse engineering[7] about 300 corpus sentences. These sentences were initially classified in terms of:

- The combination of domain concepts they expressed.
- The thematic role and top-level syntactic category used for each of these concepts.

[6]This paragraph was *not* generated by STREAK, it is shown here only for contrastive purposes.

[7]*i.e.*, analyzing how they could be incrementally generated through gradual revisions.

The resulting classes, called *realization patterns*, abstract the mapping from semantic to syntactic structure by factoring out lexical material and syntactic details. Two examples of realization patterns are given in Fig. 3. Realization patterns were then grouped into *surface decrement pairs* consisting of:

- A more complex pattern (called the *target* pattern).
- A simpler pattern (called the *source* pattern) that is structurally the closest to the target pattern among patterns with one less concept[8].

The structural transformations from source to target pattern in each surface decrement pair were then hierarchically classified, resulting in the revision rule hierarchy shown in Fig. 4-10. For example, the surface decrement pair $< R_b^2, R_b^1 >$, shown in Fig. 3, is one of the pairs from which the revision rule **Adjunctization of Range into Instrument**, shown in Fig. 10 was abstracted.

It involves displacing the **Range** argument of the source clause as an **Instrument** adjunct to accommodate a new verb and its argument. This revision rule is a sibling of the rule **Adjunctization of Created into Instrument** used to revise sentence 1 into 2 in STREAK's run shown in Fig. 1 (where the **Created** argument role "42 points" of the verb "to score" in 1 becomes an **Instrument** adjunct in 2).

The bottom level of the revision rule hierarchy specifies the *side revisions* that are orthogonal and sometimes accompany the restructuring revisions discussed up to this point. Side revisions do not make the draft more informative, but instead improve its style, conciseness and unambiguity. For example, when STREAK revises sentence (3) into (4) in the example run of Fig. 1, the **Agent** of the absorbed clause "Danny Ainge added 21 points" becomes *controlled* by the new embedding clause "Danny Ainge came off the bench" to avoid the verbose form:
? "Danny Ainge came off the bench for Danny Ainge to add 21 points".

4 Evaluation methodology

In the spectrum of possible evaluations, the evaluation presented in this paper is characterized as follows:

- Its object is the *revision rule hierarchy* acquired from the sports summary corpus. It thus does not directly evaluate the output of STREAK, but rather the special knowledge structures required by its underlying revision-based model.

[8] *i.e.*, the source pattern expresses the same concept combination than the target pattern minus one concept.

- The particular property of this revision rule hierarchy that is evaluated is *cross-domain portability*: how much of it could be re-used to generate summaries in another domain, namely the stock market?
- The basis for this evaluation is *corpus data*[9]. The original sports summary corpus from which the revision rules were acquired is used as the 'training' (or acquisition) corpus and a corpus of stock market reports taken from several newswires is used as the 'test' corpus. This test corpus comprises over 18,000 sentences.
- The evaluation procedure is *quantitative*, measuring percentages of revision rules whose target and source realization patterns are observable in the test corpus. It is also *semi-automated* through the use of the corpus search tool CREP (Duford, 1993) (as explained below).

Basic principle As explained in section 3, a revision rule is associated with a list of surface decrement pairs, each one consisting of:

- A *source* pattern whose content and linguistic form match the triggering conditions of the rule (*e.g.*, R_b^1 in Fig. 3 for the rule **Adjunctization of Range into Instrument**).
- A *target* pattern whose content and linguistic form can be derived from the source pattern by applying the rule (*e.g.*, R_b^2 in Fig. 3 for the rule **Adjunctization of Range into Instrument**).

This list of decrement pairs can thus be used as the *signature* of the revision rule to detect its usage in the test corpus. The needed evidence is the simultaneous presence of two test corpus sentences[10], each one respectively matching the source and target patterns of at least one element in this list. Requiring occurrence of the *source* pattern in the test corpus is necessary for the computation of conservative portability estimates: while it may seem that one target pattern alone is enough evidence, without the presence of the corresponding source pattern, one cannot rule out the possibility that, in the test domain, this target pattern is either a basic pattern or derived from another source pattern using another revision rule.

[9] Only the corpus analysis was performed for both domains. The implementation was *not* actually ported to the stock market domain.

[10] In general, *not* from the same report.

Realization pattern R_b^2:

- Expresses the concept pair:
  <game-result(winner,loser,score), **streak(winner,aspect,result-type,length)**>.
- Is a *target* pattern of the revision rule `Adjunctization of Range into Instrument`.

winner	**aspect**		type	**streak**	**length**			score	game-result	loser
agent	action	affected/located			location	instrument				
proper	verb	NP			PP	PP				
		det	classifier	noun		prep	NP			
							det	number	noun	PP
Utah	**extended**	**its**	**win**	**streak**	**to 6 games**	**with**	a	99-84	triumph	over Denver
Boston	**stretching**	**its**	**winning**	**spree**	**to 9 outings**	**with**	a	118-94	rout	of Utah

Realization pattern R_b^1:

- Expresses the single concept <game-result(winner,loser,score)>.
- Is a *source* pattern of the revision rule `Adjunctization of Range into Instrument`.
- Is a surface decrement of pattern R_b^2 above.

winner			score	game-result	loser
agent	action	range			
proper	support-verb	NP			
		det	number	noun	PP
Chicago	claimed	a	128-94	victory	over New Jersey
Orlando	recorded	a	101-95	triumph	against New York

Figure 3: Realization pattern examples

Partially automating the evaluation The software tool CREP[11] was developed to partially automate detection of realization patterns in a text corpus. The basic idea behind CREP is to approximate a realization pattern by a regular expression whose terminals are words or parts-of-speech tags (POS-tags). CREP will then automatically retrieve the corpus sentences matching those expressions. For example, the CREP expression C_1 below approximates the realization pattern R_b^1 shown in Fig. 3:

(C_1) `TEAM 0= (claimed|recorded)@VBD 1- SCORE 0= (victory|triumph)@NN 0= (over|against)@IN 0= TEAM`

In the expression above, '`VBD`', '`NN`' and '`IN`' are the POS-tags for past verb, singular noun and preposition (respectively), and the sub-expressions '`TEAM`' and '`SCORE`' (whose recursive definitions are not shown here) match the team names and possible final scores (respectively) in the NBA. The CREP operators '`N=`' and '`N-`' (N being an arbitrary integer) respectively specify exact and minimal distance of N words, and '`|`' encodes disjunction.

Because a realization pattern abstracts away from lexical items to capture the mapping from concepts to syntactic structure, approximating such a pattern by a regular expression of words and POS-tags involves encoding each concept of the pattern by the disjunction of its alternative lexicalizations. In a given domain, there are therefore two sources of inaccuracy for such an approximation:

- Lexical ambiguity resulting in false positives by over-generalization.
- Incomplete vocabulary resulting in false negatives by over-specialization[12].

Lexical ambiguities can be alleviated by writing more context-sensitive expressions. The vocabulary can be acquired through additional exploratory CREP runs with expressions containing wild-cards for some concept slots. Although automated corpus search using CREP expressions considerably speeds-up corpus analysis, manual intervention remains

[11] CREP was implemented (on top of FLEX, GNUS' version of LEX) and to a large extent also designed by Duford. It uses Ken Church's POS tagger.

[12] This is the case for example of C_1 above, which is a simplification of the actual expression that was used to search occurrences of R_b^1 in the test corpus (*e.g.*, C_1 is missing "win" and "rout" as alternatives for "victory").

necessary to filter out incorrect matches resulting from imperfect approximations.

Cross-domain discrepancies Basic similarities between the finance and sports domains form the basis for the portability of the revision rules. In both domains, the core facts reported are statistics compiled within a standard temporal unit (in sports, one ballgame; in finance, one stock market session) together with streaks[13] and records compiled across several such units. This correspondence is, however, imperfect. Consequently, before they can track down usage of a revision rule in the test domain, the CREP expressions approximating the signature of the rule in the acquisition domain must be *adjusted* for cross-domain discrepancies to prevent false negatives. Two major types of adjustments are necessary: lexical and thematic.

Lexical adjustments handle cases of partial mismatch between the respective vocabularies used to lexicalize matching conceptual structures in each domain. (*e.g.*,, the verb *"to rebound from"* expresses the interruption of a streak in the stock market domain, while in the basketball domain *"to break"* or *"to snap"* are preferred since *"to rebound"* is used to express a different concept).

Thematic adjustments handle cases of partial differences between corresponding conceptual structures in the acquisition and test domains. For example, while in sports `game-result` involves antagonistic teams, its financial domain counterpart `session-result` concerns only a single indicator. Consequently, the sub-expression for the `loser` role in the example CREP expression C_1 shown before, and which approximates realization pattern R_b^1 for `game-result` (shown in Fig. 3), needs to become optional in order to also approximate patterns for `session-result`. This is done using the CREP operator ? as shown below:

($C_1\prime$): `TEAM 0= (claimed|recorded)@VBD 1-SCORE 0= (victory|triumph)@NN 0= ((over|against)@IN 0= TEAM)?`

Note that it is the CREP expressions used to automatically retrieve test corpus sentence pairs attesting usage of a revision rule that require this type of adjustment and *not* the revision rule itself[14]. For example, the `Adjoin of Frequency PP to Clause` revision rule attaches a streak to a `session-result` clause *without* `loser` role *in exactly the same way* than it attaches a streak to a `game-result` *with* `loser` role. This is illustrated by the two corpus sentences below:

P_2^a: "The Chicago Bulls beat <u>the Phoenix Suns</u> 99 91 **for their 3rd straight win**"

P_2^t: "The Amex Market Value Index inched up 0.16 to 481.94 **for its sixth straight advance**"

Detailed evaluation procedure The overall procedure to test portability of a revision rule consists of considering the surface decrement pairs in the rule signature in order, and repeating the following steps:

1. Write a CREP expression for the acquisition *target* pattern.
2. Iteratively delete, replace or generalize subexpressions in the CREP expression - to gloss over thematic and lexical discrepancies between the acquisition and test domains, and prevent false negatives - until it matches some test corpus sentence(s).
3. Post-edit the file containing these matched sentences. If it contains only false positives of the sought target pattern, go back to step 2. Otherwise, proceed to step 4.
4. Repeat step (1-3) with the *source* pattern of the pair under consideration. If a valid match can also be found for this source pattern, stop: the revision rule is portable. Otherwise, start over from step 1 with the next surface decrement pair in the revision rule signature. If there is no next pair left, stop: the revision rule is considered non-portable.

Steps (2,3) constitute a general, generate-and-test procedure to detect realization patterns usage in a corpus[15]. Changing one CREP sub-expression may result in going from too specific an expression with no valid match to either: (1) a well-adjusted expression with a valid match, (2) still too specific an expression with no valid match, or (3) already too general an expression with too many matches to be manually post-edited.

It is in fact always possible to write more context-sensitive expressions, to manually edit larger no-match files, or even to consider larger test corpora in the hope of finding a match. At some point however, one has to estimate, guided by the results of previous runs, that the likelihood of finding a match is too

[13] *i.e.*, series of events with similar outcome.

[14] Some revision rules do require adjustment, but of another type (*cf.* Sect. 5).

[15] And since most generators rely on knowledge structures equivalent to realization patterns, this procedure can probably be adapted to semi-automatically evaluate the portability of virtually any corpus-based generator.

small to justify the cost of further attempts. This is why the last line in the algorithm reads "considered non-portable" as opposed to "non-portable". The algorithm guarantees the validity of positive (*i.e.,* portable) results only. Therefore, the figures presented in the next section constitute in fact a *lower-bound* estimate of the actual revision rule portability.

5 Evaluation results

The results of the evaluation are summarized in Fig. 4-10. They show the revision rule hierarchy, with portable classes highlighted in bold. The frequency of occurrence of each rule in the acquisition corpus is given below the leaves of the hierarchy.

Some rules are *same-concept portable*: they are used to attach corresponding concepts in each domain (*e.g.,* `Adjoin of Frequency PP to Clause`, as explained in Sect. 4). They could be re-used "as is" in the financial domain. Other rules, however, are only *different-concept portable*: they are used to attach altogether different concepts in each domain. This is the case for example of `Adjoin Finite Time Clause to Clause`, as illustrated by the two corpus sentences below, where the added temporal adjunct (in bold) conveys a streak in the sports sentence, but a complementary statistics in the financial one:

T_3^a: *"to lead Utah to a 119-89 trouncing of Denver* **as the Jazz defeated the Nuggets for the 12th straight time at home."**

T_3^t: *"Volume amounted to a solid 349 million shares* **as advances out-paced declines 299 to 218."**.

For different-concept portable rules, the left-hand side field specifying the concepts incorporable to the draft using this rule will need to be changed when porting the rule to the stock market domain. In Fig. 4-10, the arcs leading same-concept portable classes are full and thick, those leading to different-concept portable classes are dotted, and those leading to a non-portable classes are full but thin.

59% of all revision rule classes turned out to be same-concept portable, with another 7% different-concept portable. Remarkably, *all* eight top-level classes identified in the sports domain had instances *same-concept portable* to the financial domain, even those involving the most complex non-monotonic revisions, or those with only a few instances in the sports corpus. Among the bottom-level classes that distinguish between revision rule applications in very specific semantic and syntactic contexts, 42% are same-concept portable with another 10% different-concept portable. Finally, the correlation between high usage frequency in the acquisition corpus and portability to the test corpus is not statistically significant (*i.e.,* the hypothesis that the more common a rule, the more likely it is to be portable could *not* be confirmed on the analyzed sample). See (Robin, 1994b) for further details on the evaluation results.

There are two main stumbling blocks to portability: thematic role mismatch and side revisions. Thematic role mismatches are cases where the semantic label or syntactic sub-category of a constituent added or displaced by the rule differ in each domain (*e.g.,* `Adjunctization of Created into Instrument` *vs.* `Adjoin of Affected into Instrument`). They push portability from 92% down to 71%. Their effect could be reduced by allowing STREAK's reviser to manipulate the draft down to the surface syntactic role level (*e.g.,* in both corpora `Created` and `Affected` surface as object). Currently, the reviser stops at the thematic role level to allow STREAK to take full advantage of the syntactic processing front-end SURGE (Elhadad and Robin, 1996), which accepts such thematic structures as input.

Accompanying side revisions push portability from 71% to 52%. This suggests that the design of STREAK could be improved by keeping side revisions separate from re-structuring revisions and interleaving the applications of the two. Currently, they are integrated together at the bottom of the revision rule hierarchy.

6 Related work

Apart from STREAK, only three generation projects feature an empirical and quantitative evaluation: ANA (Kukich, 1983), KNIGHT (Lester, 1993) and IMAGENE (Van der Linden, 1993).

ANA generates short, newswire style summaries of the daily fluctuations of several stock market indexes from half-hourly updates of their values. For evaluation, Kukich measures both the conceptual and linguistic (lexical and syntactic) coverages of ANA by comparing the number of concepts and realization patterns identified during a corpus analysis with those actually implemented in the system.

KNIGHT generates natural language concept definitions from a large biological knowledge base, relying on SURGE for syntactic realization. For evaluation, Lester performs a Turing test in which a panel of human judges rates 120 sample definitions by assigning grades (from A to F) for:

- Semantic accuracy (defined as "Is the definition adequate, providing correct information and focusing on what's important?" in the instructions provided to the judges).
- Stylistic accuracy (defined as "Does the definition use good prose and is the information it

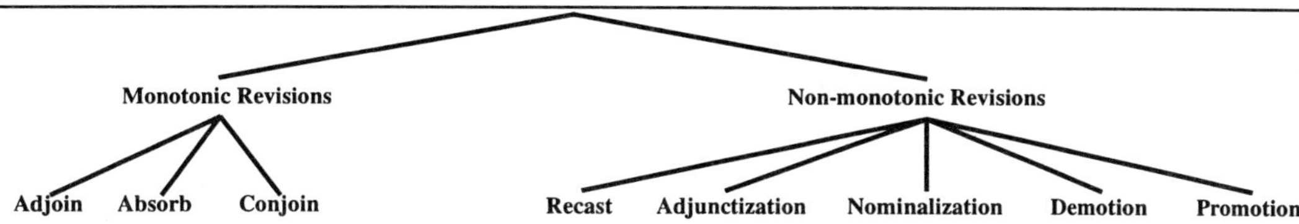

Figure 4: Revision rule hierarchy: top-levels

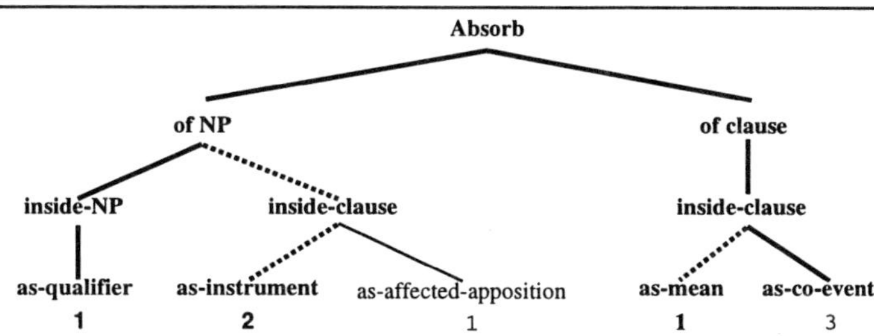

Figure 5: Absorb revision rule sub-hierarchy

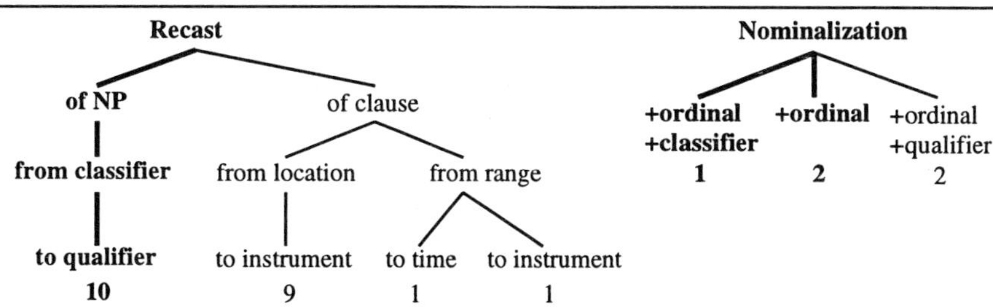

Figure 6: Recast and Nominalize revision rule sub-hierarchy

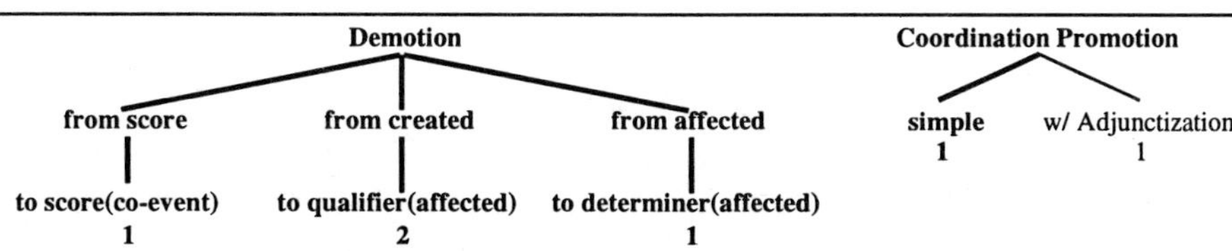

Figure 7: Demotion and Promotion revision rule sub-hierarchy

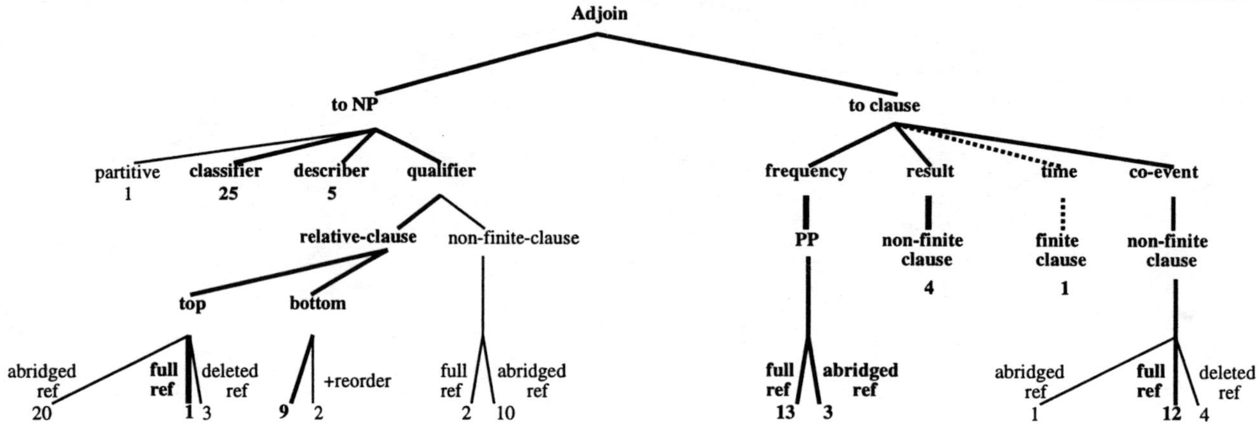

Figure 8: Adjoin revision rule sub-hierarchy

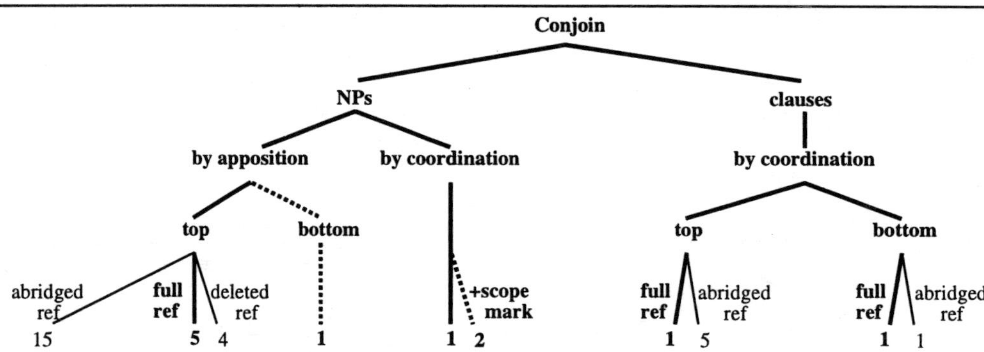

Figure 9: Conjoin revision rule sub-hierarchy

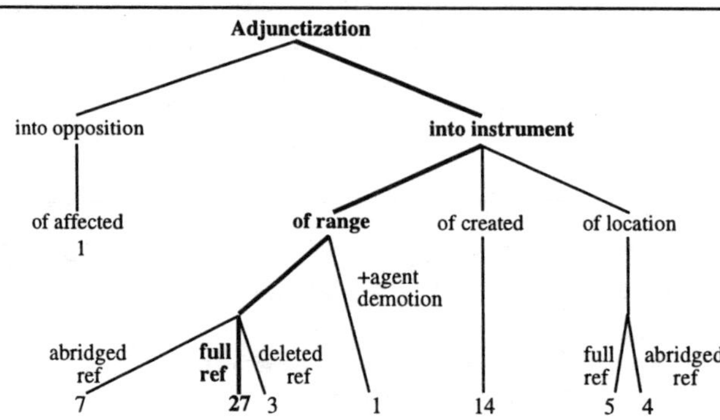

Figure 10: Adjunctization revision rule sub-hierarchy

	Object of Evaluation	Evaluated Properties	Empirical Basis	Evaluation Procedure
ANA	knowledge structures "	conceptual coverage linguistic coverage	textual corpus "	manual "
KNIGHT	output text "	semantic accuracy stylistic accuracy	human judges "	manual "
IMAGENE	output text "	stylistic accuracy stylistic robustness	textual corpus "	manual "
STREAK	knowledge structures " "	**cross-domain portability** same-domain robustness same-domain scalability	textual corpus " "	semi-automatic " "

Figure 11: Empirical evaluations in language generation

conveys well organized" in the instructions provided to the judges).

The judges did not know that half the definitions were computer-generated while the other half were written by four human domain experts. Impressively, the results show that:

- With respect to semantic accuracy, the human judges could *not* tell KNIGHT apart from the human writers.

- While as a group, humans got statistically significantly better grades for stylistic accuracy than KNIGHT, the best human writer was single-handly responsible for this difference.

IMAGENE generates instructions on how to operate household devices relying on NIGEL (Mann and Matthiessen, 1983) for syntactic realization. The implementation focuses on a very limited aspect of text generation: the realization of purpose relations. Taking as input the description of a pair <operation, purpose of the operation>, augmented by a set of features simulating the communicative context of generation, IMAGENE selects, among the many realizations of purpose generable by NIGEL (*e.g.,* fronted to-infinitive clause *vs.* trailing for-gerund clauses), the one that is most appropriate for the simulated context (*e.g.,* in the context of several operations sharing the same purpose, the latter is preferentially expressed *before* those actions than after them). IMAGENE's contextual preference rules were abstracted by analyzing an acquisition corpus of about 300 purpose clauses from cordless telephone manuals. For evaluation, Van der Linden compares the purpose realizations picked by IMAGENE to the one in the corresponding corpus text, first on the acquisition corpus and then on a test corpus of about 300 other purpose clauses from manuals for other devices than cordless telephones (ranging from clock radio to automobile). The results show a 71% match on the acquisition corpus[16] and a 52% match on the test corpus.

The table of Fig. 11 summarizes the difference on both goal and methodology between the evaluations carried out in the projects ANA, KNIGHT, IMAGENE and STREAK. In terms of goals, while Kukich and Lester evaluate the coverage or accuracy of a particular *implementation*, I instead focus on three properties inherent to the use of the revision-based generation *model* underlying STREAK: robustness (how much of other text samples from the same domain can be generated without acquiring new knowledge?) and scalability (how much more new knowledge is needed to fully cover these other samples?) discussed in (Robin and McKeown, 1995), and portability to another domain in the present paper. Van der Linden does a little bit of both by first measuring the stylistic accuracy of his system for a very restricted sub-domain, and then measuring how it degrades for a more general domain.

In itself, measuring the accuracy and coverage of a particular implementation in the sub-domain for which it was designed brings little insights about what generation approach should be adopted in future work. Indeed, even a system using mere canned text can be very accurate and attain substantial coverage if enough hand-coding effort is put into it. However, all this effort will have to be entirely duplicated each time the system is scaled up or ported to a new domain. Measuring how much of this effort duplication can be avoided when relying on revision-based generation was the very object of the three evaluations carried in the STREAK project.

[16] This imperfect match on the acquisition corpus seems to result from the *heuristic* nature of IMAGENE's stylistic preferences: individually, none of them needs to apply to the whole corpus.

In terms of methodology, the main originality of these three evaluations is the use of CREP to partially automate reverse engineering of corpus sentences. Beyond evaluation, CREP is a simple, but general and very handy tool that should prove useful to speed-up a wide range of corpora analyses.

7 Conclusion

In this paper, I presented a quantitative evaluation of the portability to the stock market domain of the revision rule hierarchy used by the system STREAK to incrementally generate newswire sports summaries. The evaluation procedure consists of searching a test corpus of stock market reports for sentence pairs whose (semantic and syntactic) structures respectively match the triggering condition and application result of each revision rule. The results show that at least 59% of all rule classes are fully portable, with at least another 7% partially portable.

Since the sports domain is not closer to the financial domain than to other quantitative domains such as meteorology, demography, business auditing or computer surveillance, these results are very encouraging with respect to the general cross-domain reusability potential of the knowledge structures used in revision-based generation. However, the present evaluation concerned only one type of such knowledge structures: revision rules. In future work, similar evaluations will be needed for the other types of knowledge structures: content selection rules, phrase planning rules and lexicalization rules.

Acknowledgements

Many thanks to Kathy McKeown for stressing the importance of empirically evaluating STREAK. The research presented in this paper is currently supported by CNPq (Brazilian Research Council) under post-doctoral research grant 150130-95.3. It started out while I was at Columbia University supported by of a joint grant from the Office of Naval Research, by the Advanced Research Projects Agency under contract N00014-89-J-1782, by National Science Foundation Grants IRT-84-51438 and GER-90-2406, and by the New York State Science and Technology Foundation under this auspices of the Columbia University CAT in High Performance Computing and Communications in Health Care, a New York State Center for Advanced Technology.

References

Duford, D. 1993. CREP: a regular expression-matching textual corpus tool. Technical Report CU-CS-005-93. Computer Science Department, Columbia University, New York.

Elhadad, M. and Robin, J. 1996. An overview of SURGE: a re-usable comprehensive syntactic realization component. Technical Report 96-03. Computer Science and Mathematics Department, Ben Gurion University, Beer Sheva, Israël.

Kukich, K. 1983. Knowledge-based report generation: a knowledge engineering approach to natural language report generation. PhD. Thesis. Department of Information Science. University of Pittsburgh.

Lester, J.C. 1993. Generating natural language explanations from large-scale knowledge bases. PhD. Thesis. Computer Science Department, University of Texas at Austin.

Mann, W.C. and Matthiessen, C. M. 1983. NIGEL: a systemic grammar for text generation. Research Report RR-83-105. ISI. Marina Del Rey, CA.

Robin, J. and McKeown, K.R. 1993. Corpus analysis for revision-based generation of complex sentences. In *Proceedings of the 11th National Conference on Artificial Intelligence*, Washington DC. (AAAI'93).

Robin, J. and McKeown, K.R. 1995. Empirically designing and evaluating a new revision-based model for summary generation. *Artificial Intelligence.* Vol 85. *Special Issue on Empirical Methods.* North-Holland.

Robin, J. 1993. A revision-based generation architecture for reporting facts in their historical context. In *New Concepts in Natural Language Generation: Planning, Realization and System.* Horacek, H. and Zock, M., Eds. Frances Pinter.

Robin, J. 1994a. Automatic generation and revision of natural language summaries providing historical background In *Proceedings of the 11th Brazilian Symposium on Artificial Intelligence*, Fortaleza, Brazil. (SBIA'94).

Robin, J. 1994b. Revision-based generation of natural language summaries providing historical background: corpus-based analysis, design, implementation and evaluation. PhD. Thesis. Available as Technical Report CU-CS-034-94. Computer Science Department, Columbia University, New York.

Van der Linden, K. and Martin, J.H. 1995. Expressing rhetorical relations in instructional texts: a case study of the purpose relation. *Computational Linguistics,* 21(1). MIT Press.

Compilation of Weighted Finite-State Transducers from Decision Trees

Richard Sproat
Bell Laboratories
700 Mountain Avenue
Murray Hill, NJ, USA
rws@bell-labs.com

Michael Riley
AT&T Research
600 Mountain Avenue
Murray Hill, NJ, USA
riley@research.att.com

Abstract

We report on a method for compiling decision trees into weighted finite-state transducers. The key assumptions are that the tree predictions specify how to rewrite symbols from an input string, and the decision at each tree node is stateable in terms of regular expressions on the input string. Each leaf node can then be treated as a separate rule where the left and right contexts are constructable from the decisions made traversing the tree from the root to the leaf. These rules are compiled into transducers using the weighted rewrite-rule rule-compilation algorithm described in (Mohri and Sproat, 1996).

1 Introduction

Much attention has been devoted recently to methods for inferring linguistic models from data. One powerful inference method that has been used in various applications are decision trees, and in particular classification and regression trees (Breiman et al., 1984).

An increasing amount of attention has also been focussed on finite-state methods for implementing linguistic models, in particular finite-state transducers and *weighted* finite-state transducers; see (Kaplan and Kay, 1994; Pereira et al., 1994, inter alia). The reason for the renewed interest in finite-state mechanisms is clear. Finite-state machines provide a mathematically well-understood computational framework for representing a wide variety of information, both in NLP and speech processing. Lexicons, phonological rules, Hidden Markov Models, and (regular) grammars are all representable as finite-state machines, and finite-state operations such as union, intersection and composition mean that information from these various sources can be combined in useful and computationally attractive ways. The reader is referred to the above-cited papers (among others) for more extensive justification.

This paper reports on a marriage of these two strands of research in the form of an algorithm for compiling the information in decision trees into weighted finite-state transducers.[1] Given this algorithm, information inferred from data and represented in a tree can be used directly in a system that represents other information, such as lexicons or grammars, in the form of finite-state machines.

2 Quick Review of Tree-Based Modeling

A general introduction to classification and regression trees ('CART') including the algorithm for growing trees from data can be found in (Breiman et al., 1984). Applications of tree-based modeling to problems in speech and NLP are discussed in (Riley, 1989; Riley, 1991; Wang and Hirschberg, 1992; Magerman, 1995, inter alia). In this section we presume that one has already trained a tree or set of trees, and we merely remind the reader of the salient points in the interpretation of those trees.

Consider the tree depicted in Figure 1, which was trained on the TIMIT database (Fisher et al., 1987), and which models the phonetic realization of the English phoneme /aa/ (/ɑ/) in various environments (Riley, 1991). When this tree is used in predicting the allophonic form of a particular instance of /aa/, one starts at the root of the tree, and asks questions about the environment in which the /aa/ is found. Each non-leaf node n, dominates two daughter nodes conventionally labeled as $2n$ and $2n+1$; the decision on whether to go left to $2n$ or right to $2n+1$ depends on the answer to the question that is being asked at node n.

[1]The work reported here can thus be seen as complementary to recent reports on methods for directly inferring transducers from data (Oncina et al., 1993; Gildea and Jurafsky, 1995).

A concrete example will serve to illustrate. Consider that we have /aa/ in some environment. The first question that is asked concerns the number of segments, including the /aa/ itself, that occur to the left of the /aa/ in the word in which /aa/ occurs. (See Table 1 for an explanation of the symbols used in Figure 1.) In this case, if the /aa/ is initial — i.e., *lseg* is 1, one goes left; if there is one or more segments to the left in the word, go right. Let us assume that this /aa/ is initial in the word, in which case we go left. The next question concerns the consonantal 'place' of articulation of the segment to the right of /aa/; if it is alveolar go left; otherwise, if it is of some other quality, or if the segment to the right of /aa/ is not a consonant, then go right. Let us assume that the segment to the right is /z/, which is alveolar, so we go left. This lands us at terminal node 4. The tree in Figure 1 shows us that in the training data 119 out of 308 occurrences of /aa/ in this environment were realized as [ao], or in other words that we can estimate the probability of /aa/ being realized as [ao] in this environment as .385. The full set of realizations at this node with estimated non-zero probabilities is as follows (see Table 2 for a relevant set of ARPABET-IPA correspondences):

phone	probability	– log prob. (weight)
ao	**0.385**	**0.95**
aa	0.289	1.24
q+aa	0.103	2.27
q+ao	0.096	2.34
ah	0.069	2.68
ax	0.058	2.84

An important point to bear in mind is that a decision tree in general is a complete description, in the sense that for any new data point, there will be some leaf node that corresponds to it. So for the tree in Figure 1, each new novel instance of /aa/ will be handled by (exactly) one leaf node in the tree, depending upon the environment in which the /aa/ finds itself.

Another important point is that each decision tree considered here has the property that its predictions specify how to rewrite a symbol (in context) in an input string. In particular, they specify a two-level mapping from a set of input symbols (phonemes) to a set of output symbols (allophones).

3 Quick Review of Rule Compilation

Work on finite-state phonology (Johnson, 1972; Koskenniemi, 1983; Kaplan and Kay, 1994) has shown that systems of rewrite rules of the familiar form $\phi \rightarrow \psi/\lambda\_\_\rho$, where ϕ, ψ, λ and ρ are regular expressions, can be represented computationally as finite-state transducers (FSTs): note that ϕ represents the rule's input rule, ψ the output, and λ and ρ, respectively, the left and right contexts.

Kaplan and Kay (1994) have presented a concrete algorithm for compiling systems of such rules into FSTs. These methods can be extended slightly to include the compilation of *probabilistic* or *weighted* rules into weighted finite-state-transducers (WFSTs — see (Pereira et al., 1994)): Mohri and Sproat (1996) describe a rule-compilation algorithm which is more efficient than the Kaplan-Kay algorithm, and which has been extended to handle weighted rules. For present purposes it is sufficient to observe that given this extended algorithm, we can allow ψ in the expression $\phi \rightarrow \psi/\lambda\_\_\rho$, to represent a weighted regular expression. The compiled transducer corresponding to that rule will replace ϕ with ψ with the appropriate weights in the context $\lambda\_\_\rho$.

4 The Tree Compilation Algorithm

The key requirements on the kind of decision trees that we can compile into WFSTs are (1) the predictions at the leaf nodes specify how to rewrite a particular symbol in an input string, and (2) the decisions at each node are stateable as regular expressions over the input string. Each leaf node represents a single rule. The regular expressions for each branch describe one aspect of the left context λ, right context ρ, or both. The left and right contexts for the rule consist of the *intersections* of the partial descriptions of these contexts defined for each branch traversed between the root and leaf node. The input ϕ is predefined for the entire tree, whereas the output ψ is defined as the union of the set of outputs, along with their weights, that are associated with the leaf node. The weighted rule belonging to the leaf node can then be compiled into a transducer using the weighted-rule-compilation algorithm referenced in the preceding section. The transducer for the entire tree can be derived by the *intersection* of the entire set of transducers associated with the leaf nodes. Note that while regular relations are not generally closed under intersection, the subset of *same-length* (or more strictly speaking *length-preserving*) relations is closed; see below.

To see how this works, let us return to the example in Figure 1. To start with, we know that this tree models the phonetic realization of /aa/, so we can immediately set ϕ to be *aa* for the whole tree. Next, consider again the traversal of the tree from the root node to leaf node 4. The first decision concerns the number of segments to the left of the /aa/ in the word, either none for the left

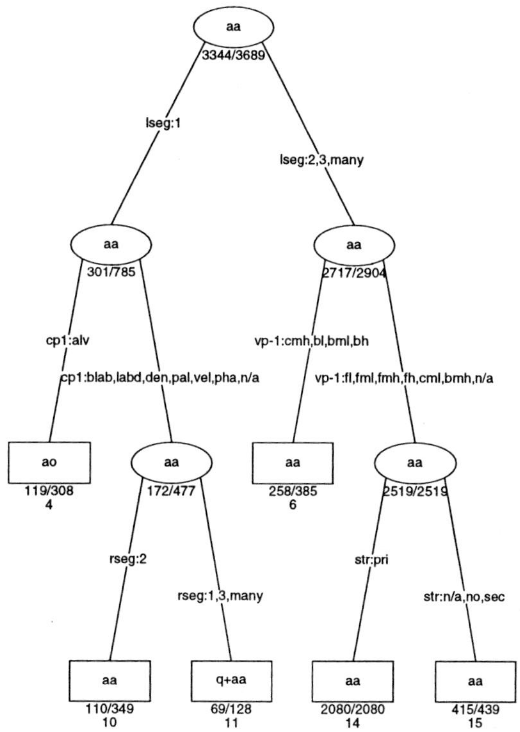

Figure 1: Tree modeling the phonetic realization of /aa/. All phones are given in ARPABET. Table 2 gives ARPABET-IPA conversions for symbols relevant to this example. See Table 1 for an explanation of other symbols

cpn	place of articulation of consonant *n* segments to the right
cp-n	place of articulation of consonant *n* segments to the left
	values: **alv**eolar; **bi**la**b**ial; **lab**io**d**ental; **den**tal; **pal**atal; **vel**ar; **pha**ryngeal;
	n/a if is a vowel, or there is no such segment
vpn	place of articulation of vowel *n* segments to the right
vp-n	place of articulation of vowel *n* segments to the left
	values: **c**entral-**m**id-**h**igh; **b**ack-**l**ow; **b**ack-**m**id-**l**ow; **b**ack-**h**igh; **f**ront-**l**ow;
	front-**m**id-**l**ow; **f**ront-**m**id-**h**igh; **f**ront-**h**igh; **c**entral-**m**id-**l**ow; **b**ack-**m**id-**h**igh
	n/a if is a consonant, or there is no such segment
lseg	number of preceding segments *including* the segment of interest *within the word*
rseg	number of following segments *including* the segment of interest *within the word*
	values: **1**, **2**, **3**, **many**
str	stress assigned to this vowel
	values: **pri**mary, **sec**ondary, **no** (zero) stress
	n/a if there is no stress mark

Table 1: Explanation of symbols in Figure 1.

aa	ɑ
ao	ɔ
ax	ə
ah	ʌ
q+aa	ʔɑ
q+ao	ʔɔ

Table 2: ARPABET-IPA conversion for symbols relevant for Figure 1.

branch, or one or more for the right branch. Assuming that we have a symbol α representing a single segment, the symbol # representing a word boundary, and allowing for the possibility of intervening optional stress marks — ′ — which do not count as segments, these two possibilities can be represented by the regular expressions for λ in (a) of Table 3.[2] At this node there is no decision based on the righthand context, so the righthand context is free. We can represent this by setting ρ at this node to be Σ^*, where Σ (conventionally) represents the entire alphabet: note that the alphabet is defined to be an alphabet of all ϕ:ψ correspondence pairs that were determined empirically to be possible.

The decision at the left daughter of the root node concerns whether or not the segment to the right is an alveolar. Assuming we have defined classes of segments *alv*, *blab*, and so forth (represented as unions of segments) we can represent the regular expression for ρ as in (b) of Table 3. In this case it is λ which is unrestricted, so we can set that at Σ^*.

We can derive the λ and ρ expressions for the rule at leaf node 4 by intersecting together the expressions for these contexts defined for each branch traversed on the way to the leaf. For leaf node 4, $\lambda = \#Opt(') \cap \Sigma^* = \#Opt(')$, and $\rho = \Sigma^* \cap Opt(')(alv) = Opt(')(alv)$.[3] The rule input ϕ has already been given as *aa*. The output ψ is defined as the union of all of the possible expressions — at the leaf node in question — that *aa* could become, with their associated weights (negative log probabilities), which we represent here as subscripted floating-point numbers:

$$\psi = ao_{0.95} \cup aa_{1.24} \cup q{+}aa_{2.27} \cup q{+}ao_{2.34} \cup ah_{2.68} \cup ax_{2.84}$$

Thus the entire weighted rule can be written as follows:

$$aa \rightarrow (ao_{0.95} \cup aa_{1.24} \cup q{+}aa_{2.27} \cup q{+}ao_{2.34} \cup ah_{2.68} \cup ax_{2.84}) / \#Opt(')\_\_\_Opt(')(alv)$$

By a similar construction, the rule at node 6, for example, would be represented as:

$$aa \rightarrow (aa_{0.40} \cup ao_{1.11}) / \ (\#(Opt(')\alpha)^{+}Opt(')) \cap (\Sigma^*((cmh) \cup (bl) \cup (bml) \cup (bh)))\_\_\_\Sigma^*$$

Each node thus represents a rule which states that a mapping occurs between the input symbol ϕ and the weighted expression ψ in the condition described by $\lambda\_\_\_\rho$. Now, in cases where ϕ finds itself in a context that is *not* subsumed by $\lambda\_\_\_\rho$, the rule behaves exactly as a two-level *surface coercion rule* (Koskenniemi, 1983): it freely allows ϕ to correspond to any ψ as specified by the alphabet of pairs. These ϕ:ψ correspondences are, however, constrained by *other* rules derived from the tree, as we shall see directly.

The interpretation of the full tree is that it represents the conjunction of all such mappings: for rules 1, 2 ... n, ϕ corresponds to ψ_1 given condition $\lambda_1\_\_\_\rho_1$ **and** ϕ corresponds to ψ_2 given condition $\lambda_2\_\_\_\rho_2$ ... **and** ϕ corresponds to ψ_n given condition $\lambda_n\_\_\_\rho_n$. But this conjunction is simply the *intersection* of the entire set of transducers defined for the leaves of the tree. Observe now that the ϕ:ψ correspondences that were left free by the rule of one leaf node, are constrained by intersection with the other leaf nodes: since, as noted above, the tree is a complete description, it follows that for any leaf node i, and for any context $\lambda\_\_\_\rho$ *not* subsumed by $\lambda_i\_\_\_\rho_i$, there is some leaf node j such that $\lambda_j\_\_\_\rho_j$ subsumes $\lambda\_\_\_\rho$. Thus, the transducers compiled for the rules at nodes 4 and 6, are intersected together, along with the rules for all the other leaf nodes. Now, as noted above, and as discussed by Kaplan and Kay (1994) regular relations — the algebraic counterpart of FSTs — are not in general closed under intersection; however, the subset of *same-length* regular relations *is* closed under intersection, since they can be thought of as finite-state *acceptors* ex-

[2] As far as possible, we use the notation of Kaplan and Kay (1994).

[3] Strictly speaking, since the λs and ρs at each branch may define expressions of different lengths, it is necessary to left-pad each λ with Σ^*, and right-pad each ρ with Σ^*. We gloss over this point here in order to make the regular expressions somewhat simpler to understand

(a)	left branch	λ	=	$\#Opt(')$
		ρ	=	Σ^*
	right branch	λ	=	$(\#Opt(')\alpha Opt(')) \cup (\#Opt(')\alpha Opt(')\alpha Opt('))\cup$ $(\#Opt(')\alpha Opt(')\alpha Opt(')(\alpha Opt('))^+)$
			=	$(Opt(')\alpha)^+Opt(')$
		ρ	=	Σ^*
(b)	left branch	λ	=	Σ^*
		ρ	=	$Opt(')(alv)$
	right branch	λ	=	Σ^*
		ρ	=	$(Opt(')(blab)) \cup (Opt(')(labd)) \cup (Opt(')(den)) \cup (Opt(')(pal))\cup$ $(Opt(')(vel)) \cup (Opt(')(pha)) \cup (Opt(')(n/a))$

Table 3: Regular-expression interpretation of the decisions involved in going from the root node to leaf node 4 in the tree in Figure 1. Note that, as per convention, superscript '+' denotes one or more instances of an expression.

pressed over *pairs* of symbols.[4] This point can be extended somewhat to include relations that involve *bounded* deletions or insertions: this is precisely the interpretation necessary for systems of two-level rules (Koskenniemi, 1983), where a single transducer expressing the entire system may be constructed via intersection of the transducers expressing the individual rules (Kaplan and Kay, 1994, pages 367–376). Indeed, our decision tree represents neither more nor less than a set of *weighted* two-level rules. Each of the symbols in the expressions for λ and ρ actually represent (sets of) pairs of symbols: thus *alv*, for example, represents all lexical alveolars paired with all of their possible surface realizations. And just as each tree represents a system of weighted two-level rules, so a set of trees — e.g., where each tree deals with the realization of a particular phone — represents a system of weighted two-level rules, where each two-level rule is compiled from each of the individual trees.

We can summarize this discussion more formally as follows. We presume a function *Compile* which given a rule returns the WFST computing that rule. The WFST for a single leaf L is thus defined as follows, where ϕ_T is the input symbol for the entire tree, ψ_L is the output expression defined at L, P_L represents the path traversed from the root node to L, p is an individual branch on that path, and λ_p and ρ_p are the expressions for λ and ρ defined at p:

$$Rule_L = Compile(\phi_T \rightarrow \psi_L / \bigcap_{p\in P_L} \lambda_p \_\_ \bigcap_{p\in P_L} \rho_p)$$

The transducer for an entire tree T is defined as:

$$Rule_T = \bigcap_{L\in T} Rule_L$$

Finally, the transducer for a forest F of trees is just:

$$Rule_F = \bigcap_{T\in F} Rule_T$$

5 Empirical Verification of the Method.

The algorithm just described has been empirically verified on the Resource Management (RM) continuous speech recognition task (Price et al., 1988). Following somewhat the discussion in (Pereira et al., 1994; Pereira and Riley, 1996), we can represent the speech recognition task as the problem of finding the best path in the composition of a grammar (language model) G, the transitive-closure of a dictionary D mapping between words and their *phonemic* representation, a model of phone realization Φ, and a weighted lattice representing the acoustic observations A.

[4] One can thus define intersection for transducers analogously with intersection for acceptors. Given two machines G_1 and G_2, with transition functions δ_1 and δ_2, one can define the transition function of G, δ, as follows: for an input-output pair (i,o), $\delta((q_1,q_2),(i,o)) = (q_1',q_2')$ if and only if $\delta_1(q_1,(i,o)) = q_1'$ and $\delta_2(q_2,(i,o)) = q_2'$.

Thus:

$$BestPath(G \circ D^* \circ \Phi \circ A) \quad (1)$$

The transducer $\Phi = \bigcap_{T \in F} Rule_T$ can be constructed out of the forest F of 40 trees, one for each phoneme, trained on the TIMIT database. The size of the trees range from 1 to 23 leaf nodes, with a total of 291 leaves for the entire forest.

The model was tested on 300 sentences from the RM task containing 2560 word tokens, and approximately 10,500 phonemes. A version of the model of recognition given in expression (1), where Φ is a transducer computed from the trees, was compared with a version where the trees were used directly following a method described in (Ljolje and Riley, 1992). The phonetic realizations and their weights were identical for both methods, thus verifying the correctness of the compilation algorithm described here.

The sizes of the compiled transducers can be quite large; in fact they were sufficiently large that instead of constructing Φ beforehand, we intersected the 40 individual transducers with the lattice D^* at runtime. Table 4 gives sizes for the entire set of phone trees: tree sizes are listed in terms of number of rules (terminal nodes) and raw size in bytes; transducer sizes are listed in terms of number of states and arcs. Note that the entire alphabet comprises 215 symbol pairs. Also given in Table 4 are the compilation times for the individual trees on a Silicon Graphics R4400 machine running at 150 MHz with 1024 Mbytes of memory. The times are somewhat slow for the larger trees, but still acceptable for off-line compilation.

While the sizes of the resulting transducers seem at first glance to be unfavorable, it is important to bear in mind that size is not the only consideration in deciding upon a particular representation. WFSTs possess several nice properties that are not shared by trees, or handwritten rulesets for that matter. In particular, once compiled into a WFST, a tree can be used in the same way as a WFST derived from any other source, such as a lexicon or a language model; a compiled WFST can be used directly in a speech recognition model such as that of (Pereira and Riley, 1996) or in a speech synthesis text-analysis model such as that of (Sproat, 1996). Use of a tree directly requires a special-purpose interpreter, which is much less flexible.

It should also be borne in mind that the size explosion evident in Table 4 also characterizes rules that are compiled from hand-built rewrite rules (Kaplan and Kay, 1994; Mohri and Sproat, 1996). For example, the text-analysis ruleset for the Bell Labs German text-to-speech (TTS) system (see (Sproat, 1996; Mohri and Sproat, 1996)) contains sets of rules for the pronunciation of various orthographic symbols. The ruleset for <a>, for example, contains 25 ordered rewrite rules. Over an alphabet of 194 symbols, this compiles, using the algorithm of (Mohri and Sproat, 1996), into a transducer containing 213,408 arcs and 1,927 states. This is 72% as many arcs and 48% as many states as the transducer for /ah/ in Table 4. The size explosion is not quite as great here, but the resulting transducer is still large compared to the original rule file, which only requires 1428 bytes of storage. Again, the advantages of representing the rules as a transducer outweigh the problems of size.[5]

6 Future Applications

We have presented a practical algorithm for converting decision trees inferred from data into weighted finite-state transducers that directly implement the models implicit in the trees, and we have empirically verified that the algorithm is correct.

Several interesting areas of application come to mind. In addition to speech recognition, where we hope to apply the phonetic realization models described above to the much larger North American Business task (Paul and Baker, 1992), there are also applications to TTS where, for example, the decision trees for prosodic phrase-boundary prediction discussed in (Wang and Hirschberg, 1992) can be compiled into transducers and used directly in the WFST-based model of text analysis used in the multi-lingual version of the Bell Laboratories TTS system, described in (Sproat, 1995; Sproat, 1996).

7 Acknowledgments

The authors wish to thank Fernando Pereira, Mehryar Mohri and two anonymous referees for useful comments.

References

Leo Breiman, Jerome H. Friedman, Richard A. Olshen, and Charles J. Stone. 1984. *Clas-*

[5] Having said this, we note that obviously one would like to decrease the size of the resulting transducers if that is possible. We are currently investigating ways to avoid precompiling the transducers beforehand, but rather to construct 'on the fly', only those portions of the transducers that are necessary for a particular intersection.

ARPABET phone	# nodes	size of tree (bytes)	# arcs	# states	time (sec)
zh	1	47	215	1	0.3
jh	2	146	675	6	0.8
aw	2	149	1,720	8	1
f	2	119	669	6	0.9
ng	2	150	645	3	0.8
oy	2	159	1,720	8	1
uh	2	126	645	3	0.9
p	3	252	6,426	90	4
ay	3	228	4,467	38	2
m	3	257	2,711	27	1
ow	3	236	3,010	14	3
sh	3	230	694	8	1
v	3	230	685	8	1
b	4	354	3,978	33	2
ch	4	353	3,010	25	4
th	4	373	1,351	11	2
dh	5	496	1,290	6	3
ey	5	480	11,510	96	27
g	6	427	372,339	3,000	21
k	6	500	6,013	85	9
aa	6	693	18,441	106	15
ah	7	855	40,135	273	110
y	7	712	9,245	43	12
ao	8	1,099	85,439	841	21
eh	8	960	16,731	167	13
er	8	894	101,765	821	31
w	8	680	118,154	1,147	51
hh	9	968	17,459	160	10
l	9	947	320,266	3,152	31
uw	9	1,318	44,868	552	28
z	9	1,045	1,987	33	5
s	10	1,060	175,901	2,032	25
ae	11	1,598	582,445	4,152	231
iy	11	1,196	695,255	9,625	103
d	12	1,414	36,067	389	38
n	16	1,899	518,066	3,827	256
r	16	1,901	131,903	680	69
ih	17	2,748	108,970	669	71
t	22	2,990	1,542,612	8,382	628
ax	23	4,281	295,954	3,966	77

Table 4: Sizes of transducers corresponding to each of the individual phone trees.

sification and Regression Trees. Wadsworth & Brooks, Pacific Grove CA.

William Fisher, Victor Zue, D. Bernstein, and David Pallet. 1987. An acoustic-phonetic data base. *Journal of the Acoustical Society of America*, 91, December. Supplement 1.

Daniel Gildea and Daniel Jurafsky. 1995. Automatic induction of finite state transducers for simple phonological rules. In *33rd Annual Meeting of the Association for Computational Linguistics*, pages 9–15, Morristown, NJ. Association for Computational Linguistics.

C. Douglas Johnson. 1972. *Formal Aspects of Phonological Description.* Mouton, Mouton, The Hague.

Ronald Kaplan and Martin Kay. 1994. Regular models of phonological rule systems. *Computational Linguistics*, 20:331–378.

Kimmo Koskenniemi. 1983. *Two-Level Morphology: a General Computational Model for Word-Form Recognition and Production.* Ph.D. thesis, University of Helsinki, Helsinki.

Andrej Ljolje and Michael D. Riley. 1992. Optimal speech recognition using phone recognition and lexical access. In *Proceedings of ICSLP*, pages 313–316, Banff, Canada, October.

David Magerman. 1995. Statistical decision-tree models for parsing. In *33rd Annual Meeting of the Association for Computational Linguistics*, pages 276–283, Morristown, NJ. Association for Computational Linguistics.

Mehryar Mohri and Richard Sproat. 1996. An efficient compiler for weighted rewrite rules. In *34rd Annual Meeting of the Association for Computational Linguistics*, Morristown, NJ. Association for Computational Linguistics.

José Oncina, Pedro García, and Enrique Vidal. 1993. Learning subsequential transducers for pattern recognition tasks. *IEEE Transactions on Pattern Analysis and Machine Intelligence*, 15:448–458.

Douglas Paul and Janet Baker. 1992. The design for the Wall Street Journal-based CSR corpus. In *Proceedings of International Conference on Spoken Language Processing*, Banff, Alberta. ICSLP.

Fernando Pereira and Michael Riley. 1996. Speech recognition by composition of weighted finite automata. CMP-LG archive paper 9603001.

Fernando Pereira, Michael Riley, and Richard Sproat. 1994. Weighted rational transductions and their application to human language processing. In *ARPA Workshop on Human Language Technology*, pages 249–254. Advanced Research Projects Agency, March 8–11.

Patty Price, William Fisher, Jared Bernstein, and David Pallett. 1988. The DARPA 1000-word Resource Management Database for continuous speech recognition. In *Proceedings of ICASSP88*, volume 1, pages 651–654, New York. ICASSP.

Michael Riley. 1989. Some applications of tree-based modelling to speech and language. In *Proceedings of the Speech and Natural Language Workshop*, pages 339–352, Cape Cod MA, October. DARPA, Morgan Kaufmann.

Michael Riley. 1991. A statistical model for generating pronunciation networks. In *Proceedings of the International Conference on Acoustics, Speech, and Signal Processing*, pages S11.1.–S11.4. ICASSP91, October.

Richard Sproat. 1995. A finite-state architecture for tokenization and grapheme-to-phoneme conversion for multilingual text analysis. In Susan Armstrong and Evelyne Tzoukermann, editors, *Proceedings of the EACL SIGDAT Workshop*, pages 65–72, Dublin, Ireland. Association for Computational Linguistics.

Richard Sproat. 1996. Multilingual text analysis for text-to-speech synthesis. In *Proceedings of the ECAI-96 Workshop on Extended Finite State Models of Language*, Budapest, Hungary. European Conference on Artificial Intelligence.

Michelle Wang and Julia Hirschberg. 1992. Automatic classification of intonational phrase boundaries. *Computer Speech and Language*, 6:175–196.

FAST PARSING USING PRUNING AND GRAMMAR SPECIALIZATION

Manny Rayner and David Carter
SRI International
Suite 23, Millers Yard
Cambridge CB2 1RQ
United Kingdom
manny@cam.sri.com, dmc@cam.sri.com

Abstract

We show how a general grammar may be automatically adapted for fast parsing of utterances from a specific domain by means of constituent pruning and grammar specialization based on explanation-based learning. These methods together give an order of magnitude increase in speed, and the coverage loss entailed by grammar specialization is reduced to approximately half that reported in previous work. Experiments described here suggest that the loss of coverage has been reduced to the point where it no longer causes significant performance degradation in the context of a real application.

1 Introduction

Suppose that we have a general grammar for English, or some other natural language; by this, we mean a grammar which encodes most of the important constructions in the language, and which is intended to be applicable to a large range of different domains and applications. The basic question attacked in this paper is the following one: can such a grammar be concretely useful if we want to process input from a *specific* domain? In particular, how can a parser that uses a general grammar achieve a level of efficiency that is practically acceptable?

The central problem is simple to state. By the very nature of its construction, a general grammar allows a great many theoretically valid analyses of almost any non-trivial sentence. However, in the context of a specific domain, most of these will be extremely implausible, and can in practice be ignored. If we want efficient parsing, we want to be able to focus our search on only a small portion of the space of theoretically valid grammatical analyses.

One possible solution is of course to dispense with the idea of using a general grammar, and simply code a new grammar for each domain. Many people do this, but one cannot help feeling that something is being missed; intuitively, there are many domain-independent grammatical constraints, which one would prefer only to need to code once. In the last ten years, there have been a number of attempts to find ways to automatically adapt a general grammar and/or parser to the sub-language defined by a suitable training corpus. For example, (Briscoe and Carroll, 1993) train an LR parser based on a general grammar to be able to distinguish between likely and unlikely sequences of parsing actions; (Andry et al., 1994) automatically infer sortal constraints, that can be used to rule out otherwise grammatical constituents; and (Grishman et al., 1984) describes methods that reduce the size of a general grammar to include only rules actually useful for parsing the training corpus.

The work reported here is a logical continuation of two specific strands of research aimed in this general direction. The first is the popular idea of *statistical tagging* e.g. (DeRose, 1988; Cutting et al., 1992; Church, 1988). Here, the basic idea is that a given small segment S of the input string may have several possible analyses; in particular, if S is a single word, it may potentially be any one of several parts of speech. However, if a substantial training corpus is available to provide reasonable estimates of the relevant parameters, the immediate context surrounding S will usually make most of the locally possible analyses of S extremely implausible. In the specific case of part-of-speech tagging, it is well-known (DeMarcken, 1990) that a large proportion of the incorrect tags can be eliminated "safely", i.e. with very low risk of eliminating correct tags. In the present paper, the statistical tagging idea is generalized to a method called "constituent pruning"; this acts on local analyses of phrases normally larger than single-word units.

Constituent pruning is a bottom-up approach, and is complemented by a second, top-down, method based on *Explanation-Based Learning* (EBL; (Mitchell et al., 1986; van Harmelen and Bundy, 1988)). This part of the paper is essentially an extension and generalization of the line of work described in (Rayner, 1988; Rayner and Samuelsson, 1990; Samuelsson and Rayner, 1991; Rayner and Samuelsson, 1994; Samuelsson, 1994b). Here, the basic idea is that grammar rules tend in any specific domain to combine much more frequently in some ways than in others. Given a sufficiently large corpus parsed by the original, general, grammar, it is possible to identify the common combinations of grammar rules and "chunk" them into "macro-rules". The result is a "specialized" grammar; this has a larger number of rules, but a simpler structure, allowing it in practice to be parsed very much more quickly using an LR-based method (Samuelsson, 1994a). The coverage of the specialized grammar is a strict subset of that of the original grammar; thus any analysis produced by the specialized grammar is guaranteed to be valid in the original one as well. The practical utility of the specialized grammar is largely determined by the loss of coverage incurred by the specialization process.

The two methods, constituent pruning and grammar specialization, are combined as follows. The rules in the original, general, grammar are divided into two sets, called *phrasal* and *non-phrasal* respectively. Phrasal rules, the majority of which define non-recursive noun phrase constructions, are used as they are; non-phrasal rules are combined using EBL into chunks, forming a specialized grammar which is then compiled further into a set of LR-tables. Parsing proceeds by interleaving constituent creation and deletion. First, the lexicon and morphology rules are used to hypothesize word analyses. Constituent pruning then removes all sufficiently unlikely edges. Next, the phrasal rules are applied bottom-up, to find all possible phrasal edges, after which unlikely edges are again pruned. Finally, the specialized grammar is used to search for full parses. The scheme is fully implemented within a version of the Spoken Language Translator system (Rayner et al., 1993; Agnäs et al., 1994), and is normally applied to input in the form of small lattices of hypotheses produced by a speech recognizer.

The rest of the paper is structured as follows. Section 2 describes the constituent pruning method. Section 3 describes the grammar specialization method, focusing on how the current work extends and improves on previous results. Section 4 describes experiments where the constituent pruning/grammar specialization method was used on sets of previously unseen speech data. Section 5 concludes and sketches further directions for research, which we are presently in the process of investigating.

2 Constituent Pruning

Before both the phrasal and full parsing stages, the constituent table (henceforth, the chart) is pruned to remove edges that are relatively unlikely to contribute to correct analyses.

For example, after the string "Show flight D L three one two" is lexically analysed, edges for "D" and "L" as individual characters are pruned because another edge, derived from a lexical entry for "D L" as an airline code, is deemed far more plausible. Similarly, edges for "one" as a determiner and as a noun are pruned because, when flanked by two other numbers, "one" is far more likely to function as a number.

Phrasal parsing then creates a number of new edges, including one for "flight D L three one two" as a noun phrase. This edge is deemed far more likely to serve as the basis for a correct full parse than any of the edges spanning substrings of this phrase; those edges, too, are therefore pruned. As a result, full parsing is very quick, and only one analysis (the correct one) is produced for the sentence. In the absence of pruning, processing takes over eight times as long and produces 37 analyses in total.

2.1 The pruning algorithm

Our algorithm estimates the probability of correctness of each edge: that is, the probability that the edge will contribute to the correct full analysis of the sentence (assuming there is one), given certain lexical and/or syntactic information about it. Values on each criterion (selection of pieces of information) are derived from training corpora by maximum likelihood estimation followed by smoothing. That is, our estimate for the probability that an edge with property P is correct is (modulo smoothing) simply the number of times edges with property P occur in *correct* analyses in training divided by the number of times such edges are *created* during the analysis process in training.

The current criteria are:

- The *left bigram* score: the probability of correctness of an edge considering only the following data about it:
  - its *tag* (corresponding to its major category symbol plus, for a few categories, some ad-

ditional distinctions derived from feature values);
  - for a lexical edge, its *word* or *semantic word class* (words with similar distributions, such as city names, are grouped into classes to overcome data sparseness); or for a phrasal edge, the name of the final (topmost) *grammar rule* that was used to create it;
  - the tag of a neighbouring edge immediately to its left. If there are several left neighbours, the one giving the highest probability is used.

- The *right bigram* score: as above, but considering right neighbours.

- The *unigram* score: the probability of correctness of an edge considering only the tree of grammar rules, with words or word classes at the leaves, that gave rise to it. For a lexical edge, this reduces to its word or word class, and its tag.

Other criteria, such as trigrams and finer-grained tags, are obviously worth investigating, and could be applied straightforwardly within the framework described here.

The minimum score derived from any of the criteria applied is deemed initially to be the score of the constituent. That is, an assumption of full statistical dependence (Yarowsky, 1994), rather than the more common full independence, is made.[1] When recognizer output is being processed, however, the estimate from each criterion is in fact multiplied by a further estimate derived from the acoustic score of the edge: that is, the score assigned by the speech recognizer to the best-scoring sentence hypothesis containing the word or word string for the edge in question. Multiplication is used here because acoustic and lexicosyntactic likelihoods for a word or constituent would appear to be more nearly fully independent than fully dependent, being based on very different kinds of information.

Next, account is taken of the connectivity of the chart. Each *vertex* of the chart is labelled with the score of the best path through the chart that visits that vertex. In accordance with the dependence assumption, the score of a path is defined as the minimum of the scores of its component edges. Then the score of each edge is recalculated to be the minimum of its existing score and the scores of its start and end vertices, on the grounds that a constituent, however intrinsically plausible, is not worth preserving if it does not occur on any plausible paths.

Finally, a pruning threshold is calculated as the score of the best path through the chart multiplied by a certain fraction. For the first pruning phase we use 1/20, and for the second, 1/150, although performance is not very sensitive to this. Any constituents scoring less than the threshold are pruned out.

2.2 Relation to other pruning methods

As the example above suggests, judicious pruning of the chart at appropriate points can greatly restrict the search space and speed up processing. Our method has points of similarity with some very recent work in Constraint Grammar[2] and is an alternative to several other, related schemes.

Firstly, a remarked earlier, it generalizes *tagging*: it not only adjudicates between possible labels for the same word, but can also use the existence of a constituent over one span of the chart as justification for pruning another constituent over another span, normally a subsumed one, as in the "D L" example. This is especially true in the second stage of pruning, when many constituents of different lengths have been created. Furthermore, it applies equally well to lattices, rather than strings, of words, and can take account of acoustic plausibility as well as syntactic considerations.

Secondly, our method is related to *beam search* (Woods, 1985). In beam search, incomplete parses of an utterance are pruned or discarded when, on

---

[1] If events $E_1, E_2, ..., E_n$ are fully independent, then the joint probability $P(E_1 \wedge ... \wedge E_n)$ is the product of $P(E_1)...P(E_n)$, but if they are maximally dependent, it is the minimum of these values. Of course, neither assumption is any more than an approximation to the truth; but assuming dependence has the advantage that the estimate of the joint probability depends much less strongly on n, and so estimates for alternative joint events can be directly compared, without any possibly tricky normalization, even if they are composed of different numbers of atomic events. This property is desirable: different (sub-)paths through a chart may span different numbers of edges, and one can imagine evaluation criteria which are only defined for some kinds of edge, or which often duplicate information supplied by other criteria. Taking minima means that the pruning of an edge results from it scoring poorly on one criterion, regardless of other, possibly good scores assigned to it by other criteria. This fits in with the fact that on the basis of local information alone it is not usually possibly to predict with confidence that a particular edge is highly *likely* to contribute to the correct analysis (since global factors will also be important) but it often is possible to spot highly *unlikely* edges. In other words, our training procedure yields far more probability estimates close to zero than close to one.

[2] Christer Samuelsson, personal communication, 8th April 1996; see (Karlsson et al., 1995) for background.

some criterion, they are significantly less plausible than other, competing parses. This pruning is fully interleaved with the parsing process. In contrast, our pruning takes place only at certain points: currently before parsing begins, and between the phrasal and full parsing stages. Potentially, as with any generate-and-test algorithm, this can mean efficiency is reduced: some paths will be explored that could in principle be pruned earlier. However, as the results in section 4 below will show, this is not in practice a serious problem, because the second pruning phase greatly reduces the search space in preparation for the potentially inefficient full parsing phase. Our method has the advantage, compared to beam search, that there is no need for any particular search order to be followed; when pruning takes place, all constituents that could have been found at the stage in question are guaranteed already to exist.

Thirdly, our method is a generalization of the strategy employed by (McCord, 1993). McCord interleaved parsing with pruning in the same way as us, but only compared constituents over the same span and with the same major category. Our comparisons are more global and therefore can result in more effective pruning.

3 Grammar specialization

As described in Section 1 above, the non-phrasal grammar rules are subjected to two phases of processing. In the first, "EBL learning" phase, a parsed training corpus is used to identify "chunks" of rules, which are combined by the EBL algorithm into single macro-rules. In the second phase, the resulting set of "chunked" rules is converted into LR table form, using the method of (Samuelsson, 1994a).

There are two main parameters that can be adjusted in the EBL learning phase. Most simply, there is the size of the training corpus; a larger training corpus means a smaller loss of coverage due to grammar specialization. (Recall that grammar specialization in general trades coverage for speed). Secondly, there is the question of how to select the rule-chunks that will be turned into macro-rules. At one limit, the whole parse-tree for each training example is turned into a single rule, resulting in a specialized grammar all of whose derivations are completely "flat". These grammars can be parsed extremely quickly, but the coverage loss is in practice unacceptably high, even with very large training corpora. At the opposite extreme, each rule-chunk consists of a single rule-application; this yields a specialized grammar identical to the original one. The challenge is to find an intermediate solution, which specializes the grammar non-trivially without losing too much coverage.

Several attempts to find good "chunking criteria" are described in the papers by Rayner and Samuelsson quoted above. In (Rayner and Samuelsson, 1994), a simple scheme is given, which creates rules corresponding to four possible units: full utterances, recursive NPs, PPs, and non-recursive NPs. A more elaborate scheme is given in (Samuelsson, 1994b), where the "chunking criteria" are learned automatically by an entropy-minimization method; the results, however, do not appear to improve on the earlier ones. In both cases, the coverage loss due to grammar specialization was about 10 to 12% using training corpora with about 5,000 examples. In practice, this is still unacceptably high for most applications.

Our current scheme is an extension of the one from (Rayner and Samuelsson, 1994), where the rule-chunks are trees of non-phrasal rules whose roots and leaves are categories of the following possible types: full utterances, utterance units, imperative VPs, NPs, relative clauses, VP modifiers and PPs. The resulting specialized grammars are forced to be non-recursive, with derivations being a maximum of six levels deep. This is enforced by imposing the following dominance hierarchy between the possible categories:

```
utterance > utterance_unit > imperative_VP
     > NP > {rel, VP_modifier} > PP
```

The precise definition of the rule-chunking criteria is quite simple, and is reproduced in the appendix.

Note that only the non-phrasal rules are used as input to the chunks from which the specialized grammar rules are constructed. This has two important advantages. Firstly, since all the phrasal rules are excluded from the specialization process, the coverage loss associated with missing combinations of phrasal rules is eliminated. As the experiments in the next section show, the resulting improvement is quite substantial. Secondly, and possibly even more importantly, the number of specialized rules produced by a given training corpus is approximately halved. The most immediate consequence is that much larger training corpora can be used before the specialized grammars produced become too large to be handled by the LR table compiler. If both phrasal and non-phrasal rules are used, we have been unable to compile tables for rules derived from training sets of over 6,000 examples (the process was killed after running for about six hours on a Sun Sparc 20/HS21, SpecINT92=131.2). Using only non-phrasal rules, compilation of the tables for a 15,000 example training set required less than two CPU-hours on the same machine.

4 Experiments

This section describes a number of experiments carried out to test the utility of the theoretical ideas presented above. The basic corpus used was a set of 16,000 utterances from the Air Travel Planning (ATIS; (Hemphill et al., 1990)) domain. All of these utterances were available in text form; 15,000 of them were used for training, with 1,000 held out for test purposes. Care was taken to ensure not just that the utterances themselves, but also the *speakers* of the utterances were disjoint between test and training data; as pointed out in (Rayner et al., 1994a), failure to observe these precautions can result in substantial spurious improvements in test data results.

The 16,000 sentence corpus was analysed by the SRI Core Language Engine (Alshawi (ed), 1992), using a lexicon extended to cover the ATIS domain (Rayner, 1994). All possible grammatical analyses of each utterance were recorded, and an interactive tool was used to allow a human judge to identify the correct and incorrect readings of each utterance. The judge was a first-year undergraduate student with a good knowledge of linguistics but no prior experience with the system; the process of judging the corpus took about two and a half person-months. The input to the EBL-based grammar-specialization process was limited to readings of corpus utterances that had been judged correct. When utterances had more than one correct reading, a preference heuristic was used to select the most plausible one.

Two sets of experiments were performed. In the first, increasingly large portions of the training set were used to train specialized grammars. The coverage loss due to grammar specialization was then measured on the 1,000 utterance test set. The experiment was carried out using both the chunking criteria from (Rayner and Samuelsson, 1994) (the "Old" scheme), and the chunking criteria described in Section 3 above (the "New" scheme). The results are presented in Table 1.

The second set of experiments tested more directly the effect of constituent pruning and grammar specialization on the Spoken Language Translator's speed and coverage; in particular, coverage was measured on the real task of translating English into Swedish, rather than the artificial one of producing a correct QLF analysis. To this end, the first 500 test-set utterances were presented in the form of speech hypothesis lattices derived by aligning and conflating the top five sentence strings produced by a version of the DECIPHER (TM) recognizer (Murveit et al., 1993). The lattices were analysed by four different versions of the parser, exploring the different combinations of turning constituent pruning on or off, and specialized versus unspecialized grammars. The specialized grammar used the "New" scheme, and had been trained on the full training set. Utterances which took more than 90 CPU seconds to process were timed out and counted as failures.

Examples	Old scheme		New scheme	
	Rules	Loss	Rules	Loss
100	100	47.8%	69	35.5%
250	181	37.6%	126	21.8%
500	281	27.6%	180	14.7%
1000	432	22.7%	249	10.8%
3000	839	14.9%	455	7.8%
5000	1101	11.2%	585	6.6%
7000	1292	10.4%	668	6.0%
11000	1550	9.8%	808	5.8%
15000	1819	8.7%	937	5.0%

Table 1: EBL rules and EBL coverage loss against number of training examples

The four sets of outputs from the parser were then translated into Swedish by the SLT transfer and generation mechanism (Agnäs et al., 1994). Finally, the four sets of candidate translations were pairwise compared in the cases where differing translations had been produced. We have found this to be an effective way of evaluating system performance. Although people differ widely in their judgements of whether a given translation can be regarded as "acceptable", it is in most cases surprisingly easy to say which of two possible translations is preferable. The last two tables summarize the results. Table 2 gives the average processing times per input lattice for each type of processing (times measured running SICStus Prolog 3#3 on a SUN Sparc 20/HS21), showing how the time is divided between the various processing phases. Table 3 shows the relative scores of the four parsing variants, measured according to the "preferable translation" criterion.

5 Conclusions and further directions

Table 2 indicates that EBL and pruning each make processing about three times faster; the combination of both gives a factor of about nine. In fact, as the detailed breakdown shows, even this underestimates the effect on the main parsing phase: when both pruning and EBL are operating, processing times for other components (morphology, pruning and preferences) become the dominant ones. As we have so

	E– P–	E+ P–	E– P+	E+ P+
Morph/lex lookup	0.53	0.54	0.54	0.49
Phrasal parsing	0.27	0.28	0.14	0.14
Pruning	–	–	0.57	0.56
Full parsing	12.42	2.61	3.04	0.26
Preferences	3.63	1.57	1.27	0.41
TOTAL	16.85	5.00	5.57	1.86

Table 2: Breakdown of average time spent on each processing phase for each type of processing (seconds per utterance)

	E– P–	E+ P–	E– P+	E+ P+
E–/P–		12–24	25–63	24–65
E+/P–	24–12		31–50	26–47
E–/P+	63–25	50–31		5–8
E+/P+	65–24	47–26	8–5	

Table 3: Comparison between translation results on the four different analysis alternatives, measured on the 500-utterance test set. The entry for a given row and column holds two figures, showing respectively the number of examples where the "row" variant produced a better translation than the "column" variant and the number where it produced a worse one. Thus for example "EBL+/pruning+" was better than "EBL–/pruning–" on 65 examples, and worse on 24.

far expended little effort on optimizing these phases of processing, it is reasonable to expect substantial further gains to be possible.

Even more interestingly, Table 3 shows that real system performance, in terms of producing a good translation, is significantly *improved* by pruning, and is not degraded by grammar specialization. (The slight improvement in coverage with EBL on is not statistically significant). Our interpretation of these results is that the technical loss of grammar coverage due to the specialization and pruning processes is more than counterbalanced by two positive effects. Firstly, fewer utterances time out due to slow processing; secondly, the reduced space of possible analyses means that the problem of selecting between different possible analyses of a given utterance becomes easier.

To sum up, the methods presented here demonstrate that it is possible to use the combined pruning and grammar specialization method to speed up the whole analysis phase by nearly an order of magnitude, without incurring any real penalty in the form of reduced coverage. We find this an exciting and significant result, and are further continuing our research in this area during the coming year. In the last two paragraphs we sketch some ongoing work.

All the results presented above pertain to English only. The first topic we have been investigating is the application of the methods described here to processing of other languages. Preliminary experiments we have carried out on the Swedish version of the CLE (Gambäck and Rayner 1992) have been encouraging; using exactly the same pruning methods and EBL chunking criteria as for English, we obtain comparable speed-ups. The loss of coverage due to grammar specialization also appears comparable, though we have not yet had time to do the work needed to verify this properly. We intend to do so soon, and also to repeat the experiments on the French version of the CLE (Rayner, Carter and Bouillon, 1996).

The second topic is a more radical departure, and can be viewed as an attempt to make interleaving of parsing and pruning the basic principle underlying the CLE's linguistic analysis process. Exploiting the "stratified" nature of the EBL-specialized grammar, we group the chunked rules by level, and apply them one level at a time, starting at the bottom. After each level, constituent pruning is used to eliminate unlikely constituents. The intent is to achieve a trainable robust parsing model, which can return a useful partial analysis when no single global analysis is found. An initial implementation exists, and is currently being tested; preliminary results here are also very positive. We expect to be able to report on this work more fully in the near future.

Acknowledgements

The work reported in this paper was funded by Telia Research AB. We would like to thank Christer Samuelsson for making the LR compiler available to us, Martin Keegan for patiently judging the results of processing 16,000 ATIS utterances, and Steve Pulman and Christer Samuelsson for helpful comments.

References

Agnäs, M-S., Alshawi, H., Bretan, I., Carter, D.M. Ceder, K., Collins, M., Crouch, R., Digalakis, V., Ekholm, B., Gambäck, B., Kaja, J., Karlgren, J., Lyberg, B., Price, P., Pulman, S., Rayner, M., Samuelsson, C. and Svensson, T. 1994. Spoken

Language Translator: First Year Report. SRI technical report CRC-043[3]

Alshawi, H. (ed.) 1992. The Core Language Engine. MIT Press.

Andry, F., M. Gawron, J. Dowding, and R. Moore. 1994. A Tool for Collecting Domain Dependent Sortal Constraints From Corpora. Proc. COLING-94, Kyoto.

Briscoe, Ted, and John Carroll. 1993. Generalized Probabilistic LR Parsing of Natural Language (Corpora) with Unification-Based Grammars. Computational Linguistics, 19:1, pp. 25-60.

Church, Ken. 1988. A stochastic parts program and noun phrase parser for unrestricted text. Proc. 1st ANLP, Austin, Tx., pp. 136-143.

Cutting, D., J. Kupiec, J. Pedersen and P. Sibun. 1992. A Practical Part-of-Speech Tagger Proc. 3rd ANLP, Trento, Italy, pp. 133-140.

DeMarcken, C.G. 1990. Parsing the LOB Corpus Proc. 28th ACL, Pittsburgh, Pa., pp. 243-251

DeRose, Steven. 1988. Grammatical Category Disambiguation by Statistical Optimization. Computational Linguistics 14, pp. 31-39

Gambäck, Björn, and Manny Rayner. "The Swedish Core Language Engine". Proc. 3rd Nordic Conference on Text Comprehension in Man and Machine, Linköping, Sweden. Also SRI Technical Report CRC-025.

Grishman, R., N. Nhan, E. Marsh and L. Hirschmann. 1984. Automated Determination of Sublanguage Usage. Proc. 22nd COLING, Stanford, pp. 96-100.

van Harmelen, Frank, and Alan Bundy. 1988. Explanation-Based Generalization = Partial Evaluation (Research Note) Artificial Intelligence 36, pp. 401–412.

Hemphill, C.T., J.J. Godfrey and G.R. Doddington. 1990. The ATIS Spoken Language Systems pilot corpus. Proc. DARPA Speech and Natural Language Workshop, Hidden Valley, Pa., pp. 96-101.

Karlsson, F., A. Voutilainen, J. Heikkilä and A. Anttila (eds). 1995. Constraint Grammar. Mouton de Gruyer, Berlin, New York.

McCord, M. 1993. Heuristics for Broad-Coverage Natural Language Parsing. Proc. 1st ARPA Workshop on Human Language Technology, Princeton, NJ. Morgan Kaufmann.

[3]All SRI Cambridge technical reports are available through WWW from `http://www.cam.sri.com`

Mitchell, T., R. Keller, and S. Kedar-Cabelli. 1986. Explanation-Based Generalization: a Unifying View. Machine Learning 1:1, pp. 47-80.

Murveit, H., Butzberger, J., Digalakis, V. and Weintraub, M. 1993. Large Vocabulary Dictation using SRI's DECIPHER(TM) Speech Recognition System: Progressive Search Techniques. Proc. Inter. Conf. on Acoust., Speech and Signal, Minneapolis, Mn.

Rayner, M. 1988. Applying Explanation-Based Generalization to Natural-Language Processing. Proc. the International Conference on Fifth Generation Computer Systems, Kyoto, pp. 1267-1274.

Rayner, M. 1994. Overview of English Linguistic Coverage. In (Agnäs et al., 1994)

Rayner, M., Alshawi, H., Bretan, I., Carter, D.M., Digalakis, V., Gambäck, B., Kaja, J., Karlgren, J., Lyberg, B., Price, P., Pulman, S. and Samuelsson, C. 1993. A Speech to Speech Translation System Built From Standard Components. Proc.1st ARPA workshop on Human Language Technology, Princeton, NJ. Morgan Kaufmann. Also SRI Technical Report CRC-031.

Rayner, M., D. Carter and P. Bouillon. 1996. Adapting the Core Language Engine to French and Spanish. Proc. NLP-IA, Moncton, New Brunswick. Also SRI Technical Report CRC-061.

Rayner, M., D. Carter, V. Digalakis and P. Price. 1994. Combining Knowledge Sources to Reorder N-Best Speech Hypothesis Lists. Proc.2nd ARPA workshop on Human Language Technology, Princeton, NJ., pp. 217-221. Morgan Kaufmann. Also SRI Technical Report CRC-044.

Rayner. M., and C. Samuelsson. 1990. Using Explanation-Based Learning to Increase Performance in a Large NL Query System. Proc. DARPA Speech and Natural Language Workshop, June 1990, pp. 251-256. Morgan Kaufmann.

Rayner, M., and C. Samuelsson. 1994. Corpus-Based Grammar Specialization for Fast Analysis. In (Agnäs et al., 1994)

Samuelsson, C. 1994. Notes on LR Parser Design. Proc. COLING-94, Kyoto, pp. 386-390.

Samuelsson, C. 1994. Grammar Specialization through Entropy Thresholds. Proc. ACL-94, Las Cruces, NM, pp. 188-195.

Samuelsson, C., and M. Rayner. 1991. Quantitative Evaluation of Explanation-Based Learning as an Optimization Tool for a Large-Scale Natural Language System. Proc. 12th IJCAI, Sydney, pp. 609-615.

Woods, W. 1985. Language Processing for Speech Understanding. Computer Speech Processing, W. Woods and F. Fallside (eds), Prentice-Hall International.

Yarowsky, D. 1994. Decision Lists for Lexical Ambiguity Resolution. Proc. ACL-94, Las Cruces, NM, pp. 88-95.

Appendix: definition of the "New" chunking rules

This appendix defines the "New" chunking rules referred to in Sections 3 and 4. There are seven types of non-phrasal constituent in the specialised grammar. We start by describing each type of constituent through examples.

Utterance: The top category.

Utterance_unit: `Utterance_ units` are minimal syntactic units capable of standing on their own: for example, declarative clauses, questions, NPs and PPs. Utterances may consist of more than one `utterance_unit`. The following is an `utterance` containing two `utterance_units`: "[Flights to Boston on Monday] [please show me the cheapest ones.]"

Imperative_VP: Since imperative verb phrases are very common in the corpus, we make them a category of their own in the specialised grammar. To generalise over possible addition of adverbials (in particular, "please" and "now"), we define the `imperative_vp` category so as to leave the adverbials outside. Thus the bracketed portion of the following utterance is an `imperative_vp`: "That's fine now [give me the fares for those flights]"

Non_phrasal_NP: All NPs which are not produced entirely by phrasal rules. The following are all `non_phrasal_NPs`: "Boston and Denver", "Flights on Sunday morning", "Cheapest fare from Boston to Denver", "The meal I'd get on that flight"

Rel: Relative clauses.

VP_modifier: VPs appearing as NP postmodifiers. The bracketed portions of the following are `VP_modifiers`: "Delta flights [arriving after seven P M]" "All flights tomorrow [ordered by arrival time]"

PP: The CLE grammar treats nominal temporal adverbials, sequences of PPs, and "A to B" constructions as PPs (cf (Rayner, 1994)). The following are examples of PPs: "Tomorrow afternoon", "From Boston to Dallas on Friday", "Denver to San Francisco Sunday"

We can now present the precise criteria which determine the chunks of rules composed to form each type of constituent. For each type of constituent in the specialised grammar, the chunk is a subtree extracted from the derivation tree of a training example (cf (Rayner and Samuelsson, 1994)); we specify the roots and leaves of the relevant subtrees. The term "phrasal tree" will be used to mean a derivation tree all of whose rule-applications are phrasal rules.

Utterance: The root of the chunk is the root of the original tree. The leaves are the nodes resulting from cutting at maximal subtrees for `utterance_units`, `non_phrasal_nps` `pps`, and maximal phrasal subtrees.

Utterance_unit: The root is the root of a maximal subtree for a constituent of type `utterance_unit`. The leaves are the nodes resulting from cutting at maximal subtrees for `imperative_vps`, `nps`, and `pps`, and maximal phrasal subtrees.

Imperative_VP: The root is the root of a maximal subtree under an application of the `S` $\rightarrow$ `VP` rule whose root is not an application of an adverbial modification rule. The leaves are the nodes resulting from cutting at maximal subtrees for `non_phrasal_np`, and `pp`, and maximal phrasal subtrees.

Non_phrasal_NP: The root is the root of a maximal non-phrasal subtree for a constituent of type `np`. The leaves are the nodes resulting from cutting at maximal subtrees for `rel`, `vp_modifier`, and `pp`, and maximal phrasal subtrees.

Rel: The root is the root of a maximal subtree for a constituent of type `rel`. The leaves are the nodes resulting from cutting at maximal subtrees for `pp`, and maximal phrasal subtrees.

VP_modifier: The root is the root of a `vp` subtree immediately dominated by an application of the `NP` $\rightarrow$ `NP VP` rule. The leaves are the nodes resulting from cutting at maximal subtrees for `pp`, and maximal phrasal subtrees.

PP: The root is the root of a maximal non-phrasal subtree for a constituent of type `pp`. The leaves are the nodes resulting from cutting at maximal phrasal subtrees.

An Efficient Compiler for Weighted Rewrite Rules

Mehryar Mohri
AT&T Research
600 Mountain Avenue
Murray Hill, 07974 NJ
mohri@research.att.com

Richard Sproat
Bell Laboratories
700 Mountain Avenue
Murray Hill, 07974 NJ
rws@bell-labs.com

Abstract

Context-dependent rewrite rules are used in many areas of natural language and speech processing. Work in computational phonology has demonstrated that, given certain conditions, such rewrite rules can be represented as finite-state transducers (FSTs). We describe a new algorithm for compiling rewrite rules into FSTs. We show the algorithm to be simpler and more efficient than existing algorithms. Further, many of our applications demand the ability to compile *weighted* rules into *weighted* FSTs, transducers generalized by providing transitions with weights. We have extended the algorithm to allow for this.

1. Motivation

Rewrite rules are used in many areas of natural language and speech processing, including syntax, morphology, and phonology[1]. In interesting applications, the number of rules can be very large. It is then crucial to give a representation of these rules that leads to efficient programs.

Finite-state transducers provide just such a compact representation (Mohri, 1994). They are used in various areas of natural language and speech processing because their increased computational power enables one to build very large machines to model interestingly complex linguistic phenomena. They also allow algebraic operations such as union, composition, and projection which are very useful in practice (Berstel, 1979; Eilenberg, 1974 1976). And, as originally shown by Johnson (1972), rewrite rules can be modeled as finite-state transducers, under the condition that no rule be allowed to apply any more than a finite number of times to its own output.

Kaplan and Kay (1994), or equivalently Karttunen (1995), provide an algorithm for compiling rewrite rules into finite-state transducers, under the condition that they do not rewrite their noncontextual part[2]. We here present a new algorithm for compiling such rewrite rules which is both simpler to understand and implement, and computationally more efficient. Clarity is important since, as pointed out by Kaplan and Kay (1994), the representation of rewrite rules by finite-state transducers involves many subtleties. Time and space efficiency of the compilation are also crucial. Using naive algorithms can be very time consuming and lead to very large machines (Liberman, 1994).

In some applications such as those related to speech processing, one needs to use *weighted* rewrite rules, namely rewrite rules to which weights are associated. These weights are then used at the final stage of applications to output the most probable analysis. Weighted rewrite rules can be compiled into *weighted* finite-state transducers, namely transducers generalized by providing transitions with a weighted output, under the same context condition. These transducers are very useful in speech processing (Pereira et al., 1994). We briefly describe how we have augmented our algorithm to handle the compilation of weighted rules into weighted finite-state transducers.

In order to set the stage for our own contribution, we start by reviewing salient aspects of the Kaplan and Kay algorithm.

[1] Parallel rewrite rules also have interesting applications in biology. In addition to their formal language theory interest, systems such as those of Aristid Lindenmayer provide rich mathematical models for biological development (Rozenberg and Salomaa, 1980).

[2] The general question of the decidability of the halting problem even for one-rule semi-Thue systems is still open. Robert McNaughton (1994) has recently made a positive conjecture about the class of the rules without *self overlap*.

$$
\begin{array}{rcl}
Prologue \circ & & \\
Id(Obligatory(\phi, <_i, >)) & = & Id(\overline{\Sigma^*_{>< \ 0} <_i \phi^0_{><} > \Sigma^*_{>< \ 0}}) \circ \\
Id(Rightcontext(\rho, <, >)) & = & Id((\overline{\Sigma^*_{>0} > \overline{\rho_{>0}\Sigma^*_{>0} - > \Sigma^*_{>0}}} \cap \overline{\overline{\Sigma^*_{>0} >} \rho_{>0}\Sigma^*_{>0} - > \Sigma^*_{>0}})_<) \circ \\
Replace & = & [Id(\Sigma^*_{<_i >_i \ 0})Opt(Id(<_a)\phi^0_{<_c >_c} \times \psi^0_{<_c >_c} Id(>_a))]^* \circ \\
Id(Leftcontext(\lambda, <, >)) & = & Id((\overline{\overline{\Sigma^*_{<0}\lambda_{<0} - \Sigma^*_{<0} <} < \Sigma^*_{<0}} \cap \overline{\Sigma^*_{<0}\lambda_{<0} - \Sigma^*_{<0} < \overline{< \Sigma^*_{<0}}})_>) \circ \\
Prologue^{-1} & &
\end{array}
\qquad (1)
$$

Figure 1: Compilation of obligatory left-to-right rules, using the KK algorithm.

2. The KK Algorithm

The rewrite rules we consider here have the following general form:

$$\phi \rightarrow \psi / \lambda \_\_ \rho \qquad (2)$$

Such rules can be interpreted in the following way: ϕ is to be replaced by ψ whenever it is preceded by λ and followed by ρ. Thus, λ and ρ represent the left and right contexts of application of the rules. In general, ϕ, ψ, λ and ρ are all regular expressions over the alphabet of the rules. Several types of rules can be considered depending on their being obligatory or optional, and on their direction of application, from left to right, right to left or simultaneous application.

Consider an obligatory rewrite rule of the form $\phi \rightarrow \psi / \lambda \_\_ \rho$, which we will assume applies left to right across the input string. Compilation of this rule in the algorithm of Kaplan and Kay (1994) (KK for short) involves composing together six transducers, see Figure 1.

We use the notations of KK. In particular, Σ denotes the alphabet, $<$ denotes the set of context labeled brackets $\{<_a, <_i, <_c\}$, $>$ the set $\{>_a, >_i, >_c\}$, and 0 an additional character representing deleted material. Subscript symbols of an expression are symbols which are allowed to freely appear anywhere in the strings represented by that expression. Given a regular expression r, $Id(r)$ is the identity transducer obtained from an automaton A representing r by adding output labels to A identical to its input labels.

The first transducer, *Prologue*, freely introduces labeled brackets from the set $\{<_a, <_i, <_c, >_a, >_i, >_c\}$ which are used by left and right context transducers. The last transducer, $Prologue^{-1}$, erases all such brackets.

In such a short space, we can of course not hope to do justice to the KK algorithm, and the reader who is not familiar with it is urged to consult their paper. However, one point that we do need to stress is the following: while the construction of *Prologue*, $Prologue^{-1}$ and *Replace* is fairly direct, construction of the other transducers is more complex, with each being derived via the application of several levels of regular operations from the original expressions in the rules. This clearly appears from the explicit expressions we have indicated for the transducers. The construction of the three other transducers involves many operations including: two intersections of automata, two distinct subtractions, and nine complementations. Each subtraction involves an intersection and a complementation algorithm[3]. So, in the whole, four intersections and eleven complementations need to be performed.

Intersection and complementation are classical automata algorithms (Aho et al., 1974; Aho et al., 1986). The complexity of intersection is quadratic. But the classical complementation algorithm requires the input automaton to be deterministic. Thus, each of these 11 operations requires first the determinization of the input. Such operations can be very costly in the case of the automata involved in the KK algorithm[4].

In the following section we briefly describe a new algorithm for compiling rewrite rules. For reasons of space, we concentrate here on the compilation of left-to-right obligatory rewrite rules. However, our methods extend straightforwardly to other modes of application (optional, right-to-left, simultaneous, batch), or kinds of rules (two-level rules) discussed by Kaplan and Kay (1994).

[3] A subtraction can of course also be performed *directly* by combining the two steps of intersection and complementation, but the corresponding algorithm has exactly the same cost as the total cost of the two operations performed consecutively.

[4] One could hope to find a more efficient way of determining the complement of an automaton that would not require determinization. However, this problem is PSPACE-complete. Indeed, the *regular expression non-universality* problem is a subproblem of complementation known to be PSPACE-complete (Garey and Johnson, 1979, page 174), (Stockmeyer and Meyer, 1973). This problem also known as *the emptiness of complement problem* has been extensively studied (Aho et al., 1974, page 410-419).

3. New Algorithm

3.1. Overview

In contrast to the KK algorithm which introduces brackets everywhere only to restrict their occurrence subsequently, our algorithm introduces context symbols just when and where they are needed. Furthermore, the number of intermediate transducers necessary in the construction of the rules is smaller than in the KK algorithm, and each of the transducers can be constructed more directly and efficiently from the primitive expressions of the rule, ϕ, ψ, λ, ρ.

A transducer corresponding to the left-to-right obligatory rule $\phi \rightarrow \psi/\lambda\_\_\_\rho$ can be obtained by composition of five transducers:

$$r \circ f \circ replace \circ l_1 \circ l_2 \qquad (3)$$

1. The transducer r introduces in a string a marker $>$ before every instance of ρ. For reasons that will become clear we will notate this as $\Sigma^*\rho \rightarrow \Sigma^* > \rho$.
2. The transducer f introduces markers $<_1$ and $<_2$ before each instance of ϕ that is followed by $>$: $(\Sigma \cup \{>\})^*\phi > \rightarrow (\Sigma \cup \{>\})^*\{<_1, <_2\}\phi >$. In other words, this transducer marks just those ϕ that occur before ρ.
3. The replacement transducer *replace* replaces ϕ with ψ in the context $<_1 \phi >$, simultaneously deleting $>$ in all positions (Figure 2). Since $>$, $<_1$, and $<_2$ need to be ignored when determining an occurrence of ϕ, there are loops over the transitions $>: \epsilon, <_1: \epsilon, <_2: \epsilon$ at all states of ϕ, or equivalently of the states of the cross product transducer $\phi \times \psi$.
4. The transducer l_1 admits only those strings in which occurrences of $<_1$ are preceded by λ and deletes $<_1$ at such occurrences: $\Sigma^*\lambda <_1 \rightarrow \Sigma^*\lambda$.
5. The transducer l_2 admits only those strings in which occurrences of $<_2$ are not preceded by λ and deletes $<_2$ at such occurrences: $\Sigma^*\overline{\lambda} <_2 \rightarrow \Sigma^*\overline{\lambda}$.

Clearly the composition of these transducers leads to the desired result. The construction of the transducer *replace* is straightforward. In the following, we show that the construction of the other four transducers is also very simple, and that it only requires the determinization of 3 automata and additional work linear (time and space) in the size of the determinized automata.

3.2. Markers

Markers of TYPE 1

Let us start by considering the problem of constructing what we shall call a TYPE 1 transducer,

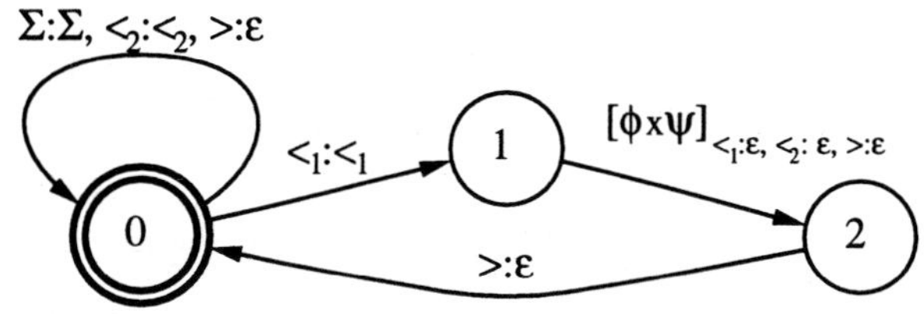

Figure 2: Replacement transducer *replace* in the obligatory left-to-right case.

which inserts a marker after all prefixes of a string that match a particular regular expression. Given a regular expression β defined on the alphabet Σ, one can construct, using classical algorithms (Aho et al., 1986), a deterministic automaton α representing $\Sigma^*\beta$. As with the KK algorithm, one can obtain from α a transducer $\chi = Id(\alpha)$ simply by assigning to each transition the same output label as the input label. We can easily transform χ into a new transducer τ such that it inserts an arbitrary marker # after each occurrence of a pattern described by β. To do so, we make final the non-final states of χ and for any final state q of χ we create a new state q', a copy of q. Thus, q' has the same transitions as q, and q' is a final state. We then make q non-final, remove the transitions leaving q and add a transition from q to q' with input label the empty word ϵ, and output #. Figures 3 and 4 illustrate the transformation of χ into τ.

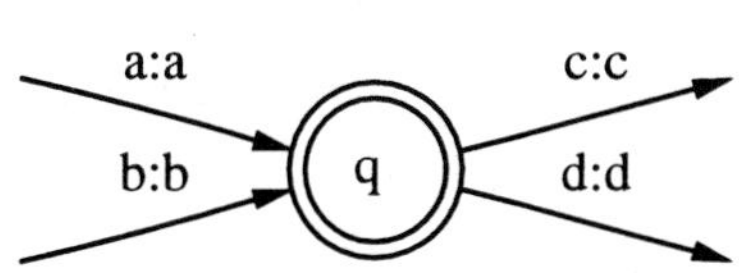

Figure 3: Final state q of χ with entering and leaving transitions.

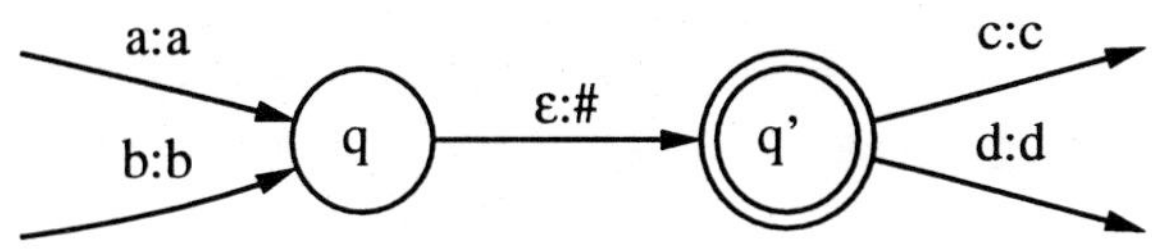

Figure 4: States and transitions of τ obtained by modifications of those of χ.

Proposition 1 *Let α be a deterministic automaton representing $\Sigma^*\beta$, then the transducer τ obtained as described above is a transducer post-marking occurrences of β in a string of Σ^* by #.*

Proof. The proof is based on the observation that a deterministic automaton representing $\Sigma^*\beta$ is necessarily complete[5]. Notice that non-deterministic automata representing $\Sigma^*\beta$ are not necessarily complete. Let q be a state of α and let $u \in \Sigma^*$ be a string reaching q[6]. Let v be a string described by the regular expression β. Then, for any $a \in \Sigma$, uav is in $\Sigma^*\beta$. Hence, uav is accepted by the automaton α, and, since α is deterministic, there exists a transition labeled with a leaving q. Thus, one can read any string $u \in \Sigma^*$ using the automaton α. Since by definition of α, the state reached when reading a prefix u' of u is final iff $u' \in \Sigma^*\beta$, by construction, the transducer τ inserts the symbol # after the prefix u' iff u' ends with a pattern of β. This ends the proof of the proposition. □

Markers of TYPE 2

In some cases, one wishes to check that any occurrence of # in a string s is preceded (or followed) by an occurrence of a pattern of β. We shall say that the corresponding transducers are of TYPE 2. They play the role of a filter. Here again, they can be defined from a deterministic automaton representing $\Sigma^*\beta$. Figure 5 illustrates the modifications to make from the automaton of figure 3. The symbols # should only appear at final states and must be erased. The loop $\# : \epsilon$ added at final states of $Id(\alpha)$ is enough for that purpose. All states of the transducer are then made final since any string conforming to this restriction is acceptable: cf. the transducer l_1 for λ above.

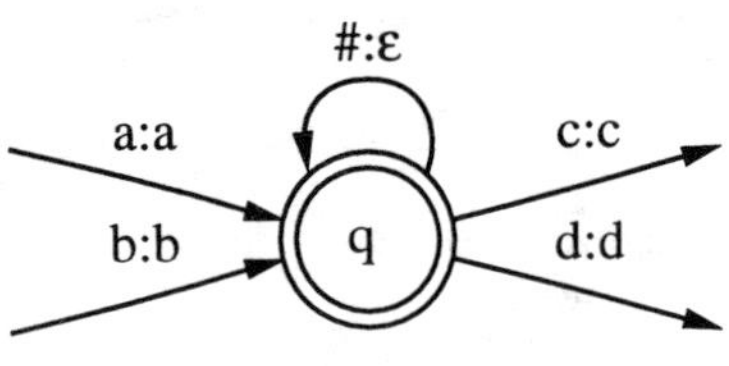

Figure 5: Filter transducer, TYPE 2.

[5] An automaton A is complete iff at any state q and for any element a of the alphabet Σ there exists at least one transition leaving q labeled with a. In the case of deterministic automata, the transition is unique.

[6] We assume all states of α accessible. This is true if α is obtained by determinization.

Markers of TYPE 3

In other cases, one wishes to check the reverse constraint, that is that occurrences of # in the string s are not preceded (or followed) by any occurrence of a pattern of β. The transformation then simply consists of adding a loop at each non-final state of $Id(\alpha)$, and of making all states final. Thus, a state such as that of figure 6 is trans-

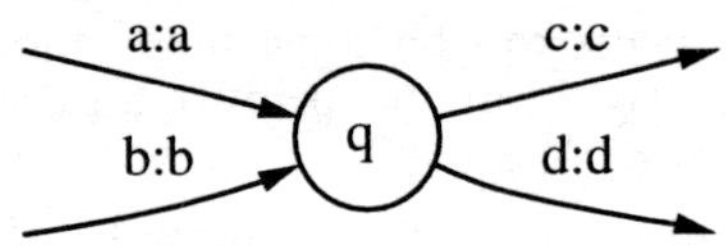

Figure 6: Non-final state q of α.

formed into that of figure 5. We shall say that the corresponding transducer is of TYPE 3: cf. the transducer l_2 for $\overline{\lambda}$.

The construction of these transducers (TYPE 1-3) can be generalized in various ways. In particular:

- One can add several alternative markers $\{\#_1, \cdots, \#_k\}$ after each occurrence of a pattern of β in a string. The result is then an automaton with transitions labeled with, for instance, $\#_1, \cdots, \#_k$ after each pattern of β: cf. transducer f for ϕ above.
- Instead of inserting a symbol, one can delete a symbol which would be necessarily present after each occurrence of a pattern of β.

For any regular expression α, define $Marker(\alpha, type, deletions, insertions)$ as the transducer of type *type* constructed as previously described from a deterministic automaton representing α, *insertions* and *deletions* being, respectively, the set of insertions and deletions the transducer makes.

Proposition 2 *For any regular expression α, $Marker(\alpha, type, deletions, insertions)$ can be constructed from a deterministic automaton representing α in linear time and space with respect to the size of this automaton.*

Proof. We proved in the previous proposition that the modifications do indeed lead to the desired transducer for TYPE 1. The proof for other cases is similar. That the construction is linear in space is clear since at most one additional transition and state is created for final or non-final states[7]. The overall time complexity of the construction is linear, since the construction of $Id(\alpha)$ is linear in the

[7] For TYPE 2 and TYPE 3, no state is added but only a transition per final or non-final state.

$$r = [reverse(Marker(\Sigma^* reverse(\rho), 1, \{>\}, \emptyset))] \quad (4)$$
$$f = [reverse(Marker((\Sigma \cup \{>\})^* reverse(\phi_> >), 1, \{<_1, <_2\}, \emptyset))] \quad (5)$$
$$l_1 = [Marker(\Sigma^* \lambda, 2, \emptyset, \{<_1\})]_{<_2:<_2} \quad (6)$$
$$l_2 = [Marker(\Sigma^* \lambda, 3, \emptyset, \{<_2\})] \quad (7)$$

Figure 7: Expressions of the r, f, l_1, and l_2 using $Marker$.

number of transitions of α and that other modifications consisting of adding new states and transitions and making states final or not are also linear. □

We just showed that $Marker(\alpha, type, deletions, insertions)$ can be constructed in a very efficient way. Figure 7 gives the expressions of the four transducers r, f, l_1, and l_2 using $Marker$.

Thus, these transducers can be constructed very efficiently from deterministic automata representing[8] $\Sigma^* reverse(\rho)$, $(\Sigma \cup \{>\})^* reverse(\phi_> >)$, and $\Sigma^*\lambda$. The construction of r and f requires two reverse operations. This is because these two transducers insert material *before* ρ or ϕ.

4. Extension to Weighted Rules

In many applications, in particular in areas related to speech, one wishes not only to give all possible analyses of some input, but also to give some measure of how likely each of the analyses is. One can then generalize replacements by considering *extended* regular expressions, namely, using the terminology of formal language theory, *rational power series* (Berstel and Reutenauer, 1988; Salomaa and Soittola, 1978).

The rational power series we consider here are functions mapping Σ^* to $\mathcal{R}_+ \cup \{\infty\}$ which can be described by regular expressions over the alphabet $(\mathcal{R}_+ \cup \{\infty\}) \times \Sigma$. $S = (4a)(2b)^*(3b)$ is an example of rational power series. It defines a function in the following way: it associates a non-null number only with the strings recognized by the regular expression ab^*b. This number is obtained by adding the coefficients involved in the recognition of the string. The value associated with $abbb$, for instance, is $(S, abbb) = 4 + 2 + 2 + 3 = 11$.

In general, such extended regular expressions can be redundant. Some strings can be matched in different ways with distinct coefficients. The value associated with those strings is then the minimum of all possible results. $S' = (2a)(3b)(4b) + (5a)(3b^*)$ matches abb with the different weights $2 + 3 + 4 = 9$ and $5 + 3 + 3 = 11$. The minimum of the two is the value associated with abb: $(S', abb) = 9$. Non-negative numbers in the definition of these power series are often interpreted as the negative logarithm of probabilities. This explains our choice of the operations: addition of the weights along the string recognition and *min*, since we are only interested in that result which has the highest probability[9].

Rewrite rules can be generalized by letting ψ be a rational power series. The result of the application of a generalized rule to a string is then a set of *weighted strings* which can be represented by a *weighted automaton*. Consider for instance the following rule, which states that an abstract nasal, denoted N, is rewritten as m in the context of a following labial:

$$N \rightarrow m / \_\_[+labial] \quad (8)$$

Now suppose that this is only *probabilistically* true, and that while ninety percent of the time N does indeed become m in this environment, about ten percent of the time in real speech it becomes n. Converting from probabilities to weights, one would say that N becomes m with weight $\alpha = -\log(0.9)$, and n with weight $\beta = -\log(0.1)$, in the stated environment. One could represent this by the following rule:

$$N \rightarrow \alpha m + \beta n / \_\_[+labial] \quad (9)$$

We define *Weighted finite-state transducers* as transducers such that in addition to input and output labels, each transition is labeled with a weight.

The result of the application of a weighted transducer to a string, or more generally to an automaton is a weighted automaton. The corresponding operation is similar to the unweighted case. However, the weight of the transducer and those of the string or automaton need to be combined too, here added, during composition (Pereira et al., 1994).

[8] As in the KK algorithm we denote by $\phi_>$ the set of the strings described by ϕ containing possibly occurrences of $>$ at any position. In the same way, subscripts such as $>:>$ for a transducer τ indicate that loops by $>:>$ are added at all states of τ. We denote by $reverse(\alpha)$ the regular expression describing exactly the reverse strings of α if α is a regular expression, or the reverse transducer of α if α is a transducer.

[9] Using the terminology of the theory of languages, the functions we consider here are power series defined on the *tropical semiring* $(\mathcal{R}_+ \cup \{\infty\}, \min, +, \infty, 0)$ (Kuich and Salomaa, 1986).

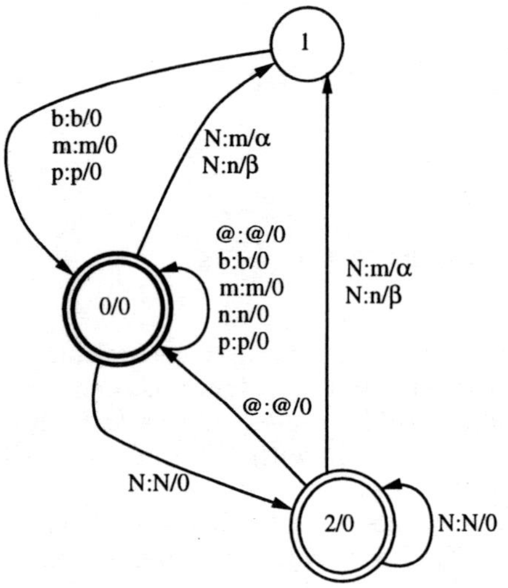

Figure 8: Transducer representing the rule 9.

We have generalized the composition operation to the weighted case by introducing this combination of weights. The algorithm we described in the previous sections can then also be used to compile weighted rewrite rules.

As an example, the obligatory rule 9 can be represented by the weighted transducer of Figure 8 [10]. The following theorem extends to the weighted case the assertion proved by Kaplan and Kay (1994).

Theorem 1 *A weighted rewrite rule of the type defined above that does not rewrite its non-contextual part can be represented by a weighted finite-state transducer.*

Proof. The construction we described in the previous section also provides a constructive proof of this theorem in the unweighted case. In case ψ is a power series, one simply needs to use in that construction a weighted finite-state transducer representing ψ. By definition of composition of weighted transducers, or multiplication of power series, the weights are then used in a way consistent with the definition of the weighted context-dependent rules. □

5. Experiments

In order to compare the performance of the algorithm presented here with KK, we timed both algorithms on the compilation of individual rules taken from the following set ($k \in [0, 10]$):

$$a \rightarrow b / \; c^k \underline{\quad\quad} \qquad (10)$$

$$a \rightarrow b / \; \underline{\quad\quad} c^k \qquad (11)$$

[10]We here use the symbol @ to denote all letters different from b, m, n, p, and N.

In other words we tested twenty two rules where the left context or the right context is varied in length from zero to ten occurrences of c. For our experiments, we used the alphabet of a realistic application, the text analyzer for the Bell Laboratories German text-to-speech system consisting of 194 labels. All tests were run on a Silicon Graphics IRIS Indigo 4000, 100 MhZ IP20 Processor, 128 Mbytes RAM, running IRIX 5.2. Figure 9 shows the relative performance of the two algorithms for the left context: apparently the performance of both algorithms is *roughly* linear in the length of the left context, but KK has a worse constant, due to the larger number of operations involved. Figure 10 shows the equivalent data for the right context. At first glance the data looks similar to that for the left context, until one notices that in Figure 10 we have plotted the time on a log scale: the KK algorithm is hyperexponential.

What is the reason for this performance degradation in the right context? The culprits turn out to be the two intersectands in the expression of $Rightcontext(\rho, <, >)$ in Figure 1. Consider for example the righthand intersectand, namely $\overline{\overline{\Sigma^*_{>0} >} \rho_{>0}\Sigma^*_{>0}- > \Sigma^*_{>0}}$, which is the complement of $\overline{\Sigma^*_{>0} >} \rho_{>0}\Sigma^*_{>0}- > \Sigma^*_{>0}$. As previously indicated, the complementation algorithm requires determinization, and the determinization of automata representing expressions of the form $\Sigma^*\alpha$, where α is a regular expression, is often very expensive, specially when the expression α is already complex, as in this case.

Figure 11 plots the behavior of determinization on the expression $\overline{\Sigma^*_{>0} >} \rho_{>0}\Sigma^*_{>0}- > \Sigma^*_{>0}$ for each of the rules in the set $a \rightarrow b / \underline{\quad\quad} c^k$, ($k \in [0, 10]$). On the horizontal axis is the number of arcs of the non-deterministic input machine, and on the vertical axis the log of the number of arcs of the deterministic machine, i.e. the machine result of the determinization algorithm without using any minimization. The perfect linearity indicates an exponential time and space behavior, and this in turn explains the observed difference in performance. In contrast, the construction of the right context machine in our algorithm involves only the single determinization of the automaton representing $\Sigma^*\rho$, and thus is much less expensive. The comparison just discussed involves a rather artificial ruleset, but the differences in performance that we have highlighted show up in real applications. Consider two sets of pronunciation rules from the Bell Laboratories German text-to-speech system: the size of the alphabet for this ruleset is 194, as noted above. The first ruleset, consisting of pronunciation rules for the orthographic vowel <ö> contains twelve rules, and the second ruleset, which deals with the orthographic

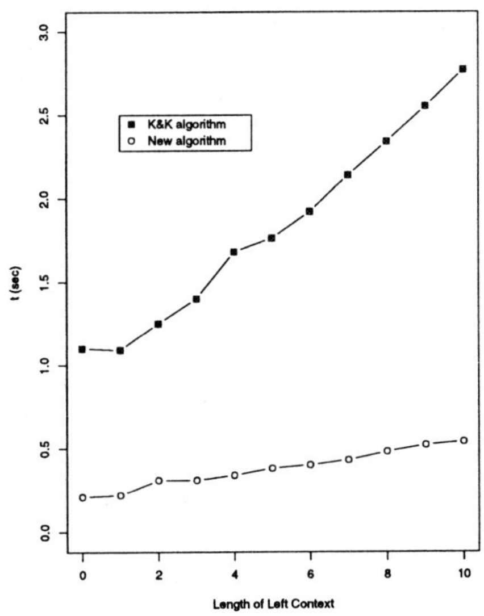

Figure 9: Compilation times for rules of the form $a \rightarrow b/\ c^k\_\_\_$, ($k \in [0, 10]$).

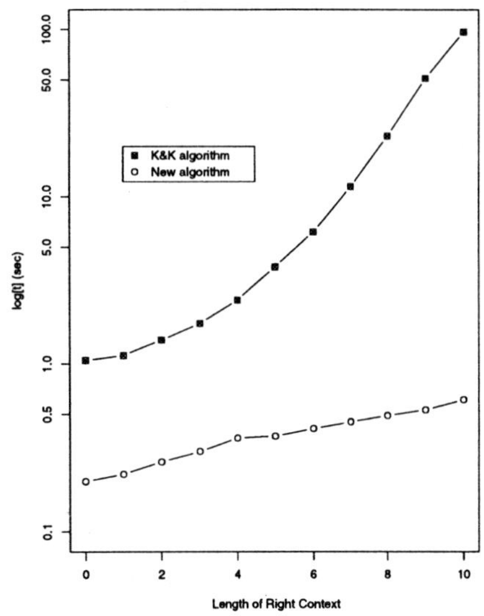

Figure 10: Compilation times for rules of the form $a \rightarrow b/\_\_\_c^k$, ($k \in [0, 10]$).

vowel <a> contains twenty five rules. In the actual application of the rule compiler to these rules, one compiles the individual rules in each ruleset one by one, and composes them together in the order written, compacts them after each composition, and derives a single transducer for each set. When done off-line, these operations of composition and compaction dominate the time corresponding to the construction of the transducer for each individual rule. The difference between the two algorithms appears still clearly for these two sets of rules. Table 1 shows for each algorithm the times in seconds for the overall construction, and the number of states and arcs of the output transducers.

Table 1: Comparison in a real example.

Rules	KK			New		
	time	space		time	space	
	(s)	states	arcs	(s)	states	arcs
<ö>	62	412	50,475	47	394	47,491
<a>	284	1,939	215,721	240	1,927	213,408

6. Conclusion

We briefly described a new algorithm for compiling context-dependent rewrite rules into finite-state transducers. Several additional methods can be used to make this algorithm even more efficient.

The automata determinizations needed for this algorithm are of a specific type. They represent expressions of the type $\Sigma^*\phi$ where ϕ is a regular expression. Given a deterministic automaton representing ϕ, such determinizations can be performed in a more efficient way using *failure functions* (Mohri, 1995). Moreover, the corresponding determinization is independent of Σ which can be very large in some applications. It only depends on the alphabet of the automaton representing ϕ.

One can devise an *on-the-fly* implementation of the composition algorithm leading to the final transducer representing a rule. Only the necessary part of the intermediate transducers is then expanded for a given input (Pereira et al., 1994).

The resulting transducer representing a rule is often subsequentiable or p-subsequentiable. It can then be determinized and minimized (Mohri, 1994). This both makes the use of the transducer time efficient and reduces its size.

We also indicated an extension of the theory of rule-compilation to the case of weighted rules, which compile into weighted finite-state transducers. Many algorithms used in the finite-state theory and in their applications to natural language processing can be extended in the same way.

To date the main serious application of this compiler has been to developing text-analyzers for text-to-speech systems at Bell Laboratories (Sproat, 1996): partial to more-or-less complete analyzers have been built for Spanish, Italian, French, Romanian, German, Russian, Mandarin and Japanese. However, we hope to also be able to use the compiler in serious applications in speech

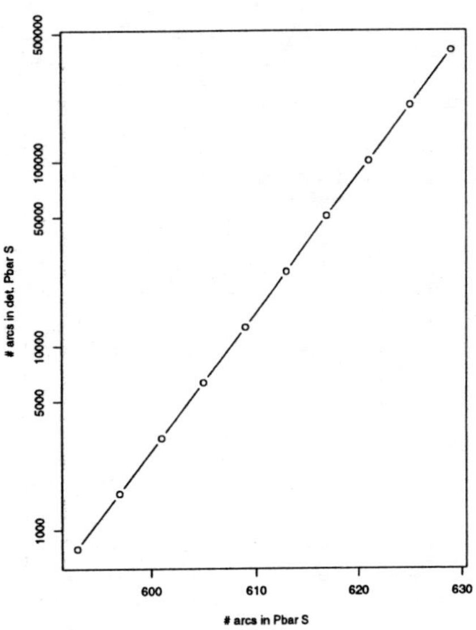

Figure 11: Number of arcs in the non-deterministic automaton τ representing $\overline{PS} = \Sigma^*_{>0} > \rho_{>0}\Sigma^*_{>0} - > \Sigma^*_{>0}$ versus the log of the number of arcs in the automaton obtained by determinization of τ.

recognition in the future.

Acknowledgements

We wish to thank several colleagues of AT&T/Bell Labs, in particular Fernando Pereira and Michael Riley for stimulating discussions about this work and Bernd Möbius for providing the German pronunciation rules cited herein.

References

Alfred V. Aho, John E. Hopcroft, and Jeffrey D. Ullman. 1974. *The design and analysis of computer algorithms.* Addison Wesley: Reading, MA.

Alfred V. Aho, Ravi Sethi, and Jeffrey D. Ullman. 1986. *Compilers, Principles, Techniques and Tools.* Addison Wesley: Reading, MA.

Jean Berstel and Christophe Reutenauer. 1988. *Rational Series and Their Languages.* Springer-Verlag: Berlin-New York.

Jean Berstel. 1979. *Transductions and Context-Free Languages.* Teubner Studienbucher: Stuttgart.

Samuel Eilenberg. 1974-1976. *Automata, Languages and Machines*, volume A-B. Academic Press.

Michael R. Garey and David S. Johnson. 1979. *Computers and Intractability.* Freeman and Company, New York.

C. Douglas Johnson. 1972. *Formal Aspects of Phonological Description.* Mouton, Mouton, The Hague.

Ronald M. Kaplan and Martin Kay. 1994. Regular models of phonological rule systems. *Computational Linguistics*, 20(3).

Lauri Karttunen. 1995. The replace operator. In *33rd Meeting of the Association for Computational Linguistics (ACL 95), Proceedings of the Conference, MIT, Cambridge, Massachussetts.* ACL.

Wener Kuich and Arto Salomaa. 1986. *Semirings, Automata, Languages.* Springer-Verlag: Berlin-New York.

Mark Liberman. 1994. Commentary on kaplan and kay. *Computational Linguistics*, 20(3).

Robert McNaughton. 1994. The uniform halting problem for one-rule semi-thue systems. Technical Report 94-18, Department of Computer Science, Rensselaer Polytechnic Institute, Troy, New York.

Mehryar Mohri. 1994. Compact representations by finite-state transducers. In *32nd Meeting of the Association for Computational Linguistics (ACL 94), Proceedings of the Conference, Las Cruces, New Mexico.* ACL.

Mehryar Mohri. 1995. Matching patterns of an automaton. *Lecture Notes in Computer Science*, 937.

Fernando C. N. Pereira, Michael Riley, and Richard Sproat. 1994. Weighted rational transductions and their application to human language processing. In *ARPA Workshop on Human Language Technology.* Advanced Research Projects Agency.

Grzegorz Rozenberg and Arto Salomaa. 1980. *The Mathematical Theory of L Systems.* Academic Press, New York.

Arto Salomaa and Matti Soittola. 1978. *Automata-Theoretic Aspects of Formal Power Series.* Springer-Verlag: Berlin-New York.

Richard Sproat. 1996. Multilingual text analysis for text-to-speech synthesis. In *Proceedings of the ECAI-96 Workshop on Extended Finite State Models of Language*, Budapest, Hungary. European Conference on Artificial Intelligence.

L. J. Stockmeyer and A. R. Meyer. 1973. Word problems requiring exponential time. In *Proceedings of the 5th Annual ACM Symposium on Theory of Computing.* Association for Computing Machinery, New York, 1-9.

Efficient Tabular LR Parsing

Mark-Jan Nederhof
Faculty of Arts
University of Groningen
P.O. Box 716
9700 AS Groningen
The Netherlands
markjan@let.rug.nl

Giorgio Satta
Dipartimento di Elettronica ed Informatica
Università di Padova
via Gradenigo, 6/A
I-35131 Padova
Italy
satta@dei.unipd.it

Abstract

We give a new treatment of tabular LR parsing, which is an alternative to Tomita's generalized LR algorithm. The advantage is twofold. Firstly, our treatment is conceptually more attractive because it uses simpler concepts, such as grammar transformations and standard tabulation techniques also know as *chart parsing*. Secondly, the static and dynamic complexity of parsing, both in space and time, is significantly reduced.

1 Introduction

The efficiency of LR(k) parsing techniques (Sippu and Soisalon-Soininen, 1990) is very attractive from the perspective of natural language processing applications. This has stimulated the computational linguistics community to develop extensions of these techniques to general context-free grammar parsing. The best-known example is *generalized* LR parsing, also known as Tomita's algorithm, described by Tomita (1986) and further investigated by, for example, Tomita (1991) and Nederhof (1994a). Despite appearances, the graph-structured stacks used to describe Tomita's algorithm differ very little from *parse tables*, or in other words, generalized LR parsing is one of the so called *tabular* parsing algorithms, among which also the CYK algorithm (Harrison, 1978) and Earley's algorithm (Earley, 1970) can be found. (Tabular parsing is also known as *chart parsing*.)

In this paper we investigate the extension of LR parsing to general context-free grammars from a more general viewpoint: tabular algorithms can often be described by the composition of two constructions. One example is given by Lang (1974) and Billot and Lang (1989): the construction of pushdown automata from grammars and the simulation of these automata by means of tabulation yield different tabular algorithms for different such constructions. Another example, on which our presentation is based, was first suggested by Leermakers (1989): a grammar is first transformed and then a standard tabular algorithm along with some filtering condition is applied using the transformed grammar. In our case, the transformation and the subsequent application of the tabular algorithm result in a new form of tabular LR parsing.

Our method is more efficient than Tomita's algorithm in two respects. First, reduce operations are implemented in an efficient way, by splitting them into several, more primitive, operations (a similar idea has been proposed by Kipps (1991) for Tomita's algorithm). Second, several paths in the computation that must be simulated separately by Tomita's algorithm are collapsed into a single computation path, using state minimization techniques. Experiments on practical grammars have indicated that there is a significant gain in efficiency, with regard to both space and time requirements.

Our grammar transformation produces a so called *cover* for the input grammar, which together with the filtering condition fully captures the specification of the method, abstracting away from algorithmic details such as data structures and control flow. Since this cover can be easily precomputed, implementing our LR parser simply amounts to running the standard tabular algorithm. This is very attractive from an application-oriented perspective, since many actual systems for natural language processing are based on these kinds of parsing algorithm.

The remainder of this paper is organized as follows. In Section 2 some preliminaries are discussed. We review the notion of LR automaton in Section 3 and introduce the notion of 2LR automaton in Section 4. Then we specify our tabular LR method in Section 5, and provide an analysis of the algorithm in Section 6. Finally, some empirical results are given in Section 7, and further discussion of our method is provided in Section 8.

2 Definitions

Throughout this paper we use standard formal language notation. We assume that the reader is familiar with context-free grammar parsing theory (Harrison, 1978).

A context-free grammar (CFG) is a 4-tuple $G = (\Sigma, N, P, S)$, where Σ and N are two finite disjoint sets of terminal and nonterminal symbols, respectively, $S \in N$ is the start symbol, and P is a finite set of rules. Each rule has the form $A \rightarrow \alpha$ with $A \in N$ and $\alpha \in V^*$, where V denotes $N \cup \Sigma$. The size of G, written $|G|$, is defined as $\sum_{(A\rightarrow\alpha)\in P} |A\alpha|$; by $|\alpha|$ we mean the length of a string of symbols α.

We generally use symbols $A, B, C, \ldots$ to range over N, symbols $a, b, c, \ldots$ to range over Σ, symbols X, Y, Z to range over V, symbols $\alpha, \beta, \gamma, \ldots$ to range over V^*, and symbols $v, w, x, \ldots$ to range over Σ^*. We write ϵ to denote the empty string.

A CFG is said to be in *binary form* if $\alpha \in \{\epsilon\} \cup V \cup N^2$ for all of its rules $A \rightarrow \alpha$. (The binary form does not limit the (weak) generative capacity of context-free grammars (Harrison, 1978).) For technical reasons, we sometimes use the *augmented* grammar associated with G, defined as $G^\dagger = (\Sigma^\dagger, N^\dagger, P^\dagger, S^\dagger)$, where $S^\dagger$, $\triangleright$ and $\triangleleft$ are fresh symbols, $\Sigma^\dagger = \Sigma \cup \{\triangleright, \triangleleft\}$, $N^\dagger = N \cup \{S^\dagger\}$ and $P^\dagger = P \cup \{S^\dagger \rightarrow \triangleright S \triangleleft\}$.

A pushdown automaton (PDA) is a 5-tuple $\mathcal{A} = (\Sigma, Q, T, q_{in}, q_{fin})$, where Σ, Q and T are finite sets of input symbols, stack symbols and transitions, respectively; $q_{in} \in Q$ is the initial stack symbol and $q_{fin} \in Q$ is the final stack symbol.[1] Each transition has the form $\delta_1 \overset{z}{\mapsto} \delta_2$, where $\delta_1, \delta_2 \in Q^*$, $1 \leq |\delta_1|$, $1 \leq |\delta_2| \leq 2$, and $z = \epsilon$ or $z = a$. We generally use symbols $q, r, s, \ldots$ to range over Q, and the symbol δ to range over Q^*.

Consider a fixed input string $v \in \Sigma^*$. A *configuration* of the automaton is a pair (δ, w) consisting of a stack $\delta \in Q^*$ and the remaining input w, which is a suffix of the input string v. The rightmost symbol of δ represents the top of the stack. The *initial* configuration has the form (q_{in}, v), where the stack is formed by the initial stack symbol. The *final* configuration has the form $(q_{in}\ q_{fin}, \epsilon)$, where the stack is formed by the final stack symbol stacked upon the initial stack symbol.

[1] We dispense with the notion of *state*, traditionally incorporated in the definition of PDA. This does not affect the power of these devices, since states can be encoded within stack symbols and transitions.

The application of a transition $\delta_1 \overset{z}{\mapsto} \delta_2$ is described as follows. If the top-most symbols of the stack are δ_1, then these symbols may be replaced by δ_2, provided that either $z = \epsilon$, or $z = a$ and a is the first symbol of the remaining input. Furthermore, if $z = a$ then a is removed from the remaining input. Formally, for a fixed PDA $\mathcal{A}$ we define the binary relation $\vdash$ on configurations as the least relation satisfying $(\delta\delta_1, w) \vdash (\delta\delta_2, w)$ if there is a transition $\delta_1 \overset{\epsilon}{\mapsto} \delta_2$, and $(\delta\delta_1, aw) \vdash (\delta\delta_2, w)$ if there is a transition $\delta_1 \overset{a}{\mapsto} \delta_2$. The recognition of a certain input v is obtained if starting from the initial configuration for that input we can reach the final configuration by repeated application of transitions, or, formally, if $(q_{in}, v) \vdash^* (q_{in}\ q_{fin}, \epsilon)$, where $\vdash^*$ denotes the reflexive and transitive closure of $\vdash$.

By a *computation* of a PDA we mean a sequence $(q_{in}, v) \vdash (\delta_1, w_1) \vdash \ldots \vdash (\delta_n, w_n)$, $n \geq 0$. A PDA is called *deterministic* if for all possible configurations at most one transition is applicable. A PDA is said to be in *binary form* if, for all transitions $\delta_1 \overset{z}{\mapsto} \delta_2$, we have $|\delta_1| \leq 2$.

3 LR automata

Let $G = (\Sigma, N, P, S)$ be a CFG. We recall the notion of LR automaton, which is a particular kind of PDA. We make use of the augmented grammar $G^\dagger = (\Sigma^\dagger, N^\dagger, P^\dagger, S^\dagger)$ introduced in Section 2.

Let $I_{\mathrm{LR}} = \{A \rightarrow \alpha \bullet \beta \mid (A \rightarrow \alpha\beta) \in P^\dagger\}$. We introduce the function *closure* from $2^{I_{\mathrm{LR}}}$ to $2^{I_{\mathrm{LR}}}$ and the function *goto* from $2^{I_{\mathrm{LR}}} \times V$ to $2^{I_{\mathrm{LR}}}$. For any $q \subseteq I_{\mathrm{LR}}$, $closure(q)$ is the smallest set such that

(i) $q \subseteq closure(q)$; and

(ii) $(B \rightarrow \alpha \bullet A\beta) \in closure(q)$ and $(A \rightarrow \gamma) \in P^\dagger$ together imply $(A \rightarrow \bullet\, \gamma) \in closure(q)$.

We then define

$$goto(q, X) = \{A \rightarrow \alpha X \bullet \beta \mid (A \rightarrow \alpha \bullet X\beta) \in closure(q)\}.$$

We construct a finite set $\mathcal{R}_{\mathrm{LR}}$ as the smallest collection of sets satisfying the conditions:

(i) $\{S^\dagger \rightarrow \triangleright \bullet S\triangleleft\} \in \mathcal{R}_{\mathrm{LR}}$; and

(ii) for every $q \in \mathcal{R}_{\mathrm{LR}}$ and $X \in V$, we have $goto(q, X) \in \mathcal{R}_{\mathrm{LR}}$, provided $goto(q, X) \neq \emptyset$.

Two elements from $\mathcal{R}_{\mathrm{LR}}$ deserve special attention: $q_{in} = \{S^\dagger \rightarrow \triangleright \bullet S\triangleleft\}$, and q_{fin}, which is defined to be the unique set in $\mathcal{R}_{\mathrm{LR}}$ containing $(S^\dagger \rightarrow \triangleright S \bullet \triangleleft)$; in other words, $q_{fin} = goto(q_{in}, S)$.

For $A \in N$, an *A-redex* is a string $q_0 q_1 q_2 \cdots q_m$, $m \geq 0$, of elements from $\mathcal{R}_{\text{LR}}$, satisfying the following conditions:

(i) $(A \rightarrow \alpha\ \bullet) \in closure(q_m)$, for some $\alpha = X_1 X_2 \cdots X_m$; and

(ii) $goto(q_{k-1}, X_k) = q_k$, for $1 \leq k \leq m$.

Note that in such an A-redex, $(A \rightarrow \bullet\ X_1 X_2 \cdots X_m) \in closure(q_0)$, and $(A \rightarrow X_1 \cdots X_k \bullet X_{k+1} \cdots X_m) \in q_k$, for $0 < k \leq m$.

The LR automaton associated with G is now introduced.

Definition 1 *$\mathcal{A}_{\text{LR}} = (\Sigma, Q_{\text{LR}}, T_{\text{LR}}, q_{in}, q_{fin})$, where $Q_{\text{LR}} = \mathcal{R}_{\text{LR}}$, $q_{in} = \{S^\dagger \rightarrow \triangleright \bullet S \triangleleft\}$, $q_{fin} = goto(q_{in}, S)$, and T_{LR} contains:*

(i) *$q \overset{a}{\mapsto} q\, q'$, for every $a \in \Sigma$ and $q, q' \in \mathcal{R}_{\text{LR}}$ such that $q' = goto(q, a)$;*

(ii) *$q\delta \overset{\epsilon}{\mapsto} q\, q'$, for every $A \in N$, A-redex $q\delta$, and $q' \in \mathcal{R}_{\text{LR}}$ such that $q' = goto(q, A)$.*

Transitions in (i) above are called *shift*, transitions in (ii) are called *reduce*.

4 2LR Automata

The automata $\mathcal{A}_{\text{LR}}$ defined in the previous section are deterministic only for a subset of the CFGs, called the LR(0) grammars (Sippu and Soisalon-Soininen, 1990), and behave nondeterministically in the general case. When designing tabular methods that simulate nondeterministic computations of $\mathcal{A}_{\text{LR}}$, two main difficulties are encountered:

- A reduce transition in $\mathcal{A}_{\text{LR}}$ is an elementary operation that removes from the stack a number of elements bounded by the size of the underlying grammar. Consequently, the time requirement of tabular simulation of $\mathcal{A}_{\text{LR}}$ computations can be onerous, for reasons pointed out by Sheil (1976) and Kipps (1991).

- The set $\mathcal{R}_{\text{LR}}$ can be exponential in the size of the grammar (Johnson, 1991). If in such a case the computations of $\mathcal{A}_{\text{LR}}$ touch upon each state, then time and space requirements of tabular simulation are obviously onerous.

The first issue above is solved here by recasting $\mathcal{A}_{\text{LR}}$ in binary form. This is done by considering each reduce transition as a sequence of "pop" operations which affect at most two stack symbols at a time. (See also Lang (1974), Villemonte de la Clergerie (1993) and Nederhof (1994a), and for LR parsing specifically Kipps (1991) and Leermakers (1992b).) The following definition introduces this new kind of automaton.

Definition 2 *$\mathcal{A}'_{\text{LR}} = (\Sigma, Q'_{\text{LR}}, T'_{\text{LR}}, q_{in}, q_{fin})$, where $Q'_{\text{LR}} = \mathcal{R}_{\text{LR}} \cup I_{\text{LR}}$, $q_{in} = \{S^\dagger \rightarrow \triangleright \bullet S \triangleleft\}$, $q_{fin} = goto(q_{in}, S)$ and T'_{LR} contains:*

(i) *$q \overset{a}{\mapsto} q\, q'$, for every $a \in \Sigma$ and $q, q' \in \mathcal{R}_{\text{LR}}$ such that $q' = goto(q, a)$;*

(ii) *$q \overset{\epsilon}{\mapsto} q\, (A \rightarrow \alpha\ \bullet)$, for every $q \in \mathcal{R}_{\text{LR}}$ and $(A \rightarrow \alpha\ \bullet) \in closure(q)$;*

(iii) *$q\, (A \rightarrow \alpha X \bullet \beta) \overset{\epsilon}{\mapsto} (A \rightarrow \alpha \bullet X\beta)$, for every $q \in \mathcal{R}_{\text{LR}}$ and $(A \rightarrow \alpha X \bullet \beta) \in q$;*

(iv) *$q\, (A \rightarrow \bullet\ \alpha) \overset{\epsilon}{\mapsto} q\, q'$, for every $q, q' \in \mathcal{R}_{\text{LR}}$ and $(A \rightarrow \alpha) \in P^\dagger$ such that $q' = goto(q, A)$.*

Transitions in (i) above are again called *shift*, transitions in (ii) are called *initiate*, those in (iii) are called *gathering*, and transitions in (iv) are called *goto*. The role of a reduce step in $\mathcal{A}_{\text{LR}}$ is taken over in $\mathcal{A}'_{\text{LR}}$ by an initiate step, a number of gathering steps, and a goto step. Observe that these steps involve the new stack symbols $(A \rightarrow \alpha \bullet \beta) \in I_{\text{LR}}$ that are distinguishable from possible stack symbols $\{A \rightarrow \alpha \bullet \beta\} \in \mathcal{R}_{\text{LR}}$.

We now turn to the second above-mentioned problem, regarding the size of set $\mathcal{R}_{\text{LR}}$. The problem is in part solved here as follows. The number of states in $\mathcal{R}_{\text{LR}}$ is considerably reduced by identifying two states if they become identical after items $A \rightarrow \alpha \bullet \beta$ from I_{LR} have been simplified to only the suffix of the right-hand side β. This is reminiscent of techniques of state minimization for finite automata (Booth, 1967), as they have been applied before to LR parsing, e.g., by Pager (1970) and Nederhof and Sarbo (1993).

Let $G^\dagger$ be the augmented grammar associated with a CFG G, and let $I_{2\text{LR}} = \{\beta \mid (A \rightarrow \alpha\beta) \in P^\dagger\}$. We define variants of the *closure* and *goto* functions from the previous section as follows. For any set $q \subseteq I_{2\text{LR}}$, $closure'(q)$ is the smallest collection of sets such that

(i) $q \subseteq closure'(q)$; and

(ii) $(A\beta) \in closure'(q)$ and $(A \rightarrow \gamma) \in P^\dagger$ together imply $(\gamma) \in closure'(q)$.

Also, we define

$$goto'(q, X) \quad = \quad \{\beta \mid (X\beta) \in closure'(q)\}.$$

We now construct a finite set $\mathcal{R}_{2\text{LR}}$ as the smallest set satisfying the conditions:

(i) $\{S\triangleleft\} \in \mathcal{R}_{2LR}$; and

(ii) for every $q \in \mathcal{R}_{2LR}$ and $X \in V$, we have $goto'(q, X) \in \mathcal{R}_{2LR}$, provided $goto'(q, X) \neq \emptyset$.

As stack symbols, we take the elements from I_{2LR} and a subset of elements from $(V \times \mathcal{R}_{2LR})$:

$$Q_{2LR} = \{(X, q) \mid \exists q'[goto'(q', X) = q]\} \cup I_{2LR}$$

In a stack symbol of the form (X, q), the X serves to record the grammar symbol that has been recognized last, cf. the symbols that formerly were found immediately before the dots.

The 2LR automaton associated with G can now be introduced.

Definition 3 $\mathcal{A}_{2LR} = (\Sigma, Q_{2LR}, T_{2LR}, q'_{in}, q'_{fin})$, *where* Q_{2LR} *is as defined above,* $q'_{in} = (\triangleright, \{S\triangleleft\})$, $q'_{fin} = (S, goto'(\{S\triangleleft\}, S))$, *and* T_{2LR} *contains:*

(i) $(X, q) \overset{a}{\mapsto} (X, q)\,(a, q')$, *for every* $a \in \Sigma$ *and* $(X, q), (a, q') \in Q_{2LR}$ *such that* $q' = goto'(q, a)$;

(ii) $(X, q) \overset{\epsilon}{\mapsto} (X, q)\,(\epsilon)$, *for every* $(X, q) \in Q_{2LR}$ *such that* $\epsilon \in closure'(q)$;

(iii) $(X, q)\,(\beta) \overset{\epsilon}{\mapsto} (X\beta)$, *for every* $(X, q) \in Q_{2LR}$ *and* $\beta \in q$;

(iv) $(X, q)\,(\alpha) \overset{\epsilon}{\mapsto} (X, q)\,(A, q')$, *for every* (X, q), $(A, q') \in Q_{2LR}$ *and* $(A \rightarrow \alpha) \in P^{\dagger}$ *such that* $q' = goto'(q, A)$.

Note that in the case of a reduce/reduce conflict with two grammar rules sharing some suffix in the right-hand side, the gathering steps of $\mathcal{A}_{2LR}$ will treat both rules simultaneously, until the parts of the right-hand sides are reached where the two rules differ. (See Leermakers (1992a) for a similar sharing of computation for common suffixes.)

An interesting fact is that the automaton $\mathcal{A}_{2LR}$ is very similar to the automaton $\mathcal{A}_{LR}$ constructed for a grammar transformed by the transformation τ_{two} given by Nederhof and Satta (1994).[2]

5 The algorithm

This section presents a tabular LR parser, which is the main result of this paper. The parser is derived from the 2LR automata introduced in the previous section. Following the general approach presented by Leermakers (1989), we simulate computations of these devices using a tabular method, a grammar transformation and a filtering function.

We make use of a tabular parsing algorithm which is basically an asynchronous version of the CYK algorithm, as presented by Harrison (1978), extended to productions of the forms $A \rightarrow B$ and $A \rightarrow \epsilon$ and with a left-to-right filtering condition. The algorithm uses a parse table consisting in a 0-indexed square array U. The indices represent positions in the input string. We define U_i to be $\bigcup_{k \leq i} U_{k,i}$.

Computation of the entries of U is moderated by a filtering process. This process makes use of a function *pred* from 2^N to 2^N, specific to a certain context-free grammar. We have a certain nonterminal A_{init} which is initially inserted in $U_{0,0}$ in order to start the recognition process.

We are now ready to give a formal specification of the tabular algorithm.

Algorithm 1 Let $G = (\Sigma, N, P, S)$ be a CFG in binary form, let *pred* be a function from 2^N to 2^N, let A_{init} be the distinguished element from N, and let $v = a_1 a_2 \cdots a_n \in \Sigma^*$ be an input string. We compute the least $(n+1) \times (n+1)$ table U such that $A_{init} \in U_{0,0}$ and

(i) $A \in U_{j-1,j}$
if $(A \rightarrow a_j) \in P$, $A \in pred(U_{j-1})$;

(ii) $A \in U_{j,j}$
if $(A \rightarrow \epsilon) \in P$, $A \in pred(U_j)$;

(iii) $A \in U_{i,j}$
if $B \in U_{i,k}$, $C \in U_{k,j}$, $(A \rightarrow BC) \in P$, $A \in pred(U_i)$;

(iv) $A \in U_{i,j}$
if $B \in U_{i,j}$, $(A \rightarrow B) \in P$, $A \in pred(U_i)$.

The string has been accepted when $S \in U_{0,n}$.

We now specify a grammar transformation, based on the definition of $\mathcal{A}_{2LR}$.

Definition 4 *Let* $\mathcal{A}_{2LR} = (\Sigma, Q_{2LR}, T_{2LR}, q'_{in}, q'_{fin})$ *be the* 2LR *automaton associated with a* CFG G. *The* **2LR cover** *associated with* G *is the* CFG $\mathcal{C}_{2LR}(G) = (\Sigma, Q_{2LR}, P_{2LR}, q'_{fin})$, *where the rules in* P_{2LR} *are given by:*

(i) $(a, q') \rightarrow a$,
for every $(X, q) \overset{a}{\mapsto} (X, q)\,(a, q') \in T_{2LR}$;

(ii) $(\epsilon) \rightarrow \epsilon$,
for every $(X, q) \overset{\epsilon}{\mapsto} (X, q)\,(\epsilon) \in T_{2LR}$;

(iii) $(X\beta) \rightarrow (X, q)\,(\beta)$,
for every $(X, q)\,(\beta) \overset{\epsilon}{\mapsto} (X\beta) \in T_{2LR}$;

[2]For the earliest mention of this transformation, we have encountered pointers to Schauerte (1973). Regrettably, we have as yet not been able to get hold of a copy of this paper.

(iv) $(A, q') \rightarrow (\alpha)$,
for every $(X, q)\ (\alpha) \overset{\epsilon}{\mapsto} (X, q)\ (A, q') \in T_{2LR}$.

Observe that there is a direct, one-to-one correspondence between transitions of $\mathcal{A}_{2LR}$ and productions of $\mathcal{C}_{2LR}(G)$.

The accompanying function *pred* is defined as follows (q, q', q'' range over the stack elements):

$$\begin{aligned} pred(\tau) \quad = \quad & \{q \mid q'q'' \overset{\epsilon}{\mapsto} q \in T_{2LR}\} \ \cup \\ & \{q \mid q' \in \tau,\ q' \overset{z}{\mapsto} q'\ q \in T_{2LR}\} \ \cup \\ & \{q \mid q' \in \tau,\ q'\ q'' \overset{\epsilon}{\mapsto} q'\ q \in T_{2LR}\}. \end{aligned}$$

The above definition implies that only the tabular equivalents of the shift, initiate and goto transitions are subject to actual filtering; the simulation of the gathering transitions does not depend on elements in τ.

Finally, the distinguished nonterminal from the cover used to initialize the table is q'_{in}. Thus we start with $(\triangleright, \{S\triangleleft\}) \in U_{0,0}$.

The 2LR cover introduces spurious ambiguity: where some grammar G would allow a certain number of parses to be found for a certain input, the grammar $\mathcal{C}_{2LR}(G)$ in general allows *more* parses. This problem is in part solved by the filtering function *pred*. The remaining spurious ambiguity is avoided by a particular way of constructing the parse trees, described in what follows.

After Algorithm 1 has recognized a given input, the set of all parse trees can be computed as $tree(q'_{fin}, 0, n)$ where the function *tree*, which determines sets of either parse trees or lists of parse trees for entries in U, is recursively defined by:

(i) $tree((a, q'), i, j)$ is the set $\{a\}$. This set contains a single parse tree consisting of a single node labelled a.

(ii) $tree(\epsilon, i, i)$ is the set $\{\epsilon\}$. This set consists of an empty list of trees.

(iii) $tree(X\beta, i, j)$ is the union of the sets $\mathcal{T}^k_{(X\beta),i,j}$, where $i \leq k \leq j$, $(\beta) \in U_{k,j}$, and there is at least one $(X, q) \in U_{i,k}$ and $(X\beta) \rightarrow (X, q)\ (\beta)$ in $\mathcal{C}_{2LR}(G)$, for some q. For each such k, select one such q. We define $\mathcal{T}^k_{(X\beta),i,j} = \{t \cdot ts \mid t \in tree((X, q), i, k) \wedge ts \in tree(\beta, k, j)\}$. Each $t \cdot ts$ is a list of trees, with head t and tail ts.

(iv) $tree((A, q'), i, j)$ is the union of the sets $\mathcal{T}^\alpha_{(A,q'),i,j}$, where $(\alpha) \in U_{i,j}$ is such that $(A, q') \rightarrow (\alpha)$ in $\mathcal{C}_{2LR}(G)$. We define $\mathcal{T}^\alpha_{(A,q'),i,j} = \{glue(A, ts) \mid ts \in tree(\alpha, i, j)\}$. The function *glue* constructs a tree from a fresh root node labelled A and the trees in list *ts* as immediate subtrees.

We emphasize that in the third clause above, one should not consider more than one q for given k in order to prevent spurious ambiguity. (In fact, for fixed X, i, k and for different q such that $(X, q) \in U_{i,k}$, $tree((X, q), i, k)$ yields the exact same set of trees.) With this proviso, the degree of ambiguity, i.e. the number of parses found by the algorithm for any input, is reduced to exactly that of the source grammar.

A practical implementation would construct the parse trees on-the-fly, attaching them to the table entries, allowing packing and sharing of subtrees (cf. the literature on *parse forests* (Tomita, 1986; Billot and Lang, 1989)). Our algorithm actually only needs one (packed) subtree for several $(X, q) \in U_{i,k}$ with fixed X, i, k but different q. The resulting parse forests would then be optimally compact, contrary to some other LR-based tabular algorithms, as pointed out by Rekers (1992), Nederhof (1993) and Nederhof (1994b).

6 Analysis of the algorithm

In this section, we investigate how the steps performed by Algorithm 1 (applied to the 2LR cover) relate to those performed by $\mathcal{A}_{2LR}$, for the same input.

We define a subrelation $\models^+$ of $\vdash^+$ as: $(\delta, uw) \models^+ (\delta\delta', w)$ if and only if $(\delta, uw) = (\delta, z_1 z_2 \cdots z_m w) \vdash (\delta\delta_1, z_2 \cdots z_m w) \vdash \ldots \vdash (\delta\delta_m, w) = (\delta\delta', w)$, for some $m \geq 1$, where $|\delta_k| > 0$ for all k, $1 \leq k \leq m$. Informally, we have $(\delta, uw) \models^+ (\delta\delta', w)$ if configuration $(\delta\delta', w)$ can be reached from (δ, uw) without the bottom-most part δ of the intermediate stacks being affected by any of the transitions; furthermore, at least one element is pushed on top of δ.

The following characterization relates the automaton $\mathcal{A}_{2LR}$ and Algorithm 1 applied to the 2LR cover. Symbol $q \in Q_{2LR}$ is eventually added to $U_{i,j}$ if and only if for some δ:

$$(q'_{in}, a_1 \ldots a_n) \vdash^* (\delta, a_{i+1} \ldots a_n) \models^+ (\delta q, a_{j+1} \ldots a_n).$$

In words, q is found in entry $U_{i,j}$ if and only if, at input position j, the automaton would push some element q on top of some lower-part of the stack δ that remains unaffected while the input from i to j is being read.

The above characterization, whose proof is not reported here, is the justification for calling the resulting algorithm tabular LR parsing. In particular, for a grammar for which $\mathcal{A}_{2LR}$ is deterministic, i.e. for an LR(0) grammar, the number of steps performed by $\mathcal{A}_{2LR}$ and the number of steps performed by the above algorithm are exactly the same. In the case of grammars which are not LR(0), the tabular LR algorithm is more efficient than for example a backtrack realisation of $\mathcal{A}_{2LR}$.

For determining the order of the time complexity of our algorithm, we look at the most expensive step, which is the computation of an element $(X\beta) \in U_{i,j}$ from two elements $(X, q) \in U_{i,k}$ and $(\beta) \in U_{k,j}$, through $(X, q)\ (\beta) \overset{\epsilon}{\mapsto} (X\beta) \in T_{2LR}$. In a straightforward realisation of the algorithm, this step can be applied $\mathcal{O}(|T_{2LR}| \cdot |v|^3)$ times (once for each i, k, j and each transition), each step taking a constant amount of time. We conclude that the time complexity of our algorithm is $\mathcal{O}(|T_{2LR}| \cdot |v|^3)$.

As far as space requirements are concerned, each set $U_{i,j}$ or U_i contains at most $|Q_{2LR}|$ elements. (One may assume an auxiliary table storing each U_i.) This results in a space complexity $\mathcal{O}(|Q_{2LR}| \cdot |v|^2)$.

The entries in the table represent single stack elements, as opposed to pairs of stack elements following Lang (1974) and Leermakers (1989). This has been investigated before by Nederhof (1994a, p. 25) and Villemonte de la Clergerie (1993, p. 155).

7 Empirical results

We have performed some experiments with Algorithm 1 applied to $\mathcal{A}_{2LR}$ and $\mathcal{A}'_{LR}$, for 4 practical context-free grammars. For $\mathcal{A}'_{LR}$ a cover was used analogous to the one in Definition 4; the filtering function remains the same.

The first grammar generates a subset of the programming language ALGOL 68 (van Wijngaarden and others, 1975). The second and third grammars generate a fragment of Dutch, and are referred to as the CORRie grammar (Vosse, 1994) and the Deltra grammar (Schoorl and Belder, 1990), respectively. These grammars were stripped of their arguments in order to convert them into context-free grammars. The fourth grammar, referred to as the Alvey grammar (Carroll, 1993), generates a fragment of English and was automatically generated from a unification-based grammar.

The test sentences have been obtained by automatic generation from the grammars, using the Grammar Workbench (Nederhof and Koster, 1992), which uses a random generator to select rules; therefore these sentences do not necessarily represent input typical of the applications for which the grammars were written. Table 1 summarizes the test material.

Our implementation is merely a prototype, which means that absolute duration of the parsing process is little indicative of the actual efficiency of more sophisticated implementations. Therefore, our measurements have been restricted to implementation-independent quantities, viz. the number of elements stored in the parse table and the number of elementary steps performed by the algorithm. In a practical implementation, such quantities will strongly influence the space and time complexity, although they do not represent the only determining factors. Furthermore, all optimizations of the time and space efficiency have been left out of consideration.

$G = (\Sigma, N, P, S)$	$\|G\|$	$\|N\|$	$\|P\|$	$\|w\|$
ALGOL 68	783	167	330	13.7
CORRie	1141	203	424	12.3
Deltra	1929	281	703	10.8
Alvey	5072	265	1484	10.7

Table 1: The test material: the four grammars and some of their dimensions, and the average length of the test sentences (20 sentences of various length for each grammar).

	$\mathcal{A}'_{LR}$		$\mathcal{A}_{2LR}$	
G	space	time	space	time
ALGOL 68	327	375	234	343
CORRie	7548	28028	5131	22414
Deltra	11772	94824	6526	70333
Alvey	599	1147	354	747

Table 2: Dynamic requirements: average space and time per sentence.

Table 2 presents the costs of parsing the test sentences. The first and third columns give the number of entries stored in table U, the second and fourth columns give the number of elementary steps that were performed.

An elementary step consists of the derivation of one element in Q'_{LR} or Q_{2LR} from one or two other elements. The elements that are used in the filtering process are counted individually. We give an example for the case of $\mathcal{A}'_{LR}$. Suppose we derive an element $q' \in U_{i,j}$ from an element $(A \rightarrow \bullet\, \alpha) \in U_{i,j}$, warranted by two elements $q_1, q_2 \in U_i$, $q_1 \neq q_2$, through *pred*, in the presence of $q_1\ (A \rightarrow \bullet\, \alpha) \overset{\epsilon}{\mapsto} q_1\ q' \in T'_{LR}$ and $q_2\ (A \rightarrow \bullet\, \alpha) \overset{\epsilon}{\mapsto} q_2\ q' \in T'_{LR}$. We then count *two* parsing steps, one for q_1 and one for q_2.

Table 2 shows that there is a significant gain in space and time efficiency when moving from $\mathcal{A}'_{LR}$ to

G	$\mathcal{A}'_{LR}$			$\mathcal{A}_{2LR}$		
	$\lvert\mathcal{R}_{LR}\rvert$	$\lvert Q'_{LR}\rvert$	$\lvert T'_{LR}\rvert$	$\lvert\mathcal{R}_{2LR}\rvert$	$\lvert Q_{2LR}\rvert$	$\lvert T_{2LR}\rvert$
ALGOL 68	434	1,217	13,844	109	724	12,387
CORRie	600	1,741	22,129	185	821	15,569
Deltra	856	2,785	54,932	260	1,089	37,510
Alvey	3,712	8,784	1,862,492	753	3,065	537,852

Table 3: Static requirements.

$\mathcal{A}_{2LR}$.

Apart from the dynamic costs of parsing, we have also measured some quantities relevant to the construction and storage of the two types of tabular LR parser. These data are given in Table 3.

We see that the number of states is strongly reduced with regard to traditional LR parsing. In the case of the Alvey grammar, moving from $|\mathcal{R}_{LR}|$ to $|\mathcal{R}_{2LR}|$ amounts to a reduction to 20.3 %. Whereas time- and space-efficient computation of $\mathcal{R}_{LR}$ for this grammar is a serious problem, computation of $\mathcal{R}_{2LR}$ will not be difficult on any modern computer. Also significant is the reduction from $|T'_{LR}|$ to $|T_{2LR}|$, especially for the larger grammars. These quantities correlate with the amount of storage needed for naive representation of the respective automata.

8 Discussion

Our treatment of tabular LR parsing has two important advantages over the one by Tomita:

- It is conceptually simpler, because we make use of simple concepts such as a grammar transformation and the well-understood CYK algorithm, instead of a complicated mechanism working on graph-structured stacks.
- Our algorithm requires fewer LR states. This leads to faster parser generation, to smaller parsers, and to reduced time and space complexity of parsing itself.

The conceptual simplicity of our formulation of tabular LR parsing allows comparison with other tabular parsing techniques, such as Earley's algorithm (Earley, 1970) and tabular left-corner parsing (Nederhof, 1993), based on implementation-independent criteria. This is in contrast to experiments reported before (e.g. by Shann (1991)), which treated tabular LR parsing differently from the other techniques.

The reduced time and space complexities reported in the previous section pertain to the tabular realisation of two parsing techniques, expressed by the automata $\mathcal{A}'_{LR}$ and $\mathcal{A}_{2LR}$. The tabular realisation of the former automata is very close to a variant of Tomita's algorithm by Kipps (1991). The objective of our experiments was to show that the automata $\mathcal{A}_{2LR}$ provide a better basis than $\mathcal{A}'_{LR}$ for tabular LR parsing with regard to space and time complexity.

Parsing algorithms that are not based on the LR technique have however been left out of consideration, and so were techniques for unification grammars and techniques incorporating finite-state processes.[3]

Theoretical considerations (Leermakers, 1989; Schabes, 1991; Nederhof, 1994b) have suggested that for natural language parsing, LR-based techniques may not necessarily be superior to other parsing techniques, although convincing empirical data to this effect has never been shown. This issue is difficult to resolve because so much of the relative efficiency of the different parsing techniques depends on particular grammars and particular input, as well as on particular implementations of the techniques. We hope the conceptual framework presented in this paper may at least partly alleviate this problem.

Acknowledgements

The first author is supported by the Dutch Organization for Scientific Research (NWO), under grant 305-00-802. Part of the present research was done while the second author was visiting the Center for Language and Speech Processing, Johns Hopkins University, Baltimore, MD.

We received kind help from John Carroll, Job Honig, Kees Koster, Theo Vosse and Hans de Vreught in finding the grammars mentioned in this paper. Generous help with locating relevant literature was provided by Anton Nijholt, Rockford Ross, and Arnd Rußmann.

[3] As remarked before by Nederhof (1993), the algorithms by Schabes (1991) and Leermakers (1989) are not really related to LR parsing, although some notation used in these papers suggests otherwise.

References

Billot, S. and B. Lang. 1989. The structure of shared forests in ambiguous parsing. In *27th Annual Meeting of the ACL*, pages 143–151.

Booth, T.L. 1967. *Sequential Machines and Automata Theory.* Wiley, New York.

Carroll, J.A. 1993. Practical unification-based parsing of natural language. Technical Report No. 314, University of Cambridge, Computer Laboratory, England. PhD thesis.

Earley, J. 1970. An efficient context-free parsing algorithm. *Communications of the ACM*, 13(2):94–102.

Harrison, M.A. 1978. *Introduction to Formal Language Theory.* Addison-Wesley.

Johnson, M. 1991. The computational complexity of GLR parsing. In Tomita (1991), chapter 3, pages 35–42.

Kipps, J.R. 1991. GLR parsing in time $\mathcal{O}(n^3)$. In Tomita (1991), chapter 4, pages 43–59.

Lang, B. 1974. Deterministic techniques for efficient non-deterministic parsers. In *Automata, Languages and Programming, 2nd Colloquium*, LNCS 14, pages 255–269, Saarbrücken. Springer-Verlag.

Leermakers, R. 1989. How to cover a grammar. In *27th Annual Meeting of the ACL*, pages 135–142.

Leermakers, R. 1992a. A recursive ascent Earley parser. *Information Processing Letters*, 41(2):87–91.

Leermakers, R. 1992b. Recursive ascent parsing: from Earley to Marcus. *Theoretical Computer Science*, 104:299–312.

Nederhof, M.J. 1993. Generalized left-corner parsing. In *Sixth Conference of the European Chapter of the ACL*, pages 305–314.

Nederhof, M.J. 1994a. *Linguistic Parsing and Program Transformations.* Ph.D. thesis, University of Nijmegen.

Nederhof, M.J. 1994b. An optimal tabular parsing algorithm. In *32nd Annual Meeting of the ACL*, pages 117–124.

Nederhof, M.J. and K. Koster. 1992. A customized grammar workbench. In J. Aarts, P. de Haan, and N. Oostdijk, editors, *English Language Corpora: Design, Analysis and Exploitation*, Papers from the thirteenth International Conference on English Language Research on Computerized Corpora, pages 163–179, Nijmegen. Rodopi.

Nederhof, M.J. and J.J. Sarbo. 1993. Increasing the applicability of LR parsing. In *Third International Workshop on Parsing Technologies*, pages 187–201.

Nederhof, M.J. and G. Satta. 1994. An extended theory of head-driven parsing. In *32nd Annual Meeting of the ACL*, pages 210–217.

Pager, D. 1970. A solution to an open problem by Knuth. *Information and Control*, 17:462–473.

Rekers, J. 1992. *Parser Generation for Interactive Environments.* Ph.D. thesis, University of Amsterdam.

Schabes, Y. 1991. Polynomial time and space shift-reduce parsing of arbitrary context-free grammars. In *29th Annual Meeting of the ACL*, pages 106–113.

Schauerte, R. 1973. Transformationen von LR(k)-grammatiken. Diplomarbeit, Universität Göttingen, Abteilung Informatik.

Schoorl, J.J. and S. Belder. 1990. Computational linguistics at Delft: A status report. Report WTM/TT 90–09, Delft University of Technology, Applied Linguistics Unit.

Shann, P. 1991. Experiments with GLR and chart parsing. In Tomita (1991), chapter 2, pages 17–34.

Sheil, B.A. 1976. Observations on context-free parsing. *Statistical Methods in Linguistics*, pages 71–109.

Sippu, S. and E. Soisalon-Soininen. 1990. *Parsing Theory, Vol. II: LR(k) and LL(k) Parsing.* Springer-Verlag.

Tomita, M. 1986. *Efficient Parsing for Natural Language.* Kluwer Academic Publishers.

Tomita, M., editor. 1991. *Generalized LR Parsing.* Kluwer Academic Publishers.

van Wijngaarden, A. et al. 1975. Revised report on the algorithmic language ALGOL 68. *Acta Informatica*, 5:1–236.

Villemonte de la Clergerie, E. 1993. *Automates à Piles et Programmation Dynamique — DyALog: Une application à la Programmation en Logique.* Ph.D. thesis, Université Paris VII.

Vosse, T.G. 1994. *The Word Connection.* Ph.D. thesis, University of Leiden.

Magic for Filter Optimization in Dynamic Bottom-up Processing

Guido Minnen*
SFB 340, University of Tübingen
Kleine Wilhelmstraße. 113
D-72074 Tübingen,
Germany
e-mail:minnen@sfs.nphil.uni-tuebingen.de

Abstract

Off-line compilation of logic grammars using *Magic* allows an incorporation of filtering into the logic underlying the grammar. The explicit definite clause characterization of filtering resulting from Magic compilation allows processor independent and logically clean optimizations of *dynamic bottom-up processing* with respect to goal-directedness. Two *filter optimizations* based on the program transformation technique of Unfolding are discussed which are of practical and theoretical interest.

1 Introduction

In natural language processing *filtering* is used to weed out those search paths that are redundant, i.e., are not going to be used in the proof tree corresponding to the natural language expression to be generated or parsed. Filter optimization often comprises an extension of a specific processing strategy such that it exploits specific knowledge about grammars and/or the computational task(s) that one is using them for. At the same time it often remains unclear how these optimizations relate to each other and what they actually mean. In this paper I show how starting from a definite clause characterization of filtering derived automatically from a logic grammar using Magic compilation, filter optimizations can be performed in a processor independent and logically clean fashion.

Magic (templates) is a general compilation technique for efficient bottom-up evaluation of logic programs developed in the deductive database community (Ramakrishnan et al., 1992). Given a logic program, Magic produces a new program in which the filtering as normally resulting from top-down evaluation is explicitly characterized through, so-called, *magic predicates*, which produce variable bindings for filtering when evaluated bottom-up. The original rules of the program are extended such that these bindings can be made effective.

As a result of the definite clause characterization of filtering, Magic brings filtering into the logic underlying the grammar. I discuss two filter optimizations. These optimizations are direction independent in the sense that they are useful for both generation and parsing. For expository reasons, though, they are presented merely on the basis of examples of generation.

Magic compilation does not limit the information that can be used for filtering. This can lead to nontermination as the tree fragments enumerated in bottom-up evaluation of magic compiled grammars are *connected* (Johnson, forthcoming). More specifically, 'magic generation' falls prey to non-termination in the face of head recursion, i.e., the generation analog of left recursion in parsing. This necessitates a *dynamic* processing strategy, i.e., memoization, extended with an abstraction function like, e.g., restriction (Shieber, 1985), to weaken filtering and a subsumption check to discard redundant results. It is shown that for a large class of grammars the subsumption check which often influences processing efficiency rather dramatically can be eliminated through fine-tuning of the magic predicates derived for a particular grammar after applying an abstraction function in an off-line fashion.

Unfolding can be used to eliminate superfluous filtering steps. Given an off-line optimization of the order in which the right-hand side categories in the rules of a logic grammar are processed (Minnen et al., 1996) the resulting processing behavior can be considered a generalization of the head corner generation approach (Shieber et al., 1990): Without the need to rely on notions such as *semantic head* and *chain rule*, a head corner behavior can be mimicked in a strict bottom-up fashion.

*url: http://www.sfs.nphil.uni-tuebingen/~minnen

2 Definite Clause Characterization of Filtering

Many approaches focus on exploiting specific knowledge about grammars and/or the computational task(s) that one is using them for by making filtering explicit and extending the processing strategy such that this information can be made effective. In generation, examples of such extended processing strategies are head corner generation with its semantic linking (Shieber et al., 1990) or bottom-up (Earley) generation with a semantic filter (Shieber, 1988). Even though these approaches often accomplish considerable improvements with respect to efficiency or termination behavior, it remains unclear how these optimizations relate to each other and what comprises the logic behind these specialized forms of filtering. By bringing filtering into the logic underlying the grammar it is possible to show in a perspicuous and logically clean way how and why filtering can be optimized in a particular fashion and how various approaches relate to each other.

2.1 Magic Compilation

Magic makes filtering explicit through characterizing it as definite clauses. Intuitively understood, filtering is reversed as binding information that normally becomes available as a result of top-down evaluation is derived by bottom-up evaluation of the definite clause characterization of filtering. The following is the basic Magic algorithm taken from Ramakrishnan et al. (1992).

> Let P be a program and $q(\bar{c})$ a query on the program. We construct a new program P^{mg}. Initially P^{mg} is empty.
>
> 1. Create a new predicate *magic_p* for each predicate p in P. The arity is that of p.
> 2. For each rule in P, add the *modified version* of the rule to P^{mg}. If rule r has head, say, $p(\bar{t})$, the modified version is obtained by adding the literal *magic_p*$(\bar{t})$ to the body.
> 3. For each rule r in P with head, say, $p(\bar{t})$, and for each literal $q_i(\bar{t_i})$ in its body, add a *magic rule* to P^{mg}. The head is *magic_q*$_i(\bar{t_i})$. The body contains the literal *magic_p*$(\bar{t})$, and all the literals that precede q_i in the rule.
> 4. Create a *seed* fact *magic_q*$(\bar{c})$ from the query.

To illustrate the algorithm I zoom in on the application of the above algorithm to one particular grammar rule. Suppose the original grammar rule looks as follows:

```
s(P0,P,VForm,SSem):-
   vp(P1,P,VForm,[CSem],SSem),
   np(P0,P1,CSem).
```

Step 2 of the algorithm results in the following modified version of the original grammar rule:

```
s(P0,P,VForm,SSem):-
   magic_s(P0,P,VForm,SSem),
   vp(P1,P,VForm,[CSem],SSem),
   np(P0,P1,CSem).
```

A magic literal is added to the right-hand side of the rule which 'guards' the application of the rule. This does not change the semantics of the original grammar as it merely serves as a way to incorporate the relevant bindings derived with the magic predicates to avoid redundant applications of a rule. Corresponding to the first right-hand side literal in the original rule step 3 derives the following magic rule:

```
magic_vp(P1,P,VForm,[CSem],SSem):-
   magic_s(P0,P,VForm,SSem).
```

It is used to derive from the guard for the original rule a guard for the rules defining the first right-hand side literal. The second right-hand side literal in the original rule leads to the following magic rule:

```
magic_np(P0,P1,CSem):-
   magic_s(P0,P,VForm,SSem),
   vp(P1,P,VForm,[CSem],SSem).
```

Finally, step 4 of the algorithm ensures that a seed is created. Assuming that the original rule is defining the start category, the query corresponding to the generation of the s "John buys Mary a book" leads to the following seed:

```
magic_s(P0,P,finite,buys(john,a(book),mary)).
```

The seed constitutes a representation of the initial bindings provided by the query that is used by the magic predicates to derive guards. Note that the creation of the seed can be delayed until run-time, i.e., the grammar does not need to be recompiled for every possible query.

2.2 Example

Magic compilation is illustrated on the basis of the simple logic grammar extract in figure 1. This grammar has been optimized automatically for generation (Minnen et al., 1996): The right-hand sides of the rules are reordered such that a simple left-to-right evaluation order constitutes the optimal evaluation order. With this grammar a simple top-down generation strategy does not terminate as a result of the head recursion in rule 3. It is necessary to use

```
(1) sentence(P0,P,decl(SSem)):-
       s(P0,P,finite,SSem).
(2) s(P0,P,VForm,SSem):-
       vp(P1,P,VForm,[CSem],SSem).
       np(P0,P1,CSem),
(3) vp(P0,P,VForm,Args,SSem):-
       vp(P0,P1,VForm,[CSem|Args],SSem),
       np(P1,P,CSem).
(4) vp(P0,P,VForm,Args,SSem):-
       v(P0,P,VForm,Args,SSem).
(5) np(P0,P,NPSem):-
       pn(P0,P,NPSem)
(6) np(P0,P,NPSem):-
       det(P0,P1,NSem,NPSem),
       n(P1,P,NSem).
(7) det([a|P],P,NSem,a(NSem)).
(8) v([buys|P],P,finite,[I,D,S],buys(S,D,I)).
(9) pn([mary|P],P,mary)
(10)n([book|P],P,book).
```

Figure 1: *Simple head-recursive grammar.*

memoization extended with an abstraction function and a subsumption check. Strict bottom-up generation is not attractive either as it is extremely inefficient: One is forced to generate all possible natural language expressions licensed by the grammar and subsequently check them against the start category. It is possible to make the process more efficient through excluding specific lexical entries with a semantic filter. The use of such a semantic filter in bottom-up evaluation requires the grammar to obey the *semantic monotonicity constraint* in order to ensure completeness(Shieber, 1988) (see below).

The 'magic-compiled grammar' in figure 2 is the result of applying the algorithm in the previous section to the head-recursive example grammar and subsequently performing two optimizations (Beeri and Ramakrishnan, 1991): All (calls to) magic predicates corresponding to lexical entries are removed. Furthermore, data-flow analysis is used to fine-tune the magic predicates for the specific processing task at hand, i.e., generation.[1] Given a user-specified *abstract query*, i.e., a specification of the intended input (Beeri and Ramakrishnan, 1991) those arguments which are not bound and which therefore serve no filtering purpose are removed. The modified versions of the original rules in the grammar are adapted accordingly. The effect of taking data-flow into account can be observed by comparing the rules for `magic_vp` and `magic_np` in the previous section with rule 12 and 14 in figure 2, respectively.

Figure 3 shows the results from generation of the `sentence` "John buys Mary a book". In the case of this example the seed looks as follows:

`magic_sentence(decl(buys(john,a(book),mary))).`

The *facts*, i.e., passive edges/items, in figure 3 resulted from *semi-naive* bottom-up evaluation (Ramakrishnan et al., 1992) which constitutes a dynamic bottom-up evaluation, where repeated derivation of facts from the same earlier derived facts (as in *naive* evaluation; Bancilhon, 1985) is blocked. (Active edges are not memoized.) The figure[2] consist of two tree structures (connected through dotted lines) of which the left one corresponds to the filtering part of the derivation. The filtering tree is reversed and derives magic facts starting from the seed in a bottom-up fashion. The tree on the right is the proof tree for the example sentence which is built up as a result of unifying in the derived magic facts when applying a particular rule. E.g., in order to derive fact 13, magic fact 2 is unified with the magic literal in the modified version of rule 2 (in addition to the facts 12 and 10). This, however, is not represented in order to keep the figure clear. Dotted lines are used to represent when 'normal' facts are combined with magic facts to derive new magic facts.

As can be reconstructed from the numbering of the facts in figure 3 the resulting processing behavior is identical to the behavior that would result from Earley generation as in Gerdemann (1991) except that the different filtering steps are performed in a bottom-up fashion. In order to obtain a generator similar to the bottom-up generator as described in Shieber (1988) the compilation process can be modified such that only lexical entries are extended with magic literals. Just like in case of Shieber's bottom-up generator, bottom-up evaluation of magic-compiled grammars produced with this Magic variant is only guaranteed to be complete in case the original grammar obeys the semantic monotonicity constraint.

[1]For expository reasons some data-flow information that does restrict processing is not taken into account. E.g., the fact that the vp literal in rule 2 is always called with a one-element list is ignored here, but see section 3.1.

[2]The numbering of the facts corresponds to the order in which they are derived. A number of lexical entries have been added to the example grammar. The facts corresponding to lexical entries are ignored. For expository reasons the phonology and semantics of lexical entries (except for vs) are abbreviated by the first letter. Furthermore the fact corresponding to the vp "buys Mary a book John" is not included.

```
(1) sentence(P0,P,decl(SSem)):-
        magic_sentence(decl(SSem)),
        s(P0,P,finite,SSem).
(2) s(P0,P,VForm,SSem):-
        magic_s(VForm,SSem),
        vp(P1,P,VForm,[CSem],SSem),
        np(P0,P1,CSem).
(3) vp(P0,P,VForm,Args,SSem):-
        magic_vp(VForm,SSem),
        vp(P0,P1,VForm,[CSem|Args],SSem),
        np(P1,P,CSem).
(4) vp(P0,P,VForm,Args,SSem):-
        magic_vp(VForm,SSem),
        v(P0,P,VForm,Args,SSem).
(5) np(P0,P,NPSem):-
        magic_np(NPSem),
        pn(P0,P,NPSem).
(6)  np(P0,P,NPSem):-
        magic_np(NPSem),
        det(P0,P1,NSem,NPSem),
        n(P1,P,NSem).
(7)  det([a|P],P,NSem,a(NSem)).
(8)  v([buys|P],P,finite,[I,D,S],buys(S,D,I)).
(9)  pn([mary|P],P,mary)
(10) n([book|P],P,book).
(11) magic_s(finite,SSem):-
        magic_sentence(decl(SSem)).
(12) magic_vp(VForm,SSem):-
        magic_s(VForm,SSem).
(13) magic_vp(VForm,SSem):-
        magic_vp(VForm,SSem).
(14) magic_np(CSem):-
        magic_s(VForm,SSem),
        vp(P1,P,VForm,[CSem],SSem).
(15) magic_np(CSem):-
        magic_vp(VForm,SSem),
        vp(P0,P1,VForm,[CSem|Args],SSem).
```

Figure 2: *Magic compiled version 1 of the grammar in figure 1.*

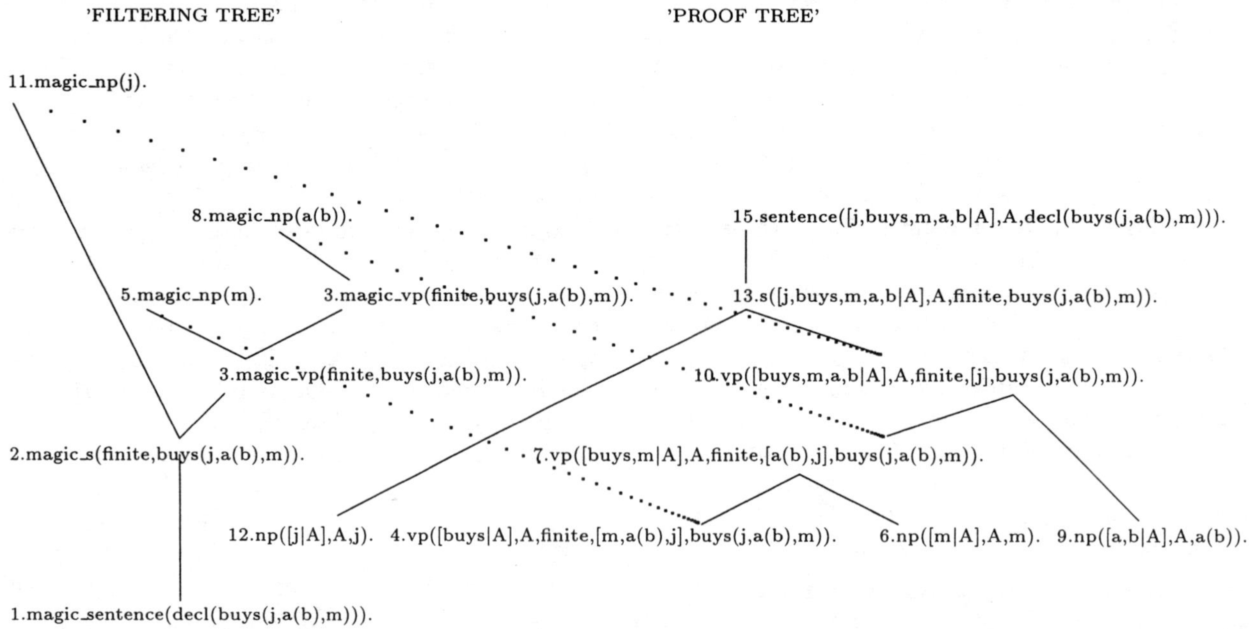

Figure 3: *'Connecting up' facts resulting from semi-naive generation of the sentence "John buys Mary a book" with the magic-compiled grammar from figure 2.*

3 Filter Optimization through Program Transformation

As a result of characterizing filtering by a definite clause representation Magic brings filtering inside of the logic underlying the grammar. This allows it to be optimized in a processor independent and logically clean fashion. I discuss two possible filter optimizations based on a program transformation technique called *unfolding* (Tamaki and Sato, 1984) also referred to as partial execution, e.g., in Pereira and Shieber (1987).

3.1 Subsumption Checking

Just like top-down evaluation of the original grammar bottom-up evaluation of its magic compiled version falls prey to non-termination in the face of head recursion. It is however possible to eliminate the subsumption check through fine-tuning the magic predicates derived for a particular grammar in an off-line fashion. In order to illustrate how the magic predicates can be adapted such that the subsumption check can be eliminated it is necessary to take a closer look at the relation between the magic predicates and the facts they derive. In figure 4 the relation between the magic predicates for the example grammar is represented by an *unfolding tree* (Pettorossi and Proietti, 1994). This, however, is not an ordinary unfolding tree as it is constructed on the basis of an *abstract seed*, i.e., a seed adorned with a specification of which arguments are to be considered bound. Note that an abstract seed can be derived from the user-specified abstract query. Only the magic part of the abstract unfolding tree is represented.

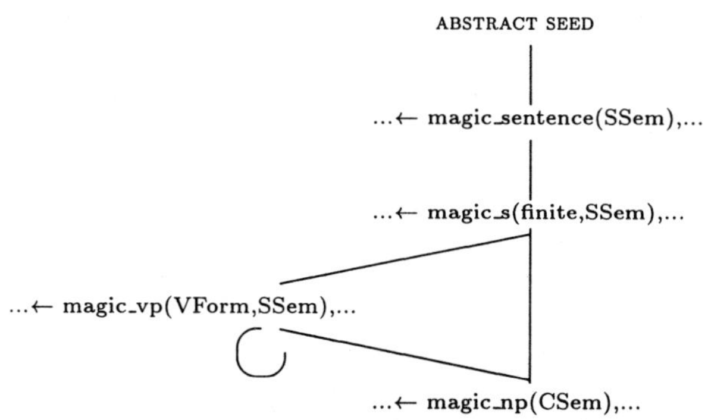

Figure 4: *Abstract unfolding tree representing the relation between the magic predicates in the compiled grammar.*

The abstract unfolding tree in figure 4 clearly shows why there exists the need for subsumption checking: Rule 13 in figure 2 produces infinitely many `magic_vp` facts. This 'cyclic' magic rule is derived from the head-recursive `vp` rule in the example grammar. There is however no reason to keep this rule in the magic-compiled grammar. It influences neither the efficiency of processing with the grammar nor the completeness of the evaluation process.

3.1.1 Off-line Abstraction

Finding these types of cycles in the magic part of the compiled grammar is in general undecidable. It is possible though to 'trim' the magic predicates by applying an abstraction function. As a result of the explicit representation of filtering we do not need to postpone abstraction until run-time, but can trim the magic predicates off-line. One can consider this as bringing abstraction into the logic as the definite clause representation of filtering is weakened such that only a mild form of connectedness results which does not affect completeness (Shieber, 1985). Consider the following magic rule:

```
magic_vp(VForm,[CSem|Args],SSem):-
   magic_vp(VForm,Args,SSem).
```

This is the rule that is derived from the head-recursive `vp` rule when the partially specified subcategorization list is considered as filtering information (cf., fn. 1). The rule builds up infinitely large subcategorization lists of which eventually only one is to be matched against the subcategorization list of, e.g., the lexical entry for "buys". Though this rule is not cyclic, it becomes cyclic upon *off-line abstraction*:

```
magic_vp(VForm,[CSem|_],SSem):-
   magic_vp(VForm,[CSem2|_],SSem).
```

Through trimming this magic rule, e.g., given a bounded term depth (Sato and Tamaki, 1984) or a restrictor (Shieber, 1985), constructing an abstract unfolding tree reveals the fact that a cycle results from the magic rule. This information can then be used to discard the culprit.

3.1.2 Indexing

Removing the direct or indirect cycles from the magic part of the compiled grammar does eliminate the necessity of subsumption checking in many cases. However, consider the magic rules 14 and 15 in figure 2. Rule 15 is more general than rule 14. Without subsumption checking this leads to spurious ambiguity: Both rules produce a magic fact with which a subject `np` can be built. A possible solution to this problem is to couple magic rules with the modified version of the original grammar rule that instigated it. To accomplish this I propose a technique that can be considered the off-line variant of an indexing technique described in Gerdemann (1991).[3] The indexing technique is illustrated on the basis of the running example: Rule 14 in figure 1 is coupled to the modified version of the original s rule that instigated it, i.e., rule 2. Both rules receive an index:

```
s(P0,P,VForm,SSem):-
    magic_s(P0,P,VForm,SSem),
    vp(P1,P,VForm,[CSem],SSem),
    np(P0,P1,CSem,index_1).

magic_np(CSem,index_1):-
   magic_s(P0,P,VForm,SSem),
   vp(P1,P,VForm,[CSem],SSem).
```

The modified versions of the rules defining nps are adapted such that they percolate up the index of the guarding magic fact that licensed its application. This is illustrated on the basis of the adapted version of rule 14:

```
np(P0,P,NPSem,INDEX):-
   magic_np(NPSem,INDEX),
   pn(P0,P,NPSem).
```

As is illustrated in section 3.3 this allows the avoidance of spurious ambiguities in the absence of subsumption check in case of the example grammar.

3.2 Redundant Filtering Steps

Unfolding can also be used to collapse filtering steps. As becomes apparent upon closer investigation of the abstract unfolding tree in figure 4 the magic predicates magic_sentence, magic_s and magic_vp provide virtually identical variable bindings to guard bottom-up application of the modified versions of the original grammar rules. Unfolding can be used to reduce the number of magic facts that are produced during processing. E.g., in figure 2 the magic_s rule:

```
magic_s(finite,SSem):-
    magic_sentence(decl(SSem)).
```

can be eliminated by unfolding the magic_s literal in the modified s rule:

```
s(P0,P,VFORM,SSem):-
    magic_s(VFORM,SSem),
    vp(P1,P,VFORM,,[CSem],SSem),
    np(P0,P1,CSem).
```

This results in the following new rule which uses the seed for filtering directly without the need for an intermediate filtering step:

```
s(P0,P,finite,SSem):-
    magic_sentence(decl(SSem)),
    vp(P1,P,finite,[CSem],SSem),
    np(P0,P1,CSem).
```

Note that the unfolding of the magic_s literal leads to the instantiation of the argument VFORM to finite. As a result of the fact that there are no other magic_s literals in the remainder of the magic-compiled grammar the magic_s rule can be discarded.

This filter optimization is reminiscent of computing the deterministic closure over the magic part of a compiled grammar (Dörre, 1993) at compile time. Performing this optimization throughout the magic part of the grammar in figure 2 not only leads to a more succinct grammar, but brings about a different processing behavior. Generation with the resulting grammar can be compared best with head corner generation (Shieber et al., 1990) (see next section).

3.3 Example

After cycle removal, incorporating relevant indexing and the collapsing of redundant magic predicates the magic-compiled grammar from figure 2 looks as displayed in figure 5. Figure 6 shows the chart resulting from generation of the sentence "John buys Mary a book".[4] The seed is identical to the one used for the example in the previous section. The *facts* in the chart resulted from *not-so-naive* bottom-up evaluation: semi-naive evaluation without subsumption checking (Ramakrishnan et al., 1992). The resulting processing behavior is similar to the behavior that would result from head corner generation except that the different filtering steps are performed in a bottom-up fashion. The head corner approach jumps top-down from pivot to pivot in order to satisfy its assumptions concerning the flow of semantic information, i.e., semantic chaining, and subsequently generates starting from the semantic head in a bottom-up fashion. In the example, the seed is used without any delay to apply the base case of the vp-procedure, thereby jumping over all intermediate chain and non-chain rules. In this respect the initial reordering of rule 2 which led to rule 2 in the final grammar in figure 5 is crucial (see section 4).

4 Dependency Constraint on Grammar

To which extent it is useful to collapse magic predicates using unfolding depends on whether the grammar has been optimized through reordering the

[3]This technique resembles an extension of Magic called *Counting* (Beeri and Ramakrishnan, 1991). However, Counting is more refined as it allows to distinguish between different levels of recursion and serves entirely different purposes.

[4]In addition to the conventions already described regarding figure 3, indices are abbreviated.

```
(1)  sentence(P0,P,decl(SSem)):-
        magic_sentence(decl(SSem)),
        s(P0,P,finite,SSem).
(2)  s(P0,P,finite,SSem):-
        magic_sentence(decl(SSem)),
        vp(P1,P,finite,[CSem],SSem),
        np(P0,P1,CSem,index_1).
(3)  vp(P0,P,finite,Args,SSem):-
        magic_sentence(decl(SSem)),
        vp(P0,P1,finite,[CSem|Args],SSem),
        np(P1,P,CSem,index_2).
(4)  vp(P0,P,finite,Args,SSem):-
        magic_sentence(decl(SSem)),
        v(P0,P,finite,Args,SSem).
(5)  np(P0,P,NPSem,INDEX):-
        magic_np(NPSem,INDEX),
        pn(P0,P,NPSem).
(6)  np(P0,P,NPSem,INDEX):-
        magic_np(NPSem,INDEX),
        det(P0,P1,NSem,NPSem),
        n(P1,P,NSem).
(7)  det([a|P],P,NSem,a(NSem)).
(8)  v([buys|P],P,finite,[I,D,S],buys(S,D,I)).
(9)  pn([mary|P],P,mary)
(10) n([book|P],P,book).
(14) magic_np(CSem,index_1):-
        magic_sentence(decl(SSem)),
        vp(P1,P,finite,[CSem],SSem).
(15) magic_np(CSem,index_2):-
        magic_sentence(decl(SSem)),
        vp(P0,P1,finite,[CSem|Args],SSem).
```

Figure 5: *Magic compiled version 2 of the grammar in figure 1.*

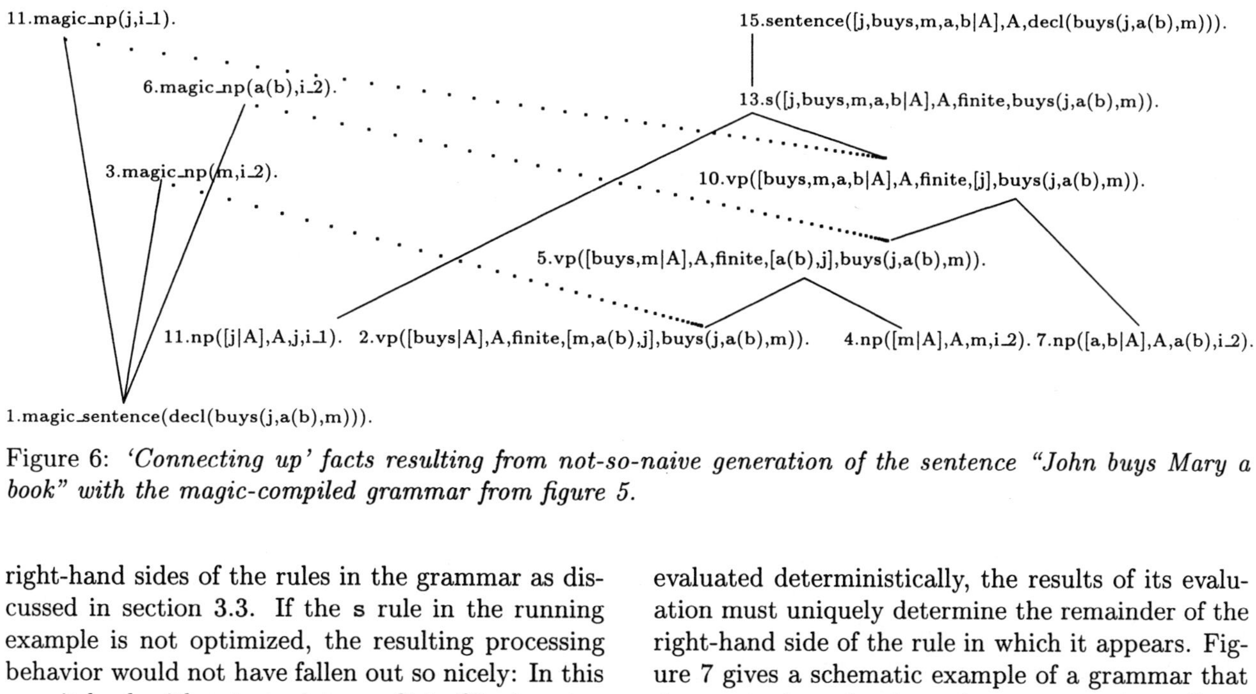

Figure 6: *'Connecting up' facts resulting from not-so-naive generation of the sentence "John buys Mary a book" with the magic-compiled grammar from figure 5.*

right-hand sides of the rules in the grammar as discussed in section 3.3. If the s rule in the running example is not optimized, the resulting processing behavior would not have fallen out so nicely: In this case it leads either to an intermediate filtering step for the non-chaining sentence rule or to the addition of the literal corresponding to the subject np to all chain and non-chain rules along the path to the semantic head.

Even when cycles are removed from the magic part of a compiled grammar and indexing is used to avoid spurious ambiguities as discussed in the previous section, subsumption checking can not always be eliminated. The grammar must be finitely ambiguous, i.e., fulfill the *off-line parsability constraint* (Shieber, 1989). Furthermore, the grammar is required to obey what I refer to as the *dependency constraint*: When a particular right-hand side literal can not be evaluated deterministically, the results of its evaluation must uniquely determine the remainder of the right-hand side of the rule in which it appears. Figure 7 gives a schematic example of a grammar that does not obey the dependency constraint. Given

```
(1)  cat_1(...):-
          magic_cat_1(Filter),
          cat_2(Filter,Dependency,...),
          cat_3(Dependency).
(2)  magic_cat_3(Filter):-
          magic_cat_1(Filter),
          cat_2(Filter,Dependency,...).
     ...
(3)  cat_2(property_1,property_2,...).
(4)  cat_2(property_1,property_2,...).
```

Figure 7: *Abstract example grammar not obeying the dependency constraint.*

a derived fact or seed `magic_cat_1(property_1)` bottom-up evaluation of the abstract grammar in figure 7 leads to spurious ambiguity. There are two possible solutions for `cat_2` as a result of the fact that the filtering resulting from the magic literal in rule 1 is too unspecific. This is not problematic as long as this nondeterminism will eventually disappear, e.g., by combining these solutions with the solutions to `cat_3`. The problem arises as a result of the fact that these solutions lead to identical filters for the evaluation of the `cat_3` literal, i.e., the solutions to `cat_2` do not uniquely determine `cat_3`.

Also with respect to the dependency constraint an optimization of the rules in the grammar is important. Through reordering the right-hand sides of the rules in the grammar the amount of nondeterminism can be drastically reduced as shown in Minnen et al. (1996). This way of following the intended semantic dependencies the dependency constraint is satisfied automatically for a large class of grammars.

5 Concluding Remarks

Magic evaluation constitutes an interesting combination of the advantages of top-down and bottom-up evaluation. It allows bottom-up filtering that achieves a goal-directedness which corresponds to dynamic top-down evaluation with abstraction and subsumption checking. For a large class of grammars in effect identical operations can be performed off-line thereby allowing for more efficient processing. Furthermore, it enables a reduction of the number of edges that need to be stored through unfolding magic predicates.

6 Acknowledgments

The presented research was sponsored by Teilprojekt B4 "From Constraints to Rules: Efficient Compilation of HPSG Grammars" of the Sonderforschungsbereich 340 of the Deutsche Forschungsgemeinschaft. The author wishes to thank Dale Gerdemann, Mark Johnson, Thilo Götz and the anonymous reviewers for valuable comments and discussion. Of course, the author is responsible for all remaining errors.

References

Francois Bancilhon. 1985. Naive Evaluation of Recursively Defined Relations. In Brodie and Mylopoulos, editors, *On Knowledge Base Management Systems - Integrating Database and AI Systems.* Springer-Verlag.

Catriel Beeri and Raghu Ramakrishnan. 1991. On the Power of Magic. *Journal of Logic Programming 10.*

Jochen Dörre. 1993. Generalizing Earley Deduction for Constraint-based Grammars. Dörre and Dorna, editors, *Computational Aspects of Constraint-Based Linguistic Description I*, DYANA-2, Deliverable R1.2.A.

Dale Gerdemann. 1991. *Parsing and Generation of Unification Grammars.* Ph.D. thesis, University of Illinois, USA.

Mark Johnson. forthcoming. *Constraint-based Natural Language Parsing.* Brown University, Richmond, USA. Draft of 6 August 1995.

Guido Minnen, Dale Gerdemann, and Erhard Hinrichs. 1996. Direct Automated Inversion of Logic Grammars. *New Generation Computing 14.*

Fernando Pereira and Stuart Shieber. 1987. *Prolog and Natural Language Analysis.* CSLI Lecture Notes, No. 10. Center for the Study of Language and Information, Chicago, USA.

Alberto Pettorossi and Maurizio Proietti. 1994. Transformations of Logic Programs: Foundations and Techniques. *Journal of Logic Programming 19/20.*

Raghu Ramakrishnan, Divesh Srivastava, and S. Sudarshan. 1992. Efficient Bottom-up Evaluation of Logic Programs. In Vandewalle, editor, *The State of the Art in Computer Systems and Software Engineering.* Kluwer Academic Publishers.

Taisuke Sato and Hisao Tamaki. 1984. Enumeration of Success Patterns in Logic Programs. *Theoretical Computer Sience 34.*

Stuart Shieber, Gertjan van Noord, Robert Moore, and Fernando Pereira. 1990. Semantic Head-driven Generation. *Computational Linguistics 16.*

Stuart Shieber. 1985. Using Restriction to Extend Parsing Algorithms for Complex Feature-based Formalisms. In *Proceedings of the 23rd Annual Meeting Association for Computational Linguistics*, Chicago, USA.

Stuart Shieber. 1988. A Uniform Architecture for Parsing and Generation. In *Proceedings of the 12th Conference on Computational Linguistics*, Budapest, Hungary.

Stuart Shieber. 1989. Parsing and Type Inference for Natural and Computer Languages. Ph.D. thesis, Stanford University, USA.

Hisao Tamaki and Taisuke Sato. 1984. Unfold/Fold Transformation of Logic Programs. In *Proceedings of the 2nd International Conference on Logic Programming*, Uppsala, Sweden.

Efficient Transformation-Based Parsing

Giorgio Satta
Dipartimento di Elettronica ed Informatica
Università di Padova
via Gradenigo, 6/A
I-35131 Padova, Italy
satta@dei.unipd.it

Eric Brill
Department of Computer Science
Johns Hopkins University
Baltimore, MD 21218-2694
brill@cs.jhu.edu

Abstract

In transformation-based parsing, a finite sequence of tree rewriting rules are checked for application to an input structure. Since in practice only a small percentage of rules are applied to any particular structure, the naive parsing algorithm is rather inefficient. We exploit this sparseness in rule applications to derive an algorithm two to three orders of magnitude faster than the standard parsing algorithm.

1 Introduction

The idea of using transformational rules in natural language analysis dates back at least to Chomsky, who attempted to define a set of transformations that would apply to a word sequence to map it from deep structure to surface structure (see (Chomsky, 1965)). Transformations have also been used in much of generative phonology to capture contextual variants in pronunciation, starting with (Chomsky and Halle, 1968). More recently, transformations have been applied to a diverse set of problems, including part of speech tagging, pronunciation network creation, prepositional phrase attachment disambiguation, and parsing, under the paradigm of transformation-based error-driven learning (see (Brill, 1993; Brill, 1995) and (Brill and Resnik, 1994)). In this paradigm, rules can be learned automatically from a training corpus, instead of being written by hand.

Transformation-based systems are typically deterministic. Each rule in an ordered list of rules is applied once wherever it can apply, then is discarded, and the next rule is processed until the last rule in the list has been processed. Since for each rule the application algorithm must check for a matching at all possible sites to see whether the rule can apply, these systems run in $O(\pi\rho n)$ time, where π is the number of rules, ρ is the cost of a single rule matching, and n is the size of the input structure. While this results in fast processing, it is possible to create much faster systems. In (Roche and Schabes, 1995), a method is described for converting a list of transformations that operates on strings into a deterministic finite state transducer, resulting in an optimal tagger in the sense that tagging requires only one state transition per word, giving a linear time tagger whose run-time is independent of the number and size of rules.

In this paper we consider transformation-based parsing, introduced in (Brill, 1993), and we improve upon the $O(\pi\rho n)$ time upper bound.. In transformation-based parsing, an ordered sequence of tree-rewriting rules (tree transformations) are applied to an initial parse structure for an input sentence, to derive the final parse structure. We observe that in most transformation-based parsers, only a small percentage of rules are actually applied, for any particular input sentence. For example, in an application of the transformation-based parser described in (Brill, 1993), $\pi = 300$ rules were learned, to be applied at each node of the initial parse structure, but the average number of rules that are successfully applied at each node is only about one. So a lot of time is spent testing whether the conditions are met for applying a transformation and finding out that they are not met. This paper presents an original algorithm for transformation-based parsing working in $O(\rho t \log(t))$ time, where t is the total number of rules applied for an input sentence. Since in practical cases t is smaller than n and we can neglect the $\log(n)$ factor, we have achieved a time improvement of a factor of π. We emphasize that π can be several hundreds large in actual systems where transformations are lexicalized.

Our result is achieved by preprocessing the transformation list, deriving a finite state, deterministic tree automaton. The algorithm then exploits the automaton in a way that obviates the need for checking the conditions of a rule when that rule will not apply, thereby greatly improving parsing run-time over the straightforward parsing algorithm. In a sense, our algorithm spends time only with rules that can be applied, as if it knew in advance which rules cannot be applied during the parsing process.

The remainder of this paper is organized as follows. In Section 2 we introduce some preliminaries, and in Section 3 we provide a representation of transformations that uses finite state, deterministic tree automata. Our algorithm is then specified in Section 4. Finally, in Section 5 we discuss related work in the existing literature.

2 Preliminaries

We review in the following subsections some terminology that is used throughout this paper.

2.1 Trees

We consider ordered trees whose nodes are assigned labels over some finite alphabet Σ; this set is denoted as Σ^T. Let $T \in \Sigma^T$. A node of T is called **leftmost** if it does not have any left sibling (a root node is a leftmost node). The **height** of T is the length of a longest path from the root to one of its leaves (a tree composed of a single node has height zero). We define $|T|$ as the number of nodes in T. A tree $T \in \Sigma^T$ is denoted as A if it consists of a single leaf node labeled by A, and as $A(T_1, T_2, \ldots, T_d)$, $d \geq 1$, if T has root labeled by A with d (ordered) children denoted by $T_1, \ldots, T_d$. Sometimes in the examples we draw trees in the usual way, indicating each node with its label.

What follows is standard terminology from the tree pattern matching literature, with the simplification that we do not use variable terms. See (Hoffmann and O'Donnell, 1982) for general definitions. Let n be a node of T. We say that a tree S **matches** T at n if there exists a one-to-one mapping from the nodes of S to the nodes of T, such that the following conditions are all satisfied: (i) if n' maps to n'', then n' and n'' have the same label; (ii) the root of S maps to n; and (iii) if n' maps to n'' and n' is not a leaf in S, then n' and n'' have the same degree and the i-th child of n' maps to the i-th child of n''. We say that T and S are **equivalent** if they match each other at the respective root nodes. In what follows trees that are equivalent are not treated as the same object. We say that a tree T' is a **subtree** of T at n if there exists a tree S that matches T at n, and T' consists of the nodes of T that are matched by some node of S and the arcs of T between two such nodes. We also say that T' is matched by S at n. In addition, T' is a **prefix** of T if n is the root of T; T' is the **suffix** of T at n if T' contains all nodes of T dominated by n.

Example 1 Let $T = B(D, C(B(D, B), C))$ and let n be the second child of T's root. $S = C(B, C)$ matches T at n. $S' = B(D, C(B), C))$ is a prefix of S and $S'' = C(B(D, B), C)$ is the suffix of T at n. □

We now introduce a tree replacement operator that will be used throughout the paper. Let S be a subtree of T and let S' be a tree having the same number of leaves as S. Let $n_1, n_2, \ldots, n_l$ and $n'_1, n'_2, \ldots, n'_l$, $l \geq 1$, be all the leaves from left to right of S and S', respectively. We write $T[S/S']$ to denote the tree obtained by embedding S' within T in place of S, through the following steps: (i) if the root of S is the i-th child of a node n_f in T, the root of S' becomes the i-th child of n_f; and (ii) the (ordered) children of n_i in T, if any, become the children of n'_i, $1 \leq i \leq l$. The root of $T[S/S']$ is the root of T if node n_f above exists, and is the root of S' otherwise.

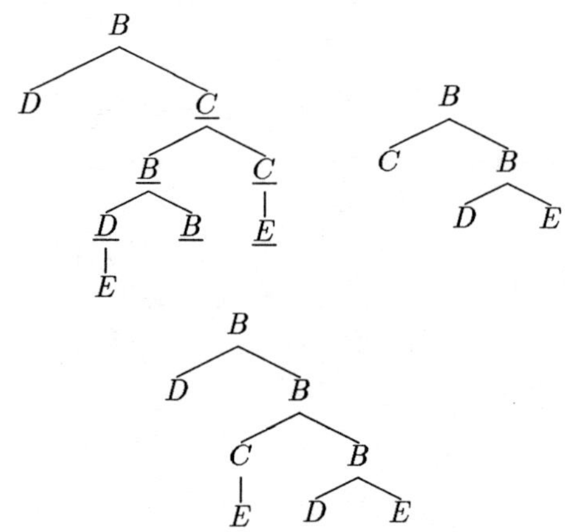

Figure 1: From left to right, top to bottom: tree T with subtree S indicated using underlined labels at its nodes; tree S' having the same number of leaves as S; tree $T[S/S']$ obtained by "replacing" S with S'.

Example 2 Figure 1 depicts trees T, S' and T' in this order. A subtree S of T is also indicated using underlined labels at nodes of T. Note that S and S' have the same number of leaves. Then we have $T' = T[S/S']$. □

2.2 Tree automata

Deterministic (bottom-up) tree automata were first introduced in (Thatcher, 1967) (called FRT there). The definition we propose here is a generalization of the canonical one to trees of any degree. Note that the transition function below is computed on a number of states that is independent of the degree of the input tree. Deterministic tree automata will be used later to implement the bottom-up tree pattern matching algorithm of (Hoffmann and O'Donnell, 1982).

Definition 1 *A deterministic tree automaton (DTA) is a 5-tuple $M = (Q, \Sigma, \delta, q_0, F)$, where Q is a finite set of states, Σ is a finite alphabet, $q_0 \in Q$ is the initial state, $F \subseteq Q$ is the set of final states and δ is a transition function mapping $Q^2 \times \Sigma$ into Q.*

Informally, a DTA M walks through a tree T by visiting its nodes in post-order, one node at a time. Every time a node is read, the current state of the device is computed on the basis of the states reached upon reading the immediate left sibling and the rightmost child of the current node, if any. In this way the decision of the DTA is affected not only by the portion of the tree below the currently read node, but also by each subtree rooted in a left sibling of the current node. This is formally stated in what follows. Let $T \in \Sigma^T$ and let n be one of its nodes, labeled by a. The state **reached** by M upon reading n is recursively specified as:

$$\hat{\delta}(T, n) \quad = \quad \delta(X, X', a), \qquad (1)$$

where $X = q_0$ if n is a leftmost node, $X = \hat{\delta}(T, n')$ if n' is the immediate left sibling of n; and $X' = q_0$ if n is a leaf node, $X' = \hat{\delta}(T, n'')$ if n'' is the rightmost child of n. The tree language recognized by M is the set

$$L(M) \quad = \quad \{T \mid \hat{\delta}(T, n) \in F,\ T \in \Sigma^T,\ n \text{ the root of } T\}. \qquad (2)$$

Example 3 Consider the infinite set $L = \{B(A, C), B(A, B(A, C)), B(A, B(A, B(A, C))), \ldots\}$ consisting of all right-branching trees with internal nodes labeled by B and with strings A^nC, $n \geq 1$ as their yields. Let $M = (Q, \{A, B, C\}, \delta, q_0, \{q_{BC}\})$ be a DTA specified as follows: $Q = \{q_0, q_A, q_{BC}, q_{-1}\}$; $\delta(q_0, q_0, A) = q_A$, $\delta(q_A, q_0, C) = \delta(q_A, q_{BC}, B) = q_{BC}$ and q_{-1} is the value of all other entries of δ. It is not difficult to see that $L(M) = L$. □

Observe that when we restrict to monadic trees, that is trees whose nodes have degree not greater than one, the above definitions correspond to the well known formalisms of deterministic finite state automata, the associated extended transition function, and the regular languages.

2.3 Transformation-based parsing

Transformation-based parsing was first introduced in (Brill, 1993). Informally, a transformation-based parser assigns to an input sentence an initial parse structure, in some uniform way. Then the parser iteratively checks an ordered sequence of tree transformations for application to the initial parse tree, in order to derive the final parse structure. This results in a deterministic, linear time parser. In order to present our algorithm, we abstract away from the assignment of the initial parse to the input, and introduce below the notion of transformation-based tree rewriting system. The formulation we give here is inspired by (Kaplan and Kay, 1994) and (Roche and Schabes, 1995). The relationship between transformation-based tree rewriting systems and standard term-rewriting systems will be discussed in the final section.

Definition 2 *A* transformation-based tree rewriting system *(TTS) is a pair $G = (\Sigma, R)$, where Σ is a finite alphabet and $R = \langle r_1, r_2, \ldots, r_\pi \rangle$, $\pi \geq 1$, is a finite sequence of tree rewriting rules having the form $Q \to Q'$, with $Q, Q' \in \Sigma^T$ and such that Q and Q' have the same number of leaves.*

If $r = (Q \to Q')$, we write lhs(r) for Q and rhs(r) for Q'. We also write lhs(R) for $\{\text{lhs}(r) \mid r \in R\}$. (Recall that we regard lhs(r_i) and lhs(r_j), $i \neq j$, as different objects, even if these trees are equivalent.) We define $|r| = |\text{lhs}(r)| + |\text{rhs}(r)|$.

The notion of transformation associated with a TTS $G = (\Sigma, R)$ is now introduced. Let $C, C' \in \Sigma^T$. For any node n of C and any rule $r = (Q \to Q')$ of G, we write

$$C \quad \stackrel{r,n}{\Longrightarrow} \quad C' \qquad (3)$$

if Q does not match C at n and $C = C'$; or if Q matches C at n and $C' = C[S/Q'_c]$, where S is the subtree of T matched by Q at n and Q'_c is a fresh copy of Q'. Let $\langle n_1, n_2, \ldots, n_t \rangle$, $t \geq 1$, be the post-ordered sequence of all nodes of C. We write

$$C \quad \stackrel{r}{\Rightarrow} \quad C' \qquad (4)$$

if $C_{i-1} \stackrel{r,n_i}{\Longrightarrow} C_i$, $1 \leq i \leq t$, $C_0 = C$ and $C_t = C'$. Finally, we define the translation induced by G on Σ^T as the map $M(G) = \{(C, C') \mid C \in \Sigma^T,\ C_{i-1} \stackrel{r_i}{\Rightarrow} C_i \text{ for } 1 \leq i \leq \pi,\ C_0 = C,\ C_\pi = C'\}$.

3 Rule representation

We develop here a representation of rule sequences that makes use of DTA and that is at the basis of the main result of this paper. Our technique improves the preprocessing phase of a bottom-up tree pattern matching algorithm presented in (Hoffmann and O'Donnell, 1982), as it will be discussed in the final section.

Let $G = (\Sigma, R)$ be a TTS, $R = \langle r_1, r_2, \ldots, r_\pi \rangle$. In what follows we construct a DTA that "detects" each subtree of an input tree that is equivalent to some tree in lhs(R). We need to introduce some additional notation. Let N be the set of all nodes from the trees in lhs(R). Call N_r the set of all root nodes (in N), N_m the set of all leftmost nodes, N_l the set of all leaf nodes, and N_a the set of all nodes labeled by $a \in \Sigma$. For each $q \in 2^N$, let $right(q) = \{n \mid n \in N,\ n' \in q,\ n \text{ has immediate left sibling } n'\}$ and let $up(q) = \{n \mid n \in N,\ n' \in q,\ n \text{ has rightmost child } n'\}$. Also, let q_0 be a fresh symbol.

Definition 3 *G is associated with a DTA $A_G = (2^N \cup \{q_0\}, \Sigma, \delta_G, q_0, F)$, where $F = \{q \mid q \in 2^N,\ (q \cap N_r) \neq \emptyset\}$ and δ_G is specified as follows:*

(i) $\delta_G(q_0, q_0, a) = N_a \cap N_m \cap N_l$;

(ii) $\delta_G(q_0, q', a) = N_a \cap N_m \cap (N_l \cup up(q'))$, *for* $q' \neq q_0$;

(iii) $\delta_G(q, q_0, a) = N_a \cap N_l \cap (N_r \cup right(q))$, *for* $q \neq q_0$;

(iv) $\delta_G(q, q', a) = N_a \cap up(q') \cap (N_r \cup right(q))$, *for* $q \neq q_0 \neq q'$.

Observe that each state of A_G simultaneously carries over the recognition of several suffixes of trees in lhs(R). These processes are started whenever A_G reads a leftmost node n with the same label as a leftmost leaf node in some tree in lhs(R) (items (i) and (ii) in Definition 3). Note also that we do not require any matching of the left siblings when we match the root of a tree in lhs(R) (items (iii) and (iv)).

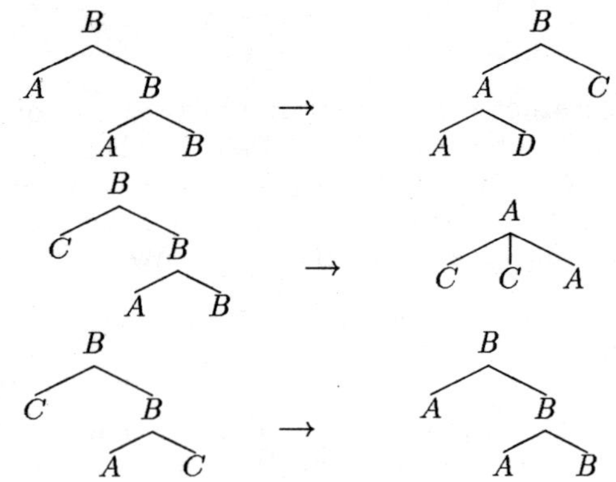

Figure 2: From top to bottom: rules r_1, r_2 and r_3 of G.

Example 4 Let $G = (\Sigma, R)$, where $\Sigma = \{A, B, C, D\}$ and $R = \langle r_1, r_2, r_3\rangle$. Rules r_i are depicted in Figure 2. We write n_{ij} to denote the j-th node in a post-order enumeration of the nodes of lhs(r_i), $1 \leq i \leq 3$ and $1 \leq j \leq 5$. (Therefore n_{35} denotes the root node of lhs(r_3) and n_{22} denotes the first child of the second child of the root node of lhs(r_2).) If we consider only the useful states, that is those states that can be reached on an actual input, the DTA $A_G = (Q, \Sigma, \delta, q_0, F)$, is specified as follows: $Q = \{q_i \mid 0 \leq i \leq 11\}$, where $q_1 = \{n_{11}, n_{12}, n_{22}, n_{32}\}$, $q_2 = \{n_{21}, n_{31}\}$, $q_3 = \{n_{13}, n_{23}\}$, $q_4 = \{n_{33}\}$, $q_5 = \{n_{14}\}$, $q_6 = \{n_{24}\}$, $q_7 = \{n_{34}\}$, $q_8 = \{n_{15}\}$, $q_9 = \{n_{35}\}$, $q_{10} = \{n_{25}\}$, $q_{11} = \emptyset$; $F = \{q_8, q_9, q_{10}\}$. The transition function δ, restricted to the useful states, is specified in Figure 3. Note that among the $2^{15}+1$ possible states, only 12 are useful. □

$$
\begin{array}{rclrcl}
\delta(q_0, q_0, A) & = & q_1 & \delta(q_0, q_0, C) & = & q_2 \\
\delta(q_1, q_0, B) & = & q_3 & \delta(q_1, q_0, C) & = & q_4 \\
\delta(q_1, q_3, B) & = & q_5 & \delta(q_2, q_3, B) & = & q_6 \\
\delta(q_2, q_4, B) & = & q_7 & \delta(q_0, q_5, B) & = & q_8 \\
\delta(q_0, q_6, B) & = & q_9 & \delta(q_0, q_7, B) & = & q_{10}
\end{array}
$$

Figure 3: Transition function of G. For all $(q, q', a) \in Q^2 \times \Sigma$ not indicated above, $\delta(q, q', a) = q_{11}$.

Although the number of states of A_G is exponential in $|N|$, in practical cases most of these states are never reached by the automaton on an actual input, and can therefore be ignored. This happens whenever there are few pairs of suffix trees of trees in lhs(R) that share a common prefix tree but no tree in the pair matches the other at the root node. This is discussed at length in (Hoffmann and O'Donnell, 1982), where an upper bound on the number of useful states is provided.

The following lemma provides a characterization of A_G that will be used later.

Lemma 1 *Let n be a node of $T \in \Sigma^T$ and let n' be the root node of $r \in R$. Tree* lhs(r) *matches T at n if and only if $n' \in \hat{\delta}_G(T, n)$.*

Proof (outline). The statement can be shown by proving the following claim. Let m be a node in T and m' be a node in lhs(r). Call $m_1, \ldots, m_k = m$, $k \geq 1$, the ordered sequence of the left siblings of m, with m included, and call $m'_1, \ldots, m'_{k'} = m'$, $k' \geq 1$, the ordered sequence of the left siblings of m', with m' included. If $m' \notin N_r$, then the two following conditions are equivalent:

- $m' \in \hat{\delta}_G(T, m)$;
- $k = k'$ and, for $1 \leq i \leq k$, the suffix of lhs(r) at m'_i matches T at m_i.

The claim can be shown by induction on the position of m' in a post-order enumeration of the nodes of lhs(r). The lemma then follows from the specification of set F and the treatment of set N_r in items (iii) and (iv) in Definition 3. □

We also need a function mapping $F \times \{1..(\pi+1)\}$ into $\{1..\pi\} \cup \{\perp\}$, specified as ($\min \emptyset = \perp$):

$$
\begin{array}{rcl}
next(q, i) & = & \min\{j \mid i \leq j \leq \pi, \text{ lhs}(r_j) \text{ has} \\
& & \text{root node in } q\}. \qquad (5)
\end{array}
$$

Assume that $q \in F$ is reached by A_G upon reading a node n (in some tree). In the next section $next(q, i)$ is used to select the index of the rule that should be next applied at node n, after the first $i-1$ rules of R have been considered.

4 The algorithm

We present a translation algorithm for TTS that can immediately be converted into a transformation-based parsing algorithm. We use all definitions introduced in the previous sections. To simplify the presentation, we first make the assumption that the order in which we apply several instances of the same rule to a given tree does not affect the outcome. Later we will deal with the general case.

4.1 Order-free case

We start with an important property that is used by the algorithm below and that can be easily shown (see also (Hoffmann and O'Donnell, 1982)). Let $G = (\Sigma, R)$ be a TTS and let h_G be the maximum height of a tree in lhs(R). Given trees T and S, S a subtree of T, we write *local*(T, S) to denote the set of all nodes of S and the first h_G proper ancestors of the root of S in T (when these nodes are defined).

Lemma 2 *Assume that* lhs(r), $r \in R$, *matches a tree T at some node n. Let $T \stackrel{r,n}{\Longrightarrow} T'$ and let S be the copy of* rhs(r) *used in the rewriting. For every node n' not included in local(T', S), we have $\hat{\delta}_G(T, n') = \hat{\delta}_G(T', n')$.* □

We precede the specification of the method with an informal presentation. The following three data structures are used. An associative list *state* associates each node n of the rewritten input tree with the state reached by A_G upon reading n. If n is no longer a node of the rewritten input tree, *state* associates n with the emptyset. A set *rule*(i) is associated with each rule r_i, containing some of the nodes of the rewritten input tree at which lhs(r_i) matches. A heap data structure H is also used to order the indices of the non-empty sets *rule*(i) according to the priority of the associated rules in the rule sequence. All the above data structures are updated by a procedure called *update*.

To compute the translation $M(G)$ we first visit the input tree with A_G and initialize our data structures in the following way. For each node n, *state* is assigned a state of A_G as specified above. If rule r_i must be applied first at n, n is added to *rule*(i) and H is updated. We then enter a main loop and retrieve elements from the heap. When i is retrieved, rule r_i is considered for application at each node n in *rule*(i). It is important to observe that, since some rewriting of the input tree might have occurred in between the time n has been inserted in *rule*(i) and the time i is retrieved from H, it could be that the current rule r_i can no longer be applied at n. Information in *state* is used to detect these cases. Crucial to the efficiency of our algorithm, each time a rule is applied only a small portion of the current tree needs to be reread by A_G, in order to update our data structures, as specified by Lemma 2 above. Finally, the main loop is exited when the heap is empty.

Algorithm 1 Let $G = (\Sigma, R)$ be a TTS, $R = \langle r_1, r_2, \ldots, r_\pi \rangle$ and let $T \in \Sigma^T$ be an input tree. Let $A_G = (2^N \cup \{q_0\}, \Sigma, \delta_G, q_0, F)$ be the DTA associated with G and $\hat{\delta}_G$ the reached state function. Let also i be an integer valued variable, *state* be an associative array, *rule*(i) be an initially empty set, for $1 \le i \le \pi$, and let H be a heap data structure. ($n \to$ *rule*(i) adds n to *rule*(i); $i \to H$ inserts i in H; $i \leftarrow H$ assigns to i the least element in H, if H is not empty.) The algorithm is specified in Figure 4. □

Example 4 (continued) We describe a run of Algorithm 1 working with the sample TTS $G = (\Sigma, R)$ previously specified (see Figure 2).

```
proc update(oldset, newset, j)
for each node n ∈ oldset
    state(n) ← ∅
for each node n ∈ newset do
    state(n) ← δ̂_G(C, n)
    if state(n) ∈ F and next(state(n), j) ≠⊥ then do
      if rule(next(state(n), j)) = ∅
        then next(state(n), j) → H
      n → rule(next(state(n), j))
    od
od

main
C ← T; i ← 1
update(∅, nodes of C, i)
while H not empty do
    i ← H
    for each node n ∈ rule(i) s.t. the root of lhs(r_i)
      is in state(n) do
      S ← the subtree of C matched by lhs(r_i) at n
      S' ← copy of rhs(r_i)
      C ← C[S/S']
      update(nodes of S, local(C, S'), i + 1)
    od
od
return C.
```

Figure 4: Translation algorithm computing $M(G)$ for a TTS G.

Let $C_i \in \Sigma^T$, $1 \le i \le 3$, be as depicted in Figure 5. We write m_{ij} to denote the j-th node in a post-order enumeration of the nodes of C_i, $1 \le i \le 3$ and $1 \le j \le 7$. Assume that C_1 is the input tree.

After the first call to procedure *update*, we have $state(m_{17}) = q_{10} = \{n_{25}\}$ and $state(m_{16}) = q_8 = \{n_{15}\}$; no other final state is associated with a node of C_1. We also have that $rule(1) = \{m_{16}\}$, $rule(2) = \{m_{17}\}$, $rule(3) = \emptyset$ and H contains indices 1 and 2.

Index 1 is then retrieved from H and the only node in *rule*(1), i.e., m_{16}, is considered. Since the root of lhs(r_1), i.e., node n_{15}, belongs to q_8, m_{16} passes the test in the head of the for-statement in the main program. Then r_1 is applied to C_1, yielding C_2. Observe that $m_{11} = m_{21}$ and $m_{17} = m_{27}$; all the remaining nodes of C_2 are fresh nodes.

The next call to *update*, associated with the application of r_1, updates the associative list *state* in such a way that $state(m_{27}) = q_9 = \{n_{35}\}$, and no other final state is associated with a node of C_2. Also, we now have $rule(1) = \{m_{16}\}$, $rule(2) = \{m_{27}\}$ (recall that $m_{17} = m_{27}$), $rule(3) = \{m_{27}\}$, and H contains indices 2 and 3.

Index 2 is next retrieved from H and node m_{27} is considered. However, at this point the root of lhs(r_2), i.e., node n_{25}, does no longer belong to $state(m_{27})$, indicating that r_2 is no longer applicable to that node. The body of the for-statement in the

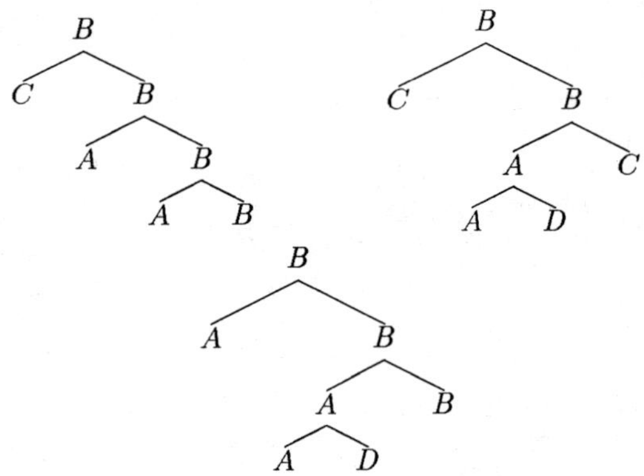

Figure 5: From left to right, top to bottom: trees C_1, C_2 and C_3. In the sample TTS G we have $(C_1, C_3) \in M(G)$, since $C_1 \overset{r_1}{\Rightarrow} C_2 \overset{r_2}{\Rightarrow} C_2 \overset{r_3}{\Rightarrow} C_3$.

main program is not executed this time.

Finally, index 3 is retrieved from H and node m_{27} is again considered, this time for the application of rule r_3. Since the root of $\mathrm{lhs}(r_3)$, i.e., node n_{35}, belongs to $state(m_{27})$, r_3 is applied to C_2 at node m_{27}, yielding C_3. Data structures are again updated by a call to procedure *update* with the second parameter equal to 4. Then state q_8 is associated with node m_{37}, the root node of C_3. Despite of the fact that $q_8 \in F$, we now have $next(q_8, 4) = \bot$. Therefore rule r_1 is not considered for application to C_3. Since H is now empty, the computation terminates returning C_3. □

The results in Lemma 1 and Lemma 2 can be used to show that, in the main program, a node n passes the test in the head of the for-statement if and only if $\mathrm{lhs}(r_i)$ matches C at n. The correctness of Algorithm 1 then follows from the definition of the heap data structure.

We now turn to computational complexity issues. Let $\rho = \max_{1 \leq i \leq \pi} |r_i|$. For $T \in \Sigma^T$, let also $t(T)$ be the total number of rules that are successfully applied on a run of Algorithm 1 on input T, counting repetitions.

Theorem 1 *The running time of Algorithm* 1 *on input tree* T *is* $O(|T| + \rho t(T) \log(t(T)))$.

Proof. We can implement our data structures in such a way that each of the primitive access operations that are executed by the algorithm takes a constant amount of time.

Consider each instance of the membership of a node n in a set $rule(i)$ and represent it as a pair (n, i). We call *active* each pair (n, i) such that $\mathrm{lhs}(r_i)$ matches C at n at the time i is retrieved from H. As already mentioned, these pairs pass the test in the head of the for-loop in the main program. The number of active pairs is therefore $t(T)$. All remaining pairs are called *dead*. Note that an active pair (n, i) can turn at most $|\mathrm{lhs}(r_i)| + h_R$ active pairs into dead ones, through a call to the procedure *update*. Hence the total number of dead pairs must be $O(\rho t(T))$. We conclude that the number of pairs totally instantiated by the algorithm is $O(\rho t(T))$.

It is easy to see that the number of pairs totally instantiated by the algorithm is also a bound on the number of indices inserted in or retrieved from the heap. Then the time spent by the algorithm with the heap is $O(\rho t(T) \log(t(T)))$ (see for instance (Cormen, Leiserson, and Rivest, 1990)). The first call to the procedure *update* in the main program takes time proportional to $|T|$. All remaining operations of the algorithm will now be charged to some active pair.

For each active pair, the body of the for-loop in the main program and the body of the *update* procedure are executed, taking an amount of time $O(\rho)$. For each dead pair, only the test in the head of the for-loop is executed, taking a constant amount of time. This time is charged to the active node that turned the pair under consideration into a dead one. In this way each active node is charged an extra amount of time $O(\rho)$.

Every operation executed by the algorithm has been considered in the above analysis. We can then conclude that the running time of Algorithm 1 is $O(|T| + \rho t(T) \log(t(T)))$. □

Let us compare the above result with the time performance of the standard algorithm for transformation-based parsing. The standard algorithm checks each rule in R for application to an initial parse tree T, trying to match the left-hand side of the current rule at each node of T. Using the notation of Theorem 1, the running time is then $O(\pi\rho|T|)$. In practical applications, $t(T)$ and $|T|$ are very close (of the order of the length of the input string). Therefore we have achieved a time improvement of a factor of $\pi / \log(t(T))$. We emphasize that π might be several hundreds large if the learned transformations are lexicalized. Therefore we have improved the asymptotic time complexity of transformation-based parsing of a factor between two to three orders of magnitude.

4.2 Order-dependent parsing

We consider here the general case for the TTS translation problem, in which the order of application of several instances of rule r to a tree can affect the final result of the rewriting. In this case rule r is called *critical*. According to the definition of translation induced by a TTS, a critical rule should always be applied in post-order w.r.t. the nodes of the tree to be rewritten. The solution we propose here for critical rules is based on a preprocessing of the rule sequence of the system.

We informally describe the technique presented below. Assume that a critical rule r is to be applied at several matching nodes of a tree C. We partition the matching nodes into two sets. The first set contains all the nodes n at which the matching of lhs(r) overlaps with a second matching at a node n' dominated by n. All the remaining matching nodes are inserted in the second set. Then rule r is applied to the nodes of the second set. After that, the nodes in the first set are in turn partitioned according to the above criterion, and the process is iterated until all the matching nodes have been considered for application of r. This is more precisely stated in what follows.

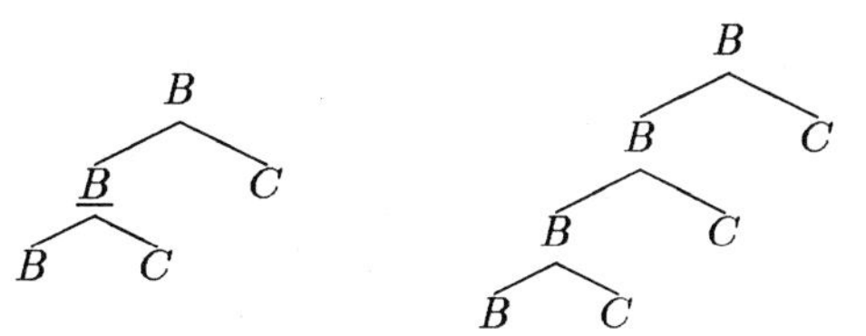

Figure 6: From left to right: trees Q and Q_p. Node p of Q is indicated by underlying its label.

We start with some additional notation. Let $r = (Q \rightarrow Q')$ be a tree-rewriting rule. Also, let p be a node of Q and let S be the suffix of Q at p. We say that p is *periodic* if (i) p is not the root of Q; and (ii) S matches Q at the root node. It is easy to see that the fact that lhs(r) has some periodic node is a necessary condition for r to be critical. Let the root of S be the i-th child of a node n_f in Q, and let Q_c be a copy of Q. We write Q_p to denote the tree obtained starting from Q by excising S and by letting the root of Q_c be the new i-th child of n_f. Finally, call n_1 the root of Q_p and n_2 the root of Q.

Example 5 Figure 6 depicts trees Q and Q_p. The periodic node p of Q under consideration is indicated by underlying its label. □

Let us assume that rule r is critical and that p is the only periodic node in Q. We add Q_p to set lhs(R) and construct A_G accordingly. Algorithm 1 should then be modified as follows. We call *p-chain* any sequence of one or more subtrees of C, all matched by Q, that partially overlap in C. Let n be a node of C and let $q = state(n)$. Assume that $n_2 \in q$ and call S the subtree of C at n matched by Q (S exists by Lemma 1). We distinguish two possible cases.

Case 1: If $n_1 \in q$, then we know that Q also matches some portion of C that overlaps with S (at the node matched by the periodic node p of Q). In this case S belongs to a p-chain consisting of at least two subtrees and S is not the bottom-most subtree in the p-chain.

Case 2: If $n_1 \notin q$, then we know that S is the bottom-most subtree in a p-chain.

Let i be the index of rule r under consideration. We use an additional set $chain(i)$. Each node n of C such that $n_2 \in state(n)$ is then inserted in $chain(i)$ if $state(n)$ satisfies Case 1 above, and is inserted in $rule(i)$ otherwise. Note that $chain(i)$ is non-empty only in case $rule(i)$ is such. Whenever i is retrieved from H, we process each node n in $rule(i)$, as usual. But when we update our data structures with the procedure *update*, we also look for matchings of lhs(r_i) at nodes of C in $chain(i)$. The overall effect of this is that each p-chain is considered in a bottom-up fashion in the application of r. This is compatible with the post-order application requirement.

The above technique can be applied for each periodic node in a critical rule, and for each critical rule of G. This only affects the size of A_G, not the time requirements of Algorithm 1. In fact, the proposed preprocessing can at worst double h_G.

5 Discussion

In this section we relate our work with the existing literature and further discuss our result.

There are several alternative ways in which one could see transformation-based rewriting systems. TTS's are closely related to a class of graph rewriting systems called neighbourhood-controlled embedding graph grammars (NCE grammars; see (Janssens and Rozenberg, 1982)). In fact our definition of the $\stackrel{r,n}{\Longrightarrow}$ relation and of the underlying [/] operator has been inspired by similar definitions in the NCE formalism. Apart from the restriction to tree rewriting, the main difference between NCE grammars and TTS's is that in the latter formalism the productions are totally ordered, therefore there is no recursion.

Ordered trees can also be seen as ground terms. If we extend the alphabet Σ with variable symbols, we can redefine the $\stackrel{r,n}{\Longrightarrow}$ relation through variable substitution. In this way a TTS becomes a particular kind of term-rewriting system. The idea of imposing a total order on the rules of a term-rewriting system can be found in the literature, but in these cases all rules are reconsidered for application at each step in the rewriting, using their priority (see for instance the priority term-rewriting systems (Baeten, Bergstra, and Klop, 1987)). Therefore these systems allow recursion. There are cases in which a critical rule in a TTS does not give rise to order-dependency in rewriting. Methods for deciding the confluency property for a term-rewriting system with critical pairs (see (Dershowitz and Jouannaud, 1990) for definitions and an overview) can also be used to detect the above cases for TTS.

As already pointed out, the translation problem investigated here is closely related with the standard tree pattern matching problem. Our automata A_G (Definition 3) can be seen as an abstraction of the bottom-up tree pattern matching algorithm presented in (Hoffmann and O'Donnell, 1982). While that result uses a representation of the pattern set (our set lhs(R)) requiring an amount of space which is exponential in the degree of the pattern trees, as an improvement, our transition function does not depend on this parameter. However, in the worst case the space requirements of both algorithm are exponential in the number of nodes in lhs(R) (see the analysis in (Hoffmann and O'Donnell, 1982)). As already discussed in Section 3, the worst case condition is hardly met in natural language applications.

Polynomial space requirements can be guaranteed if one switches to top-down tree pattern matching algorithms. One such a method is reported in (Hoffmann and O'Donnell, 1982), but in this case the running-time of Algorithm 1 cannot be maintained. Faster top-down matching algorithms have been reported in (Kosaraju, 1989) and (Dubiner, Galil, and Magen, 1994), but these methods seems impractical, due to very large hidden constants.

A tree-based extension of the very fast algorithm described in (Roche and Schabes, 1995) is in principle possible for transformation-based parsing, but is likely to result in huge space requirements and seems impractical. The algorithm presented here might then be a good compromise between fast parsing and reasonable space requirements.

When restricted to monadic trees, our automaton A_G comes down to the finite state device used in the well-known string pattern matching algorithm of Aho and Corasick (see (Aho and Corasick, 1975)), requiring linear space only. If space requirements are of primary importance or when the rule set is very large, our method can then be considered for string-based transformation rewriting as an alternative to the already mentioned method in (Roche and Schabes, 1995), which is faster but has more onerous space requirements.

Acknowledgements

The present research was done while the first author was visiting the Center for Language and Speech Processing, Johns Hopkins University, Baltimore, MD. The second author is also a member of the Center for Language and Speech Processing. This work was funded in part by NSF grant IRI-9502312. The authors are indebted with Alberto Apostolico, Rao Kosaraju, Fernando Pereira and Murat Saraclar for technical discussions on topics related to this paper. The authors whish to thank an anonymous referee for having pointed out important connections between TTS and term-rewriting systems.

References

Aho, A. V. and M. Corasick. 1975. Efficient string matching: An aid to bibliographic search. *Communications of the Association for Computing Machinery*, 18(6):333–340.

Baeten, J., J. Bergstra, and J. Klop. 1987. Priority rewrite systems. In *Proc. Second International Conference on Rewriting Techniques and Applications, LNCS 256*, pages 83–94, Berlin, Germany. Springer-Verlag.

Brill, E. 1993. Automatic grammar induction and parsing free text: A transformation-based approach. In *Proceedings of the 31st Meeting of the Association of Computational Linguistics*, Columbus, Oh.

Brill, E. 1995. Transformation-based error-driven learning and natural language processing: A case study in part of speech tagging. *Computational Linguistics.*

Brill, E. and P. Resnik. 1994. A transformation-based approach to prepositional phrase attachment disambiguation. In *Proceedings of the Fifteenth International Conference on Computational Linguistics (COLING-1994)*, Kyoto, Japan.

Chomsky, N. 1965. *Aspects of the Theory of Syntax.* The MIT Press, Cambridge, MA.

Chomsky, N. and M. Halle. 1968. *The Sound Pattern of English.* Harper and Row.

Cormen, T. H., C. E. Leiserson, and R. L. Rivest. 1990. *Introduction to Algorithms.* The MIT Press, Cambridge, MA.

Dershowitz, N. and J. Jouannaud. 1990. Rewrite systems. In J. Van Leeuwen, editor, *Handbook of Theoretical Computer Science*, volume B. Elsevier and The MIT Press, Amsterdam, The Netherlands and Cambridge, MA, chapter 6, pages 243–320.

Dubiner, M., Z. Galil, and E. Magen. 1994. Faster tree pattern matching. *Journal of the Association for Computing Machinery*, 41(2):205–213.

Hoffmann, C. M. and M. J. O'Donnell. 1982. Pattern matching in trees. *Journal of the Association for Computing Machinery*, 29(1):68–95.

Janssens, D. and G. Rozenberg. 1982. Graph grammars with neighbourhood-controlled embedding. *Theoretical Computer Science*, 21:55–74.

Kaplan, R. M. and M. Kay. 1994. Regular models of phonological rule sistems. *Computational Linguistics*, 20(3):331–378.

Kosaraju, S. R. 1989. Efficient tree-pattern matching. In *Proceedings of the 30 Conference on Foundations of Computer Science (FOCS)*, pages 178–183.

Roche, E. and Y. Schabes. 1995. Deterministic part of speech tagging with finite state transducers. *Computational Linguistics.*

Thatcher, J. W. 1967. Characterizing derivation trees of context-free grammars through a generalization of finite automata theory. *Journal of Computer and System Science*, 1:317–322.

Resolving Anaphors in Embedded Sentences

Saliha Azzam
University of Sheffield
Department of Computer Science
Regent Court
211 Portobello Street
Sheffield S1 4DP U.K.
S.Azzam@dcs.shef.ac.uk

Abstract

We propose an algorithm to resolve anaphors, tackling mainly the problem of intrasentential antecedents. We base our methodology on the fact that such antecedents are likely to occur in embedded sentences. Sidner's focusing mechanism is used as the basic algorithm in a more complete approach. The proposed algorithm has been tested and implemented as a part of a conceptual analyser, mainly to process pronouns. Details of an evaluation are given.

1 Introduction

Intrasentential antecedents, i.e., antecedents occurring in the same sentence as the anaphor, are a crucial issue for the anaphora resolution method. The main problem is to determine the constraints that intrasentential phrases must respect in anaphoric relations. These constraints are used to determine relations between a given anaphor and its antecedents. Until now, this kind of constraint has been tackled mainly in terms of syntactic aspects, see (Lappin and Leass, 1994) (Merlo, 1993) and (Hobbs, 1985). We propose to consider new kinds of criteria that combine semantic restrictions with sentence structure.

One of these criteria is, for example, the way in which the verb meaning influences the sentence structure, then the way in which the sentence structure influences the anaphoric relations between intrasentential phrases. The structure we studied is the embedded sentence structure. Indeed, an important assumption we have made is that embedded sentences favour the occurrence of intrasentential antecedents. We exploit the focusing mechanism proposed by Sidner (Sidner, 1979) (Sidner, 1981) (Sidner, 1983) extending and refining her algorithms. The algorithm is designed for anaphors generally, even if we focus mainly on pronouns in this paper. Indeed, the distinction between different kinds of anaphors is made at the level of anaphor interpretation rules. These resolution rule aspects will not be developed here; though they have been developed in the literature, e.g., see (Carter, 1987), and (Sidner, 1981) (Sidner, 1983). We focus more on the mechanisms that handle these different kinds of rules.

We first present how intrasentential antecedents occur in embedded sentences. We recall the main ideas of the focusing approach, then expand on the main hypotheses which led the design of the anaphora resolution algorithm.

2 Intrasentential Antecedents

2.1 Embedded sentences and elementary events

An embedded sentence contains either more than one verb or a verb and derivations of other verbs (see sentence 1 with verbs *said* and *forming*).

> 1) Three of the world's leading advertising groups, Agence Havas S.A. of France, Young & Rubicam of the U.S. and Dentsu Inc. of Japan, said they are forming a global advertising joint venture.

Broadly speaking embedded sentences concern more than one fact. In sentence 1 there is the fact of saying something and that of forming a joint venture. We call such a fact an elementary event (EE hereafter). Thus an embedded sentence will contain several EEs.

Factors that influence embedded sentences are mainly semantic features of verbs. For example the verb *to say*, that takes a sentence complement favours an introduction of a new fact, i.e., "to say something", and the related fact. There are other classes of verbs such as *want to*, *hope that*, and so on. In the following, subordinate phrases, like relative or causal sentences, will be also considered as embedded ones.

2.2 Embedded sentences with intrasentential antecedents

First of all, we will distinguish the Possessive, Reciprocal and Reflexive pronouns (PRR hereafter) from the other pronouns (non-PRR hereafter).

On the basis of 120 articles, of 4 sentences on average, containing 332 pronouns altogether, we made the following assumption (1):

Assumption : non-PRR pronouns can have intrasentential antecedents, only if these pronouns occur in an embedded sentence.

The statistics below show that of 262 non-PRR pronouns, there are 244 having intrasentential antecedents, all of which occur in embedded sentences and none in a "simple" sentence. The remaining 18 non-PRR pronouns have intersentential antecedents.

Pronouns	332
non-PRR	262
With intrasentential antecedents in an embedded sentence	244
With intrasentential in a simple sentence	0
With intersentential antecedents	18

Our assumption means that, while the PRR pronouns may find their antecedents in an non embedded sentence (e.g., sentences 2 and 3) the non-PRR pronouns can not.

2) Vulcan made *its* initial Investment in Telescan in May, 1992.
3) The agencies HCM and DYR are *themselves* joint ventures.

Without jumping to conclusions, we cannot avoid making a parallel with the topological relations defined in the binding theory (Chomsky, 1980), between two coreferring phrases in the syntactic tree level. Assumption 1 redefines these relations in an informal and less rigorous way, at the semantic level, i.e., considering semantic parameters such as the type of verbs that introduce embedded sentences.

2.3 Using Sidner's Focusing Approach

To resolve anaphors one of the most suitable existing approaches when dealing with anaphor issues in a conceptual analysis process is the focusing approach proposed by Sidner. However, this mechanism is not suitable for intrasentential cases. We propose to exploit its main advantages in order to build our anaphora resolution mechanism extending it to deal also with intrasentential antecedents.

We describe the main elements of the focusing approach that are necessary to understand our method, without going into great detail, see (Sidner, 1979) (Sidner, 1981) (Sidner, 1983). Sidner proposed a methodology, modelling the way "focus" of attention and anaphor resolution influence one another. Using pronouns reflects what the speaker has focused on in the previous sentence, so that the focus is that phrase which the pronouns refer to. The resolution is organised through the following processes:

- The expected focus algorithm that selects an initial focus called the "expected focus". This selection may be "confirmed" or "rejected" in subsequent sentences. The expected focus is generally chosen on the basis of the verb semantic categories. There is a preference in terms of thematic position: the "theme" (as used by Gruber and Anderson, 1976 for the notion of the object case of a verb) is the first, followed by the goal, the instrument and the location ordered according to their occurrence in the sentence; the final item is the agent that is selected when no other role suits.
- The anaphora interpreter uses the state of the focus and a set of algorithms associated with each anaphor type to determine which element of the data structures is the antecedent. Each algorithm is a filter containing several interpretation rules (IR).

  Each IR in the algorithm appropriate to an anaphor suggests one or several antecedents depending on the focus and on the anaphor type.
- An evaluation of the proposed antecedents is performed using different kinds of criteria (syntax, semantics, inferential, etc.)
- The focusing algorithm makes use of data structures, i.e., the focus registers that represent the state of the focus: the current focus (CF) representation, alternate focus list (AFL) that contains the other phrases of the sentence and the focus stack (FS). A parallel structure to the CF is also set to deal with the agentive pronouns. The focusing algorithm updates the state of the focus after each sentence anaphor (except the first sentence). After the first sentence, it confirms or rejects the predicted focus taking into account the results of anaphor interpretation. In the case of rejection, it determines which phrase is to move into focus.

This is a brief example (Sidner 1983) :

a Alfred and Zohar liked to play baseball.

b *They* played it every day after school before dinner.

c After *their* game, Alfred and Zohar had ice cream cones.

d *They* tasted really good.

- In a) the expected focus is "baseball" (the theme)
- In b) "it" refers to "baseball" (CF). "they" refers to Alfred and Zohar (AF)
- The focusing algorithm confirms the CF.
- In d) "they" refers to "ice cream cones" in AFL.
- The focusing algorithm decides that since no anaphor refers to the CF, the CF is stacked and

"ice cream cones" is the new CF (focus movement).

We call a basic focusing cycle the cycle that includes :

- the focusing algorithm
- followed by the interpretation of anaphors,
- then by the evaluation of the proposed antecedents.

2.4 What needs to be improved in the focusing approach?

2.4.1 Intrasentential antecedents

The focusing approach always prefers the previous sentences' entities as antecedents to the current sentences. In fact only previous sentence entities are present in the focus registers. Thus phrases of the current sentence can not be proposed as antecedents. This problem has already been underlined, see (Carter, 1987) in particular who proposed augmenting the focus registers with the entities of the current sentence. For example in sentence 4 while the focus algorithm would propose only "John" as an antecedent for "him", in Carter's method "Bill" will also be proposed.

> 4) John walked into the room. He told Bill someone wanted to see *him*.

2.4.2 Initial Anaphors

The focusing mechanism fails in the expected focus algorithm when encountering anaphors occurring in the first sentence of a text, which we call initial anaphors, such as *They* in sentence (1). The problem with initial anaphors is that the focus registers cannot be initialised or may be wrongly filled if there are anaphors inside the first sentence of the text. It is clear that taking the sentence in its classical meaning as the unit of processing in the focusing approach, is not suitable when sentences are embedded.

We will focus on the mechanisms and algorithmic aspects of the resolution (how to fill the registers, how to structure algorithms, etc.) and not on the rule aspects, like how IRs decide to choose *Bill* and not *John* (sentence 4).

3 Our Solution

As stated above, embedded sentences include several elementary events (EEs). EEs are represented as conceptual entities in our work. We consider that such successive EEs involve the same context that is introduced by several successive short sentences. Moreover, our assumption states that when non-PRR anaphors have intrasentential antecedents, they occur in embedded sentences. Starting with these considerations, the algorithm is governed by the hypotheses expanded below.

3.1 Main hypotheses

First hypothesis : EE is the unit of processing in the basic focusing cycle.

An EE is the unit of processing in our resolution algorithm instead of the sentence. The basic focusing cycle is applied on each EE in turn and not sentence by sentence. Notice that a simple sentence coincides with its EE.

Second hypothesis : The "initial" EE of a well formed first sentence does not contain non-PRR pronouns just as an initial simple sentence cannot.

For example, in the splitting of sentence 1 into two EEs (see below), EE1 does not contain non-PRR pronouns because it is the initial EE of the whole discourse.

> EE1) "Three of the world's leading advertising groups, Agence Havas S.A. of France, Young & Rubicam of the U.S. and Dentsu Inc. of Japan, said"
> EE2) "they are forming a global advertising joint venture."

Third hypothesis : PRR pronouns require special treatment.

PRR could refer to intrasentential antecedents in simple sentences (such as in those of sentences 3 and 4). An initial EE could then contain an anaphor of the PRR type. Our approach is to add a special phase that resolves first the PRRs occurring in the initial EE before applying the expected focusing algorithm on the same initial EE. In all other cases, PRRs are treated equally to other pronouns.

This early resolution relies on the fact that the PRR pronouns may refer to the agent, as in sentence 3, as well as to the complement phrases. However the ambiguity will not be huge at this first level of the treatment. Syntactic and semantic features can easily be used to resolve these anaphors. This relies also on the fact that the subject of the initial EE cannot be a pronoun (second hypothesis).

Having mentioned this particular case of PRR in initial EE, we now expand on the whole algorithm of resolution.

3.2 The Algorithm

In the following, remember that what we called the basic focusing cycle is the following successive steps :

- applying the resolution rules,
- applying the focusing algorithm, i.e., updating the focus registers
- the evaluation of the proposed antecedents for each anaphor.

The algorithm is based on the decomposition of the sentence into EEs and the application of the basic focusing cycle on each EE in turn and not sentence by sentence.

The complete steps are given below (see also figure 1):

Step 1 Split the sentence, i.e., its semantic representation, into EEs.

Step 2 Apply the expected focus algorithm to the first EE.

Step 3 Perform the basic focusing cycle for every anaphor of all the EEs of the current sentence.

Step 4 Perform a collective evaluation (i.e., evaluation that involves all the anaphors of the sentence), when all the anaphors of the current sentence are processed.

Step 5 Process the next sentence until all the sentences are processed:

- split the sentence into EEs
- apply Step 3 then Step 4.

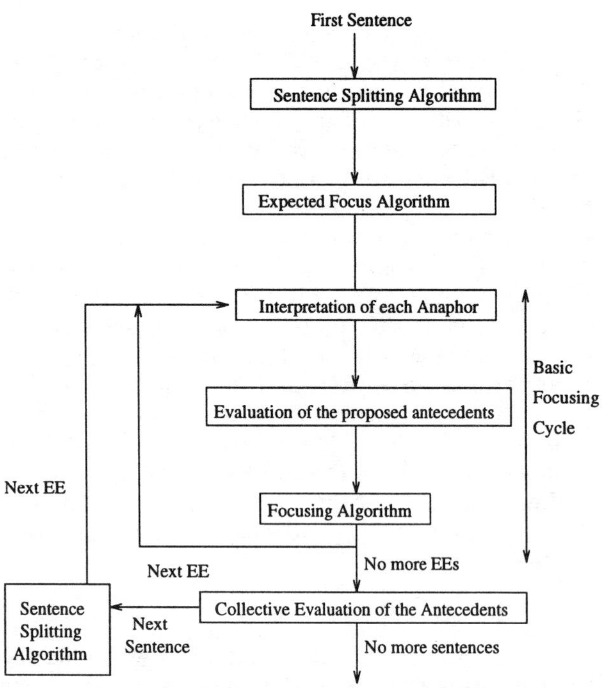

Figure 1: The Algorithm

Main Results :

1. Intrasentential antecedents are taken into account when applying the focusing algorithm. For example, in sentence 1, the intrasentential antecedent *Bill* will be taken into account, because EE1 would be processed beforehand by the expected focusing algorithm.
2. The problem of initial anaphors is then resolved. The expected focusing algorithm is applied only on the initial EE which must not contain anaphors.

3.3 Examples and results

To illustrate the algorithm, let's consider the following sentence :

> Lafarge Coppee said it would buy 10 percent in National Gypsum, the number two plasterboard company in the US, a purchase which allows it to be present on the world's biggest plasterboard market.

At the conceptual level, there are 3 EEs. They are involved respectively by the *said*, *buy*, and *allows* verbs. They correspond respectively to the following surface sentences:

EE1 "Lafarge Coppee said"

EE2 "it would buy 10 percent in National Gypsum, the number two plasterboard company in the US"

EE3 "a purchase which allows it to be present on the world's biggest plasterboard market."

Consider the algorithm :

- the expected focusing algorithm is applied to the first EE, EE1, which contains non-PRR anaphors.
- the other phases of the algorithm, i.e., the basic focusing cycle, are applied to the subsequent EEs :
  - EE2 contains only one pronoun *it*, which is resolved by the basic focusing cycle
  - *it* in EE3 will be resolved in the same way.

The anaphora resolution has been implemented as a part of a conceptual analyser (Azzam, 1995a). It dealt particularly with pronouns. It has been tested on a set of 120 news reports. We made two kinds of algorithm evaluations: the evaluation of the implemented procedure and an evaluation by hand. For the implementation the success rate of resolution was 70%. The main cases of failure are related to the non implemented aspects like the treatment of coordination ambiguities and the appositions, or other anaphoric phenomena, like ellipsis.

For the second evaluation which concerns the real evaluation of the approach,i.e., without going into the practical issues concerning implementation, the success rate was 95%. The main cases of failure were due to the cases that were not considered by the algorithm, like for example the pronouns occurring before their antecedents , i.e., cataphors. Such cases occur for example in sentences 5 and 6 pointed out by Hobbs (Hobbs, 1985) to discuss the cases that are not handled easily in the literature.

> 5) Mary sacked out in *his* apartment before *Sam* could kick her out.
> 6) Girls who *he* has dated say that *Sam* is charming.

Our algorithm fails in resolving *his* in 5, because the algorithm searches only for the entities that precede the anaphor in the text. The same applies for *he* in 6. However improving our algorithm to process classical cases of cataphors, such as that in sentence 6, should not require major modifications, only a change in the order in which the EEs are searched.

For example, to process pronouns of the sentence 6 split into two EES (see below), the algorithm must consider EE2 before EE1. This means applying the step 2 of the algorithm to EE2, then step 3 to EE1. The sentence 5 should require specific treatment, though.

> EE1) "that *Sam* is charming"
> EE2) "Girls who *he* has dated say"

Hobbs also pointed out the cases of "picture noun" examples, as in sentences 7 and 8:

> 7) John saw a picture of him.
> 8) John's father's portrait of him.

In 7 our algorithm is successful, i.e., it will not identify *him* with *John* because of our previous assumption (section 2.2). However our algorithm would fail in 8 because the non-PRR pronoun *him* could refer to *John* which occurs in the same EE.

Notice that Hobbs' (Hobbs, 1985) remark that "the more deeply the pronoun is embedded and the more elaborate the construction it occurs in, the more acceptable the non reflexive" is consistent with our assumption.

For example in the embedded sentence 9 where either the reflexive (himself) or non reflexive pronouns (him) may be used, it is more natural to make use of *him*.

> 9) John claimed that the picture of him hanging in the post office was a fraud.

4 The Conceptual Level

We comment here on the main aspects of the conceptual analysis that are related to the anaphora resolution process. They concern mainly the way of splitting embedded sentences and the problems of determining the theme and of managing the other ambiguities and the several readings.

The conceptual analyser's strategy consists of a continuous step-by-step translation of the original natural language sentences into conceptual structures (CS hereafter). This translation uses the results of the syntactic analysis (syntactic tree). It is a progressive substitution of the NL terms located in the syntactic tree with concepts and templates of the conceptual representation language. Triggering rules are evoked by words of the sentence and allow the activation of well-formed CS templates when the syntactico-semantic filter is unified with the syntactic tree. The values caught by the filter variables are the arguments of the CS roles, i.e., they fill the CS roles. If they are anaphors, they are considered to be unbound variables and result in unfilled roles in the CS. The anaphora resolution aims therefore at filling the unfilled roles with the corresponding antecedents.

4.1 Splitting into EEs

The splitting of a sentence in EE is done on the corresponding CS. A minimal CS is a template comprising a predicate that identifies the basic type of the represented event and a set of roles or predicate cases.
For example, the sentence "to say that they agree to form a joint venture" is represented, in a simplified way, with three templates, corresponding to the predicates:

- *move* information (from "to say"),
- *produce* an agreement (from "to agree"),
- *produce* a joint venture (from "to form").

Given that one template at the semantic level represents an elementary event, the splitting is implicitly already done when these templates are created in the triggering phase. Indeed, the syntactico-semantic filter of the triggering rules takes into account the semantic features of words (mainly verbs) for recognising in the surface sentence those that are able to trigger an elementary event.

4.2 Determining the theme

Gruber and Anderson characterise the theme as follows: if a verb describes a change to some entity, whether of position, activity, class or possession, then the theme is the changed entity, (Gruber, 1976) and (Anderson, 1977). As Carter (Carter, 1987) demonstrated, this definition of Gruber and Anderson is sufficient to apply the focusing mechanism. This assumption is particularly apt when we dispose of a conceptual representation. Indeed, to determine the thematic roles, we established a set of thematic rules that affect for a given predicative occurrence, its thematic functions according to the predicate type, the role type and the argument's semantic class.

4.3 Managing other ambiguities

An important aspect appears when one designs a concrete system, namely how to make other disambiguation processes cohabit. In the conceptual analyser, the general disambiguation module (GDM) deals with other ambiguities, like prepositional phrase attachment. It coordinates the treatment of different kinds of ambiguities. This is necessary because the conceptual structures (CS) on which the rules are performed could be incomplete because of other types of ambiguities not being resolved. For example, if the CF of the sentence is a PP object that is not attached yet in the CS the thematic rules fail to fill the CF. The GDM ensures that every disambiguation module intervenes only if previous ambiguities have already been resolved. The process of co-ordinating ambiguity processing is fully expanded in (Azzam, 1995b).

4.4 Multiple readings

When dealing with ambiguities, another important aspect is managing multiple readings. At a certain point when the GDM calls the anaphora module to deal with a given anaphor, the status of the conceptual analysis could be characterised by the following parameters :

- The set of conceptual structures for the current reading Ri on which the resolution is performed, given that several readings could arise from previous ambiguity processing.
- The set of conceptual structures of the current sentence Si where the anaphor occurs;
- The set of conceptual structures of the current elementary event EEi where the anaphor occurs after the Si splitting.
- The state of the focus (content of the registers), SFi

The main assumption is that the anaphora resolution algorithm always applies to a single state, (Ri, Si , EEi, SFi) when resolving a given anaphor (Step 3) :

a If several antecedents are still possible after the individual evaluation of the anaphor, Ri is then duplicated, in Rij, as many times as there are possibilities.

b When performing the collective evaluation of all Si anaphors, every inconsistent Rij is suppressed.

c The result is a set of readings (Rij, Sj , EEj, SFi).

5 Conclusion

We have proposed a methodology to resolve anaphors occurring in embedded sentences. The main idea of the methodology is the use of other kinds of restrictions between the anaphor and its antecedents than the syntactic ones. We demonstrated that anaphors with intrasentential antecedents are closely related to embedded sentences and we showed how to exploit this data to design the anaphora resolution methodology. Mainly, we exploited Sidner's focusing mechanism, refining the classical unit of processing, that is the sentence, to that of the elementary event. The algorithm has been implemented (in Common Lisp, Sun Sparc) to deal with pronouns as a part of a deep analyser. The main advantages of the proposed algorithm is that it is independent from the knowledge representation language used and the deep understanding approach in which it is integrated. Thus, it could be set up in any conceptual analyser, as long as a semantic representation of the text is available. Moreover Sidner's approach does not impose its own formalisms (syntactic or semantic) for its application. The improvement of the proposed algorithm requires dealing with special cases of anaphors such as cataphors and also with specific cases which are not easily handled in the literature. For example, we saw that a solution to processing cataphors could be to reconsider the order in which the conceptual structures (elementary events beforehand) are searched.

6 Acknowledgements

This work has been supported by the European Community Grant LE1-2238 (AVENTINUS project).

References

Anderson, S.R. 1977. Formal syntax. In Wasow and Akmajian, editors, *Comment on the paper by Wasow in Culicover.* Academic Press, pages 361–376.

Azzam, Saliha. 1995a. *Computation of Ambiguities (Anaphors and PPs) in NL texts. CLAM : The prototype.* Ph.D. thesis, Paris Sorbonne University.

Azzam, Saliha. 1995b. Anaphors, pps and disambiguation process for conceptual analysis. In *14th International Joint Conference on Artificial Intelligence (IJCAI'95).* San Mateo (CA): Morgan Kaufmann.

Carter, David. 1987. *Interpreting Anaphors in natural language texts.* Chichester : Ellis Horwood.

Gruber, J.S. 1976. *Lexical structures in syntax and semantics.* North-Holland.

Hobbs, Jerry. 1985. Resolving pronoun references. In B. Grosz K. Sparck-Jones B. Webber, editor, *Readings in Natural Language*, volume 44. Morgan Kaufmann Publishers Los Altos California, pages 311–338.

Lappin, S. and H.J. Leass. 1994. An algorithm for pronominal anaphora resolution. *Computational Linguistics*, 20:535–561.

Merlo, P. 1993. For an incremental computation of intrasentential coreference. In *the 13th International Joint Conference on Artificial Intelligence (IJCAI'93)*, pages 1216–1221. San Mateo (CA): Morgan Kaufmann.

Sidner, C. 1979. Toward a computation of intrasentential coreference. Technical Report TR-537, MIT. Artificial Intelligence Laboratory.

Sidner, C. 1981. Focusing for interpretation of pronouns. *American Journal of Computational Linguistics*, 7:217–231.

Sidner, C. 1983. Focusing in the comprehension of definite anaphora. In Brady. M and Berwick R.C, editors, *Computational Models of Discourse*. Cambridge (MA) : The MIT Press.

Functional Centering

Michael Strube & Udo Hahn
Freiburg University
Computational Linguistics Lab
Europaplatz 1, D-79085 Freiburg, Germany
{strube,hahn}@coling.uni-freiburg.de

Abstract

Based on empirical evidence from a free word order language (German) we propose a fundamental revision of the principles guiding the ordering of discourse entities in the forward-looking centers within the centering model. We claim that grammatical role criteria should be replaced by indicators of the functional information structure of the utterances, i.e., the distinction between context-bound and unbound discourse elements. This claim is backed up by an empirical evaluation of functional centering.

1 Introduction

The centering model has evolved as a methodology for the description and explanation of the local coherence of discourse (Grosz et al., 1983; 1995), with focus on pronominal and nominal anaphora. Though several cross-linguistic studies have been carried out (cf. the enumeration in Grosz et al. (1995)), an almost canonical scheme for the ordering on the forward-looking centers has emerged, one that reflects well-known regularities of fixed word order languages such as English. With the exception of Walker et al. (1990; 1994) for Japanese, Turan (1995) for Turkish, Rambow (1993) for German and Cote (1996) for English, only *grammatical roles* are considered and the (partial) ordering in Table 1[1] is taken for granted.

subject > dir-object > indir-object > complement(s) > adjunct(s)

Table 1: Grammatical Role Based Ranking on the C_f

[1]Table 1 contains the most explicit ordering of grammatical roles we are aware of and has been taken from Brennan et al. (1987). Often, the distinction between complements and adjuncts is collapsed into the category "others" (c.f., e.g., Grosz et al. (1995)).

Our work on the resolution of anaphora (Strube & Hahn, 1995; Hahn & Strube, 1996) and textual ellipsis (Hahn et al., 1996), however, is based on German, a free word order language, in which grammatical role information is far less predictive for the organization of centers. Rather, for establishing proper referential relations, the *functional information structure* of the utterances becomes crucial (different perspectives on functional analysis are brought forward in Daneš (1974b) and Dahl (1974)). We share the notion of functional information structure as developed by Daneš (1974a). He distinguishes between two crucial dichotomies, viz. *given information* vs. *new information* (constituting the *information structure* of utterances) on the one hand, and *theme* vs. *rheme* on the other (constituting the *thematic structure* of utterances; cf. Halliday & Hasan (1976, pp.325-6)). Daneš refers to a definition given by Halliday (1967) to avoid the confusion likely to arise in the use of these terms: "[...] while *given* means *what you were talking about* (or *what I was talking about before*), *theme* means *what I am talking about (now)* [...]" Halliday (1967, p.212). Daneš concludes that the distinction between *given information* and *theme* is justified, while the distinction between *new information* and *rheme* is not. Thus, we arrive at a trichotomy between *given information*, *theme* and *rheme* (the latter being equivalent to *new information*). We here subscribe to these considerations, too, and will return in Section 3 to these notions in order to rephrase them more explicitly by using the terminology of the centering model.

In this paper, we intend to make two contributions to the centering approach. The first one, the introduction of functional notions of information structure in the centering model, is methodological in nature. The second one concerns an empirical issue in that we demonstrate how a functional model of centering can successfully be applied to the analysis of several forms of anaphoric text phenomena.

At the methodological level, we develop arguments that (at least for free word order languages) grammatical role indicators should be replaced by functional role patterns to more adequately account for the ordering of discourse entities in center lists. In Section 3 we elaborate on the particular information structure criteria underlying a function-based center ordering. We also make a second, even more general methodological claim for which we have gathered some preliminary, though still not conclusive evidence. Based on a re-evaluation of empirical arguments discussed in the literature on centering, we stipulate that exchanging grammatical by functional criteria is also a reasonable strategy for fixed word order languages. Grammatical role constraints can indeed be rephrased by functional ones, which is simply due to the fact that grammatical roles and the information structure patterns, as we define them, coincide in these kinds of languages. Hence, the proposal we make seems more general than the ones currently under discussion in that, given a functional framework, fixed and free word order languages can be accounted for by the same ordering principles. As a consequence, we argue against Walker et al.'s (1994, p.227) stipulation, which assumes that the C_f ranking is the only parameter of the centering theory which is language-dependent. Instead, we claim that *functional centering* constraints for the C_f ranking are possibly universal.

The second major contribution of this paper is related to the unified treatment of specific text phenomena. It consists of an equally balanced treatment of intersentential (pro)nominal anaphora and textual ellipsis (also called functional or partial anaphora). The latter phenomenon (cf. the examples given in the next section), in particular, is usually only sketchily dealt with in the centering literature, e.g., by asserting that the entity in question "is realized but not directly realized" (Grosz et al., 1995, p.217). Furthermore, the distinction between those two kinds of realization is generally delegated to the underlying semantic theory. We will develop arguments how to locate elliptical discourse entities and resolve textual ellipsis properly at the center level. The ordering constraints we supply account for all of the above mentioned types of anaphora in a precise way, including (pro)nominal anaphora (Strube & Hahn, 1995; Hahn & Strube, 1996). This claim will be validated by a substantial body of empirical data (cf. Section 4).

2 Types of Anaphora Considered

Text phenomena, e.g., textual forms of ellipsis and anaphora, are a challenging issue for the design of parsers for text understanding systems, since imperfect recognition facilities either result in referentially incoherent or invalid text knowledge representations. At the conceptual level, textual ellipsis relates a quasi-anaphoric expression to its extrasentential antecedent by conceptual attributes (or roles) associated with that antecedent (see, e.g., the relation between *"Akkus" (accumulator)* and *"316LT"*, a particular notebook, in (1b) and (1a)). Thus, it complements the phenomenon of nominal anaphora, where an anaphoric expression is related to its antecedent in terms of conceptual generalization (as, e.g., *"Rechner" (computer)* in (1c) refers to *"316LT"* in (1a) mediated by the textual ellipsis in (1b)). The resolution of text-level nominal (and pronominal) anaphora contributes to the construction of referentially valid text knowledge bases, while the resolution of textual ellipsis yields referentially coherent text knowledge bases.

(1) a. Ein Reserve-Batteriepack versorgt den *316LT* ca. 2 Minuten mit Strom.
(A reserve battery pack – supplies – the *316LT* – for approximately 2 minutes – with power.)

b. Der Status des *Akkus* wird dem Anwender angezeigt.
(The status of the *accumulator* – is – to the user – indicated.)

c. Ca. 30 Minuten vor der *Entleerung* beginnt der *Rechner* 5 Sekunden zu beepen.
(Approximately 30 minutes – before the *discharge* – starts – the *computer* – for 5 seconds – to beep.)

d. 5 Minuten bevor *er* sich ausschaltet, fängt die Low-Battery-LED an zu blinken.
(5 minutes – before – *it* – itself – turns off – begins – the low-battery-LED – to flash.)

In the case of textual ellipsis, the missing conceptual link between two discourse elements occurring in adjacent utterances must be inferred in order to establish the local coherence of the discourse (for an early statement of that idea, cf. Clark (1975)). In the surface form of utterance (1b) the information is missing that *"Akkus" (accumulator)* links up with *"316LT"*. This relation can only be made explicit if conceptual knowledge about the domain, *viz.* the relation *part-of* between the concepts ACCUMULATOR and 316LT, is available (see Hahn et al. (1996) for a more detailed treatment of text ellipsis resolution).

3 Principles of Functional Centering

Within the framework of the centering model (Grosz et al., 1995), we distinguish each utterance's backward-looking center ($C_b(U_n)$) and its forward-looking centers ($C_f(U_n)$). The ranking imposed on the elements of the C_f reflects the assumption that the most highly ranked element of $C_f(U_n)$ – the preferred center $C_p(U_n)$ – is the most preferred antecedent of an anaphoric or elliptical expression in U_{n+1}, while the remaining elements are partially ordered according to decreasing preference for establishing referential links. Hence, the most important single construct of the centering model is the ordering of the list of forward-looking centers (Walker et al., 1994).

The main difference between Grosz et al.'s work and our proposal concerns the criteria for ranking the forward-looking centers. While Grosz et al. assume that *grammatical roles* are the major determinant for the ranking on the C_f, we claim that for languages with relatively free word order (such as German), it is the *functional information structure (IS)* of the utterance in terms of the context-boundedness or unboundedness of discourse elements. The centering data structures and the notion of context-boundedness can be used to redefine Daneš' (1974a) trichotomy between *given information*, *theme* and *new information* (*rheme*). The $C_b(U_n)$, the most highly ranked element of $C_f(U_{n-1})$ realized in U_n, corresponds to the element which represents the *given* information. The *theme* of U_n is represented by the preferred center $C_p(U_n)$, the most highly ranked element of $C_f(U_n)$. The *theme/rheme hierarchy* of U_n is represented by $C_f(U_n)$ which – in our approach – is partly determined by the $C_f(U_{n-1})$: the rhematic elements of U_n are the ones not contained in $C_f(U_{n-1})$ (unbound discourse elements); they express the *new information* in U_n. The ones contained in $C_f(U_{n-1})$ and $C_f(U_n)$ (bound discourse elements) are thematic, with the theme/rheme hierarchy corresponding to the ranking in the C_fs. The distinction between context-bound and unbound elements is important for the ranking on the C_f, since bound elements are generally ranked higher than any other non-anaphoric elements (cf. also Hajičová et al. (1992)).

An alternative definition of *theme* and *rheme* in the context of the centering approach is proposed by Rambow (1993). In his approach the *theme* corresponds to the C_b and the *theme/rheme hierarchy* can be derived from those elements of $C_f(U_{n-1})$ that are realized in U_n. Rambow does not distinguish, however, between the *information structure* and the *thematic structure* of utterances, which leads to problems when a change of the criteria for recognizing the thematic structure is envisaged. Our approach is flexible enough to accomodate other conceptions of *theme/rheme* as defined, e.g., by Hajičová et al. (1995), since this change affects only the thematic but not the information structure of utterances.

bound element(s) $\succ_{IS_{base}}$ unbound element(s)
anaphora $\succ_{IS_{bound}}$ (possessive pronoun *xor* elliptical antecedent) $\succ_{IS_{bound}}$ (elliptical expression *xor* head of anaphoric expression)
nom head$_1$ $>_{prec}$ nom head$_2$ $>_{prec}$ ... $>_{prec}$ nom head$_n$

Table 2: Functional Ranking Constraints on the C_f

The rules holding for the ranking on the C_f, derived from a German language corpus, are summarized in Table 2. They are organized into three layers[2]. At the top level, $\succ_{IS_{base}}$ denotes the basic relation for the overall ranking of information structure *(IS)* patterns. Accordingly, any *context-bound* expression in the utterance U_{n-1} is given the highest preference as a potential antecedent of an anaphoric or elliptical expression in U_n while any unbound expression is ranked next to context-bound expressions.

The second relation depicted in Table 2, $\succ_{IS_{bound}}$, denotes preference relations dealing exclusively with multiple occurrences of (resolved) anaphora, i.e., *bound elements*, in the preceding utterance. $\succ_{IS_{bound}}$ distinguishes among *different forms* of *context-bound elements* (viz., anaphora, possessive pronouns and textual ellipses) and their associated preference order. The final element of $\succ_{IS_{bound}}$ is either the elliptical expression or the head of an anaphoric expression which is used as a possessive determiner, a Saxon genitive, a prepositional or a genitival attribute (cf. the ellipsis in (2c): *"die Ladezeit" (the charge time)* vs. *"seine Ladezeit" (its charge time)* or *"die Ladezeit des Akkus" (the accumulator's charge time)*).

For illustration purposes, consider text fragment (1) and the corresponding C_b/C_f data in Table 3[3]: In (1d) the pronoun *"er" (it)* might be resolved to *"Akku" (accumulator)* or *"Rechner" (computer)*, since both fulfill the agreement condition for pronoun resolution. Now, *"der Rechner" (computer)* figures as a nominal anaphor, already resolved to DELL-316LT, while *"Akku" (accumulator)* is only the antecedent of the elliptical expression *"der Entleerung" (discharge)*. Therefore, the preferred antecedent of *"er" (it)* is determined as *Rechner (computer)*.

The bottom level of Table 2 specifies $>_{prec}$ which covers the preference order for multiple occurrences of the *same type* of any information structure pattern, e.g., the occurrence of two anaphora or two unbound elements (all heads in an utterance are ordered by linear precedence relative to their text position). In sentence (2b), two nominal anaphors occur, *"Akku" (accumulator)* and *"Rechner" (computer)*. The textual ellipsis *"Ladezeit" (charge time)* in (2c) has to be resolved to the most preferred element of the C_f of (2b), *viz.* the entity denoted by *"Akku" (accumulator)* (cf. Table 4). Note that *"Rechner" (computer)* is the subject of the sentence, though it is not the preferred antecedent, since *"Akku" (accumulator)* precedes *"Rechner" (computer)* and is anaphoric as well.

[2]Disregarding coordinations, the ordering we propose induces a *strict* ordering on the entities in a center list.

[3]*Minuten (minutes)* is excluded from the C_f for reasons concerning the processing of complex sentences (cf. Strube (1996)).

(1a)	Cb:	DELL-316LT: 316LT	CONTINUE
	Cf:	[DELL-316LT: 316LT, RESERVE-BATTERY-PACK: Reserve-Batteriepack, TIME-UNIT-PAIR: 2 Minuten, POWER: Strom]	
(1b)	Cb:	DELL-316LT: —	CONTINUE
	Cf:	[DELL-316LT: —, ACCU: Akku, STATUS: Status, USER: Anwender]	
(1c)	Cb:	DELL-316LT: Rechner	CONTINUE
	Cf:	[DELL-316LT: Rechner, ACCU: —, DISCHARGE: Entleerung, TIME-UNIT-PAIR: 30 Minuten, TIME-UNIT-PAIR: 5 Sekunden]	
(1d)	Cb:	DELL-316LT: er	CONTINUE
	Cf:	[DELL-316LT: er, LOW-BATTERY-LED: Low-Battery-LED	

Table 3: Centering Data for Text Fragment (1)

(2a)	Cb:	DELL-316LT: 316LT	CONTINUE
	Cf:	[DELL-316LT: 316LT, NIMH-ACCU: NiMH-Akku]	
(2b)	Cb:	DELL-316LT: Rechner	RETAIN
	Cf:	[NIMH-ACCU: Akku, DELL-316LT: Rechner, TIME-UNIT-PAIR: 4 Stunden, POWER: Strom]	
(2c)	Cb:	NIMH-ACCU: —	SMOOTH-SHIFT
	Cf:	[NIMH-ACCU: —, CHARGE-TIME: Ladezeit, TIME-UNIT-PAIR: 1,5 Stunden]	

Table 4: Centering Data for Text Fragment (2)

(2) a. Der *316LT* wird mit einem *NiMH-Akku* bestückt.
(The *316LT* is – with a *NiMH-accumulator* – equipped.)

b. Durch diesen neuartigen *Akku* wird der *Rechner* für ca. 4 Stunden mit Strom versorgt.
(Because of this new type of *accumulator* – is the *computer* – for approximately 4 hours – with power – provided.)

c. Darüberhinaus ist die *Ladezeit* mit 1,5 Stunden sehr kurz.
(Also – is – the *charge time* of 1.5 hours – quite short.)

Given these basic relations, we may formulate the composite relation $>_{IS}$ (Table 5). It states the conditions for the comprehensive ordering of items on C_f (x and y denote lexical heads).

$>_{IS}$:= { (x, y) |
if x and y both represent the same type of IS pattern
then the relation $>_{prec}$ applies to x and y
else if x and y both represent different forms of bound elements
then the relation $>_{IS_{bound}}$ applies to x and y
else the relation $>_{IS_{base}}$ applies to x and y }

Table 5: Information Structure Relation

4 Evaluation

In this section, we first describe the empirical and methodological framework in which our evaluation experiments were embedded, and then turn to a discussion of evaluation results and the conclusions we draw from the data.

4.1 Evaluation Framework

The test set for our evaluation experiment consisted of three different text sorts: 15 product reviews from the information technology *(IT)* domain (one of the two main corpora at our lab), one article from the German news magazine *Der Spiegel*, and the first two chapters of a short story by the German writer *Heiner Müller*[4]. The evaluation was carried out manually in order to circumvent error chaining[5]. Table 6 summarizes the total numbers of anaphors, textual ellipses, utterances and words in the test set.

	anaphors	ellipses	utterances	words
IT	308	294	451	5542
Spiegel	102	25	82	1468
Müller	153	20	87	867
Σ	563	339	620	7877

Table 6: Test Set

Given this test set, we compared three major approaches to centering, *viz.* the original model whose ordering principles are based on grammatical role indicators only (the so-called *canonical* model) as characterized by Table 1, an "intermediate" model which can be considered a *naive* approach to free word order languages, and, of course, the *functional* model based on information structure constraints as stated in Table 2. For reasons discussed below, augmented versions of the naive and the canonical approaches will also be considered. They are characterized by the additional

[4]Liebesgeschichte. In Heiner Müller. *Geschichten aus der Produktion 2*. Berlin: Rotbuch Verlag, pp. 57-63.

[5]A performance evaluation of the current anaphora and ellipsis resolution capacities of our system is reported in Hahn et al. (1996).

constraint that elliptical antecedents are ranked higher than elliptical expressions (short: "ante > express").

For the evaluation of a centering algorithm on naturally occurring text it is necessary to specify how to deal with complex sentences. In particular, methods for the interaction between intra- and intersentential anaphora resolution have to be defined, since the centering model is concerned only with the latter case (see Suri & McCoy (1994)). We use an approach as described by Strube (1996) for the evaluation.

Since most of the anaphors in these texts are nominal anaphors, the resolution of which is much more restricted than that of pronominal anaphors, the rate of success for the whole anaphora resolution process is not significant enough for a proper evaluation of the functional constraints. The reason for this lies in the fact that nominal anaphors are far more constrained by conceptual criteria than pronominal anaphors. So the chance to properly resolve a nominal anaphor, even at lower ranked positions in the center lists, is greater than for pronominal anaphors. While we shift our evaluation criteria away from simple anaphora resolution success data to structural conditions based on the proper ordering of center lists (in particular, we focus on the most highly ranked item of the forward-looking centers) these criteria compensate for the high proportion of nominal anaphora that occur in our test sets. The types of centering transitions we make use of (cf. Table 7) are taken from Walker et al. (1994).

	$C_b(U_n) = C_b(U_{n-1})$ OR $C_b(U_{n-1})$ undef.	$C_b(U_n) \neq C_b(U_{n-1})$
$C_b(U_n) = C_p(U_n)$	CONTINUE	SMOOTH-SHIFT
$C_b(U_n) \neq C_p(U_n)$	RETAIN	ROUGH-SHIFT

Table 7: Transition Types

4.2 Evaluation Results

In Table 8 we give the numbers of centering transitions between the utterances in the three test sets. The first column contains those which are generated by the *naive* approach (such a proposal was made by Gordon et al. (1993) as well as by Rambow (1993) who, nevertheless, restricts it to the German middlefield only). We simply ranked the elements of C_f according to their text position. While it is usually assumed that the elliptical expression ranks above its antecedent (Grosz et al., 1995, p.217), we assume the contrary. The second column contains the results of this modification with respect to the *naive* approach. In the third column of Table 8 we give the numbers of transitions which are generated by the *canonical* constraints as stated by Grosz et al. (1995, p.214, 217). The fourth column supplies the results of the same modification as was used for the naive approach, *viz.* elliptical antecedents are ranked higher than elliptical expressions. The fifth column shows the results which are generated by the *functional* constraints from Table 2.

First, we examine the error data for anaphora resolution for the five cases. All approaches have 99 errors in common. These are due to underspecifications at different levels, e.g., the failure to account for prepositional anaphors (16), plural anaphors (8), anaphors which refer to a member of a set (14), sentence anaphors (21), and anaphors which refer to the global focus (12). Only 6 errors of the functional approach are directly caused by an inappropriate ordering of the C_f, while the naive approach leads to 10 errors and the canonical to 7. When the antecedent of an elliptical expression is ranked above the elliptical expression itself the error rate of these two augmented approaches increases to 12 and 9, respectively.

We now turn to the distribution of transition types for the different approaches. The centering model assumes a preference order among these transitions, e.g., CONTINUE ranks above RETAIN and RETAIN ranks above SHIFT. This preference order reflects the presumed inference load put on the hearer or speaker to *coherently* decode or encode a discourse. Since the functional approach generates a larger amount of CONTINUE transitions, we interpret this as a first rough indication that this approach provides for more efficient processing than its competitors.

But this reasoning is not entirely conclusive. Counting single occurrences of transition types, in general, does not reveal the entire validity of the center lists. Instead, considering adjacent transition pairs gives a more reliable picture, since depending on the text sort considered (e.g., technical *vs.* news magazine *vs.* literary texts) certain sequences of transition types may be entirely plausible, though they include transitions which, when viewed in isolation, seem to imply considerable inferencing load (cf. Table 8). For instance, a CONTINUE transition which follows a CONTINUE transition is a sequence which requires the lowest processing costs. But a CONTINUE transition which follows a RETAIN transition implies higher processing costs than a SMOOTH-SHIFT transition following a RETAIN transition. This is due to the fact that a RETAIN transition ideally predicts a SMOOTH-SHIFT in the following utterance. In this case the SMOOTH-SHIFT is the "least effort" transition, because only the first element of the C_f of the preceding utterance has to be checked to perform the SMOOTH-SHIFT transition, while in the case of CONTINUE at least one more check has to be performed. Hence, we claim that no one particular centering transition is preferred over another. Instead, we postulate that some *centering transition pairs* are preferred over others. Following this

	Transition Types	naive	naive & ante > express	canonical	canonical & ante > express	functional
IT	CONTINUE	49	167	102	197	309
	RETAIN	269	158	226	131	25
	SMOOTH-SHIFT	32	41	24	35	51
	ROUGH-SHIFT	39	23	37	26	4
	Errors	69	70	68	69	67
Spiegel	CONTINUE	17	28	37	43	50
	RETAIN	42	32	28	23	12
	SMOOTH-SHIFT	9	9	7	8	13
	ROUGH-SHIFT	7	6	3	1	0
	Errors	18	19	16	17	16
Müller	CONTINUE	31	31	32	32	36
	RETAIN	19	19	18	18	15
	SMOOTH-SHIFT	15	17	15	16	18
	ROUGH-SHIFT	14	12	14	13	10
	Errors	22	22	22	22	22
Σ	CONTINUE	97	226	171	272	395
	RETAIN	330	209	272	172	52
	SMOOTH-SHIFT	56	67	46	59	82
	ROUGH-SHIFT	60	41	54	40	14
	Errors (specific errors)	109 (10)	111 (12)	106 (7)	108 (9)	105 (6)

Table 8: Numbers of Centering Transitions

line of argumentation, we here propose to classify all occurrences of centering transition pairs with respect to the costs they imply. The cost-based evaluation of different C_f orderings refers to evaluation criteria which form an intrinsic part of the centering model[6].

Transition pairs hold for two immediately successive utterances. We distinguish between two types of transition pairs, *cheap* ones and *expensive* ones. We call a transition pair *cheap* if the *backward-looking center* of the current utterance is correctly predicted by the *preferred center* of the immediately preceding utterance, i.e., $C_b(U_i) = C_p(U_{i-1}), i = 2 \ldots n$. Transition pairs are called *expensive* if the *backward-looking center* of the current utterance is not correctly predicted by the *preferred center* of the immediately preceding utterance, i.e., $C_b(U_i) \neq C_p(U_{i-1}), i = 2 \ldots n$. Table 9 contains a detailed synopsis of cheap and expensive transition pairs. In particular, chains of the RETAIN transition in passages where the C_b does not change (passages with constant theme) show that the canonical ordering constraints for the *forward-looking centers* are not appropriate.

The numbers of centering transition pairs generated by the different approaches are shown in Table 10. In general, the functional approach shows the best results, while the naive and the canonical approaches work reasonably well for the literary text, but exhibit a poor performance for the texts from the IT domain and the news magazine. The results for the latter approaches become only slightly more positive with the modification of ranking the antecedent of a textual ellipsis above the elliptical expression, but they do not compare to the results of the functional approach.

We were also interested in finding out whether the functional ordering we propose possibly "includes" the grammatical role based criteria discussed so far. We, therefore, re-evaluated the examples already annotated with C_b/C_f data available in the literature (for the English language, we considered all examples from Grosz et al. (1995) and Brennan et al. (1987); for Japanese we took the data from Walker et al. (1994)). Surprisingly enough, all examples of Grosz et al. (1995) passed the test successfully. Only with respect to the troublesome *Alfa Romeo driving* scenario (cf. Brennan et al. (1987, p.157)) our constraints fail to properly rank the elements of the third sentence C_f of that example.[7] Note also that these results were achieved without having recourse to extra constraints, e.g., the shared property constraint to account for anaphora parallelism (Kameyama, 1986).

We applied our constraints to Japanese examples in the same way. Again we abandoned all extra constraints set up in these studies, e.g., the Zero Topic Assignment (ZTA) rule and the special role of empathy

[6] As a consequence of this postulate, we have to redefine Rule 2 of the Centering Constraints (Grosz et al., 1995, p.215) appropriately, which gives an informal characterization of a preference for sequences of CONTINUE over sequences of RETAIN and, similarly, sequences of RETAIN over sequences of SHIFT. Our specification for the case of text interpretation says that cheap transitions are preferred over expensive ones, with cheap and expensive transitions as defined in Table 9.

[7] In essence, the very specific problem addressed by that example seems to be that *Friedman* has not been previously introduced in the local discourse segment and is only accessible via the global focus.

	CONTINUE	RETAIN	SMOOTH-SHIFT	ROUGH-SHIFT
–	**cheap**	expensive	–	–
CONTINUE	**cheap**	**cheap**	expensive	expensive
RETAIN	expensive	expensive	**cheap**	expensive
SMOOTH-SHIFT	**cheap**	expensive	expensive	expensive
ROUGH-SHIFT	expensive	expensive	**cheap**	expensive

Table 9: Costs for Transition Pairs

	cost type	naive	naive & ante > express	canonical	canonical & ante > express	functional
IT	cheap	72	180	129	236	321
	expensive	317	209	260	153	68
Spiegel	cheap	25	36	45	51	62
	expensive	50	39	30	24	13
Müller	cheap	45	48	46	48	55
	expensive	34	31	33	31	24
Σ	cheap	142	264	220	335	438
	expensive	401	279	323	208	105

Table 10: Cost Values for Centering Transition Pair Types

verbs (Walker et al., 1994). However, the results our constraints generate are the same as those generated by Walker et al. including these model extensions. Only a single problematic case remains, *viz.* example (30) of Walker et al. (1994, p.214) causes the same problems they described (discourse-initial utterance, semantic or world knowledge should be available). Even for the crucial examples (32)-(36) of Walker et al. (1994, p.216-221) our constraints generate the same C_fs as Walker et al.'s constraints with ZTA.

To summarize the results of our empirical evaluation, we first claim that our proposal based on functional criteria leads to substantially better and — with respect to the inference load placed on the text understander, whether human or machine — more plausible results for languages with free word order than the structural constraints given by Grosz et al. (1995) and those underlying a naive approach. We base these observations on an evaluation approach which considers transition pairs in terms of the inference load specific pairs imply. Second, we have gathered some evidence, still far from being conclusive, that the functional constraints on centering seem to incorporate the structural constraints for English and the modified structural constraints for Japanese. Hence, we hypothesize that functional constraints on centering might constitute a general mechanism for treating free and fixed word order languages by the same descriptive mechanism. This claim, however, has to be further substantiated by additional cross-linguistic empirical studies.

5 Comparison with Related Approaches

The centering model (Grosz et al., 1983; 1995) is concerned with the interactions between the local coherence of discourse and the choices of referring expressions. Crucial for the centering model is the way the forward-looking centers are organized. Despite several cross-linguistic studies a kind of "standard" has emerged based on the study of English (cf. Table 1 in Section 1). Only few of these cross-linguistic studies have led to changes in the basic order of discourse entities, the work of Walker et al. (1990; 1994) being the most far reaching exception. They consider the role of expressive means in Japanese to indicate topic status and the speaker's perspective, thus introducing *functional* notions, viz. TOPIC and EMPATHY, into the discussion. German, the object language we deal with, is also a free word order language like Japanese (possibly even more constrained). Our basic revision of the ordering scheme completely abandons grammatical role information and replaces it with entirely functional notions reflecting the information structure of the utterances in the discourse. Interestingly enough, several extra assumptions introduced to account, e.g., for anaphora parallelism (e.g., the shared property constraint formulated by Kameyama (1986)) can be eliminated without affecting the correctness of anaphora resolutions. Rambow (1993) has presented a theme/rheme distinction within the centering model to which we fully subscribe. His proposal concerning the centering analysis of German (already referred to as the "naive" approach; cf. Section 4) is limited, however, to the German middlefield and, hence, incomplete.

A common topic of criticism relating to focusing approaches to anaphora resolution has been the diversity of data structures they require, which are likely to hide the underlying linguistic regularities. Focusing algorithms prefer the discourse element already in focus for anaphora resolution, thus considering context-boundedness, too. But the items of the focus lists are either ordered by thematic roles (Sidner,

1983) or grammatical roles (Suri & McCoy, 1994; Dahl & Ball, 1990)). Dahl & Ball (1990) improve the focusing mechanism by simplifying its data structures and, thus, their proposal is more closely related to the centering model than any other focusing mechanism. But their approach still relies upon grammatical information for the ordering of the centering list, while we use only the functional information structure as the guiding principle.

6 Conclusion

In this paper, we provided an account for ordering the forward-looking centers which is entirely based on functional notions, grounded on the information structure of utterances in a discourse. We motivated our proposal by the constraints which hold for a free word order language such as German and derived our results from data-intensive empirical studies of (real-world) expository texts. We have gathered preliminary evidence that the functional ordering of discourse entities in the centers seems to coincide with the grammatical roles of fixed word order languages. We also augmented the ordering criteria of the forward-looking center such that it accounts not only for (pro)nominal but also for functional anaphora (textual ellipsis), an issue that, so far, has only been sketchily dealt with in the centering framework. The extensions we propose have been validated by the empirical analysis of real-world expository texts of considerable length. We thus follow methodological principles of corpus-based studies that have been successfully exercised in the work of Passonneau (1993). Still open are proper descriptions of deictic expressions, proper names (cf. the *Alfa Romeo driving* scenario), and plural or generic definite noun phrases. An anaphora resolution module and an ellipsis handler based on this functional centering model has been implemented as part of a comprehensive text parser for German.

Acknowledgments. We would like to thank our colleagues in the $\mathcal{CLIF}$ group for fruitful discussions and Jon Alcantara (Cambridge, UK) for re-reading the final version via Internet. This work has been funded by *LGFG Baden-Württemberg* (M. Strube).

References

Brennan, S. E., M. W. Friedman & C. J. Pollard (1987). A centering approach to pronouns. In *Proc. of ACL-87*, pp. 155–162.

Clark, H. H. (1975). Bridging. In *Proc. of TINLAP-1*, pp. 169–174.

Cote, S. (1996). Ranking forward-looking centers. In E. Prince, A. Joshi & M. Walker (Eds.), *Centering in Discourse*. Oxford: Oxford University Press (to appear).

Dahl, D. A. & C. N. Ball (1990). Reference resolution in PUNDIT. In P. Saint-Dizier & S. Szpakowicz (Eds.), *Logic and Logic Grammars for Language Processing*, pp. 168–184. Chichester, U.K.: Ellis Horwood.

Dahl, Ö. (Ed.) (1974). *Topic and Comment, Contextual Boundness, and Focus*. Hamburg: Buske.

Daneš, F. (1974a). Functional sentence perspective and the organization of the text. In F. Daneš (Ed.), *Papers on Functional Sentence Perspective*, pp. 106–128. Prague: Academia.

Daneš, F. (Ed.) (1974b). *Papers on Functional Sentence Perspective*. Prague: Academia.

Gordon, P. C., B. J. Grosz & L. A. Gilliom (1993). Pronouns, names, and the centering of attention in discourse. *Cognitive Science*, 17:311–347.

Grosz, B. J., A. K. Joshi & S. Weinstein (1983). Providing a unified account of definite noun phrases in discourse. In *Proc. of ACL-83*, pp. 44–50.

Grosz, B. J., A. K. Joshi & S. Weinstein (1995). Centering: A framework for modeling the local coherence of discourse. *Computational Linguistics*, 21(2):203–225.

Hahn, U. & M. Strube (1996). Incremental centering and center ambiguity. In *Proc. of the 18th Annual Conference of the Cognitive Science Society. La Jolla, CA*.

Hahn, U., M. Strube & K. Markert (1996). Bridging textual ellipses. In *Proc. of COLING-96*.

Hajičová, E., V. Kuboň & P. Kuboň (1992). Stock of shared knowledge: A tool for solving pronominal anaphora. In *Proc. of COLING-92*, Vol. 1, pp. 127–133.

Hajičová, E., H. Skoumalová & P. Sgall (1995). An automatic procedure for topic-focus identification. *Computational Linguistics*, 21(1):81–94.

Halliday, M. A. K. (1967). Notes on transitivity and theme in English, Part 2. *Journal of Linguistics*, 3:199–244.

Halliday, M. A. K. & R. Hasan (1976). *Cohesion in English*. London: Longman.

Kameyama, M. (1986). A property-sharing constraint in centering. In *Proc. of ACL-86*, pp. 200–206.

Passonneau, R. J. (1993). Getting and keeping the center of attention. In M. Bates & R. Weischedel (Eds.), *Challenges in Natural Language Processing*, pp. 179–227. Cambridge, UK: Cambridge University Press.

Rambow, O. (1993). Pragmatic aspects of scrambling and topicalization in German. In *IRCS Workshop on Centering in Discourse. Univ. of Pennsylvania, 1993*.

Sidner, C. L. (1983). Focusing in the comprehension of definite anaphora. In M. Brady & R. Berwick (Eds.), *Computational Models of Discourse*, pp. 267–330. Cambridge, MA: MIT Press.

Strube, M. (1996). Processing complex sentences in the centering framework. In *this volume*.

Strube, M. & U. Hahn (1995). *ParseTalk* about sentence- and text-level anaphora. In *Proc. of EACL-95*, pp. 237–244.

Suri, L. Z. & K. F. McCoy (1994). RAFT/RAPR and centering: A comparison and discussion of problems related to processing complex sentences. *Computational Linguistics*, 20(2):301–317.

Turan, U. (1995). *Null vs. Overt Subjects in Turkish: A Centering Approach*. (Ph.D. thesis). University of Pennsylvania.

Walker, M. A., M. Iida & S. Cote (1990). Centering in Japanese discourse. In *Proc. of COLING-90, Appendix*, 6pp.

Walker, M. A., M. Iida & S. Cote (1994). Japanese discourse and the process of centering. *Computational Linguistics*, 20(2):193–233.

Mechanisms for Mixed-Initiative Human–Computer Collaborative Discourse

Curry I. Guinn

Department of Computer Science
Duke University
Box 90129
Durham, NC 27708
cig@cs.duke.edu

Center for Digital Systems Engineering
Research Triangle Institute
Box 12194
Research Triangle Park, NC 27709
cig@rti.org

Abstract

In this paper, we examine mechanisms for automatic dialogue initiative setting. We show how to incorporate initiative changing in a task-oriented human–computer dialogue system, and we evaluate the effects of initiative both analytically and via computer–computer dialogue simulation.

1 Motivation: Initiative in Task-Oriented Dialogues

Efficient human–computer dialogue requires immediate utterance-by-utterance accommodation to the needs of the interaction. The participants must continuously focus all concerns on the goals of the task and avoid extraneous paths. This means that the **dialogue initiative** should always pass immediately to the participant who is best able to handle the current task. An agent is said to have *dialogue initiative* over a mutual goal when that agent controls how that goal will be solved by the collaborators. In the implemented voice dialogue system "The Circuit Fix-it Shop" (Smith et al., 1992; Smith and Hipp, 1995), the dialogue fragment given in Figure 1 occurs between a human user and a computer collaborator. Utterances 2 and 4 indicate that the computer is directing the search for the missing wire in the faulty circuit. However, in Utterance 5 the user takes the initiative and suggests a different wire than has been proposed by the computer. In this paper we will present a theory explaining how initiative changes between participants and how computational agents can evaluate who should be in control of solving a goal.

1	U	The LED is displaying an alternately flashing one and the top corner of a seven.
2	C	There is supposed to be a wire between connector nine nine and connector one zero zero.
3	U	It is there.
4	C	There is supposed to be a wire between connector nine eight and connector one zero two.
5	U	There is no wire on connector **one zero four**. [*emphasis mine*]
6	C	There is supposed to be a wire between connector one zero four and connector one zero two.

Table 1: A Dialogue Fragment in the Circuit Fix-it Shoppe Domain

2 Automating Dialogue Initiative

Many implemented dialogue systems are question-answer systems with fixed initiative where one agent is in control and the other agent is passive (the master-slave assumption). For instance, in the LADDER system (Hendrix et al., 1978) the user has the initiative while the computer is passive. In contrast, the VODIS system (Young and Proctor, 1989) has the computer taking the initiative while the user is passive. Some dialogue systems (like GUS (Bobrow et al., 1977)) allow for a more mixed-initiative interaction; however, the places where the user can take the initiative are limited and defined *a priori*. The dialogue model of Smith (1995) allows for either the computer or the user to assume degrees of initiative; however, Smith presents no algorithm for the computer to change initiative during a dialogue. Our model of mixed-initiative dialogue allows either participant to be in control of the dialogue at any point in time.

Like Smith (1995) we believe that *the level of initiative in the dialogue should mirror the level of initiative in the task* (which is a corollary to Grosz's

(1978) *the structure of a dialog mirrors the structure of the underlying task*). Unlike previous research in dialogue initiative, however, we attach an initiative level to **each goal** in the task tree. Thus an agent may have initiative over one goal but not another. As goals get pushed and popped from the problem-solving stack, initiative changes accordingly. Thus many initiative changes are done implicitly based on which goal is being solved.

2.1 The Setting of Initiative Levels

In our model of dialogue, initiative levels for each goal are defined during the interaction based on 1) explicit and implicit initiative-changing utterances and 2) competency evaluation.

Explicit and Implicit Initiative-Changing Utterances Several researchers (Whittaker and Stenton, 1988; Walker and Whittaker, 1990) have noted that dialogue control can be exchanged through overt cues in the discourse. Our model concentrates on two specific dialogue cues: questions and answers. When an agent A_1 asks another agent A_2 to satisfy a goal G, agent A_2 gains initiative over goal G *and all subgoals of* G *until agent* A_2 *passes control of one of those subgoals back to agent* A_1. A similar initiative-setting mechanism is fired if agent A_1 announces that it cannot satisfy goal G. When a goal has been answered (satisfied) the problem-solving stack is popped. The initiative will now belong to whomever the initiative is for the goal on top of the stack.[1]. In the following human-computer dialogue gathered by Smith and Hipp(Smith and Hipp, 1995),

U: How do I fix this circuit?
C: What is the LED displaying?
U: Nothing.
C: What is the switch at?
U: Where is the switch?
C: In the lower left corner.
U: The switch is down.
C: Put the switch up.

all initiative changes can be accounted for by explicit initiative-changing utterances or by popping of the problem-solving stack due to goal resolution as illustrated in Figure 1.

Competency Evaluation for Initiative Setting How does an agent decide whether to ask its collaborator for help? An obvious approach is to ask for help when the agent is unable to satisfy a goal on its own. This approach is the basic mechanism for several dialogue systems (Young et al., 1989; Smith and Hipp, 1995; Guinn, 1994). An additional approach is to ask the collaborator for help if it is believed that the collaborator has a better chance of solving the goal (or solving it more efficiently). Such an evaluation requires knowledge of the collaborating agent's capabilities as well as an understanding of the agent's own capabilities.

Our methodology for evaluating competency involves a probabilistic examination of the search space of the problem domain. In the process of solving a goal, there may be many branches that can be taken in an attempt to prove a goal. Rather than selecting a branch at random, intelligent behavior involves evaluating (by some criteria) each possible branch that may lead toward the solution of a goal to determine which branch is more likely to lead to a solution. In this evaluation, certain important **factors** are examined to weight various branches. For example, during a medical exam, a patient may complain of dizziness, nausea, fever, headache, and itchy feet. The doctor may know of thousands of possible diseases, conditions, allergies, etc. To narrow the search, the doctor will try to find a pathology that accounts for these symptoms. There may be some diseases that account for all 5 symptoms, others that might account for 4 out of the 5 symptoms, and so on. In this manner, the practitioner sorts and prunes his list of possible pathologies. Competency evaluation will be based on how likely an agent's branch will be successful (based on a weighted factor analysis) and how likely the collaborator's branch will be successful (based on a weighted factor analysis and a probabilistic model of the collaborator's knowledge).

In Section 3 we will sketch out how this calculation is made, present several mode selection schemes based on this factor analysis, and show the results of analytical evaluation of these schemes. In Section 4 we will present the methodology and results of using these schemes in a simulated dialogue environment.

3 Mathematical Analysis of Efficiency

Our model of best-first search assumes that for each goal there exists a set of n factors, $f_1, \ldots, f_n$, which are used to guide the search through the problem-solving space. Associated with each factor are two weights, w_i, which is the percentage of times a successful branch will have that factor and x_i which is the percentage of all branches that satisfy f_i. If an agent, a, knows $q_1^a, \ldots, q_n^a$ percentage of the knowledge concerning factors $f_1, \ldots, f_n$, respectively, and assuming independence of factors, using Bayes' rule an agent can calculate the success likelihood of each

[1]Since each participant is carrying out initiative evaluation independently, there may be conflicts on who should be in control. Numerous researchers have studied how negotiation may be used to resolve these conflicts (Guinn, 1994; Guinn, 1993a; Lambert and Carberry, 1992; McRoy, 1993; Sidner, 1993)

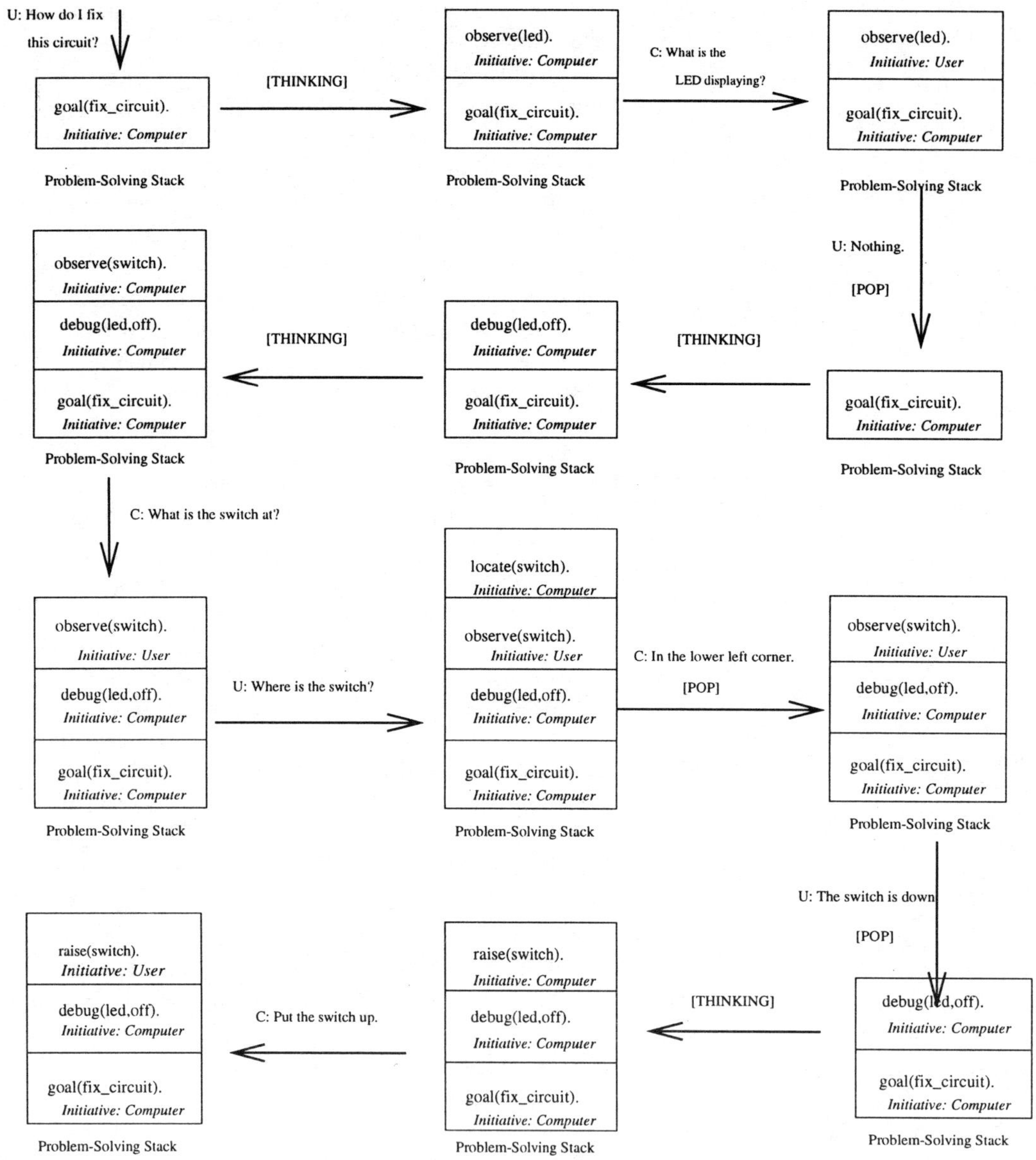

Figure 1: Tracking Initiative via Explicit Initiative-Changing Utterances and Problem-Solving Stack Manipulation

possible branch of a goal G that it knows:

$$p(b) = 1 - \prod_{i=1}^{n} 1 - F(i)w_i \frac{(1/k)}{x_i} \qquad (1)$$

where b is a branch out of a list of k branches and $F(i) = 1$ if the agent knows branch b satisfies factor f_i and $F(i) = x_i(1-q_i^a)$ otherwise. [Note: $x_i(1-q_i^a)$ is the probability that the branch satisfies factor f_i but the agent does not know this fact.] We define the sorted list of branches for a goal G that an agent knows, $[b_1^a, \ldots, b_k^a]$, where for each b_i^a, $p(b_i^a)$ is the likelihood that branch b_i^a will result in success where $p(b_i^a) >= p(b_j^a), \forall i < j$.

3.1 Efficiency Analysis of Dialogue Initiative

For efficient initiative-setting, it is also necessary to establish the likelihood of success for one's collaborator's 1st-ranked branch, 2nd-ranked branch, and so on. This calculation is difficult because the agent does not have direct access to its collaborator's knowledge. Again, we will rely on a probabilistic analysis. Assume that the agent does not know exactly what is in the collaborator's knowledge but does know the *degree* to which the collaborator knows about the factors related to a goal. Thus, in the medical domain, the agent may know that the collaborator knows more about diseases that account for dizziness and nausea, less about diseases that cause fever and headache, and nothing about diseases that cause itchy feet. For computational purposes these degrees of knowledge for each factor can be quantified: the agent, a, may know percentage q^a of the knowledge about diseases that cause dizziness while the collaborator, c, knows percentage q^c of the knowledge about these diseases. Suppose the agent has 1) a user model that states that the collaborator knows percentages $q_1^c, q_2^c, \ldots, q_n^c$ about factors $f_1, f_2, \ldots, f_n$, respectively and 2) a model of the domain which states the approximate number of branches, $\mathcal{N}$. Assuming independence, the expected number of branches which satisfy all n factors is $ExpAllN = \mathcal{N}\prod_{i=1}^{n} x_i$. Given that a branch satisfies all n factors, the likelihood that the collaborator will know that branch is $\prod_{i=1}^{n} q_i^c$. Therefore, the expected number of branches for which the collaborator knows all n factors is $ExpAllN \prod_{i=1}^{n} q_i^c$. The probability that one of these branches is a success-producing branch is $1-\prod_{i=1}^{n} 1-w_i\frac{(1/k)}{x_i}$ (from Equation 1). By computing similar probabilities for each combination of factors, the agent can compute the likelihood that the collaborator's first branch will be a successful branch, and so on. A more detailed account of this evaluation is given by Guinn (1993b; 1994).

We have investigated four initiative-setting schemes using this analysis. These schemes do not necessarily correspond to any observable human-human or human-computer dialogue behavior. Rather, they provide a means for exploring proposed dialogue initiative schemes.

Random In Random mode, one agent is given initiative at random in the event of a conflict. This scheme provides a baseline for initiative setting algorithms. Hopefully, a proposed algorithm will do better than Random.

SingleSelection In SingleSelection mode, the more knowledgeable agent (defined by which agent has the greater total percentage of knowledge) is given initiative. The initiative is set throughout the dialogue. Once a leader is chosen, the participants act in a master-slave fashion.

Continuous In Continuous mode, the more knowledgeable agent (defined by which agent's first-ranked branch is more likely to succeed) is initially given initiative. If that branch fails, this agent's second-ranked branch is compared to the other agent's first-ranked branch with the winner gaining initiative. In general if Agent 1 is working on its ith-ranked branch and Agent 2 is working on its jth-ranked branch, we compare $p^{A_1}(b_i^{A_1})$ to $p^{A_2}(b_j^{A_2})$.

Oracle In Oracle mode, an all-knowing mediator selects the agent that has the correct branch ranked highest in its list of branches. This scheme is an upper bound on the effectiveness of initiative setting schemes. No initiative setting algorithm can do better.

As knowledge is varied between participants we see some significant differences between the various strategies. Figure 2 summarizes this analysis. The x and y axis represent the amount of knowledge that each agent is given[2], and the z axis represents the percentage of branches explored from a single goal. SingleSelection and Continuous modes perform significantly better than Random mode. On average Continuous mode results in 40% less branches searched per goal than Random. Continuous mode

[2]This distribution is normalized to insure that all the knowledge is distributed between each agent. Agent 1 will have $q_1 + (1-q_1)(1-q_2)\frac{q_1}{q_1+q_2}$ percent of the knowledge while Agent 2 will have $q_2 + (1-q_1)(1-q_2)\frac{q_2}{q_1+q_2}$ percent of the knowledge. If $q_1 + q_2 = 0$, then set $q_1 = q_2 = 0.5$.

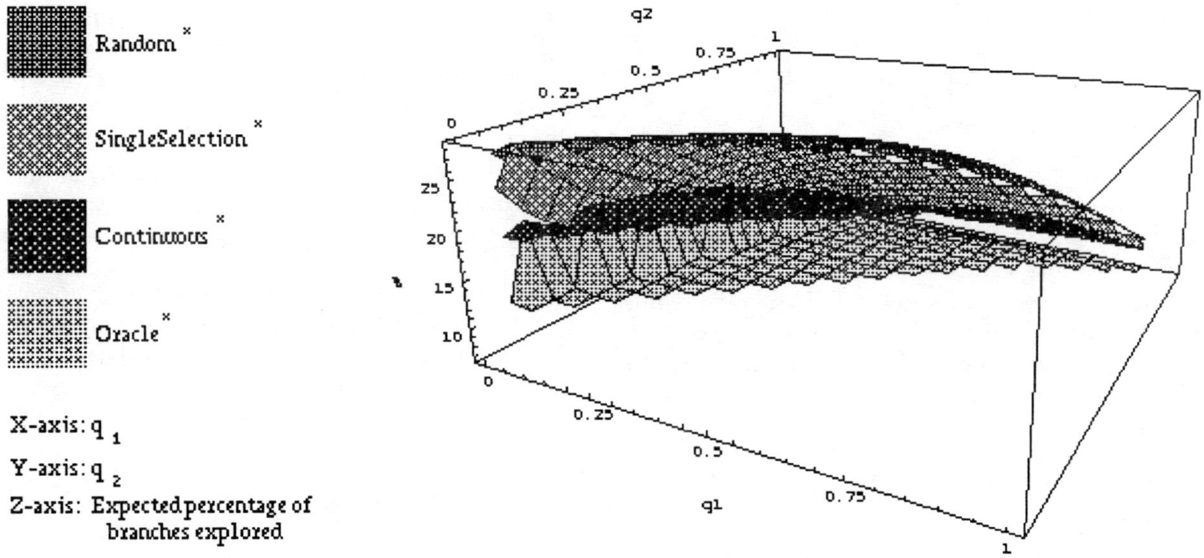

Figure 2: An Analytical Comparison of Dialogue Initiative-Setting Schemes

performs between 15-20% better than SingleSelection. The large gap between Oracle and Continuous is due to the fact that Continuous initiative selection is only using limited probabilistic information about the knowledge of each agent.

4 Computer Simulations

The dialogue model outlined in this paper has been implemented, and computer–computer dialogues have been carried out to evaluate the model and judge the effectiveness of various dialogue initiative schemes. In a methodology similar to that used by Power (1979), Carletta (1992) and Walker (1993), knowledge is distributed by a random process between agents, and the resulting interaction between these collaborating agents is observed. This methodology allows investigators to test different aspects of a dialogue theory. Details of this experimental strategy are given by Guinn (1995).

4.1 The Usage of Computer-Computer Dialogues

The use of computer-computer simulations to study and build human-computer dialogue systems is controversial. Since we are building computational models of dialogue, it is perfectly reasonable to explore these computational models through computer-computer simulations. The difficulty lies in what these simulations say about human-computer or computer-computer dialogues. This author argues that computer-computer simulations are one layer in the multi-layer process of building human-computer dialogue systems. Computer-computer simulations allow us to evaluate our computational models and explore issues that can not be resolved analytically. These simulations can help us prune out some mechanisms and suggest mechanisms that may work well in a human-computer system. For instance, if the dialogues that result in a computer-computer conversation are incoherent to a human observer, this suggests that the dialogue mechanisms employed may be inappropriate for a human-computer system. On the other hand, if the resulting dialogues are coherent and exhibit features that are desired in a human-computer system, this suggests that these mechanisms may work well in a human-computer system. The final test, of course, must be in the implementation of a human-computer dialogue system. The scarcity of such systems suggests that it is an extremely expensive process to build a functional human-computer dialogue system, and computer-computer simulations can assist in reducing these costs.

4.2 Simulation Results

A murder mystery domain was created with 22 suspects. An annotated example dialogue from a computer–computer collaboration in this domain is presented in Figure 3. Agents were given partial information through a random process. By using either Random mode or Continuous mode, we can evaluate the effect of those mechanisms in this experimental environment. Table 2 presents results computed from 5008 collaborations where the agents

Speaker	Utterance
Watson	Who is the murderer of Lord Dunsmore?[a]
Holmes	Is it the case that Suspect16 is the murderer of Lord Dunsmore?
Watson	Is it the case that Suspect16 had a motive to murder Lord Dunsmore?
Holmes	Suspect16 had a motive to murder Lord Dunsmore.
Watson	Is it the case that Suspect16 had access to the poison?
Holmes	I am unable to determine whether Suspect16 had access to the poison.
Watson	I am unable to determine whether Suspect16 is the murderer of Lord Dunsmore.
Holmes	I am unable to determine whether Suspect16 is the murderer of Lord Dunsmore.
Holmes	Who is the murderer of Lord Dunsmore?[b]
Watson	Is it the case that Suspect10 is the murderer of Lord Dunsmore?
Holmes	Is it the case that Suspect10 had a motive to murder Lord Dunsmore?
Watson	Suspect10 had a motive to murder Lord Dunsmore.
Holmes	Is it the case that Suspect10 had access to the poison?
Watson	Suspect10 had access to the poison.
Holmes	Is it the case that Suspect10 had an opportunity to administer the poison?
Watson	I am unable to determine whether Suspect10 had an opportunity to administer the poison.
Holmes	I am unable to determine whether Suspect10 is the murderer of Lord Dunsmore.
Watson	I am unable to determine whether Suspect10 is the murderer of Lord Dunsmore.
Watson	Is it the case that Suspect9 is the murderer of Lord Dunsmore?
Holmes	Is it the case that Suspect7 is the murderer of Lord Dunsmore?[c]
Watson	I have proven that Suspect9 has a motive to murder Lord Dunsmore and Suspect9 had access to the poison.[d]
Holmes	I have proven that Suspect7 had access to the poison, Suspect7 had an opportunity to administer the poison, and Suspect7 has a criminal disposition.[e]
Watson	Suspect7 is the murderer of Lord Dunsmore.[f]

[a] Watson gives control of the investigation over to Holmes. Each participant uses the Continuous Mode algorithm to determine who should be in control.

[b] Holmes is giving up control of directing the investigation here.

[c] Holmes is challenging Watson's investigative choice.

[d] Watson negotiates for his choice.

[e] Holmes negotiates for his choice.

[f] Watson now has enough information to prove that Suspect7 is the murderer.

Figure 3: A Sample Dialogue

had to communicate to solve the task.

	Random	Continuous
Times (secs)	82.398	44.528
# of Utterances	39.921	26.650
Suspects Examined	6.188	3.412

Table 2: Data on 5008 Non-trivial Dialogues from the Murder Mystery Domain

5 Extension to Human–Computer Dialogues

Currently, two spoken-dialogue human-computer systems are being developed using the underlying algorithms described in this paper. The Duke Programming Tutor instructs introductory computer science students how to write simple Pascal programs by providing multiple modes of input and output (voice/text/graphics) (Bierman et al., 1996). The Advanced Maintenance Assistant and Trainer (AMAT) currently being developed by Research Triangle Institute for the U.S. Army allows a maintenance trainee to converse with a computer assistant in the diagnosis and repair of a *virtual* M1A1 tank. While still in prototype development, preliminary results suggest that the algorithms that were successful for efficient computer–computer collaboration are capable of participating in *coherent* human–machine interaction. Extensive testing remains to be done to determine the actual gains in efficiency due to various mechanisms.

One tenet of our theory is that proper initiative setting requires an effective user model. There are several mechanisms we are exploring in acquiring the kind of user model information necessary for the previously described dialogue mode algorithms. Stereotypes (Rich, 1979; Chin, 1989) are a valuable tool in domains where user classification is possible and relevant. For instance, in the domain of military equipment maintenance, users can be easily classified by rank, years of experience, equipment familiarity and so on. An additional source of user model information can be dynamically obtained in environments where the user interacts for an extended period of time. A tutoring/training system has the advantage of knowing exactly what lessons a student has taken and how well the student did on individual lessons and questions. Dynamically modifying the user model based on on-going problem solving is difficult. One mechanism that may prove particularly effective is negotiating problem-solving strategies (Guinn, 1994). The quality of a collaborator's negotiation reflects the quality of its underlying knowledge. There is a tradeoff in that negotiation is expensive, both in terms of time and computational complexity. Thus, a synthesis of user modeling techniques will probably be required for effective and efficient collaboration.

6 Acknowledgements

Work on this project has been supported by grants from the National Science Foundation (NSF-IRI-92-21842), the Office of Naval Research (N00014-94-1-0938), and ACT II funding from STRICOM for the Combat Service Support Battlelab.

References

A. Bierman, C. Guinn, M. Fulkerson, G. Keim, Z. Liang, D Melamed, and K Rajagopalan. 1996. Goal-Oriented multimedia dialogue with variable initiative. In *submitted for publication.*

D.G. Bobrow, R.M. Kaplan, M. Kay, D.A. Norman, H. Thompson, and T. Winograd. 1977. GUS, a frame driven dialog system. *Artificial Intelligence*, 8:155–173.

J. Carletta. 1992. Planning to fail, not failing to plan: Risk-taking and recovery in task-oriented dialogue. In *Proceedings of the 14th International Conference on Computational Linguistics (COLING-92)*, pages 896–900, Nantes, France.

D.N. Chin. 1989. KNOME: Modeling what the user knows in UC. In A. Kobsa and W. Wahlster, editors, *User Models in Dialog Systems*, pages 74–107. Springer-Verlag, New York.

B. J. Grosz. 1978. Discourse analysis. In D. Walker, editor, *Understanding Spoken Language*, chapter IX, pages 235–268. Elsevier, North-Holland, New York, NY.

C.I. Guinn. 1993a. Conflict resolution in collaborative discourse. In *Computational Models of Conflict Management in Cooperative Problem Solving, Workshop Proceedings from the 13th International Joint Conference on Artificial Intelligence*, Chambery, France, August.

Curry I. Guinn. 1993b. A computational model of dialogue initiative in collaborative discourse. *Human-Computer Collaboration: Reconciling Theory, Synthesizing Practice, Papers from the 1993 Fall Symposium Series, Technical Report FS-93-05.*

Curry I. Guinn. 1994. *Meta-Dialogue Behaviors: Improving the Efficiency of Human–Machine Dialogue — A Computational Model of Variable Initiative and Negotiation in Collaborative Problem-Solving.* Ph.D. thesis, Duke University.

Curry I. Guinn. 1995. The role of computer–computer dialogues in human–computer dialogue system development. *AAAI Spring Symposium on Empirical Methods in Discourse Interpretation and Generation, Technical Report SS-95-06.*

G.G. Hendrix, E.D. Sacerdoti, D. Sagalowicz, and J. Slocum. 1978. Developing a natural language interface to complex data. *ACM Transactions on Database Systems*, pages 105–147, June.

L. Lambert and S. Carberry. 1992. Modeling negotiation subdialogues. *Proceedings of the 30th Annual Meeting of the Association for Computational Linguistics*, pages 193–200.

S. McRoy. 1993. Misunderstanding and the negotiation of meaning. *Human-Computer Collaboration: Reconciling Theory, Synthesizing Practice, Papers from the 1993 Fall Symposium Series, AAAI Technical Report FS-93-05*, September.

R. Power. 1979. The organization of purposeful dialogues. *Linguistics*, 17.

E. Rich. 1979. User modeling via stereotypes. *Cognitive Science*, 3:329–354.

C. L. Sidner. 1993. The role of negotiation in collaborative activity. *Human-Computer Collaboration: Reconciling Theory, Synthesizing Practice, Papers from the 1993 Fall Symposium Series, AAAI Technical Report FS-93-05*, September.

R.W. Smith and D.R. Hipp. 1995. *Spoken Natural Language Dialog Systems: A Practical Approach.* Oxford University Press, New York.

R.W. Smith, D.R. Hipp, and A.W Biermann. 1992. A dialog control algorithm and its performance. In *Proceedings of the 3rd Conference on Applied Natural Language Processing.*

M. Walker and S Whittaker. 1990. Mixed initiative in dialogue: An investigation into discourse segmentation. In *Proceedings of the 28th Annual Meeting of the Association for Computational Linguistics*, pages 70–78.

M. A. Walker. 1993. *Informational Redundancy and Resource Bounds in Dialogue.* Ph.D. thesis, University of Pennsylvania.

S. Whittaker and P. Stenton. 1988. Cues and control in expert-client dialogues. In *Proceedings of the 26th Annual Meeting of the Association for Computational Linguistics*, pages 123–130.

S.J. Young and C.E. Proctor. 1989. The design and implementation of dialogue control in voice operated database inquiry systems. *Computer Speech and Language*, 3:329–353.

S.R. Young, A.G. Hauptmann, W.H. Ward, E.T. Smith, and P. Werner. 1989. High level knowledge sources in usable speech recognition systems. *Communications of the ACM*, pages 183–194, August.

A Prosodic Analysis of Discourse Segments in Direction-Giving Monologues

Julia Hirschberg
AT&T Laboratories, 2C-409
600 Mountain Avenue
Murray Hill, NJ 07974

Christine H. Nakatani*
Harvard University
33 Oxford Street
Cambridge, MA 02138

Abstract

This paper reports on corpus-based research into the relationship between intonational variation and discourse structure. We examine the effects of speaking style (read versus spontaneous) and of discourse segmentation method (text-alone versus text-and-speech) on the nature of this relationship. We also compare the acoustic-prosodic features of initial, medial, and final utterances in a discourse segment.

1 Introduction

This paper presents empirical support for the assumption long held by computational linguists, that intonation can provide valuable cues for discourse processing. The relationship between intonational variation and discourse structure has been explored in a new corpus of direction-giving monologues. We examine the effects of speaking style (read versus spontaneous) and of discourse segmentation method (text-alone versus text-and-speech) on the nature of this relationship. We also compare the acoustic-prosodic features of initial, medial, and final utterances in a discourse segment. A better understanding of the role of intonation in conveying discourse structure will enable improvements in the naturalness of intonational variation in text-to-speech systems as well as in algorithms for recognizing discourse structure in speech-understanding systems.

2 Theoretical and Empirical Foundations

It has long been assumed in computational linguistics that discourse structure plays an important role in Natural Language Understanding tasks such as identifying speaker intentions and resolving anaphoric reference. Previous research has found that discourse structural information can be inferred from orthographic cues in text, such as paragraphing and punctuation; from linguistic cues in text or speech, such as CUE PHRASES[1] (Cohen, 1984; Reichman, 1985; Grosz and Sidner, 1986; Passonneau and Litman, 1993; Passonneau and Litman, to appear) and other lexical cues (Hinkelman and Allen, 1989); from variation in referring expressions (Linde, 1979; Levy, 1984; Grosz and Sidner, 1986; Webber, 1988; Song and Cohen, 1991; Passonneau and Litman, 1993), tense, and aspect (Schubert and Hwang, 1990; Song and Cohen, 1991); from knowledge of the domain, especially for task-oriented discourses (Grosz, 1978); and from speaker intentions (Carberry, 1990; Litman and Hirschberg, 1990; Lochbaum, 1994). Recent methods for automatic recognition of discourse structure from text have incorporated thesaurus-based and other information retrieval techniques to identify changes in topic (Morris and Hirst, 1991; Yarowsky, 1991; Iwańska et al., 1991; Hearst, 1994; Reynar, 1994).

Parallel investigations on prosodic/acoustic cues to discourse structure have investigated the contributions of features such as pitch range, pausal duration, amplitude, speaking rate, and intonational contour to signaling topic change. Variation in pitch range has often been seen as conveying 'topic structure' in discourse. Brown et al. (1980) found that subjects typically started new topics relatively high in their pitch range and finished topics by compressing their range. Silverman (1987) found that manipulation of pitch range alone, or in conjunction with pausal duration between utterances, facilitated the disambiguation of ambiguous topic structures. Avesani and Vayra (1988) also found variation in pitch range in professional recordings which appeared to correlate with topic structure, and Ayers (1992) found that pitch range correlates with hierarchical topic structure more closely in read than spontaneous conversational speech. Duration of pause between utterances or phrases has also been identi-

*The second author was partially supported by NSF Grants No. IRI-90-09018, No. IRI-93-08173, and No. CDA-94-01024 at Harvard University and by AT&T Bell Laboratories.

[1] Also called DISCOURSE MARKERS or DISCOURSE PARTICLES, these are items such as *now*, *first*, and *by the way*, which explicitly mark discourse structure.

fied as an indicator of topic structure, with longer pauses marking major topic shifts (Lehiste, 1979; Brown, Currie, and Kenworthy, 1980; Avesani and Vayra, 1988; Passonneau and Litman, 1993); Woodbury (1987), however, found no such correlation in his data. Amplitude was also found to increase at the start of a new topic and decrease at the end (Brown, Currie, and Kenworthy, 1980). Swerts and colleagues (1992) found that melody and duration can pre-signal the end of a discourse unit, in addition to marking the discourse-unit-final utterance itself. And speaking rate has been found to correlate with structural variation; in several studies (Lehiste, 1980; Brubaker, 1972; Butterworth, 1975) segment-initial utterances exhibited slower rates, and segment-final, faster rates. Swerts and Ostendorf (1995), however, report negative rate results.

In general, these studies have lacked an independently-motivated notion of discourse structure. With few exceptions, they rely on intuitive analyses of topic structure; operational definitions of discourse-level properties (e.g., interpreting paragraph breaks as discourse segment boundaries); or 'theory-neutral' discourse segmentations, where subjects are given instructions to simply mark changes in topic. Recent studies have focused on the question of whether discourse structure itself can be empirically determined in a reliable manner, a prerequisite to investigating linguistic cues to its existence. An intention-based theory of discourse was used in (Hirschberg and Grosz, 1992; Grosz and Hirschberg, 1992) to identify intonational correlates of discourse structure in news stories read by a professional speaker. Discourse structural elements were determined by experts in the Grosz and Sidner (1986) theory of discourse structure, based on either text alone or text and speech. This study revealed strong correlations of aspects of pitch range, amplitude, and timing with features of global and local structure for both segmentation methods. Passonneau and Litman (to appear) analyzed correlations of pause, as well as cue phrases and referential relations, with discourse structure; their segmenters were asked to identify speakers' communicative "actions". The present study addresses issues of speaking style and segmentation method while exploring in more detail than previous studies the prosodic parameters that characterize initial, medial, and final utterances in a discourse segment.

3 Methods

3.1 The Boston Directions Corpus

The current investigation of discourse and intonation is based on analysis of a corpus of spontaneous and read speech, the Boston Directions Corpus.[2] This corpus comprises elicited monologues produced by multiple non-professional speakers, who were given written instructions to perform a series of nine increasingly complex direction-giving tasks. Speakers first explained simple routes such as getting from one station to another on the subway, and progressed gradually to the most complex task of planning a round-trip journey from Harvard Square to several Boston tourist sights. Thus, the tasks were designed to require increasing levels of planning complexity. The speakers were provided with various maps, and could write notes to themselves as well as trace routes on the maps. For the duration of the experiment, the speakers were in face-to-face contact with a silent partner (a confederate) who traced on her map the routes described by the speakers. The speech was subsequently orthographically transcribed, with false starts and other speech errors repaired or omitted; subjects returned several weeks after their first recording to read aloud from transcriptions of their own directions.

3.2 Acoustic-Prosodic Analysis

For this paper, the spontaneous and read recordings for one male speaker were acoustically analyzed; fundamental frequency and energy were calculated using Entropic speech analysis software. The prosodic transcription, a more abstract representation of the intonational prominences, phrasing, and melodic contours, was obtained by hand-labeling. We employed the ToBI standard for prosodic transcription (Pitrelli, Beckman, and Hirschberg, 1994), which is based upon Pierrehumbert's theory of American English intonation (Pierrehumbert, 1980). The ToBI transcription provided us with a breakdown of the speech sample into minor or INTERMEDIATE PHRASES (Pierrehumbert, 1980; Beckman and Pierrehumbert, 1986). This level of prosodic phrase served as our primary unit of analysis for measuring both speech and discourse properties. The portion of the corpus we report on consists of 494 and 552 intermediate phrases for read and spontaneous speech, respectively.

3.3 Discourse Segmentation

In our research, the Grosz and Sidner (1986) theory of discourse structure, hereafter G&S, provides a foundation for segmenting discourses into constituent parts. According to this model, at least three components of discourse structure must be distinguished. The utterances composing the discourse divide into segments that may be embedded relative to one another. These segments and the embedding relationships between them form the LINGUISTIC STRUCTURE. The embedding relationships reflect changes in the ATTENTIONAL STATE, the dynamic record of the entities and attributes that are salient during a particular part of the discourse. Changes in linguistic structure, and hence atten-

[2]The Boston Directions Corpus was designed and collected in collaboration with Barbara Grosz.

tional state, depend on the discourse's INTENTIONAL STRUCTURE; this structure comprises the intentions or DISCOURSE SEGMENT PURPOSES (DSPs) underlying the discourse and relations between DSPs.

Two methods of discourse segmentation were employed by subjects who had expertise in the G&S theory. Following Hirschberg and Grosz (1992), three subjects labeled from text alone (group T) and three labeled from text and speech (group S). Other than this difference in input modality, all subjects received identical written instructions. The text for each task was presented with line breaks corresponding to intermediate phrase boundaries (i.e., ToBI BREAK INDICES of level 3 or higher (Pitrelli, Beckman, and Hirschberg, 1994)). In the instructions, subjects were essentially asked to analyze the linguistic and intentional structures by segmenting the discourse, identifying the DSPs, and specifying the hierarchical relationships among segments.

4 Results

4.1 Discourse Segmentation

4.1.1 Raw Agreement

Labels on which all labelers in the group agreed are termed the CONSENSUS LABELS.[3] The consensus labels for segment-initial (SBEG), segment-final (SF), and segment-medial (SCONT, defined as neither SBEG nor SF) phrase labels are given in Table 1.[4]

Table 1: Percentage of Consensus Labels by Segment Boundary Type

	SBEG	SF	SCONT	Total
READ (N=494)				
Text alone (T)	14%	11%	32%	57%
Text & Speech (S)	18%	14%	49%	80%
SPON (N=552)				
Text alone (T)	13%	10%	40%	61%
Text & Speech (S)	15%	13%	54%	81%

Note that group T and group S segmentations differ significantly, in contrast to earlier findings of Hirschberg and Grosz (1992) on a corpus of read-aloud news stories and in support of informal findings of Swerts (1995). Table 1 shows that group S produced significantly more consensus boundaries for both read ($p<.001$, χ=58.8, df=1) and spontaneous ($p<.001$, χ=55.4, df=1) speech than did group T. When the read and spontaneous data are pooled, group S agreed upon significantly more SBEG boundaries ($p<.05$, χ=4.7, df=1) as well as SF boundaries ($p<.05$, χ=4.4, df=1) than did group T. Further, it is not the case that text-alone segmenters simply chose to place fewer boundaries in the discourse; if this were so, then we would expect a high percentage of SCONT consensus labels where no SBEGs or SFs were identified. Instead, we find that the number of consensus SCONTs was significantly higher for text-and-speech labelings than for text-alone ($p<.001$, χ=49.1, df=1). It appears that the speech signal can help disambiguate among alternate segmentations of the same text. Finally, the data in Table 1 show that spontaneous speech can be segmented as reliably as its read counterpart, contrary to Ayer's results (1992).

[3] Use of consensus labels is a conservative measure of labeler agreement. Results in (Passonneau and Litman, 1993) and (Swerts, 1995) show that with a larger number of labelers, notions of BOUNDARY STRENGTH can be employed.

[4] Consensus percentages for the three types in Table 1 do not necessarily sum to the total consensus agreement percentage, since a phrase is both segment-initial and segment-final when it makes up a segment by itself.

4.1.2 Inter-labeler Reliability

Comparisons of inter-labeler reliability, that is, the reproducibility of a coding scheme given multiple labelers, provide another perspective on the segmentation data. How best to measure inter-labeler reliability for discourse segmentation tasks, especially for hierarchical segmentation, is an open research question (Passonneau and Litman, to appear; Carletta, 1995; Flammia and Zue, 1995; Rotondo, 1984; Swerts, 1995). For comparative purposes, we explored several measures proposed in the literature, namely, COCHRAN'S Q and the KAPPA (κ) COEFFICIENT (Siegel and Castellan, 1988). Cochran's Q, originally proposed in (Hirschberg and Grosz, 1992) to measure the likelihood that similarity among labelings was due to chance, was not useful in the current study; all tests of similarity using this metric (pairwise, or comparing all labelers) gave probability near zero. We concluded that this statistic did not serve, for example, to capture the differences observed between labelings from text alone versus labelings from text and speech.

Recent discourse annotation studies (Isard and Carletta, 1995; Flammia and Zue, 1995) have measured reliability using the κ coefficient, which factors out chance agreement taking the expected distribution of categories into account. This coefficient is defined as

$$\kappa = \frac{P_O - P_E}{1 - P_E}$$

where P_O represents the observed agreement and P_E represents the expected agreement. Typically, values of .7 or higher for this measure provide evidence of good reliability, while values of .8 or greater indicate high reliability. Isard and Carletta (1995) report pairwise κ scores ranging from .43 to .68 in a study of naive and expert classifications of types of 'moves' in the Map Task dialogues. For theory-neutral discourse segmentations of information-seeking dialogues, Flammia (Flammia and Zue, 1995) reports an average pairwise κ

of .45 for five labelers and of .68 for the three most similar labelers.

An important issue in applying the κ coefficient is how one calculates the expected agreement using prior distributions of categories. We first calculated the prior probabilities for our data based simply on the distribution of SBEG versus non-SBEG labels for all labelers on one of the nine direction-giving tasks in this study, with separate calculations for the read and spontaneous versions. This task, which represented about 8% of the data for both speaking styles, was chosen because it was midway in planning complexity and in length among all the tasks. Using these distributions, we calculated κ coefficients for each pair of labelers in each condition for the remaining eight tasks in our corpus. The observed percentage of SBEG labels, prior distribution for SBEG, average of the pairwise κ scores, and standard deviations for those scores are presented in Table 2.

Table 2: Comparison of Average κ Coefficients for SBEGs

	% SBEG	P_E	Avg. κ	s.d.
READ				
Text alone	.38	.53	.56	.08
Text & Speech	.35	.55	.81	.01
SPON				
Text alone	.39	.52	.63	.04
Text & Speech	.35	.55	.80	.03

The average κ scores for group T segmenters indicate weak inter-labeler reliability. In contrast, average κ scores for group S are .8 or better, indicating a high degree of inter-labeler reliability. Thus, application of this somewhat stricter reliability metric confirms that the availability of speech critically influences how listeners perceive discourse structure.

The calculation of reliability for SBEG versus non-SBEG labeling in effect tests the similarity of linearized segmentations and does not speak to the issue of how similar the labelings are in terms of hierarchical structure. Flammia has proposed a method for generalizing the use of the κ coefficient for hierarchical segmentation that gives an upper-bound estimate on inter-labeler agreement.[5] We applied this metric to our segmentation data, calculating weighted averages for pairwise κ scores averaged for each task. Results for each condition, together with the lowest and highest average κ scores over the tasks, are presented in Table 3.

[5] Flammia uses a flexible definition of segment match to calculate pairwise observed agreement: roughly, a segment in one segmentation is matched if both its SBEG and SF correspond to segment boundary locations in the other segmentation.

Table 3: Comparison of Weighted Average κ Coefficients and Extra for Each Condition Using Flammia's Metric

	% Weighted Average	Low	High
READ			
Text alone	0.51	.22	.67
Text & Speech	0.70	.48	.87
SPON			
Text alone	0.53	.19	.60
Text & Speech	0.74	.63	1.00

Once again, averaged scores of .7 or better for text-and-speech labelings, for both speaking styles, indicate markedly higher inter-labeler reliability than do scores for text-alone labelings, which averaged .51 and .53.

4.2 Intonational Features of Segments

4.2.1 Phrase Classes and Features

For purposes of intonational analysis, we take advantage of the high degree of agreement among our discourse labelers and include in each segment boundary class (SBEG, SF, and SCONT) only the phrases whose classification all subjects agreed upon. We term these the CONSENSUS-LABELED PHRASES, and compare their features to those of all phrases not in the relevant class (i.e., non-consensus-labeled phrases and consensus-labeled phrases of the other types). Note that there were one-third fewer consensus-labeled phrases for text-alone labelings than for text-and-speech (see Table 1). We examined the following acoustic and prosodic features of SBEG, SCONT, and SF consensus-labeled phrases: f0 maximum and f0 average;[6] rms (energy) maximum and rms average; speaking rate (measured in syllables per second); and duration of preceding and subsequent silent pauses. As for the segmentation analyses, we compared intonational correlates of segment boundary types not only for group S versus group T, but also for spontaneous versus read speech. While correlates *have* been identified in read speech, they have been observed in spontaneous speech only rarely and descriptively.

[6] We calculated f0 maximum in two ways: as simple f0 peak within the intermediate phrase and also as f0 maximum measured at the rms maximum of the sonorant portion of the nuclear-accented syllable in the intermediate phrase (HIGH F0 in the ToBI framework (Pitrelli, Beckman, and Hirschberg, 1994)). The latter measure proved more robust, so we report results based on this metric. The same applies to measurement of rms maximum. Average f0 and rms were calculated over the entire intermediate phrase.

Table 4: Acoustic-Prosodic Correlates of Consensus Labelings from Text Alone

	Max F0 (at HighF0)	Avg F0 (phrasal)	Max RMS (at HighF0)	Avg RMS (phrasal)	Rate	Preceding Pause	Subsequent Pause
SBEG							
Read	higher	higher	higher	higher		longer	shorter
Spon	higher	higher	higher	higher		longer	shorter
SCONT							
Read	lower	lower*†	lower*†	lower		shorter†	shorter†
Spon	lower				slower†	shorter†	shorter†
SF							
Read	lower	lower	lower	lower	faster*†	shorter	longer
Spon	lower	lower	lower	lower	faster†	shorter	longer

Table 5: Acoustic-Prosodic Correlates of Consensus Labelings from Text and Speech

	Max F0 (at HighF0)	Avg F0 (phrasal)	Max RMS (at HighF0)	Avg RMS (phrasal)	Rate	Preceding Pause	Subsequent Pause
SBEG							
Read	higher	higher	higher	higher		longer	shorter
Spon	higher	higher	higher	higher		longer	shorter
SCONT							
Read	lower	lower†		lower		shorter†	shorter†
Spon	lower				slower†	shorter†	shorter†
SF							
Read	lower	lower	lower	lower	faster*	shorter	longer
Spon	lower	lower	lower	lower	faster	shorter	longer

4.2.2 Global Intonational Correlates

We found strong correlations for consensus SBEG, SCONT, and SF phrases for all conditions. Results for group T are given in Table 4, and for group S, in Table 5.[7]

Consensus SBEG phrases in all conditions possess significantly higher maximum and average f0, higher maximum and average rms, shorter subsequent pause, and longer preceding pause. For consensus SCONT phrases, we found some differences between read and spontaneous speech for both labeling methods. Features for group T included significantly lower f0 maximum and average and lower rms maximum and average for read speech, but only lower f0 maximum for the spontaneous condition. Group S features for SCONT were identical to group T except for the absence of a correlation for maximum rms. While SCONT phrases for both speaking styles exhibited significantly shorter preceding and subsequent pauses than other phrases, only the spontaneous condition showed a significantly slower rate. For consensus SF phrases, we again found similar patterns for both speaking styles and both labeling methods, namely lower f0 maximum and average, lower rms maximum and average, faster speaking rate, shorter preceding pauses, and longer subsequent pauses.

While it may appear somewhat surprising that results for both labeling methods match so closely, in fact, correlations for text-and-speech labels presented in Table 5 were almost invariably statistically stronger than those for text-alone labels presented in Table 4. These more robust results for text-and-speech labelings occur even though the data set of consensus labels is considerably larger than the data set of consensus text-alone labelings.

4.2.3 Local Intonational Correlates

With a view toward automatically segmenting a spoken discourse, we would like to directly classify phrases of all three discourse categories. But SCONT and SF phrases exhibit similar prominence features and appear distinct from each other only in terms of timing differences. A second issue is whether such classification can be done 'on-line.' To address both of these issues, we made *pairwise* comparisons of consensus-labeled phrase groups using measures of *relative change* in acoustic-prosodic parameters over a local window of two consecutive phrases. Table 6 presents significant findings on relative changes in f0, loudness (measured in decibels), and speaking rate, from prior to current intermedi-

[7]T-tests were used to test for statistical significance of difference in the means of two classes of phrases. Results reported are significant at the .005 level or better, except where '*' indicates significance at the .03 level or better. Results were calculated using one-tailed t-tests, except where '†' indicates a two-tailed test.

Table 6: Acoustic-Prosodic Change from Preceding Phrase for Consensus Labelings from Text and Speech

	Max F0 Change (at HighF0s)	Max DB Change (at HighF0s)	Rate Change
SBEG versus SCONT			
Read	increase	increase	
Spon	increase	increase	
SCONT versus SF			
Read	increase*	increase*	
Spon		increase	
SBEG versus SF			
Read	increase	increase	
Spon	increase	increase	decrease*†

ate phrase.[8]

First, note that SBEG is distinguished from both SCONT and SF in terms of f0 change and db change from prior phrase; that is, while SBEG phrases are distinguished on a variety of measures from all other phrases (including non-consensus-labeled phrases) in Table 5, this table shows that SBEGs are also distinguishable directly from each of the other consensus-labeled categories. Second, while SCONT and SF appear to share prominence features in Table 5, Table 6 reveals differences between SCONT and SF in amount of f0 and db change. Thus, in addition to lending themselves to on-line processing, local measures may also capture valuable prominence cues to distinguish between segment-medial and segment-final phrases.

5 Conclusion

Although this paper reports results from only a single speaker, the findings are promising. We have demonstrated that a theory-based method for discourse analysis can provide reliable segmentations of spontaneous as well as read speech. In addition, the availability of speech in the text-and-speech labeling method led to significantly higher reliability scores. The stronger correlations found for intonational features of the text-and-speech labelings suggest not only that discourse labelers make use of prosody in their analyses, but also that obtaining such data can lead to more robust modeling of the relationship between intonation and discourse structure.

The following preliminary results can be considered for incorporation in such a model. First, segment-initial utterances differ from medial and final utterances in both prominence and rhythmic properties. Segment-medial and segment-final utterances are distinguished more clearly by rhythmic features, primarily pause. Finally, all correlations found for global parameters can also be computed based on relative change in acoustic-prosodic parameters in a window of two phrases.

Ongoing research is addressing the development of automatic classification algorithms for discourse boundary type; the role of prosody in conveying hierarchical relationships among discourse segments; individual speaker differences; and discourse segmentation methods that can be used by naive subjects.

[8]We present results only for text-and-speech labelings; results for text-alone were quite similar. Note that 'increase' means that there is a significantly greater increase in f0, rms, or rate from prior to current phrase for category 1 than for category 2 of the comparison, and 'decrease' means that there is a significantly greater decrease. T-tests again were one-tailed unless marked by †, and significance levels were .002 or better except those marked by *, which were at .01 or better.

References

Avesani, Cinzia and Mario Vayra. 1988. Discorso, segmenti di discorso e un' ipotesi sull' intonazione. In *Corso di stampa negli Atti del Convegno Internazionale "Sull'Interpunzione"*, Vallecchi, Firenze, Maggio, pages 8–53.

Ayers, Gayle M. 1992. Discourse functions of pitch range in spontaneous and read speech. Paper presented at the Linguistic Society of America Annual Meeting.

Beckman, Mary and Janet Pierrehumbert. 1986. Intonational structure in Japanese and English. *Phonology Yearbook*, 3:15–70.

Brown, G., K. Currie, and J. Kenworthy. 1980. *Questions of Intonation.* University Park Press, Baltimore.

Brubaker, R. S. 1972. Rate and pause characteristics of oral reading. *Journal of Psycholinguistic Research*, 1(2):141–147.

Butterworth, B. 1975. Hesitation and semantic planning in speech. *Journal of Psycholinguistic Research*, 4:75–87.

Carberry, Sandra. 1990. *Plan Recognition in Natural Language Dialogue.* MIT Press, Cambridge MA.

Carletta, Jean C. 1996. Assessing agreement on classification tasks: the kappa statistic. *Computational Linguistics*, 22(2), To appear.

Cohen, Robin. 1984. A computational theory of the function of clue words in argument understanding. In *Proceedings of the 10th International Conference on Computational Linguistics*, pages 251–255, Stanford.

Flammia, Giovanni and Victor Zue. 1995. Empirical evaluation of human performance and agreement in parsing discourse constituents in spoken dialogue. In *Proceedings of EUROSPEECH-95*, Volume 3, pages 1965–1968. Madrid.

Grosz, B. and J. Hirschberg. 1992. Some intonational characteristics of discourse structure. In *Proceedings of the 2nd International Conference on Spoken Language Processing*, pages 429-432, Banff, October.

Grosz, Barbara. 1978. Discourse analysis. In D. Walker, editor, *Understanding Spoken Language*. Elsevier, pages 235–268.

Grosz, Barbara J. and Candace L. Sidner. 1986. Attention, intentions, and the structure of discourse. *Computational Linguistics*, 12(3):175–204.

Hearst, Marti A. 1994. *Context and Structure in Automated Full-Text Information Access*. Ph.D. thesis, University of California at Berkeley. Available as Report No. UCB/CSD-94/836.

Hinkelman, E. and J. Allen. 1989. Two constraints on speech act ambiguity. In *Proceedings of the 27th Annual Meeting of the Association for Computational Linguistics*, pages 212–219, Vancouver.

Hirschberg, J. and B. Grosz. 1992. Intonational features of local and global discourse structure. In *Proceedings of the Speech and Natural Language Workshop*, pages 441–446, Harriman NY, DARPA, Morgan Kaufmann, February.

Isard, Amy and Jean Carletta. 1995. Transaction and action coding in the map task corpus. Research paper HCRC/RP–65, March, Human Communication Research Centre, University of Edinburgh, Edinburgh.

Iwańska, Lucja, Douglas Appelt, Damaris Ayuso, Kathy Dahlgren, Bonnie Glover Stalls, Ralph Grishman, George Krupka, Christine Montgomery, and Ellen Riloff. 1991. Computational aspects of discourse in the context of Muc-3. In *Proceedings of the Third Message Understanding Conference (Muc-3)*, pages 256–282, San Mateo, CA, Morgan Kaufmann, May.

Lehiste, I. 1979. Perception of sentence and paragraph boundaries. In B. Lindblom and S. Oehman, editors, *Frontiers of Speech Research*. Academic Press, London, pages 191–201.

Lehiste, I. 1980. Phonetic characteristics of discourse. Paper presented at the Meeting of the Committee on Speech Research, Acoustical Society of Japan.

Levy, Elena. 1984. *Communicating Thematic Structure in Narrative Discourse: The Use of Referring Terms and Gestures*. Ph.D. thesis, The University of Chicago, Chicago, June.

Linde, C. 1979. Focus of attention and the choice of pronouns in discourse. In T. Givon, editor, *Syntax and Semantics, Vol. 12: Discourse and Syntax*. The Academic Press, New York, pages 337–354.

Litman, Diane and Julia Hirschberg. 1990. Disambiguating cue phrases in text and speech. In *Proceedings of the 13th International Conference on Computational Linguistics*, pages 251–256, Helsinki, August.

Lochbaum, Karen. 1994. *Using Collaborative Plans to Model the Intentional Structure of Discourse*. Ph.D. thesis, Harvard University. Available as Tech Report TR-25-94.

Morris, J. and G. Hirst. 1991. Lexical cohesion computed by thesaural relations as an indicator of the structure of text. *Computational Linguistics*, 17:21–48.

Passonneau, R. and D. Litman. 1993. Feasibility of automated discourse segmentation. In *Proceedings of the 31st Annual Meeting of the Association for Computational Linguistics*, pages 148-155, Columbus.

Passonneau, Rebecca J. and Diane J. Litman. To Appear. Empirical analysis of three dimensions of spoken discourse: Segmentation, coherence and linguistic devices. In E. Hovy and D. Scott, editors, *Burning Issues in Discourse*. Springer Verlag.

Pierrehumbert, Janet B. 1980. *The Phonology and Phonetics of English Intonation*. Ph.D. thesis, Massachusetts Institute of Technology, September. Distributed by the Indiana University Linguistics Club.

Pitrelli, John, Mary Beckman, and Julia Hirschberg. 1994. Evaluation of prosodic transcription labeling reliability in the ToBI framework. In *Proceedings of the 3rd International Conference on Spoken Language Processing*, volume 2, pages 123–126, Yokohama.

Reichman, R. 1985. *Getting Computers to Talk Like You and Me: Discourse Context, Focus, and Semantics*. Bradford. The Massachusetts Institute of Technology, Cambridge.

Reynar, Jeffrey C. 1994. An automatic method of finding topic boundaries. In *Proceedings of the Student Session of the 32nd Annual Meeting of the Association for Computational Linguistics*, pages 331–333. Las Cruces, NM.

Rotondo, John A. 1984. Clustering analysis of subjective partitions of text. *Discourse Processes*, 7:69–88.

Schubert, L. K. and C. H. Hwang. 1990. Picking reference events from tense trees. In *Proceedings of the Speech and Natural Language Workshop*, pages 34–41, Hidden Valley PA. DARPA.

Siegel, S. and Jr. Castellan, N. John. 1988. *Nonparametric Statistics for the Behavioral Sciences.* McGraw-Hill, New York, second edition.

Silverman, K. 1987. *The Structure and Processing of Fundamental Frequency Contours.* Ph.D. thesis, Cambridge University, Cambridge UK.

Song, F. and R. Cohen. 1991. Tense interpretation in the context of narrative. In *Proceedings of the 9th National Conference of the American Association for Artificial Intelligence*, pages 131–136.

Swerts, M., R. Gelyukens, and J. Terken. 1992. Prosodic correlates of discourse units in spontaneous speech. In *Proceedings of the International Conference on Spoken Language Processing*, pages 421–428, Banff, Canada, October.

Swerts, Marc. 1995. Combining statistical and phonetic analyses of spontaneous discourse segmentation. In *Proceedings of the XIIth International Congress of Phonetic Sciences*, volume 4, pages 208–211, Stockholm, August.

Swerts, Marc and Mari Ostendorf. 1995. Discourse prosody in human-machine interactions. In *Proceedings ESCA Workshop on Spoken Dialogue Systems: Theories and Applications*, pages 205–208, Visgo, Denmark, May/June.

Webber, B. 1988. Discourse deixis: Reference to discourse segments. In *Proceedings of the 26th Annual Meeting of the Association for Computational Linguistics*, pages 113–122, Buffalo.

Woodbury, Anthony C. 1987. Rhetorical structure in a central Alaskan Yupik Eskimo traditional narrative. In J. Sherzer and A. Woodbury, editors, *Native American Discourse: Poetics and Rhetoric*, pages 176–239, Cambridge University Press, Cambridge UK.

Yarowsky, David. 1991. Personal communication, December.

An Information Structural Approach to Spoken Language Generation

Scott Prevost
The Media Laboratory
Massachusetts Institute of Technology
20 Ames Street
Cambridge, Massachusetts 02139-4307 USA
prevost@media.mit.edu

Abstract

This paper presents an architecture for the generation of spoken monologues with contextually appropriate intonation. A two-tiered *information structure* representation is used in the high-level content planning and sentence planning stages of generation to produce efficient, coherent speech that makes certain discourse relationships, such as explicit contrasts, appropriately salient. The system is able to produce appropriate intonational patterns that cannot be generated by other systems which rely solely on word class and given/new distinctions.

1 Introduction

While research on generating coherent *written* text has flourished within the computational linguistics and artificial intelligence communities, research on the generation of *spoken* language, and particularly intonation, has received somewhat less attention. In this paper, we argue that commonly employed models of text organization, such as schemata and rhetorical structure theory (RST), do not adequately address many of the issues involved in generating *spoken* language. Such approaches fail to consider contextually bound focal distinctions that are manifest through a variety of different linguistic and paralinguistic devices, depending on the language.

In order to account for such distinctions of focus, we employ a two-tiered *information structure* representation as a framework for maintaining local coherence in the generation of natural language. The higher tier, which delineates the *theme*, that which links the utterance to prior utterances, and the *rheme*, that which forms the core contribution of the utterance to the discourse, is instrumental in determining the high-level organization of information within a discourse segment. Dividing semantic representations into their thematic and rhematic parts allows propositions to be presented in a way that maximizes the shared material between utterances.

The lower tier in the information structure representation specifies the semantic material that is in "focus" within themes and rhemes. Material may be in focus for a variety of reasons, such as to emphasize its "new" status in the discourse, or to contrast it with other salient material. Such focal distinctions may affect the linguistic presentation of information. For example, the it-cleft in (1) may mark *John* as standing in contrast to some other recently mentioned person. Similarly, in (2), the pitch accent on *red* may mark the referenced car as standing in contrast to some other car inferable from the discourse context.[1]

(1) It was John who spoke first.

(2) Q: Which car did Mary drive?
A: (MARY drove)$_{th}$ (the RED car.)$_{rh}$
L+H* LH(%) H* LL$

By appealing to the notion that the simple rise-fall tune (H* LL%) very often accompanies the rhematic material in an utterance and the rise-fall-rise tune often accompanies the thematic material (Steedman, 1991; Prevost and Steedman, 1994), we present a spoken language generation architecture for producing short spoken monologues with contextually appropriate intonation.

2 Information Structure

Information Structure refers to the organization of information within an utterance. In particular, it

[1] In this example, and throughout the remainder of the paper, the intonation contour is informally noted by placing prosodic phrases in parentheses and marking pitch accented words with capital letters. The tunes are more formally annotated with a variant of (Pierrehumbert, 1980) notation described in (Prevost, 1995). Three different pause lengths are associated with boundaries in the modified notation. '(%)' marks intra-utterance boundaries with very little pausing, '%' marks intra-utterance boundaries associated with clauses demarcated by commas, and '$' marks utterance-final boundaries. For the purposes of generation and synthesis, these distinctions are crucial.

(3) Q: I know the AMERICAN amplifier produces MUDDY treble,
(But WHAT) (does the BRITISH amplifier produce?)
L+H* L(H%) H* LL$

A: (The BRITISH amplifier produces) (CLEAN treble.)

(The	BRITISH L+H* *theme-focus*	amplifier produces) L(H%)	(CLEAN H* *rheme-focus*	treble.) LL$
	Theme		*Rheme*	

(4) Q: I know the AMERICAN amplifier produces MUDDY treble,
(But WHAT) (produces CLEAN treble?)
L+H* L(H%) H* LL$

A: (The	BRITISH H* *rheme-focus*	amplifier) L(L%)	(produces	CLEAN L+H* *theme-focus*	treble.) LH$
	Rheme			*Theme*	

defines how the information conveyed by a sentence is related to the knowledge of the interlocutors and the structure of their discourse. Sentences conveying the same propositional content in different contexts need not share the same information structure. That is, information structure refers to how the semantic content of an utterance is packaged, and amounts to instructions for updating the models of the discourse participants. The realization of information structure in a sentence, however, differs from language to language. In English, for example, intonation carries much of the burden of information structure, while languages with freer word order, such as Catalan (Engdahl and Vallduví, 1994) and Turkish (Hoffman, 1995) convey information structure syntactically.

2.1 Information Structure and Intonation

The relationship between intonational structure and information structure is illustrated by (3) and (4). In each of these examples, the answer contains the same string words but different intonational patterns and information structural representations. The theme of each utterance is considered to be represented by the material repeated from the question. That is, the theme of the answer is what links it to the question and defines what the utterance is about. The rheme of each utterance is considered to be represented by the material that is new or forms the core contribution of the utterance to the discourse. By mapping the rise-fall tune (H* LL%) onto rhemes and the rise-fall-rise tune (L+H* LH%) onto themes (Steedman, 1991; Prevost and Steedman, 1994), we can easily identify the string of words over which these two prominent tunes occur directly from the information structure. While this mapping is certainly overly simplistic, the results presented in Section 4.3 demonstrate its appropriateness for the class of simple declarative sentences under investigation.

Knowing the strings of words to which these two tunes are to be assigned, however, does not provide enough information to determine the location of the pitch accents (H* and L+H*) within the tunes. Moreover, the simple mapping described above does not account for the frequently occurring cases in which thematic material bears no pitch accents and is consequently unmarked intonationally. Previous approaches to the problem of determining where to place accents have utilized heuristics based on "givenness." That is, content-bearing words (e.g. nouns and verbs) which had not been previously mentioned (or whose roots had not been previously mentioned) were assigned accents, while function words were de-accented (Davis and Hirschberg, 1988; Hirschberg, 1990). While these heuristics account for a broad range of intonational possibilities, they fail to account for accentual patterns that serve to contrast entities or propositions that were previously "given" in the discourse. Consider, for example the intonational pattern in (5), in which the pitch accent on *amplifier* in the response cannot be attributed to its being "new" to the discourse.

(5) Q: Do critics prefer the BRITISH amplifier
L* H
or the AMERICAN amplifier?
H* LL$
A: They prefer the AMERICAN amplifier.
H* LL$

For the determination of pitch accent placement, we rely on a secondary tier of information structure which identifies focused properties within themes and rhemes. The theme-foci and the rheme-foci mark the information that differentiates properties or entities in the current utterance from properties or entities established in prior utterances. Consequently, the semantic material bearing "new" information is considered to be in focus. Furthermore, the focus may include semantic material that serves to contrast an entity or proposition from alternative entities or propositions already established in the discourse. While the types of pitch accents (H* or L+H*) are determined by the theme/rheme delineation and the aforementioned mapping onto tunes, the locations of pitch accents are determined by the assignment of foci within the theme and rheme, as illustrated in (3) and (4). Note that it is in precisely those cases where thematic material, which is "given" by default, does not contrast with any other previously established properties or entities that this material is intonationally unmarked, as in (6).

(6) Q: Which amplifier does Scott PREFER?
H* LL$
A: (He prefers)$_{th}$ (the BRITISH amplifier.)$_{rh}$
H* LL$

2.2 Contrastive Focus Algorithm

The determination of contrastive focus, and consequently the determination of pitch accent locations, is based on the premise that each object in the knowledge base is associated with a set of alternatives from which it must be distinguished if reference is to succeed. The set of alternatives is determined by the hierarchical structure of the knowledge base. For the present implementation, only properties with the same parent or grandparent class are considered to be alternatives to one another.

Given an entity x and a referring expression for x, the contrastive focus feature for its semantic representation is computed on the basis of the contrastive focus algorithm described in (7), (8) and (9). The data structures and notational conventions are given below.

(7) *DElist*: a collection of discourse entities that have been evoked in prior discourse, ordered by recency. The list may be limited to some size k so that only the k most recent discourse entities pushed onto the list are retrievable.

$ASet(x)$: the set of alternatives for object x, i.e. those objects that belong to the same class as x, as defined in the knowledge base.

$RSet(x, S)$: the set of alternatives for object x as restricted by the referring expressions in *DElist* and the set of properties S.

$CSet(x, S)$: the subset of properties of S to be accented for contrastive purposes.

$Props(x)$: a list of properties for object x, ordered by the grammar so that nominal properties take precedence over adjectival properties.

The algorithm, which assigns contrastive focus in both thematic and rhematic constituents, begins by isolating the discourse entities in the given constituent. For each such entity x, the structures defined above are initialized as follows:

(8) $Props(x) := [P \mid P(x)$ is true in KB $]$
$ASet(x) := \{y \mid alt(x, y)\}$, x's alternatives
$RSet(x, \{\}) := \{x\} \cup \{y \mid y \in ASet(x)\ \&\ y \in DElist\}$, evoked alternatives
$CSet(x, \{\}) := \{\}$

The algorithm appears in pseudo-code in (9).[2]

(9)
```
S := {}
for each P in Props(x)
    RSet(x, S ∪ {P}) :=
        {y | y ∈ RSet(x, S) & P(y)}
    if RSet(x, S ∪ {P}) = RSet(x, S) then
        % no restrictions were made
        % based on property P.
        CSet(x, S ∪ {P}) := CSet(x, S)
    else
        % property P eliminated some
        % members of the RSet.
        CSet(x, S ∪ {P}) := CSet(x, S) ∪ {P}
    endif
    S := S ∪ {P}
endfor
```

In other words, given an object x, a list of its properties and a set of alternatives, the set of alternatives is restricted by including in the initial *RSet* only x and those objects that are explicitly referenced in the prior discourse. Initially, the set of properties to be contrasted (*CSet*) is empty. Then, for each property of x in turn, the *RSet* is restricted to include only those objects satisfying the given property in the knowledge base. If imposing this restriction on the *RSet* for a given property decreases the cardinality of the *RSet*, then the property serves to distinguish x from other salient alternatives evoked in the prior discourse, and is therefore added to the contrast set. Conversely, if imposing the restriction on the *RSet* for a given property does not change the *RSet*, the property is *not* necessary for distinguishing x from its alternatives, and is not added to the *CSet*.

Based on this contrastive focus algorithm and the mapping between information structure and intonation described above, we can view information structure as the representational bridge between discourse and intonational variability. The following sections elucidate how such a formalism can be integrated into the computational task of generating spoken language.

[2] An in-depth discussion of the algorithm and numerous examples are presented in (Prevost, 1995).

3 Generation Architecture

The task of natural language generation (NLG) has often been divided into three stages: content planning, in which high-level goals are satisfied and discourse structure is determined, sentence planning, in which high-level abstract semantic representations are mapped onto representations that more fully constrain the possible sentential realizations (Rambow and Korelsky, 1992; Reiter and Mellish, 1992; Meteer, 1991), and surface generation, in which the high-level propositions are converted into sentences.

The selection and organization of propositions and their divisions into theme and rheme are determined by the content planner, which maintains discourse coherence by stipulating that semantic information must be shared between consecutive utterances whenever possible. That is, the content planner ensures that the theme of an utterance links it to material in prior utterances.

The process of determining foci within themes and rhemes can be divided into two tasks: determining which discourse *entities* or *propositions* are in focus, and determining how their linguistic realizations should be marked to convey that focus. The first of these tasks can be handled in the content phase of the NLG model described above. The second of these tasks, however, relies on information, such as the construction of referring expressions, that is often considered the domain of the sentence planning stage. For example, although two discourse entities e_1 and e_2 can be determined to stand in contrast to one another by appealing only to the discourse model and the salient pool of knowledge, the method of contrastively distinguishing between them by the placement of pitch accents cannot be resolved until the choice of referring expressions has been made. Since referring expressions are generally taken to be in the domain of the sentence planner (Dale and Haddock, 1991), the present approach resolves issues of contrastive focus assignment at the sentence processing stage as well.

During the content generation phase, the content of the utterance is planned based on the previous discourse. While template-based systems (McKeown, 1985) have been widely used, rhetorical structure theory (RST) approaches (Mann and Thompson, 1986; Hovy, 1993), which organize texts by identifying rhetorical relations between clause-level propositions from a knowledge base, have recently flourished. Sibun (Sibun, 1991) offers yet another alternative in which propositions are linked to one another not by rhetorical relations or pre-planned templates, but rather by physical and spatial properties represented in the knowledge-base.

The present framework for organizing the content of a monologue is a hybrid of the template and RST approaches. The implementation, which is presented in the following section, produces descriptions of objects from a knowledge base with context-appropriate intonation that makes proper distinctions of contrast between alternative, salient discourse entities. Certain constraints, such as the requirement that objects be identified or defined at the beginning of a description, are reminiscent of McKeown's schemata. Rather than imposing strict rules on the order in which information is presented, the order is determined by domain specific knowledge, the communicative intentions of the speaker, and beliefs about the hearer's knowledge. Finally, the system includes a set of rhetorical constraints that may rearrange the order of presentation for information in order to make certain rhetorical relationships salient. While this approach has proven effective in the present implementation, further research is required to determine its usefulness for a broader range of discourse types.

4 The Prolog Implementation

The monologue generation program produces text and contextually-appropriate intonation contours to describe an object from the knowledge base. The system exhibits the ability to intonationally contrast alternative entities and properties that have been explicitly evoked in the discourse even when they occur with several intervening sentences.

4.1 Content Generation

The architecture for the monologue generation program is shown in Figure 1, in which arrows represent the computational flow and lines represent dependencies among modules. The remainder of this section contains a description of the computational path through the system with respect to a single example. The input to the program is a goal to describe an object from the knowledge base, which in this case contains a variety of facts about hypothetical stereo components. In addition, the input provides a communicative intention for the goal which may affect its ultimate realization, as shown in (10). For example, given the goal `describe(x)`, the intention `persuade-to-buy(hearer,x)` may result in a radically different monologue than the intention `persuade-to-sell(hearer,x)`.

(10) *Goal:* `describe e1`
Input: `generate(intention(bel(h1, good-to-buy(e1)))`

Information from the knowledge base is selected to be included in the output by a set of relations that determines the degree to which knowledge base facts and rules support the communicative intention of the speaker. For example, suppose the system "believes" that conveying the proposition in (11) moderately supports the intention of making hearer `h1` want to buy `e1`, and further that the rule in (12) is known by `h1`.

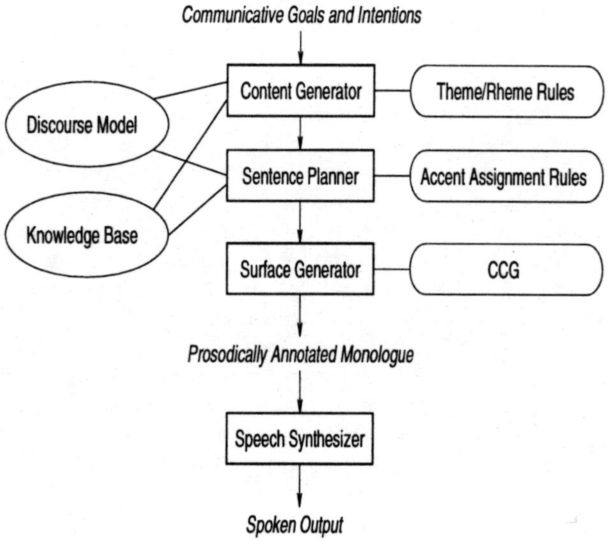

Figure 1: An Architecture for Monologue Generation

```
(11) bel(h1, holds(rating(X, powerful)))
```

```
(12) holds(rating(X, powerful)) :-
       holds(produce(X, Y)),
       holds(isa(Y, watts-per-channel)),
       holds(amount(Y, Z)),
       number(Z),
       Z >= 100.
```

The program then consults the facts in the knowledge base, verifies that the property does indeed hold and consequently includes the corresponding facts in the set of properties to be conveyed to the hearer, as shown in (13).

```
(13) holds(produce(e1, e7)).
     holds(isa(e7, watts-per-channel)).
     holds(amount(e7, 100)).
```

The content generator starts with a simple description template that specifies that an object is to be explicitly identified or defined before other propositions concerning it are put forth. Other relevant propositions concerning the object in question are then linearly organized according to beliefs about how well they contribute to the overall intention. Finally, a small set of rhetorical predicates rearranges the linear ordering of propositions so that sets of sentences that stand in some interesting rhetorical relationship to one another will be realized together in the output. These rhetorical predicates employ information structure to assist in maintaining the coherence of the output. For example, the *conjunction* predicate specifies that propositions sharing the same theme or rheme be realized together in order to avoid excessive topic shifting. The *contrast* predicate specifies that pairs of themes or rhemes that explicitly contrast with one another be realized together. The result is a set of properties roughly ordered by the degree to which they support the given intention, as shown in (14).

```
(14) holds(defn(isa(e1,amplifier)))
     holds(design(e1,solid-state),pres)
     holds(cost(e1,e9),pres)
     holds(produce(e1,e7),pres)
     holds(contrast(praise(e4,e1),
                    revile(e5,e1)),past)
```

The top-level propositions shown in (14) were selected by the program because the hearer (`h1`) is believed to be interested in the design of the amplifier and the reviews the amplifier has received. Moreover, the belief that the hearer is interested in buying an expensive, powerful amplifier justifies including information about its cost and power rating. Different sets of propositions would be generated for other (perhaps thriftier) hearers. Additionally, note that the propositions `praise(e4,e1)` and `revile(e5,e1)` are combined into the larger proposition `contrast(praise(e4,e1),revile(e5,e1))`. This is accomplished by the rhetorical constraints that determine the two propositions to be contrastive because `e4` and `e5` belong to the same set of alternative *entities* in the knowledge base and `praise` and `revile` belong to the same set of alternative *propositions* in the knowledge base.

The next phase of content generation recognizes the dependency relationships between the properties to be conveyed based on shared discourse entities. This phase, which represents an extension of the rhetorical constraints, arranges propositions to ensure that consecutive utterances share semantic material (cf. (McKeown et al., 1994)). This rule, which in effect imposes a strong bias for Centering Theory's *continue* and *retain* transitions (Grosz et al., 1986) determines the theme-rheme segmentation for each proposition.

4.2 Sentence Planning

After the coherence constraints from the previous section are applied, the sentence planner is responsible for making decisions concerning the form in which propositions are realized. This is accomplished by the following simple set of rules. First, Definitional `isa` properties are realized by the matrix verb. Other `isa` properties are realized by nouns or noun phrases. Top-level properties (such as those in (14)) are realized by the matrix verb. Finally, embedded properties (those evoked for building referring expressions for discourse entities) are realized by adjectival modifiers if possible and otherwise by relative clauses.

While there are certainly a number of linguistically interesting aspects to the sentence planner, the most important aspect for the present purposes is the determination of theme-foci and rheme-foci. The focus assignment algorithm employed by the sentence planner, which has access to both the discourse model and the knowledge base, works as follows. First, each property or discourse entity in the semantic and information structural representations is marked as either previously mentioned or new to the discourse. This assignment is made with respect to two data structures, the discourse entity list (DEList), which tracks the succession of entities through the discourse, and a similar structure for evoked properties. Certain aspects of the semantic form are considered unaccentable because they correspond to the interpretations of closed-class items such as function words. Items that are assigned focus based on their "newness" are assigned the $\circ$ focus operator, as shown in (15).

(15)	Semantics:	$defn(isa(\circ e1, \circ c1))$
	Theme:	$\circ e1$
	Rheme:	$\lambda x.isa(x, \circ c1)$
	Supporting Props:	$isa(c1, \circ amplifier)$
		$\circ design(c1, \circ solidstate)$

The second step in the focus assignment algorithm checks for the presence of contrasting propositions in the ISStore, a structure that stores a history of information structure representations. Propositions are considered contrastive if they contain two contrasting pairs of discourse entities, or if they contain one contrasting pair of discourse entities as well as contrasting functors.

Discourse entities are determined to be contrastive if they belong to the same set of alternatives in the knowledge base, where such sets are inferred from the `isa`-links that define class hierarchies. While the present implementation only considers entities with the same parent or grandparent class to be alternatives for the purposes of contrastive stress, a graduated approach that entails degrees of contrastiveness may also be possible.

The effects of the focus assignment algorithm are easily shown by examining the generation of an utterance that contrasts with the utterance shown in (15). That is, suppose the generation program has finished generating the output corresponding to the examples in (10) through (15) and is assigned the new goal of describing entity `e2`, a different amplifier. After applying the second step on the focus assignment algorithm, contrasting discourse entities are marked with the $\bullet$ contrastive focus operator, as shown in (16). Since `e1` and `e2` are both instances of the class **`amplifiers`** and `c1` and `c2` both describe the class **`amplifiers`** itself, these two pairs of discourse entities are considered to stand in contrastive relationships.

(16)	Semantics:	$defn(isa(\bullet e2, \bullet c2))$
	Theme:	$\bullet e2$
	Rheme:	$\lambda x.isa(x, \bullet c2)$
	Supporting Props:	$class(c2, amplifier)$
		$design(c2, \circ tube)$

While the previous step of the algorithm determined which abstract discourse entities and properties stand in contrast, the third step uses the contrastive focus algorithm described in Section 2 to determine which elements need to be contrastively focused for reference to succeed. This algorithm determines the minimal set of properties of an entity that must be "focused" in order to distinguish it from other salient entities. For example, although the representation in (16) specifies that `e2` stands in contrast to some other entity, it is the property of `e2` having a tube design rather than a solid-state design that needs to be conveyed to the hearer. After applying the third step of the focus assignment to (16), the result appears as shown in (17), with "tube" contrastively focused as desired.

(17)	Semantics:	$defn(isa(\bullet e2, \bullet c2))$
	Theme:	$\bullet e2$
	Rheme:	$\lambda x.isa(x, \bullet c2)$
	Supporting Props:	$isa(c2, amplifier)$
		$design(c2, \bullet tube)$

The final step in the sentence planning phase of generation is to compute a representation that can serve as input to a surface form generator based on Combinatory Categorial Grammar (CCG) (Steedman, 1991), as shown in (18).[3]

(18) **Theme:** $np(3, s)$:
$(e1\hat{\ }S)\hat{\ }def(e1, \bullet x5(e1)\&S)@u/rh$
Rheme: s :
$(act\hat{\ }pres)\hat{\ }indef(c1, (amplifier(c1)\&$
$\bullet tube(c1))\&isa(e1, c1))\backslash np(3, s) : e1@rh$

4.3 Results

Given the focus-marked output of the sentence planner, the surface generation module consults a CCG grammar which encodes the information structure/intonation mapping and dictates the generation of both the syntactic and prosodic constituents. The result is a string of words and the appropriate prosodic annotations, as shown in (19). The output of this module is easily translated into a form suitable for a speech synthesizer, which produces spoken output with the desired intonation.[4]

(19) The X5 is a TUBE amplifier.
$L{+}H^*_c$ L(H%) H^*_c LL$

The modules described above and shown in Figure 1 are implemented in Quintus Prolog. The system produces the types of output shown in (20) and

[3] A complete description of the CCG generator can be found in (Prevost and Steedman, 1993). CCG was chosen as the grammatical formalism because it licenses non-traditional syntactic constituents that are congruent with the bracketings imposed by information structure and intonational phrasing, as illustrated in (3).

[4] The system currently uses the AT&T Bell Laboratories TTS system, but the implementation is easily adaptable to other synthesizers.

(21), which should be interpreted as a single (two paragraph) monologue satisfying a goal to describe two different objects.[5] Note that both paragraphs include very similar types of information, but radically different intonational contours, due to the discourse context. In fact, if the intonational patterns of the two examples are interchanged, the resulting speech sounds highly unnatural.

(20) a. Describe the x4.
b. The X4
L+H* L(H%)
is a SOLID-state AMPLIFIER.
H* H* LL$
It COSTS EIGHT HUNDRED DOLLARS,
H* H* H* H* LL%
and PRODUCES
H*
ONE hundred watts-per-CHANNEL.
H* H* LL$
It was PRAISED by STEREOFOOL,
H^*_c $!H^*_c$ LH%
an AUDIO JOURNAL,
H* H* LH%
but was REVILED by AUDIOFAD,
H^*_c $!H^*_c$ LH%
ANOTHER audio journal.
H* LL$

(21) a. Describe the x5.
b. The X5 is a TUBE amplifier.
$L+H^*_c$ L(H%) H^*_c LL$
IT costs NINE hundred dollars,
$L+H^*_c$ L(H%) H^*_c LH%
produces TWO hundred watts-per-channel.
H^*_c LH%
and was praised
by Stereofool AND Audiofad.
H^*_c LL$

Several aspects of the output shown above are worth noting. Initially, the program assumes that the hearer has no specific knowledge of any particular objects in the knowledge base. Note however, that every proposition put forth by the generator is assumed to be incorporated into the hearer's set of beliefs. Consequently, the descriptive phrase "an audio journal," which is new information in the first paragraph, is omitted from the second. Additionally, when presenting the proposition '*Audiofad is an audio journal*,' the generator is able to recognize the similarity with the corresponding proposition about Stereofool (i.e. both propositions are abstractions over the single variable open proposition '*X is an audio journal*'). The program therefore interjects the *other* property and produces "another audio journal."

Several aspects of the contrastive intonational effects in these examples also deserve attention. Because of the content generator's use of the rhetorical contrast predicate, items are eligible to receive stress in order to convey contrast before the contrasting items are even mentioned. This phenomenon is clearly illustrated by the clause "PRAISED by STEREOFOOL" in (20), which is contrastively stressed before "REVILED by AUDIOFAD" is uttered. Such situations are produced only when the contrasting propositions are gathered by the content planner in a single invocation of the generator and identified as contrastive when the rhetorical predicates are applied. Moreover, unlike systems that rely solely on word class and given/new distinctions for determining accentual patterns, the system is able to produce contrastive accents on pronouns despite their "given" status, as shown in (21).

5 Conclusions

The generation architecture described above and implemented in Quintus Prolog produces paragraph-length, spoken monologues concerning objects in a simple knowledge base. The architecture relies on a mapping between a two-tiered information structure representation and intonational tunes to produce speech that makes appropriate contrastive distinctions prosodically. The process of natural language generation, in accordance with much of the recent literature in the field, is divided into three processes: high-level content planning, sentence planning, and surface generation. Two points concerning the role of intonation in the generation process are emphasized. First, since intonational phrasing is dependent on the division of utterances into theme and rheme, and since this division relates consecutive sentences to one another, matters of information structure (and hence intonational phrasing) must be largely resolved during the high-level planning phase. Second, since accentual decisions are made with respect to the particular linguistic realizations of discourse properties and entities (e.g. the choice of referring expressions), these matters cannot be fully resolved until the sentence planning phase.

6 Acknowledgments

The author is grateful for the advice and helpful suggestions of Mark Steedman, Justine Cassell, Kathy McKeown, Aravind Joshi, Ellen Prince, Mark Liberman, Matthew Stone, Beryl Hoffman and Kris Thórisson as well as the anonymous ACL reviewers. Without the AT&T Bell Laboratories TTS system, and the patient advice on its use from Julia Hirschberg and Richard Sproat, this work would not have been possible. This research was funded by NSF grants IRI91-17110 and IRI95-04372 and the generous sponsors of the MIT Media Laboratory.

[5] The implementation assigns slightly higher pitch to accents bearing the subscript c (e.g. H^*_c), which mark contrastive focus as determined by the algorithm describe above and in (Prevost, 1995).

References

Bolinger, D. (1989). *Intonation and Its Uses*. Stanford University Press.

Culicover, P. and Rochemont, M. (1983). Stress and focus in English. *Language*, 59:123–165.

Dale, R. and Haddock, N. (1991). Content determination in the generation of referring expressions. *Computational Intelligence*, 7(4):252–265.

Davis, J. and Hirschberg, J. (1988). Assigning intonational features in synthesized spoken discourse. In *Proceedings of the 26th Annual Meeting of the Association for Computational Linguistics*, pages 187–193, Buffalo.

Engdahl, E. and Vallduví, E. (1994). Information packaging and grammar architecture: A constraint-based approach. In Engdahl, E., editor, *Integrating Information Structure into Constraint-Based and Categorial Approaches (DYANA-2 Report R.1.3.B)*. CLLI, Amsterdam.

Grosz, B. J., Joshi, A. K., and Weinstein, S. (1986). Towards a computational theory of discourse interpretation. Unpublished manuscript.

Gussenhoven, C. (1983b). *On the Grammar and Semantics of Sentence Accent*. Foris, Dodrecht.

Halliday, M. (1970). Language structure and language function. In Lyons, J., editor, *New Horizons in Linguistics*, pages 140–165. Penguin.

Hirschberg, J. (1990). Accent and discourse context: Assigning pitch accent in synthetic speech. In *Proceedings of the Eighth National Conference on Artificial Intelligence*, pages 952–957.

Hoffman, B. (1995). *The Computational Analysis of the Syntax and Interpretation of 'Free' Word Order in Turkish*. PhD thesis, University of Pennsylvania, Philadelphia.

Hovy, E. (1993). Automated discourse generation using discourse structure relations. *Artificial Intelligence*, 63:341–385.

Mann, W. and Thompson, S. (1986). Rhetorical structure theory: Description and construction of text structures. In Kempen, G., editor, *Natural Language Generation: New Results in Artificial Intelligence, Psychology and Linguistics*, pages 279–300. Kluwer Academic Publishers, Boston.

McKeown, K., Kukich, K., and Shaw, J. (1994). Practical issues in automatic documentation generation. In *Proceedings of the Fourth ACL Conference on Applied Natural Language Processing*, pages 7–14, Stuttgart. Association for Computational Linguistics.

McKeown, K. R. (1985). *Text Generation: Using Discourse Strategies and Focus Constraints to Generate Natural Language Text*. Cambridge University Press, Cambridge.

Meteer, M. (1991). Bridging the generation gap between text planning and linguistic realization. *Computational Intelligence*, 7(4):296–304.

Pierrehumbert, J. (1980). *The Phonology and Phonetics of English Intonation*. PhD thesis, Massachusetts Institute of Technology. Distributed by Indiana University Linguistics Club, Bloomington, IN.

Prevost, S. (1995). *A Semantics of Contrast and Information Structure for Specifying Intonation in Spoken Language Generation*. PhD Thesis, University of Pennsylvania.

Prevost, S. and Steedman, M. (1993). Generating contextually appropriate intonation. In *Proceedings of the 6th Conference of the European Chapter of the Association for Computational Linguistics*, pages 332–340, Utrecht.

Prevost, S. and Steedman, M. (1994). Specifying intonation from context for speech synthesis. *Speech Communication*, 15:139–153.

Rambow, O. and Korelsky, T. (1992). Applied text generation. In *Proceedings of the Third Conference on Applied Natural Language Processing (ANLP-1992)*, pages 40–47.

Reiter, E. and Mellish, C. (1992). Using classification to generate text. In *Proceedings of the 30th Annual Meeting of the Association for Computational Linguistics*, pages 265–272.

Robin, J. (1993). A revision-based generation architecture for reporting facts in their historical context. In Horacek, H. and Zock, M., editors, *New Concepts in Natural Language Generation: Planning, Realization and Systems*, pages 238–265. Pinter Publishers, New York.

Rochemont, M. (1986). *Focus in Generative Grammar*. John Benjamins, Philadelphia.

Sibun, P. (1991). *The Local Organization and Incremental Generation of Text*. PhD thesis, University of Massachusetts.

Steedman, M. (1991a). Structure and intonation. *Language*, pages 260–296.

The Rhythm of Lexical Stress in Prose

Doug Beeferman
School of Computer Science
Carnegie Mellon University
Pittsburgh, PA 15213, USA
dougb+@cs.cmu.edu

Abstract

"Prose rhythm" is a widely observed but scarcely quantified phenomenon. We describe an information-theoretic model for measuring the regularity of lexical stress in English texts, and use it in combination with trigram language models to demonstrate a relationship between the probability of word sequences in English and the amount of rhythm present in them. We find that the stream of lexical stress in text from the Wall Street Journal has an entropy rate of less than 0.75 bits per syllable for common sentences. We observe that the average number of syllables per word is greater for rarer word sequences, and to normalize for this effect we run control experiments to show that the choice of word order contributes significantly to stress regularity, and increasingly with lexical probability.

1 Introduction

Rhythm inheres in creative output, asserting itself as the meter in music, the iambs and trochees of poetry, and the uniformity in distances between objects in art and architecture. More subtly there is widely believed to be rhythm in English prose, reflecting the arrangement of words, whether deliberate or subconscious, to enhance the perceived acoustic signal or reduce the burden of remembrance for the reader or author.

In this paper we describe an information-theoretic model based on lexical stress that substantiates this common perception and relates stress regularity in written speech (which we shall equate with the intuitive notion of "rhythm") to the probability of the text itself. By computing the *stress entropy rate* for both a set of *Wall Street Journal* sentences and a version of the corpus with randomized intra-sentential word order, we also find that word order contributes significantly to rhythm, particularly within highly probable sentences. We regard this as a first step in quantifying the extent to which metrical properties influence syntactic choice in writing.

1.1 Basics

In speech production, syllables are emitted as pulses of sound synchronized with movements of the musculature in the rib cage. Degrees of stress arise from variations in the amount of energy expended by the speaker to contract these muscles, and from other factors such as intonation. Perceptually stress is more abstractly defined, and it is often associated with "peaks of prominence" in some representation of the acoustic input signal (Ochsner, 1989).

Stress as a lexical property, the primary concern of this paper, is a function that maps a word to a sequence of discrete levels of physical stress, approximating the relative emphasis given each syllable when the word is pronounced. Phonologists distinguish between three levels of lexical stress in English: *primary*, *secondary*, and what we shall call *weak* for lack of a better substitute for *unstressed*. For the purposes of this paper we shall regard stresses as symbols fused serially in time by the writer or speaker, with words acting as building blocks of predefined stress sequences that may be arranged arbitrarily but never broken apart.

The *culminative* property of stress states that every content word has exactly one primary-stressed syllable, and that whatever syllables remain are subordinate to it. Monosyllabic function words such as *the* and *of* usually receive weak stress, while content words get one strong stress and possibly many secondary and weak stresses.

It has been widely observed that strong and weak tend to alternate at "rhythmically ideal disyllabic distances" (Kager, 1989a). "Ideal" here is a complex function involving production, perception, and many unknowns. Our concern is not to pinpoint this ideal, nor to answer precisely why it is sought by speakers and writers, but to gauge *to what extent* it is sought.

We seek to investigate, for example, whether the avoidance of primary stress *clash*, the placement of two or more strongly stressed syllables in succession, influences syntactic choice. In the Wall Street Journal corpus we find such sentences as "The **fol**-low-ing **is**-sues **re**-cent-ly were **filed** with the Se-**cur**-i-ties and Ex-**change** Com-**mis**-sion". The phrase "recently were filed" can be syntactically permuted as "were filed recently", but this clashes *filed* with the first syllable of *recently*. The chosen sentence avoids consecutive primary stresses. Kager postulates with a decidedly information theoretic undertone that the resulting binary alternation is "simply the maximal degree of rhythmic organization compatible with the requirement that adjacent stresses are to be avoided." (Kager, 1989a)

Certainly we are not proposing that a hard decision based only on metrical properties of the output is made to resolve syntactic choice ambiguity, in the case above or in general. Clearly semantic emphasis has its say in the decision. But it is our belief that rhythm makes a nontrivial contribution, and that the tools of statistics and information theory will help us to estimate it formally. Words are the building blocks. How much do their selection (diction) and their arrangement (syntax) act to enhance rhythm?

1.2 Past models and quantifications

Lexical stress is a well-studied subject at the intra-word level. Rules governing how to map a word's orthographic or phonetic transcription to a sequence of stress values have been searched for and studied from rules-based, statistical, and connectionist perspectives.

Word-external stress regularity has been denied this level of attention. Patterns in phrases and compound words have been studied by Halle (Halle and Vergnaud, 1987) and others, who observe and reformulate such phenomena as the emphasis of the penultimate constituent in a compound noun (*National Center for* Supercomputing *Applications*, for example.) Treatment of *lexical* stress across word boundaries is scarce in the literature, however. Though prose rhythm inquiry is more than a hundred years old (Ochsner, 1989), it has largely been dismissed by the linguistic community as irrelevant to formal models, as a mere curiosity for literary analysis. This is partly because formal methods of inquiry have failed to present a compelling case for the existence of regularity (Harding, 1976).

Past attempts to quantify prose rhythm may be classified as perception-oriented or signal-oriented. In both cases the studies have typically focussed on regularities in the distance between peaks of prominence, or interstress intervals, either perceived by a human subject or measured in the signal. The former class of experiments relies on the subjective segmentation of utterances by a necessarily limited number of participants—subjects tapping out the rhythms they perceive in a waveform on a recording device, for example (Kager, 1989b). To say nothing of the psychoacoustic biases this methodology introduces, it relies on too little data for anything but a sterile set of means and variances.

Signal analysis, too, has not yet been applied to very large speech corpora for the purpose of investigating prose rhythm, though the technology now exists to lend efficiency to such studies. The experiments have been of smaller scope and geared toward detecting isochrony, regularity in absolute *time*. Jassem *et al.*(Jassem, Hill, and Witten, 1984) use statistical techniques such as regression to analyze the duration of what they term *rhythm units*. Jassem postulates that speech is composed of extra-syllable *narrow* rhythm units with roughly fixed duration independent of the number of syllable constituents, surrounded by variable-length *anacruses*. Abercrombie (Abercrombie, 1967) views speech as composed of metrical *feet* of variable length that begin with and are conceptually highlighted by a single stressed syllable.

Many experiments lead to the common conclusion that English is *stress-timed*, that there is some regularity in the absolute duration between strong stress events. In contrast to postulated syllable-timed languages like French in which we find exactly the inverse effect, speakers of English tend to expand and to contract syllable streams so that the duration between bounding primary stresses matches the other intervals in the utterance. It is unpleasant for production and perception alike, however, when too many weak-stressed syllables are forced into such an interval, or when this amount of "padding" varies wildly from one interval to the next. Prose rhythm analysts so far have not considered the syllable stream independent from syllabic, phonemic, or interstress duration. In particular they haven't measured the regularity of the purely lexical stream. They have instead continually re-answered questions concerning isochrony.

Given that speech can be divided into interstress units of roughly equal duration, we believe the more interesting question is whether a speaker or writer modifies his diction and syntax to fit a regular number of *syllables* into each unit. This question can only be answered by a lexical approach, an approach that pleasingly lends itself to efficient experimentation with very large amounts of data.

2 Stress entropy rate

We regard every syllable as having either strong or weak stress, and we employ a purely lexical, context independent mapping, a pronunciation dictionary [1], to tell us which syllables in a word receive which level of stress. We base our experiments on a binary-valued symbol set $\Sigma_1 = \{W, S\}$ and on a ternary-valued symbol set $\Sigma_2 = \{W, S, P\}$, where 'W' indicates weak stress, 'S' indicates strong stress,

[1] We use the 116,000-entry *CMU Pronouncing Dictionary version 0.4* for all experiments in this paper.

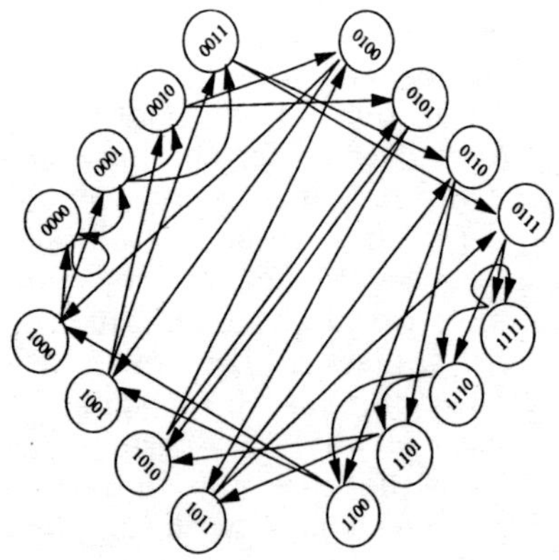

Figure 2: A 5-gram model viewed as a first-order Markov chain

and 'P' indicates a pause. Abstractly the dictionary maps words to sequences of symbols from {primary, secondary, unstressed}, which we interpret by downsampling to our binary system—primary stress is strong, non-stress is weak, and secondary stress ('2') we allow to be either weak or strong depending on the experiment we are conducting.

We represent a sentence as the concatenation of the stress sequences of its constituent words, with 'P' symbols (for the Σ_2 experiments) breaking the stream where natural pauses occur.

Traditional approaches to lexical language modeling provide insight on our analogous problem, in which the input is a stream of syllables rather than words and the values are drawn from a vocabulary Σ of stress levels. We wish to create a model that yields approximate values for probabilities of the form $p(s_k | s_0, s_1, \ldots, s_{k-1})$, where $s_i \in \Sigma$ is the stress symbol at syllable i in the text. A model with separate parameters for each history is prohibitively large, as the number of possible histories grows exponentially with the length of the input; and for the same reason it is impossible to train on limited data. Consequently we partition the history space into equivalence classes, and the stochastic n-gram approach that has served lexical language modeling so well treats two histories as equivalent if they end in the same $n-1$ symbols.

As Figure 2 demonstrates, an n-gram model is simply a stationary Markov chain of order $k = n - 1$, or equivalently a first-order Markov chain whose states are labeled with tuples from Σ^k.

To gauge the regularity and compressibility of the training data we can calculate the *entropy rate* of the stochastic process as approximated by our model, an upper bound on the expected number of bits needed to encode each symbol in the best possible encoding. Techniques for computing the entropy rate of a stationary Markov chain are well known in information theory (Cover and Thomas, 1991). If $\{X_i\}$ is a Markov chain with stationary distribution μ and transition matrix P, then its entropy rate is $H(\mathcal{X}) = -\sum_{i,j} \mu_i p_{ij} \log p_{ij}$.

The probabilities in P can be trained by accumulating, for each $(s_1, s_2, \ldots, s_k) \in \Sigma^k$, the k-gram count in $C(s_1, s_2, \ldots, s_k)$ in the training data, and normalizing by the $(k-1)$-gram count $C(s_1, s_2, \ldots, s_{k-1})$.

The stationary distribution μ satisfies $\mu P = \mu$, or equivalently $\mu_k = \sum_j \mu_j p_{j,k}$ (Parzen, 1962). In general finding μ for a large state space requires an eigenvector computation, but in the special case of an n-gram model it can be shown that the value in μ corresponding to the state $(s_1, s_2, \ldots, s_k)$ is simply the k-gram frequency $C(s_1, s_2, \ldots, s_k)/N$, where N is the number of symbols in the data.[2] We therefore can compute the entropy rate of a stress sequence in time linear in both the amount of data and the size of the state space. This efficiency will enable us to experiment with values of n as large as seven; for larger values the amount of training data, not time, is the limiting factor.

3 Methodology

The training procedure entails simply counting the number of occurrences of each n-gram for the training data and computing the stress entropy rate by the method described. As we treat each sentence as an independent event, no cross-sentence n-grams are kept: only those that fit between sentence boundaries are counted.

3.1 The meaning of stress entropy rate

We regard these experiments as computing the entropy rate of a Markov chain, estimated from training data, that approximately models the emission of symbols from a random source. The entropy rate bounds how compressible the training sequence is, and not precisely how predictable unseen sequences from the same source would be. To measure the efficacy of these models in prediction it would be necessary to divide the corpus, train a model on one subset, and measure the entropy rate of the other with respect to the trained model. Compression can take place off-line, after the entire training set is read, while prediction cannot "cheat" in this manner.

But we claim that our results predict how effective prediction would be, for the small state space in our Markov model and the huge amount of training data translate to very good state coverage. In language modeling, unseen words and unseen n-grams are a serious problem, and are typically combatted with smoothing techniques such as the backoff model and the discounting formula offered by Good and Turing. In our case, unseen "words" never occur, for

[2] This ignores edge effects, for $\sum_s C(s_1, s_2, \ldots, s_k) = N - k + 1$, but this discrepancy is negligible when N is very large.

Lis	ten	to	me	close	ly	I'll	en	deav	or	to	ex	plain	/
S	W	S	S	S	W	S	W	S	W	S	W	S	P

what	sep	ar	ates	a	char	la	tan	from	a	Char	le	magne	.
W	S	W	2	W	S	W	W	S	W	S	W	2	P

Figure 1: A song lyric exemplifies a highly regular stress stream (from the musical *Pippin* by Stephen Schwartz.)

the tiniest of realistic training sets will cover the binary or ternary vocabulary. Coverage of the n-gram set is complete for our prose training texts for n as high as eight; nor do singleton states (counts that occur only once), which are the bases of Turing's estimate of the frequency of untrained states in new data, occur until $n = 7$.

3.2 Lexicalizing stress

Lexical stress is the "backbone of speech rhythm" and the primary tool for its analysis. (Baum, 1952) While the precise acoustical prominences of syllables within an utterance are subject to certain word-external hierarchical constraints observed by Halle (Halle and Vergnaud, 1987) and others, lexical stress is a local property. The stress patterns of individual words within a phrase or sentence are generally context independent.

One source of error in our method is the ambiguity for words with multiple phonetic transcriptions that differ in stress assignment. Highly accurate techniques for part-of-speech labeling could be used for stress pattern disambiguation when the ambiguity is purely lexical, but often the choice, in both production and perception, is dialectal. It would be straightforward to divide among all alternatives the count for each n-gram that includes a word with multiple stress patterns, but in the absence of reliable frequency information to weight each pattern we chose simply to use the pronunciation listed first in the dictionary, which is judged by the lexicographer to be the most popular. Very little accuracy is lost in making this assumption. Of the 115,966 words in the dictionary, 4635 have more than one pronunciation; of these, 1269 have more than one distinct stress pattern; of these, 525 have different primary stress placements. This smallest class has a few common words (such as "refuse" used as a noun and as a verb), but most either occur infrequently in text (obscure proper nouns, for example), or have a primary pronunciation that is overwhelmingly more common than the rest.

4 Experiments

The efficiency of the n-gram training procedure allowed us to exploit a wealth of data—over 60 million syllables—from 38 million words of *Wall Street Journal* text. We discarded sentences not completely covered by the pronunciation dictionary, leaving 36.1 million words and 60.7 million syllables for experimentation.

Our first experiments used the binary Σ_1 alphabet. The maximum entropy rate possible for this process is one bit per syllable, and given the unigram distribution of stress values in the data (55.2% are primary), an upper bound of slightly over 0.99 bits can be computed. Examining the 4-gram frequencies for the entire corpus (Figure 3a) sharpens this substantially, yielding an entropy rate estimate of 0.846 bits per syllable. Most frequent among the 4-grams are the patterns WSWS and SWSW, consistent with the principle of binary alternation mentioned in section 1.

The 4-gram estimate matches quite closely with the estimate of 0.852 bits that can be derived from the distribution of word stress patterns excerpted in Figure 3b. But both measures overestimate the entropy rate by ignoring longer-range dependencies that become evident when we use larger values of n. For $n = 6$ we obtain a rate of 0.795 bits per syllable over the entire corpus.

Since we had several thousand times more data than is needed to make reliable estimates of stress entropy rate for values of n less than 7, it was practical to subdivide the corpus according to some criterion, and calculate the stress entropy rate for each subset as well as for the whole. We chose to divide at the sentence level and to partition the 1.59 million sentences in the data based on a likelihood measure suitable for testing the hypothesis from section 1.

A lexical trigram backoff-smoothed language model was trained on separate data to estimate the language *perplexity* of each sentence in the corpus. Sentence perplexity $PP(S)$ is the inverse of sentence probability normalized for length, $1/P(S)^{\frac{1}{|S|}}$, where $P(S)$ is the probability of the sentence according to the language model and $|S|$ is its word count. This measure gauges the average "surprise" after revealing each word in the sentence as judged by the trigram model. The question of whether more probable word sequences are also more rhythmic can be approximated by asking whether sentences with lower perplexity have lower stress entropy rate.

Each sentence in the corpus was assigned to one of one hundred bins according to its perplexity—sentences with perplexity between 0 and 10 were assigned to the first bin; between 10 and 20, the sec-

(a)

WWWW:	0.78%	WSWW:	6.91%	SWWW:	2.96%	SSWW:	3.94%
WWWS:	2.94%	WSWS:	11.00%	SWWS:	7.80%	SSWS:	8.59%
WWSW:	6.97%	WSSW:	6.16%	SWSW:	11.21%	SSSW:	6.25%
WWSS:	3.71%	WSSS:	6.06%	SWSS:	8.48%	SSSS:	6.27%

(b)

S	45.87%
SW	18.94%
W	9.54%
SWW	5.74%
WS	5.14%
WSW	4.54%

Figure 3: (a) The corpus frequencies of all binary stress 4-grams (based on 60.7 million syllables), with secondary stress mapped to "weak" (W). (b) The corpus frequencies of the top six lexical stress patterns.

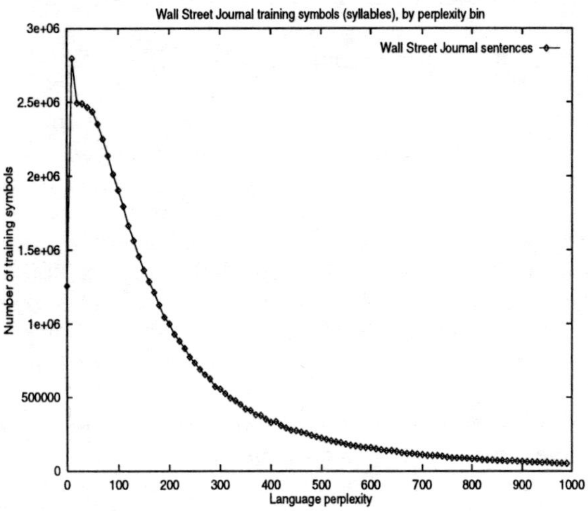

Figure 4: The amount of training data, in syllables, in each perplexity bin. The bin at perplexity level *pp* contains all sentences in the corpus with perplexity no less than *pp* and no greater than *pp* + 10. The smallest count (at bin 990) is 50662.

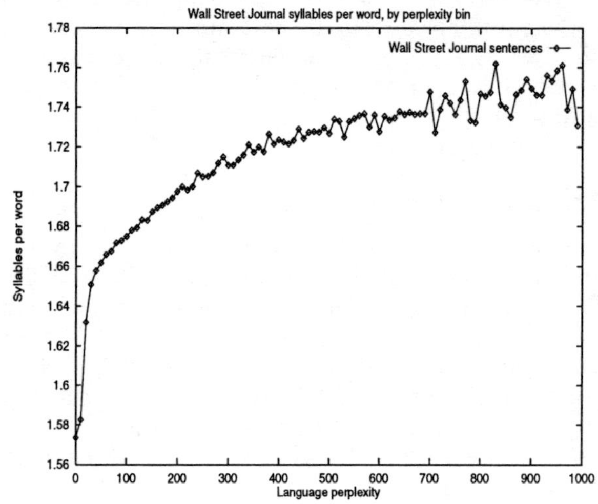

Figure 5: The average number of syllables per word for each perplexity bin.

ond; and so on. Sentences with perplexity greater than 1000, which numbered roughly 106 thousand out of 1.59 million, were discarded from all experiments, as 10-unit bins at that level captured too little data for statistical significance. A histogram showing the amount of training data (in syllables) per perplexity bin is given in Figure 4.

It is crucial to detect and understand potential sources of bias in the methodology so far. It is clear that the perplexity bins are well trained, but not yet that they are comparable with each other. Figure 5 shows the average number of syllables per word in sentences that appear in each bin. That this function is roughly increasing agrees with our intuition that sequences with longer words are rarer. But it biases our perplexity bins at the extremes. Early bins, with sequences that have a small syllable rate per word (1.57 in the 0 bin, for example), are predisposed to a lower stress entropy rate since primary stresses, which occur roughly once per word, are more frequent. Later bins are also likely to be prejudiced in that direction, for the inverse reason: The increasing frequency of multisyllabic words makes it more and more fashionable to transit to a weak-stressed syllable following a primary stress, sharpening the probability distribution and decreasing entropy.

This is verified when we run the stress entropy rate computation for each bin. The results for n-gram models of orders 3 through 7, for the case in which secondary lexical stress is mapped to the "weak" level, are shown in Figure 6.

All of the rates calculated are substantially less than a bit, but this only reflects the stress regularity inherent in the vocabulary and in word selection, and says nothing about word arrangement. The atomic elements in the text stream, the words, contribute regularity independently. To determine how much is contributed by the way they are glued together, we need to remove the bias of word choice.

For this reason we settled on a model size, $n = 6$, and performed a variety of experiments with both the original corpus and with a control set that contained exactly the same bins with exactly the same sentences, but mixed up. Each sentence in the control set was permuted with a pseudorandom sequence of swaps based on an insensitive function of the original; that is to say, identical sentences in the

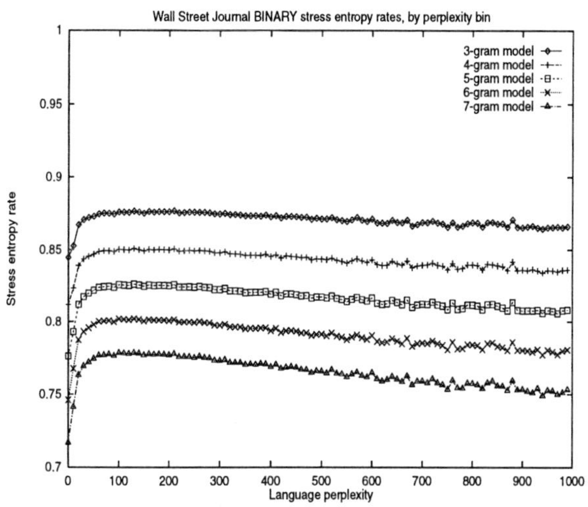

Figure 6: n-gram stress entropy rates for Σ_1, weak secondary stress

corpus were shuffled the same way and sentences differing by only one word were shuffled similarly. This allowed us to keep steady the effects of multiple copies of the same sentence in the same perplexity bin. More importantly, these tests hold everything constant—diction, syllable count, syllable rate per word—except for syntax, the arrangement of the chosen words within the sentence. Comparing the unrandomized results with this control experiment allows us, therefore, to factor out everything *but* word order. In particular, subtracting the stress entropy rates of the original sentences from the rates of the randomized sentences gives us a figure, relative entropy, that estimates how many bits we save by knowing the proper word order given the word choice. The results for these tests for weak and strong secondary stress are shown in Figures 7 and 8, including the difference curves between the randomized-word and original entropy rates.

The consistently positive difference function demonstrates that there *is* some extra stress regularity to be had with proper word order, about a hundredth of a bit on average. The difference is small indeed, but its consistency over hundreds of well-trained data points puts the observation on statistically solid ground.

The negative slopes of the difference curves suggests a more interesting conclusion: As sentence perplexity increases, the gap in stress entropy rate between syntactic sentences and randomly permuted sentences narrows. Restated inversely, using entropy rates for randomly permuted sentences as a baseline, sentences with higher sequence probability are relatively more rhythmical in the sense of our definition from section 1.

To supplement the Σ_1 binary vocabulary tests we ran the same experiments with $\Sigma_2 = \{0, 1, P\}$, introducing a pause symbol to examine how stress behaves near phrase boundaries. Commas, dashes, semicolons, colons, ellipses, and all sentence-terminating punctuation in the text, which were removed in the Σ_1 tests, were mapped to a single pause symbol for Σ_2. Pauses in the text arise not only from semantic constraints but also from physiological limitations. These include the "breath groups" of syllables that influence both vocalized and written production. (Ochsner, 1989). The results for these experiments are shown in Figures 9 and 10. Expectedly, adding the symbol increases the confusion and hence the entropy, but the rates remain less than a bit. The maximum possible rate for a ternary sequence is $\log_2 3 \approx 1.58$.

The experiments in this section were repeated with a larger perplexity interval that partitioned the corpus into 20 bins, each covering 50 units of perplexity. The resulting curves mirrored the finer-grain curves presented here.

5 Conclusions and future work

We have quantified lexical stress regularity, measured it in a large sample of written English prose, and shown there to be a significant contribution from word order that increases with lexical perplexity.

This contribution was measured by comparing the entropy rate of lexical stress in natural sentences with randomly permuted versions of the same. Randomizing the word order in this way yields a fairly crude baseline, as it produces asyntactic sequences in which, for example, single-syllable function words can unnaturally clash. To correct for this we modified the randomization algorithm to permute only open-class words and to fix in place determiners, particles, pronouns, and other closed-class words. We found the entropy rates to be consistently midway between the fully randomized and unrandomized values. But even this constrained randomization is weaker than what we'd like. Ideally we should factor out semantics as well as word choice, comparing each sentence in the corpus with its grammatical variations. While this is a difficult experiment to do automatically, we're hoping to approximate it using a natural language generation system based on link grammar under development by the author.

Also, we're currently testing other data sources such as the Switchboard corpus of telephone speech (Godfrey, Holliman, and McDaniel, 1992) to measure the effects of rhythm in more spontaneous and grammatically relaxed texts.

6 Acknowledgments

Comments from John Lafferty, Georg Niklfeld, and Frank Dellaert contributed greatly to this paper. The work was supported in part by an ARPA AASERT award, number DAAH04-95-1-0475.

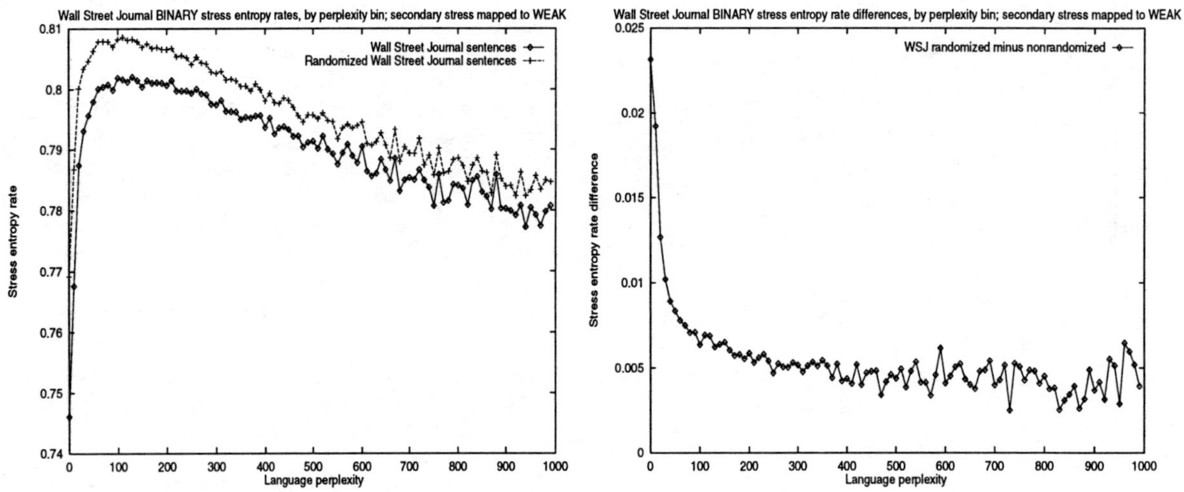

Figure 7: 6-gram stress entropy rates and difference curve for Σ_1, weak secondary stress

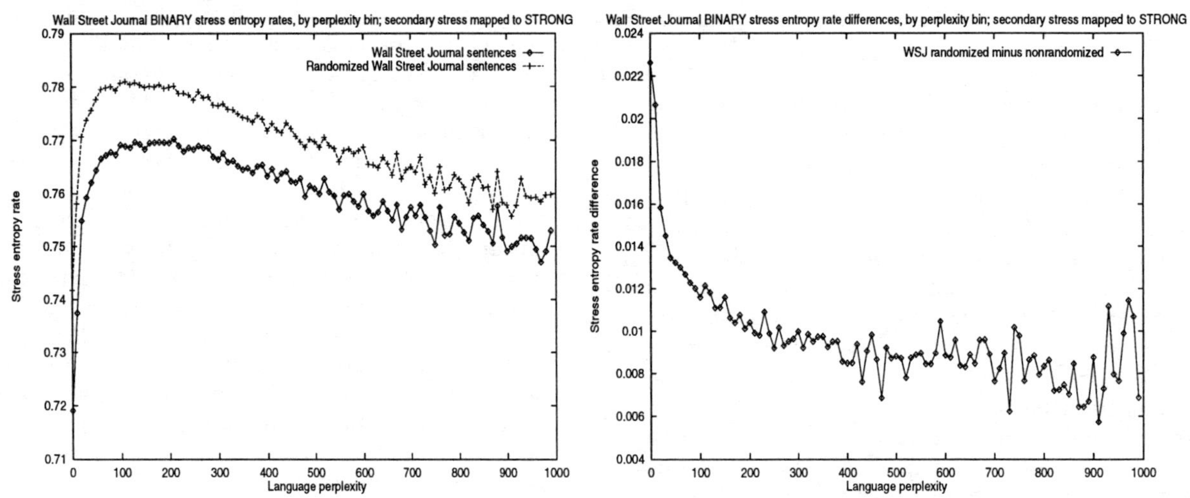

Figure 8: 6-gram entropy rates and difference curve for Σ_1, strong secondary stress

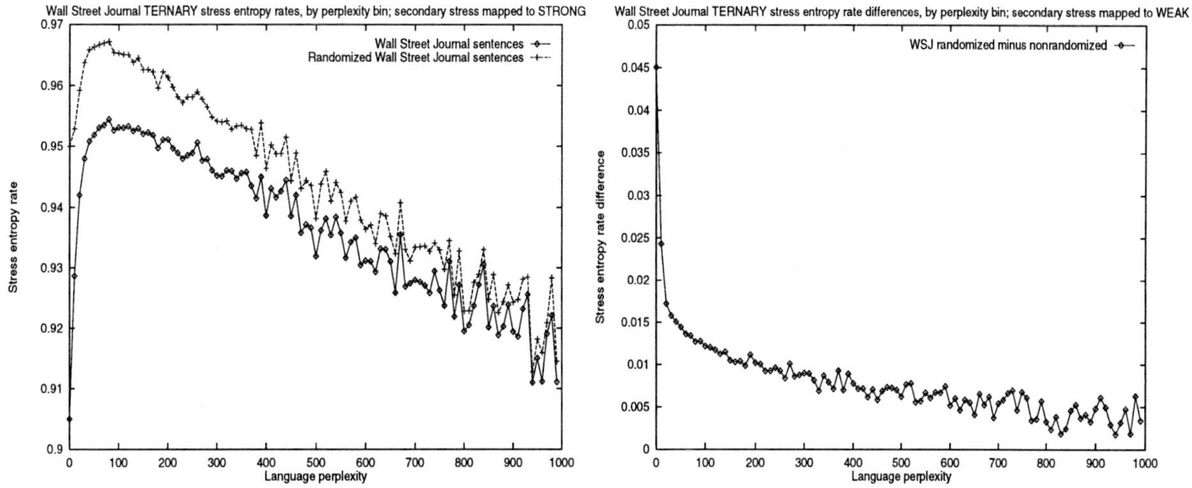

Figure 9: 6-gram entropy rates and difference curve for Σ_2, weak secondary stress

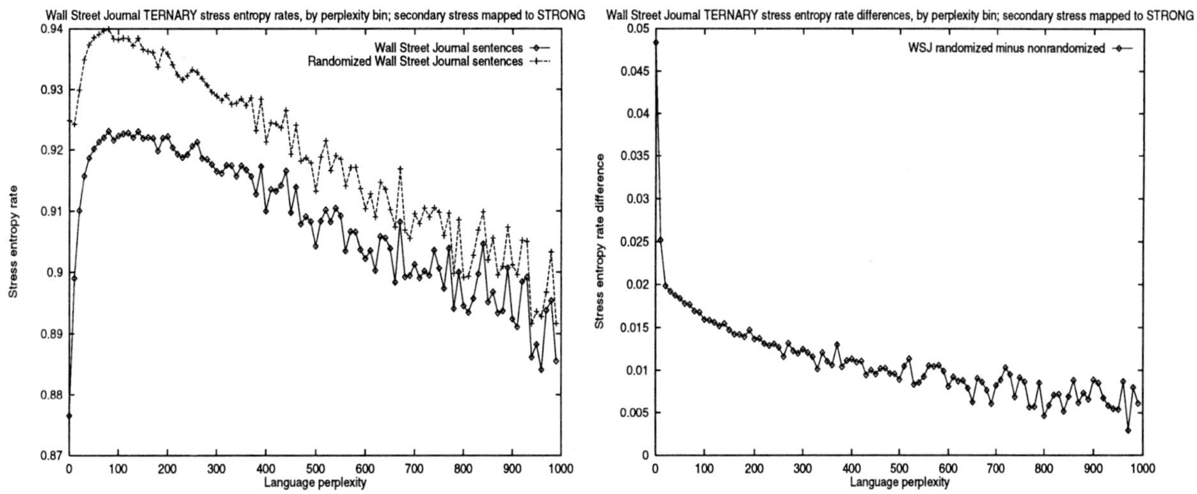

Figure 10: 6-gram entropy rates and difference curve for Σ_2, strong secondary stress

References

Abercrombie, D. 1967. *Elements of general phonetics.* Edinburgh University Press.

Baum, P. F. 1952. *The Other Harmony of Prose.* Duke University Press.

Cover, T. M. and J. A. Thomas. 1991. *Elements of information theory.* John Wiley & Sons, Inc.

Godfrey, J., E. Holliman, and J. McDaniel. 1992. Switchboard: Telephone speech corpus for research development. In *Proc. ICASSP-92*, pages I–517–520.

Halle, M. and J. Vergnaud. 1987. *An essay on stress.* The MIT Press.

Harding, D. W. 1976. *Words into rhythm: English speech rhythm in verse and prose.* Cambridge University Press.

Jassem, W., D. R. Hill, and I. H. Witten. 1984. Isochrony in English speech: its statistical validity and linguistic relevance. In D. Gibbon and H. Richter, editors, *Intonation, rhythm, and accent: Studies in Discourse Phonology.* Walter de Gruyter, pages 203–225.

Kager, R. 1989a. *A metrical theory of stress and destressing in English and Dutch.* Foris Publications.

Kager, R. 1989b. *The rhythm of English prose.* Foris Publications.

Ochsner, R. S. 1989. *Rhythm and writing.* The Whitson Publishing Company.

Parzen, E. 1962. *Stochastic processes.* Holden-Day.

An Empirical Study of Smoothing Techniques for Language Modeling

Stanley F. Chen
Harvard University
Aiken Computation Laboratory
33 Oxford St.
Cambridge, MA 02138
sfc@eecs.harvard.edu

Joshua Goodman
Harvard University
Aiken Computation Laboratory
33 Oxford St.
Cambridge, MA 02138
goodman@eecs.harvard.edu

Abstract

We present an extensive empirical comparison of several smoothing techniques in the domain of language modeling, including those described by Jelinek and Mercer (1980), Katz (1987), and Church and Gale (1991). We investigate for the first time how factors such as training data size, corpus (*e.g.*, Brown versus Wall Street Journal), and n-gram order (bigram versus trigram) affect the relative performance of these methods, which we measure through the cross-entropy of test data. In addition, we introduce two novel smoothing techniques, one a variation of Jelinek-Mercer smoothing and one a very simple linear interpolation technique, both of which outperform existing methods.

1 Introduction

Smoothing is a technique essential in the construction of n-gram language models, a staple in speech recognition (Bahl, Jelinek, and Mercer, 1983) as well as many other domains (Church, 1988; Brown et al., 1990; Kernighan, Church, and Gale, 1990). A *language model* is a probability distribution over strings $P(s)$ that attempts to reflect the frequency with which each string s occurs as a sentence in natural text. Language models are used in speech recognition to resolve acoustically ambiguous utterances. For example, if we have that $P(\textit{it takes two}) \gg P(\textit{it takes too})$, then we know *ceteris paribus* to prefer the former transcription over the latter.

While smoothing is a central issue in language modeling, the literature lacks a definitive comparison between the many existing techniques. Previous studies (Nadas, 1984; Katz, 1987; Church and Gale, 1991; MacKay and Peto, 1995) only compare a small number of methods (typically two) on a single corpus and using a single training data size. As a result, it is currently difficult for a researcher to intelligently choose between smoothing schemes.

In this work, we carry out an extensive empirical comparison of the most widely used smoothing techniques, including those described by Jelinek and Mercer (1980), Katz (1987), and Church and Gale (1991). We carry out experiments over many training data sizes on varied corpora using both bigram and trigram models. We demonstrate that the relative performance of techniques depends greatly on training data size and n-gram order. For example, for bigram models produced from large training sets Church-Gale smoothing has superior performance, while Katz smoothing performs best on bigram models produced from smaller data. For the methods with parameters that can be tuned to improve performance, we perform an automated search for optimal values and show that sub-optimal parameter selection can significantly decrease performance. To our knowledge, this is the first smoothing work that systematically investigates any of these issues.

In addition, we introduce two novel smoothing techniques: the first belonging to the class of smoothing models described by Jelinek and Mercer, the second a very simple linear interpolation method. While being relatively simple to implement, we show that these methods yield good performance in bigram models and superior performance in trigram models.

We take the performance of a method m to be its cross-entropy on test data

$$\frac{1}{N_T} \sum_{i=1}^{l_T} - \log_2 P_m(t_i)$$

where $P_m(t_i)$ denotes the language model produced with method m and where the test data T is composed of sentences $(t_1, \ldots, t_{l_T})$ and contains a total of N_T words. The entropy is inversely related to the average probability a model assigns to sentences in the test data, and it is generally assumed that lower entropy correlates with better performance in applications.

1.1 Smoothing n-gram Models

In n-gram language modeling, the probability of a string $P(s)$ is expressed as the product of the probabilities of the words that compose the string, with each word probability conditional on the identity of the last $n-1$ words, *i.e.*, if $s = w_1 \cdots w_l$ we have

$$P(s) = \prod_{i=1}^{l} P(w_i|w_1^{i-1}) \approx \prod_{i=1}^{l} P(w_i|w_{i-n+1}^{i-1}) \quad (1)$$

where w_i^j denotes the words $w_i \cdots w_j$. Typically, n is taken to be two or three, corresponding to a *bigram* or *trigram* model, respectively.[1]

Consider the case $n = 2$. To estimate the probabilities $P(w_i|w_{i-1})$ in equation (1), one can acquire a large corpus of text, which we refer to as *training data*, and take

$$\begin{aligned} P_{\text{ML}}(w_i|w_{i-1}) &= \frac{P(w_{i-1}w_i)}{P(w_{i-1})} \\ &= \frac{c(w_{i-1}w_i)/N_S}{c(w_{i-1})/N_S} \\ &= \frac{c(w_{i-1}w_i)}{c(w_{i-1})} \end{aligned}$$

where $c(\alpha)$ denotes the number of times the string α occurs in the text and N_S denotes the total number of words. This is called the *maximum likelihood* (ML) estimate for $P(w_i|w_{i-1})$.

While intuitive, the maximum likelihood estimate is a poor one when the amount of training data is small compared to the size of the model being built, as is generally the case in language modeling. For example, consider the situation where a pair of words, or *bigram*, say *burnish the*, doesn't occur in the training data. Then, we have $P_{\text{ML}}(\textit{the}|\textit{burnish}) = 0$, which is clearly inaccurate as this probability should be larger than zero. A zero bigram probability can lead to errors in speech recognition, as it disallows the bigram regardless of how informative the acoustic signal is. The term *smoothing* describes techniques for adjusting the maximum likelihood estimate to hopefully produce more accurate probabilities.

As an example, one simple smoothing technique is to pretend each bigram occurs once more than it actually did (Lidstone, 1920; Johnson, 1932; Jeffreys, 1948), yielding

$$P_{+1}(w_i|w_{i-1}) = \frac{c(w_{i-1}w_i) + 1}{c(w_{i-1}) + |V|}$$

where V is the vocabulary, the set of all words being considered. This has the desirable quality of preventing zero bigram probabilities. However, this scheme has the flaw of assigning the same probability to say, *burnish the* and *burnish thou* (assuming neither occurred in the training data), even though intuitively the former seems more likely because the word *the* is much more common than *thou*.

To address this, another smoothing technique is to *interpolate* the bigram model with a unigram model $P_{\text{ML}}(w_i) = c(w_i)/N_S$, a model that reflects how often each word occurs in the training data. For example, we can take

$$P_{\text{interp}}(w_i|w_{i-1}) = \lambda P_{\text{ML}}(w_i|w_{i-1}) + (1-\lambda)P_{\text{ML}}(w_i)$$

getting the behavior that bigrams involving common words are assigned higher probabilities (Jelinek and Mercer, 1980).

2 Previous Work

The simplest type of smoothing used in practice is *additive* smoothing (Lidstone, 1920; Johnson, 1932; Jeffreys, 1948), where we take

$$P_{\text{add}}(w_i|w_{i-n+1}^{i-1}) = \frac{c(w_{i-n+1}^{i}) + \delta}{c(w_{i-n+1}^{i-1}) + \delta|V|} \quad (2)$$

and where Lidstone and Jeffreys advocate $\delta = 1$. Gale and Church (1990; 1994) have argued that this method generally performs poorly.

The Good-Turing estimate (Good, 1953) is central to many smoothing techniques. It is not used directly for n-gram smoothing because, like additive smoothing, it does not perform the interpolation of lower- and higher-order models essential for good performance. Good-Turing states that an n-gram that occurs r times should be treated as if it had occurred r^* times, where

$$r^* = (r+1)\frac{n_{r+1}}{n_r}$$

and where n_r is the number of n-grams that occur exactly r times in the training data.

Katz smoothing (1987) extends the intuitions of Good-Turing by adding the interpolation of higher-order models with lower-order models. It is perhaps the most widely used smoothing technique in speech recognition.

Church and Gale (1991) describe a smoothing method that combines the Good-Turing estimate with *bucketing*, the technique of partitioning a set of n-grams into disjoint groups, where each group is characterized independently through a set of parameters. Like Katz, models are defined recursively in terms of lower-order models. Each n-gram is assigned to one of several buckets based on its frequency predicted from lower-order models. Each bucket is treated as a separate distribution and Good-Turing estimation is performed within each, giving corrected counts that are normalized to yield probabilities.

[1] To make the term $P(w_i|w_{i-n+1}^{i-1})$ meaningful for $i < n$, one can pad the beginning of the string with a distinguished token. In this work, we assume there are $n-1$ such distinguished tokens preceding each sentence.

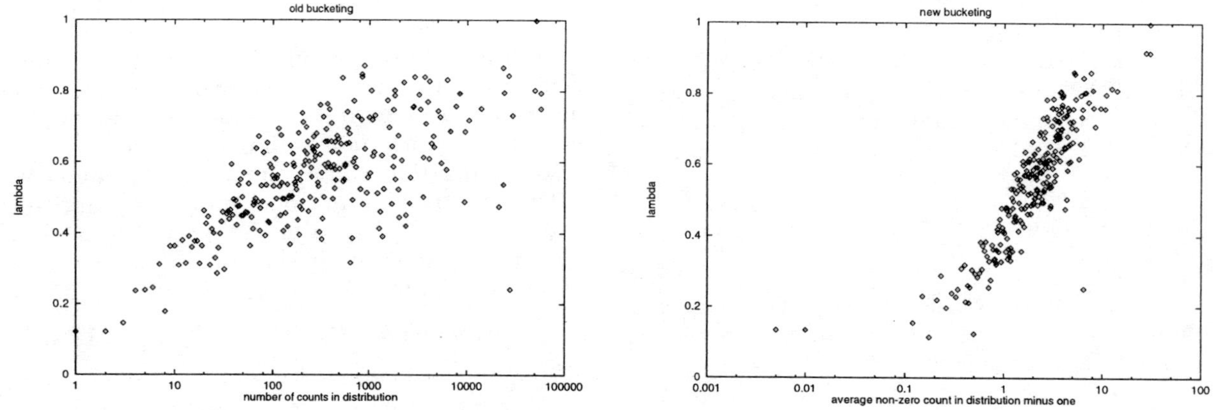

Figure 1: λ values for old and new bucketing schemes for Jelinek-Mercer smoothing; each point represents a single bucket

The other smoothing technique besides Katz smoothing widely used in speech recognition is due to Jelinek and Mercer (1980). They present a class of smoothing models that involve linear interpolation, *e.g.*, Brown et al. (1992) take

$$\begin{aligned} P_{\text{interp}}(w_i|w_{i-n+1}^{i-1}) = \\ \lambda_{w_{i-n+1}^{i-1}}\, P_{\text{ML}}(w_i|w_{i-n+1}^{i-1}) + \\ (1-\lambda_{w_{i-n+1}^{i-1}})\, P_{\text{interp}}(w_i|w_{i-n+2}^{i-1}) \end{aligned} \quad (3)$$

That is, the maximum likelihood estimate is interpolated with the smoothed lower-order distribution, which is defined analogously. Training a distinct $\lambda_{w_{i-n+1}^{i-1}}$ for each w_{i-n+1}^{i-1} is not generally felicitous; Bahl, Jelinek, and Mercer (1983) suggest partitioning the $\lambda_{w_{i-n+1}^{i-1}}$ into buckets according to $c(w_{i-n+1}^{i-1})$, where all $\lambda_{w_{i-n+1}^{i-1}}$ in the same bucket are constrained to have the same value.

To yield meaningful results, the data used to estimate the $\lambda_{w_{i-n+1}^{i-1}}$ need to be disjoint from the data used to calculate P_{ML}.[2] In *held-out interpolation*, one reserves a section of the training data for this purpose. Alternatively, Jelinek and Mercer describe a technique called *deleted interpolation* where different parts of the training data rotate in training either P_{ML} or the $\lambda_{w_{i-n+1}^{i-1}}$; the results are then averaged.

Several smoothing techniques are motivated within a Bayesian framework, including work by Nadas (1984) and MacKay and Peto (1995).

3 Novel Smoothing Techniques

Of the great many novel methods that we have tried, two techniques have performed especially well.

[2]When the same data is used to estimate both, setting all $\lambda_{w_{i-n+1}^{i-1}}$ to one yields the optimal result.

3.1 Method *average-count*

This scheme is an instance of Jelinek-Mercer smoothing. Referring to equation (3), recall that Bahl et al. suggest bucketing the $\lambda_{w_{i-n+1}^{i-1}}$ according to $c(w_{i-n+1}^{i-1})$. We have found that partitioning the $\lambda_{w_{i-n+1}^{i-1}}$ according to the average number of counts per non-zero element $\frac{c(w_{i-n+1}^{i-1})}{|w_i : c(w_{i-n+1}^{i})>0|}$ yields better results.

Intuitively, the less sparse the data for estimating $P_{\text{ML}}(w_i|w_{i-n+1}^{i-1})$, the larger $\lambda_{w_{i-n+1}^{i-1}}$ should be. While larger $c(w_{i-n+1}^{i-1})$ generally correspond to less sparse distributions, this quantity ignores the allocation of counts between words. For example, we would consider a distribution with ten counts distributed evenly among ten words to be much more sparse than a distribution with ten counts all on a single word. The average number of counts per word seems to more directly express the concept of sparseness.

In Figure 1, we graph the value of λ assigned to each bucket under the original and new bucketing schemes on identical data. Notice that the new bucketing scheme results in a much tighter plot, indicating that it is better at grouping together distributions with similar behavior.

3.2 Method *one-count*

This technique combines two intuitions. First, MacKay and Peto (1995) argue that a reasonable form for a smoothed distribution is

$$P_{\text{one}}(w_i|w_{i-n+1}^{i-1}) = \frac{c(w_{i-n+1}^{i}) + \alpha P_{\text{one}}(w_i|w_{i-n+2}^{i-1})}{c(w_{i-n+1}^{i-1}) + \alpha}$$

The parameter α can be thought of as the number of counts being added to the given distribution, where the new counts are distributed as in the lower-order distribution. Secondly, the Good-Turing estimate can be interpreted as stating that the number of these extra counts should be proportional to the number of words with exactly one count in the given distribution. We have found that taking

$$\alpha = \gamma \left[n_1(w_{i-n+1}^{i-1}) + \beta \right] \qquad (4)$$

works well, where

$$n_1(w_{i-n+1}^{i-1}) = |w_i : c(w_{i-n+1}^{i}) = 1|$$

is the number of words with one count, and where β and γ are constants.

4 Experimental Methodology

4.1 Data

We used the Penn treebank and TIPSTER corpora distributed by the Linguistic Data Consortium. From the treebank, we extracted text from the tagged Brown corpus, yielding about one million words. From TIPSTER, we used the Associated Press (AP), Wall Street Journal (WSJ), and San Jose Mercury News (SJM) data, yielding 123, 84, and 43 million words respectively. We created two distinct vocabularies, one for the Brown corpus and one for the TIPSTER data. The former vocabulary contains all 53,850 words occurring in Brown; the latter vocabulary consists of the 65,173 words occurring at least 70 times in TIPSTER.

For each experiment, we selected three segments of held-out data along with the segment of training data. One held-out segment was used as the test data for performance evaluation, and the other two were used as development test data for optimizing the parameters of each smoothing method. Each piece of held-out data was chosen to be roughly 50,000 words. This decision does not reflect practice very well, as when the training data size is less than 50,000 words it is not realistic to have so much development test data available. However, we made this decision to prevent us having to optimize the training versus held-out data tradeoff for each data size. In addition, the development test data is used to optimize typically very few parameters, so in practice small held-out sets are generally adequate, and perhaps can be avoided altogether with techniques such as deleted estimation.

4.2 Smoothing Implementations

In this section, we discuss the details of our implementations of various smoothing techniques. Due to space limitations, these descriptions are not comprehensive; a more complete discussion is presented in Chen (1996). The titles of the following sections include the mnemonic we use to refer to the implementations in later sections. Unless otherwise specified, for those smoothing models defined recursively in terms of lower-order models, we end the recursion by taking the $n = 0$ distribution to be the uniform distribution $P_{\text{unif}}(w_i) = 1/|V|$. For each method, we highlight the parameters (*e.g.*, λ_n and δ below) that can be tuned to optimize performance. Parameter values are determined through training on held-out data.

4.2.1 Baseline Smoothing (`interp-baseline`)

For our baseline smoothing method, we use an instance of Jelinek-Mercer smoothing where we constrain all $\lambda_{w_{i-n+1}^{i-1}}$ to be equal to a single value λ_n for each n, *i.e.*,

$$\begin{aligned} P_{\text{base}}(w_i|w_{i-n+1}^{i-1}) &= \lambda_n \, P_{\text{ML}}(w_i|w_{i-n+1}^{i-1}) + \\ & \quad (1-\lambda_n) \, P_{\text{base}}(w_i|w_{i-n+2}^{i-1}) \end{aligned}$$

4.2.2 Additive Smoothing (`plus-one` and `plus-delta`)

We consider two versions of additive smoothing. Referring to equation (2), we fix $\delta = 1$ in `plus-one` smoothing. In `plus-delta`, we consider any δ.

4.2.3 Katz Smoothing (`katz`)

While the original paper (Katz, 1987) uses a single parameter k, we instead use a different k for each $n > 1$, k_n. We smooth the unigram distribution using additive smoothing with parameter δ.

4.2.4 Church-Gale Smoothing (`church-gale`)

To smooth the counts n_r needed for the Good-Turing estimate, we use the technique described by Gale and Sampson (1995). We smooth the unigram distribution using Good-Turing without any bucketing.

Instead of the bucketing scheme described in the original paper, we use a scheme analogous to the one described by Bahl, Jelinek, and Mercer (1983). We make the assumption that whether a bucket is large enough for accurate Good-Turing estimation depends on how many n-grams with non-zero counts occur in it. Thus, instead of partitioning the space of $P(w_{i-1})P(w_i)$ values in some uniform way as was done by Church and Gale, we partition the space so that at least $c_{\min}$ non-zero n-grams fall in each bucket.

Finally, the original paper describes only bigram smoothing in detail; extending this method to trigram smoothing is ambiguous. In particular, it is unclear whether to bucket trigrams according to $P(w_{i-2}^{i-1})P(w_i)$ or $P(w_{i-2}^{i-1})P(w_i|w_{i-1})$. We chose the former; while the latter may yield better performance, our belief is that it is much more difficult to implement and that it requires a great deal more computation.

4.2.5 Jelinek-Mercer Smoothing (`interp-held-out` and `interp-del-int`)

We implemented two versions of Jelinek-Mercer smoothing differing only in what data is used to train the λ's. We bucket the $\lambda_{w_{i-n+1}^{i-1}}$ according to $c(w_{i-n+1}^{i-1})$ as suggested by Bahl et al. Similar to our Church-Gale implementation, we choose buckets to ensure that at least c_{min} words in the data used to train the λ's fall in each bucket.

In **interp-held-out**, the λ's are trained using held-out interpolation on one of the development test sets. In **interp-del-int**, the λ's are trained using the *relaxed deleted interpolation* technique described by Jelinek and Mercer, where one word is deleted at a time. In **interp-del-int**, we bucket an n-gram according to its count before deletion, as this turned out to significantly improve performance.

4.2.6 Novel Smoothing Methods (new-avg-count and new-one-count)

The implementation **new-avg-count**, corresponding to smoothing method *average-count*, is identical to **interp-held-out** except that we use the novel bucketing scheme described in section 3.1. In the implementation **new-one-count**, we have different parameters β_n and γ_n in equation (4) for each n.

5 Results

In Figure 2, we display the performance of the **interp-baseline** method for bigram and trigram models on TIPSTER, Brown, and the WSJ subset of TIPSTER. In Figures 3–6, we display the relative performance of various smoothing techniques with respect to the baseline method on these corpora, as measured by difference in entropy. In the graphs on the left of Figures 2–4, each point represents an average over ten runs; the error bars represent the empirical standard deviation over these runs. Due to resource limitations, we only performed multiple runs for data sets of 50,000 sentences or less. Each point on the graphs on the right represents a single run, but we consider sizes up to the amount of data available. The graphs on the bottom of Figures 3–4 are close-ups of the graphs above, focusing on those algorithms that perform better than the baseline. To give an idea of how these cross-entropy differences translate to perplexity, each 0.014 bits correspond roughly to a 1% change in perplexity.

In each run except as noted below, optimal values for the parameters of the given technique were searched for using Powell's search algorithm as realized in *Numerical Recipes in C* (Press et al., 1988, pp. 309–317). Parameters were chosen to optimize the cross-entropy of one of the development test sets associated with the given training set. To constrain the search, we searched only those parameters that were found to affect performance significantly, as verified through preliminary experiments over several data sizes. For **katz** and **church-gale**, we did not perform the parameter search for training sets over 50,000 sentences due to resource constraints, and instead manually extrapolated parameter values from optimal values found on smaller data sizes. We ran **interp-del-int** only on sizes up to 50,000 sentences due to time constraints.

Method	Lines
`interp-baseline`[3]	400
`plus-one`	40
`plus-delta`	40
`katz`	300
`church-gale`	1000
`interp-held-out`	400
`interp-del-int`	400
`new-avg-count`	400
`new-one-count`	50

Table 1: Implementation difficulty of various methods in terms of lines of C++ code

From these graphs, we see that additive smoothing performs poorly and that methods **katz** and **interp-held-out** consistently perform well. Our implementation **church-gale** performs poorly except on large bigram training sets, where it performs the best. The novel methods **new-avg-count** and **new-one-count** perform well uniformly across training data sizes, and are superior for trigram models. Notice that while performance is relatively consistent across corpora, it varies widely with respect to training set size and n-gram order.

The method **interp-del-int** performs significantly worse than **interp-held-out**, though they differ only in the data used to train the λ's. However, we delete one word at a time in **interp-del-int**; we hypothesize that deleting larger chunks would lead to more similar performance.

In Figure 7, we show how the values of the parameters δ and c_{min} affect the performance of methods **katz** and **new-avg-count**, respectively, over several training data sizes. Notice that poor parameter setting can lead to very significant losses in performance, and that optimal parameter settings depend on training set size.

To give an informal estimate of the difficulty of implementation of each method, in Table 1 we display the number of lines of C++ code in each implementation excluding the core code common across techniques.

6 Discussion

To our knowledge, this is the first empirical comparison of smoothing techniques in language modeling of such scope: no other study has used multiple training data sizes, corpora, or has performed parameter optimization. We show that in order to completely

[3]To implement the baseline method, we just used the `interp-held-out` code as it is a special case. Written anew, it probably would have been about 50 lines.

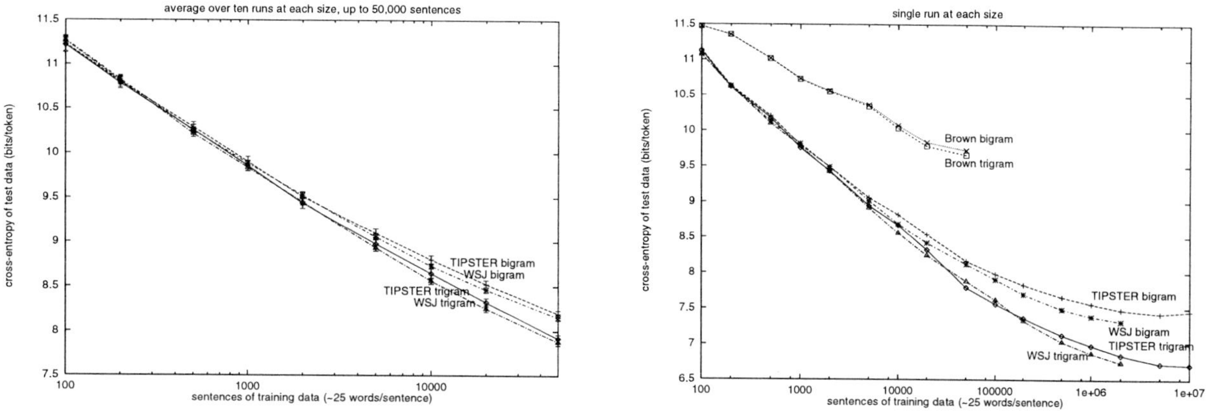

Figure 2: Baseline cross-entropy on test data; graph on left displays averages over ten runs for training sets up to 50,000 sentences, graph on right displays single runs for training sets up to 10,000,000 sentences

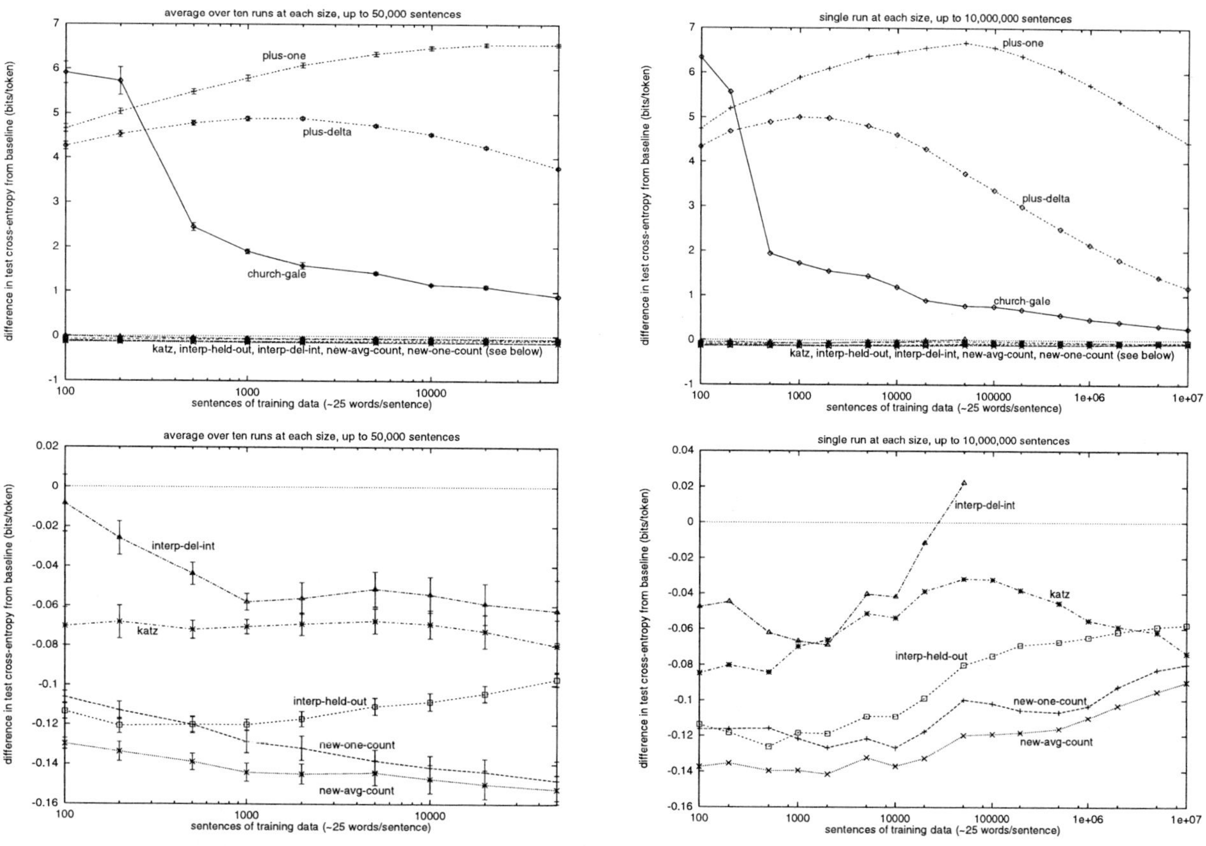

Figure 3: Trigram model on TIPSTER data; relative performance of various methods with respect to baseline; graphs on left display averages over ten runs for training sets up to 50,000 sentences, graphs on right display single runs for training sets up to 10,000,000 sentences; top graphs show all algorithms, bottom graphs zoom in on those methods that perform better than the baseline method

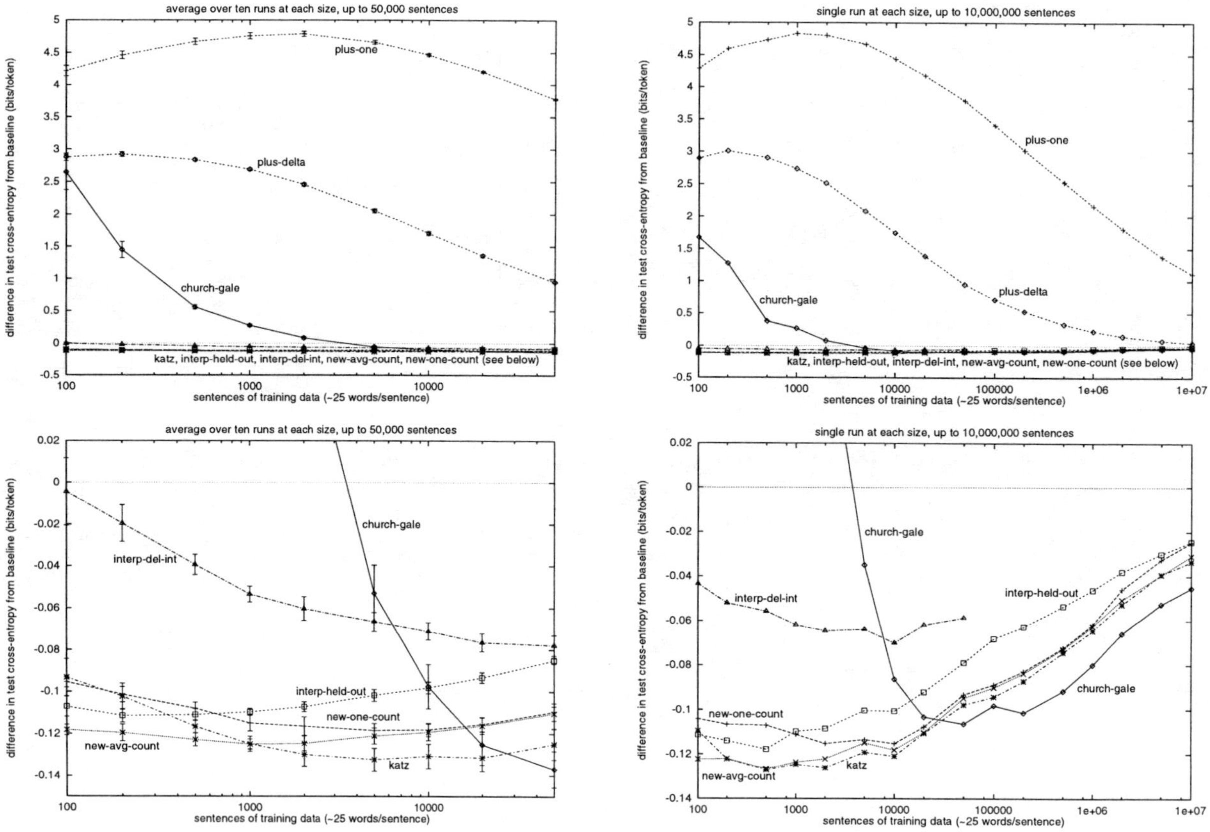

Figure 4: Bigram model on TIPSTER data; relative performance of various methods with respect to baseline; graphs on left display averages over ten runs for training sets up to 50,000 sentences, graphs on right display single runs for training sets up to 10,000,000 sentences; top graphs show all algorithms, bottom graphs zoom in on those methods that perform better than the baseline method

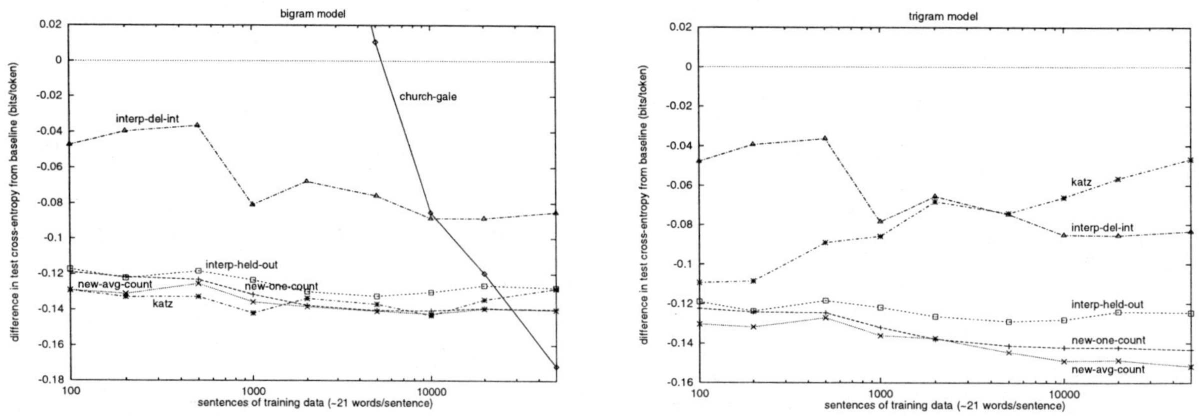

Figure 5: Bigram and trigram models on Brown corpus; relative performance of various methods with respect to baseline

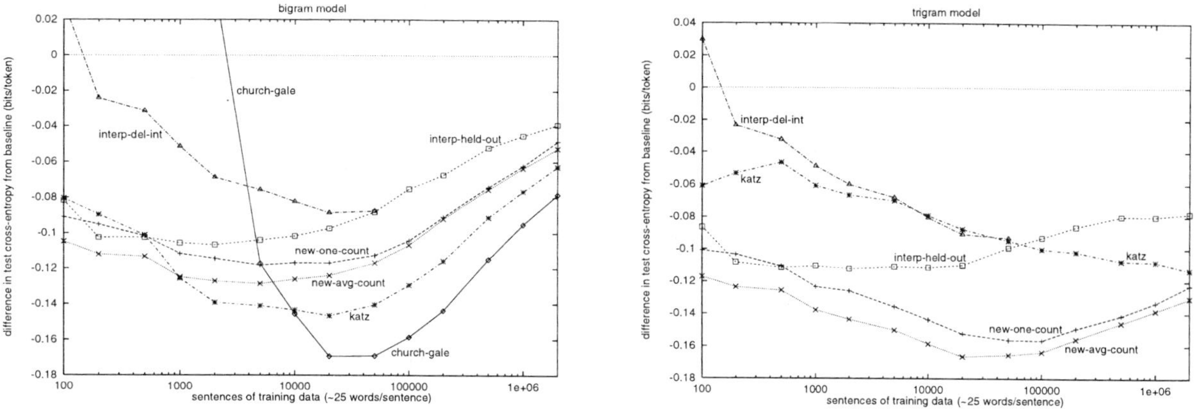

Figure 6: Bigram and trigram models on Wall Street Journal corpus; relative performance of various methods with respect to baseline

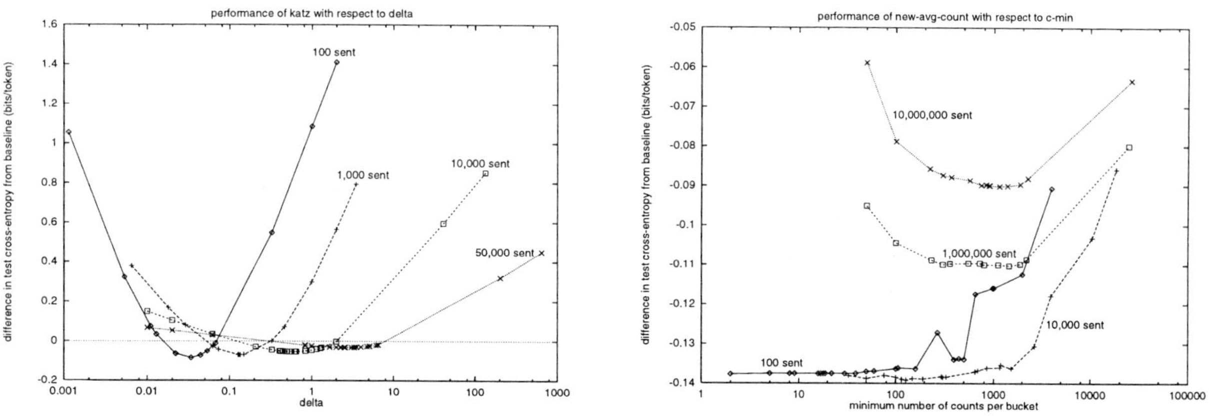

Figure 7: Performance of **katz** and **new-avg-count** with respect to parameters δ and $c_{\min}$, respectively

characterize the relative performance of two techniques, it is necessary to consider multiple training set sizes and to try both bigram and trigram models. Multiple runs should be performed whenever possible to discover whether any calculated differences are statistically significant. Furthermore, we show that sub-optimal parameter selection can also significantly affect relative performance.

We find that the two most widely used techniques, Katz smoothing and Jelinek-Mercer smoothing, perform consistently well across training set sizes for both bigram and trigram models, with Katz smoothing performing better on trigram models produced from large training sets and on bigram models in general. These results question the generality of the previous reference result concerning Katz smoothing: Katz (1987) reported that his method slightly outperforms an unspecified version of Jelinek-Mercer smoothing on a single training set of 750,000 words. Furthermore, we show that Church-Gale smoothing, which previously had not been compared with common smoothing techniques, outperforms all existing methods on bigram models produced from large training sets. Finally, we find that our novel methods *average-count* and *one-count* are superior to existing methods for trigram models and perform well on bigram models; method *one-count* yields marginally worse performance but is extremely easy to implement.

In this study, we measure performance solely through the cross-entropy of test data; it would be interesting to see how these cross-entropy differences correlate with performance in end applications such as speech recognition. In addition, it would be interesting to see whether these results extend to fields other than language modeling where smoothing is used, such as prepositional phrase attachment (Collins and Brooks, 1995), part-of-speech tagging (Church, 1988), and stochastic parsing (Magerman, 1994).

Acknowledgements

The authors would like to thank Stuart Shieber and the anonymous reviewers for their comments on previous versions of this paper. We would also like to thank William Gale and Geoffrey Sampson for supplying us with code for "Good-Turing frequency estimation without tears." This research was supported by the National Science Foundation under Grant No. IRI-93-50192 and Grant No. CDA-94-01024. The second author was also supported by a National Science Foundation Graduate Student Fellowship.

References

Bahl, Lalit R., Frederick Jelinek, and Robert L. Mercer. 1983. A maximum likelihood approach to continuous speech recognition. *IEEE Transactions on Pattern Analysis and Machine Intelligence*, PAMI-5(2):179–190, March.

Brown, Peter F., John Cocke, Stephen A. DellaPietra, Vincent J. DellaPietra, Frederick Jelinek, John D. Lafferty, Robert L. Mercer, and Paul S. Roossin. 1990. A statistical approach to machine translation. *Computational Linguistics*, 16(2):79–85, June.

Brown, Peter F., Stephen A. DellaPietra, Vincent J. DellaPietra, Jennifer C. Lai, and Robert L. Mercer. 1992. An estimate of an upper bound for the entropy of English. *Computational Linguistics*, 18(1):31–40, March.

Chen, Stanley F. 1996. *Building Probabilistic Models for Natural Language*. Ph.D. thesis, Harvard University. In preparation.

Church, Kenneth. 1988. A stochastic parts program and noun phrase parser for unrestricted text. In *Proceedings of the Second Conference on Applied Natural Language Processing*, pages 136–143.

Church, Kenneth W. and William A. Gale. 1991. A comparison of the enhanced Good-Turing and deleted estimation methods for estimating probabilities of English bigrams. *Computer Speech and Language*, 5:19–54.

Collins, Michael and James Brooks. 1995. Prepositional phrase attachment through a backed-off model. In David Yarowsky and Kenneth Church, editors, *Proceedings of the Third Workshop on Very Large Corpora*, pages 27–38, Cambridge, MA, June.

Gale, William A. and Kenneth W. Church. 1990. Estimation procedures for language context: poor estimates are worse than none. In *COMPSTAT, Proceedings in Computational Statistics, 9th Symposium*, pages 69–74, Dubrovnik, Yugoslavia, September.

Gale, William A. and Kenneth W. Church. 1994. What's wrong with adding one? In N. Oostdijk and P. de Haan, editors, *Corpus-Based Research into Language*. Rodolpi, Amsterdam.

Gale, William A. and Geoffrey Sampson. 1995. Good-Turing frequency estimation without tears. *Journal of Quantitative Linguistics*, 2(3). To appear.

Good, I.J. 1953. The population frequencies of species and the estimation of population parameters. *Biometrika*, 40(3 and 4):237–264.

Jeffreys, H. 1948. *Theory of Probability*. Clarendon Press, Oxford, second edition.

Jelinek, Frederick and Robert L. Mercer. 1980. Interpolated estimation of Markov source parameters from sparse data. In *Proceedings of the Workshop on Pattern Recognition in Practice*, Amsterdam, The Netherlands: North-Holland, May.

Johnson, W.E. 1932. Probability: deductive and inductive problems. *Mind*, 41:421–423.

Katz, Slava M. 1987. Estimation of probabilities from sparse data for the language model component of a speech recognizer. *IEEE Transactions on Acoustics, Speech and Signal Processing*, ASSP-35(3):400–401, March.

Kernighan, M.D., K.W. Church, and W.A. Gale. 1990. A spelling correction program based on a noisy channel model. In *Proceedings of the Thirteenth International Conference on Computational Linguistics*, pages 205–210.

Lidstone, G.J. 1920. Note on the general case of the Bayes-Laplace formula for inductive or *a posteriori* probabilities. *Transactions of the Faculty of Actuaries*, 8:182–192.

MacKay, David J. C. and Linda C. Peto. 1995. A hierarchical Dirichlet language model. *Natural Language Engineering*, 1(3):1–19.

Magerman, David M. 1994. *Natural Language Parsing as Statistical Pattern Recognition*. Ph.D. thesis, Stanford University, February.

Nadas, Arthur. 1984. Estimation of probabilities in the language model of the IBM speech recognition system. *IEEE Transactions on Acoustics, Speech and Signal Processing*, ASSP-32(4):859–861, August.

Press, W.H., B.P. Flannery, S.A. Teukolsky, and W.T. Vetterling. 1988. *Numerical Recipes in C*. Cambridge University Press, Cambridge.

Minimizing Manual Annotation Cost In Supervised Training From Corpora

Sean P. Engelson and **Ido Dagan**
Department of Mathematics and Computer Science
Bar-Ilan University
52900 Ramat Gan, Israel
{engelson,dagan}@bimacs.cs.biu.ac.il

Abstract

Corpus-based methods for natural language processing often use supervised training, requiring expensive manual annotation of training corpora. This paper investigates methods for reducing annotation cost by *sample selection*. In this approach, during training the learning program examines many unlabeled examples and selects for labeling (annotation) only those that are most informative at each stage. This avoids redundantly annotating examples that contribute little new information. This paper extends our previous work on *committee-based sample selection* for probabilistic classifiers. We describe a family of methods for committee-based sample selection, and report experimental results for the task of stochastic part-of-speech tagging. We find that all variants achieve a significant reduction in annotation cost, though their computational efficiency differs. In particular, the simplest method, which has no parameters to tune, gives excellent results. We also show that sample selection yields a significant reduction in the size of the model used by the tagger.

1 Introduction

Many corpus-based methods for natural language processing (NLP) are based on supervised training—acquiring information from a manually annotated corpus. Therefore, reducing annotation cost is an important research goal for statistical NLP. The ultimate reduction in annotation cost is achieved by unsupervised training methods, which do not require an annotated corpus at all (Kupiec, 1992; Merialdo, 1994; Elworthy, 1994). It has been shown, however, that some supervised training prior to the unsupervised phase is often beneficial. Indeed, fully unsupervised training may not be feasible for certain tasks. This paper investigates an approach for optimizing the supervised training (learning) phase, which reduces the annotation effort required to achieve a desired level of accuracy of the trained model.

In this paper, we investigate and extend the *committee-based sample selection* approach to minimizing training cost (Dagan and Engelson, 1995). When using sample selection, a learning program examines many unlabeled (not annotated) examples, selecting for labeling only those that are most informative for the learner at each stage of training (Seung, Opper, and Sompolinsky, 1992; Freund et al., 1993; Lewis and Gale, 1994; Cohn, Atlas, and Ladner, 1994). This avoids redundantly annotating many examples that contribute roughly the same information to the learner.

Our work focuses on sample selection for training probabilistic classifiers. In statistical NLP, probabilistic classifiers are often used to select a preferred analysis of the linguistic structure of a text (for example, its syntactic structure (Black et al., 1993), word categories (Church, 1988), or word senses (Gale, Church, and Yarowsky, 1993)). As a representative task for probabilistic classification in NLP, we experiment in this paper with sample selection for the popular and well-understood method of stochastic part-of-speech tagging using Hidden Markov Models.

We first review the basic approach of committee-based sample selection and its application to part-of-speech tagging. This basic approach gives rise to a family of algorithms (including the original algorithm described in (Dagan and Engelson, 1995)) which we then describe. First, we describe the 'simplest' committee-based selection algorithm, which has no parameters to tune. We then generalize the selection scheme, allowing more options to adapt and tune the approach for specific tasks. The paper compares the performance of several instantiations of the general scheme, including a *batch* selection method similar to that of Lewis and Gale (1994). In particular, we found that the simplest version of the method achieves a significant reduction in annotation cost, comparable to that of other versions.

We also evaluate the computational efficiency of the different variants, and the number of unlabeled examples they consume. Finally, we study the effect of sample selection on the size of the model acquired by the learner.

2 Probabilistic Classification

This section presents the framework and terminology assumed for probabilistic classification, as well as its instantiation for stochastic bigram part-of-speech tagging.

A *probabilistic classifier* classifies input examples e by classes $c \in C$, where C is a known set of possible classes. Classification is based on a score function, $F_M(c, e)$, which assigns a score to each possible class of an example. The classifier then assigns the example to the class with the highest score. F_M is determined by a probabilistic model M. In many applications, F_M is the conditional probability function, $P_M(c|e)$, specifying the probability of each class given the example, but other score functions that correlate with the likelihood of the class are often used.

In stochastic part-of-speech tagging, the model assumed is a Hidden Markov Model (HMM), and input examples are sentences. The class c, to which a sentence is assigned is a sequence of the parts of speech (tags) for the words in the sentence. The score function is typically the joint (or conditional) probability of the sentence and the tag sequence[1]. The tagger then assigns the sentence to the tag sequence which is most probable according to the HMM.

The probabilistic model M, and thus the score function F_M, are defined by a set of parameters, $\{\alpha_i\}$. During training, the values of the parameters are estimated from a set of statistics, S, extracted from a training set of annotated examples. We denote a particular model by $M = \{a_i\}$, where each a_i is a specific value for the corresponding α_i.

In bigram part-of-speech tagging the HMM model M contains three types of parameters: *transition probabilities* $P(t_i \rightarrow t_j)$ giving the probability of tag t_j occuring after tag t_i, *lexical probabilities* $P(t|w)$ giving the probability of tag t labeling word w, and *tag probabilities* $P(t)$ giving the marginal probability of a tag occurring.[2] The values of these parameters are estimated from a tagged corpus which provides a training set of labeled examples (see Section 4.1).

3 Evaluating Example Uncertainty

A sample selection method needs to evaluate the expected usefulness, or information gain, of learning from a given example. The methods we investigate approach this evaluation implicitly, measuring an example's informativeness as the uncertainty in its classification given the current training data (Seung, Opper, and Sompolinsky, 1992; Lewis and Gale, 1994; MacKay, 1992). The reasoning is that if an example's classification is uncertain given current training data then the example is likely to contain unknown information useful for classifying similar examples in the future.

We investigate the *committee-based* method, where the learning algorithm evaluates an example by giving it to a *committee* containing several variant models, all 'consistent' with the training data seen so far. The more the committee members agree on the classification of the example, the greater our certainty in its classification. This is because when the training data entails a specific classification with high certainty, most (in a probabilistic sense) classifiers consistent with the data will produce that classification.

The committee-based approach was first proposed in a theoretical context for learning binary non-probabilistic classifiers (Seung, Opper, and Sompolinsky, 1992; Freund et al., 1993). In this paper, we extend our previous work (Dagan and Engelson, 1995) where we applied the basic idea of the committee-based approach to probabilistic classification. Taking a Bayesian perspective, the posterior probability of a model, $P(M|S)$, is determined given statistics S from the training set (and some prior distribution for the models). Committee members are then generated by drawing models randomly from $P(M|S)$. An example is selected for labeling if the committee members largely disagree on its classification. This procedure assumes that one can sample from the models' posterior distribution, at least approximately.

To illustrate the generation of committee-members, consider a model containing a single binomial parameter α (the probability of a success), with estimated value a. The statistics S for such a model are given by N, the number of trials, and x, the number of successes in those trials.

Given N and x, the 'best' parameter value may be estimated by one of several estimation methods. For example, the maximum likelihood estimate for α is $a = \frac{x}{N}$, giving the model $M = \{a\} = \{\frac{x}{N}\}$. When generating a committee of models, however, we are not interested in the 'best' model, but rather in sampling the distribution of models given the statistics. For our example, we need to sample the posterior density of estimates for α, namely $P(\alpha = a|S)$. Sampling this distribution yields a set of estimates scattered around $\frac{x}{N}$ (assuming a uniform prior), whose variance decreases as N increases. In other words, the more statistics there are for estimating the parameter, the more similar are the parameter values used by different committee members.

For models with multiple parameters, parame-

[1]This gives the Viterbi model (Merialdo, 1994), which we use here.

[2]This version of the method uses Bayes' theorem ($P(w_i|t_i) \propto \frac{P(t_i|w_i)}{P(t_i)}$) (Church, 1988).

ter estimates for different committee members differ more when they are based on low training counts, and they agree more when based on high counts. Selecting examples on which the committee members disagree contributes statistics to currently uncertain parameters whose uncertainty *also* affects classification.

It may sometimes be difficult to sample $P(M|S)$ due to parameter interdependence. Fortunately, models used in natural language processing often assume independence between most model parameters. In such cases it is possible to generate committee members by sampling the posterior distribution for each independent group of parameters separately.

4 Bigram Part-Of-Speech Tagging

4.1 Sampling model parameters

In order to generate committee members for bigram tagging, we sample the posterior distributions for transition probabilities, $P(t_i \rightarrow t_j)$, and for lexical probabilities, $P(t|w)$ (as described in Section 2).

Both types of the parameters we sample have the form of multinomial distributions. Each multinomial random variable corresponds to a conditioning event and its values are given by the corresponding set of conditioned events. For example, a transition probability parameter $P(t_i \rightarrow t_j)$ has conditioning event t_i and conditioned event t_j.

Let $\{u_i\}$ denote the set of possible values of a given multinomial variable, and let $S = \{n_i\}$ denote a set of statistics extracted from the training set for that variable, where n_i is the number of times that the value u_i appears in the training set for the variable, defining $N = \sum_i n_i$. The parameters whose posterior distributions we wish to estimate are $\alpha_i = P(u_i)$.

The maximum likelihood estimate for each of the multinomial's distribution parameters, α_i, is $\hat{\alpha}_i = \frac{n_i}{N}$. In practice, this estimator is usually smoothed in some way to compensate for data sparseness. Such smoothing typically reduces slightly the estimates for values with positive counts and gives small positive estimates for values with a zero count. For simplicity, we describe here the approximation of $P(\alpha_i = a_i|S)$ for the unsmoothed estimator[3].

We approximate the posterior $P(\alpha_i = a_i|S)$ by first assuming that the multinomial is a collection of independent binomials, each of which corresponds to a single value u_i of the multinomial; we then normalize the values so that they sum to 1. For each such binomial, we approximate $P(\alpha_i = a_i|S)$ as a truncated normal distribution (restricted to [0,1]), with estimated mean $\mu = \frac{n_i}{N}$ and variance $\sigma^2 = \frac{\mu(1-\mu)}{N}$. [4]

To generate a particular multinomial distribution, we randomly choose values for the binomial parameters α_i from their approximated posterior distributions (using the simple sampling method given in (Press et al., 1988, p. 214)), and renormalize them so that they sum to 1. Finally, to generate a random HMM given statistics S, we choose values independently for the parameters of each multinomial, since all the different multinomials in an HMM are independent.

4.2 Examples in bigram training

Typically, concept learning problems are formulated such that there is a set of training examples that are independent of each other. When training a bigram model (indeed, any HMM), this is not true, as each word is dependent on that before it. This problem is solved by considering each sentence as an individual example. More generally, it is possible to break the text at any point where tagging is unambiguous. We thus use unambiguous words (those with only one possible part of speech) as example boundaries in bigram tagging. This allows us to train on smaller examples, focusing training more on the truly informative parts of the corpus.

5 Selection Algorithms

Within the committee-based paradigm there exist different methods for selecting informative examples. Previous research in sample selection has used either *sequential* selection (Seung, Opper, and Sompolinsky, 1992; Freund et al., 1993; Dagan and Engelson, 1995), or *batch* selection (Lewis and Catlett, 1994; Lewis and Gale, 1994). We describe here general algorithms for both sequential and batch selection.

Sequential selection examines unlabeled examples as they are supplied, one by one, and measures the disagreement in their classification by the committee. Those examples determined to be sufficiently informative are selected for training. Most simply, we can use a committee of size two and select an example when the two models disagree on its classification. This gives the following, parameter-free, **two member sequential selection algorithm**, executed for each unlabeled input example e:

1. Draw 2 models randomly from $P(M|S)$, where S are statistics acquired from previously labeled examples;

[3]In the implementation we smooth the MLE by interpolation with a uniform probability distribution, following Merialdo (1994). Approximate adaptation of $P(\alpha_i = a_i|S)$ to the smoothed version of the estimator is simple.

[4]The normal approximation, while easy to implement, can be avoided. The posterior probability $P(\alpha_i = a_i|S)$ for the multinomial is given exactly by the Dirichlet distribution (Johnson, 1972) (which reduces to the Beta distribution in the binomial case). In this work we assumed a uniform prior distribution for each model parameter; we have not addressed the question of how to best choose a prior for this problem.

2. Classify e by each model, giving classifications c_1 and c_2;
3. If $c_1 \neq c_2$, select e for annotation;
4. If e is selected, get its correct label and update S accordingly.

This basic algorithm needs no parameters. If desired, it is possible to tune the frequency of selection, by changing the variance of $P(M|S)$ (or the variance of $P(\alpha_i = a_i|S)$ for each parameter), where larger variances increase the rate of disagreement among the committee members. We implemented this effect by employing a temperature parameter t, used as a multiplier of the variance of the posterior parameter distribution.

A more general algorithm results from allowing (i) a larger number of committee members, k, in order to sample $P(M|S)$ more precisely, and (ii) more refined example selection criteria. This gives the following **general sequential selection algorithm**, executed for each unlabeled input example e:

1. Draw k models $\{M_i\}$ randomly from $P(M|S)$ (possibly using a temperature t);
2. Classify e by each model M_i giving classifications $\{c_i\}$;
3. Measure the disagreement D over $\{c_i\}$;
4. Decide whether to select e for annotation, based on the value of D;
5. If e is selected, get its correct label and update S accordingly.

It is easy to see that two member sequential selection is a special case of general sequential selection, where any disagreement is considered sufficient for selection. In order to instantiate the general algorithm for larger committees, we need to define (i) a measure for disagreement (Step 3), and (ii) a selection criterion (Step 4).

Our approach to measuring disagreement is to use the *vote entropy*, the entropy of the distribution of classifications assigned to an example ('voted for') by the committee members. Denoting the number of committee members assigning c to e by $V(c,e)$, the vote entropy is:

$$D = -\frac{1}{\log k} \sum_c \frac{V(c,e)}{k} \log \frac{V(c,e)}{k}$$

(Dividing by $\log k$ normalizes the scale for the number of committee members.) Vote entropy is maximized when all committee members disagree, and is zero when they all agree.

In bigram tagging, each example consists of a sequence of several words. In our system, we measure D separately for each word, and use the average entropy over the word sequence as a measurement of disagreement for the example. We use the average entropy rather than the entropy over the entire sequence, because the number of committee members is small with respect to the total number of possible tag sequences. Note that we do not look at the entropy of the distribution given by each single model to the possible tags (classes), since we are only interested in the uncertainty of the final classification (see the discussion in Section 7).

We consider two alternative selection criteria (for Step 4). The simplest is *thresholded selection*, in which an example is selected for annotation if its vote entropy exceeds some threshold θ. The other alternative is *randomized selection*, in which an example is selected for annotation based on the flip of a coin biased according to the vote entropy—a higher vote entropy entailing a higher probability of selection. We define the selection probability as a linear function of vote entropy: $p = gD$, where g is an *entropy gain* parameter. The selection method we used in our earlier work (Dagan and Engelson, 1995) is randomized sequential selection using this linear selection probability model, with parameters k, t and g.

An alternative to sequential selection is *batch selection*. Rather than evaluating examples individually for their informativeness a large batch of examples is examined, and the m best are selected for annotation. The **batch selection algorithm**, executed for each batch B of N examples, is as follows:

1. For each example e in B:
   (a) Draw k models randomly from $P(M|S)$;
   (b) Classify e by each model, giving classifications $\{c_i\}$;
   (c) Measure the disagreement D_e for e over $\{c_i\}$;
2. Select for annotation the m examples from B with the highest D_e;
3. Update S by the statistics of the selected examples.

This procedure is repeated sequentially for successive batches of N examples, returning to the start of the corpus at the end. If N is equal to the size of the corpus, batch selection selects the m globally best examples in the corpus at each stage (as in (Lewis and Catlett, 1994)). On the other hand, as N decreases, batch selection becomes closer to sequential selection.

6 Experimental Results

This section presents results of applying committee-based sample selection to bigram part-of-speech tagging, as compared with complete training on all examples in the corpus. Evaluation was performed using the University of Pennsylvania tagged corpus from the ACL/DCI CD-ROM I. For ease of implementation, we used a complete (closed) lexicon which contains all the words in the corpus.

The committee-based sampling algorithm was initialized using the first 1,000 words from the corpus,

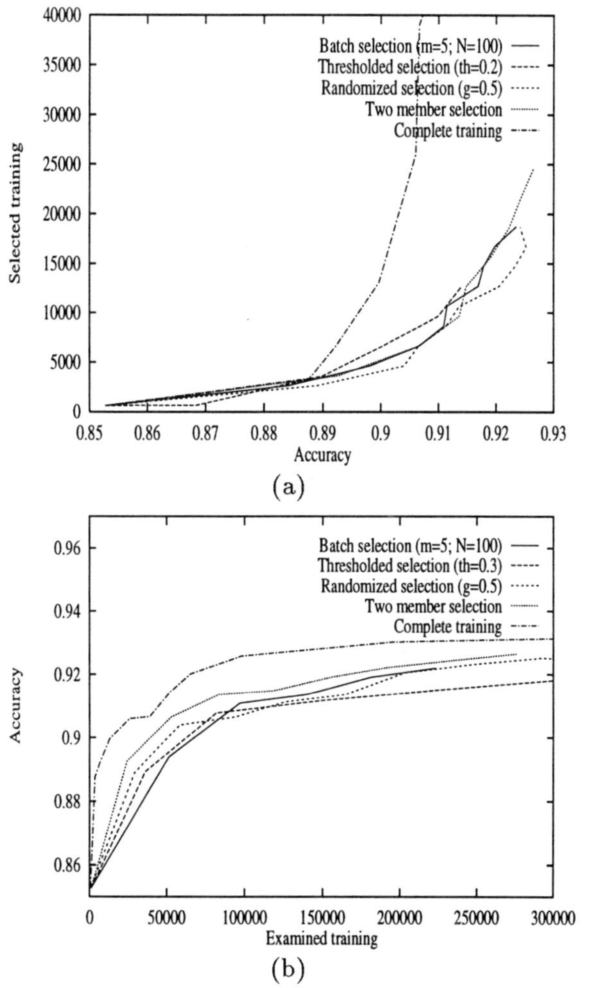

Figure 1: Training versus accuracy. In batch, random, and thresholded runs, $k = 5$ and $t = 50$. (a) Number of ambiguous words selected for labeling versus classification accuracy achieved. (b) Accuracy versus number of words examined from the corpus (both labeled and unlabeled).

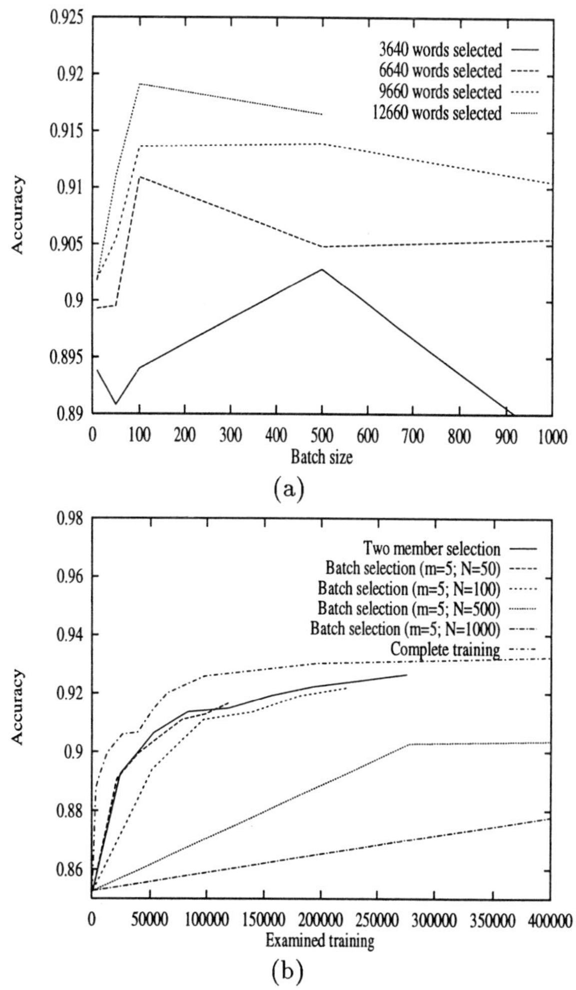

Figure 2: Evaluating batch selection, for $m = 5$. (a) Accuracy achieved versus batch size at different numbers of selected training words. (b) Accuracy versus number of words examined from the corpus for different batch sizes.

and then sequentially examined the following examples in the corpus for possible labeling. The training set consisted of the first million words in the corpus, with sentence ordering randomized to compensate for inhomogeneity in corpus composition. The test set was a separate portion of the corpus, consisting of 20,000 words. We compare the amount of training required by different selection methods to achieve a given tagging accuracy on the test set, where both the amount of training and tagging accuracy are measured over ambiguous words.[5]

The effectiveness of randomized committee-based selection for part-of-speech tagging, with 5 and 10 committee members, was demonstrated in (Dagan and Engelson, 1995). Here we present and compare results for batch, randomized, thresholded, and two member committee-based selection.

Figure 1 presents the results of comparing the several selection methods against each other. The plots shown are for the best parameter settings that we found through manual tuning for each method. Figure 1(a) shows the advantage that sample selection gives with regard to annotation cost. For example, complete training requires annotated examples containing 98,000 ambiguous words to achieve a 92.6% accuracy (beyond the scale of the graph), while the selective methods require only 18,000–25,000 ambiguous words to achieve this accuracy. We also find

[5]Note that most other work on tagging has measured accuracy over all words, not just ambiguous ones. Complete training of our system on 1,000,000 words gave us an accuracy of 93.5% over ambiguous words, which corresponds to an accuracy of 95.9% over all words in the test set, comparable to other published results on bigram tagging.

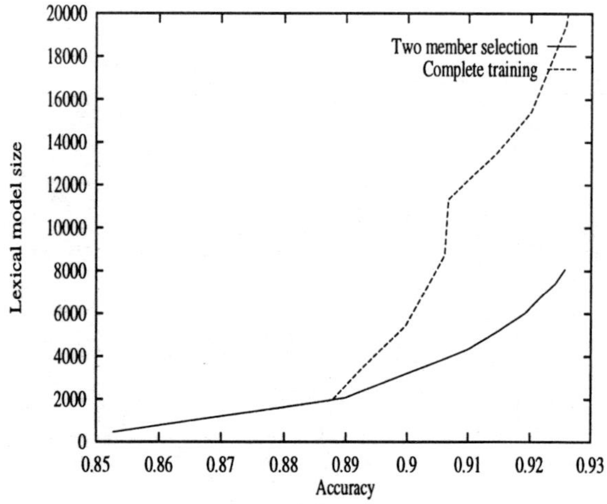

(a)

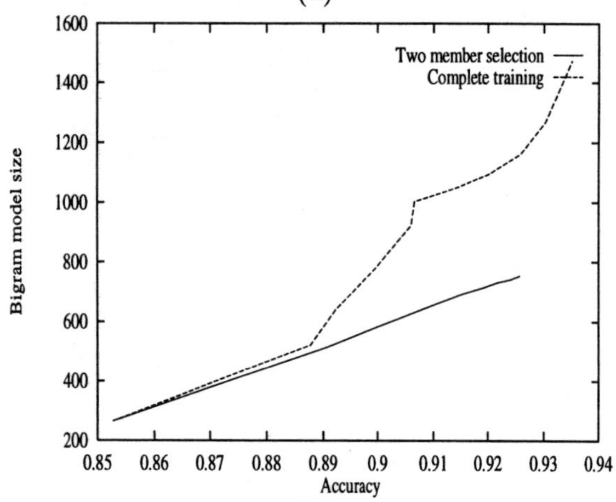

(b)

Figure 3: The size of the trained model, measured by the number of frequency counts > 0, plotted (y-axis) versus classification accuracy achieved (x-axis). (a) Lexical counts (freq(t, w)) (b) Bigram counts (freq($t_1 \rightarrow t_2$)).

that, to a first approximation, all selection methods considered give similar results. Thus, it seems that a refined choice of the selection method is not crucial for achieving large reductions in annotation cost.

This equivalence of the different methods also largely holds with respect to computational efficiency. Figure 1(b) plots classification accuracy versus number of words *examined*, instead of those *selected*. We see that while all selective methods are less efficient in terms of examples examined than complete training, they are comparable to each other. Two member selection seems to have a clear, though small, advantage.

In Figure 2 we investigate further the properties of batch selection. Figure 2(a) shows that accuracy increases with batch size only up to a point, and then starts to decrease. This result is in line with theoretical difficulties with batch selection (Freund et al., 1993) in that batch selection does not account for the distribution of input examples. Hence, once batch size increases past a point, the input distribution has too little influence on which examples are selected, and hence classification accuracy decreases. Furthermore, as batch size increases, computational efficiency, in terms of the number of examples examined to attain a given accuracy, decreases tremendously (Figure 2(b)).

The ability of committee-based selection to focus on the more informative parts of the training corpus is analyzed in Figure 3. Here we examined the number of lexical and bigram counts that were stored (i.e, were non-zero) during training, using the two member selection algorithm and complete training. As the graphs show, the sample selection method achieves the same accuracy as complete training with fewer lexical and bigram counts. This means that many counts in the data are less useful for correct tagging, as replacing them with smoothed estimates works just as well.[6] Committee-based selection ignores such counts, focusing on parameters which improve the model. This behavior has the practical advantage of reducing the size of the model significantly (by a factor of three here). Also, the average count is lower in a model constructed by selective training than in a fully trained model, suggesting that the selection method avoids using examples which increase the counts for already known parameters.

7 Discussion

Why does committee-based sample selection work? Consider the properties of those examples that are selected for training. In general, a selected training example will contribute data to several statistics, which in turn will improve the estimates of several parameter values. An *informative* example is therefore one whose contribution to the statistics leads to a significantly useful improvement of model parameter estimates. Model parameters for which acquiring additional statistics is most beneficial can be characterized by the following three properties:

1. The current estimate of the parameter is uncertain due to insufficient statistics in the training set. Additional statistics would bring the estimate closer to the true value.

2. Classification of examples is sensitive to changes in the current estimate of the parameter. Otherwise, even if the current value of the parameter is very uncertain, acquiring additional statistics will not change the resulting classifications.

3. The parameter affects classification for a large proportion of examples in the input. Parame-

[6]As noted above, we smooth the MLE estimates by interpolation with a uniform probability distribution (Merialdo, 1994).

ters that affect only few examples have low overall utility.

The committee-based selection algorithms work because they tend to select examples that affect parameters with the above three properties. Property 1 is addressed by randomly drawing the parameter values for committee members from the posterior distribution given the current statistics. When the statistics for a parameter are insufficient, the variance of the posterior distribution of the estimates is large, and hence there will be large differences in the values of the parameter chosen for different committee members. Note that property 1 is not addressed when uncertainty in classification is only judged relative to a *single* model[7] (as in, eg, (Lewis and Gale, 1994)).

Property 2 is addressed by selecting examples for which committee members highly disagree in *classification* (rather than measuring disagreement in parameter estimates). Committee-based selection thus addresses properties 1 and 2 simultaneously: it acquires statistics just when uncertainty in current parameter estimates entails uncertainty regarding the *appropriate* classification of the example. Our results show that this effect is achieved even when using only two committee members to sample the space of likely classifications. By *appropriate* classification we mean the classification given by a perfectly-trained model, that is, one with accurate parameter values.

Note that this type of uncertainty regarding the identity of the *appropriate* classification, is different than uncertainty regarding the *correctness* of the classification itself. For example, sufficient statistics may yield an accurate 0.51 probability estimate for a class c in a given example, making it certain that c is the appropriate classification. However, the certainty that c is the *correct* classification is low, since there is a 0.49 chance that c is the wrong class for the example. A single model can be used to estimate only the second type of uncertainty, which does not correlate directly with the utility of additional training.

Finally, property 3 is addressed by independently examining input examples which are drawn from the input distribution. In this way, we implicitly model the distribution of model parameters used for classifying input examples. Such modeling is absent in batch selection, and we hypothesize that this is the reason for its lower effectiveness.

8 Conclusions

Annotating large textual corpora for training natural language models is a costly process. We propose reducing this cost significantly using committee-based sample selection, which reduces redundant annotation of examples that contribute little new information. The method can be applied in a semi-interactive process, in which the system selects several new examples for annotation at a time and updates its statistics after receiving their labels from the user. The implicit modeling of uncertainty makes the selection system generally applicable and quite simple to implement.

Our experimental study of variants of the selection method suggests several practical conclusions. First, it was found that the simplest version of the committee-based method, using a two-member committee, yields reduction in annotation cost comparable to that of the multi-member committee. The two-member version is simpler to implement, has no parameters to tune and is computationally more efficient. Second, we generalized the selection scheme giving several alternatives for optimizing the method for a specific task. For bigram tagging, comparative evaluation of the different variants of the method showed similar large reductions in annotation cost, suggesting the robustness of the committee-based approach. Third, sequential selection, which implicitly models the expected utility of an example relative to the example distribution, worked in general better than batch selection. The latter was found to work well only for small batch sizes, where the method mimics sequential selection. Increasing batch size (approaching 'pure' batch selection) reduces both accuracy and efficiency. Finally, we studied the effect of sample selection on the size of the trained model, showing a significant reduction in model size.

8.1 Further research

Our results suggest applying committee-based sample selection to other statistical NLP tasks which rely on estimating probabilistic parameters from an annotated corpus. Statistical methods for these tasks typically assign a probability estimate, or some other statistical score, to each alternative analysis (a word sense, a category label, a parse tree, etc.), and then select the analysis with the highest score. The score is usually computed as a function of the estimates of several 'atomic' parameters, often binomials or multinomials, such as:

- In word sense disambiguation (Hearst, 1991; Gale, Church, and Yarowsky, 1993): $P(s|f)$, where s is a specific sense of the ambiguous word in question w, and f is a feature of occurrences of w. Common features are words in the context of w or morphological attributes of it.
- In prepositional-phrase (PP) attachment (Hindle and Rooth, 1993): $P(a|f)$, where a is a possible attachment, such as an attachment to a head verb or noun, and f is a feature, or a combination of features, of the attachment. Com-

[7] The use of a single model is also criticized in (Cohn, Atlas, and Ladner, 1994).

mon features are the words involved in the attachment, such as the head verb or noun, the preposition, and the head word of the PP.

- In statistical parsing (Black et al., 1993): $P(r|h)$, the probability of applying the rule r at a certain stage of the top down derivation of the parse tree given the history h of the derivation process.
- In text categorization (Lewis and Gale, 1994; Iwayama and Tokunaga, 1994): $P(t|C)$, where t is a term in the document to be categorized, and C is a candidate category label.

Applying committee-based selection to supervised training for such tasks can be done analogously to its application in the current paper[8]. Furthermore, committee-based selection may be attempted also for training non-probabilistic classifiers, where explicit modeling of information gain is typically impossible. In such contexts, committee members might be generated by randomly varying some of the decisions made in the learning algorithm.

Another important area for future work is in developing sample selection methods which are independent of the eventual learning method to be applied. This would be of considerable advantage in developing selectively annotated corpora for general research use. Recent work on heterogeneous uncertainty sampling (Lewis and Catlett, 1994) supports this idea, using one type of model for example selection and a different type for classification.

Acknowledgments. We thank Yoav Freund and Yishay Mansour for helpful discussions. The first author gratefully acknowledges the support of the Fulbright Foundation.

References

Black, Ezra, Fred Jelinek, John Lafferty, David Magerman, Robert Mercer, and Salim Roukos. 1993. Towards history-based grammars: using richer models for probabilistic parsing. In *Proc. of the Annual Meeting of the ACL*, pages 31–37.

Church, Kenneth W. 1988. A stochastic parts program and noun phrase parser for unrestricted text. In *Proc. of ACL Conference on Applied Natural Language Processing.*

Cohn, David, Les Atlas, and Richard Ladner. 1994. Improving generalization with active learning. *Machine Learning*, 15:201–221.

[8]Measuring disagreement in full syntactic parsing is complicated. It may be approached by similar methods to those used for parsing evaluation, which measure the disagreement between the parser's output and the correct parse.

Dagan, Ido and Sean Engelson. 1995. Committee-based sampling for training probabilistic classifiers. In *Proc. Int'l Conference on Machine Learning*, July.

Elworthy, David. 1994. Does Baum-Welch re-estimation improve taggers? In *Proc. of ACL Conference on Applied Natural Language Processing*, pages 53–58.

Freund, Y., H. S. Seung, E. Shamir, and N. Tishby. 1993. Information, prediction, and query by committee. In *Advances in Neural Information Processing*, volume 5. Morgan Kaufmann.

Gale, William, Kenneth Church, and David Yarowsky. 1993. A method for disambiguating word senses in a large corpus. *Computers and the Humanities*, 26:415–439.

Hearst, Marti. 1991. Noun homograph disambiguation using local context in large text corpora. In *Proc. of the Annual Conference of the UW Center for the New OED and Text Research*, pages 1–22.

Hindle, Donald and Mats Rooth. 1993. Structural ambiguity and lexical relations. *Computational Linguistics*, 19(1):103–120.

Iwayama, M. and T. Tokunaga. 1994. A probabilistic model for text categorization based on a single random variable with multiple values. In *Proceedings of the 4th Conference on Applied Natural Language Processing.*

Johnson, Norman L. 1972. *Continuous Multivariate Distributions.* John Wiley & Sons, New York.

Kupiec, Julian. 1992. Robust part-of-speech tagging using a hidden makov model. *Computer Speech and Language*, 6:225–242.

Lewis, David D. and Jason Catlett. 1994. Heterogeneous uncertainty sampling for supervised learning. In *Proc. Int'l Conference on Machine Learning.*

Lewis, David D. and William A. Gale. 1994. A sequential algorithm for training text classifiers. In *Proc. of the ACM SIGIR Conference.*

MacKay, David J. C. 1992. Information-based objective functions for active data selection. *Neural Computation*, 4.

Merialdo, Bernard. 1994. Tagging text with a probabilistic model. *Computational Linguistics*, 20(2):155–172.

Press, William H., Brian P. Flannery, Saul A. Teukolsky, and William T. Vetterling. 1988. *Numerical Recipes in C.* Cambridge University Press.

Seung, H. S., M. Opper, and H. Sompolinsky. 1992. Query by committee. In *Proc. ACM Workshop on Computational Learning Theory.*

Unsupervised Learning of Word-Category Guessing Rules

Andrei Mikheev

HCRC Language Technology Group
University of Edinburgh
2 Buccleuch Place
Edinburgh EH8 9LW, Scotland, UK
: Andrei.Mikheev@ed.ac.uk

Abstract

Words unknown to the lexicon present a substantial problem to part-of-speech tagging. In this paper we present a technique for fully unsupervised statistical acquisition of rules which guess possible parts-of-speech for unknown words. Three complementary sets of word-guessing rules are induced from the lexicon and a raw corpus: prefix morphological rules, suffix morphological rules and ending-guessing rules. The learning was performed on the Brown Corpus data and rule-sets, with a highly competitive performance, were produced and compared with the state-of-the-art.

1 Introduction

Words unknown to the lexicon present a substantial problem to part-of-speech (POS) tagging of real-world texts. Taggers assign a single POS-tag to a word-token, provided that it is known what parts-of-speech this word can take on in principle. So, first words are looked up in the lexicon. However, 3 to 5% of word tokens are usually missing in the lexicon when tagging real-world texts. This is where word-POS guessers take their place — they employ the analysis of word features, e.g. word leading and trailing characters, to figure out its possible POS categories. A set of rules which on the basis of ending characters of unknown words, assign them with sets of possible POS-tags is supplied with the Xerox tagger (Kupiec, 1992). A similar approach was taken in (Weischedel et al., 1993) where an unknown word was guessed given the probabilities for an unknown word to be of a particular POS, its capitalisation feature and its ending. In (Brill, 1995) a system of rules which uses both ending-guessing and more morphologically motivated rules is described. The best of these methods are reported to achieve 82–85% of tagging accuracy on unknown words, e.g. (Brill, 1995; Weischedel et al., 1993).

The major topic in the development of word-POS guessers is the strategy which is to be used for the acquisition of the guessing rules. A rule-based tagger described in (Voutilainen, 1995) is equipped with a set of guessing rules which has been hand-crafted using knowledge of English morphology and intuition. A more appealing approach is an empirical automatic acquisition of such rules using available lexical resources. In (Zhang&Kim, 1990) a system for the automated learning of morphological word-formation rules is described. This system divides a string into three regions and from training examples infers their correspondence to underlying morphological features. Brill (Brill, 1995) outlines a transformation-based learner which learns guessing rules from a pre-tagged training corpus. A statistical-based suffix learner is presented in (Schmid, 1994). From a pre-tagged training corpus it constructs the suffix tree where every suffix is associated with its information measure. Although the learning process in these and some other systems is fully unsupervised and the accuracy of obtained rules reaches current state-of-the-art, they require specially prepared training data — a pre-tagged training corpus, training examples, etc.

In this paper we describe a new fully automatic technique for learning part-of-speech guessing rules. This technique does not require specially prepared training data and employs fully unsupervised statistical learning using the lexicon supplied with the tagger and word-frequencies obtained from a raw corpus. The learning is implemented as a two-staged process with feedback. First, setting certain parameters a set of guessing rules is acquired, then it is evaluated and the results of evaluation are used for re-acquisition of a better tuned rule-set.

2 Guessing Rules Acquisition

As was pointed out above, one of the requirements in many techniques for automatic learning of part-of-speech guessing rules is specially prepared training data — a pre-tagged training corpus, training examples, etc. In our approach we decided to reuse the data which come naturally with a tagger, viz. the lexicon. Another source of information which is used and which is not prepared specially for the task is a text corpus. Unlike other approaches we don't require the corpus to be pre-annotated but use it in its raw form. In our experiments we used the lexicon and word-frequencies derived from the

Brown Corpus (Francis&Kucera, 1982). There are a number of reasons for choosing the Brown Corpus data for training. The most important ones are that the Brown Corpus provides a model of general multi-domain language use, so general language regularities can be induced from it, and second, many taggers come with data trained on the Brown Corpus which is useful for comparison and evaluation. This, however, by no means restricts the described technique to that or any other tag-set, lexicon or corpus. Moreover, despite the fact that the training is performed on a particular lexicon and a particular corpus, the obtained guessing rules suppose to be domain and corpus independent and the only training-dependent feature is the tag-set in use.

The acquisition of word-POS guessing rules is a three-step procedure which includes the *rule extraction*, *rule scoring* and *rule merging* phases. At the rule extraction phase, three sets of word-guessing rules (morphological prefix guessing rules, morphological suffix guessing rules and ending-guessing rules) are extracted from the lexicon and cleaned from coincidental cases. At the scoring phase, each rule is scored in accordance with its accuracy of guessing and the best scored rules are included into the final rule-sets. At the merging phase, rules which have not scored high enough to be included into the final rule-sets are merged into more general rules, then re-scored and depending on their score added to the final rule-sets.

2.1 Rule Extraction Phase

2.1.1 Extraction of Morphological Rules.

Morphological word-guessing rules describe how one word can be guessed given that another word is known. For example, the rule: **[un (VBD VBN) (JJ)]** says that prefixing the string "un" to a word, which can act as past form of verb (VBD) and participle (VBN), produces an adjective (JJ). For instance, by applying this rule to the word "undeveloped", we first segment the prefix "un" and if the remaining part "developed" is found in the lexicon as **(VBD VBN)**, we conclude that the word "undeveloped" is an adjective (JJ). The first POS-set in a guessing rule is called the *initial class* (I-class) and the POS-set of the guessed word is called the *resulting class* (R-class). In the example above **(VBD VBN)** is the I-class of the rule and **(JJ)** is the R-class.

In English, as in many other languages, morphological word formation is realised by affixation: prefixation and suffixation. Although sometimes the affixation is not just a straightforward concatenation of the affix with the stem[1], the majority of cases clearly obey simple concatenative regularities. So, we decided first to concentrate only on simple concatenative cases. There are two kinds of morphological rules to be learned: suffix rules (A^s) — rules which are applied to the tail of a word, and prefix rules (A^p) — rules which are applied to the beginning of a word. For example:

A^s : **[ed (NN VB) (JJ VBD VBN)]**

says that if by stripping the suffix "ed" from an unknown word we produce a word with the POS-class **(NN VB)**, the unknown word is of the class – **(JJ VBD VBN)**. This rule works, for instance, for **[book →booked]**, **[water →watered]**, etc. To extract such rules a special operator ∇ is applied to every pair of words from the lexicon. It tries to segment an affix by leftmost string subtraction for suffixes and rightmost string subtraction for prefixes. If the subtraction results in an non-empty string it creates a morphological rule by storing the POS-class of the shorter word as the I-class and the POS-class of the longer word as the R-class. For example:

[booked (JJ VBD VBN)] ∇ **[book (NN VB)]** →
A^s : **[ed (NN VB) (JJ VBD VBN)]**

[undeveloped (JJ)] ∇ **[developed (VBD VBN)]** →
A^p : **[un (VBD VBN) (JJ)]**

The ∇ operator is applied to all possible lexicon-entry pairs and if a rule produced by such an application has already been extracted from another pair, its frequency count (f) is incremented. Thus two different sets of guessing rules — prefix and suffix morphological rules together with their frequencies — are produced. Next, from these sets of guessing rules we need to cut out infrequent rules which might bias the further learning process. To do that we eliminate all the rules with the frequency f less than a certain threshold θ[2]. Such filtering reduces the rule-sets more than tenfold and does not leave clearly coincidental cases among the rules.

2.1.2 Extraction of Ending Guessing Rules.

Unlike morphological guessing rules, ending-guessing rules do not require the main form of an unknown word to be listed in the lexicon. These rules guess a POS-class for a word just on the basis of its ending characters and without looking up its stem in the lexicon. Such rules are able to cover more unknown words than morphological guessing rules but their accuracy will not be as high. For example, an ending-guessing rule

A^e: **[ing - (JJ NN VBG)]**

says that if a word ends with "ing" it can be an adjective, a noun or a gerund. Unlike a morphological rule, this rule does not ask to check whether the substring preceeding the "ing"-ending is a word with a particular POS-tag. Thus an ending-guessing rule looks exactly like a morphological rule apart from the I-class which is always void.

To collect such rules we set the upper limit on the ending length equal to five characters and thus collect from the lexicon all possible word-endings of length 1, 2, 3, 4 and 5, together with the POS-classes of the words where these endings were detected to appear. This is done by the operator Δ. For example, from the word **[different (JJ)]** the Δ operator will produce five ending-guessing rules: **[t - (JJ)]**; **[nt - (JJ)]**; **[ent - (JJ)]**; **[rent - (JJ)]**; **[erent - (JJ)]**. The Δ operator is applied to each entry in the lexicon in the

[1] consider an example: try – tried.

[2] usually we set this threshold quite low: 2–4.

way described for the ∇ operator of the morphological rules and then infrequent rules with $f < \theta$ are filtered out.

2.2 Rule Scoring Phase

Of course, not all acquired rules are equally good as plausible guesses about word-classes: some rules are more accurate in their guessings and some rules are more frequent in their application. So, for every acquired rule we need to estimate whether it is an effective rule which is worth retaining in the final rule-set. For such estimation we perform a statistical experiment as follows: for every rule we calculate the number of times this rule was applied to a word token from a raw corpus and the number of times it gave the right answer. Note that the task of the rule is not to disambiguate a word's POS but to provide *all* and *only* possible POSs it can take on. If the rule is correct in the majority of times it was applied it is obviously a good rule. If the rule is wrong most of the times it is a bad rule which should not be included into the final rule-set.

To perform this experiment we take one-by-one each rule from the rule-sets produced at the rule extraction phase, take each word token from the corpus and guess its POS-set using the rule if the rule is applicable to the word. For example, if a guessing rule strips a particular suffix and a current word from the corpus does not have this suffix, we classify these word and rule as incompatible and the rule as not applicable to that word. If the rule is applicable to the word we perform look-up in the lexicon for this word and then compare the result of the guess with the information listed in the lexicon. If the guessed POS-set is the same as the POS-set stated in the lexicon, we count it as success, otherwise it is failure. The value of a guessing rule, thus, closely correlates with its *estimated proportion of success* ($\hat{p}$) which is the proportion of all positive outcomes (x) of the rule application to the total number of the trials (n), which are, in fact, attempts to apply the rule to all the compatible words in the corpus. We also smooth $\hat{p}$ so as not to have zeros in positive or negative outcome probabilities: $\hat{p} = \frac{x+0.5}{n+1}$

$\hat{p}$ estimate is a good indicator of rule accuracy. However, it frequently suffers from large *estimation error* due to insufficient training data. For example, if a rule was detected to work just twice and the total number of observations was also two, its estimate $\hat{p}$ is very high (1, or 0.83 for the smoothed version) but clearly this is not a very reliable estimate because of the tiny size of the sample. Several smoothing methods have been proposed to reduce the estimation error. For different reasons all these smoothing methods are not very suitable in our case. In our approach we tackle this problem by calculating the *lower confidence limit* π_L for the rule estimate. This can be seen as the minimal expected value of $\hat{p}$ for the rule if we were to draw a large number of samples. Thus with certain confidence α we can assume that if we used more training data, the rule estimate $\hat{p}$ would be no worse than the π_L limit. The lower confidence limit π_L is calculated as:

$$\pi_L = \hat{p} - z_{(1-\alpha)/2} * s_p = \hat{p} - z_{(1-\alpha)/2} * \sqrt{\frac{\hat{p}(1-\hat{p})}{n}}$$

This function favours the rules with higher estimates obtained over larger samples. Even if one rule has a high estimate but that estimate was obtained over a small sample, another rule with a lower estimate but over a large sample might be valued higher. Note also that since $\hat{p}$ itself is smoothed we will not have zeros in positive ($\hat{p}$) or negative ($1-\hat{p}$) outcome probabilities. This estimation of the rule value in fact resembles that used by (Tzoukermann et al., 1995) for scoring POS-disambiguation rules for the French tagger. The main difference between the two functions is that there the z value was implicitly assumed to be 1 which corresponds to the confidence of 68%. A more standard approach is to adopt a rather high confidence value in the range of 90-95%. We adopted 90% confidence for which $z_{(1-0.90)/2} = z_{0.05} = 1.65$. Thus we can calculate the score for the ith rule as: $\hat{p}_i - 1.65 * \sqrt{\frac{\hat{p}_i(1-\hat{p}_i)}{n_i}}$

Another important consideration for scoring a word-guessing rule is that the longer the affix or ending of the rule the more confident we are that it is not a coincidental one, even on small samples. For example, if the estimate for the word-ending "o" was obtained over a sample of 5 words and the estimate for the word-ending "fulness" was also obtained over a sample of 5 words, the later case is more representative even though the sample size is the same. Thus we need to adjust the estimation error in accordance with the length of the affix or ending. A good way to do that is to divide it by a value which increases along with the increase of the length. After several experiments we obtained:

$$score_i = \hat{p}_i - 1.65 * \sqrt{\frac{\hat{p}_i(1-\hat{p}_i)}{n_i}} / (1 + \log(|S_i|))$$

When the length of the affix or ending is 1 the estimation error is not changed since log(1) is 0. For the rules with the affix or ending length of 2 the estimation error is reduced by $1 + \log(2) = 1.3$, for the length 3 this will be $1 + \log(3) = 1.48$, etc. The longer the length the smaller the sample which will be considered representative enough for a confident rule estimation. Setting the threshold θ_s at a certain level lets only the rules whose score is higher than the threshold to be included into the final rule-sets. The method for setting up this threshold is based on empirical evaluations of the rule-sets and is described in Section 3.

2.3 Rule Merging Phase

Rules which have scored lower than the threshold θ_s can be merged into more general rules which if scored above the threshold are also included into the final rule-sets. We can merge two rules which have scored below the threshold and have the same affix (or ending) and the initial class (I)[3]. The score of the resulting rule will be higher than the scores of the merged rules since the number of positive observations increases and the number of the trials remains the same. After a successful application of the merging, the resulting rule substitutes the two merged ones. To perform such rule-merging over a rule-set, first, the rules which have not been included into the final set are sorted by their score and best-scored rules are merged first. This is done recursively until the score of the resulting rule does not exceed the threshold in which case it is added to the final rule-set. This process is applied until no merges can be done to the rules which have scored below the threshold.

3 Direct Evaluation Stage

There are two important questions which arise at the rule acquisition stage - how to choose the scoring threshold θ_s and what is the performance of the rule-sets produced with different thresholds. The task of assigning a set of POS-tags to a word is actually quite similar to the task of document categorisation where a document should be assigned with a set of descriptors which represent its contents. The performance of such assignment can be measured in:

recall - the percentage of POSs which were assigned correctly by the guesser to a word;

precision - the percentage of POSs the guesser assigned correctly over the total number of POSs it assigned to the word;

coverage - the proportion of words which the guesser was able to classify, but not necessarily correctly;

In our experiments we measured word precision and word recall (micro-average). There were two types of data in use at this stage. First, we evaluated the guessing rules against the actual lexicon: every word from the lexicon, except for closed-class words and words shorter than five characters[4], was guessed by the different guessing strategies and the results were compared with the information the word had in the lexicon. In the other evaluation experiment we measured the performance of the guessing rules against the training corpus. For every word we computed its metrics exactly as in the previous experiment. Then we multiplied these results by the corpus frequency of this particular word and averaged them. Thus the most frequent words had the greatest influence on the aggreagte measures.

First, we concentrated on finding the best thresholds θ_s for the rule-sets. To do that for each rule-set produced using different thresholds we recorded the three metrics and chose the set with the best aggregate. In Table 1 some results of that experiment are shown. The best thresholds were detected: for ending rules – 75 points, for suffix rules – 60, and for prefix rules – 80. One can notice a slight difference in the results obtained over the lexicon and the corpus. The corpus results are better because the training technique explicitly targeted the rule-sets to the most frequent cases of the corpus rather than the lexicon. In average ending-guessing rules were detected to cover over 96% of the unknown words. The precision of 74% roughly can be interpreted as that for words which take on three different POSs in their POS-class, the ending-guessing rules will assign four, but in 95% of the times (recall) the three required POSs will be among the four assigned by the guess. In comparison with the Xerox word-ending guesser taken as the base-line model we detect a substantial increase in the precision by about 22% and a cheerful increase in coverage by about 6%. This means that the Xerox guesser creates more ambiguity for the disambiguator, assigning five instead of three POSs in the example above. It can also handle 6% less unknown words which, in fact, might decrease its performance even lower. In comparison with the ending-guessing rules, the morphological rules have much better precision and hence better accuracy of guessing. Virtually almost every word which can be guessed by the morphological rules is guessed exactly correct (97% recall and 97% precision). Not surprisingly, the coverage of morphological rules is much lower than that of the ending-guessing ones – for the suffix rules it is less than 40% and for the prefix rules about 5-6%.

After obtaining the optimal rule-sets we performed the same experiment on a word-sample which was not included into the training lexicon and corpus. We gathered about three thousand words from the lexicon developed for the Wall Street Journal corpus[5] and collected frequencies of these words in this corpus. At this experiment we obtained similar metrics apart from the coverage which dropped about 0.5% for Ending 75 and Xerox rule-sets and 7% for the Suffix 60 rule-set. This, actually, did not come as a surprise, since many main forms required by the suffix rules were missing in the lexicon.

In the next experiment we evaluated whether the morphological rules add any improvement if they are used in conjunction with the ending-guessing rules. We also evaluated in detail whether a conjunctive application with the Xerox guesser would boost the performance. As in the previous experiment we measured the precision, recall and coverage both on the lexicon and on the corpus. Table 2 demonstrates some results of this experiment. The first part of the table shows that when the Xerox guesser is applied before the E_{75} guesser we measure a drop in the performance. When the Xerox guesser is applied after the E_{75} guesser no sufficient changes to the performance are noticed. This actually proves that the E_{75} rule-set fully supercedes the Xerox rule-set. The second part of the table shows that the cascading application of the morphological rule-sets together with the ending-guessing rules increases the over-

[3]For ending-guessing rules this is always true, so only the ending itself counts.

[4]the actual size of the filtered lexicon was 47,659 entries out of 53,015 entries of the original lexicon.

[5]these words were not listed in the training lexicon

all precision of the guessing by a further 5%. This makes the improvements against the base-line Xerox guesser 28% in precision and 7% in coverage.

4 Tagging Unknown Words

The direct evaluation of the rule-sets gave us the grounds for the comparison and selection of the best performing guessing rule-sets. The task of unknown word guessing is, however, a subtask of the overall part-of-speech tagging process. Thus we are mostly interested in how the advantage of one rule-set over another will affect the tagging performance. So, we performed an independent evaluation of the impact of the word guessers on tagging accuracy. In this evaluation we tried two different taggers. First, we used a tagger which was a C++ re-implementation of the LISP implemented HMM Xerox tagger described in (Kupiec, 1992). The other tagger was the rule-based tagger of Brill (Brill, 1995). Both of the taggers come with data and word-guessing components pre-trained on the Brown Corpus[6]. This, actually gave us the search-space of four combinations: the Xerox tagger equipped with the original Xerox guesser, Brill's tagger with its original guesser, the Xerox tagger with our cascading $P_{80}+S_{60}+E_{75}$ guesser and Brill's tagger with the cascading guesser. For words which failed to be guessed by the guessing rules we applied the standard method of classifying them as common nouns (NN) if they are not capitalised inside a sentence and proper nouns (NP) otherwise. As the base-line result we measured the performance of the taggers with all known words on the same word sample.

In the evaluation of tagging accuracy on unknown words we pay attention to two metrics. First we measure the accuracy of tagging solely on unknown words:

$$UnkownScore = \frac{CorrectlyTaggedUnkownWords}{TotalUnknownWords}$$

This metric gives us the exact measure of how the tagger has done on unknown words. In this case, however, we do not account for the known words which were mis-tagged because of the guessers. To put a perspective on that aspect we measure the overall tagging performance:

$$TotalScore = \frac{CorrectlyTaggedWords}{TotalWords}$$

Since the Brown Corpus model is a general language model, it, in principle, does not put restrictions on the type of text it can be used for, although its performance might be slightly lower than that of a model specialised for this particular sublanguage. Here we want to stress that our primary task was not to evaluate the taggers themselves but rather their performance with the word-guessing modules. So we did not worry too much about tuning the taggers for the texts and used the Brown Corpus model instead. We tagged several texts of different origins, except from the Brown Corpus. These texts were not seen at the training phase which means that neither the taggers nor the guessers had been trained on these texts and they naturally had words unknown to the lexicon. For each text we performed two tagging experiments. In the first experiment we tagged the text with the Brown Corpus lexicon supplied with the taggers and hence had only those unknown words which naturally occur in this text. In the second experiment we tagged the same text with the lexicon which contained only closed-class[7] and short[8] words. This small lexicon contained only 5,456 entries out of 53,015 entries of the original Brown Corpus lexicon. All other words were considered as unknown and had to be guessed by the guessers.

We obtained quite stable results in these experiments. Here is a typical example of tagging a text of 5970 words. This text was detected to have 347 unknown words. First, we tagged the text by the four different combinations of the taggers with the word-guessers using the full-fledged lexicon. The results of this tagging are summarised in Table 3. When using the Xerox tagger with its original guesser, 63 unknown words were incorrectly tagged and the accuracy on the unknown words was measured at 81.8%. When the Xerox tagger was equipped with our cascading guesser its accuracy on unknown words increased by almost 9% upto 90.5%. The same situation was detected with Brill's tagger which in general was slightly more accurate than the Xerox one[9]. The cascading guesser performed better than Brill's original guesser by about 8% boosting the performance on the unknown words from 84.5%[10] to 92.2%. The accuracy of the taggers on the set of 347 unknown words when they were made known to the lexicon was detected at 98.5% for both taggers.

In the second experiment we tagged the same text in the same way but with the small lexicon. Out of 5,970 words of the text, 2,215 were unknown to the small lexicon. The results of this tagging are summarised in Table 4. The accuracy of the taggers on the 2,215 unknown words when they were made known to the lexicon was much lower than in the previous experiment — 90.3% for the Xerox tagger and 91.5% for Brill's tagger. Naturally, the performance of the guessers was also lower than in the previous experiment plus the fact that many "semi-closed" class adverbs like "however", "instead", etc., were missing in the small lexicon. The accuracy of the tagging on unknown words dropped by about 5% in general. The best results on unknown words were again obtained on the cascading guesser (86%–87.45%) and Brill's tagger again did better then the Xerox one by 1.5%.

Two types of mis-taggings caused by the guessers

[6]Since Brill's tagger was trained on the Penn tag-set (Marcus et al., 1993) we provided an additional mapping.

[7]articles, prepositions, conjunctions, etc.

[8]shorter than 5 characters

[9]This, however, was not an entirely fair comparison because of the differences in the tag-sets in use by the taggers. The Xerox tagger was trained on the original Brown Corpus tag-set which makes more distinctions between categories than the Penn Brown Corpus tag-set.

[10]This figure agrees with the 85% quoted by Brill (Brill, 1994).

occured. The first type is when guessers provided broader POS-classes for unknown words and the tagger had difficulties with the disambiguation of such broader classes. This is especially the case with the "ing" words which, in general, can act as nouns, adjectives and gerunds and only direct lexicalization can restrict the search space, as in the case with the word "going" which cannot be an adjective but only a noun and a gerund. The second type of mistagging was caused by wrong assignments of POSs by the guesser. Usually this is the case with irregular words like, for example, "cattle" which was wrongly guessed as a singular noun (NN) but in fact is a plural noun (NNS).

5 Discussion and Conclusion

We presented a technique for fully unsupervised statistical acquisition of rules which guess possible parts-of-speech for words unknown to the lexicon. This technique does not require specially prepared training data and uses for training the lexicon and word frequencies collected from a raw corpus. Using these training data three types of guessing rules are learned: prefix morphological rules, suffix morphological rules and ending-guessing rules. To select best performing guessing rule-sets we suggested an evaluation methodology, which is solely dedicated to the performance of part-of-speech guessers.

Evaluation of tagging accuracy on unknown words using texts unseen by the guessers and the taggers at the training phase showed that tagging with the automatically induced cascading guesser was consistently more accurate than previously quoted results known to the author (85%). The cascading guesser outperformed the guesser supplied with the Xerox tagger by about 8-9% and the guesser supplied with Brill's tagger by about 6-7%. Tagging accuracy on unknown words using the cascading guesser was detected at 90-92% when tagging with the full-fledged lexicon and 86–88% when tagging with the closed-class and short word lexicon. When the unknown words were made known to the lexicon the accuracy of tagging was detected at 96-98% and 90-92% respectively. This makes the accuracy drop caused by the cascading guesser to be less than 6% in general. Another important conclusion from the evaluation experiments is that the morphological guessing rules do improve the guessing performance. Since they are more accurate than ending-guessing rules they are applied before ending-guessing rules and improve the precision of the guessings by about 5%. This, actually, results in about 2% higher accuracy of tagging on unknown words.

The acquired guessing rules employed in our cascading guesser are, in fact, of a standard nature and in that form or another are used in other POS-guessers. There are, however, a few points which make the rule-sets acquired by the presented here technique more accurate:

- the learning of such rules is done from the lexicon rather than tagged corpus, because the guesser's task is akin to the lexicon lookup;
- there is a well-tuned statistical scoring procedure which accounts for rule features and frequency distribution;
- there is an empirical way to determine an optimum collection of rules, since acquired rules are subject to rigorous direct evaluation in terms of precision, recall and coverage;
- rules are applied cascadingly using the most accurate rules first.

One of the most important issues in the induction of guessing rule-sets is the choice right data for training. In our approach, guessing rules are extracted from the lexicon and the actual corpus frequencies of word-usage then allow for discrimination between rules which are no longer productive (but have left their imprint on the basic lexicon) and rules that are productive in real-life texts. Thus the major factor in the learning process is the lexicon. Since guessing rules are meant to capture general language regularities the lexicon should be as general as possible (list *all* possible POSs for a word) and as large as possible. The corresponding corpus should include most of the words from the lexicon and be large enough to obtain reliable estimates of word-frequency distribution. Our experiments with the lexicon and word frequencies derived from the Brown Corpus, which can be considered as a general model of English, resulted in guessing rule-sets which proved to be domain and corpus independent[11], producing similar results on test texts of different origin.

Although in general the performance of the cascading guesser is only 6% worse than the lookup of a general language lexicon there is room for improvement. First, in the extraction of the morphological rules we did not attempt to model non-concatenative cases. In English, however, since most of letter mutations occur in the last letter of the main word it is possible to account for it. So our next goal is to extract morphological rules with one letter mutations at the end. This would account for cases like "try - tries", "reduce - reducing", "advise - advisable". We expect it to increase the coverage of thesuffix morphological rules and hence contribute to the overall guessing accuracy. Another avenue for improvement is to provide the guessing rules with the probabilities of emission of POSs from their resulting POS-classes. This information can be compiled automatically and also might improve the accuracy of tagging unknown words.

The described rule acquisition and evaluation methods are implemented as a modular set of C++ and AWK tools, and the guesser is easily extendable to sub-language specific regularities and retrainable to new tag-sets and other languages, provided that these languages have affixational morphology. Both the software and the produced guessing rule-sets are available by contacting the author.

[11] but tag-set dependent

6 Acknowledgements

Some of the research reported here was funded as part of EPSRC project IED4/1/5808 "Integrated Language Database". I would also like to thank Chris Brew for helpful discussions on the issues related to this paper.

References

E. Brill 1994. Some Advances in Transformation-Based Part of Speech Tagging. In *Proceedings of the Twelfth National Conference on Artificial Intelligence (AAAAI-94)*, Seattle, WA.

E. Brill 1995. Transformation-based error-driven learning and Natural Language processing: a case study in part-of-speech tagging. In *Computational Linguistics* 21(4) pp. 543–565.

W. Francis and H. Kucera 1982. Frequency Analysis of English Usage. Houghton Mifflin, Boston 1982.

J. Kupiec 1992. Robust Part-of-Speech Tagging Using a Hidden Markov Model. In *Computer Speech and Language*

M. Marcus, M.A. Marcinkiewicz, and B. Santorini 1993. Building a Large Annotated Corpus of English: The Penn Treebank. In *Computational Linguistics*, vol 19/2 pp.313-329

H. Schmid 1994. Part of Speech Tagging with Neural Networks. In *Proceedings of the International Conference on Computational Linguistics*, pp.172-176, Kyoto, Japan.

E. Tzoukermann, D.R. Radev, and W.A. Gale 1995. Combining Linguistic Knowledge and Statistical Learning in French Part of Speech Tagging. In *EACL SIGDAT Workshop*, pp.51-59, Dublin, Ireland

A. Voutilainen 1995. A Syntax-Based Part-of-Speech Analyser In *Proceedings of the Seventh Conference of European Chapter of the Association for Computational Linguistics (EACL)* pp.157-164, Dublin, Ireland

R. Weischedel, M. Meteer, R. Schwartz, L. Ramshaw and J. Palmucci 1993. Coping with ambiguity and unknown words through probabilistic models. In *Computational Linguistics*, vol 19/2 pp.359-382

Byoung-Tak Zhang and Yung-Taek Kim 1990. Morphological Analysis and Synthesis by Automated Discovery and Acquisition of Linguistic Rules. In *Proceedings of the 13th International Conference on Computational Linguistics*, pp.431-435, Helsinki, Finland.

Measure	Test	Xerox	Ending 75	Suffix 60	Prefix 80
Recall	Lexicon	0.956313	0.945726	0.95761	0.955748
	Corpus	0.944526	0.952016	0.97352	0.978515
Precision	Lexicon	0.460761	0.675122	0.919796	0.922534
	Corpus	0.523965	0.745339	0.979351	0.977633
Coverage	Lexicon	0.917698	0.977089	0.37597	0.049558
	Corpus	0.893275	0.96104	0.320996	0.058372

Table 1: Results obtained at the evaluation of the acquired rule-sets over the training lexicon and the training corpus. Guessing rule-sets produced using different confidence thresholds were compared. Best-scored rule-sets detected: Prefix 80 - prefix morphological rules which scored over 80 points, Suffix 60 - suffix morphological rules which scored over 60 points and Ending 75 - ending-guessing rules which scored over 75 points. As the base-line model was taken the ending guesser developed by Xerox (X).

Guessing Strategy	Lexicon Precision	Lexicon Recall	Lexicon Coverage	Corpus Precision	Corpus Recall	Corpus Coverage
Xerox (X)	0.460761	0.956331	0.917698	0.523965	0.944526	0.893275
Ending 75 (E_{75})	**0.675122**	0.945726	0.977089	**0.745339**	0.952016	0.96104
X+E_{75}	0.470249	0.95783	0.989843	0.519715	0.949789	0.969023
E_{75}+X	0.670741	0.943319	0.989843	0.743932	0.951541	0.969023
P_{80}+E_{75}	0.687126	0.946208	0.977488	0.748922	0.951563	0.96104
S_{60}+E_{75}	0.734143	0.945015	0.979686	0.792901	0.951015	0.963289
P_{80}+S_{60}+E_{75}	**0.745504**	0.945445	0.980086	**0.796252**	0.950562	0.963289

Table 2: Results of the cascading application of the rule-sets over the training lexicon and training corpus. P_{80} - prefix rule-set scored over 80 points, S_{60} - suffix rule-set scored over 60 points, E_{75} - ending-guessing rule-set scored over 75 points. As the base-line model was taken the ending guesser developed by Xerox (X). The first part of the table shows that the E_{75} rule-set outperforms and fully supercedes the Xerox rule-set. The second part of the table shows that the cascading application of the morphological rule-sets together with the ending-guessing rules increases the performance by about 5% in precision.

Tagger	Guessing strategy	Total words	Unkn. words	Total mistag.	Unkn. mistag.	Total Score	Unkn. Score
Xerox	Xerox	5,970	347	324	63	94.3%	81.8%
Xerox	P_{80} +S_{60} +E_{75}	5,970	347	292	33	95.1%	90.5%
Brill	Brill	5,970	347	246	54	95.9%	84.5%
Brill	P_{80} +S_{60} +E_{75}	5,970	347	219	27	96.3%	92.2%

Table 3: This table shows the results of tagging a text with 347 unknown words by four different combinations of two taggers and three word-guessing modules using the Brown Corpus model. The accuracy of tagging the unknown words when they were made known to the lexicon was detected at 98.5% for both taggers.

Tagger	Guessing strategy	Total words	Unkn. words	Total mistag.	Unkn. mistag.	Total Score	Unkn. Score
Xerox	Xerox	5,970	2215	556	516	90.7%	76.7%
Xerox	P_{80} +S_{60} +E_{75}	5,970	2215	332	309	94.44%	86.05%
Brill	Brill	5,970	2215	464	410	93.1%	81.5%
Brill	P_{80} +S_{60} +E_{75}	5,970	2215	327	287	94.52%	87.45%

Table 4: This table shows the results of tagging the same as in Table 3 text by four different combinations of two taggers and three word-guessing modules using the Brown Corpus model and the lexicon which contained only closed-class and short words. The accuracy of tagging the unknown words when they were made known to the lexicon was detected at 90.3% for the Xerox tagger and at 91.5% for Brill's tagger.

Linguistic Structure as Composition and Perturbation

Carl de Marcken
MIT AI Laboratory, NE43-769
545 Technology Square
Cambridge, MA, 02139, USA
cgdemarc@ai.mit.edu

Abstract

This paper discusses the problem of learning language from unprocessed text and speech signals, concentrating on the problem of learning a lexicon. In particular, it argues for a representation of language in which linguistic parameters like words are built by perturbing a composition of existing parameters. The power of the representation is demonstrated by several examples in text segmentation and compression, acquisition of a lexicon from raw speech, and the acquisition of mappings between text and artificial representations of meaning.

1 Motivation

Language is a robust and necessarily redundant communication mechanism. Its redundancies commonly manifest themselves as predictable patterns in speech and text signals, and it is largely these patterns that enable text and speech compression. Naturally, many patterns in text and speech reflect interesting properties of language. For example, *the* is both an unusually frequent sequence of letters and an English word. This suggests using compression as a means of acquiring underlying properties of language from surface signals. The general methodology of language-learning-by-compression is not new. Some notable early proponents included Chomsky (1955), Solomonoff (1960) and Harris (1968), and compression has been used as the basis for a wide variety of computer programs that attack unsupervised learning in language; see (Olivier, 1968; Wolff, 1982; Ellison, 1992; Stolcke, 1994; Chen, 1995; Cartwright and Brent, 1994) among others.

1.1 Patterns and Language

Unfortunately, while surface patterns often reflect interesting linguistic mechanisms and parameters, they do not always do so. Three classes of examples serve to illustrate this.

1.1.1 Extralinguistic Patterns

The sequence *it was a dark and stormy night* is a pattern in the sense it occurs in text far more frequently than the frequencies of its letters would suggest, but that does not make it a lexical or grammatical primitive: it is the product of a complex mixture of linguistic and extra-linguistic processes. Such patterns can be indistinguishable from desired ones. For example, in the Brown corpus (Francis and Kucera, 1982) *scratching her nose* occurs 5 times, a corpus-specific idiosyncrasy. This phrase has the same structure as the idiom *kicking the bucket.* It is difficult to imagine any induction algorithm learning *kicking the bucket* from this corpus without also (mistakenly) learning *scratching her nose.*

1.1.2 The Definition of Interesting

This discussion presumes there is a set of desired patterns to extract from input signals. What is this set? For example, is *kicking the bucket* a proper lexical unit? The answer depends on factors external to the unsupervised learning framework. For the purposes of machine translation or information retrieval this sequence is an important idiom, but with respect to speech recognition it is unremarkable. Similar questions could be asked of subword units like syllables. Plainly, the answers depends on the learning context, and not on the signal itself.

1.1.3 The Definition of Pattern

Any statistical definition of pattern depends on an underlying model. For instance, the sequence *the dog* occurs much more frequently than one would expect given an independence assumption about letters. But for a model with knowledge of syntax and word frequencies, there is nothing remarkable about the phrase. Since all existing models have flaws, patterns will always be learned that are artifacts of imperfections in the learning algorithm.

These examples seem to imply that unsupervised induction will never converge to ideal grammars and lexicons. While there is truth to this, the rest of this paper describes a representation of language that bypasses many of the apparent difficulties.

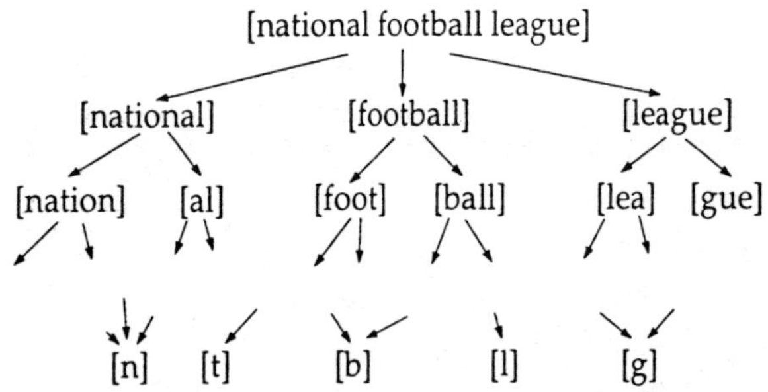

Figure 1: A compositional representation.

Code	Length	Components
$000 = c_{of}$	2	c_o, c_f
$001 = c_{the}$	3	c_t, c_h, c_e
$010 = c_{in}$	2	c_i, c_n
$0110 = c_{some}$	4	c_s, c_o, c_m, c_e
$0111 = c_{someofthe}$	3	$c_{some}, c_{of}, c_{the}$
$10000 = \dots$	...	...

Figure 2: A coding of the first few words of a hypothetical lexicon. The first two columns can be coded succinctly, leaving the cost of pointers to component words as the dominant cost of both the lexicon and the representation of the input.

2 A Compositional Representation

The examples in sections 1.1.1 and 1.1.2 seem to imply that any unsupervised language learning program that returns only one segmentation of the input is bound to make many mistakes. And section 1.1.3 implies that the decisions about linguistic units must be made relative to their representations. Both problems can be solved if linguistic units (for now, words in the lexicon) are built by composition of other units. For example, *kicking the bucket* might be built by composing *kicking*, *the* and *bucket*.[1] Of course, if a word is merely the composition of its parts, there is nothing interesting about it and no reason to include it in the lexicon. So the motivation for including a word in the lexicon must be that it function differently from its parts. Thus a word is a perturbation of a composition.

In the case of *kicking the bucket* the perturbation is one of both meaning and frequency. For *scratching her nose* the perturbation may just be frequency.[2] This is a very natural representation from the viewpoint of language. It correctly predicts that both phrases inherit their sound and syntax from their component words. At the same time it leaves open the possibility that idiosyncratic information will be attached to the whole, as with the meaning of *kicking the bucket*. This structure is very much like the class hierarchy of a modern programming language. It is not the same thing as a context-free grammar, since each word does not act in the same way as the default composition of its components.

Figure 1 illustrates a recursive decomposition (under concatenation) of the phrase *national football league*. The phrase is broken into three words, each of which are also decomposed in the lexicon. This process bottoms out in the terminal characters. This is a real decomposition achieved by a program described in section 4. Not shown are the perturbations (in this case merely frequency changes) that distinguish each word from its parts. This general framework extends to other perturbations. For example, the word *wanna* is naturally thought of as a composition of *want* and *to* with a sound change. And in speech the three different words *to*, *two* and *too* may well inherit the sound of a common ancestor while introducing new syntactic and semantic properties.

2.1 Coding

Of course, for this representation to be more than an intuition both the composition and perturbation operators must be exactly specified. In particular, a code must be designed that enables a word (or a sentence) to be expressed in terms of its parts. As a simple example, suppose that the composition operator is concatenation, that terminals are characters, and that the only perturbation operator is the ability to express the frequency of a word independently of the frequency of its parts. Then to code either a sentence of the input or a (nonterminal) word in the lexicon, the number of component words in the representation must be written, followed by a code for each component word. Naturally, each word in the lexicon must be associated with its code, and under a near-optimal coding scheme like a Huffman code, the code length will be related to the frequency of the word. Thus, associating a word with a code substitutes for writing down the frequency of a word. Furthermore, if words are written down in order of decreasing frequency, a Huffman code for a large lexicon can be specified using a negligible number of bits. This and the near-negligible cost of writing down word lengths will not be discussed further. Figure 2 presents a portion of an encoding of a hypothetical lexicon.

2.2 MDL

Given a coding scheme and a particular lexicon (and a parsing algorithm) it is in theory possible to calculate the minimum length encoding of a given input.

[1] A simple composition operator is concatenation, but in section 6 a more interesting one is discussed.

[2] Naturally, an unsupervised learning algorithm with no access to meaning will not treat them differently.

Part of the encoding will be devoted to the lexicon, the rest to representing the input in terms of the lexicon. The lexicon that minimizes the combined description length of the lexicon and the input maximally compresses the input. In the sense of Rissanen's minimum description-length (MDL) principle (Rissanen, 1978; Rissanen, 1989) this lexicon is the theory that best explains the data, and one can hope that the patterns in the lexicon reflect the underlying mechanisms and parameters of the language that generated the input.

2.3 Properties of the Representation

Representing words in the lexicon as perturbations of compositions has a number of desirable properties.

- The choice of composition and perturbation operators captures a particular detailed theory of language. They can be used, for instance, to reference sophisticated phonological and morphological mechanisms.
- The length of the description of a word is a measure of its linguistic plausibility, and can serve as a buffer against learning unnatural coincidences.
- Coincidences like *scratching her nose* do not exclude desired structure, since they are further broken down into components that they inherit properties from.
- Structure is shared: the words *blackbird* and *blackberry* can share the common substructure associated with *black*, such as its sound and meaning. As a consequence, data is pooled for estimation, and representations are compact.
- Common irregular forms are compiled out. For example, if *went* is represented in terms of *go* (presumably to save the cost of unnecessarily reproducing syntactic and semantic properties) the complex sound change need only be represented once, not every time *went* is used.
- Since parameters (words) have compact representations, they are cheap from a description length standpoint, and many can be included in the lexicon. This allows learning algorithms to fit detailed statistical properties of the data.

This coding scheme is very similar to that found in popular dictionary-based compression schemes like LZ78 (Ziv and Lempel, 1978). It is capable of compressing a sequence of identical characters of length n to size $\mathcal{O}(\log n)$. However, in contrast to compression schemes like LZ78 that use deterministic rules to add parameters to the dictionary (and do not arrive at linguistically plausible parameters), it is possible to perform more sophisticated searches in this representation.

```
Start with lexicon of terminals.
Iterate
   Iterate (EM)
      Parse input and words using current lexicon.
      Use word counts to update frequencies.
   Add words to the lexicon.
   Iterate (EM)
      Parse input and words using current lexicon.
      Use word counts to update frequencies.
   Delete words from the lexicon.
```

Figure 3: An iterative search algorithm. Two iterations of the inner loops are usually sufficient for convergence, and for the tests described in this paper after 10 iterations of the outer loop there is little change in the lexicon in terms of either compression performance or structure.

3 A Search Algorithm

Since the class of possible lexicons is infinite, the minimization of description length is necessarily heuristic. Given a fixed lexicon, the expectation-maximization algorithm (Dempster et al., 1977) can be used to arrive at a (locally) optimal set of frequencies and codelengths for the words in the lexicon. For composition by concatenation, the algorithm reduces to the special case of the Baum-Welch procedure (Baum et al., 1970) discussed in (Deligne and Bimbot, 1995). In general, however, the parsing and reestimation involved in EM can be considerably more complicated. To update the structure of the lexicon, words can be added or deleted from it if this is predicted to reduce the description length of the input. This algorithm is summarized in figure 3.[3]

3.1 Adding and Deleting Words

For words to be added to the lexicon, two things are needed. The first is a means of hypothesizing candidate new words. The second is a means of evaluating candidates. One reasonable means of generating candidates is to look at pairs (or triples) of words that are composed in the parses of words and sentences of the input. Since words are built by composing other words and act like their composition, a new word can be created from such a pair and substituted in place of the pair wherever the pair appears. For example, if *water* and *melon* are frequently composed, then a good candidate for a new word is *water* $\circ$ *melon* = *watermelon*, where $\circ$ is the concatenation

[3] For the composition operators and test sets we have looked at, using single (Viterbi) parses produces almost exactly the same results (in terms of both compression and lexical structure) as summing probabilities over multiple parses.

operator. In order to evaluate whether the addition of such a new word is likely to reduce the description length of the input, it is necessary to record during the EM step the extra statistics of how many times the composed pairs occur in parses.

The effect on description length of adding a new word can not be exactly computed. Its addition will not only affect other words, but may also cause other words to be added or deleted. Furthermore, it is more computationally efficient to add and delete many words simultaneously, and this complicates the estimation of the change in description length. Fortunately, simple approximations of the change are adequate. For example, if Viterbi analyses are being used then the new word *watermelon* will completely take the place of all compositions of *water* and *melon*. This reduces the counts of *water* and *melon* accordingly, though they are each used once in the representation of *watermelon*. If it is assumed that no other word counts change, these assumptions allow one to predict the counts and probabilities of all words after the change. Since the codelength of a word w with probability $p(w)$ is approximately $-\log p(w)$, the total estimated change in description length of adding a new word W to a lexicon L is

$$\begin{aligned}\Delta &\approx -c'(W)\log p'(W) + \text{d.l.(changes)} + \\ &\quad \sum_{w \in L}(-c'(w)\log p'(w) + c(w)\log p(w))\end{aligned}$$

where $c(w)$ is the count of the word w, primes indicated counts and probabilities after the change and d.l.(changes) represents the cost of writing down the perturbations involved in the representation of W. If $\Delta < 0$ the word is predicted to reduce the total description length and is added to the lexicon. Similar heuristics can be used to estimate the benefit of deleting words.[4]

3.2 Search Properties

A significant source of problems in traditional grammar induction techniques is local minima (de Marcken, 1995a; Pereira and Schabes, 1992; Carroll and Charniak, 1992). The search algorithm described above avoids many of these problems. The reason is that hidden structure is largely a "compile-time" phenomena. During parsing all that is important about a word is its surface form and codelength. The internal representation does not matter. Therefore, the internal representation is free to reorganize at any time; it has been decoupled. This allows structure to be built bottom up or for structure to emerge inside already existing parameters. Furthermore, since parameters (words) encode surface patterns, it is relatively easy to determine when they are useful, and their use is limited. They usually do not have competing roles, in contrast, for instance, to hidden nodes in neural networks. And since there are no fixed number of parameters, when words do start to have multiple disparate uses, they can be split with common substructure shared. Finally, since add and delete cycles can compensate for initial mistakes, inexact heuristics can be used for adding and deleting words.

4 Concatenation Results

The simplest reasonable instantiation of the composition-and-perturbation framework is with the concatenation operator and frequency perturbation. This instantiation is easily tested on problems of text segmentation and compression. Given a text document, the search algorithm can be used to learn a lexicon that minimizes its description length. For testing purposes, spaces will be removed from input text and true words will be defined to be minimal sequences bordered by spaces in the original input). The search algorithm parses the input as it compresses it, and can therefore output a segmentation of the input in terms of words drawn from the lexicon. These words are themselves decomposed in the lexicon, and can be considered to form a tree that terminates in the characters of the sentence. This tree can have no more than $\mathcal{O}(n)$ nodes for a sentence with n characters, though there are $\mathcal{O}(n^2)$ possible "true words" in the input sentence; thus, the tree contains considerable information. Define *recall* to be the percentage of true words that occur at some level of the segmentation-tree. Define *crossing-bracket* to be the percentage of true words that violate the segmentation-tree structure.[5]

The search algorithm was applied to two texts, a lowercase version of the million-word Brown corpus with spaces and punctuation removed, and 4 million characters of Chinese news articles in a two-byte/character format. In the case of the Chinese, which contains no inherent separators like spaces, segmentation performance is measured relative to another computer segmentation program that had access to a (human-created) lexicon. The algorithm was given the raw encoding and had to deduce the internal two-byte structure. In the case of the Brown corpus, word recall was 90.5% and crossing-brackets was 1.7%. For the Chinese word recall was 96.9% and crossing-brackets was 1.3%. In the case of both English and Chinese, most of the unfound words were words that occurred only once in the corpus. Thus, the algorithm has done an extremely good job of learning words and properly using them to segment the input. Furthermore, the crossing-bracket

[4] See (de Marcken, 1995b) for more detailed discussion of these estimations. The actual formulas used in the tests presented in this paper are slightly more complicated than presented here.

[5] The true word *moon* in the input *[the][moon]* is a crossing-bracket violation of *them* in the segmentation tree *[[them][o][on]]*.

Rank	Word
0	[s]
1	[the]
2	[and]
3	[a]
4	[of]
5	[in]
6	[to]
500	[students]
501	[material]
502	[um]
503	[words]
504	[period]
505	[class]
506	[question]
5000	[[ing][them]]
5001	[[mon][k]]
5002	[[re][lax]]
5003	[[rig][id]]
5004	[[connect][ed]]
5005	[[i][k]]
5006	[[hu][t]]
26000	[[pleural][blood][supply]]
26001	[[anordinary][happy][family]]
26002	[[f][eas][ibility][of]]
26003	[[lunar][brightness][distribution]]
26004	[[primarily][diff][using]]
26005	[[sodium][tri][polyphosphate]]
26006	[[charcoal][broil][ed]]

Figure 4: Sections of the lexicon learned from the Brown corpus, ranked by frequency. The words in the less-frequent half are listed with their first-level decomposition. Word 5000 causes crossing-bracket violations, and words 26002 and 26006 have internal structure that causes recall violations.

measure indicates that the algorithm has made very few clear mistakes. Of course, the hierarchical lexical representation does not make a commitment to what levels are "true words" and which are not; about 5 times more internal nodes exist than true words. Experiments in section 5 demonstrate that for most applications this is not only not a problem, but desirable. Figure 4 displays some of the lexicon learned from the Brown corpus.

The algorithm was also run as a compressor on a lower-case version of the Brown corpus with spaces and punctuation left in. All bits necessary for exactly reproducing the input were counted. Compression performance is 2.12 bits/char, significantly lower than popular algorithms like *gzip* (2.95 bits/char). This is the best text compression result on this corpus that we are aware of, and should not be confused with lower figures that do not include the cost of parameters. Furthermore, because the compressed text is stored in terms of linguistic units like words, it can be searched, indexed, and parsed without decompression.

5 Learning Meanings

Unsupervised learning algorithms are rarely used in isolation. The goal of this work has been to explain how linguistic units like words can be learned, so that other processes can make use of these units. In this section a means of learning the mappings between words and artificial representations of meanings is described. The composition-and-perturbation encompasses this application neatly.

Imagine that text utterances are paired with representations of meaning,[6] and that the goal is to find the minimum-length description of both the text and the meaning. If there is mutual information between the meaning and text portions of the input, then better compression is achieved if the two streams are compressed simultaneously. If a text word can have some associated meaning, then writing down that word to account for some portion of text also accounts for some portion of the meaning of that text. The remaining meaning can be written down more succinctly. Thus, there is an incentive to associate meaning with sound, although of course the association pays a price in the description of the lexicon.

Although it is obviously a naive simplification, many of the interesting properties of the compositional representation surface even when meanings are treating as sets of arbitrary symbols. A word is now both a character sequence and a set of symbols. The composition operator concatenates the characters and unions the meaning symbols. Of course, there must be some way to alter the default meaning of a word. One way to do this is to explicitly write out any symbols that are present in the word's meaning but not in its components, or *vice versa*. Thus, the word *red* {RED} might be represented as *r* ∘ *e* ∘ *d*+RED. Given an existing word *berry* {BERRY}, the red berry *cranberry* {RED BERRY} can be represented *c* ∘ *r* ∘ *a* ∘ *n* ∘ *berry* {BERRY}+RED.

5.1 Results

To test the algorithm's ability to infer word meanings, 10,000 utterances from an unsegmented textual database of mothers' speech to children were paired with representations of meaning, constructed by assigning a unique symbol to each root word in the vocabulary. For example, the sentence *and what is he painting a picture of?* is paired with the unordered meaning AND WHAT BE HE PAINT A PICTURE OF. In the first experiment, the algorithm received these pairs with no noise or ambiguity, using an encoding of meaning symbols such that each symbol's length was 10 bits. After 8 iterations of training without meaning and then a further 8 iterations with, the text sequences were parsed again without access to the true meaning. The meanings

[6]This framework is easily extended to handle multiple ambiguous meanings (with and without priors) and noise, but these extensions will not be discussed here.

of the resulting word sequences were compared with the true meanings. Symbol accuracy was 98.9%, recall was 93.6%. Used to differentiate the true meaning from the meanings of the previous 20 sentences, the program selected correctly 89.1% of the time, or ranked the true meaning tied for first 10.8% of the time.

A second test was performed in which the algorithm received three possible meanings for each utterance, the true one and also the meaning of the two surrounding utterances. A uniform prior was used. Symbol accuracy was again 98.9%, recall was 75.3%.

The final lexicon includes extended phrases, but meanings tend to filter down to the proper level. For instance, although the words ***duck***, ***ducks***, ***the ducks*** and ***duckdrink*** all exist and contain the meaning DUCK, the symbol is only written into the description of ***duck***. All others inherit it. Similar results hold for similar experiments on the Brown corpus. For example, ***scratching her nose*** inherits its meaning completely from its parts, while ***kicking the bucket*** does not. This is exactly the result argued for in the motivation section of this paper, and illustrates why occasional extra words in the lexicon are not a problem for most applications.

6 Other Applications and Current Work

We have performed other experiments using this representation and search algorithm, on tasks in unsupervised learning from speech and grammar induction.

Figure 5 contains a small portion of a lexicon learned from 55,000 utterances of continuous speech by multiple speakers. The utterances are taken from dictated Wall Street Journal articles. The concatenation operators was used with phonemes as terminals. A second layer was added to the framework to map from phonemes to speech; these extensions are described in more detail in (de Marcken, 1995b). The sound model of each phoneme was learned separately using supervised training on different, segmented speech. Although the phoneme model is extremely poor, many words are recognizable, and this is the first significant lexicon learned directly from spoken speech without supervision.

If the composition operator makes use of context, then the representation extends naturally to a more powerful form of context-free grammars, where composition is tree-insertion. In particular, if each word is associated with a part-of-speech, and parts of speech are permissible terminals in the lexicon, then "words" become production rules. For example, a word might be $VP \rightarrow$ *take off NP* and represented in terms of the composition of $VP \rightarrow V\ P\ NP$, $V \rightarrow$ *take* and $P \rightarrow$ *off*. Furthermore, $VP \rightarrow V\ P\ NP$ may be represented in terms of $VP \rightarrow V\ PP$ and $PP \rightarrow P\ NP$. In this way syntactic structure emerges in the internal representation of words. This sort of grammar offers significant advantages over context-free grammars in that non-independent rule expansions can be accounted for. We are currently looking at various methods for automatically acquiring parts of speech; in initial experiments some of the first such classes learned are the class of vowels, of consonants, and of verb endings.

Rank	w	rep(w)
5392	[wɔrmr]	[[wɔr]mr]
5393	[θauzn]	[θ[auzn]]
5394	[təhɪd]	[[təh]ɪd]
5395	[ɛktɪd]	[ɛk[tɪd]]
5396	[ʌniɨn]	[ʌn[iɨn]]
5397	[mɛliɨndalrz]	[[mɛliɨndalr]z]
8948	[aidiɨz]	[[ai]diɨz]
8949	[sɨkrti]	[sɨk[rti]]
8950	[lɔŋtaim]	[[lɔŋ][taim]]
8951	[sɛkgɪn]	[[sɛk][gɪn]]
8952	[wʌnpʌ]	[[wʌn]pʌ]
8953	[vɛndčr]	[v[ɛn][dčr]]
8954	[əlɪmɪnei]	[ə[lɪmɪn][ei]]
8955	[mɛliɨŋ]	[[mɛl]i[ɨŋ]]
8956	[bɛliɨndal]	[bɛ[liɨndal]]
9164	[gouldmɨnsæks]	[[goul]d[mɨn]s[æks]]
9165	[kmpšutr]	[[kmp][šut]r]
9166	[gavrmɨn]	[ga[vrmɨn]]
9167	[oublzəhuou]	[[oubl][zəhuou]]
9168	[mɨnɨstreišɨn]	[[mɨn]ɨ[streišɨn]]
9169	[tǰɛrɨn]	[[tǰɛ]r[ɨn]]
9170	[hʌblhəhwou]	[[hʌbl][həhwou]]
9171	[sʌmpðɨŋ]	[s[ʌmp][ðɨŋ]]
9172	[prplouzl]	[[pr][plou]zl]
9173	[bouskgi]	[[bou][skg]i]
9174	[kgɛdǰɨl]	[[kgɛ][dǰɨ]l]
9175	[gouldmaiɨnz]	[[goul]d[maiɨnz]]
9176	[kɔrpreitɪd]	[[kɔrpr][eitɪd]]

Figure 5: Some words from a lexicon learned from 55,000 utterances of continuous, dictated Wall Street Journal articles. Although many words are seemingly random, words representing *million dollars*, *Goldman-Sachs*, *thousand*, etc. are learned. Furthermore, as word 8950 (*long time*) shows, they are often properly decomposed into components.

7 Conclusions

No previous unsupervised language-learning procedure has produced structures that match so closely with linguistic intuitions. We take this as a vindication of the perturbation-of-compositions representation. Its ability to capture the statistical and linguistic idiosyncrasies of large structures without sacrificing the obvious regularities within them makes it a valuable tool for a wide variety of induction problems.

References

Leonard E. Baum, Ted Petrie, George Soules, and Norman Weiss. 1970. A maximization technique occurring in the statistical analysis of probabalistic functions in markov chains. *Annals of Mathematical Statistics*, 41:164–171.

Glenn Carroll and Eugene Charniak. 1992. Learning probabalistic dependency grammars from labelled text. In *Working Notes, Fall Symposium Series, AAAI*, pages 25–31.

Timothy Andrew Cartwright and Michael R. Brent. 1994. Segmenting speech without a lexicon: Evidence for a bootstrapping model of lexical acquisition. In *Proc. of the 16th Annual Meeting of the Cognitive Science Society*, Hillsdale, New Jersey.

Stanley F. Chen. 1995. Bayesian grammar induction for language modeling. In *Proc. 32nd Annual Meeting of the Association for Computational Linguistics*, pages 228–235, Cambridge, Massachusetts.

Noam A. Chomsky. 1955. *The Logical Structure of Linguistic Theory.* Plenum Press, New York.

Carl de Marcken. 1995a. Lexical heads, phrase structure and the induction of grammar. In *Third Workshop on Very Large Corpora*, Cambridge, Massachusetts.

Carl de Marcken. 1995b. The unsupervised acquisition of a lexicon from continuous speech. Memo A.I. Memo 1558, MIT Artificial Intelligence Lab., Cambridge, Massachusetts.

Sabine Deligne and Frédéric Bimbot. 1995. Language modeling by variable length sequences: Theoretical formulation and evaluation of multigrams. In *Proceedings of the International Conference on Speech and Signal Processing*, volume 1, pages 169–172.

A. P. Dempster, N. M. Liard, and D. B. Rubin. 1977. Maximum liklihood from incomplete data via the EM algorithm. *Journal of the Royal Statistical Society*, B(39):1–38.

T. Mark Ellison. 1992. *The Machine Learning of Phonological Structure.* Ph.D. thesis, University of Western Australia.

W. N. Francis and H. Kucera. 1982. *Frequency analysis of English usage: lexicon and grammar.* Houghton-Mifflin, Boston.

Zellig Harris. 1968. *Mathematical Structure of Language.* Wiley, New York.

Donald Cort Olivier. 1968. *Stochastic Grammars and Language Acquisition Mechanisms.* Ph.D. thesis, Harvard University, Cambridge, Massachusetts.

Fernando Pereira and Yves Schabes. 1992. Inside-outside reestimation from partially bracketed corpora. In *Proc. 29th Annual Meeting of the Association for Computational Linguistics*, pages 128–135, Berkeley, California.

Jorma Rissanen. 1978. Modeling by shortest data description. *Automatica*, 14:465–471.

Jorma Rissanen. 1989. *Stochastic Complexity in Statistical Inquiry.* World Scientific, Singapore.

R. J. Solomonoff. 1960. The mechanization of linguistic learning. In *Proceedings of the 2nd International Conference on Cybernetics*, pages 180–193.

Andreas Stolcke. 1994. *Bayesian Learning of Probabalistic Language Models.* Ph.D. thesis, University of California at Berkeley, Berkeley, CA.

J. Gerald Wolff. 1982. Language acquisition, data compression and generalization. *Language and Communication*, 2(1):57–89.

J. Ziv and A. Lempel. 1978. Compression of individual sequences by variable rate coding. *IEEE Transactions on Information Theory*, 24:530–536.

Generating an LTAG out of a principle-based hierarchical representation

Marie-Hélène Candito
TALANA and UFRL, Université Paris 7
2, place Jussieu, Tour centrale 8ème étage pièce 801
75251 Paris cedex 05 FRANCE
marie-helene.candito@linguist.jussieu.fr

Abstract

Lexicalized Tree Adjoining Grammars have proved useful for NLP. However, numerous redundancy problems face LTAGs developers, as highlighted by Vijay-Shanker and Schabes (92).

We present and a tool that automatically generates the tree families of an LTAG. It starts from a compact hierarchical organization of syntactic descriptions that is linguistically motivated and carries out all the relevant combinations of linguistic phenomena.

1 Lexicalized TAGs

Lexicalized Tree Adjoining Grammar (LTAG) is a formalism integrating lexicon and grammar (Joshi, 87; Schabes et al., 88), which has proved useful for NLP. Linguists have developed over the years sizeable LTAG grammars, especially for English (XTAG group, 95) and French (Abeillé, 91).

In this formalism, the lexical items are associated with elementary trees representing their maximal projection. Features structures are associated with the trees, that are combined with substitution and adjunction. Adjunction allows the extended domain of locality of the formalism : all trees anchored by a predicate contain nodes for all its arguments.

Such a lexicalized formalism needs a practical organization. LTAGs consist of a morphological lexicon, a syntactic lexicon of lemmas and a set of tree schemata, i.e. trees in which the lexical anchor is missing. In the syntactic lexicon, lemmas select the tree schemata they can anchor[1].

The set of tree schemata forms the syntactic part of the grammar. The tree schemata selected by predicative items are grouped into families, and collectively selected. A tree family contains the different possible trees for a given canonical subcategorization. Along with the "canonical" trees, a family contains the ones that would be transformationally related in a movement-base approach. These are first the trees where a "redistribution" of the syntactic function of the arguments has occurred, for instance the passive trees, or middle (for French) or dative shift (for English), leading to an "actual subcategorization" different from the canonical one. Secondly, a family may contain the trees with extracted argument (or cliticized in French).

In the syntactic lexicon, a particular lemma may select a family only partially. For instance a lemma might select the transitive family, ruling out the passive trees. On the other hand, the features appearing in the tree schemata are common to every lemma selecting these trees. The idiosyncratic features (attached to the anchor or upper in the tree) are introduced in the syntactic lexicon.

2 Development and maintenance problems with LTAGs

This extreme lexicalization entails that a sizeable LTAG comprises hundreds of elementary trees (over 600 for the cited large grammars). And as highlighted by Vijay-Shanker and Schabes (92), information on syntactic structures and associated features equations is repeated in dozens of tree schemata (hundreds for subject-verb agreement for instance).

Redundancy makes the tasks of LTAG writing, extending or updating very difficult, especially because all combinations of phenomena must be handled. And, in addition to the practical problem of grammar storage, redundancy makes it hard to get a clear vision of the theoretical and practical choices on which the grammar is based.

3 Existing solutions

A few solutions have been proposed for the problems described above. They use two main devices for lexicon representation : inheritance networks and lexical rules. But for LTAG representation, inheritance networks have to include phrase-structure information also, and lexical rules become "lexico-syntactic rules". Vijay-Shanker and Schabes, (92) have first proposed a scheme for LTAG representation. Implemented work is also described in (Becker, 93; 95) and (Evans et al., 95).

The three cited solutions give an efficient representation (without redundancy) of an LTAG, but have in our opinion two major deficiencies. First these solutions use inheritance networks and lexical rules in a purely technical way. They give no principle about the form of the hierarchy or the lexical rules, whereas we

[1] At grammar use, the words of the sentence to be parsed are associated with the relevant tree schemata to form complete lexicalized trees.

believe that addressing the practical problem of redundancy should give the opportunity of formalizing the well-formedness of elementary trees and of tree families. And second, the *generative* aspect of these solutions is not developed. Certainly the lexical rules are proposed as a tool for generation of new schemata or new classes in a inheritance network. But the *automatic* triggering, ordering and bounding of the lexical rules is not discussed[2].

4 Proposed solution : a principle-based representation and a generation system

We propose a system for the writing and/or the updating of an LTAG. It comprises a principled and hierarchical representation of lexico-syntactic structures. Using this hierarchy and principles of well-formedness, the tool carries out automatically the relevant crossings of linguistic phenomena to generate the tree families.

This solution not only addresses the problem of redundancy but also gives a more principle-based representation of an LTAG. The implementation of the principles gives a real generative power to the tool.

Due to a lack of space we cannot develop all the aspects of this work[3]. After a brief description of the organization of the syntactic hierarchy, we will focus on the use of partial descriptions of trees.

4.1 Organization of the hierarchy

The proposed organization of the hierarchy follows from the linguistic principles of well-formedness of elementary TAG trees, mainly the predicate-arguments co-occurrence principle (Kroch and Joshi, 85; Abeillé, 91) : the trees for a predicative item contain positions for all its arguments.

But for a given predicate, we expect the canonical arguments to remain constant through redistribution of functions. The canonical subject (argument 0) in a passive construction, even when unexpressed, is still an argument of the predicate. So the principle should be a principle of predicate-*functions* co-occurrence : the trees for a predicative item contain positions for all the functions of its actual subcategorization.

This reformulated principle presupposes the definition of an actual subcategorization, given the canonical subcategorization of a predicate. This presupposition and the predicate-functions co-occurrence principle are fulfilled by organizing the hierarchy along the three following dimensions :

dimension 1 : canonical subcategorization frame
This dimension defines the types of canonical subcategorization. Its classes contain information on the arguments of a predicate, their index, their possible categories and their canonical syntactic function.

dimension 2 : redistribution of syntactic functions
This dimension defines the types of redistribution of functions (including the case of no redistribution at all). The association of a canonical subcategorization frame and a compatible redistribution gives an actual subcategorization, namely a list of argument-function pairs, that have to be locally realized.

dimension 3 : syntactic realizations of functions
It expresses the way the different syntactic functions are positioned at the phrase-structure level (in canonical, cliticized, extracted position...).

These three dimensions constitute the core hierarchy. Out of this syntactic database and following principles of well-formedness the generator creates elementary trees. This is a two-steps process : it first creates some *terminal classes* with inherited properties only - they are totally defined by their list of super-classes. Then it translates these terminal classes into the relevant elementary tree schemata, in the XTAG[4] format, so that they can be used for parsing.

Tree schemata generation respects the predicate-functions co-occurrence principle. Their corresponding terminal classes are created first by associating a canonical subcat (dimension 1) with a compatible redistribution, including the case of no redistribution (dimension 2). Then for each function defined in the actual subcat, exactly one realization of function is picked up in dimension 3.

The generation is made family by family. This is simply achieved by fixing the canonical subcat frame (dimension 1), At the development stage, generation can also be done following other criterions. For instance, all passive trees or all trees with extracted complements can be generated.

4.2 Formal choices : monotonic inheritance network and partial descriptions of trees

The generation process described above is quite powerful in the context of LTAGs, because it carries out automatically all the relevant crossings of linguistic phenomena. These crossings are precisely the major source of redundancy in LTAGs. Because of this generative device, we do not need to introduce lexico-syntactic rules, and thus we do not have to face the problems of ordering and bounding their application.

Further, as was mentioned in section 1, lexical idiosyncrasies are handled in the syntactic lexicon, and not in the set of tree schemata. So to represent hierarchically this set, we do not think that nonmonotonicity is linguistically justified. We have thus chosen monotonicity, which gives more transparency and improves declarativity. We follow here

[2]Becker (93) gives a linguistic principle for the bounding of his meta-rules, but has no solution for the application of this principle.

[3]A fuller description of the work can be found in (Candito, to appear)

[4]XTAG (Paroubek et al., 92) is a tool for writing and using LTAGs, including among other things a tree editor and a syntactic parser.

Vijay-Shanker and Schabes (92) and use partial descriptions of trees (Rogers and Vijay-Shanker, 94)[5].

A partial description is a set of constraints that characterizes a set of trees. Adding information to the description reduces monotonically the set of satisfying trees. The partial descriptions of Rogers and Vijay-Shanker (94) use three relations : left-of, parent and dominance (represented with a dashed line). A dominance link can be further specified as a path of length superior or equal to zero. These links are obviously useful to underspecify a relation between two nodes at a general level, that will be specified at an either lower or lateral level. Figure 1 shows a partial description representing a sentence with a nominal subject in canonical position, giving no other information about possible other complements. The underspecified link between the S and V nodes allows for either presence or absence of a cliticized complement on the verb. In the case of a clitic, the path between the S and V nodes can be specified with the description of figure 2. Then, if we have the information that the nodes labelled respectively S and V of figures 1 and 2 are the same, the conjunction of the two descriptions is equivalent to the description of figure 3.

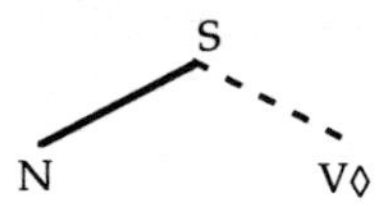

Figure 1

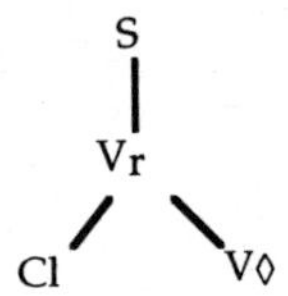

Figure 2

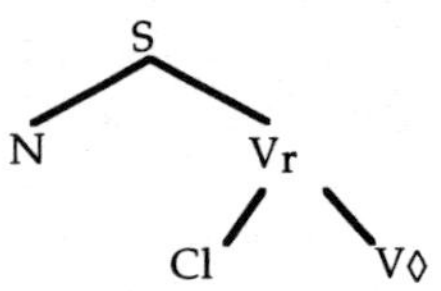

Figure 3

This example shows the declarativity obtained with partial descriptions that use large dominance links. The inheritance of descriptions of figure 1 and 2 is order independent. Without large dominance links, an order of inheritance of the classes describing a subject in canonical position and a cliticized complement should be predefined.

In the hierarchy of syntactic descriptions we propose, the partial description associated with a class is the unification of the own description of the class with all inherited partial descriptions. Identity of nodes is stated in our system by "naming" both nodes in the same way, since in descriptions of trees, nodes are referred to by constants. Two nodes, in two conjunct descriptions, referred to by the same constant are the same node. Equality of nodes can also be inferred, mainly using the fact that a tree node has only one direct parent node.

We have added atomic features associated with each constant, such as category, index, canonical syntactic function and actual syntactic function. In the conjunction of two descriptions, the identification of two nodes known to be the same requires the unification of such features. In case of failure, the whole conjunction leads to an unsatisfiable description.

A terminal class is translated into its corresponding elementary tree(s) by taking the minimal satisfying tree(s) of the partial description of the class[6].

4.3 Application to the French LTAG

The tool was used to generate tree families of the French grammar, using a hand-written hierarchy of syntactic descriptions. This task is facilitated by the guidelines given on the form of the hierarchy. Out of about 90 hand-written classes, the tool generates 730 trees for the 17 families for verbs without sentential complements[7], 400 of which were present in the pre-existing grammar. We have added phenomena such as some causative constructions or free order of complements.

The proposed type of hierarchy is meant to be universal, and we are currently working on its application to Italian.

5 References

A. Abeillé. 1991. Une grammaire lexicalisée d'Arbres Adjoints pour le français, PhD thesis, Univ. Paris 7.

T. Becker. 1993. HyTAG : a new type of Tree Adjoining Grammars for Hybrid Syntactic Representation of Free Order Languages, PhD thesis, Univ. of Saarbrücken.

T. Becker. 1994. Patterns in Metarules. Proc. of TAG+3.

M-H. Candito. To appear. A principle-based hierarchical representation of LTAGs. Proc. of COLING'96, Copenhagen.

R. Evans, G. Gazdar and D. Weir. 1995. Encoding Lexicalized Tree Adjoining Grammar with a Nonmonotonic Inheritance Hierarchy. Proc. of ACL'95, Boston.

A. Joshi. 1987. Introduction to Tree Adjoining Grammar, in A. Manaster Ramer (ed), *The Mathematics of Language*, J. Benjamins, pp. 87-114.

A. Kroch and A. Joshi. 1985. The linguistic relevance of Tree Adjoining Grammars. Technical report, Univ. of Pennsylvania.

P. Paroubek, Y. Schabes and A. Joshi. 1992. XTAG - A graphical Workbench for developing Tree Adjoining Grammars. Proc. of 3-ANLP, Trento.

J. Rogers and K. Vijay-Shanker. 1992. Reasoning with descriptions of trees. Proc. ACL'92, pp. 72-80.

J. Rogers and K. Vijay-Shanker. 1994. Obtaining trees from their descriptions : an application to Tree-Adjoining Grammars. Computational Intelligence, vol. 10, N° 4.

Y. Schabes, A. Abeillé and A. Joshi. 1988. Parsing strategies with lexicalized grammars : Tree Adjoining Grammars. Proc. of COLING'88, Budapest, vol. 2.

K. Vijay-Shanker and Y. Schabes. 1992. Structure Sharing in Lexicalized Tree Adjoining Grammar. Proc. of COLING'92, Nantes, pp. 205-211.

XTAG research group. 1995. A lexicalized TAG for English, Technical Report IRCS 95-03, Univ. of Pennsylvania.

[5] Vijay-Shanker & Schabes (92) have used the partial descriptions introduced in (Rogers & Vijay-Shanker, 92), but we have used the more recent version of (Rogers & Vijay-Shanker, 94). The difference lies principally in the definition of quasi-trees, first seen as partial models of trees and later as distinguished sets of constraints.

[6] Intuitively the remaining underspecified links are taken to be path of minimal length. See Rogers and Vijay-Shanker (94).

[7] By the time of conference, we will be able to give figures for the families with sentential complements also.

Using Parsed Corpora for Structural Disambiguation in the TRAINS Domain

Mark Core
Department of Computer Science
University of Rochester
Rochester, New York 14627
mcore@cs.rochester.edu

Abstract

This paper describes a prototype disambiguation module, KANKEI, which was tested on two corpora of the TRAINS project. In ambiguous verb phrases of form V ... NP PP or V ... NP adverb(s), the two corpora have very different PP and adverb attachment patterns; in the first, the correct attachment is to the VP 88.7% of the time, while in the second, the correct attachment is to the NP 73.5% of the time. KANKEI uses various n-gram patterns of the phrase heads around these ambiguities, and assigns parse trees (with these ambiguities) a score based on a linear combination of the frequencies with which these patterns appear with NP and VP attachments in the TRAINS corpora. Unlike previous statistical disambiguation systems, this technique thus combines evidence from bigrams, trigrams, and the 4-gram around an ambiguous attachment. In the current experiments, equal weights are used for simplicity but results are still good on the TRAINS corpora (92.2% and 92.4% accuracy). Despite the large statistical differences in attachment preferences in the two corpora, training on the first corpus and testing on the second gives an accuracy of 90.9%.

1 Introduction

The goal of the TRAINS project is to build a computerized planning assistant that can interact conversationally with its user. The current version of this planning assistant, TRAINS 95, is described in (Allen et al., 1995); it passes speech input onto a parser whose chart is used by the dialog manager and other higher-level reasoning components. The planning problems handled involve moving several trains from given starting locations to specified destinations on a map display (showing a network of rail lines in the eastern United States). The 95 dialogs are a corpus of people's utterances to the TRAINS 95 system; they contain 773 instances of PP or adverb postmodifiers that can attach to either NPs or VPs. Many of these cases were unambiguous, as there was no NP following the VP, or the NP did not follow a verb. Only 275 utterances contained ambiguous constructions and in 73.5% of these, the correct PP/adverb attachment was to the NP.

One goal of the TRAINS project is to enhance the TRAINS 95 system sufficiently to handle the more complex TRAINS 91-93 dialogs. This corpus was created between 1991 and 1993 from discussions between humans on transportation problems involving trains. The dialogs deal with time constraints and the added complexity of using engines to pick up boxcars and commodities to accomplish delivery goals. This corpus contains 3201 instances of PP or adverb postmodifiers that can attach to either NPs or VPs. 1573 of these examples contained both an NP and a VP to which the postmodifier could attach. The postmodifier attached to the VP in 88.7% of these examples. On average, a postmodifier attachment ambiguity appears in the 91-93 dialogs after about 54 words, which is more frequent than the 74 word average of the 95 dialogs. This suggests that a disambiguation module is going to become necessary for the TRAINS system. This is especially true since some of the methods used by TRAINS 95 to recover from parse errors will not work in a more complex domain. For instance in the 95 dialogs, a PP of form *at city-name* can be assumed to give the current location of an engine that is to be moved. However, this is not true of the 91-93 dialogs where actions such as *load* often take *at city-name* as adjuncts.

2 Methodology

KANKEI[1] is a first attempt at a TRAINS disambiguation module. Like the systems in (Hindle and Rooth, 1993) and (Collins and Brooks, 1995), KANKEI records attachment statistics on informa-

[1] From the Japanese word, kankei, meaning "relation."

tion extracted from a corpus. This information consists of phrase head patterns around the possible locations of PP/adverb attachments. Figure 1 shows how the format of these patterns allows for combinations including a verb, NP-head (rightmost NP before the postmodifier), and either the preposition and head noun in the PP, or one or more adverbs.[2] These patterns are similar to ones used by the disambiguation system in (Collins and Brooks, 1995) and (Brill and Resnik, 1994) except that Brill and Resnik form rules from these patterns while KANKEI and the system of Collins and Brooks use the attachment statistics of multiple patterns. While KANKEI combines the statistics of multiple patterns to make a disambiguation decision, Collins and Brooks' model is a backed-off model that uses 4-gram statistics where possible, 3-gram statistics where possible if no 4-gram statistics are available, and bigram statistics otherwise.

verb NP-head (preposition obj-head | adverb1 adverb2)

Figure 1: Format of an attachment pattern

Most items in this specification are optional. The only requirement is that patterns have at least two items: a preposition or adverb and a verb or NP-head. The singular forms of nouns and the base forms of verbs are used. These patterns (with hyphens separating the items) form keys to two hash tables; one records attachments to NPs while the other records attachments to VPs. Numbers are stored under these keys to record how often such a pattern was seen in a not necessarily ambiguous VP or NP attachment. Sentence 1 instantiates the longest possible pattern, a 4-gram that here consists of *need*, *orange*, *in*, and *Elmira*.

`1) I need the oranges in Elmira.`

The TRAINS corpora are much too small for KANKEI to rely only on the full pattern of phrase heads around an ambiguous attachment. While searching for attachment statistics for sentence 1, KANKEI will check its hash tables for the key *need-orange-in-Elmira*. If it relied entirely on full patterns, then if the pattern had not been seen, KANKEI would have to randomly guess the attachment. Such a technique will be referred to as *full matching*. Normally KANKEI will do *partial matching*, i.e., if it cannot find a pattern such as *need-orange-in-Elmira*, it will look for smaller partial patterns which here would be: *need-in*, *orange-in*, *orange-in-Elmira*, *need-in-Elmira*, and *need-orange-in*. The frequency with which NP and VP attachment occurs for these patterns is totaled to see if one attachment is preferred. Currently, we count partial patterns equally, but in future refinements we would like to choose weights more judiciously. For instance, we would expect shorter patterns such as *need-in* to carry less weight than longer ones. The need to choose weights is a drawback of the approach. However, the intuition is that one source of evidence is insufficient for proper disambiguation. Future work needs to further test this hypothesis.

The statistics used by KANKEI for partial or full matching can be obtained in various ways. One is to use the same kinds of full and partial pattern matching in training as are used in disambiguation. This is called *comprehensive training*. Another method, called *raw training*, is to record only full patterns for ambiguous and unambiguous attachments in the corpus. (Note that full patterns can be as small as bigrams, such as when an adverb follows an NP acting as a subject.) Although raw training only collects a subset of the data collected by comprehensive training, it still gives KANKEI some flexibility when disambiguating phrases. If the full pattern of an ambiguity has not been seen, KANKEI can test whether a partial pattern of this ambiguous attachment occurred as an unambiguous attachment in the training corpus.

Like the disambiguation system of (Brill and Resnik, 1994), KANKEI can also use word classes for some of the words appearing in its patterns. The rudimentary set of noun word classes used in this project is composed of **city** and **commodity** classes and a **train** class including cars and engines.

3 Measure of Success

One hope of this project is to make generalizations across corpora of different domains. Thus, experiments included trials where the 91-93 dialogs were used to predict the 95 dialogs[3] and vice versa. Experiments on the effect of training and testing KANKEI on the same set of dialogs used cross validation; several trials were run with a different part of the corpus being held out each time. In all these cases, the use of partial patterns and word classes was varied in an attempt to determine their effect.

Word Classes	Yes	Yes	Yes	Yes
Raw Training	Yes	Yes	No	Yes
P. Matching	Yes	Yes	No	No
Default Guess	VP	NP	NP	NP
% by Default	7.6	3.6	42.3	43.0
% Accuracy	90.9	87.6	86.9	85.5

Table 1: Results of training with the 93 dialogs and testing on the 95 dialogs

Tables 1, 2, and 3 show the results for the best parameter settings from these experiments.

[2]Examples of trailing adverb pairs are *first off* and *right now*.

[3]91-93 dialogs were used for training and the 95 dialogs for testing.

Word Classes	Yes	Yes	No	Yes	No
Raw Training	No	No	No	Yes	No
P. Matching	Yes	Yes	Yes	Yes	Yes
Default Guess	NP	VP	VP	VP	NP
% by Default	3.9	3.6	5.1	9.5	4.0
% Accuracy	92.4	92.0	92.0	91.6	90.9

Table 2: Results of training and testing on the 95 dialogs

Word Classes	Yes	No	Yes	Yes
Raw Training	No	No	Yes	No
P. Matching	Yes	Yes	No	No
Default Guess	VP	VP	VP	VP
% by Default	7.2	8.8	42.9	42.7
% Accuracy	92.2	91.3	91.0	91.0

Table 3: Results of training and testing on the 93 dialogs

The rows labeled *% by Default* give the portion of the total success rate (last row) accounted for by KANKEI's default guess. The results of training on the 95 data and testing on the 93 data are not shown because the best results were no better than always attaching to the VP. Notice that all of these results involve either word classes or partial patterns. There is a difference of at least 30 attachments (1.9% accuracy) between the best results in these tables and the results that did not use word classes or partial patterns. Thus, it appears that at least one of these methods of generalization is needed for this high-dimensional space. The 93 dialogs predicted attachments in the 95 test data with a success rate of 90.9% which suggests that KANKEI is capable of making generalizations that are independent of the corpus from which they were drawn. The overall accuracy is high: the 95 data was able to predict itself with an accuracy of 92.2%, while the 93 data predicted itself with an accuracy of 92.4%.

4 Discussion and Future Work

The results for the TRAINS corpora are encouraging. We would also like to explore how KANKEI performs in a more general domain such as the Wall Street Journal corpus from the Penn Treebank. We could then compare results with Collins and Brooks' disambiguation system which was also tested using the Penn Treebank's Wall Street Journal corpus.

Weighting the n-grams in a nonuniform manner should improve accuracy on the TRAINS corpora as well as in more general domains. (Alshawi and Carter, 1994) address a related problem, weighting scores from different disambiguation systems to obtain a single rating for a parse tree. They achieved good results using a hill climbing technique to explore the space of possible weights. Another possible technique for combining evidence is the maximum-entropy technique of (Wu, 1993). We are also considering using logical forms (instead of word and word classes) in collocation patterns.

The integration of KANKEI with the TRAINS parser needs to be completed. As a first attempt, when the TRAINS parser tries to extend the arcs associated with the rules: VP -> VP (PP|ADV) and NP -> NP (PP|ADV), KANKEI will adjust the probabilities of these arcs based on attachment statistics.[4] Ultimately, the TRAINS disambiguation module will contain functions measuring rule habituation and distance effects. Then it will become necessary to weight the scores of each disambiguation technique according to its effectiveness. The ability to adjust probabilities based on evidence seen is an advantage over rule-based approaches. This advantage is obtained at the expense of storing all the patterns seen.

Acknowledgments

This work was supported in part by National Science Foundation grant IRI-95033312. Len Schubert's supervision and many helpful suggestions are gratefully acknowledged. Thanks also to James Allen for his helpful comments.

References

James Allen, George Ferguson, Bradford Miller, and Eric Ringger. 1995. Spoken dialogue and interactive planning. In *Proc. of the ARPA Spoken Language Technology Workshop*, Austin, TX.

Hiyan Alshawi and David Carter. 1994. Training and scaling preference functions. *Computational Linguistics*, 20(4):635–648.

Eric Brill and Philip Resnik. 1994. A rule-based approach to prepositional phrase attachment disambiguation. In *Proc. of 15th International Conference on Computational Linguistics*, Kyoto, Japan.

Michael Collins and James Brooks. 1995. Prepositional phrase attachment through a backed-off model. In *Proc. of the 3rd Workshop on Very Large Corpora*, pages 27–38, Boston, MA.

Donald Hindle and Mats Rooth. 1993. Structural amiguity and lexical relations. *Computational Linguistics*, 19(1):103–120.

Dekai Wu. 1993. Estimating probability distributions over hypotheses with variable unification. In *Proc. of the 11th National Conference on Artificial Intelligence*, pages 790–795, Washington D.C.

[4] The TRAINS parser is probabilistic although the probabilities are parse scores not formal probabilities.

Subdeletion in Verb Phrase Ellipsis

Paul G. Donecker
Villanova University
800 Lancaster Avenue
Villanova, PA 19085
donecker@monet.vill.edu

Abstract

This paper stems from an ongoing research project[1] on verb phrase ellipsis. The project's goals are to implement a verb phrase ellipsis resolution algorithm, automatically test the algorithm on corpus data, then automatically evaluate the algorithm against human-generated answers. The paper will establish the current status of the algorithm based on this automatic evaluation, categorizing current problem situations. An algorithm to handle one of these problems, the case of subdeletion, will be described and evaluated. The algorithm attempts to detect and solve subdeletion by locating adjuncts of similar types in a verb phrase ellipsis and corresponding antecedent.

1. Introduction

A verb phrase ellipsis (VPE) exists when a sentence has an auxiliary verb but no verb phrase (VP). For example, in the sentence "Gather ye rosebuds while ye may," "may" is the beginning of a VPE. Its antecedent is "gather ye rosebuds." The research described in this paper is part of a project to automate the resolution of VPE occurrences, and also to automate the evaluation of the success of the VPE resolution (Hardt 1995).

Based on these evaluations of the algorithm, several distinct categories of error situations have been determined. We have focused on errors in which the program selects the correct head verb as antecedent. These cases can be divided into the following categories: 1) too much material included from the antecedent, 2) not enough much material included from the antecedent, 3) discontinuous antecedents, and 4) miscellaneous.

For a subset of case 1, subdeletion, an algorithm derived from (Lappin and McCord, 1990) is evaluated in regard to the Brown Corpus.

2. Background

Previous studies on evaluating discourse processing (e.g., Walker, 1989; Hobbs, 1978) have involved subjectively examining test cases to determine correctness. With the development of resources such as the Penn Treebank (Marcus, Santorini, and Marcinkiewicz, 1993), it has become possible to automate empirical tests of discourse processing systems to obtain a more objective measure of their success. Towards this end, an algorithm was implemented in a Common Lisp program called VPEAL (Verb Phrase Ellipsis Antecedent Locator) (Hardt, 1995), drawing on the Penn Treebank as input. The portion of the Penn Treebank examined--the Brown Corpus, about a million words--contains about 400 VPEs.

Furthermore, to automatically evaluate the algorithm, utilities were developed to automatically test the output of VPEAL for correctness. The most recent version of VPEAL contained 18 sub-parts for ranking and choosing antecedents. Testing the program's performance involved finding the percentage of correct antecedents found by any or all of these algorithms. This was achieved by having human coders read plain text versions of the parsed passages, marking what they felt to be the antecedent. Antecedents selected by VPEAL were considered correct if they matched the antecedents selected by the coders.

The remainder of this paper will describe the categories of errors observed, then describe an approach to reducing one category of errors.

3. Categories of Errors

The most recent version of VPEAL correctly selects 257 out of 380 antecedents from the Brown Corpus. We have divided the categories into the following categories:

A. Incorrect verb: 90 cases. In these cases, VPEAL selected an incorrect head verb for the

[1] This research was supported in part by NSF Career Grant, no. IRI-9502257.

antecedent. The causes of these errors are being evaluated.

B. Incorrect antecedent but correct verb: 33 cases. VPEAL selected the correct verb to head the antecedent, but the selected antecedent was either incomplete or included incorrect information. These cases can be further divided into: 1) too much material included from the antecedent, 2) not enough much material included from the antecedent, 3) discontinuous antecedents, and 4) miscellaneous. These subcategories are described below.

1. Too much material is included from the antecedent: 11 cases.

Example (excerpt from Penn Treebank):
produce humorous effects in his novels and tales as they did in the writing of Longstreet and Hooper and Harris
VPE: did
VPEAL's antecedent: produce humorous effects in his novels and tales
Coder's antecedent: produce humorous effects

Normally, an entire verb phrase is selected as the antecedent. In these cases, though, part of the selected antecedent was not required by the VPE. The most common situation (6 cases), as in the above example, was subdeletion--when the VPE structure contains a noun phrase or prepositional phrase which substitutes for a corresponding structure in the antecedent verb phrase.

2. Not enough material is included from the antecedent: 10 cases.

Example (excerpt from Penn Treebank):
But even if we can not see the repulsive characteristics in this new image of America, foreigners can
VPE: can
VPEAL's antecedent: see the repulsive characteristics
Coder's antecedent: see the repulsive characteristics in this new image of America

By default, only text contained by the selected verb phrase is included in the antecedent. In these cases, however, human coders have selected text that is adjacent to but not parsed as contained by the verb phrase as part of the antecedent. It can be argued that these errors are not the fault of the VPEAL algorithm--that if text is parsed as not being a part of the verb phrase then it should still not be included when the verb phrase is chosen as the antecedent. If the above prepositional phrase "in this new image of America" were parsed as part of the verb phrase-- as indeed it should have been--then the algorithm would have derived the correct antecedent.

3. Discontinuous antecedents--the correct antecedent is split into two parts: 5 cases.

Example (excerpt from Penn Treebank):
representing as I do today my wife
VPE: do
VPEAL's antecedent: representing
Coder's antecedent: representing my wife

This situation is similar to B2 in that the antecedent is incorrect because text not contained by the selected verb phrase should be included in the antecedent. In these cases, however, the reason the omitted text is not contained by the antecedent verb phrase is that an interposing phrase (in the example above, the VPE itself) occurs in the middle of the antecedent.

4. Miscellaneous: 7 cases.

4. Improving Performance in the Case of Subdeletion

In this section an algorithm is described to reduce the errors in error category B1 caused by subdeletion. Subdeletion is probably the most straightforward of the error categories. The problem category occurred when prepositional phrases and noun phrases in the antecedent verb phrases were unnecessary because of analogous phrases adjacent to the VPE. The proposed solution was to check whether the VPE has a sister node that is a prepositional phrase or noun phrase. If it does, and a phrase of the same type exists as a sister node to the head verb in the antecedent, then the phrase in the antecedent is removed. This is essentially the strategy outlined by Lappin and McCord (1990). Following are the specific steps to implementing the algorithm:

1. Check if there are any prepositional phrases or noun phrases that are sister nodes to the antecedent head verb.

2. Check if there are any prepositional phrases or noun phrases that are sister nodes to the VPE head verb.

3. If a prepositional phrase or noun phrase is found in step 1, and a phrase of the same type is found

in step 2, then remove the phrase found in step 1 from the antecedent.

For example, refer to the example from error case B.1. Step 1 would locate the noun phrase "humorous effects" and the prepositional phrase "in his novels and tales" as sister nodes to the antecedent head verb "produce."

Step 2 would locate the prepositional phrase "in the writing of Longstreet and Hooper and Harris" as a sister node to the VPE head verb "did."

Step 3 would determine that a prepositional phrase exists after both the antecedent's head verb and the VPE and therefore would delete "in his novels and tales" from the antecedent, resulting in the correct antecedent, "produce humorous effects."

This algorithm will correctly handle the 6 cases of subdeletion in the Brown Corpus. However, examples can be constructed for which this algorithm does not account. In the sentence "Julie drove to school on Friday, and Laura did on Saturday," for example, the VPE is "did" and the correct antecedent is "drove to school." In this example, two prepositional phrases--"to school" and "on Friday"--follow the antecedent's head verb "drove." A prepositional phrase, "on Saturday," also exists following the VPE's head verb. Following the above algorithm, both prepositional phrases "to school" and "on Friday" would be deleted, resulting in an incorrect antecedent. The algorithm makes no provisions for cases containing multiple prepositional phrases and noun phrases. Fortunately, such situations seem rare, as none were found in the Brown Corpus.

More significantly, the algorithm also assumes that analogous phrases following the antecedent and VPE always implies subdeletion. That is, it assumes that prepositional phrases or noun phrases following the VPE always implies that like phrases should be deleted from the antecedent. Again, it is possible to imagine a counterexample, for example, "Dad stayed in the Hilton like Mom did in Pittsburgh." Here, the above algorithm would incorrectly remove the prepositional phrase "in the Hilton."

The expectation was that these counter examples would be less frequent than the cases in which the algorithm would correctly remove unwanted text. A manual sampling of VPEs in the Brown Corpus showed this to be true. When the algorithm was implemented, however, the number of correct answers improved to 258, an increase of 1. In addition to solving the 6 cases of subdeletion, the algorithm introduced 5 errors; each of these new errors involved a noun phrase or prepositional phrase in the VPE that did not require the deletion of a counterpart in the antecedent. For example, one of the newly introduced errors occurred in the fragment "...creaking in the fog as it had for thirty years." The prepositional phrase "for thirty years" in the VPE caused the removal of the phrase "in the fog" from the antecedent, even though the phrases are not parallel in meaning.

These results imply that the structure of a sentence alone is insufficient to detect subdeletion. It is possible, however, that a larger sample of relevant examples would suggest the best choice (to delete or not to delete) in the absence of additional information. Towards these ends, other corpora in the Penn Treebank will be examined with VPEAL. Also, newer versions of the Treebank include semantic tags to adjunct phrases which will aid in preventing the misidentification of subdeletion described above.

5. Conclusion

Improving the results of the VPEAL program is an iterative process. We have categorized the errors occurring in VPEAL. An algorithm for solving the error category of subdeletion was described and examined. Potential problem situations for the algorithm were also presented. Empirical evaluation of the algorithm indicates that a purely syntactic approach to detecting subdeletion is probably insufficient. Additional approaches to the problem of subdeletion were suggested. Other cases of errors will be likewise evaluated.

Bibliography

Hardt, Daniel. 1995. An empirical approach to VP ellipsis.

Hobbs, Jerry. 1978. Resolving pronoun references. Lingua, 44:311-388.

Lappin, Shalom and Michael McCord. 1990. Anaphora Resolution in Slot Grammar. Computational Linguistics, 16(4).

Marcus, Mitchell P., Beatrice Santorini, and Mary Ann Marcinkiewicz. 1993. Building a large annotated corpus of english: The penn treebank. Computational Linguistics, 19(2).

Walker, Marilyn. 1989. Evaluating discourse processing algorithms. In Proceedings, 27th Annual Meeting of the ACL, Vancouver, Canada.

Using textual clues to improve metaphor processing

Stéphane Ferrari
LIMSI-CNRS
PO Box 133
F-91403 Orsay cédex, FRANCE
ferrari@limsi.fr

Abstract

In this paper, we propose a textual clue approach to help metaphor detection, in order to improve the semantic processing of this figure. The previous works in the domain studied the semantic regularities only, overlooking an obvious set of regularities. A corpus-based analysis shows the existence of surface regularities related to metaphors. These clues can be characterized by syntactic structures and lexical markers. We present an object oriented model for representing the textual clues that were found. This representation is designed to help the choice of a semantic processing, in terms of possible non-literal meanings. A prototype implementing this model is currently under development, within an incremental approach allowing step-by-step evaluations. [1]

1 Introduction

Metaphor is a frequently used figure of speech, reflecting common cognitive processes. Most of the previous works in Natural Language Understanding (NLU) looked for regularities only on the semantic side of this figure, as shown in a brief overview in section 2. This resulted in complex semantic processings, not based on any previous robust detection, or requiring large and exhaustive knowledge bases. Our aim is to provide NLU systems with a set of heuristics for choosing the most adequate semantic processing, as well as to give some probabilistic clues for disambiguating the possibly multiple meaning representations.

A corpus-based analysis we made showed the existence of textual clues in relation with the metaphors. These clues, mostly lexical markers combined with syntactic structures, are easy to spot, and can provide a first set of detection heuristics. We propose, in section 3, an object oriented model for representing these clues and their properties, in order to integrate them in a NLU system. For each class, attributes give information for spoting the clues, and, when possible, the source and the target of the metaphor, using the results of a syntactic parsing. A prototype, STK, partially implementing the model, is currently under development, within an incremental approach. It is already used to evaluate the clues relevance.

In conclusion, we will discuss how the model can help chosing the adequate semantic analysis to process at the sentence level or disambiguating multiple meaning representations, providing probabilities for non-literal meanings.

2 Classical methods: a brief overview

The classical NLU points of view of metaphor have pointed out the multiple kinds of relations between what is called the source and the target of the metaphor, but rarely discuss the problem of detecting the figure that bears the metaphor. For our purpose, we choose to present these approaches in two main groups, depending on how they initiate the semantic processing.

The previous works led to a classification introduced by Dan Fass (Fass, 1991). In the *comparison view*, the metaphor corresponds to an analogy between the structures representing the source and the target of the figure, as in Gentner's works (Gentner, 1988) and their implementation (Falkenhainer et al., 1989). The *interaction view*, as in Hobbs (Hobbs, 1991), points at the novelty brought by the metaphor. Fass also distinguishes a *selection restrictions violations view* presenting the metaphor as a kind of anomaly. We would argue that the two previous views already considered metaphor as a kind of anomaly. Indeed, the semantic analysis proposed for dealing with metaphors were processed depending on the results of another, say a "classical" one[2].

[1]This work takes part in a research project sponsored by the AUPELF-UREF (Francophone Agency For Education and Research)

[2]We prefer to call it a *classical* rather than *literal meanings* processing because it can deal with some conventional metaphors, even if not explicitly mentioned.

Thereby, detecting a metaphor meant detecting an anomaly in the meaning representation issued from such a classical analysis.

Fass proposed a method for discriminating literal meanings, metaphors, metonymies and "anomalies", merging different points of view (Fass, 1991). In this approach, multiple semantic analysis can be processed, resulting in possibly multiple meaning representations. In (Prince and Sabah, 1992), a method to overcome similar kinds of ambiguities reveal the difficulties encountered if no previous detection is made. James Martin's approach (Martin, 1992), called the *conventional view* by Fass, is based on Lakoff's theory on cognitive metaphors (Lakoff and Johnson, 1980). It requires a specific knowledge representation base and also results in multiple representation meanings. Detecting a metaphor is meaningless here, and conventional metaphoric meanings can be viewed as polysemies. Martin revealed at least that the heuristic of the ill-formness of meaning representations issued from classical analysis is not sufficient at all to deal with all the possible metaphors.

In our point of view, all the previous approaches were founded. The main remaining problem, however, is to choose an adequate processing when confronted with a metaphor, and thus, to detect the metaphors before trying to build their meaning representation. This can be partially solved using textual clues.

3 Textual clues: object oriented description

If the classical views of the metaphor overlook the textual clues, in other domains, especially those concerning explanation, they have been wisely reintroduced. In (Pery-Woodley, 1990), Pery-Woodley shows the existence of such clues related to the explanatory discourse. They can help in generating explanations in natural language as well as in modelling the student in a intelligent tutoring system (Daniel et al., 1992). A corpus of 26 explanatory texts in French, of about 200 words each, has been collected under a shared research project between psychologists and computer scientists, in order to study metaphors and analogies in teaching. The analysis we made showed the existence of textual clues in relation with metaphoric contexts and analogies (e.g. "like", "such as", "illustrated by"). They can be characterized by syntactic regularities (e.g. the comparative is used in structures such as "less than", "more than"; the identification is made through attributes or appositions, ...). They also involve lexical markers (e.g. "literaly", "illustrating", "metaphorically",). These properties, already found in the previous works, can help detecting the clues themselves. Studying the relation between the syntactic regularities and the lexical markers, one can observe that the first build the ground where to find the second. We thus propose an object-oriented model for representing these clues. A generic textual clue can thereby be described by the two following attributes:

- the *Surface Syntactic Pattern* representing the syntactic regularity, with a label on the item where to find the lexical marker
- the *Lexical Marker* itself

Typically, the word "metaphor" itself can be used as a lexical marker in expressions such as *"to extend the conventional metaphor, pruning such a tree means to generalize"*. On the other hand, "metaphor" will not be a marker if used as the subject of the sentence, like in this one. Thus, describing the syntactic regularities surrounding a lexical marker improves its relevance as a marker. We propose to represent this relevance for probabilistic purposes. Each clue that was found is currently evaluated on a large corpus (about 450,000 words). The frequencies of use of the lexical markers in metaphoric contexts are represented in the relevance attribute (see example below).

The syntactic structures may also give information about the source and the target of the metaphor. For instance, in the sentence *"Yesterday, at home, Peter threw himself on the dessert like a lion."*, the subject inherits the properties of speed and voracity of a lion attacking its victim. It is here possible to spot the source and the target of the metaphor using the syntactic properties of the comparison. Two attributes are added to textual clues related to metaphors, corresponding to the elements of the sentence bearing the source and the target.

Example of textual clue representations

type metaphor-analogy

name B.2.2.2

comment *comparison involving the meaning of a marker, adjective, attribute of the object, object before the verb*

SSP GN_0 GN_1 V_1 Adj_0 [*prep*] GN_2

LM Adj_0: pareil *(meaning "similar")*

target GN_1

source GN_2

LM relevance (15/28)
number of occurrences 28
conventional metaphors 3
new metaphors 2
metaphoric contexts 12
total 15

Notations: *GN* and *GV* stand for nominal or verbal groups, *Adj* and *Adv* for adjectives and adverbs, and *prep* for prepositions.

The model has been partially implemented in a tool, STK, for detecting the textual clues related to metaphors and adding specific marks when found. In its current version, STK allows us to tokenize, tag, and search for lexical markers on large corpora. The tagger we use is the one developped by Eric Brill (Brill, 1992) with a set of tags indicating the grammatical categories as well as other information such as the number and the gender for nouns and adjectives. It is evaluated under GRACE[3] protocol for corpus-oriented tools assigning grammatical categories. It is currently used for the evaluation of the textual clues that were found. The latter can be easily retrieved using STK, avoiding lexical ambiguities. They are then analyzed by hand, in order to determine their relevance attribute. In the previous example of textual clue, the relevance values are issued from this corpus-based analysis.

4 Conclusion, perspectives

Classical approaches to the metaphor in NLU revealed multiple underlying processes. We therefore focussed our study on how to help detecting metaphors in order to chose the most adequate semantic processing. Textual clues can give information about the figures that bear the metaphor, which are easy to spot. Indeed, they can be found using the results of syntactic parsing. We proposed an object-oriented model to represent these clues and their multiple properties.

If textual clues give information about possible non-literal meanings, metaphors and analogies, one may argue they do not allow for a robust detection. Indeed, a textual clue is not sufficient to prove the presence of such figures of speech. The relevance of each clue can be used to help disambiguating multiple meaning representation when it occurs. This must not be the only disambiguation tool, but when no other is avalaible, it provides NLU systems with a probabilistic method.

Our future works will focuss on the study of the relation between the metaphors introduced by a clue and others that are not conventional. The guideline is that novel metaphors not introduced by a clue at the sentence level may have been introduced previously in the text.

References

Brill, E. (1992). A simple rule-based part of speech tagger. In *Proceedings of the Third Conference on Applied Natural Language Processing*, Trento. ACL.

Daniel, M., Nicaud, L., Prince, V., and Pery-Woodley, M. (1992). Apport du style Linguistique la Modélisation Cognitive de l'Élève. *Lecture Notes in Computer Sciences*, 608:252–260. Proceedings of the International Conference on Intelligent Tutoring Systems (ITS-92), Montréal.

Falkenhainer, B., Forbus, K., and Gentner, D. (1989). The Structure-Mapping Engine: Algorithm and Examples. *Artificial Intelligence*, 41:1–63.

Fass, D. (1991). met : A Method for Discriminating Metonymy and Metaphor by Computer. *Computational Linguistics*, 17(1):49–90.

Fass, D., Hinkelman, E., and Martin, J., editors. *Proceedings of the IJCAI Workshop on Computational Approaches to Non-Literal Language*, Sydney, Australia. 1991.

Gentner, D. (1988). *Analogical Inference and Analogical Access*, In: *Analogica*, chapter 3, pages 63–88. Edited by Prieditis A., Pitman Publishing, London, Morgan Kaufmann Publishers, Inc., Los Altos, California.

Hobbs, J. (1991). Metaphor and abduction. In (Fass et al.,), pages 52–61.

Lakoff, G. and Johnson, M. (1980). *Metaphors we live by.* University of Chicago Press, Chicago, U.S.A.

Martin, J. (1992). Computer Understanding of Conventional Metaphoric Language. *Cognitive Science*, 16:233–270.

Pery-Woodley, M. (1990). Textual clues for user modeling in an intelligent tutoring system. Master's thesis, University of Manchester, England, Great-Britain.

Prince, V. and Sabah, G. (1992). Coping with Vague and Fuzzy Words: A Multi-Expert Natural Language System which Overcomes Ambiguities. In *Acts of PRICAI'92*, Seoul, Corea. September, 1992.

[3]GRACE stands for "Grammars and Resources for Corpora Analysis and their Evaluation". It is a national research project for the development of tools for French language processing.

On Reversing the Generation Process in Optimality Theory

J. Eric Fosler
U.C. Berkeley and International Computer Science Institute
1947 Center Street, Suite 600, Berkeley, CA 94704
fosler@icsi.berkeley.edu

Abstract

Optimality Theory, a constraint-based phonology and morphology paradigm, has allowed linguists to make elegant analyses of many phenomena, including infixation and reduplication. In this work-in-progress, we build on the work of Ellison (1994) to investigate the possibility of using OT as a parsing tool that derives underlying forms from surface forms.

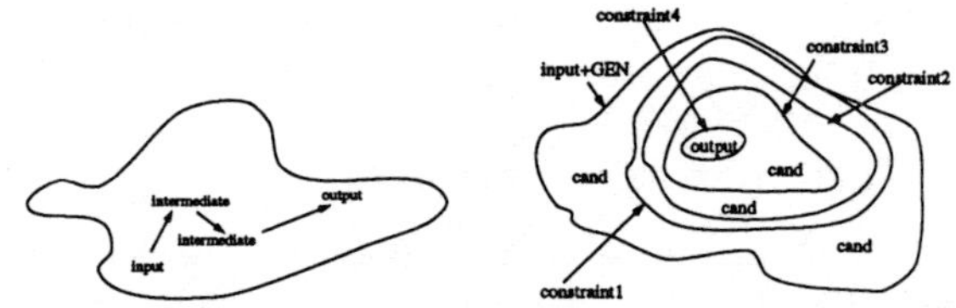

a. Derivational Phonology b. Optimality Theory

Figure 1: Search Spaces Within Different Paradigms

1 Introduction

Optimality Theory (Prince and Smolensky, 1993) is a constraint-based phonological and morphological system that allows violable constraints in deriving output surface forms from underlying forms. In OT a system of constraints selects an "optimal" surface output from a set of candidates. The methodology allows succinct analyses of phenomena such as infixation and reduplication that were difficult to describe under sets of transformational rules.

Several computational methods for OT have been produced within the short amount of time since Prince and Smolensky's paper (Ellison, 1994; Tesar, 1995; Hammond, 1995). These systems were designed as generation systems, deriving surface forms from an underlying lexicon. There have, however, been no computational models of OT parsers that derive underlying forms from the surface form.[1] In this work, we lay the theoretical groundwork for using OT as a parsing tool.

2 Comparing Derivational Methods to Optimality Theory

In traditional computational phonology/morphology systems such as two-level phonology (Koskenniemi, 1983), grammars that generate surface forms are invertible, allowing parsing back into underlying forms. In a derivational framework, the grammar converts underlying forms to surface outputs via transformations; the input and output share the same space (Figure 1a). In the one-level version of OT that most computational methods use, the space is populated with candidate outputs created by a generator function GEN operating on input strings. The search narrows in on an optimal output (Figure 1b) using evaluation constraints in a process called EVAL; successively smaller boundaries are cut out by the constraints until only one candidate remains. It is easy to see why the derivational method can be run backward: it just retraces derivational links in the graph. It is not obvious, though, how the input can be found from the search space in OT.

3 Tagalog Infixation

Infixation has traditionally been a difficult problem for computational models that use two-level phonology (Sproat, 1992). Infixation in Tagalog, however, has been modeled using OT (McCarthy and Prince, 1995). In Tagalog, the *um* affix can appear as a prefix, or "move" slightly into the word to which it is attaching (French, 1988).

Root	with *um*	Gloss
alis	um-alis	"leave"
sulat	s-um-ulat	"write"
gradwet	gr-um-adwet	"graduate"

McCarthy and Prince analyze *um* as a prefix, which moves into a word to reduce the number of coda consonants. They postulate two competing constraints, ALIGN-PREFIX and the higher-ranked NOCODA. ALIGN-PREFIX states that the prefix should remain as close to the front of the word as possible. NOCODA penalizes syllables with coda consonants.

In the OT derivation of *grumadwet* from *um+gradwet* (Figure 2), the winning candidate violates NOCODA twice, while the first two candidates violate it three times. The final candidate is pruned since it violates the ALIGN constraint more times than the winner.

[1] Some of the computational work in OT confusingly uses the term "parsing" to refer to generation.

	Candidates	NoCoda	Align
	um.grad.wet	* * *!	
	gum.rad.wet	* * *!	*
√	gru.mad.wet	**	**
	gra.dum.wet	**	* * *!*

Figure 2: OT Evaluation for Tagalog Infixation

```
(Morpheme Structure)  / PPWWWWWWW \ | / WPPWWWWWW \ | / WWPPWWWWW \
(Syllable Structure)  | NCOONCONC | | | ONCONCONC | | | OONONCONC |
(Phoneme Structure)   \ umgradwet / | \ gumradwet / | \ grumadwet /
                           Cand1           Cand2           Cand3
```

Figure 3: Candidate outputs for um+gradwet in an FST

4 Ellison's Conversion Method

Ellison (1994) provides a paradigm for converting Optimality Theory constraints into Finite State Transducers. He requires that EVAL constraints output binary marks when ranking candidates and be describable as a regular language; the output of GEN must also be describable by a regular language. As Ellison points out, most constraints can be reformulated to be binary. He is able to build FST representations for the constraints that he considers, showing them to be regular.

For the Tagalog example, GEN will output the regular language shown in Figure 3 for the first three candidates (*umgradwet*, *gumradwet*, and *grumadwet*).[2] Each candidate consists of segments associated with a syllable structure position and a morpheme structure marker.[3]

We now consider the ALIGN-PREFIX constraint, restricting the prefix to occur as early in the word as possible. This is encoded as an FST that writes marks on an output "Harmony Marks" tape. A "1" is written for any word (W) morphological material that precedes prefix (P) material, and a "0" is written for any other segment.

```
(Harmony Marks)       / 1 *  0 +  0 * \   / 0 * \
(Morpheme Structure)  | W    P    W   | | | W   |
(Syllable Structure)  | •    •    •   | | | •   |
(Phoneme Structure)   \ •    •    •   /   \ •   /
```

Figure 4: ALIGN-PREFIX FST Regular Language

The regular language generated by this FST (Figure 4) has a very simple structure. Any Ws before Ps on the Morpheme Structure tape get a harmony violation mark. Taking the product of this language with the optimal candidate scores the candidate (Figure 5). The harmony marks include two non-harmonic marks (i.e. "1"s); in the OT tableau in Figure 2, we see that ALIGN also gives two marks to the optimal candidate.

We can encode a similar FST for NOCODA. This FST examines the syllable structure tape to give harmony marks (Figure 6)— codas (Cs) get a harmony violation mark, onsets (O) and nuclei (N) are unmarked. As in the OT tableau, the winning candidate (Figure 7) violates NOCODA twice.

[2]For brevity, we are not considering other candidates.

[3]We have extended Ellison's work by adding a third tape that marks segments as belonging to the prefix or to the word.

```
(Harmony Marks)       / 1 1 0 0 0 0 0 0 0 \
(Morpheme Structure)  | W W P P W W W W W |
(Syllable Structure)  | O O N O N C O N C |
(Phoneme Structure)   \ g r u m a d w e t /
```

Figure 5: Scoring of grumadwet by ALIGN-PREFIX

```
(Harmony Marks)       / 1 | 0 | 0 \ *
(Morpheme Structure)  | • | • | • |
(Syllable Structure)  | O | N | C |
(Phoneme Structure)   \ • | • | • /
```

Figure 6: Regular Language generated by NOCODA

Once the OT constraints are represented as FSTs, combining all of the EVAL constraints into one transducer is a straightforward product. Ellison augments the product procedure so that harmony marks are concatenated by the resulting transducer.

We have used two different types of harmony marks in the ALIGN-PREFIX and NOCODA FSTs, representing the ranking of the two rules as suggested by McCarthy and Prince. The higher-ranked NOCODA constraint outputs "2" marks while ALIGN-PREFIX outputs "1" marks.[4] Harmonic comparisons between the candidates will consider the candidates with the smallest number of "2" marks first, followed by the smallest number of "1" marks. Marks are not added together, rather, the count of each type of mark is the deciding factor in evaluation.[5]

The output of GEN and the constraints of EVAL are combined into a single transducer by taking the product of all of the FSTs. For the Tagalog example, the output rankings for the candidates are shown in Figure 8. Using the harmonic marks to prune the resulting transducer reveals the optimal candidate (Figure 9).

5 Extensions to Parsing

Ellison's approach gives us an elegant method of performing OT generation using finite state automata. Nevertheless, the system cannot parse the output string back into underlying surface forms. In a derivational paradigm (Figure 1a) , the input and output forms are enclosed in the same space. The derivational grammar is a transform that one can invert using FSTs, searching for the input using the output.

Ellison's FSTs transform output candidates to harmony marks; even so, the inversion of these FSTs are useless. The crucial point is that GEN hides the surface-form-to-candidate mapping; in Ellison's system the EVAL portion of the system only combines with the *output* of GEN, so the mapping is lost. For invertability it is critical that the FST have access to both input and output forms.

In the version of OT (one-level OT) Ellison incorporated into his system, outputs of GEN are constrained

[4]Ellison uses only one type of mark and determines rank ordering from the relative positions of marks for each output segment. These two methods are equivalent.

[5]One "2" is worse than two "1"s.

```
(Harmony Marks)       / 0 0 0 0 0 2 0 0 2 \
(Morpheme Structure)  | W W P P W W W W W |
(Syllable Structure)  | O O N O N C O N C |
(Phoneme Structure)   \ g r u m a d w e t /
```

Figure 7: Scoring of grumadwet by NOCODA

(Harmony Marks)	00200000000200000020	01002000000200000020	01010000000200000020
(Morpheme Structure)	P P W W W W W W W	W P P W W W W W W	W W P P W W W W W
(Syllable Structure)	N C O O N C O N C	O N C O N C O N C	O O N O N C O N C
(Phoneme Structure)	u m g r a d w e t	g u m r a d w e t	g r u m a d w e t

Figure 8: Output of OT-FST System

(Harmony Marks)	10100000000002000002
(Morpheme Structure)	W W P P W W W W W
(Syllable Structure)	O O N O N C O N C
(Phoneme Structure)	g r u m a d w e t

Figure 9: Pruned Output of OT-FST System

to be similar to the input. McCarthy & Prince (1994) abandon this constraint principle, and use ***faithfulness*** constraints in EVAL to achieve the same effect within "modern" two-level OT. This will be a critical move for the OT-FST paradigm.

In two-level OT, GEN generates all strings; faithfulness constraints in EVAL minimize the inserted and deleted material between underlying and candidate surface forms. By specifically modeling the faithfulness constraints, we now allow the FST to have access to the input-output correspondences crucial for searching for underlying forms. The remaining question, however, is whether faithfulness constraints *can* be modeled by regular grammars. Several formulations of two-level OT faithfulness constraints are discussed by McCarthy and Prince (1994) and Orgun (1994). To illustrate the flavor of these constraints and how they might be regularizable, we consider two constraints, CORR and MATCH (named for their similarity to Orgun's constraints). For our Tagalog example, we add two tapes for the underlying word and prefix forms (Figure 10). The CORR constraint requires that for every element in the surface phoneme string there is a segment in the underlying word or prefix, and vice versa. MATCH constrains the surface string phoneme to match[6] those in the word and prefix, and vice versa (Figure 11). Using these constraints, the OT-FSTs should be able to generate and parse in the Tagalog example.

(Morpheme Structure)	W W P P W W W W W
(Syllable Structure)	O O N O N C O N C
(Surface Phoneme Structure)	g r u m a d w e t
(Word Phonemes)	(g r a d w e t)
(Prefix Phonemes)	(u m)

Figure 10: Adding Word and Prefix Tapes

The additional computational complexity for implementing this type of system may be quite large; the search space for determining unknown strings at parse time will make for a slow implementation unless suitable heuristics are found for searching over each type of string. Systems of this type are likely to become even more complex as more information such as moraic structure is added. We envision that these heuristics will be based on the harmony mark scoring of the FST, but the exact nature of this is left to future work.

6 Conclusions & Future Work

Current Computational Optimality Theory systems provide solutions for OT generation, but deriving underlying forms from surface forms is not possible within these

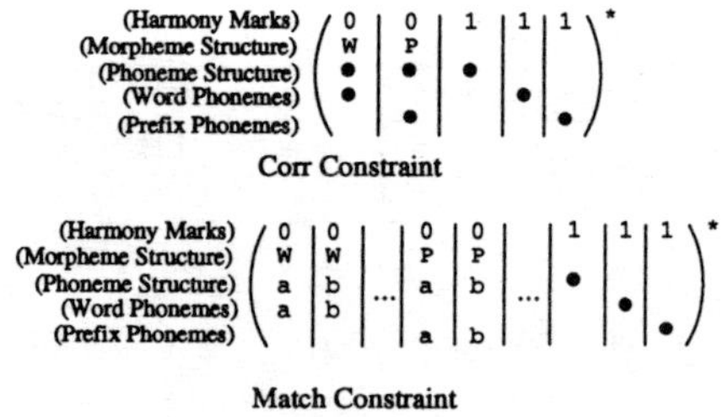

Figure 11: Faithfulness Constraints

systems. In order to extend any generation system to an OT parsing system, two-level Optimality Theory should be a critical component, since it moves the hidden relationship between input and output out of GEN and into EVAL. With two-level OT, the mapping from input to output can be directly operated upon by computational theories.

We have proposed using two-level OT to extend Ellison's technique for representing constraints as finite state transducers. By explicitly representing the input-to-output mapping using two-level OT, we have laid the theoretical groundwork for recovering underlying forms from surface forms.

In future work, we will implement the extensions to Ellison's algorithm allowing us to morphologically analyze cases like the Tagalog example. Search complexity will, however, be an issue in the implementation of the system; after an initial brute-force implementation, work must be focused on determining how the harmony marks can be used to heuristically guide the parser search.

Acknowledgments

We would like to thank Dan Jurafsky, Orhan Orgun, Sharon Inkelas, Nelson Morgan, Su-Lin Wu, and three anonymous ACL reviewers for comments, suggestions, and support.

References

T.M. Ellison. Phonological derivation in optimality theory. In *COLING-94*, 1994.

K. French. *Insights into Tagalog: Reduplication, Infixation, and Stress from Nonlinear Phonology.* M.A. Thesis, Summer Institute of Linguistics and University of Texas, Arlington, 1988.

M. Hammond. Syllable parsing in English and French. Rutgers Optimality Archive, 1995.

L. Karttunen. Kimmo: A general morphological processor. In *Texas Linguistics Forum 22*, 1983.

K. Koskenniemi. *Two-Level Morphology: A General Computational Model for Word-Form Recognition and Production.* Ph.D. thesis, University of Helsinki, 1983.

J. McCarthy and A. Prince. Prosodic morphology, parts 1 and 2. Prosodic Morphology Workshop, OTS, Utrecht, 1994.

J. McCarthy and A. Prince. Prosodic morphology. In J. Goldsmith, editor, *Handbook of Phonological Theory*, pages 318–366. Basil Blackwell Ltd., 1995.

O. Orgun. Containment: Why and why not. Unpublished ms., U. of California-Berkeley, Department of Linguistics, July 1994.

A. Prince and P. Smolensky. Optimality theory. Unpublished ms., Rutgers University, 1993.

R. Sproat. *Morphology and Computation.* MIT Press, Cambridge, MA, 1992.

B. Tesar. *Computational Optimality Theory.* Ph.D. Thesis, U. of Colorado-Boulder, Department of Computer Science, 1995.

[6]Here we mean *be identical to*; this definition can be extended with features and underspecified elements.

A Synopsis of Learning to Recognize Names Across Languages

Anthony F. Gallippi
University of Southern California
University Park, EEB 234
Los Angeles, CA 90089
USA
gallippi@aludra.usc.edu

Abstract

The development of natural language processing (NLP) systems that perform machine translation (MT) and information retrieval (IR) has highlighted the need for the automatic recognition of proper names. While various name recognizers have been developed, they suffer from being too limited; some only recognize one name class, and all are language specific. This work develops an approach to multilingual name recognition that uses machine learning and a portable framework to simplify the porting task by maximizing reuse and automation.

1 Introduction

Proper names represent a unique challenge for MT and IR systems. They are not found in dictionaries, are very large in number, come and go every day, and appear in many alias forms. For these reasons, list based matching schemes do not achieve desired performance levels. Hand coded heuristics can be developed to achieve high accuracy, however this approach lacks portability. Much human effort is needed to port the system to a new domain.

A desirable approach is one that maximizes *reuse* and minimizes human effort. This paper presents an approach to proper name recognition that uses machine learning and a language independent framework. Knowledge incorporated into the framework is based on a set of measurable linguistic characteristics, or *features*. Some of this knowledge is constant across languages. The rest can be generated automatically through machine learning techniques.

Whether a phrase (or word) is a proper name, and what type of proper name it is (company name, location name, person name, date, other) depends on (1) the internal structure of the phrase, and (2) the surrounding context.

Internal: "Mr. Brandon"
Context: "The new company, Safetek, will make air bags."

The person title "Mr." reliably shows "Mr. Brandon" to be a person name. "Safetek" can be recognized as a company name by utilizing the preceding contextual phrase and appositive "The new company,".

The recognition task can be broken down into *delimitation* and *classification*. Delimitation is the determination of the boundaries of the proper name, while classification serves to provide a more specific category.

Original:	John Smith , chairman of Safetek , announced his resignation yesterday.
Delimit:	<PN> John Smith </PN> , chairman of <PN> Safetek </PN> , announced his resignation yesterday.
Classify:	<person> John Smith </person> , chairman of <company> Safetek </company> , announced his resignation yesterday.

During the delimit step, proper name boundaries are identified. Next, the delimited names are categorized.

2 Method

The approach taken here is to utilize a data-driven knowledge acquisition strategy based on decision trees which uses contextual information. This differs from other approaches (Farwell *et al.*, 1994; Kitani & Mitamura, 1994; McDonald, 1993; Rau, 1992) which attempt to achieve this task by: (1) hand-coded heuristics, (2) list-based matching schemes, (3) human-generated knowledge bases, and (4) combinations thereof.

Delimitation occurs through the application of phrasal templates. These templates, built by hand, use logical operators (AND, OR, etc.) to combine features strongly associated with proper names, including: proper noun, ampersand, hyphen, and comma. In addition, ambiguities with delimitation are handled by including other predictive features within the templates.

To acquire the knowledge required for classification, each word is tagged with all of its associated features. Various types of features indicate the type of name: parts of speech (POS), designators,

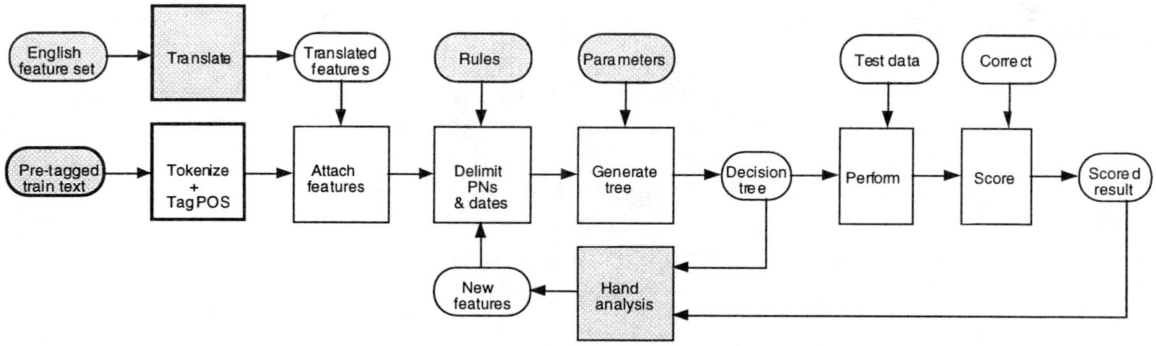

Figure 1. Multilingual development system.

morphology, syntax, semantics, and more. Designators are features which alone provide strong evidence for or against a particular name type. Examples include "Co." (company), "Dr." (person), and "County" (location).

Features are derived through automated and manual techniques. On-line lists can quickly provide useful features such as cities, family names, nationalities, etc. Proven POS taggers (Farwell *et al.*, 1994; Brill, 1992; Matsumoto *et al.*, 1992) predetermine POS features. Other features are derived through statistical measures and hand analysis.

A decision tree is built (for each name class) from the initial feature set using a recursive partitioning algorithm (Quinlan, 1986; Breiman *et al.*, 1984) that uses the following function as its splitting criterion:

$$-p*\log2(p) - (1-p)*\log2(1-p) \quad (1)$$

where p represents the proportion of names within a tree node belonging to the class for which the tree is built. The feature which minimizes the weighted sum of this function across both child nodes resulting from a split is chosen. A multitree approach was chosen over learning a single tree for all name classes because it allows for the straightforward association of features within the tree with specific name classes, and facilitates troubleshooting. Once built, the trees are all applied individually, and then the results are merged. Trees typically contained 100 or more nodes.

In order to work with another language, the following resources are needed: (1) pre-tagged training text in the new language using same tags as before, (2) a tokenizer for non-token languages, (3) a POS tagger (plus translation of the tags to a standard POS convention), and (4) translation of designators and lexical (list-based) features.

Figure 1 shows the working development system. The starting point is training text which has been pre-tagged with the locations of all proper names. The tokenizer separates punctuation from words. For non-token languages (no spaces between words), it also separates contiguous characters into constituent words. The POS tagger (Brill, 1992; Farwell *et. al.*, 1994; Matsumoto *et al.*, 1992) attaches parts of speech. The set of derived features is attached. Names are delimited using a set of POS based hand-coded templates. A decision tree is built based on the existing feature set and the specified level of context to be considered. The generated tree is applied to test data and scored. Hand analysis of results leads to the discovery of new features. The new features are added to the tokenized training text, and the process repeats.

Language-specific modules are highlighted with bold borders. Feature translation occurs through the utilization of: on-line resources, dictionaries, atlases, bilingual speakers, etc. The remainder is constant across languages: a language independent core, and an optimally derived feature set for English. Parts of the development system that are executed by hand appear shaded. Everything else is automatic.

3 Experiment

The system was first built for English and then ported to Spanish and Japanese. For English, the training text consisted of 50 messages obtained from the English Joint Ventures (EJV) domain MUC-5 corpus of the US Advanced Research Projects Agency (ARPA). This data was hand-tagged with the locations of companies, persons, locations, dates, and "other". The test set consisted of 10 new messages from the same corpus.

Experimental results were obtained by applying the generated trees to test texts. Proper names which are voted into more than one class are handled by choosing the highest priority class. Priorities are determined based on the independent accuracy of each tree. The metrics used were recall (R), precision (P), and an averaging measure, P&R, defined as:

$$P\&R = 2*P*R/(P+R) \quad (2)$$

Obtained results for English compare to the English results of Rau (1992) and McDonald (1993). The weighted average of P&R for companies, persons, locations, and dates is 94.0% (see Table 2).

The date grammar is rather small in comparison to other name classes, hence the performance for dates was perfect. Locations, by contrast, exhibited the lowest performance. This can be attributed mainly to: (1) locations are commonly associated with commas, which can create ambiguities with delimitation, and (2) locations made up a small percentage of all names in the training set, which could have resulted in overfitting of the built tree to the training data.

Three experiments were conducted for Spanish. First, the *English* trees, generated from the feature set optimized for *English*, are applied to the *Spanish* text (E-E-S). In the second experiment, new Spanish-specific trees are generated from the feature set optimized for English and applied to the Spanish test text (S-E-S). The third experiment proceeds like the second, except that minor adjustments and additions are made to the feature set with the goal of improving performance (S-S-S).

The additional resources required for the first Spanish experiment (E-E-S) are a Spanish POS tagger (Farwell *et al.,* 1994) and also the translated feature set (including POS) optimally derived for English. The second and third Spanish experiments (S-E-S, S-S-S) require in addition pre-tagged Spanish training text using the same tags as for English.

The additional features derived for S-S-S are shown in Table 1 (FN/LN=given/family name, NNP=proper noun, DE="de"). Only a few new features allows for significant performance improvement.

Table 1. Spanish specific features for S-S-S.

Type	Feature	Instances	How many
List	Companies	"IBM", "AT&T", ...	100
	Keyword	"del" (OF THE)	1
Template	Person	< FN DE LN >	1
	Person	< FN DE NNP >	1
	Date	< Num OF MM >	1
	Date	< Num OF MM OF Num >	1

The same three experiments are being conducted for Japanese. The first two, E-E-J and J-E-J, have been completed; J-J-J is in progress. Table 2 summarizes performance results and compares them to other work.

Acknowledgments

The author would like to offer special thanks and gratitude to Eduard Hovy for all of his support, direction, and encouragement from the onset of this work. Thanks also to Kevin Knight for his early suggestions, and to the Information Sciences Institute for use of their facilities and resources.

Table 2. Performance comparison to other work.

System	Language	Class	R	P	P&R
Rau	English	Com	NA	95	NA
PNF (McDonald)	English	Com Pers Loc Date	NA	NA	"Near 100%"
Panglyzer	Spanish	NA	NA	80	NA
MAJESTY	Japanese	Com Pers Loc	84.3 93.1 92.6	81.4 98.6 96.8	82.8 95.8 94.7
MNR (Gallippi)	English	Com Pers Loc Date (Avg)	97.6 98.2 85.7 100	91.6 100 91.7 100	94.5 99.1 88.6 100 94.0
MNR	Spanish	Com Pers Loc Date (Avg)	74.1 97.4 93.1 100	90.9 79.2 87.5 100	81.6 87.4 89.4 100 89.2
MNR	Japanese	Com Pers Loc Date (Avg)	60.0 86.5 80.4 90.0	60.0 84.9 82.1 94.7	60.0 85.7 81.3 92.3 83.1

References

Breiman, L., Friedman, J.H., Olshen, R.A., and Stone, C.J. 1984. *Classification and Regression Trees.* Wadsworth International Group.

Brill, E. 1992. A Simple Rule-Based Part of Speech Tagger. In *Proceedings of the Third Conference on Applied Natural Language Processing, ACL.*

Farwell, D., Helmreich, S., Jin, W., Casper, M., Hargrave, J., Molina-Salgado, H., and Weng, F. 1994. Panglyzer: Spanish Language Analysis System. In *Proceedings of the Conference of the Association of Machine Translation in the Americas (ATMA).* Columbia, MD.

Kitani, T. and Mitamura, T. 1994. An Accurate Morphological Analysis and Proper Name Identification for Japanese Text Processing. In *Transactions of Information Processing Society of Japan*, Vol. 35, No. 3, pp. 404-413.

Matsumoto, Y., Kurohashi, S., Taegi, H. and Nagao, M. 1992. *JUMAN Users' Manual Version 0.8*, Nagao Laboratory, Kyoto University.

McDonald, D. 1993. Internal and External Evidence in the Identification and Semantic Categorization of Proper Names. In *Proceedings of the SINGLEX workshop on "Acquisition of Lexical Knowledge from Text"*, pp. 32-43.

Quinlan, J.R. 1986. Induction of Decision Trees. In *Machine Learning*, pp. 81-106.

An Application of WordNet to Prepositional Attachment

Sanda M. Harabagiu
University of Southern California
Department of Electrical Engineering-Systems
Los Angeles, CA 90089-2562
harabagi@usc.edu

Abstract

This paper presents a method for word sense disambiguation and coherence understanding of prepositional relations. The method relies on information provided by WordNet 1.5. We first classify prepositional attachments according to semantic equivalence of phrase heads and then apply inferential heuristics for understanding the validity of prepositional structures.

1 Problem description

In this paper, we address the problem of disambiguation and understanding prepositional attachment. The arguments of prepositional relations are automatically categorized into semantically equivalent classes of WordNet (Miller and Teibel, 1991) concepts. Then by applying inferential heuristics on each class, we establish semantic connections between arguments that explain the validity of that prepositional structure. The method uses information provided by WordNet, such as semantic relations and textual glosses.

We have collected prepositional relations from the Wall Street Journal tagged articles of the PENN TREEBANK. Here, we focus on preposition `of`, the most frequently used preposition in the corpus.

2 Classes of prepositional relations

Since most of the prepositional attachments obey the principle of locality (Wertmer, 1991), we considered only the case of prepositional phrases preceded by noun or verb phrases. We scanned the corpus and filtered the phrase heads to create $\mathcal{C}$, an ad hoc collection of sequences $<$ *noun prep noun* $>$ and $<$ *verb prep noun* $>$. This collection is divided into classes of prepositional relations, using the following definitions:

Definition 1: Two prepositional structures $<$ $noun_1$ *prep* $noun_2$ $>$ and $<$ $noun_3$ *prep* $noun_4$ $>$ belong to the same class if one of the following conditions holds:

- $noun_1$, and $noun_2$ are hypernym/hyponym of $noun_3$, and $noun_4$ respectively, or
- $noun_1$, and $noun_2$ have a common hypernym/hyponym and with $noun_3$, and $noun_4$, respectively.

A particular case is when $noun_1$ ($noun_2$) and $noun_3$ ($noun_4$) are synonyms.

Definition 2: Two prepositional structures $<$ $verb_1$ *prep* $noun_1$ $>$ and $<$ $verb_2$ *prep* $noun_2$ $>$ belong to the same class if one of the following conditions holds:

- $verb_1$, and $noun_1$ are hypernym/hyponym of $verb_2$, and $noun_2$, respectively or
- $verb_1$, and $noun_1$ have a common hypernym/hyponym with $verb_2$, and $noun_2$, respectively.

A particular case is when the verbs or the nouns are synonyms, respectively.

The main benefit and reason for grouping prepositional relations into classes is the possibility to disambiguate the words surrounding prepositions. When classes of prepositional structures are identified, two possibilities arise:

1. A class contains at least two prepositional sequences from the collection $\mathcal{C}$. In this case, all sequences in that class are disambiguated, because for each pair ($<$ $noun_i$ *prep* $noun_j$ $>$, $<$ $noun_k$ *prep* $noun_q$ $>$), $noun_i$ and $noun_k$ (and $noun_j$ and $noun_q$ respectively) are in one of the following relations:
   (a) they are synonyms, and point to one synset that is their meaning.
   (b) they belong to synsets that are in hypernym/hyponym relation.
   (c) they belong to synsets that have a common hypernym/hyponym.

   In cases (a), (b) and (c), since words are associated to synsets, their meanings are disambiguated. The same applies for classes of prepositional sequences $<$ *verb prep noun* $>$.

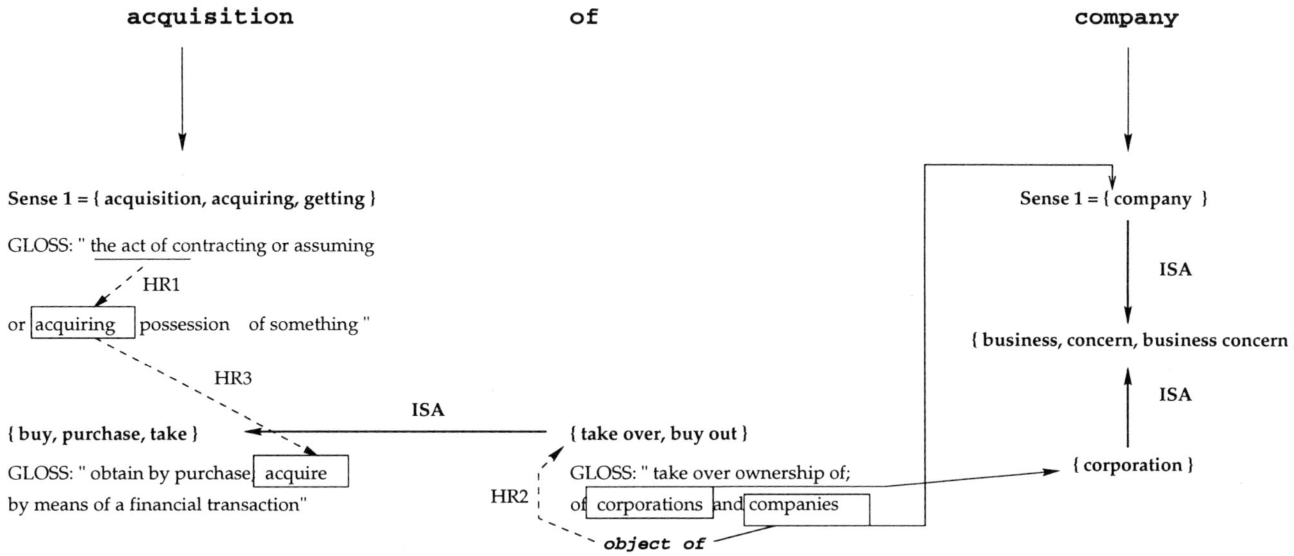

Figure 1: WordNet application of prepositional selection constraints

2. A class contains only one sequence. We disregard these classes from our study, since in this class it is not possible to disambiguate the words.

The collection $\mathcal{C}$ has 9511 < *noun of noun* > sequences, out of which 2158 have at least one of the nouns tagged as a proper noun. 602 of these sequences have both nouns tagged as proper nouns. Due to the fact that WordNet's coverage of proper nouns is rather sparse, only 34% of these sequences were disambiguated. Successful cases are < *House of Representatives* >, < *University of Pennsylvania* > or < *Museum of Art* >. Sequences that couldn't be disambiguated comprise < *Aerospaciale of France* > or < *Kennedy of Massachusetts* >. A small disambiguation rate of 28% covers the rest of the 1566 sequences relating a proper noun to a common noun. A successful disambiguation occurred for < *hundreds of Californians* > or < *corporation of Vancouver* >. Sequences like < *aftermath of Iran-Contra* > or < *acquisition of Merryl Linch* > weren't disambiguated. The results of the disambiguation of the rest of 7353 sequences comprising only common nouns are more encouraging. A total of 473 classes were devised, out of which 131 had only one element, yielding a disambiguation rate of 72.3%. The number of elements in a class varies from 2 to 68.

Now that we found disambiguated classes of prepositional structures, we provide some heuristics to better understand why the prepositional relations are valid. These heuristics are possible inferences performed on WordNet.

3 Selectional Heuristics on WordNet

In this section we focus on semantic connections between the words of prepositional structures. Consider for example `acquisition of company`. Figure 1 illustrates some of the relevant semantic connections that can be drawn from WordNet when analyzing this prepositional structure.

We note that noun `acquisition` is semantically connected to the verb `acquire`, which is related to the concept { `buy, purchase, take`}, a hypernym of { `take over, buy out`}. Typical objects for `buy out` are `corporations` and `companies`, both hypernyms of `concern`. Thus, at a more abstract level, we understand `acquisition of company` as an action performed on a typical object. Such relations hold for an entire class of prepositional structures.

What we want is to have a mechanism that extracts the essence of such semantic connections, and be able to provide the inference that the elements of this class are all sequences of < $noun_i$ *prep* $noun_j$ >, with $noun_j$ always an object of the action described by $noun_i$.

Our approach to establish semantic paths is based on inferential heuristics on WordNet. Using several heuristics one can find common properties of a prepositional class. The classification procedure disambiguates both nouns as follows: the word `acquisition` has four senses in WordNet , but it is found in its synset number 1. The word `company` appears in its synset number 1. The gloss of `acquisition` satisfies the prerequisite of HR1:

Heuristic Rule 1 (HR1) If the textual gloss of a noun concept begins with the expression `the act of` followed by the gerund of a verb, then the respective noun concept describes an action represented by the verb from the gloss.

This heuristic applies 831 times in WordNet, showing that nouns like `accomplishment`, `dispatch` or `subsidization` describe actions.

Nr.crt.	Features for < $N1$ > of < $N2$ >	Example
1	$N2$ is the object of the action described by $N1$	acquisition of company
2	$N2$ is the agent of the action described by $N1$	approval of authorities
3	$N1$ is the agent of the action with object $N2$	author of paper
4	$N1$ is the agent of the action with purpose the action described by $N2$	activists of support
5	$N1$ is the object of an action whose agent is $N2$	record of athlete
6	$N2$ describes the action with the theme $N1$	allegations of fraud
7	$N1$ is the location of the activity described by $N2$	place of business
8	$N1$ describes an action occurring at the time described by $N2$	acquisition of 1995
9	$N1$ is the consequence of a phenomenon described by $N2$	impact of earthquake
10	$N1$ is the output of an action described by $N2$	result of study

Table 1: Distribution of prepositions in the Wall Street Journal articles from PENN Treebank

Thus `acquisition` is a description of any of the verbal expressions `contract possession`, `assume possession` and `acquire possession`.

The role of `company` is recovered using another heuristic:

Heuristic Rule 2 (HR2) The gloss of a verb may contain multiple textual explanations for that concept, which are separated by semicolons. If one such explanation takes one of the forms:

- of $noun_1$
- of $noun_1$ and $noun_2$
- of $noun_1$ or $noun_2$

then $noun_1$ and $noun_2$ respectively are objects of that verb.

Heuristic HR2 applies 134 times in WordNet, providing objects for such verbs as `generalize`, `exfoliate` or `laicize`.

The noun `company` is recognized as an object of the synset {`take over, buy out`}, and so is `corporation`. Both of them are hyponyms of {`business, concern, business concern`}, which fills in the object role of {`business, concern, business concern`}. Because of that, both `company` and `corporation` from the gloss of {`take over, buy out`} are disambiguated and point to their first corresponding synsets. Due to the inheritance property, `company` is an object of any hypernyms of {`take over, buy out`}. One such hypernym, {`buy, purchase, take`} also meets the requirements of HR3:

Heuristic Rule 3 (HR3) If a verb concept has another verb at the beginning of its gloss, then that verb describes the same action, but in a more specific context.

Therefore, `acquire` is a definition of {`buy, purchase, take`}, that has `company` as an object and involves a financial transaction. These three heuristics operate throughout all the sequences of the class comprising < *acquisition of company* >, < *addition of business* >, < *formation of group* > or < *beginning of service* >

We conclude that for this class of prepositional relations, $noun_2$ is the object of the action described by $noun_1$.

4 A case study

Table 1 illustrates the semantic relations observed in WordNet for some of the classes of prepositional relations with preposition `of`, when both arguments are nouns. We applied a number of 28 heuristics on 45 disambiguated classes.

5 Conclusions

This paper proposes a method of extracting and validating semantic relations for prepositional attachment. The method is appealing because it uses WordNet (which is publicly available and applicable to broad English) and is scalable. A plausible explanation of prepositional attachment may be provided and the lexical disambiguation of the phrase heads is possible. The method may be improved by using additional attachment locations as provided by the transformations proposed in (Brill and Resnik, 1994).

References

Eric Brill and Philip Resnik. 1994. A Rule-Based Approach to Prepositional Phrase Attachment Disambiguation. In *Proceedings of COLING-94*.

George Miller and Daniel Teibel. 1991. A proposal for lexical disambiguation. In *Proceedings of the DARPA Speech and Natural Language Workshop*, pages 395–399, Washington, D.C.

Philip Resnik. 1995. Disambiguating Noun Grouping with Respect to WordNet Senses. In *Proceedings of the Third Workshop on Very Large Corpora*, pages 54–68, MIT, Cambridge,Massachusets, June.

Stefan Wermter. 1991. Integration of Semantic and Syntactic Constraints for Structural Noun Phrase Disambiguation. In *Proceedings of IJCAI-91*,pages 1486–1491.

Towards Testing the Syntax of Punctuation

Bernard Jones*
Centre for Cognitive Science
University of Edinburgh
2 Buccleuch Place
Edinburgh EH8 9LW
United Kingdom
bernie@cogsci.ed.ac.uk

Abstract

Little work has been done in NLP on the subject of punctuation, owing mainly to a lack of a good theory on which computational treatments could be based. This paper described early work in progress to try to construct such a theory. Two approaches to finding the syntactic function of punctuation marks are discussed, and procedures are described by which the results from these approaches can be tested and evaluated both against each other as well as against other work. Suggestions are made for the use of these results, and for future work.

1 Background

The field of punctuation has been almost completely ignored within Natural Language Processing, with perhaps the exception of the sentence-final full-stop (period). This is because there is no coherent theory of punctuation on which a computational treatment could be based. As a result, most contemporary systems simply strip out punctuation in input text, and do not put any marks into generated texts.

Intuitively, this seems very wrong, since punctuation is such an integral part of many written languages. If text in the real world (a newspaper, for example) were to appear without any punctuation marks, it would appear very stilted, ambiguous or infantile. Therefore it is likely that any computational system that ignores these extra textual cues will suffer a degradation in performance, or at the very least a great restriction in the class of linguistic data it is able to process.

Several studies have already shown the potential for using punctuation within NLP. Dale (1991) has shown the benefits of using punctuation in the fields of discourse structure and semantics, and Jones (1994) has shown in the field of syntax that using a grammar that includes punctuation yields around two orders of magnitude fewer parses than one which does not. Further work has been carried out in this area, particularly by Briscoe and Carroll (1995), to show more accurately the contribution that usage of punctuation can make to the syntactic analysis of text.

The main problem with these studies is that there is little available in terms of a theory of punctuation on which computational treatments could be based, and so they have somewhat ad hoc, idiosyncratic treatments. The only account of punctuation available is that of Nunberg (1990), which although it provides a useful basis for a theory is a little too vague to be used as the basis of any implementation.

Therefore it seems necessary to develop a new theory of punctuation, that is suitable for computational implementation. Some work has already been carried out, showing the variety of punctuation marks and their orthographic interaction (Jones, 1995), but this paper describes the continuation of this research to determine the true syntactic function of punctuation marks in text.

There are two possible angles to the problem of the syntactic function of punctuation: an observational one, and a theoretical one. Both approaches were adopted, in order to be be able to evaluate the results of each approach against those of the other, and in the hope that the results of both approaches could be combined. Thus the approaches are described one after the other here.

2 Corpus-based Approach

The best data source for observation of grammatical punctuation usage is a large, parsed corpus. It ensures a wide range of real language is covered, and because of its size it should minimise the effect of any

* This work was carried out under an award from the (UK) ESRC. Thanks are also due to Lex Holt, Henry Thompson, Ted Briscoe and anonymous reviewers.

errors or idiosyncrasies on the part of editors, parsers and transcribers. Since these corpora are almost all hand-produced, some errors and idiosyncrasies are inevitable — one important part of the analysis is therefore to identify possible instances of these, and if they are clear, to remove them from the results.

The corpus chosen was the Dow Jones section of the Penn Treebank (size: 1.95 million words). The bracketings were analysed so that each node with a punctuation mark as its immediate daughter is reported, with its other daughters abbreviated to their categories, as in (1) – (3).

(1) [NP [NP the following] :] ⟹ [NP = NP :]

(2) [S [PP In Edinburgh] , [S ...]] ⟹ [S = PP , S]

(3) [NP [NP Bob] , [NP ...) ,] ⟹ [NP = NP , NP ,]

In this fashion each sentence was broken down into a set of such category-patterns, resulting in a set of different category-patterns for each punctuation symbol, which were then processed to extract the underlying rule patterns which represent all the ways that punctuation behaves in this corpus, and are good indicators of how the punctuation marks might behave in the rest of language.

There were 12,700 unique category-patterns extracted from the corpus for the five most common marks of point punctuation, ranging from 9,320 for the comma to 425 for the dash. These were then reduced to just 137 underlying rule-patterns for the colon, semicolon, dash, comma, full-stop.

Even some of these underlying rule-patterns, however, were questionable since their incidence is very low (maybe once in the whole corpus) or their form is so linguistically strange so as to call into doubt their correctness (possibly idiosyncratic misparses), as in (4).

(4) [ADVP = PP , NP]

Therefore all the patterns were checked against the original corpus to recover the original sentences. The sentences for patterns with low incidence and those whose correctness was questionable were carefully examined to determine whether there was any justification for a particular rule-pattern, given the content of the sentence.

For example, the NP=NP:VP rule-pattern was removed since all the verb phrases occurring in this pattern were imperative ones, which can legitimately act as sentences (5). Therefore instances of this rule application were covered by the NP=NP:S rule-pattern. A detailed account of the removal of idiosyncratic, incorrect and exceptional rule-patterns, with justifications, is reported in (Jones, 1996).

(5) [...] the show's distributor, Viacom Inc, is giving an ultimatum: either sign new long-term commitments to buy future episodes or risk losing "Cosby" to a competitor.

After this further pruning procedure, the number of rule-patterns was reduced to just 79, more than half of which related to the comma. It was now possible to postulate some generalisations about the use of the various punctuation marks from this reduced set of rule-patterns.

These generalised punctuation rules, described in more detail in (Jones, 1996), are given below for colons (6), semicolons (7), full-stops (8), dashes (9,10), commas (11), basic quotation(12) and stress-markers (13–15).

(6) $\mathcal{X} = \mathcal{X}$: { NP | S | ADJP } $\mathcal{X}$:{NP, S}

(7) $\mathcal{S} = \mathcal{S}$; $\mathcal{S}$ $\mathcal{S}$:{NP, S, VP, PP}

(8) **T** = * .

(9) $\mathcal{D} = \mathcal{D}$ – $\mathcal{D}$ – $\mathcal{D}$:{NP, S, VP, PP, ADJP}

(10) $\mathcal{E} = \mathcal{E}$ – { NP | S | VP | PP } – $\mathcal{E}$:{NP, S }

(11) $\mathcal{C} = \mathcal{C}$, * $\mathcal{C}$:{NP, S, VP, PP, ADJP, ADVP}
$\mathcal{C}$ = * , $\mathcal{C}$

(12) $\mathcal{Q}$ = " $\mathcal{Q}$ " $\mathcal{Q}$: *

(13) $\mathcal{Z} = \mathcal{Z}$? $\mathcal{Z}$: *

(14) $\mathcal{Y} = \mathcal{Y}$! $\mathcal{Y}$: *

(15) $\mathcal{W} = \mathcal{W}$ ... $\mathcal{W}$: *

3 A Theoretical Approach

The theoretical starting point is that punctuation seems to occur at a phrasal level, i.e. it comes immediately before or after a phrasal level lexical item (e.g. a noun phrase). However, this is a rather general definition, so we need to examine the problem more exactly.

Punctuation could occur adjacent to any complex structure. However, we want to prevent occurrences such as (16). Conversely, punctuation could only occur adjacent to maximal level phrases (e.g. NP, VP). However, this rules out correct cases like (17).

(16) The, new toy ...

(17) He does, surprisingly, like fish.

Clearly we need something stricter than the first approach, but more relaxed than the second. The notion of headedness seems to be involved, so we can postulate that only non-head structures can have punctuation attached. This system still does not rule out examples like (18) however, so further refinement is necessary. The answer seems to be to look at the level of head daughter and mother categories under X-bar theory (Jackendoff, 1977). Attachment of punctuation to the non-head daughter only seems to be legal when mother and head-daughter are of the same bar level (and indeed more often than not they are identical categories), regardless of what that bar level is.

(18) the, big, man

From this theoretical approach it appears that punctuation could be described as being adjunctive (i.e. those phrases to which punctuation is attached serve an adjunctive function). Furthermore, conjunctive uses of punctuation (19,20), conventionally regarded as being distinct from other more grammatical uses (the adjunctive ones), can also be made to function via the theoretical principles formed here.

(19) dogs, cats, fish and mice

(20) most, or many, examples ...

4 Testing — Work in Progress

The next stage of this research is to test the results of both these approaches to see if they work, and also to compare their results. Since the results of the two studies do not seem incompatible, it should prove possible to combine them, and it will be interesting to see if the results from using the combined approaches differ at all from the results of using the approaches individually. It will also be useful to compare the results with those of studies that have a less formal basis for their treatments of punctuation, e.g. (Briscoe and Carroll, 1995).

For this reason the best way to test the results of these approaches to punctuation's role in syntax is to incorporate them into otherwise identical grammars and study the coverage of the grammars in parsing and the quality and accuracy of the parses. For ease of comparison with other studies, the best parsing framework to use will be the Alvey Tools' Grammar Development Environment (GDE) (Carroll et al., 1991), which allows for rapid prototyping and easy analysis of parses. The corpus of sentences to run the grammars over should ideally be large, and consist mainly of real text from external sources. To avoid dealing with idiosyncratic tagging of words, and over-complicated sentences, we shall follow Briscoe and Carroll (1995) rather than Jones (1994) and use 35,000 prepared sentences from the Susanne corpus rather than using the Spoken English Corpus.

5 Further Work

The theoretical approach not only seems to confirm the reality of the generalised punctuation rules derived observationally, since they all seem to have an adjunctive nature, but it also gives us a framework with which those generalised rules could be included in proper, linguistically-based, grammars. Results of testing will show whether either of the approaches are better on their own, and how they perform when they are combnined, and will, hopefully, show an improvement in performance over the ad-hoc methods used previously. The development of a theory of punctuation can then progress with investigations into the semantic function of punctuation marks, to ultimately form a theory that will be of great use to the NLP community.

References

Edward Briscoe and John Carroll. 1995. Developing and Evaluating a Probabilistic LR Parser of Part-of-Speech and Punctuation Labels. In *Proceedings of the ACL/SIGPARSE 4th International Workshop on Parsing Technologies*, pages 48–58, Prague

John Carroll, Edward Briscoe and Claire Grover. 1991. A Development Environment for Large Natural Language Grammars. Technical Report 233, Cambridge University Computer Laboratory.

Robert Dale. 1991. Exploring the Role of Punctuation in the Signalling of Discourse Structure. In *Proceedings of the Workshop on Text Representation and Domain Modelling*, pages 110–120, Technical University Berlin.

Ray Jackendoff. 1977. X-bar Syntax: A Study of Phrase Structure. MIT Press, Cambridge, MA.

Bernard Jones. 1994. Exploring the Role of Punctuation in Parsing Real Text. In *Proceedings of the 15th International Conference on Computational Linguistics (COLING-94)*, pages 421–425, Kyoto, Japan, August.

Bernard Jones. 1995. Exploring the Variety and Use of Punctuation. In *Proceedings of the 17th Annual Cognitive Science Conference*, pages 619–624, Pittsburgh, Pennsylvania, July.

Bernard Jones. 1996. Towards a Syntactic Account of Punctuation. To appear in *Proceedings of the 16th International Conference on Computational Linguistics (COLING-96)*, Copenhagen, Denmark, August.

Geoffrey Nunberg. 1990. The Linguistics of Punctuation. CSLI Lecture Notes **18**, Stanford, California.

Using Terminological Knowledge Representation Languages to Manage Linguistic Resources

Pamela W. Jordan
Intelligent Systems Program
University of Pittsburgh
Pittsburgh PA 15260
jordan@isp.pitt.edu

Abstract

I examine how terminological languages can be used to manage linguistic data during NL research and development. In particular, I consider the lexical semantics task of characterizing semantic verb classes and show how the language can be extended to flag inconsistencies in verb class definitions, identify the need for new verb classes, and identify appropriate linguistic hypotheses for a new verb's behavior.

1 Introduction

Problems with consistency and completeness can arise when writing a wide-coverage grammar or analyzing lexical data since both tasks involve working with large amounts of data. Since terminological knowledge representation languages have been valuable for managing data in other applications such as a software information system that manages a large knowledge base of plans (Devanbu and Litman, 1991), it is worthwhile considering how these languages can be used in linguistic data management tasks. In addition to inheritance, terminological systems provide a criterial semantics for links and automatic classification which inserts a new concept into a taxonomy so that it directly links to concepts more general than it and more specific than it (Woods and Schmolze, 1992).

Terminological languages have been used in NLP applications for lexical representation (Burkert, 1995), and grammar representation (Brachman and Schmolze, 1991), and to assist in the acquisition and maintenance of domain specific lexical semantics knowledge (Ayuso et al., 1987). Here I explore additional linguistic data management tasks. In particular I examine how a terminological language such as Classic (Brachman et al., 1991) can assist a lexical semanticist with the management of verb classes. In conclusion, I discuss ways in which terminological languages can be used during grammar writing.

Consider the tasks that confront a lexical semanticist. The regular participation of verbs belonging to a particular semantic class in a limited number of syntactic alternations is crucial in lexical semantics. A popular research direction assumes that the syntactic behavior of a verb is systematically influenced by its meaning (Levin, 1993; Hale and Keyser, 1987) and that any set of verbs whose members pattern together with respect to syntactic alternations should form a semantically coherent class (Levin, 1993). Once such a class is identified, the meaning component that the member verbs share can be identified. This gives further insight into lexical representation for the words in the class (Levin, 1993).

Terminological languages can support three important functions in this domain. First, the process of representing the system in a taxonomic logic can serve as a check on the rigor and precision of the original account. Once the account is represented, the terminological system can flag inconsistencies. Second, the classifier can identify an existing verb class that might explain an unassigned verb's behavior. That is, given a set of syntactically analyzed sentences that exemplify the syntactic alternations allowed and disallowed for that verb, the classifier will provide appropriate linguistic hypotheses. Third, the classifier can identify the need for new verb classes by flagging verbs that are not members of any existing, defined verb classes. Together, these functions provide tools for the lexical semanticist that are potentially very useful.

The second and third of these three functions can be provided in two steps: (1) classifying each alternation for a particular verb according to the type of semantic mapping allowed for the verb and its arguments; and (2) either identifying the verb class that has the given pattern of classified alternations or using the pattern to form the definition of a new verb class.

2 Sentence Classification

The usual practice in investigating the alternation patterning of a verb is to construct example sentences in which simple, illustrative noun phrases are used as arguments of a verb. The sentences in (1) exemplify two familiar alternations of *give*.

(1) a. John gave Mary a book

b. John gave a book to Mary.

Such sentences exemplify an alternation that belongs to the alternation pattern of their verb.[1] I will call this the *alternation type* of the test sentence.

To determine the alternation type of a test sentence, the sentence must be syntactically analyzed so that its grammatical functions (e.g. subject, object) are marked. Then, given semantic feature information about the words filling those grammatical functions (GFs), and information about the possible argument structures for the verb in the sentence and the semantic feature restrictions on these arguments, it is possible to find the argument structures appropriate to the input sentence. Consider the sentences and descriptions shown below for *pour*:

(2) a. [Mary_{subj}] poured [Tina_{obj}] [a glass of milk_{io}].

b. [Mary_{subj}] poured [a glass of milk_{obj}] for [Tina_{ppo}].

$pour_1$: subj → $\text{agent}_{[volitional]}$
obj → $\text{recipient}_{[volitional]}$
io → $\text{patient}_{[liquid]}$
$pour_2$: subj → $\text{agent}_{[volitional]}$
obj → $\text{patient}_{[liquid]}$
ppo → $\text{recipient}_{[volitional]}$

Given the semantic type restrictions and the GFs, $pour_1$ describes (2a) and $pour_2$, (2b). The mapping from the GFs to the appropriate argument structure is similar to lexical rules in the LFG syntactic theory except that here I semantically type the arguments. To indicate the alternation types for these sentences, I call sentence (2a) a benefactive-ditransitive and sentence (2b) a benefactive-transitive.

Classifying a sentence by its alternation type requires linguistic and world knowledge. World knowledge is used in the definitions of nouns and verbs in the lexicon and describes high-level entities, such as events, and animate and inanimate objects. Properties (such as LIQUID) are used to define specialized entities. For example, the property NON-CONSUMABLE (SMALL CAPITALS indicate Classic concepts in my implementation) specializes a LIQUID-ENTITY to define PAINT and distinguish it from WATER, which has the property that it is CONSUMABLE. Specialized EVENT entities are used in the definition of verbs in the lexicon and represent the argument structures for the verbs.

The linguistic knowledge needed to support sentence classification includes the definitions of (1) verb types such as intransitive, transitive and ditransitive; (2) verb definitions; and (3) concepts that define the links between the GFs and verb argument structures as represented by events.

[1] In the examples that I will consider, and in most examples used by linguists to test alternation patterns, there will only be one verb; this is the verb to be tested.

Verb types (SUBCATEGORIZATIONs) are defined according to the GFs found in the sentence. For example, (2a) classifies as DITRANSITIVE and (2b) as a specialized TRANSITIVE with a PP. Once the verb type is identified, verb definitions (VERBs) are needed to provide the argument structures. A VERB can have multiple senses which are instances of EVENTs, for example the verb "pour" can have the senses *pour* or *prepare*, with the required arguments shown below.[2] Note that $pour_1$ and $pour_2$ in (2) are subcategorizations of *prepare*.

pour: $\text{pourer}_{[volitional]}$
$\text{pouree}_{[inanimate-container]}$
$\text{poured}_{[inanimate-substance]}$
prepare: $\text{preparer}_{[volitional]}$
$\text{preparee}_{[liquid]}$
$\text{prepared}_{[volitional]}$

For a sentence to classify as a particular ALTERNATION, a legal linking must exist between an EVENT and the SUBCATEGORIZATION. Linking involves restricting the fillers of the GFs in the SUBCATEGORIZATION to be the same as the arguments in an EVENT. In Classic, the **same-as** restriction is limited so that either both attributes must be filled already with the same instance or the concept must already be known as a LEGAL-LINKING. Because of this I created a test (written in LISP) to identify a LEGAL-LINKING. The test inputs are the sentence predicate and GF fillers arranged in the order of the event arguments against which they are to be tested. A linking is legal when at least one of the events associated with the verb can be linked in the indicated way, and all the required arguments are filled.

Once a sentence passes the linking test, and classifies as a particular ALTERNATION, a rule associated with the ALTERNATION classifies it as a specialization of the concept. This causes the EVENT arguments to be filled with the appropriate GF fillers from the SUBCATEGORIZATION. A side-effect of the alternation classification is that the EVENT classifies as a specialized EVENT and indicates which sense of the verb is used in the sentence.

3 Semantic Class Classification

The semantic class of the verb can be identified once the example sentences are classified by their alternation type. Specialized VERB-CLASSes are defined by their good and bad alternations. Note that VERB defines one verb whereas VERB-CLASS describes a set of verbs (e.g. spray/load class). Which ALTERNATIONs are associated with a VERB-CLASS is a matter of linguistic evidence; the linguist discovers these associations by testing examples for grammaticality. To assist in this task, I provide two tests, **have-instances-of** and **have-no-instances-of**.

[2] For generality in the implementation, I use $\text{arg}_1 \ldots \text{arg}_n$ for all event definitions instead of agent ... patient or preparer ... preparee.

The **have-instances-of** test for an ALTERNATION searches a corpus of good sentences or bad sentences and tests whether at least one instance of the specified ALTERNATION, for example a benefactive-ditransitive, is present.

A bad sentence with all the required verb arguments will classify as an ALTERNATION despite the ungrammatical syntactic realization, while a bad sentence with missing required arguments will only classify as a SUBCATEGORIZATION. The **have-no-instances-of** test for a SUBCATEGORIZATION searches a corpus of bad sentences and tests whether at least one instance of the specified SUBCATEGORIZATION, for example TRANSITIVE, is present as the most specific classification.

4 Discussion

The ultimate test of this approach is in how well it will scale up. The linguist may choose to add knowledge as it is needed or may prefer to do this work in batches. To support the batch approach, it may be useful to extract detailed subcategorization information from English learner's dictionaries. Also it will be necessary to decide what semantic features are needed to restrict the fillers of the argument structures. Finally, there is the problem of collecting complete sets of example sentences for a verb. In general, a corpus of tagged sentences is inadequate since it rarely includes negative examples and is not guaranteed to exhibit the full range of alternations. In applications where a domain specific corpus is available (e.g. the Kant MT project (Mitamura et al., 1993)), the full range of relevant alternations is more likely. However, the lack of negative examples still poses a problem and would require the project linguist to create appropriate negative examples or manually adjust the class definitions for further differentiation.

While I have focused on a lexical research tool, an area I will explore in future work is how classification could be used in grammar writing. One task for which a terminological language is appropriate is flagging inconsistent rules. When writing and maintaining a large grammar, inconsistent rules is one type of grammar writing bug that occurs. For example, the following three rules are inconsistent since feature$_1$ of NP and feature$_1$ of VP would not unify in rule 1 given the values assigned in 2 and 3.

1) S → NP VP
<NP feature$_1$ > = <VP feature$_1$ >
2) NP → det N
<N feature$_1$ > = +
<NP> = <N>
3) VP → V
<V feature$_1$ > = −
<VP> = <V>

5 Conclusion

I have shown how a terminological language, such as Classic, can be used to manage lexical semantics data during analysis with two minor extensions. First, a test to identify LEGAL-LINKINGS is necessary since this cannot be directly expressed in the language and second, set membership tests, **have-instances-of** and **have-no-instances-of** are necessary since this type of expressiveness is not provided in Classic. While the solution of several knowledge acquisition issues would result in a friendlier tool for a linguistics researcher, the tool still performs a useful function.

References

Damaris M. Ayuso, Varda Shaked, and Ralph Weischedel. 1987. An environment for acquiring semantic information. In *Proceedings of 25th ACL*, pages 32–40.

Ronald J. Brachman and James Schmolze. 1991. An overview of the KL-ONE knowledge representation system. *Cognitive Science*, 9:171–216.

Ronald J. Brachman, Deborah L. McGuinness, Peter F. Patel-Schneider, and Lori A. Resnik. 1991. Living with CLASSIC: When and how to use a KL-ONE-like language. In John F. Sowa, editor, *Principles of Semantic Networks*, pages 401–456. Morgan Kaufmann, San Mateo, CA.

Gerrit Burkert. 1995. Lexical semantics and terminological knowledge representation. In Patrick Saint-Dizier and Evelyne Viegas, editors, *Computational Lexical Semantics*. Cambridge University Press.

Premkumar Devanbu and Diane J. Litman. 1991. Plan-based terminological reasoning. In James F. Allen, Richard Fikes, and Erik Sandewall, editors, *KR'91: Principles of Knowledge Representation and Reasoning*, pages 128–138. Morgan Kaufmann, San Mateo, CA.

K. L. Hale and S. J. Keyser. 1987. A view from the middle. Center for Cognitive Science, MIT. Lexicon Project Working Papers 10.

B. Levin. 1993. *English verb classes and alternations: a preliminary investigation.* University of Chicago Press.

T. Mitamura, E. Nyberg, and J. Carbonell. 1993. Automated corpus analysis and the acquisition of large, multi-lingual knowledge bases for MT. In *Proceedings of TMI-93.*

William A. Woods and James G. Schmolze. 1992. The KL-ONE family. In Fritz Lehmann, editor, *Semantic Networks in Artificial Intelligence*, pages 133–177. Pergamon Press, Oxford.

Transitivity and Foregrounding in News Articles: experiments in information retrieval and automatic summarising

Roderick Kay and Ruth Aylett
Information Technology Institute
University of Salford
Manchester M5 4WT
United Kingdom
{rnk,R.Aylett}@iti.salford.ac.uk

Abstract

This paper describes an on-going study which applies the concept of transitivity to news discourse for text processing tasks. The complex notion of transitivity is defined and the relationship between transitivity and information foregrounding is explained. A sample corpus of news articles has been coded for transitivity. The corpus is being used in two text processing experiments.

1 Introduction

The basic hypothesis of this study is that the degree of transitivity associated with a clause indicates the level of importance of a clause in a narrative text. For this assumption to form the basis of a practical implementation, transitivity must be objectively defined and the definition must be able to be processed automatically.

The notion of transitivity clearly has many implications for text processing, in particular information retrieval and automatic summarising, because it can be used to grade information in a document according to importance. In an information retrieval context, it means that a transitivity index could influence a decision about the relevance of a document to a query. In automatic summarising, it means that less important information could be *sieved* according to transitivity, leaving only the most important information to form the basis of a summary.

News discourse was chosen because it is narrative based and therefore broadly applicable to the notion of transitivity. There has also been extensive research in the structural characteristics of this text type (Duszak, 1995) (Kay and Aylett, 1994) (Bell, 1991). However, the study poses a challenge in the sense that the notion of transitivity has previously been exemplified with relatively simple sentences presenting action sequences. A central question is how well the concept can be transferred to a domain which, although narrative based, diverges into commentary and analysis.

2 Definition of Transitivity

Transitivity is usually considered to be a property of an entire clause (Hopper and Thompson, 1980). It is, broadly, the notion that an activity is transferred from an agent to a patient. It is therefore inherently linked with a clause containing two participants in which an action is highly effective.

The concept of transitivity has been defined in terms of the following parameters:

A. Participants	h	2 or more participants
	l	1 participant
B. Kinesis	h	action
	l	non-action
C. Aspect	h	telic
	l	atelic
D. Punctuality	h	punctual
	l	non-punctual
E. Volitionality	h	volitional
	l	non-volitional
F. Affirmation	h	affirmative
	l	negative
G. Mode	h	realis
	l	irrealis
H. Agency	h	A high in potency
	l	A low in potency
I. Affectedness of O	h	O totally affected
	l	O not affected
J. Individuation of O	h	O highly individuated
	l	O non-individuated

h=high, l=low

Each component of transitivity contributes to the overall effectiveness or 'intensity' with which an action is transferred from one participant to another.

A. There must be at least two participants for an action to be transferred.
B. Transferable actions can be contrasted with non-transferable states, e.g. he pushed her; he thought about her.
C. An action is either wholly or partially completed according to whether it is telic or atelic, e.g. I played the piano; I am playing the piano.
D. Punctual actions have no transitional phase between start and end point, having a greater effect

on their patients, e.g. he kicked the door; he opened the door.
E. An action is more effective if it is volitional, e.g. he bought the present; he forgot the present.
F. An affirmative action has greater transitivity than a negative action, e.g. he called the boy; he didn't call the boy.
G. An action which is realis (occurring in the real world) is more effective than an action which is irrealis (occurring in a non-real contingency world), e.g. they attacked the enemy; they might attack the enemy.
H. Participants high in agency transfer an action more effectively than participants low in agency, e.g. he shocked me; the price shocked me.
I. A patient is wholly or partially affected, e.g. I washed the dishes; I washed some of the dishes.
J. Individuation refers to the distinctiveness of the object from the agent and of the object from its own background. The following properties contribute to the individuation of an object.

INDIVIDUATED	NON-INDIVIDUATED
proper	common
human, animate	inanimate
concrete	abstract
singular	plural
count	mass
referential, definite	non-referential

Based on these components, clauses can be classified as more or less transitive. In English, as a whole, transitivity is indicated by a cluster of features associated with a clause.

The concept of foreground and background information is based on the idea that in narrative discourse some parts are more essential than others. Certain sections of a narrative are crucially linked with the temporal sequence of events which form the backbone of a text. This material is normally foregrounded. In contrast, the contextual information relating to characters and environment is backgrounded.

3 Transitivity and Text Processing

The relationship between transitivity and foregrounding has potential for text processing, in particular, information retrieval and automatic summarising. If it is possible to identify which clauses are central to a text, the information can be used to contribute to a relevance assessment or as the basis for a derived summary.

3.1 Information Retrieval

The standard model of text retrieval is based on the identification of matching query/document terms which are weighted according to their distribution throughout a text database. This model has also been enhanced by a number of linguistic techniques: expansion of query/document terms according to thesaurus relations, synonyms, etc.

The proposal for this study is to code matching query/document terms for the transitivity value of the clause in which they occur, as a starting point for producing comparative term weights based on linguistic features. Terms which are less central to a discourse will, on this basis, be given lower scores because they occur in low transitivity clauses. The net result will be to produce a document ranking order which more closely represents the importance of the documents to a user. There is also potential for producing a transitivity index for an entire document as well as for individual clauses so that this measure could also feature in a relevance assessment.

3.2 Automatic Summarising

The fundamental task in automatic summarising is to identify the most important sections of a text so that these can be extracted and possibly modified to provide a summary. The notion of transitivity provides a measure against which clauses can be scored. The highest scoring clauses, either above a threshold value or on a comparative basis, can then be identified as the basic clauses of a summary. These can either be extracted *raw* or in context with pronominal references resolved and any logical antecedents included. A previous study in this area (Decker, 1985) extracted clauses and sentences on the basis of syntactic patterns which broadly correlate with certain features of transitivity. The present study focuses on the semantic features of transitivity rather than associated syntax.

4 Experimental Procedure

The feasibility of using transitivity as a tool in text processing will be assessed by two experiments using the same corpus. Clauses in the corpus must be hand-coded for transitivity. The difficulties encountered in this process will determine the basis for future automation. For the information retrieval task, only the clauses containing query/document matching terms will be coded for transitivity. For the automatic summarising experiment all sentences within a text will be coded.

For the information retrieval experiment, ten queries are put to a newspaper database: a demonstration system running on WAIS (Wide Area Information Server), carrying two weeks of articles from the Times newspaper from 1993 and 1994. The results of the queries are downloaded in their initial ranked order (ranked by a host ranking algorithm) and re-ranked by a serial batch processor written in C++. The processor identifies the transitivity features associated with each matching clause and produces a ranked output of documents based on the weights assigned to each clause in which the search terms occur. The weights assigned to each clause are numerically equivalent to the number of transitivity features associated with each clause. The total transitivity weight for an entire document is the sum of clause weights normalised by document length.

The output dataset consists of a total of 185 news articles, an average of 18.5 per batch. Each set of articles is ranked by volunteers. The articles are ranked for their degree of relevance to a query in two ways: on a scale of one to ten; and comparatively, by the degree of relevance of an article against all other articles. All terms are treated as equal so that discrimination between documents is based purely on accumulative transitivity scores. The performance of the ranking technique is evaluated according to two precision measures: the Spearman rank correlation coefficient (rho) and the CRE (Coefficient of Ranking Effectiveness) (Noreault et al. , 1977).

For the automatic summarising experiment, ten articles are taken from the corpus at random. Summaries are produced by extracting clauses according to transitivity scores. In the initial implementation, transitivity scores will be equal to the number of transitivity features associated with the main clause of each sentence. The selection of sentences for a summary will be based, initially, on comparative transitivity scores and a reduction factor which will determine the number of sentences selected based on the length of a document.

Summaries will be analysed and assessed by volunteers for coverage, in terms of the original text, and comprehensibility as a separate text. The summaries will be compared against summaries of the same texts compiled by the syntactic technique mentioned previously and also against summaries consisting of the first paragraph of each news article.

The study is currently at the end of the coding stage for the information retrieval experiment.

References

A. Bell. 1991. The language of news media. *Basil Blackwell, Oxford*

N. Decker. 1985. The use of syntactic clues in discourse processing. *Proceedings of the 23rd meeting of the ACL*, pages 315–323.

A. Duszak. 1995. On variation in news-text prototypes: some evidence from English, Polish, and German. *Discourse Processes*, 19: 465–483.

G. Green. 1979. Organization, goals and comprehensibility in narratives: news writing, a case study. *Technical Report 132*, The Centre for the study of Reading, University of Illinois at Urbana-Champaign.

R. Kay, R. Aylett. 1994. A text grammar for news reports. *Working papers in Language and Linguistics, No 2*, European Studies Research Institute, University of Salford.

P. Hopper, S. Thompson. 1980. Transitivity in grammar in discourse. *Language*, 56: 251–299.

T. Noreault, M. Koll, M. McGill. 1977. Automatic ranked output from Boolean searches in SIRE. *Journal of the American Society for Information Science*, 27(6): 333-339.

The Selection of the Most Probable Dependency Structure in Japanese Using Mutual Information

Eduardo de Paiva Alves
University of Electro-Communications
1-5-1 Chofugaoka Chofushi Tokyo Japan
ealves@phaeton.cs.uec.ac.jp

Abstract

We use a statistical method to select the most probable structure or parse for a given sentence. It takes as input the dependency structures generated for the sentence by a dependency grammar, finds all triple of modifier, particle and modificant relations, calculates mutual information of each relation and chooses the structure for which the product of the mutual information of its relations is the highest.

1 Introduction

Computer Aided Instruction (CAI) systems are important and effective tools, especially for teaching foreign languages. Many students of Japanese as a foreign language are aware of the Computer Assisted TEchnical Reading System (CATERS) that provides helpful information for reading texts in science and technology fields (Kano and Yamamoto, 1995).

One of the difficulties in learning Japanese lies in recognizing dependency relations in Japanese sentences. This is because the language allows relatively free word orders. Take an example from a leading newspaper:

全国的な実態調査にもとづいた原因の速やかな究明を期待したい
We would like to expect a prompt study of the causes, based on a national investigation

To understand this sentence it is necessary to know that 実態調査に (investigation) modifies もとづいた (based) but not 期待したい (expect); もとづいた (based) modifies 究明 (study) but not 原因 (cause). CATERS is useful because it provides such information through several user-friendly functions.

As effective as it is for foreign students, however, the texts in CATERS are fixed and the dependency structure of every sentence in them is all hand-coded. This inability to handle new text poses a serious problem in its general applicability and extensibility.

This paper describes a method for selecting the right or most probable structure for a Japanese sentence among multiple probable structures generated by Restricted Dependency Grammar (RDG) (Fukumoto, 1992). If this method works, then its results will be quite valuable for facilitating the development of new texts for CAI systems like CATERS.

2 Background

As pointed out earlier, the dependency relation of elements in Japanese sentences are fairly complicated due to relatively free word orders. RDG is designed to determine dependency relations among words and phrases in sentences. To do so, it classifies the phrases according to grammatical categories and syntactic attributes. However, it fails to reject semantically unacceptable dependency structures. The inevitable consequence is that RDG often produces multiple parses even for a simple sentence.

Kurohashi and Nagao (1993) try to determine the dependency relations of a sentence by means of using sample sentences. When the sentence is structurally ambiguous, they determine its structure by comparing it to structurally similar patterns taken from a manually generated set of examples and calculating similarity values.

Our method, on the contrary, uses a statistical approach to select the most probable structure or parse of a given sentence. It takes as input dependency structures generated by RDG for a sentence, finds all of modifier-particle-modificant relations, calculates their mutual information and chooses the structure for which the product of the mutual information of its relations is the highest.

In order to calculate the mutual information for any modifier-particle-modificant pattern, we use the Conceptual Dictionary[1] (CD) to build a taxonomic hierarchy of the modifiers which occur

[1] The Co-occurrence Dictionary and Conceptual Dictionary used in the process are part of a set of machine readable Japanese dictionaries compiled by the Japan Electronic Dictionary Research Institute (EDR, 1993). The Conceptual Dictionary is a set of graphs consisting of 400,000 concepts and a number of taxonomic as well as functional relations between them. The Co-occurrence Dictionary consist of a list of 1,100,000 dependency relations (modifier, particle and modificant) taken from a corpus. Each entry includes syntactic information, concept identifiers (a numerical code) and the number of occurrences in the corpus.

with the particle-modificant sub-pattern in the Co-occurrence Dictionary (COD). The mutual information for any pattern is the maximum mutual information between the sub-pattern and the concepts in the taxonomic hierarchy which generalize the modifier in the pattern.

Resnik and Hearst (1993) use a similar approach to calculate preferences for prepositional phrase attachment. While they use data on word groups, our method directly uses word co-occurrence data to estimate the preferences using the CD to identify the most adequate grouping for each relation.

While Kurohashi and Nagao compare the sentence with a single sample of patterns, we use all occurrences of the pattern in COD to calculate the mutual information. Our approach automatically extracts the occurrences from the dictionary as well as builds the taxonomic hierarchy. Unlike Kurohashi and Nagao (1993), which uses only verb and adjective patterns, we cover all dependency relations.

3 Selecting the Most Probable Structure

RDG identifies all possible dependency structures which consist of modifier-modificant relations between elements in a sentence. The arcs in the following example show modifier-modificant relations which can be combined into six different dependency structures.

Our objective is to develop a method to automatically select the correct dependency structures accurately or at least those which have the highest probability of being correct. We evaluate the various possible structures according to the mutual information between modifiers and particle-modificants. In some cases there is no particle and the modificant directly precedes the modifier (see example in section 3.2). To calculate the mutual information for each relation, we obtain form the COD the conceptual identifiers (a numerical code) for the modifiers that appear with the particle-modificant and the number of their occurrences in the corpus. If the pattern is not present, backing off, we search this information for the modificant only. For each of those concept identifiers we obtain from the CD all generalizers (concept identifiers that express a similar meaning in a more general way) and build a taxonomic hierarchy with them. Using the number of occurrences obtained, we calculate the mutual information for the concepts in the taxonomic hierarchy. We also build a taxonomic hierarchy for the modifier that appears with the particle-modificant in the sentence. Then comparing these two taxonomic hierarchies (one for the modifiers in the COD, one for the modifiers in the sentence), we look for the concept identifier common to both hierarchies that has the highest mutual information. This is the mutual information for the relation itself. For each dependency structure we calculate a score by multiplying the mutual information for all ambiguous relations (the non-ambiguous do not contribute to the evaluation). The dependency structure with highest probability of being correct is the one with the highest score. Since all structures have the same number of relations, this multiplication reflects the likelyhood of the structure.

3.1 The Algorithm

The process described above is written in an algorithmic form as follows:

1. Select the ambiguous relations (those with more than one modificant) for each structure.
2. Search COD for the particle-modificant sub-pattern, in the corresponding positions. If there is no entry, search for the modificant only.
3. Obtain from the COD the concept identifiers for the modificant (there may be multiple meanings) and the concept identifiers with the number of their occurrences in the corpus for the modifiers which occur with the particle-modificant pattern.
4. For each modificant concept identifier, build a taxonomic hierarchy with its modifiers using CD to find the generalizer for each concept identifier.
5. Calculate the mutual information [2]

   for all the concept identifiers in the taxonomic hierarchies.
6. For the modifiers in the sentence, extract their concept identifiers from COD and build the taxonomic hierarchies using CD to find the generalizers for each concept identifier.
7. For each relation (modifier-particle-modificant pattern), search the concept identifier that generalizes the modifier word and has maximum mutual information. This value is the mutual information for the relation.
8. For each dependency structure, multiply the mutual information of its ambiguous dependency relations to obtain the score for that structure.
9. Arrange the structures according to their scores.

---

[2]The mutual information tells how much information one outcome gives about the other and is given by the formula:

$$I(w_1, w_2) = ln\left(\frac{P(w_1, w_2)}{P(w_1)P(w_2)}\right) \tag{1}$$

3.2 Examples

The following figure shows the output from RDG for a given sentence. The arrows in the figure indicate the dependency relations.

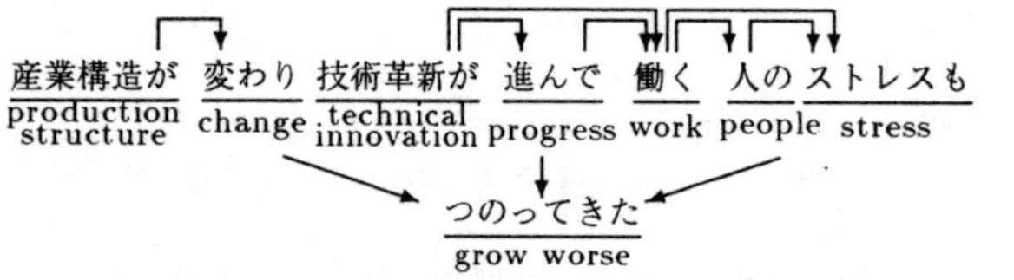

The ambiguous relations are 技術革新 が進んで, 技術革新 が働く, 働く 人, 働く ストレス, 進んで 働く and 進んでつのって. Accordingly the occurrences for the modificants in these relations (が進む, が働く, 働く, 進む, and つのる) are extracted from COD, obtaining a list of modifier concept identifiers with the number of their occurrences. Note that in the pattern 働く 人 and 働く ストレス the modificant precedes the modifier. The following figure shows some modifiers for 働く (work) with their number of occurrences.

人	女性	母親	意欲	自分	者	工場	主婦	事情	作業員
person	woman	mother	drive	each	person	factory	wife	fact	worker
32	18	6	6	3	3	3	2	2	2

Next, the taxonomic hierarchy for each particle-modificant is built and the mutual information calculated for each concept identifier. An extract of the hierarchy for 働く is shown in the following figure.

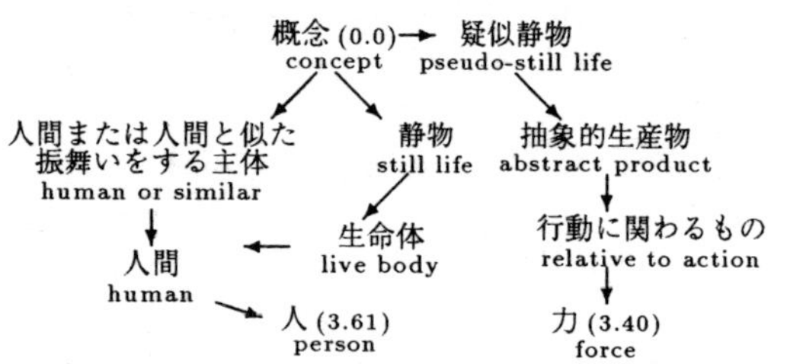

Next the generalizers for (革新, 人, and ストレス) are searched in the hierarchies for their modificants to obtain the mutual information for the relations. For 働く人 (working person) it happened to be the concept 人 (person) itself with mutual information of 3.61. For 働くストレス (working stress) the match occurred for 力 (force) giving a mutual information of 0.69.

Multiply the mutual information for all the dependency relations in each structure. For the example sentence the mutual information for the ambiguous relations are as follows:

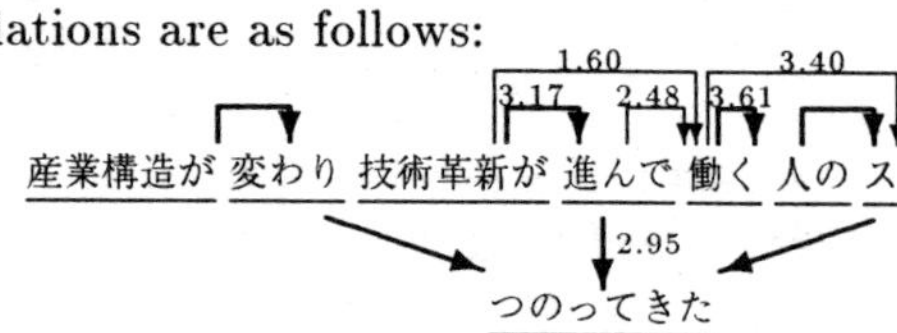

From this the algorithm selects the parse with highest score which is drawn in thick lines. The next figure shows the result for the first example sentence.

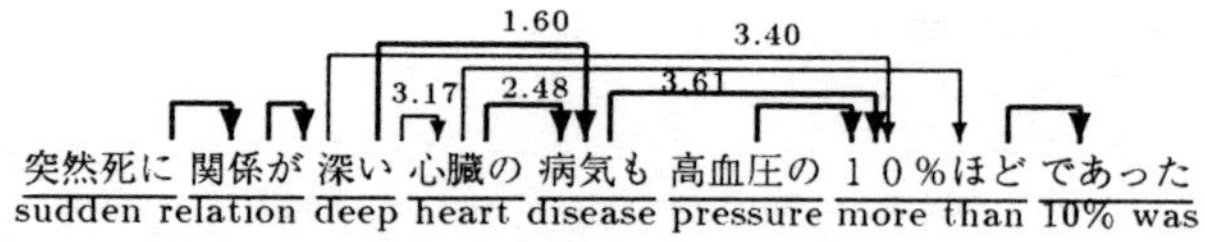

4 Results and Evaluation

We have applied our method to 35 sentences taken from a leading newspaper and included with RDG software. The average number of dependency structures per sentence is 8.68. The method we used selected the correct structures for 25 sentences. The correct structures for 8 sentences were found as the second most probable structure by the method.

In another experiment, we parsed 70 sentences using a grammar similar to the one used in Kurohashi and Nagao (1993). Our method selected the most likely relation among the multiple generated in 95% of the cases.

Although the size of the test data is small, we say that our method provided a way to identify the most probable structure more efficiently than RDG. Since the sentences used are extracted from a newspaper, it's also general in its applicability. Therefore it can be used in preparing teaching materials such as the structures used by a CAI system such as CATERS, saving the instructor of hand-coding them. In future work we shall extract the co-occurrences directly from the corpora, and use other grouping techniques to replace the CD.

5 Acknowledgments

I am thankful to my thesis advisor Dr. T. Furugori and the anonymous referees for their suggestions and comments.

References

Fukumoto, F.; Sano H., Saitoh, Y.; and Fukumoto J. 1992. A Framework for Dependency Grammar based on the word's modifiability level - Restricted Dependency Grammar. In *Trans. IPS Japan*, 33(10), (in Japanese).

Resnik,P. and Hearst M. 1993. Structural Ambiguity and Conceptual Relations. In *Proceedings of the Workshop on Very Large Corpora: Academic and Industrial Perspectives*. Ohio State University.

Japan Electronic Dictionary Research Institute, Ltd. 1993. *EDR Electronic Dictionary Specifications Guide* (in Japanese).

Kano, C. and Yamamoto, H. 1995. A System for Reading Scientific and Technical Texts, Classroom, Instruction and Evaluation. In *Jinbunkagaku to computer* 27(1) (in Japanese).

Kurohashi, S., and Nagao, M. 1993. Structural Disambiguation in Japanese by Evaluating Case Structures based on Examples in Case Frame Dictionary. In *Proceedings of IWPT93*.

Incremental Parser Generation for Tree Adjoining Grammars*

Anoop Sarkar
University of Pennsylvania
Department of Computer and Information Science
200 S. 33rd St., Philadelphia PA 19104-6389, USA
anoop@linc.cis.upenn.edu

Abstract

This paper describes the incremental generation of parse tables for the LR-type parsing of Tree Adjoining Languages (TALs). The algorithm presented handles modifications to the input grammar by updating the parser generated so far. In this paper, a lazy generation of LR-type parsers for TALs is defined in which parse tables are created by need while parsing. We then describe an incremental parser generator for TALs which responds to modification of the input grammar by updating parse tables built so far.

1 LR Parser Generation

Tree Adjoining Grammars (TAGs) are tree rewriting systems which combine trees with the single operation of *adjoining*. (Schabes and Vijay-Shanker, 1990) describes the construction of an LR parsing algorithm for TAGs[1]. Parser generation here is taken to be the construction of LR(0) tables (i.e., without any lookahead) for a particular TAG[2]. The moves made by the parser can be explained by an automaton which is weakly equivalent to TAGs called Bottom-Up Embedded Pushdown Automata (BEPDA) (Schabes and Vijay-Shanker, 1990)[3]. Storage in a BEPDA is a sequence of stacks, where new stacks can be introduced above and below the top stack in the automaton. Recognition of adjunction is equivalent to the **unwrap** move shown in Fig. 1.

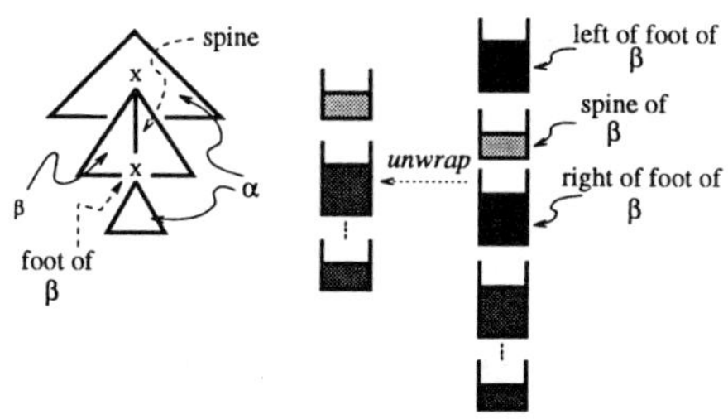

Figure 1: Recognition of adjunction in a BEPDA.

The LR parser (of (Schabes and Vijay-Shanker, 1990)) uses a parsing table and a sequence of stacks (Fig. 1) to parse the input. The parsing table encodes the actions taken by the parser as follows (using two *GOTO* functions):

- **Shift** to a new state, pushed onto a new stack which appears on top of the current sequence of stacks. The current input token is removed.
- **Resume Right** when the parser has reached right and below a node (in a dotted tree, explained below) on which an auxiliary tree has been adjoined. The $GOTO_{foot}$ function encodes the proper state such that the string to the right of the footnode can be recognized.
- **Reduce Root**, the parser executes an unwrap move to recognize adjunction (Fig. 1). The proper state for the parser after adjunction is given by the $GOTO_{right}$ function.
- **Accept** and **Error** functions as in conventional LR parsing.

There are four positions for a dot associated with a symbol in a dotted tree: left above, left below, right below and right above. A dotted tree has one such dotted symbol. The tree traversal in Fig. 2 scans the frontier of the tree from left to right while trying to recognize possible adjunctions between the

*This work is partially supported by NSF grant NSF-STC SBR 8920230 ARPA grant N00014-94 and ARO grant DAAH04-94-G0426. Thanks to Breck Baldwin, Dania Egedi, Jason Eisner, B. Srinivas and the three anonymous reviewers for their valuable comments.

[1] Familiarity with TAGs and their parsing techniques is assumed throughout the paper, see (Schabes and Joshi, 1991) for an introduction. We assume that our definition of TAG does not have the *substitution* operation. See (Aho et al., 1986) for details on LR parsing.

[2] The algorithm described here can be extended to use SLR(1) tables (Schabes and Vijay-Shanker, 1990).

[3] Note that the LR(0) tables considered here are deterministic and hence correspond to a subset of the TALs. Techniques developed in (Tomita, 1986) can be used to resolve nondeterminism in the parser.

above and below positions of the dot. Adjunction on a node is recorded by marking it with an asterisk[4].

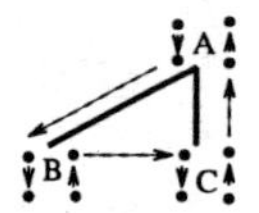

Figure 2: Left to right dotted tree traversal.

The parse table is built as a finite state automaton (FSA) with each state defined to be a set of dotted trees. The closure operations on states in the parse table are defined in Fig. 3. All the states in the parse table must be closed under these operations[5].

The FSA is built as follows: in state 0 put all the initial trees with the dot left and above the root. The state is then closed. New states are built by three transitions: $s_i\{^\bullet a\} \xrightarrow{a} s_j\{a^\bullet\}$, a is a terminal symbol; $s_i\{A_\bullet\} \xrightarrow{\beta_{right}} s_j\{A^\bullet\}$, β can adjoin at node A; $s_i\{_\bullet A\} \xrightarrow{\beta_{foot}} s_j\{A_\bullet\}$, A is a footnode. Entries in the parse table are determined as follows:

- a **shift** for each transition in the FSA.
- **resume right** iff there is a node $B*$ with the dot right and below it.
- **reduce root** iff there is a rootnode in an auxiliary tree with the dot right and above it.
- **accept** and **error** with the usual interpretation.

The items created in each state before closure applies are called the **kernels** of each state in the FSA. The initial trees with the dot left and above the root form the kernel for state 0.

2 Lazy Parser Generation

The algorithm described so far assumes that the parse table is precompiled before the parser is used. Lazy parser generation generates only those parts of the parser that become necessary during actual parsing. The approach is an extension of the algorithm for CFGs given in (Heering et al., 1990; Heering et al., 1989). To modify the LR parsing strategy given earlier we move the closure and computation of transitions from the table generation stage to the LR parser. The lazy technique expands a kernel state only when the parser, looking at the current input, indicates so. For example, a TAG and corresponding FSA is shown in Fig. 4 (*na* rules out adjunction at a node)[6]. Computation of closure and transitions in the state occurs while parsing as in Fig. 5 which is the result of the LR parser expanding the FSA in Fig. 4 while parsing the string *aec*.

The modified parse function checks the type of the state and may expand the kernel states while parsing a sentence. Memory use in the lazy technique is greater as the FSA is needed during parsing *and* parser generation.

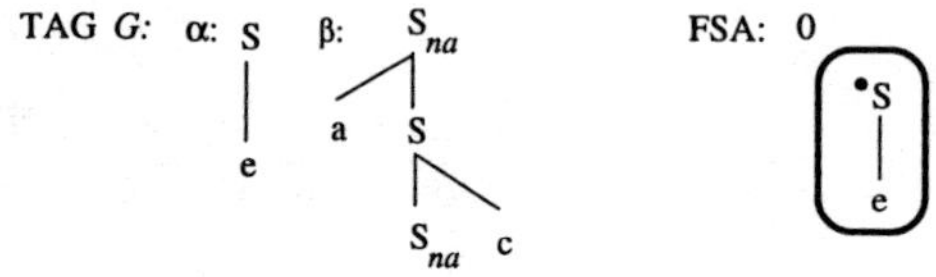

Figure 4: TAG G where $L(G) = \{a^n e c^n\}$ and corresponding FSA after lazy parse table generation.

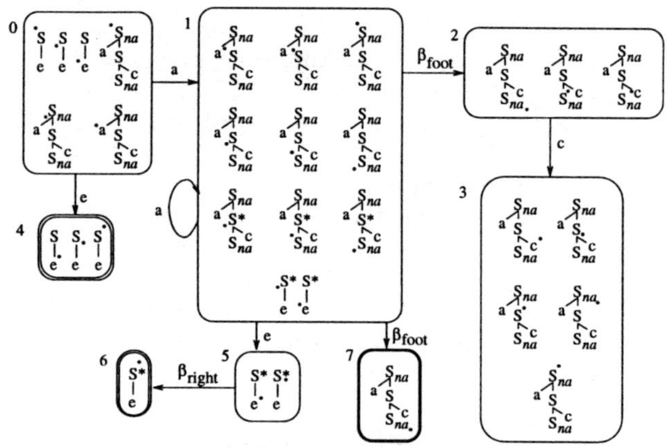

Figure 5: The FSA after parsing the string *aec*.

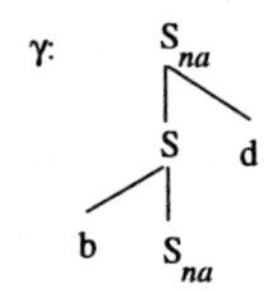

Figure 6: New tree added to G with $L(G) = \{a^n b^m e c^n d^m\}$

3 Incremental Parser Generation

An incremental parser generator responds to grammar updates by throwing away only that information from the FSA of the old grammar that is inconsistent in the updated grammar. Incremental behaviour is obtained by selecting the states in the parse table affected by the change in the grammar and returning them to their kernel form (i.e. remove items added by the closure operations). The parse table FSA will now become a disconnected graph. The lazy parser will expand the states using the new grammar. All states in the disconnected graph are kept as the lazy parser will reconnect with those states (when the transitions between states are computed) that are unaffected by the change in the grammar. Consider

[4] For example, $B*$. This differs from the usual notation for marking a footnode with an asterisk.

[5] Fig. 5 is a partial FSA for the grammar in Fig. 4.

[6] Unexpanded kernel states are marked with a bold-faced outline, acceptance states with double-lines.

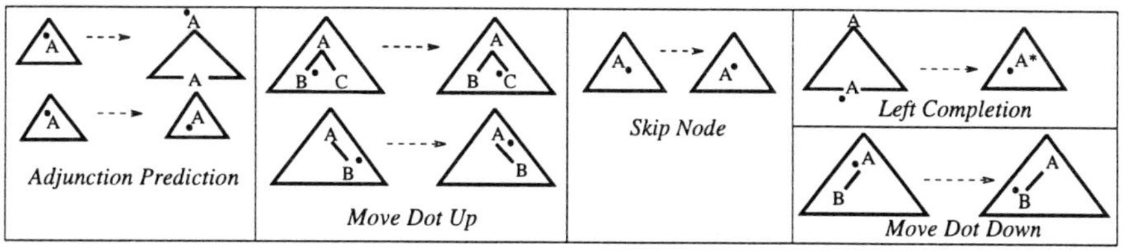

Figure 3: Closure Operations.

the addition of a tree to the grammar (deletion will be similar).

- for an initial tree α return state 0 to kernel form adding α with the dot left and above the root node. Also return all states where a possible *Left Completion* on α can occur to their kernel form.
- for an auxiliary tree β return all states where a possible *Adjunction Prediction* on β can occur and all states with a β_{right} transition to their kernel form.

For example, the addition of the tree in Fig. 6 causes the FSA to fragment into the disconnected graph in Fig. 7. It is crucial to keep the disconnected states around; consider the re-expansion of a single state in Fig. 8. All states compatible with the modified grammar are eventually reused.

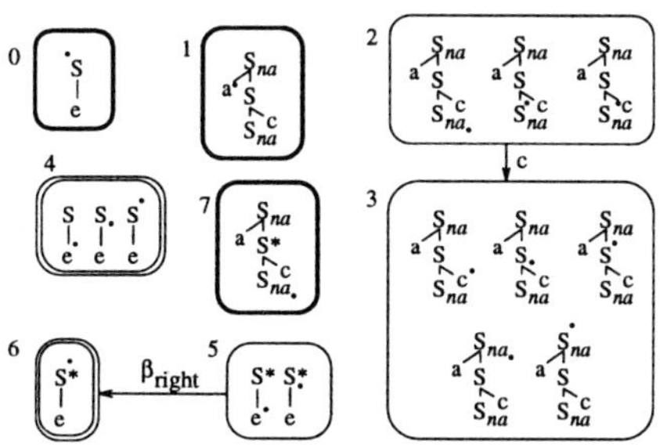

Figure 7: The parse table after the addition of γ.

The approach presented above causes certain states to become unreachable from the start state[7]. Frequent modifications of a grammar can cause many unreachable states. A *garbage collection* scheme defined in (Heering et al., 1990) can be used here which avoids overregeneration by retaining unreachable states.

4 Conclusion

What we have described above is work in progress in implementing an LR-type parser for a wide-coverage lexicalized grammar of English using TAGs (XTAG Group, 1995). Incremental parser generation allows the addition and deletion of elementary trees from a TAG without recompilation of the parse table for the updated grammar. This allows precompilation of top-down dependencies such as the prediction of adjunction while having the flexibility given by Earley-style parsers.

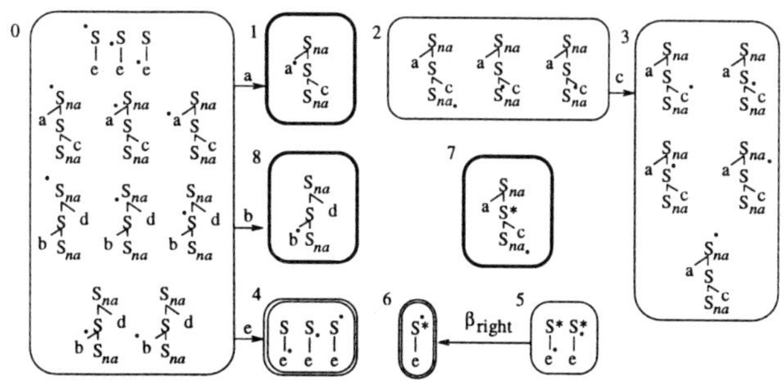

Figure 8: The parse table after expansion of state 0 with the modified grammar.

[7]Quantitative results on the performance of the algorithm presented are forthcoming.

References

Aho, Alfred V., Ravi Sethi and Jeffrey D. Ullman, *Compilers: Principles, Techniques and Tools*, Addison Wesley, Reading, MA, 1986.

Heering, Jan, Paul Klint and Jan Rekers, Incremental Generation of Parsers, In *IEEE Transactions on Software Engineering*, vol. 16, no. 12, pp. 1344-1350, 1990.

Heering, Jan, Paul Klint and Jan Rekers, Incremental Generation of Parsers, In *ACM SIGPLAN Notices (SIGPLAN '89 Conference on Programming Language Design and Implementation)*, vol. 24, no. 7, pp. 179–191, 1989.

Schabes, Yves and K. Vijay-Shanker, Deterministic Left to Right Parsing of Tree Adjoining Languages, In *28th Meeting of the Association for Computational Linguistics (ACL '90)*, Pittsburgh, PA, 1990.

Schabes, Yves and Aravind K. Joshi, Parsing with Lexicalized Tree Adjoining Grammars, In Tomita, Masaru (ed.) *Current Issues in Parsing Technologies*, Kluwer Academic, Dordrecht, The Netherlands, 1991.

Tomita, Masaru, *Efficient Parsing for Natural Language: A Fast Algorithm for Practical Systems*, Kluwer Academic, Dordrecht, The Netherlands, 1986.

XTAG Research Group, *A Lexicalized Tree Adjoining Grammar for English*, IRCS Technical Report 95-03, University of Pennsylvania, Philadelphia, PA. 1995.

Processing Complex Sentences in the Centering Framework

Michael Strube
Freiburg University
(CLIF) Computational Linguistics Lab
Europaplatz 1, D-79085 Freiburg, Germany
strube@coling.uni-freiburg.de

Abstract

We extend the centering model for the resolution of intra-sentential anaphora and specify how to handle complex sentences. An empirical evaluation indicates that the functional information structure guides the search for an antecedent within the sentence.

1 Introduction

The centering model (Grosz et al., 1995) focuses on the resolution of inter-sentential anaphora. Since intra-sentential anaphora occur at high rates in real-world texts, the model has to be extended for the resolution of anaphora at the sentence level. However, the centering framework is not fully specified to handle complex sentences (Suri & McCoy, 1994). This underspecification corresponds to the lack of a precise definition of the expression *utterance*, a term always used but intentionally left undefined[1]. Therefore, the centering algorithms currently under discussion are not able to handle naturally occurring discourse. Possible strategies for treating sentence-level anaphora within the centering framework are

1. processing sentences linearly one clause at a time (as suggested by Grosz et al. (1995)),
2. preference for sentence-external antecedents which are proposed by the centering mechanism,
3. preference for sentence-internal antecedents which are filtered by the usual binding criteria,
4. a mixed-mode which prefers only a particular set of sentence-internal over sentence-external antecedents (e.g. Suri & McCoy (1994)).

The question arises as to which strategy fits best for the interaction between the resolution of intra- and inter-sentential anaphora. In my contribution, evidence for a mixed-mode strategy is brought forward, which favors a particular set of sentence-internal antecedents given by functional criteria.

[1]Cf. the sketchy statements by Brennan et al. (1987, p.155): "[...] U is an utterance (not necessarily a full clause) [...]", and by Grosz et al. (1995, p.209): "U need not to be a full clause."

2 Constraints on Sentential Anaphora

Our studies on German texts have revealed that the functional information structure of the sentence, considered in terms of the context-boundedness of discourse elements, is the major determinant for the ranking on the *forward-looking-centers* ($C_f(U_n)$) (Strube & Hahn, 1996). Hence, context-bound discourse elements are generally ranked higher in the C_f than any other non-anaphoric element. The functional information structure has impact not only on the resolution of inter-sentential anaphora, but also on the resolution of intra-sentential anaphora. Hence, the most preferred antecedent of an intra-sentential anaphor is a phrase which is also anaphoric. Consider sentences (1) and (2) and the corresponding centering data in Table 1 (C_b: backward-looking center; the first element of the pairs denotes the discourse entity, the second element the surface). In sentence (1), a nominal anaphor occurs, *der T3100SX* (a particular notebook). In sentence (2), another nominal anaphor appears, *der Rechner (the computer)*, which is resolved to T3100SX from the previous sentence. In the matrix clause, the pronoun *er (it)* co-specifies the already resolved anaphor *der Rechner* in the subordinate clause.

(1) Ist der Resume-Modus aktiviert, schaltet sich der *T3100SX* selbständig ab.
(If the resume mode is active, – switches – itself – the *T3100SX* – automatically – off.)

(2) Bei späterem Einschalten des *Rechners* arbeitet *er* sofort an der alten Stelle weiter.
(The – later – turning on – of the *computer* – it – resumes working – at exactly the same place.)

(1)	**Cb:**	T3100SX: T3100SX
	Cf:	[T3100SX: T3100SX]
(2)	**Cb:**	T3100SX: er
	Cf:	[T3100SX: er, TURN-ON: Einschalten, PLACE: Stelle]

Table 1: Centering Data for Sentences (1) and (2)

This example illustrates our hypothesis that intra-sentential anaphors preferably co-specify context-bound discourse elements. In order to empirically strenghten this argument, we have examined several texts of different types: 15 texts from the information technology (IT) domain, one text from the German news magazine *Der Spiegel*, and the first chapters of a short story by the German writer *Heiner Müller*[2] (cf. Table 2). In the texts, 65 intra-sentential anaphors oc-

	text ana.	sent. ana.	anaphors	words
IT	284	24	308	5542
Spiegel	90	12	102	1468
Müller	124	29	153	867
Σ	498	65	563	7877

Table 2: Distribution of Anaphors in the Text Corpus

cur, 58 of them (89,2%) have an antecedent which is a resolved anaphor, while only 32 of them (49,2%) have an antecedent which is the subject of the matrix clause (cf. Table 3). These data indicate that an approach based on grammatical roles (Suri & McCoy, 1994) is inappropriate for the German language, while an approach based on the functional information structure seems preferable. In addition, we maintain that exchanging grammatical with functional criteria is also a reasonable strategy for fixed word order languages. They can be rephrased in terms of functional criteria, simply due to the fact that grammatical roles and the information structure patterns we defined, unless marked, coincide in these languages.

	cont.-bound	¬ bound	subj.	¬ subj.
IT	20	4	16	8
Spiegel	10	2	6	6
Müller	28	1	10	19
Σ	58	7	32	33

Table 3: Types of Intra-Sentential Antecedents

Since the strategy described above is valid only for complex sentences which consist of a matrix clause and one or more subordinate clauses, compound sentences which consist of main clauses must be considered. Each of these sentences is processed by our algorithm in linear order, one clause at a time with the usual centering operations. Compound sentences which consist of multiple full clauses also have multiple C_b/C_f data.

Now, we are able to define the expression *utterance* in a satisfactory manner: An utterance *U* is a simple sentence, a complex sentence, or each full clause of a compound sentence[3]. The C_f of an utterance is computed only with respect to the matrix clause. Given these findings, complex sentences can be processed at three stages (2a-2c; transitions from one stage to the next occur only when a suitable antecedent has not been found at the previous stage):

[2]Liebesgeschichte. In Heiner Müller, *Geschichten aus der Produktion* 2, Berlin: Rotbuch Verlag, pp.57-63.

[3]We do not consider dialogues with elliptical utterances.

1. For resolving an anaphor in the first clause of U_n, propose the elements of $C_f(U_{n-1})$ in the given order.
2. For resolving an anaphor in a subsequent clause of U_n,
   (a) propose already context-bound elements of U_n from left to right[4].
   (b) propose the elements of $C_f(U_{n-1})$ in the given order.
   (c) propose all elements of U_n not yet checked from left to right.
3. Compute the $C_f(U_n)$, considering only the elements of the matrix clause of U_n.

3 Evaluation

In order to evaluate the functional approach to the resolution of intra-sentential anaphora within the centering model, we compared it to the other approaches mentioned in Section 1, employing the test set referred to in Table 2. Note that we tried to eliminate error chaining and false positives (for some remarks on evaluating discourse processing algorithms, cf. Walker (1989); we consider her results as a starting point for our proposal).

First, we examine the errors which all strategies have in common (for the success rate, cf. Table 4). 99 errors are caused by underspecification at different levels, e.g., prepositional anaphors (16), plural anaphors (8), anaphors which refer to a member of a set (14), sentence anaphors (21), and anaphors which refer to a global focus (12) are not yet included in the mechanism. In 9 cases, any strategy will choose the false antecedent.

The most interesting cases are the ones for which the performance of the different strategies varies. The linear approach generates 40 additional errors in the anaphora resolution, which are caused only by the ordering strategy to process each clause of sentences with the centering mechanism. The approach which prefers inter-sentential anaphora causes 60 additional errors. Note that this strategy performs remarkably well at first sight. For 44 of the errors it chooses an inter-sentential antecedent which is, on the surface, identical to the correct intra-sentential antecedent. We count these 44 resolutions as false positives, since the anaphor has been resolved to the false discourse entity. The approach which prefers intra-sentential antecedents causes 27 additional errors. These errors occur whenever an inter-sentential anaphor can be resolved with an incorrect intra-sentential antecedent.

[4]We abstract here from the syntactic criteria for filtering out some elements of the current sentence by applying binding criteria (Strube & Hahn, 1995). Syntactic constraints like control phenomena override the preferences given by the context.

	N	linear		extra > intra		intra > extra		functional	
IT	308	237	(76,9%)	229	(74,3%)	240	(77,9%)	247	(80,2%)
Spiegel	102	82	(80,4%)	76	(74,5%)	82	(80,4%)	86	(84,3%)
Müller	153	105	(68,8%)	99	(64,7%)	115	(75,3%)	128	(83,7%)
Σ	563	424	(75,3%)	404	(71,8%)	437	(77,6%)	461	(81,9%)

Table 4: Success Rate without Semantic Constraints

The functional approach causes only 3 additional errors. These errors occur whenever the antecedent of an intra-sentential anaphor is not bound by the context (which is possible but rare) and when the anaphor can be resolved at the text level.

The results change slightly if semantic/conceptual constraints (type and further admissibility constraints) on anaphora are considered. 22 errors of the linear approach, 8 errors of the approach which prefers inter-sentential antecedents, and 12 errors of the approach which prefers inter-sentential antecedents can be avoided. Only 6 errors of the functional approach can be avoided by incorporating semantic criteria. This might constitute a cognitively valid argument for the functional approach – the better the strategy, the lower the influence of semantics or world knowledge on anaphora resolution.

To summarize the results of our empirical evaluation, we claim that our proposal based on functional criteria leads to substantively better results for languages with free word order than the linear approach suggested by Grosz et al. (1995) and the two approaches which prefer inter-sentential or intra-sentential antecedents.

4 Comparison to Related Work

Crucial for the evaluation of the centering model (Grosz et al., 1995) and its applicability to naturally occurring discourse is the lack of a specification concerning how to handle complex sentences and intra-sentential anaphora. Grosz et al. suggest the processing of sentences linearly one clause at a time. We have shown that such an approach is not appropriate for some types of complex sentences. Suri & McCoy (1994) argue in the same manner, but we consider the functional approach for languages with free word order superior to their grammatical criteria, while, for languages with fixed word order, both approaches should give the same results. Hence, our approach seems to be more generally applicable. Other approaches which integrate the resolution of sentence- and text-level anaphora are based on salience metrics (Hajičová et al., 1992; Lappin & Leass, 1994). We consider such metrics to be a method which detracts from the exact linguistic specifications as we propose them.

At first sight, grammar theories like GB (Chomsky, 1981) or HPSG (Pollard & Sag, 1994), are the best choice for resolving anaphora at the sentence-level. But these grammar theories only give filters for excluding some elements from consideration. Neither gives any preference for a particular antecedent at the sentence-level, nor do they consider text anaphora.

5 Conclusions

In this paper, we gave a specification for handling complex sentences in the centering model based on the functional information structure of utterances in discourse. We motivated our proposal by the constraints which hold for a free word order language (German) and derived our results from data-intensive empirical studies of real texts of different types.

Some issues remain open: the evaluation of the functional approach for languages with fixed word order, a fine-grained analysis of subordinate clauses as Suri & McCoy (1994) presented for *SX because SY* clauses, and, in general, the solution for the cases which cause errors in our evaluation.

Acknowledgments. This work has been funded by *LGFG Baden-Württemberg*. I would like to thank my colleagues in the $\mathcal{CLIF}$ group for fruitful discussions. I would also like to thank Jon Alcantara (Cambridge) who kindly took the role of the native speaker via Internet.

References

Brennan, S. E., M. W. Friedman & C. J. Pollard (1987). A centering approach to pronouns. In *Proc. of ACL-87*, pp. 155–162.

Chomsky, N. (1981). *Lectures on Government and Binding*. Dordrecht: Foris.

Grosz, B. J., A. K. Joshi & S. Weinstein (1995). Centering: A framework for modeling the local coherence of discourse. *Computational Linguistics*, 21(2):203–225.

Hajičová, E., V. Kuboň & P. Kuboň (1992). Stock of shared knowledge: A tool for solving pronominal anaphora. In *Proc. of COLING-92*, Vol. 1, pp. 127–133.

Lappin, S. & H. J. Leass (1994). An algorithm for pronominal anaphora resolution. *Computational Linguistics*, 20(4):535–561.

Pollard, C. & I. V. Sag (1994). *Head-Driven Phrase Structure Grammar*. Chicago, ILL: Chicago Univ. Press.

Strube, M. & U. Hahn (1995). *ParseTalk* about sentence- and text-level anaphora. In *Proc. of EACL-95*, pp. 237–244.

Strube, M. & U. Hahn (1996). Functional centering. In *this volume*.

Suri, L. Z. & K. F. McCoy (1994). RAFT/RAPR and centering: A comparison and discussion of problems related to processing complex sentences. *Computational Linguistics*, 20(2):301–317.

Walker, M. A. (1989). Evaluating discourse processing algorithms. In *Proc. of ACL-89*, pp. 251–261.

Maximizing Top-down Constraints for Unification-based Systems

Noriko Tomuro
School of Computer Science, Telecommunications and Information Systems
DePaul University
Chicago, IL 60604
cphdnt@ted.cs.depaul.edu

Abstract

A left-corner parsing algorithm with top-down filtering has been reported to show very efficient performance for unification-based systems. However, due to the non-termination of parsing with left-recursive grammars, top-down constraints must be weakened. In this paper, a general method of maximizing top-down constraints is proposed. The method provides a procedure to dynamically compute **restrictor**, a minimum set of features involved in an infinite loop for every propagation path; thus top-down constraints are maximally propagated.

1 Introduction

A left-corner parsing algorithm with top-down filtering has been reported to show very efficient performance for unification-based systems (Carroll, 1994). In particular, top-down filtering seems to be very effective in increasing parse efficiency (Shann, 1991). Ideally all top-down expectation should be propagated down to the input word so that unsuccessful rule applications are pruned at the earliest time. However, in the context of unification-based parsing, left-recursive grammars have the formal power of a Turing machine, therefore detection of all infinite loops due to left-recursion is impossible (Shieber, 1992). So, top-down constraints must be weakened in order for parsing to be guaranteed to terminate.

In order to solve the nontermination problem, Shieber (1985) proposes *restrictor*, a statically predefined set of features to consider in propagation, and *restriction*, a filtering function which removes the features not in *restrictor* from top-down expectation. However, not only does this approach fail to provide a method to automatically generate the restrictor set, it may weaken the predicative power of top-down expectation more than necessary: a globally defined *restrictor* can only specify the least common features for all propagation paths.

In this paper, a general method of maximizing top-down constraints is proposed. The method provides a procedure to dynamically compute **restrictor**, a minimum set of features involved in an infinite loop, for every propagation path. Features in this set are selected by the *detection function*, and will be ignored in top-down propagation. Using **restrictor**, only the relevant features particular to the propagation path are ignored, thus top-down constraints are maximally propagated.

2 Notation

We use notation from the PATR-II formalism (Shieber, 1986) and (Shieber, 1992). Directed acyclic graphs (dags) are adopted as the representation model. The symbol $\doteq$ is used to represent the equality relation in the unification equations, and the symbol $\cdot$ used in the form of $p1 \cdot p2$ represents the path concatenation of $p1$ and $p2$.

The *subsumption* relation is defined as "Dag D *subsumes* dag D' if D is more general than D'." The *unification* of D and D' is notated by $D \sqcup D'$.

The extraction function $D/p1$ extracts the subdag under path $p1$ for a given D, and the embedding function $D \setminus p1$ injects D into the enclosing dag D' such that $D'/p1 = D$. The filtering function ρ is similar to (Shieber, 1992): $\rho(D)$ returns a copy of D in which some features may be removed. Note that in this paper **restrictor** specifies the features to be removed by ρ, whereas in (Shieber, 1985, 1992) restrictor specifies the features to be retained by restriction which is equivalent to ρ.

3 Top-down Propagation

Top-down propagation can be precomputed to form a *reachability table*. Each entry in the table is a compiled dag which represents the relation between a non-terminal category and a rule used to rewrite the constituents in the *reachability* relation (i.e., reflexive, transitive closure of the left-corner path).

For example, consider the following fragment of a grammar used in the syntax/semantics integrated system called LINK (Lytinen, 1992):

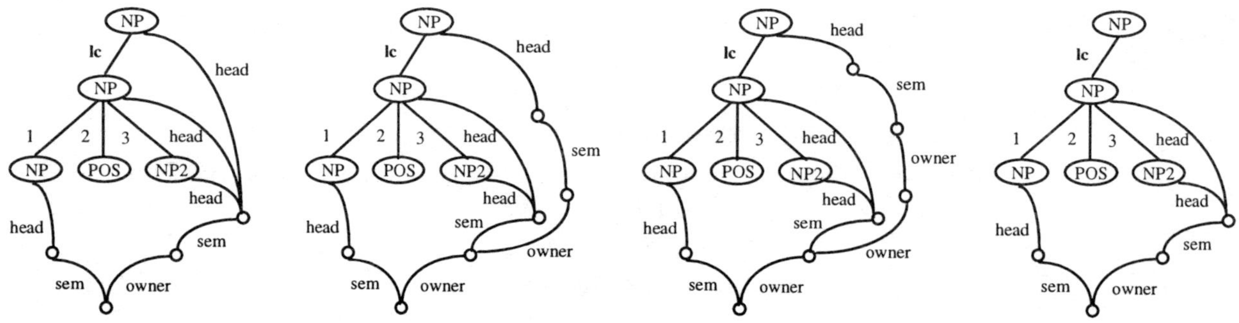

D(1) D(2) D(3) D(4)

Figure 1: DAGs used in the example

$$r1: NP_0 \rightarrow NP_1 \ POS \ NP2$$
$$\langle NP_0 \ head \rangle = \langle NP2 \ head \rangle$$
$$\langle NP_0 \ head \ sem \ owner \rangle = \langle NP_1 \ head \ sem \rangle$$

(This rule is used to parse phrases such as "Kris's desk".)

The dag $D(1)$ in Figure 1[1] represents the initial application of $r1$ to the category NP. Note that the subdag under the **lc** arc is the rule used to rewrite the constituent on the left-corner path, and the paths from the top node represent which top-down constraints are propagated to the lower level.

Top-down propagation works as follows: given a dag D that represents a reachability relation and a rule dag R whose left-hand side category (i.e., root) is the same as D's left-corner category (i.e., under its (**lc** 1) path), the resulting dag is $D1 = \rho(D') \sqcup (R \setminus \mathbf{lc})$, where D' is a copy of D in which all the numbered arcs and **lc** arc are deleted and the subdag which used to be under the (**lc** 1) path is promoted to lie under the **lc** arc. Dags after the next two recursive applications of $r1$ ($D(2)$ and $D(3)$ respectively[2]) are shown in Figure 1.

Notice the filtering function ρ is applied only to D'. In the case when $\rho(D') = nil$, the top node in $D1$ will have no connections to the rule dag under the **lc** arc. This means no top-down constraints are propagated to the lower level, therefore the parsing becomes pure bottom-up.

In many unification-based systems, subsumption is used to avoid redundancy: a dag is recorded in the table if it is not subsumed by any other one. Therefore, if a newly created dag is incompatible or more general than existing dags, rule application continues. In the above example, $D(2)$ is incompatible with $D(1)$ and therefore gets entered into the table. The *owner* arc keeps extending in the subsequent recursive applications (as in $D(3)$), thus the propagation goes into an infinite loop.

[1] Category symbols are directly indicated in the dag nodes for simplicity.

[2] In this case, ρ is assumed to be an identity function.

3.1 Proposed Method

Let A be a dag created by the first application of the rule R and B be a dag created by the second application during the top-down propagation.[3] In the proposed method, A and B are first checked for subsumption. If B is subsumed by A, the propagation for this path terminates. Otherwise a possible loop is detected. The detection function (described in the next subsection) is called on A and B and selected features are added to the **restrictor** set.[4] Then, using the updated **restrictor**, propagation is re-done from A.

When R is applied again yielding B', while B' is not subsumed by A, the following process is repeated: if B' is incompatible with A, the detection function is called on A and B' and propagation is re-done from A. If B' is more general than A, then A is replaced by B' (thereby keeping the most general dag for the path) and propagation is re-done from B'. Otherwise the process stops for this propagation path. Thus, the propagation will terminate when enough features are detected, or when **restrictor** includes all the (finite number of) features in the grammar.[5]

In the example, when the detection function is called on $D(1)$ and $D(2)$ after the first recursive application, the feature *owner* is selected and added to **restrictor**. After the propagation is re-done from $D(1)$, the resulting dag $D(4)$ becomes more general than $D(1)$.[6] Then $D(1)$ is replaced by $D(4)$, and the propagation is re-done once again. This time it results the same $D(4)$, therefore the propagation

[3] In the case of indirect recursion, there are some intervening rule applications between A and B.

[4] A separate **restrictor** must be kept for each propagation path.

[5] In reality, category feature will never be in **restrictor** because the same rule R is applied to derive both A and B'.

[6] Remember $D(4) = \rho(D(1)') \sqcup (r1 \setminus \mathbf{lc})$ where ρ filters out *owner* arc.

terminates.

3.2 Detection Function

The detection function compares two dags X and Y by checking every constraint (unification equation) x in X with any inconsistent or more general constraint y in Y. If such a constraint is found, the function selects a path in x or y and detects its last arc/feature as being involved in the possible loop.[7]

If x is the path constraint $p1 \doteq p2$ where $p1$ and $p2$ are paths of length ≥ 1, features may be detected in the following cases:[8]

- (case 1) If both $p1$ and $p2$ exist in Y, and there exists a more general constraint y in Y in the form $p1 \cdot p3 \doteq p2 \cdot p3$ (length of $p3$ is also ≥ 1), the path $p3$ is selected;
- (case 2) If both $p1$ and $p2$ exist in Y, but the subdag under $p1$ and the subdag under $p2$ do not unify, or if neither $p1$ nor $p2$ exists in Y, whichever of $p1$ or $p2$ does not contain the **lc** arc, or either if they both contain the **lc** arc, is selected; and
- (case 3) If either $p1$ or $p2$ does not exist in Y, the one which does not exist in Y is selected.

If x is the constant constraint $p1 \doteq c$ (where c is some constant), features may be detected in the following cases:

- (case 4) If there exists an incompatible constraint y of the form $p1 \doteq d$ where $d \neq c$ in Y, or if there is no path $p1$ in Y, $p1$ is selected; and
- (case 5) If there exists an incompatible constraint y of the form $p1 \cdot p2 \doteq c$, then $p2$ is selected.

4 Related Work

A similar solution to the nontermination problem with unification grammars in Prolog is proposed in (Samuelsson, 1993). In this method, an operation called anti-unification (often referred to as *generalization* as the counterpart of unification) is applied to the root and leaf terms of a cyclic propagation, and the resulting term is stored in the reachablity table as the result of applying restriction on both terms. Another approach taken in (Haas, 1989) eliminates the cyclic propagation by replacing the features in the root and leaf terms with new variables.

The method proposed in this paper is more general than the above approaches: if the selection ordering is imposed in the detection function, features in **restrictor** can be collected incrementally as the cyclic propagations are repeated. Thus, this method is able to create a less restrictive **restrictor** than these other approaches.

[7] This scheme may be rather conservative.

[8] Note the cases in this section do **not** represent all possible situations.

5 Discussion and Future Work

The proposed method has an obvious difficulty: the complexity caused by the repeated propagations could become overwhelming for some grammars. However, in the experiment on LINK system using a fairly broad grammar (over 130 rules), precompilation terminated with only a marginally longer processing time.

In the experiment, all features (around 40 syntactic/semantic features) except for one in the example in this paper were able to be used in propagation. In the preliminary analysis, the number of edges entered into the chart has decreased by 30% compared to when only the category feature (i.e., context-free backbone) was used in propagation.

For future work, we intend to apply the proposed method to other grammars. By doing the empirical analysis of precompilation and parse efficiency for different grammars, we will be able to conclude the practical applicability of the proposed method. We also indend to do more exhaustive case analysis and investigate the selection ordering of the detection function. Although the current definition covers most cases, it is by no means complete.

References

Carroll, J. (1994). Relating complexity to practical performance in parsing with wide-coverage unification grammars. In *Proceedings of the 32nd Annual Meeting of the Association for Computational Linguistics*, pp. 287-293.

Haas, A. (1989). A parsing algorithm for unification grammar, *Computational Linguistics*, **15**(4), pp. 219-232.

Lytinen, S. (1992). A unification-based, integrated natural language processing system. *Computers and Mathematics with Applications*, **23**(6-9), pp. 403-418.

Samuelsson, C. (1993). Avoiding non-termination in unification grammars. In *Proceedings of Natural Language Understanding and Logic Programming IV*, Nara, Japan.

Shann, P. (1991). Experiments with GLR and chart parsing. In Tomita, M. *Generalized LR Parsing.* Boston: Kluwer Academic Publishers, p. 17-34.

Shieber, S. (1985). Using restriction to extend parsing algorithms for complex-feature-based formalisms. In *Proceedings of the 23rd Annual Meeting of the Association for Computational Linguistics*, Chicago, IL, pp. 145-152.

Shieber, S. (1986). *An Introduction to Unification-Based Approaches to Grammar.* Stanford, CA: Center for the Study of Language and Information.

Shieber, S. (1992). *Constraint-based Grammar Formalisms.* Cambridge, MA: MIT Press.